THE PAPERS OF
ZEBULON BAIRD VANCE

Zebulon B. Vance at the age of thirty-six

The Papers of
Zebulon Baird Vance

Edited by

FRONTIS W. JOHNSTON

VOLUME ONE

1843-1862

RALEIGH

STATE DEPARTMENT OF ARCHIVES AND HISTORY

1963

CONTENTS

FOREWORD

The publication of the first volume of *The Papers of Zebulon Baird Vance* during the observance of the Civil War Centennial is an appropriate memorial to North Carolina's War Governor. The original papers have been available to scholars doing research in this period, but the printed volumes will enable persons interested in the field of Civil War history to have the Vance materials readily accessible.

A word of explanation concerning the form used in footnotes is in order. Because of unavoidable delays between the time the documentary section of the volume was set in type and the time the front matter was completed, it was not possible to follow the style now uniformly used by the State Department of Archives and History. The index was prepared by Mrs. Mary A. Holloway of the staff of the Division of Publications.

The Department wishes to express its appreciation to Dr. Frontis W. Johnston, Editor of the series. It is hoped that additional volumes will be published within the next few years.

Memory F. Blackwelder, *Editor*

February 1, 1963

PREFACE

In editing these papers, I have made no alterations in spelling, capitalization, or punctuation. Many of the letters were written by semi-illiterate persons and grammatical mistakes are very numerous. I have not used the designation "[sic]" because of the manifest impracticality of employing it with material of this kind. Although it is sometimes very difficult to be certain of details in the letters, special efforts have been made to print them just as they were written. A key for determining the nature and present location of the original manuscripts included in this volume is provided on another page.

A complete list of persons to whom I owe thanks for aid of some sort in the preparation of these papers for publication would be too long for inclusion here. But I cannot omit naming a few to whom I owe gratitude of a particular sort. The North Carolina Department of Archives and History, where the major portions of the Vance papers are deposited, has co-operated in the venture over a period of many years and is providing the funds for the publication of this volume. Mr. D. L. Corbitt, formerly Head of the Division of Publications, was especially helpful and patient—perhaps too patient—from the beginning. Dr. Christopher Crittenden, the Director, and numerous persons in the search room, gave cheerful and unfailing help from their wide knowledge and experience. Mrs. Memory F. Blackwelder, the present Editor for the Department, has directed the final details and has expedited publication by agreeing that the biographical sketch of Vance could be ended in 1865, a point well beyond the period of time covered by the letters in this volume. The sketch will be completed when the post-war letters are published.

Equally co-operative and valuable has been the aid rendered by Dr. James W. Patton and his staff at the Southern Historical Collection of the University of North Carolina, where much of the editing was done. The State Library in Raleigh, the Duke University Library, the Library of Congress, and the National Archives have also courteously supplied valuable materials. Finally, individuals in many places, especially in Asheville, North Carolina, have willingly given help on particular phases of the work.

My sincere thanks are due to the Research Fund of the Carnegie Foundation which helped me initiate the project years ago, and to Davidson College for occasional grants which have helped me carry it on.

Davidson College   Frontis W. Johnston
Davidson, North Carolina
March 27, 1963

LISTS OF LETTERS

Letters Written by Zebulon B. Vance Printed in this Volume

Place	Date	Written to
University of North Carolina	Aug. 12, [1851]	Martha E. Weaver
University of North Carolina	Sept. 14, [1851]	John M. Davidson
University of North Carolina	Sept. 24, [1851]	Martha E. Weaver
Chapel Hill	Feb. 8, [18]52	Martha E. Weaver
[University of North Carolina]	[1852]	Kate E. Smith
Asheville	Sept. 6, 1854	Kate E. Smith
House of Commons	Dec. 15, 1854	Editor, Raleigh *Register*
House of Commons	Feb. 2, 1855	Editor, Raleigh *Register*
Asheville	July 6, 1857	David L. Swain
Asheville	Feb. 19, 1858	David F. Caldwell
Asheville	April 2, 1858	Robert B. Davidson
Asheville	May 25, 1858	Margaret Mitchell
Asheville	Aug. 30, 1858	David L. Swain
Washington [D. C.]	Feb. 10, 1859	Jane Smith
Asheville	Aug. 16, [1859]	David Coleman
Asheville	Aug. 17, [1859]	David Coleman
Asheville	Aug. 18, [18]59	David Coleman
Asheville	[Aug. 22, 1859]	David Coleman
Asheville	Aug. 22, [18]59	James F. E. Hardy
		John W. Woodfin
Asheville	Aug. 22, 1859	John E. Brown
Asheville	Aug. 29, [1859]	David Coleman
Washington [D. C.]	Dec. 11, 1860	William Dickson
[Washington, D. C.]	Dec. 26, 1860	Walter W. Lenoir
Washington [D. C.]	Jan. 9, 1861	George N. Folk
Washington [D. C.]	Jan. 19, 1861	Thomas G. Walton
Statesville	May 18, [1861]	Mrs. Z. B. Vance
Suffolk, Virginia	June 19, [1861]	Mrs. Z. B. Vance
Suffolk, Virginia	June 29, 1861	Mrs. Z. B. Vance
Suffolk, Virginia	July 21, 1861	Mrs. Z. B. Vance
Morehead City	Sept. 15, 1861	Mrs. Z. B. Vance
Morehead City	Sept. 18, 1861	N. G. Allman
Carolina City	Oct. 13, 1861	Mrs. Z. B. Vance
Fort Macon	Oct. 17, 1861	Mrs. Z. B. Vance
New Bern	March 4, [1862]	Allen T. Davidson
Kinston	March 17, 1862	Lawrence O'B. Branch
Kinston	March 17, 1862	Editor, the *Standard*
Kinston	March 20, [1862]	Mrs. Z. B. Vance
Kinston	March 23, 1862	Mrs. Z. B. Vance
Kinston	April 3, [18]62	Secretary of War
Kinston	April 18, 1862	North Carolina Newspapers
Kinston	April 28, [1862]	William W. Holden
Kinston	April 29, 1862	*North Carolina Standard*
Headquarters 26th Regiment	May 2, 1862	Secretary of War
Kinston	May 17, [1862]	George W. Randolph
Kinston	May 25, [1862]	Mrs. Z. B. Vance
Kinston	May 28, 1862	Editor, the *Standard*
Kinston	June 15, 1862	George W. Randolph
Kinston	June 16, 1862	Editors, the *Observer*
Kinston	June 18, [1862]	Mrs. Z. B. Vance
Richmond [Virginia]	July 4, [1862]	George W. Randolph
Drewry's Bluff, Virginia	July 26, [1862]	Secretary of War
Petersburg [Virginia]	Aug. 8, [1862]	Mrs. Z. B. Vance
Raleigh	Aug. 17, [1862]	William A. Graham
Asheville	Aug. 25, [1862]	David L. Swain

Raleigh	Sept. 11, 1862	Peter Mallett
Raleigh	Sept. 11, 1862	George W. Randolph
Raleigh	Sept. 13, 1862	George W. Randolph
Raleigh	Sept. 18, 1862	Duncan K. McRae
Raleigh	Sept. 18, [1862]	Weldon N. Edwards
Raleigh	Sept. 24, 1862	Samuel P. Moore
Raleigh	Oct. 1, 1862	John M. Worth
Raleigh	Oct. 8, 1862	Sheriff of Wake County
Raleigh	Oct. 10, 1862	Peter Mallett
Raleigh	Oct. 10, [18]62	George W. Randolph
Raleigh	Oct. 10, 1862	John M. Worth
Raleigh	Oct. 10, [18]62	Francis L. Fries
		Henry W. Fries
Raleigh	Oct. 15, 1862	George W. Randolph
Raleigh	Oct. 25, 1862	Jefferson Davis
Raleigh	Oct. 29, 1862	Edward Stanly
[Raleigh]	[Nov. 1, 1862]	John White
Raleigh	Nov. 8, 1862	Lucius B. Northrop
Raleigh	Nov. 11, 1862	Jefferson Davis
Raleigh	Nov. 12, 1862	Jefferson Davis
Raleigh	Nov. 13, 1862	Christopher G. Memminger
Raleigh	Nov. [15], 1862	John White
Raleigh	Nov. 15, 1862	Stephen R. Mallory
Raleigh	Nov. 19, 1862	Gustavus W. Smith
Raleigh	Nov. 20, 1862	James A. Seddon
Raleigh	Nov. 21, [1862]	Stephen R. Mallory
Raleigh	Nov. 22, 1862	Joseph E. Brown
Raleigh	Nov. 24, 1862	Edward Stanly
Raleigh	Nov. 25, 1862	Jefferson Davis
Raleigh	Dec. 6, 1862	James A. Seddon
Raleigh	Dec. 6, [1862]	Governor John Letcher
[Raleigh]	[Dec. 19, 1862]	W. M. Shipp
Raleigh	Dec. 24, 1862	Jefferson Davis
Raleigh	Dec. 26, 1862	Abraham C. Myers
Raleigh	Dec. 30, [18]62	Matthias Manly

Letters Written to Zebulon B. Vance Printed in this Volume

Place	*Date*	*Written by*
Lapland	June 11, 1843	Mira M. Vance
[Lapland]	[1843]	Robert B. Vance
[Lapland]	June 18, 1843	David Vance
[Quaker Meadows]	[April 25, 1852]	Charles McDowell
Charleston, South Carolina	Oct. 26, 1852	Henry R. Dickson
Asheville	July 30, 1853	David Rankin
[Asheville]	[July 9, 1855]	James S. T. Baird
Asheville	Aug. 15, 1859	David Coleman
Asheville	Aug. 16, [1859]	David Coleman
Asheville	Aug. 17, 1859	David Coleman
Asheville	Aug. 18, 1859	David Coleman
	[Aug. 22, 1859]	John D. Hyman
Asheville	Aug. 22, 1859	James F. E. Hardy
		John W. Woodfin
Asheville	Aug. 27, 1859	David Coleman
Asheville	Aug. 29, 1859	David Coleman
Asheville	Dec. 24, 1859	W. Caleb Brown
Asheville	March 6, 1860	Harriette Vance
Asheville	April 16, 1860	Robert B. Vance
Limestone	May 17, 1860	William J. Brown
Wilkes County	Dec. 17, 1860	B. F. Eller

Fort Defiance	Jan. 7, 1861	Walter W. Lenoir
Knoxville, Tennessee	Jan. 13, [18]61	John J. Baxter
Greensboro	Jan. 13, 1861	David F. Caldwell
Columbus	Jan. 14, 1861	J. M. Hamilton
Rutherfordton	Jan. 15, 1861	George W. Logan
Rutherfordton	Jan. 16, 1860 [1861]	Robert G. Twitty
Asheville	Jan. 21, 1861	Robert B. Vance
Hominy Creek	Jan. 27, 1861	James C. L. Gudger
[Ivy P. O.]	Jan. 28, 1861	Samuel O. Deaver
Ivy Bend	Jan. 28, 1861	Joseph P. Eller
Webster	Feb. 1, 1861	William L. Love
Lenoir	Feb. 4, 1861	Calvin C. Jones
Jacks Creek	Feb. 5, 1861	John W. McElroy
Lenoir	Feb. 5, 1860[1861]	Walter W. Lenoir
Murfreesboro	April 26, 1861	William N. H. Smith
Asheville	May 28, 1861	Robert B. Vance
Reems Creek	June 9, 1861	James A. Reagan
Raleigh	June 13, 1861	Augustus S. Merrimon
Raleigh	Aug. 27, 1861	James G. Martin
Briar Creek	March 25, [1862]	Abner Carmichael
Raleigh	April 23, 1862	James G. Martin
Raleigh	April 26, 1862	James G. Martin
Raleigh	May 5, 1862	James G. Martin
Kittrell	June 4, 1862	Alpheus M. Erwin
Raleigh	June 18, 1862	Henry W. Miller
Richmond [Virginia]	Aug. 1, 1862	Secretary of War
Chapel Hill	Aug. 15, 1862	David L. Swain
Richmond, Virginia	Aug. 27, 1862	Otis F. Manson
Fayetteville	Aug. 28, 1862	Jesse G. Shepherd
Richmond, Virginia	Sept. 1, 1862	Thomas M. Garrett
Richmond [Virginia]	Sept. 2, 1862	Richard H. Battle, Jr.
Pleasantville	Sept. 2, 1862	David S. Reid
Richmond [Virginia]	Sept. 5, 1862	William N. H. Smith
Frederick, Maryland	Sept. 9, 1862	Duncan K. McRae
Frederick, Maryland	Sept. 9, 1862	Thomas Ruffin, Jr.
Rutherford C[oun]ty	Sept. 11, 1862	Tolivar Davis
Camp Holmes	Sept. 11, 1862	Peter Mallett
Drewry's Bluff, Virginia	Sept. 12, 1862	John R. Winston
Palmyra	Sept. 13, 1862	Samuel F. Patterson
Swansboro	Sept. 15, 1862	Lotte W. Humphrey
Chapel Hill	Sept. 15, 1862	David L. Swain
Charlotte	Sept. 16, [18]62	William J. Yates
Asheboro	Sept. 16, [18]62	Jonathan Worth
Richmond [Virginia]	Sept. 16, 1862	Isaac M. St. John
Richmond, Virginia	Sept. 17, 1862	Samuel P. Moore
Richmond [Virginia]	Sept. 17, 1862	Abraham C. Myers
Headquarters 26th Regiment	Sept. 18, 1862	James D. McIver
Asheville	Sept. 18, 1862	Augustus S. Merrimon
Colerain	Sept. 18, 1862	John Pool
Fort St. Philip	Sept. 19, 1862	John A. Richardson
Smithfield	Sept. 19, 1862	Henry B. Watson
Wilmington	Sept. 19, 1862	John M. Worth
White Oak	Sept. 20, 1862	Jason H. Carson
New Hanover County	Sept. 20, 1862	T. J. Corbett
Edgefield	Sept. 21, 1862	Mary A. Buie
Jam[e]stown	Sept. 21, 1862	T. M. Shoffner
Salisbury	Sept. 22, [18]62	Nathaniel Boyden
Cottage Hill	Sept. 22, 1862	John H. Robeson
Wainsville	Sept. 23, 1862	P. H. Roane
Smithfield	Sept. 23, 1862	Henry A. Gilliam
Fairfield	Sept. 23, 1862	William S. Carter
Fayetteville	Sept. 24, 1862	John M. Rose

Knoxville [Tennessee]	Sept. 25, 1862	Lawrence M. Allen
Columbus	Sept. 25, 1862	Anonymous
Columbus	Sept. 25, 1862	James E. Hannon
———	[Sept. 26, 1862]	Eugene Grissom
Olive	Sept. 26, 1862	W. W. Allen
Greensboro	Sept. 26, 1862	Calvin H. Wiley
Thompsonville	Sept. 27, [18]62	John Thompson
Petersburg, Virginia	Sept. 27, 1862	Leonidas L. Polk
Salem	Sept. 29, 1862	Elias A. Vogler
Bunker Hill, Virginia	Sept. 29, 1862	William D. Pender
Waughtown	Sept. 29, 1862	John P. Nissen
Zollicoffer, Tennessee	Sept. 30, 1862	Robert M. Henry
Huntsville	Sept. [?], 1862	Richard C. Puryear
Richmond, Virginia	Oct. 3, 1862	E. W. Johns
Drewry's Bluff, Virginia	Oct. 5, 1862	Robert D. Lunsford
Winchester, Virginia	Oct. 5, [18]62	Stephen D. Thurston
Asheboro	Oct. 7, 1862	John M. Worth
Martinsburg, Virginia	Oct. 7, 1862	Rufus Barringer
Camp Holmes	Oct. 10, 1862	James C. McRae
New Garden	Oct. 10, 1862	Nereus Mendenhall
Staunton [Virginia]	Oct. 11, 1862	Edward Warren
Winchester, Virginia	Oct. 11, 1862	Samuel H. Walkup
Salem	Oct. 13, 1862	Francis L. Fries
		Henry W. Fries
Kinston	Oct. 13, 1862	Annie Terry
Richmond [Virginia]	Oct. 17, 1862	John H. Reagan
Richmond [Virginia]	Oct. 17, 1862	Jefferson Davis
Greensboro	Oct. 18, 1862	Richard Sterling
Asheville	Oct. 20, 1862	Augustus S. Merrimon
New Bern	Oct. 21, 1862	Edward Stanly
Petersburg, Virginia	Oct. 22, 1862	Samuel G. French
Pleasant Hill	Oct. 25, 1862	Hal W. Ayer
———	Oct. 26, [18]62	James Rhodes and Others
Richmond, Virginia	Oct. 27, 1862	Jefferson Davis
Lumberton	Oct. 27, 1862	James Sinclair
Lumberton	Oct. 27, 1862	James Sinclair
Goldsboro	Oct. 31, 1862	John H. Peebles
Whiteville	Oct. 31, 1862	John A. Maultsby
Richmond, Virginia	Nov. 1, 1862	George W. Randolph
Lewisville	Nov. 1, 1862	John H. Kinyoun
Lexington	Nov. 1, 1862	John Michael
Fayetteville	Nov. 1, 1862	William Poisson
Richmond [Virginia]	Nov. 1, 1862	Jefferson Davis
Richmond [Virginia]	Nov. 2, 1862	Lucius B. Northrop
———	Nov. 2, [1862]	John L. Webb
Caldwell County	Nov. 3, 1862	Elender Gibson
Bald Creek	Nov. 3, 1862	James R. Ncill
Greensboro	Nov. 3, 1862	Calvin H. Wiley
Franklin	Nov. 3, 1862	David W. Siler
Kinston	Nov. 3, [18]62	Thomas J. Jarvis
Marion	Nov. 4, [18]62	Robert L. Abernethy
Mt. Airy	Nov. 4, 1862	Samuel Forkner
Richmond [Virginia]	Nov. 4, [1862]	Stephen R. Mallory
Mouth of Wilson, Virginia	Nov. 5, 1862	John L. Pugh
———	Nov. 5, 1862	Lydia A. Bolton
Richmond, Virginia	Nov. 5, 1862	Otis F. Manson
Salisbury	Nov. 6, 1862	William A. Houck
Asheboro	Nov. 6, 1862	John M. Worth
	Nov. 6, 1862	Cass A. Marlow
	Nov. 6, 1862	Archibald Curlee
Salem	Nov. 6, 1862	Hal W. Ayer
New Market	Nov. 6, 1862	W. A. H. Comer

Pine Hall	Nov. 7, 1862	Mrs. M. B. Moore
New Bern	Nov. 7, 1862	Edward Stanly
Knoxville, Tennessee	Nov. 9, 1862	Arthur A. Deweese
Rutherford County	Nov. 9, 1862	James M. Edwards
Goldsboro	Nov. 9, 1862	Theophilus Edwards
Asheville	Nov. 9, [18]62	Ervin Sluder
Macon County	Nov. 9, 1862	A. L. Corpening
Pittsborough	Nov. 10, 1862	Thomas Miller
Hendersonville	Nov. 10, 1862	Alexander H. Jones
Richmond [Virginia]	Nov. 10, 1862	Richard Morton
Wilson	Nov. 10, 1862	Solomon S. Satchwell
Bethania	Nov. 10, 1862	Hal W. Ayer
Greene Co[unty]	Nov. 10, 1862	Henry H. Best
Stocksville	Nov. 10, 1862	Robert V. Blackstock
Richmond, Virginia	Nov. 10, 1862	George W. Randolph
Hendersonville	Nov. 12, 1862	David M. Stradley
Wilson	Nov. 12, 1862	Amos J. Battle
Whauley	Nov. 12, 1862	Samuel J. Guy
Asheville	Nov. 13, 1862	William R. Young
Scotland Neck	Nov. 13, 1862	Richard H. Smith
Henderson	Nov. 13, 1862	A. J. Rogers
[Wilmington]	[Nov. 13, 1862]	John Dawson
Wilmington	Nov. 13, 1862	Avon E. Hall
Madison C[ourt] H[ouse], Virginia	Nov. 13, 1862	William J. Clarke
Granville County	Nov. 13, 1862	N. A. Waller
Wilmington	Nov. 14, 1862	Joseph H. Flanner
Strausburg, Virginia	Nov. 14, 1862	Duncan K. McRae
[Franklin]	Nov. 15, 1862	Cannada Henderson
Culpepper, Virginia	Nov. 15, 1862	Charles M. Andrews
Charleston [South Carolina]	Nov. 15, 1862	Thomas M. Crossan
Wilson	Nov. 15, 1862	Joseph J. Lawrence
Petersburg, Virginia	Nov. 15, 1862	Samuel G. French
Fort Fisher	Nov. 17, 1862	William Lamb
Rutherfordton	Nov. 17, 1862	George W. Logan
Oak Dale	Nov. 17, 1862	Fenner B. Satterthwaite
Trinity College	Nov. 17, 1862	Braxton Craven
———————	Nov. 17, 1862	Murdock J. McSween
Anderson's Store	Nov. 18, 1862	Celluda F. Pattilo
———————	Nov. 18, 1862	Young Jordan
Lenoir	Nov. 18, 1862	Richard N. Price
Franklin, Virginia	Nov. 18, 1862	Edward Cantwell
Randolph Co[unty]	Nov. 18, 1862	Martha Coletrane
Richmond, Virginia	Nov. 18[1], 1862	George W. Randolph
Mt. Airy	Nov. 18, 1862	Samuel Forkner
Clinton	Nov. 19, 1862	Arthur J. Hill
Asheville	Nov. 19, [18]62	John D. Hyman
Yadkin County	Nov. 21, 1862	Elizabeth Chamberlain
Trenton	Nov. 21, 1862	S. Sidney Carter
Charlotte	Nov. 22, 1862	D. T. Ramseur
———————	Nov. 22, 1862	John Roberts
Marion	Nov. 22, [18]62	Robert L. Abernethy
Knoxville [Tennessee]	Nov. 22, 1862	William H. Thomas
[Weldon]	Nov. 22, 1862	Joseph J. Williams and Others
Brunswick County	Nov. 23, 1862	Charlotte Rowell
Petersburg, Virginia	Nov. 24, 1862	Samuel G. French
Asheville	Nov. 24, 1862	John W. McElroy
Chapel Hill	Nov. 25, 1862	David L. Swain
Mocksville	Nov. 25, 1862	Allen A. Harbin
Wilmington	Nov. 25, 1862	Sewall L. Fremont

Place	Date	Name
Richland Valley	Nov. 25, 1862	John B. Fitzgerald
————————	Nov. 25, 1862	W. F. Bason
Richmond [Virginia]	Nov. 26, 1862	Jefferson Davis
Wilmington	Nov. 26, 1862	Stephen D. Wallace
Raleigh	Nov. 26, 1862	Charles W. Garrett
Warrenton	Nov. 26, 1862	S. P. Arrington
Goldsboro	Nov. 27, 1862	John D. Whitford
————————	Nov. 27, [18]62	William H. Oliver
Wilmington	Nov. 28, 1862	Oscar G. Parsley
New Bern	Nov. 28, 1862	Asa I. Smith
Iredell Co[unty]	Nov. 29, 1862	Jamima A. Thomas
Morganton	Nov. 30, 1862	Augustus S. Merrimon
Hanover Junction, Virginia	Dec. 1, 1862	Joseph R. Blanton
Hendersonville	Dec. 1, 1862	S. W. Taylor
Richmond [Virginia]	Dec. 1, 1862	Abraham C. Myers
Richmond, Virginia	Dec. 3, 1862	James A. Seddon
Morganton	Dec. 4, 1862	Tod R. Caldwell
Marion	Dec. 6, 1862	Sidney B. Erwin
Wilmington	Dec. 6, 1862	Duncan K. McRae
Wilmington	Dec. 6, 1862	John McLaurin
Wilmington	Dec. 6, 1862	W. H. C. Whiting
Cypress Creek	Dec. 7, 1862	Sarah F. Smith
Wilkes County	Dec. 7, 1862	William N. Pierce
Moorsboro	Dec. 7, 1862	W. B. Lovelace
Richmond [Virginia]	Dec. 8, 1862	Abraham C. Myers
[Burke County]	Dec. 8, 1862	S. C. Wilson and Others
Flat Rock	Dec. 8, 1862	Henry T. Farmer
Fredericksburg, Virginia	Dec. 9, 1862	Robert H. Gray
Richmond, Virginia	Dec. 10, 1862	John A. Campbell
Richmond [Virginia]	Dec. 10, [1862]	Duncan K. McRae
Edenton	Dec. [?], 1862	Catherine White
Edenton	Dec. 12, 1862	R. S. Mitchell
Fort Fisher	Dec. 12, 1862	George Tait
New Garden	Dec. 13, 1862	Nereus Mendenhall
Jefferson	Dec. 13, 1862	Alexander Dickson
Richmond, Virginia	Dec. 15, 1862	William P. Johnston
Ashe County	Dec. 15, 1862	J. A. Reves
Richmond [Virginia]	Dec. 18, 1862	S. Cooper
Fredericksburg [Virginia]	Dec. 19, 1862	Hamilton C. Jones, Jr.
Monroe	Dec. 19, 1862	George Richards
Fredericksburg, Virginia	Dec. 20, [18]62	John F. Miller
Burnsville	Dec. 26, 1862	John W. McElroy
Lumberton	Dec. 26, 1862	Giles Leitch
Richmond, Virginia	[Dec. 27, 1862]	James A. Seddon
Fredericksburg, Virginia	Dec. 28, 1862	James R. Waugh
Camp French	Dec. 29, 1862	Thomas Lilly
Palermo	Dec. 31, 1862	James G. Ramsay
Drewry's Bluff [Virginia]	Dec. [?], 1862	Officers of Second N. C. Battalion

Miscellaneous Documents Printed in this Volume

LETTERS

By	Place	Date	Written to
David Coleman	Asheville	Aug. 22, 1859	James F. E. Hardy John W. Woodfin
David Coleman	_____	[Aug. 22, 1859]	John W. Woodfin
Washington M. Hardy	Asheville	Aug. 25, 1859	John D. Hyman

PROCLAMATIONS

[Raleigh]	[Sept. 18, 1862]
Raleigh	Oct. 15, 1862
[Raleigh]	[Nov. 15, 1862]
[Raleigh]	[Nov. 26, 1862]
[Raleigh]	[Dec. 26, 1862]

MEMORANDUM

Place	Date	Written to
Raleigh	[Nov. 10, 1862]	John White

List of Operatives at the C. S. Armory, Asheville

LIST OF ILLUSTRATIONS

SYMBOLS

A. L. S. Autograph Letter Signed   L. S. Letter Signed

ZEBULON BAIRD VANCE

There is much in the race we spring from, affecting both the individual and the community. The physical and mental traits we derive from our ancestors are not more marked and important in directing our destinies than are the prejudices, aspirations and traditions we drink in from childhood. No profound observer of human nature will ever estimate the capacities or conduct of a people without first looking at their genealogical table and noting the blood that flows in their veins.[1]

The blood that flowed in the veins of Zeb Vance is historically traceable for several generations before his birth. According to a mixture of genealogy and tradition common among ancestor-conscious American families, the Vance family, then known as Vans and DeVaux, was of Norman origin. But the more proximate and much more reliable historical evidence confines the blood that flowed in Vance's veins to the Scotch-Irish, German, and Scottish pioneers who settled among the hills and valleys of western North Carolina, some of them just before and some of them just after the War of the Revolution.[2]

The Scotch-Irish strain was represented by the first American Vance, Andrew, a son of John Vance of Ireland, who migrated to Pennsylvania early in the eighteenth century. Andrew's son, Samuel Vance, was born in Ireland but about 1743 moved to Frederick County, Virginia, where he was living near Winchester when David, the eldest of his five sons, was born in 1745. Just before the Revolution both father and son left Frederick County and moved southward, Samuel to Washington County, near Abingdon, Virginia, and David to that part of Rowan County, North Carolina, which afterwards became Burke County, where he settled along the upper reaches of the Catawba River, near the future town of Morganton, and became the progenitor of the Vance family in North Carolina.[3]

The German element in Zeb Vance's ancestry is represented by Priscilla Brank, a daughter of Robert Brank, who also had settled along the Catawba. Priscilla Brank was born in Rowan County in 1756, was married to David Vance in Burke County about 1775, bore her husband eight children, and died in 1836. She was a

[1] Zebulon B. Vance, *Sketches of North Carolina* (Norfolk, 1875), p. 19 (cited hereafter as Vance, *Sketches*).

[2] Clement Dowd, *Life of Zebulon B. Vance* (Charlotte, 1897), chap. I (written by Robert B. Vance, brother of Zebulon Vance), *passim* (cited hereafter as Dowd, *Life of Vance*).

[3] There is substantial genealogical material on the Vance family in Colonel Allen T. Davidson and General Theodore F. Davidson Papers, State Department of Archives and History, Raleigh, N. C. (cited hereafter as Davidson Papers). Additional family material in the form of a typescript entitled "The Vance Family," compiled in 1929 by Anne Plummer Johnston, has been kindly furnished me by Mrs. Zeb. Vance of Macon, Georgia, through the co-operation of her relatives in Pineola, N. C.

quiet, soft-spoken lady whose son thought her chief qualities to have been humility, piety, and charity.[4]

David Vance was following his twin professions of surveyor and teacher when the Revolution began. Embracing the cause of the colonies with enthusiasm, in 1776 he was commissioned an ensign in the Second Regiment of the North Carolina Continental Line, was later promoted to a lieutenancy, served under Washington at Brandywine, Germantown, and Monmouth, and shivered and starved through that dreary winter of 1777-1778 at Valley Forge. In 1778 he was ordered to return to North Carolina, where during the campaigns of 1780 and 1781 he was constantly engaged in the partisan warfare which characterized the struggle on the southern frontier. The climax of his service came at King's Mountain, where he commanded a company, and of which he afterwards wrote an interesting account.[5]

After the close of the Revolution David Vance bore a useful and conspicuous part in public service. In 1786, 1790, and 1791, he represented Burke County in the General Assembly of North Carolina. Sometime before 1790 he moved across the Blue Ridge mountain range and settled in the little valley of Reems Creek, about a dozen miles north of what was soon to become the town of Asheville in a new county, Buncombe, which he had helped to create as a member of the legislature and of which he became the first clerk of court. Here he followed his profession of surveyor in addition to his farming activities, became Colonel of the Militia, and acquired large and valuable tracts of land. On the Reems Creek tract of 898 acres he erected a simple farmhouse in which he lived with his family of eight children until his death in 1813.[6]

The second son of David and Priscilla Vance, David II, succeeded to the name, the virtues, and the residence of his father. Although he enlisted in the War of 1812 he saw no active service in it and, except for this incident, lived the quiet life of a farmer and merchant. His death in 1844, at the age of fifty-two, deprived his seven living children of his care and guidance during the most formative years of their lives and imposed the grave task of direct-

---

[4] David Vance II to his sister, Mrs. Jane Davidson, February 3, 1836, Z. B. Vance Papers, State Department of Archives and History, Raleigh, N. C. (cited hereafter as Z. B. Vance Papers); A. T. Davidson to R. B. Davidson, October 15, 1890, Davidson Papers. The will of Priscilla Brank Vance, dated May 2, and October 7, 1835, is on file in Records of Wills, Buncombe County, Book A, pp. 38-40.

[5] John Preston Arthur, *Western North Carolina: A History (From 1730 to 1913)* (Raleigh, 1914), p. 99 (cited hereafter as Arthur, *Western North Carolina*); David Vance, *Narrative of the Battle of King's Mountain* (Greensboro, 1891) (cited hereafter as Vance, *Narrative*).

[6] David Vance II to his sister, Jean Vance Davidson, February 7, 1813, Davidson Papers; Theodore F. Davidson's sketch of David Vance in Vance, *Narrative*, pp. 41-50.

ing their education and shaping their characters upon their mother.

It is the unanimous testimony of all who knew her that Mira Margaret Baird was a remarkable woman.[7] Her father, Zebulon Baird, was a Scottish trader who came to Buncombe County in the summer of 1793 and who remained prominent in both business and politics until his death in 1827. Her mother was Hannah Erwin of Burke County, whose father was also locally prominent in politics and the first clerk of court of Burke County. The Bairds were noted for their ready wit and their fine business qualities, and these appeared in a notable degree in the mother of Zebulon Baird Vance. Though her formal education was limited, she studiously cultivated her mind and taste by reading and she fostered in her children a literary taste which was steadily developed by her habit of reading aloud in the family circle, where her natural elocution and her constant and kindly humor elevated these sessions into eloquence. Married to David Vance on January 2, 1825, she bore him eight children and, after nineteen years of married life, was left a widow with a large family and no means of support save a mountain farm in which she had nothing but dower in a much-embarrassed estate. Yet, as her distinguished son summarized it at the time of her death in 1878, "with this she reared respectably and educated tolerably all of them, not only without debt but actually increasing her property."[8]

If, as Zeb Vance wrote in 1875, "there is much in the race we spring from," what were the qualities of mind and character which he inherited from his own immediate ancestors? Certainly his paternal ancestors contributed solid qualities of character later in evidence in their distinguished grandson. They were characters of impressive personality, practical common sense, love of learning, and deep piety. They furnished to him a family tradition of courage and conviction, intensity of purpose, vigor of intellect, and above all that spirit of democracy which marked his intellectual and moral character throughout his life. From the Bairds he got his native wit and sparkle, his dynamic personality which fascinated and captured his own generation. From his mother he received whatever of business acumen and sense of family solidarity he displayed in later life. Her kindly humor was passed on, enhanced, in her son. Her love of reading and

---

[7] *Memoir of Mrs. Margarett M. Vance, and Mrs. Harriette Espy Vance* (Raleigh, 1878) (cited hereafter as *Memoir*); R. B. Vance in Dowd, *Life of Vance*, pp. 8-9. In the *Memoir* the name of Zebulon B. Vance's mother is given as cited, but in her will, dated September 7, 1878, she is Mira Margaret Vance. Record of Wills, Madison County, pp. 56-57, the courthouse at Marshall, N. C.

[8] Z. B. Vance to Cornelia P. Spencer, October, 21, 1878, Cornelia Phillips Spencer Papers, State Department of Archives and History, Raleigh, N. C. (cited hereafter as Spencer Papers).

her taste for literature was manifested in him throughout his life.
From both sides he inherited a family tradition worthy of his
own sober pride. If there were not the refinements and outward
manifestations of culture which may have been found in greater
degree in the more aristocratic east, there were excellent tastes
and elevated instincts which a frontier environment could never
entirely obliterate. Above all there was received from both sides
of the family a sense of public duty and a tradition of public
service. His immediate ancestors had served thirteen terms in
the North Carolina House of Commons and six terms in the
North Carolina Senate. His two grandfathers had served for more
than a score of years as the first clerks of court of their respective
counties. In addition, his ancestors had enlisted in both wars in
which his country had been involved at the time of his own
birth; his uncle had been a United States Congressman; his
brother was to serve eight years as clerk of court and six terms
in the United States House of Representatives, as well as shorter
terms in the State legislature and in the United States Treasury
Department. The career of Zebulon Baird Vance in both war and
public office must have appeared to him but a fulfillment of
family tradition.

Zebulon Baird Vance was the third child and second son of
David Vance II and Mira Margaret Baird Vance. His birth, on
May 13, 1830, occurred in the old homestead on Reems Creek
built by his grandfather, David Vance I, about twelve miles
north of Asheville.[9] Reems Creek flowed out of the Craggy Range
to the east and emptied into the French Broad River a few miles
west of the Vance homestead. Described by Vance as "that lov[e]-
liest of all the valleys I ever beheld," his first boyhood home was
surrounded by some of the noblest mountain scenery on the
continent. Throughout his life the glory and the grandeur of
the Appalachians held Vance's imagination, inspiring many
eloquent passages in his speeches and providing the bases for a
passionate and abiding devotion to the land of his birth.[10]

Thus on a small farm, in the unrestrained freedom of a simple
mountain community, the boy Zeb, as he was always called, passed
the early years of his life. Big physically, with a strong and
healthy body, he was sociable, affable, and witty, yet possessing
a dignity that commanded respect. Stories of his humor and
mischievousness are legion, but all testify to his basic courage and
truthfulness as much as to his wit.

Very few facts about Vance's early education have come
down to the present generation; scant information that has

[9] Mira Margaret Baird Vance to Margaret Davidson, September 14, 1830, Z. B.
Vance Papers.
[10] Vance, Sketches, passim.

survived is clouded with stories of madcap pranks and schoolboy wit. His early studies appear to have been pursued in a haphazard fashion, for educational opportunities were few. Zeb's first school was at Flat Creek, about twelve miles from the Vance homestead, and he and his older brother, Robert Brank Vance, were sent there when Zeb was six years old. They boarded at Nehemiah Blackstock's and to "Uncle Miah" and his son, Robert Vance Blackstock, are historians indebted for most of the stories and anecdotes which illustrate and enliven their knowledge of the boyhood of Zeb Vance. His first teacher was Matthew Woodson, who moved his school from Flat Creek to a point a few miles from Lapland (now Marshall), whither David Vance had moved his young family about 1837. Later Zeb attended a school in that neighborhood taught by Jane Hughey. Thus, wandering from one makeshift school to another during a period of seven years, young Zeb managed somehow or other to pick up the rudiments of learning. These early studies appear to have been extremely desultory and to have had but little influence on either his mental or moral development. There is no evidence that any of his early teachers made any decided impression on his mind or character.[11]

In 1843, at the age of thirteen, Zeb was sent to Washington College, near Jonesboro, in East Tennessee. Though it was called a college, its eighty students were scarcely at today's high school level. At Washington Zeb displayed a fondness for debate and a talent for speaking, but before the year was over his studies were interrupted by the sudden death of his father, on January 14, 1844.[12] In spite of the calamity that occasioned it, Vance's withdrawal from Washington College proved a fortunate circumstance for him. Two influences destined to have important consequences in shaping his mind and character were thereby introduced into his education. One was the home teaching of his mother; the other was the University of North Carolina.

The death of David Vance II left his widow with seven children and but slender means of support.[13] Determined to subordinate everything to the education of these children, and finding it beyond her financial ability to educate them away from home, Mira Vance bought a home in Asheville, moved up the French Broad from the mountain isolation of Lapland, and put her children in school. But she herself took the chief part in directing

---

[11] R. B. Vance in Dowd, *Life of Vance*, chap. II.

[12] Howard Ernest Carr, *Washington College. A Study of an Attempt to Provide Higher Education in Eastern Tennessee* (Knoxville, 1935); David Vance *et als.* to Z. B. Vance, June 11, 1843, Z. B. Vance Papers.

[13] David Vance II did not leave a will, but the settlement of his estate is recorded in Madison County Records, Minute Docket, Book C, pp. 254, 285-286, 328, 338, during various dates in 1844.

their studies, and she was their best teacher. The basis for their instruction was the library of about 500 volumes left to the family by her husband's brother, Dr. Robert Brank Vance, together with the smaller library which had been the pride of her husband's father, David Vance I.[14] Most of the great histories of Greece and Rome were there, together with the best of English literature and, of course, the Bible. To classics such as these Zeb Vance was introduced at an early and impressionable age in the nightly gatherings around his mother's knees, and testimony as to the long-term results of his mother's instruction comes from Zeb Vance himself. "Notwithstanding her own imperfect education," he wrote in 1878, "she was extremely literary in her tastes, and fostered this inclination in her children. She was the most correct and impressive reader I ever heard off the stage; and I am satisfied that whatever of elocution I have came from her."[15]

The years between 1844, when he left Washington College, and 1851, when he entered the University of North Carolina, are the obscure years of Vance's mature life. They were also the aimless years, years he later described as bordering on being wild ones. For a brief time in this interval he clerked at a hotel at Warm Springs,[16] on the French Broad near the Tennessee line, but the worst feature of most of the period was that he had nothing to do. If ambition was never wholly abandoned during these years, it was never channeled until it was reawakened by his falling in love. Most probably he met Harriette Espy upon one of her numerous visits in Asheville at the homes of Nicholas W. Woodfin and John W. Woodfin, lawyers and famers of Asheville, who had married sisters, Eliza and Mira McDowell, respectively, of Quaker Meadows in Burke County. Their father, Captain Charles McDowell, who was a kinsman of Harriette Espy's mother, had adopted Hattie when she was left an orphan in infancy, and had reared her in the gracious surroundings of his own home as his daughter. Auburn-haired, petite, refined, and educated, her steady influence helped to change the course of Vance's life, and gave it direction and purpose at a critical time. She was a perfect balance for a talented but scatterbrained youth.[17]

In December, 1850, Vance began to read law with John W. Woodfin in private study with another student, Augustus S.

[14] The will of David Vance I, dated August 28, 1811, and January 12, 1813, is in the Davidson Papers.
[15] Z. B. Vance to Cornelia P. Spencer, October 21, 1878, Spencer Papers.
[16] Dowd, *Life of Vance*, p. 12.
[17] Franklin Brevard McDowell, *(The) Broad Axe and the Forge; or A Narrative of Unity Church Neighborhood, From Colonial Times Until the Close of the Confederate War* (Charlotte, 1897), p. 5.

Merrimon, an able and aspiring mountain boy whose ambitions were to clash with those of Vance in later years. Vance's effort lasted only a few months, and the result was not satisfactory. In his diary Merrimon[18] pictures Zeb Vance in 1850 as "of more than ordinary talent," manly, gentlemanly, and "full of life and fun." If Merrimon, sober and literal-minded as he was, could not imagine how "some men can drink and loaf about the streets," thinking it contrary to human nature, Vance could easily believe that these habits were a part of human nature itself. Unable to resist the allurements of the village loafers whose delight in Zeb's company outweighed their sympathy with his ambitions, Vance found it impossible to concentrate on his studies. From the prospect of failure he was rescued by the spurs of ambition and of love. In the spring of 1851, after a trip to Morganton to see Hattie Espy, he made up his mind to turn from his idle habits, shake off his former associations, and seek admission to the University of North Carolina. Financial difficulties seemed to interfere, but in a manly letter to President David L. Swain, a former schoolmate sweetheart of his mother, he successfully applied for a loan to finance one year at the University, where he could take a partial course and at the same time pursue legal studies conducted by Judges William H. Battle and Samuel F. Phillips. So it was that, in July, 1851, Vance, wearing "home-made shoes and clothes about 3 inches between pants and shoes showing his hairy ankles," appeared in Chapel Hill.[19]

From the very first he adhered faithfully to his resolution to stay out of trouble and apply himself to his studies. There are numerous stories of his wit and popularity, as well as of amusingly mischievous incidents, but there is plenty of solid evidence to show that he but stated the truth when he wrote his cousin: "But the scales have fallen from my eyes John, and I have taken to real hard confinement & study."[20] Although never a brilliant scholar, he was endowed with a mind of "wonderful quickness and brightness," with keen perception, a retentive memory, and remarkable powers of concentration. In the Dialectic Society he was introduced to parliamentary procedure and gained experience in the arts of debate and the management of men. In these activities he soon developed a natural propensity for repartee, an aptness of illustration, and an eloquence of speech that made

[18] Augustus Summerfield Merrimon, *A Memoir: Augustus Summerfield Merrimon* (n.d., n.p.), December 5, 1850, through July 27, 1851 (cited hereafter as Merrimon, *A Memoir*).

[19] Kemp Plummer Battle in Dowd, *Life of Vance*, chap. III.

[20] Z. B. Vance to John Mitchell Davidson, September 14, 1851, a copy, Z. B. Vance Papers.

him a formidable adversary for the most experienced debaters in any forum.[21]

But the year spent at the University of North Carolina did much more for Vance than prepare him for law and politics. It introduced him to a world of larger vision and broader culture than any he had previously known, and his active mind and spirit were quick to respond to its influences. The faculty of the University, though small in number, was strong in ability, scholarship, and force of character. The contact between its members and the students was personal and intimate. For Dr. Elisha Mitchell he conceived a genuine affection and always spoke of him as his "dear friend." He became intimate with the family of Dr. James Phillips, professor of mathematics, with whose sons, Samuel and Charles, and daughter, Cornelia, afterwards Mrs. James M. Spencer, he formed ties of friendship which continued throughout their lives. In the family of Judge Battle, Vance found two young men about his own age to whom he became bound by the closest ties of sympathy and affection. They were Kemp P. Battle and his brother Richard—the former was throughout life his personal friend and adviser; the latter was his personal secretary during part of the war governorship and the one who made the memorial address on Vance at the dedication of the Raleigh monument in 1900.[22] But of all Vance's associations at Chapel Hill the most important was his friendship with the President, David L. Swain. The ground for their intimacy was already well prepared. Both were natives of Buncombe County and in both local attachments were strongly developed, and their families had long been neighbors. The friendship formed between the two, founded as it was on mutual respect and affection, was deep and abiding, and is best expressed in the eloquent words which shine through the Memorial Oration on Swain which Vance delivered at the University after Swain's death.[23] Years after his student days, in a crisis in his own career and in the life of the State whose executive he then was, Vance wrote: "I feel, Sir, in many respects as a son towards you. . . ."[24] This was the basis of Vance's feeling that it was an honor for himself that

---

[21] Reminiscences of numerous college mates are recorded in the Battle Family Papers, Southern Historical Collection, University of North Carolina, Chapel Hill, N. C., under 1896 dates. See specifically J. J. Slade to K. P. Battle, December 7, 1896, J. W. Wilson to K. P. Battle, December 8, 1896, and Charles Phillips to K. P. Battle, December 11, 1896.

[22] Richard H. Battle, (Address at) *The Ceremonies Attending the Unveiling of the Bronze Statue of Zeb. B. Vance, L. L. D., in Capitol Square, Raleigh, N. C., August 22, 1900* (Raleigh, 1900) (cited hereafter as Battle, Address).

[23] Zebulon B. Vance, *Life and Character of Hon. David L. Swain* . . . (Durham, 1878) (cited hereafter as Vance, *Swain*).

[24] Z. B. Vance to David L. Swain, January 2, 1864, David L. Swain Papers, State Department of Archives and History, Raleigh, N. C.

he was allowed "to be on terms of confidential intimacy with him from my first entrance into the University until his death."[25] How often must Vance have echoed the sentiment he expressed to Mrs. Spencer as he prepared to take his seat in the United States Senate in 1879: "I have often thanked God for leading my steps when a youth to Chapel Hill where I formed such lasting friendships as have been a blessing to my life. . . . The thing that has been of the most benefit to me all my life is the fact that I was a student at the University of North Carolina."[26]

His law studies had progressed so well that by the time of the Christmas holidays he was able to go to Raleigh and obtain from the Supreme Court his license to practice in the county courts. This timing was fortunate for him, for in the spring of 1852 there occurred a vacancy in the solicitorship of Buncombe County, and Vance's friends urged his election to the vacancy. His competitor was his erstwhile fellow law student, Augustus S. Merrimon. On March 29, 1852, at a meeting of the Court of Pleas and Quarter Sessions at Asheville, Zeb Vance was elected to his first public office. The Court was composed of friends and neighbors of his family and it chose him by a vote of eleven to eight. The next day Vance qualified as attorney and was sworn in as solicitor.[27] His duties were not only to prosecute offenders against the criminal law but also to advise the justices in their management of the county's finances. His public career had begun with ambition's first reward.

But ambition had been only one of the twin spurs which had prodded Vance to serious study. The other spur was love and it, too, was soon rewarded. On August 3, 1853, at Quaker Meadows, near Morganton, within sight of the home of his great-grandfather Brank and near the spot where his grandfather David Vance I had lived, Zeb Vance was married to Harriette Espy. Two years Vance's junior, Hattie Espy was the daughter of Rev. Thomas Espy, a Presbyterian minister, and his wife, Sarah Louise Tate of Burke County, both of whom died before the child was two years of age. "Slight, erect and graceful in figure, with much vivacity and sweetness of manner, and an unusual strength and quickness of mind," Hattie's chief characteristics were unaffected piety, simple, unquestioning faith, steadfastness of principle, and devotion to duty. From her father she inherited a deeply religious nature and from early childhood she was a

---

[25] Vance, *Swain*, p. 13.

[26] Z. B. Vance to Cornelia P. Spencer, quoted in *The University of North Carolina Record*, No. 18, February, 1903.

[27] Minutes of the Court of Pleas and Quarter Sessions, Clerk's Office, Buncombe County Courthouse, Asheville, N. C., Minute Docket, Book C, p. 635, March 29, 30, 1852.

devout, faithful, and orthodox member of the Presbyterian church. Though naturally high-spirited and quick-tempered, she bore through all her life great physical suffering with uncomplaining resignation to the will of Providence. Utterly devoted to "Husband," as she called Zeb, she had the happy faculty of inspiring love and affection in all with whom she came in intimate contact.[28]

Receiving his Superior Court license in 1853, Vance began his law practice before the courts of the Seventh Judicial District, an extensive circuit composed of thirteen large mountain counties, stretching from Cleveland and Burke on the east to the Tennessee line on the west. In this thinly settled region, without industrial enterprise or lucrative commerce, money was scarce, business was dull, and a lawyer's fees were "trifling." Not a single county in the district yielded enough business to support a bar and all the lawyers, therefore, old and young alike, despite the hardships, discomforts, and dangers, rode the circuit regularly, attending both the County Courts and the Superior Courts. But to Vance this arduous labor, though attended with meager financial reward, had attractions of another sort: Court days were occasions when the people of the counties came together to trade, exchange news, and above all to talk politics, and the lawyer who was ambitious of political preferment found it advantageous to attend and mingle freely with the people.

The first Superior Court session which Vance attended began at Asheville in October, 1853. For almost five years, or until he entered Congress in 1858, Vance rode this circuit faithfully. In the Superior Courts precision and dignity usually prevailed, but in the County Courts, which alternated with the Superior Courts, it was often an unseemly scramble for the ear of the court and the verdict of the jury, in which ambitious lawyers seized every opportunity to deliver stirring stump speeches on current political topics. Vance reveled in these conditions and largely by means of his genius for popularity he laid the basis for an enduring public career.[29]

In the Seventh Judicial Circuit Vance came into contact with a strong and vigorous bar. Among a dozen older leaders the Woodfin brothers, John Baxter, W. W. Avery, and Burgess S. Gaither were the most prominent. About Vance's age was a younger group of great professional promise, including Marcus

---

[28] *Memoir*. Most of this description is drawn from an article in the *Memoir* by Cornelia Phillips Spencer.

[29] Merrimon, *A Memoir*, includes many descriptive comments on the courts of this circuit during the decade of the 'fifties. See also Arthur, *Western North Carolina*, chap. XV, and MS. address of Z. B. Vance before the Georgetown College Law School, 1884, which is in the handwriting of Mrs. Vance with interlineations by Vance himself, Z. B. Vance Papers.

Erwin, David Coleman and, of course, Augustus S. Merrimon, who was beyond question Vance's ablest and most successful rival. Most of these men were more profound students of the law than was Vance, but he possessed other qualities which none of these could match. With the uncultured crowds that frequented the courts and from which the juries were drawn, ready wit, broad humor, sharp invective, apposite anecdote, and boisterous eloquence were indispensable to success, and in the use of these weapons none of his contemporaries could equal Zeb Vance. Years later he confessed that he had cultivated "the rough and unpolished ways which I so early affected as stepping stones to popularity among a rude mountain people."[30]

During the first five years of his career at the bar Vance practiced alone but, in anticipation of a political career in which he was becoming more and more interested, in 1857 he formed a partnership with William Caleb Brown which continued until Vance entered the Confederate Army in 1861.[31] After the War, when Vance moved to Charlotte, he formed a partnership with General Robert D. Johnston and Major Clement Dowd. General Johnston soon withdrew and the firm became Vance and Dowd. It so continued until 1872 when Dowd withdrew and Vance entered into partnership with Armistead Burwell. Vance's legal career came to an end in 1876 with his third election to the governorship, so that he was in active practice for only about fifteen of the forty-two years of his mature life.

Of Vance as a lawyer a layman hesitates to write. It is difficult to form a correct estimate of a lawyer at best; in the case of Vance it is particularly so. None of his addresses to juries or his arguments before courts has been preserved, and the records of important cases in which he appeared are too meager to be of much service. His reputation as a lawyer, therefore, rests largely upon tradition, and tradition concerns itself so exclusively with the superficialities of his career at the bar as to be almost worthless.

Nevertheless some conclusions can be drawn with fair certainty. The first is that to Vance the profession of the law was never a passion; it was primarily a preparation for politics, which was a passion. Law, therefore, never called forth the fullest exertion of his powers. Vance never had the ambitions of a lawyer; he never yearned, as did most lawyers, for a place on the bench as the highest reward of his profession. One cannot imagine him as

[30] Z. B. Vance to Cornelia P. Spencer, February 27, 1869, Spencer Papers.
[31] The William Caleb Brown Notebooks and Diaries in the W. Vance Brown Papers, State Department of Archives and History, Raleigh, N. C., furnish many details of the law partnership.

a judge. Neither office work nor Supreme Court practice ever made any appeal to his interest or taste. These matters took too much technical and precise learning and he could not endure such fetters; hence he would attend the County Courts and wrestle with the juries and send his partner to the Supreme Court. Nevertheless it can be asserted as a second certainty that Vance held an exalted opinion of law as a profession in itself. He thought there were "no grand civic displays in history more impressive than those presented by great events in legal transactions," and that such incidents represented "the summit of human glory" for civilized mankind.[32]

But it will not do to dismiss Vance as an effective lawyer. The trustworthy testimony of one who was his partner for six years admits that he was not a methodical student and certainly never a legal scholar, but insists that Vance had a competent knowledge of the law, was thoroughly acquainted with its fundamental principles, and was quite capable of sustaining a legal argument. If he was not always diligent in the preparation of cases, when the trial of a case had once begun he was all attention. Nothing escaped him; he literally absorbed the testimony of witnesses, even to the smallest details. Moreover, when posted on a case, Vance talked like a lawyer, recalling definitions and decisions with great facility and precision. But it was before the jury rather than before the judge that Vance's wonderful personal charm, his exhaustless flow of wit and humor, his pointed repartee, his rugged eloquence, and his remarkable power of arraying evidence and interpreting facts, of penetrating and laying bare hidden human motives, and of analyzing character, came into full and sometimes spectacular display. He understood people better than he understood the law; he knew the mental habits and points of view of his countrymen who composed the juries. He never addressed them as inferiors or as a subordinate part of the machinery of the court, but as "the great bulwark of personal rights and as the fortress and shield of the weak and the unfortunate." He appears to have had some of the qualities to have made a great lawyer—especially a great trial lawyer—but politics lured him away at an early age, and the law took a back seat.[33] He returned to it only when the verdict of bullets or of ballots separated him from his real profession—politics.

When Vance actively entered State politics in 1854 the party situation was very confused. Throughout the years of his youth—from 1836 to 1850—the Whig Party held political supremacy in

---

[32] Z. B. Vance, Georgetown College Address, Z. B. Vance Papers.
[33] The best account of Vance as a lawyer is by one of his law partners, Clement Dowd, in Dowd, *Life of Vance*, chap. IX.

North Carolina, but by 1854 it was fast approaching dissolution.[34] It had been in power too long for its own good and was suffering from the arrogance of continual success. Out of touch with the "plain people," it lacked the solid support of grass roots foundations in an age of expanding democracy.[35] The issues of free and equal suffrage and of the basis of representation began the split of the Party into factions; the question of the extension of slavery into the territories completed the dissolution. Thus 1854 found the Democrats united, aggressive, confident; the Whigs divided, bewildered, discouraged. A steady exodus of two classes of Whigs from the Party was continuing: those uneasy about southern interests, who followed the example of Thomas L. Clingman, representative in Congress from the mountain district who abandoned the Whig Party in 1852, and carried the mountain district, for twenty years a Whig stronghold, with him into the Democratic fold; and young men who resented the domination of the Whig Party by the old leaders and anticipated greater opportunities for political advancement in the more open atmosphere of the Democratic Party.[36]

For an ambitious young politician, seeking mere personal advancement, therefore, the Whig Party of 1854 had few inducements to offer. Yet it was to the Whig Party that Vance committed his political fortunes, though under no illusions as to the future of the Party. Although he fully endorsed its policies as to State affairs, he was chiefly attracted to it because of its strong Union proclivities. Convinced that the Democratic Party fostered a dangerous sectionalism, he was firm in his belief that he was "doing God a service"[37] in opposing it. It was a matter of principle that made Zeb Vance a Whig in 1854.

Running "as a regular built, old fashioned Whig,"[38] therefore, Vance announced his candidacy for the House of Commons in the *Asheville News* of April 27, 1854, more than three months before election day. His opponent was Daniel Reynolds, an elderly man who, like Vance, was a Whig, but a Whig of a different faction. Although the two rivals were in accord on State matters they were far apart on national issues. Vance stood with his party in accepting the Compromise of 1850 as a final

[34] Raleigh *Register*, September 13, 1854; William Kenneth Boyd, *History of North Carolina*, 2 vols. (Chicago and New York, 1919), II, 288.
[35] *Asheville News*, March 2, April 27, 1854.
[36] P. K. Rounsaville to W. A. Graham, January 5, 1855, William A. Graham Papers, Southern Historical Collection, University of North Carolina, Chapel Hill, N. C. (cited hereafter as Graham Papers); Joseph Gregoire deRoulhac Hamilton, *Party Politics in North Carolina, 1835-1860* (Durham, 1916), p. 163.
[37] Z. B. Vance to David F. Caldwell, February 19, 1858, Zebulon B. Vance Papers, Duke Manuscript Collection, Duke University Library, Durham, N. C. (cited hereafter as Z. B. Vance Papers, Duke).
[38] Z. B. Vance to "Cousin Kate," September 6, 1854, Z. B. Vance Papers.

solution of the slavery question; Reynolds stood with the Democrats in advocating the Kansas-Nebraska Bill. This important difference grew in significance in view of the fact that the legislature to which they sought a seat would elect two United States senators. Prominent among the candidates was their fellow Buncombe man, Thomas L. Clingman, who hoped to draw support from the pro-slavery Whigs as well as from his new Democratic associates, who, he felt, owed him election as a reward for his abandonment of his former Whig allegiance. Reynolds announced that he would support Clingman. Thus he bid for the support of the Democrats, who then decided to put up no candidate of their own. Vance announced that as a good party man he would support the nominee of the Whig caucus. So, "hungering and thirsting after the equivocal honors of politics," Vance "put in with unparalleled impudence," [39] and, after a strenuous campaign, won the election by a vote of 688 to 579, carrying nine of the eleven precincts in the County. [40]

The legislature, which met on November 20, 1854, was certainly one of the ablest in the history of North Carolina, but the chief interest of its sessions as it affects the fortunes of Zeb Vance lies in the personal and political associations that it enabled him to form among its members, a number of whom were afterwards intimately connected with him in his public career. Chief among these were Patrick H. Winston, Jr., James Madison Leach, Samuel F. Phillips, Josiah Turner, Jr., Thomas Settle, Jr., John A. Gilmer, and, above all William A. Graham, undoubtedly the State's most distinguished citizen and who became during the War Vance's most trusted adviser.

In the legislature the Democrats were in firm control of both houses and Vance's committee appointments, with the exception of the one to the education committee, were unimportant. Two matters of the session particularly engaged his attention. One was the bill to charter the Greenville and French Broad Railroad Company; the other a bill to change the basis of the distribution of the common school fund.

Vance vigorously supported the proposal for the French Broad Railroad, which asked for no State aid but which was opposed by many on the ground that it would injure the North Carolina Railroad, and made his first speech in a legislative body in its cause. [41] As a member of the committee on education Vance was the chief spokesman for the West in its effort to change the basis of distribution of the common school fund from a federal popula-

---

[39] Z. B. Vance to "Cousin Kate," September 6, 1854, Z. B. Vance Papers.

[40] *Asheville News,* August 10, 1854.

[41] Raleigh *Register,* January 17, 1855; *Private Laws of North Carolina, 1854-'55,* chap. 229 (cited hereafter as *Laws of N. C.,* or as *Public Laws of N. C.,* and as *Private Laws of N. C.,* with appropriate dates).

tion basis to a white population basis. His attempt to change the basis met with failure because the slaveholding counties, whether Whig or Democratic, were unalterably opposed.[42]

The legislature of 1854 also debated the great national issue of slavery in the territories, and Vance's earliest position with regard to this question is revealed. On November 26, 1854, Thomas Settle, Jr., a Democrat, introduced a series of resolutions setting forth the extreme southern position on the question. The resolutions declared that the Kansas-Nebraska Bill embraced "the true principle in relation to the power of the federal government on the subject of slavery in the territories"; that on that principle "all Southern men ought to unite"; that North Carolina should "resist any further encroachments on her constitutional rights"; that the repeal of the Fugitive Slave Law, or the refusal of the federal government to enforce its execution in good faith would "amount to a virtual dissolution of the Union," which would make it the "duty of this State to take such measures as may be required for her safety and security"; that if either of these contingencies should occur during a recess of the General Assembly "the Governor be requested to convene that body, to the end that the rights of the State may be maintained." [43]

Though Vance did not participate in these resolutions by debate, his attitude on the question is revealed by his votes. A motion to table, for which he voted, having been lost, a motion to "heartily approve the course of the Senator and Representatives from this State who supported said bill [Kansas-Nebraska] as it was finally passed," was made. Although the senator thus endorsed was the Whig, George E. Badger, whom Vance was supporting for re-election, Vance voted against the motion, which, however, was adopted by a vote of 72 to 34.[44] His votes here are the first evidences of his attitude on the great questions of slavery and secession which were rapidly plunging the country into division, and it was an attitude which he consistently maintained throughout the crises of the decade. The obvious irony is that in 1876 it fell to Vance, by then a Democrat, to defend the action of North Carolina in afterwards implementing the very principles enunciated in these resolutions of Settle against their author, then running as the Republican candidate for governor against Vance.

---

[42] Raleigh *Register*, December 20, 1854.

[43] *Journals of the Senate and House of Commons of the General Assembly of the State of North Carolina, at its Session of 1854-'55* (Raleigh, 1855), pp. 59-60, November 28, 1854 (cited hereafter as *Senate Journal* and *House Journal*, with appropriate dates).

[44] *House Journal, 1854-'55*, pp. 59-60.

About the only satisfaction Vance got in 1854 was the failure of Clingman to be elected a senator.

After the 1854-1855 legislative session the Whig Party practically ceased to exist as an effective political organization. In North Carolina many Whigs went over to the Democrats on the slavery and free suffrage issues; others, unwilling to affiliate with their old political opponents, gradually came to act with the American, or Know-Nothing, Party. Vance pursued the latter course, though one shrewd Buncombe observer believed that as late as 1856 a "very large majority of our people still profess to belong to the Whig party." [45] Perhaps Vance had foreseen that this would be the only course open to the old-line Union Whigs, for in the legislature he voted against a resolution denouncing the secrecy of the Know-Nothing Party as "anti-republication and dangerous in its tendencies." [46] Consequently, from 1856 to 1860, though still calling himself a Whig, he was in full association with the Know-Nothings. Though the Party appeared to make great headway for a time, this "bastard coalition of Whigs, disaffected democrats and the odds and ends and scrapings of all parties" [47] had little more cohesion than the Whigs had possessed. Though it claimed 600 members in Asheville, there were soon many withdrawals as well as assertions that such extravagant claims were humbug.[48] But Vance's heart was somehow never in the new party, and years later he confessed that one reason why he opposed the Ku Klux Klan was that "it was a secret society, and I never belonged to but one in my life and that was the Know Nothings, and they went up as they deserved to do." [49] In the west all who opposed the Democratic Party accepted Vance as their leader in their efforts to break the hold which the Democrats, under Clingman, had gained on the mountain section.

With ambition whetted by his taste of active politics Vance, when the legislature adjourned in the spring of 1855, secured a half interest in the *Asheville Spectator,* the leading Whig paper in North Carolina, whose motto was "We join ourselves to no party that does not carry the flag and keep step to the music of the Union." Becoming co-editor with John D. Hyman, his friend and supporter in the editorial policy, he struck out directly at his Democratic opponents. Though only a copy or so of the *Spectator* while Vance was editor has survived, something is learned of its

---

[45] John D. Hyman to William A. Graham, October 8, 1856, Graham Papers.

[46] *House Journal, 1854-'55,* pp. 280-281.

[47] Haywood W. Guion to J. F. Hoke, April 5, 1855, John F. Hoke Papers, Southern Historical Collection, University of North Carolina, Chapel Hill, N. C.

[48] *Asheville News,* June 28, 1855.

[49] Quoted in the Hillsborough *Recorder* from *The Charlotte Democrat,* March 21, 1871.

policies and methods from its chief rival, the Democratic *Asheville News*.[50]

According to that journal, Vance became notorious as "a Know Nothing of 'the straitest sect' and his zeal and bitterness in advocacy of his creed,—are they not recorded in the columns of the Spectator, of which paper he has been an editor for more than a year past?" [51] The venture was neither a financial nor a political success, and Vance withdrew after his defeat in the election of 1856.

On May 24, 1856, David Coleman announced that he would seek re-election as a Democrat to the North Carolina Senate; one week later Vance announced his own candidacy as a Know-Nothing. The district was strongly Democratic and Vance's already difficult task was complicated by the taint of Know-Nothingism, an association odious to many but one which Vance found it difficult to deny, since the county convention had endorsed him as "an able champion of American principles," and since without the support of the Know-Nothings his cause was hopeless.[52] He was also on the defensive because western Whigs did not like his straight party votes on the free suffrage issue.

The campaign was conducted by a series of joint debates with Coleman, held in the rough and tumble style characteristic of the time and the section.[53] The debates turned largely upon technicalities of their votes on the free-suffrage and ad valorem issues, raised by Vance to obscure his Know-Nothing connection, but with his own party disrupted and with the Democrats strongly united Vance went down to defeat. His personal strength was nevertheless indicated by the fact that Coleman's majority was only 318, that Vance carried one of four counties in the district while John A. Gilmer, Know-Nothing candidate for governor, was defeated in all of them, and by the fact that Coleman's majority of over 700 in 1854 had been more than cut in half.[54]

The Eighth Congressional District, commonly known as the "mountain district," embraced fifteen of the western counties, including Buncombe. Regarded as a Whig stronghold for twenty years before 1853, it had since followed Clingman when he left the Whig Party for the Democratic in that year. In 1857 Clingman's re-election seemed so certain that the opposition found difficulty in inducing anyone to make the race against him. The Know-Nothing district convention in Morganton had been poorly

[50] *Asheville News*, March 15, 1855.
[51] *Asheville News*, June 5, 1856.
[52] *Asheville News*, June 5, July 31, 1856.
[53] *Asheville News*, June 26, 1856.
[54] *Asheville News*, August 13, 1856.

attended and revealed Vance's party to be weak, scattered, and without organization or leadership.[55]

Finally, about a month before the election, William J. Wilson, of Haywood County, announced himself by issuing an address in which he attacked Clingman but made himself ridiculous even to the Know-Nothings, who had been inclined to support him until he repudiated the principles of both parties. The *Spectator* of July 17 was "perfectly satisfied that the American party cannot, and will not, under any circumstances support him." The paper followed with an appeal to all who opposed Clingman and the Democrats "to vote for our good and well-tried citizen, Z. B. Vance. In doing this we will show that we are sincere in what we profess."[56] It admitted that at so late a date there could be no campaign and no chance of victory, "yet it becomes you to keep up an organization and maintain your strength, however weak your enemies may say it is."[57] The hostile *Asheville News* regarded the maneuver as "a scheme of a small clique to push Mr. Vance ahead" and "give him prominence for the future."[58]

The result was another Clingman victory,[59] this time by the largest majority he had ever won. Under the circumstances Vance could have expected no other verdict and had to take what consolation he could from having been the sacrifice to "keep up an organization" and attain "prominence for the future."

The future arrived the next year. In 1858 Clingman, after a decade in the House, reached the goal of his ambitions with an appointment to fill the unexpired term of Senator Asa Biggs. This left a vacancy in the large western district. The prospects seemed strong that the Democrats would easily elect a successor to Clingman. Their hold on the district seemed secure and, furthermore, the Know-Nothing Party of Vance and his associates was weak, being handicapped by its secrecy and suspected as to its motives. By the middle of May the details of the special election now made necessary had not been clarified: It was reported that W. W. Avery and David Coleman would run for the Democrats and that probably William F. McKesson of Burke would oppose them for the American Party. "Things touching this election however have not yet fully developed themselves. The Americans seem to have

---

[55] *Asheville News*, May 28, 1857.

[56] *Asheville Spectator* as quoted in the *Asheville News*, July 23, 1857.

[57] *Asheville Spectator* as quoted in the *Asheville News*, July 23, 1857.

[58] *Asheville News*, July 30, 1857.

[59] The vote was: Clingman 8,673, Vance 3,211, Wilson 446. Vance did not carry a single county but was strongest in Wilkes, Buncombe, and Macon. *Asheville News*, August 20, 1857.

lost their zeal and I fear that vigorous efforts will not be made to secure a member of Congress from this District."[60]

Into this confused situation Vance plunged with reckless zeal, against the advice of family and friends, many of whom regarded his effort as a joke.[61] When Coleman withdrew, the Democrats united around William Waightstill Avery, who was not only a veteran politician from a prominent and distinguished Burke family, but was an able and experienced leader in his own right, having served three terms in the House of Commons and having been Speaker of the North Carolina Senate in 1856. Democratic observers, remembering that their majority had been more than 5,000 only a year before, predicted Avery's election "beyond a peradventure." [62]

But Vance's campaign was marked by an intensity and versatility never shown before. Avery was a thoroughly equipped debater but he had to meet wit and repartee from a subtle, original, and relentless, though not always dignified, opponent. Vance, improving with each speech, denounced with persistent passion the growing secessionist tendency of Democrats and made repeated and eloquent appeals for the Union. Before the contest was over in August "a new star of the first magnitude had risen in the mountains. . . . In one way or another . . . he had, to use the language of his ardent followers, 'Set the mountains on fire,' and he confounded the Democratic leaders by carrying the district by 2,049 majority."[63] Vance could hardly be blamed for taking great pride in such an unexpected victory.[64]

The victory over Avery sent Vance to Washington in December, 1858, for the Second Session of the Thirty-fifth Congress. He went as a convinced and bitter opponent of the Democratic Party, then in control of the administration. In the very year he entered Congress he explained to a political friend how he had been reared in steadfast conservatism.

> I thus learned to oppose *democracy*, ever the antipodes of conservatism, which from its very nature drew into its embrace, the factions, the fragments, the odds & ends of every ism in the land. And from that day to the present, the sectionalism which it has engendered & fostered with paternal care, the wild, reckless, lawless, violent & dangerous spirit which characterizes it, and the reeking, loathsome corruption which has made it smell to high heaven, & a stench among the nations, has but day by day, confirmed me in the opinion that I was doing God

---

[60] Augustus S. Merrimon to David F. Caldwell, May 16, 1858, David Franklin Caldwell Papers, Southern Historical Collection, University of North Carolina, Chapel Hill, N. C.

[61] Battle, Address, p. 17.

[62] *Asheville News*, June 17, 1858.

[63] Battle, Address, pp. 17, 18.

[64] Z. B. Vance to John Evans Brown, August 22, 1859, Z. B. Vance Papers.

a service in opposing it to the full extent of my abilities! I think so yet. I believe most firmly, that the Democratic party, with some of good, combines so many of the elements of death & destruction, that it has not only already brought us to our present dangerous pass, but will eventually overthrow us entirely & irredeemably. . . . "I stand" *therefore,* opposed to Democracy, & shall so stand till democracy amends or I grow corrupt—[65]

A northern colleague confirmed this devotion when he described Vance, with whom he served on a congressional committee, as "strong in integrity, wondrous in vitality . . ." and "a strict Federalist after an intense Union pattern. His voice was never heard at Washington for disunion." [66]

On only one of the familiar and divisive public questions of the day did Vance speak during his first Congress. His first speech came on February 7, 1859, and presented orthodox conservative views on the tariff, public lands, and pensions. On the tariff question, Vance disclaimed any theoretical approach but favored raising the low rates of the existing bill because of the need for revenue. He favored retrenchment and economy, except in pensions for the veterans of the War of 1812, opposed the Homestead Bill, and argued that public lands should provide a principal source for governmental revenue.[67]

Congress had no more than adjourned in early March, 1859, before David Coleman, his old rival of 1856, announced himself as the Democratic challenger for Vance's seat. Vance now had a record to defend and some more mature awareness of the passionate sectional issues of the period. As a result his speeches were usually on a higher and more serious plane than some had been in the contest of 1858 with Avery. Coleman attacked Vance's voting record and charged him with having co-operated with the Republicans.[68] Vance vigorously defended himself in what he described as "a hot and furious canvass, twice over the district." [69] Coleman, reserved, sensitive, and dignified, was offended by Vance's excited words and gestures at Waynesville and, after Vance had won the election by a majority of 1,695, challenged him to a duel. Fortunately mutual friends were able to bring about a peaceful reconciliation.[70]

The Thirty-Sixth Congress (1859-1861), the last before the division of the Union, produced some famous political struggles

[65] Z. B. Vance to David F. Caldwell, February 19, 1858, Z. B. Vance Papers, Duke.
[66] Samuel S. Cox, *Three Decades of Federal Legislation* (Providence, 1888) pp. 93, 308.
[67] *Congressional Globe,* 35 Congress, 2 session, part II, Appendix, pp. 85-87 (February 7, 1859) (cited hereafter as *Cong. Globe,* with the appropriate identification).
[68] David Coleman to Z. B. Vance, August 16, 17, 1859, Z. B. Vance Papers.
[69] Z. B. Vance to John Evans Brown, August 22, 1859, Z. B. Vance Papers.
[70] David Coleman to Z. B. Vance, August 17, 1859, and J. F. E. Hardy and J. W. Woodfin to Z. B. Vance and David Coleman, August 22, 1859, Z. B. Vance Papers.

which were previews of the future crisis but in which Vance played only routine roles. Not only was he the youngest member and without experience but distinguished participation on committees or on the floor was precluded by his party situation. As one of twenty-seven members of the American Party, all but four of whom were from the South, he was part of a minority that only rarely could employ its mathematical position as custodian of the balance of power. There were 109 Republicans, 88 administration Democrats, and 13 anti-Lecompton Democrats. Even if the Democratic factions united they could not possibly win without the aid of the "South Americans." During the celebrated forty-four ballot struggle over the speakership Vance voted for twelve different individuals, of whom six were Americans and six were Democrats, but thirty-six of his forty-four votes were for Americans. On two occasions he spoke briefly to explain his votes for Democrats.[71] At home he was criticized for helping make possible the election of a Republican by his refusal to support the caucus nominee of the Democrats.[72]

Throughout the critical political events of 1860 Vance remained a powerful influence on behalf of Union. He welcomed the nomination of John Pool for the governorship by the Whig Convention in February on a platform of Union, and in May he attended the National Convention of the Constitutional Union Party, made up mostly of border State Old-Line Union Whigs, which resulted in the nomination of Senator Bell of Tennessee for the presidency on a similar Union plank. In the State campaign, as in the national one, no candidate openly advocated secession, but the Democrats, under the leadership of Governor Ellis, included many increasingly active secessionists.[73] In numerous public meetings Vance won a permanent reputation as a speaker of unparalleled magnetism. Especially at Salisbury, on October 11, were his efforts praised by an enthusiastic Union press.[74] Such efforts almost succeeded in carrying the State for Bell, who was defeated by Breckinridge in North Carolina by a plurality of fewer than 4,000 votes and by a majority of fewer than 1,000.[75]

The election of Lincoln was a shock to most North Carolinians. Because of it the legislature which met on November 19 was dominated by a crisis psychology. Governor John W. Ellis had been re-elected and the question of secession, especially after

---

[71] *Cong. Globe,* 36 Congress, 1 session, part I, *passim,* especially pp. 1-3, 269, 286, 348, 611, 644, 654.

[72] *Asheville News,* January 26, February 16, 1860.

[73] The best account of the 1860-1861 political crisis in North Carolina is in Joseph Carlyle Sitterson, *The Secession Movement in North Carolina* (Chapel Hill, 1939), chaps. VIII and IX (cited hereafter as Sitterson, *N. C. Secession*).

[74] Battle, Address, pp. 20-22; *Fayetteville Observer,* October 22, 1860.

[75] Sitterson, *N. C. Secession,* p. 175.

South Carolina withdrew from the Union in December, was freely discussed. Although it is probable that the majority of citizens at no time favored secession because of the election of Lincoln, the legislature, on January 29, 1861, authorized a vote of the people on the question of calling a convention to consider it.[76] Vance favored the convention because he was persuaded that the unionists would dominate it,[77] but on February 28 the convention was defeated by a majority of 651 in a total vote of 93,995. Although this was a defeat for the secessionists, their cause was not lost. The failure of the Peace Convention in Washington and the nature of Lincoln's inaugural address gave them renewed hope which events at Sumter justified.

In his ardent pleas for the Union during the winter and spring of 1860-1861 Vance never denied the legal right of secession, but only its wisdom under prevailing circumstances. The firing on Fort Sumter and Lincoln's call for troops altered the circumstances. Vividly Vance has described how he changed his plea:

> For myself, I will say that I was canvassing for the Union with all my strength; I was addressing a large and excited crowd, large numbers of whom were armed, and literally had my arm extended upward in pleading for peace and the Union of our Fathers, when the telegraphic news was announced of the firing on Sumter and [the] President's call for seventy-five thousand volunteers. When my hand came down from that impassioned gesticulation, it fell slowly and sadly by the side of a Secessionist. I immediately, with altered voice and manner, called upon the assembled multitude to volunteer, not to fight against but for South Carolina.[78]

Declining all overtures, Vance refused to be a candidate for the Confederate Congress and, "in obedience . . . to patriotic instincts," raised a military company and on May 4, two weeks before the formal secession of North Carolina, marched off to war as Captain Zeb Vance. By June the "Rough and Ready Guards" had become Company F in the Fourteenth North Carolina Regiment and was sent to Suffolk, Virginia, as a part of the defense of the vital Norfolk area.[79] At the end of August Vance was elected colonel[80] of the Twenty-Sixth North Carolina Regiment

---

[76] *Laws of N. C., 1860-61,* pp. 27-31.

[77] Z. B. Vance to G. N. Folk, January 9, 1861, Winston *Western Sentinel,* February 1, 1861.

[78] Z. B. Vance, *The Political and Social South During the War,* a lecture delivered before the Andrew Post, No. 15, of the Grand Army, in Boston, December 8, 1886 (cited hereafter as Vance, *Political and Social South*). Also quoted in Dowd, *Life of Vance,* p. 441.

[79] R. B. Vance in Dowd, *Life of Vance,* chap. VI; Z. B. Vance to Mrs. Z. B. Vance, June 19, 29, July 21, 1861, Z. B. Vance Papers.

[80] North Carolina Adjutant General James G. Martin to Z. B. Vance, August 27, 1861, War Department Collection of Confederate Records, Office of the Secretary of War, Letters Received, National Archives, Washington, D. C. (cited hereafter as War Department Collection of Confederate Records, National Archives, Washington, D. C.).

and took command of it in September at Fort Macon, on Beaufort Inlet, then threatened with attack after a successful Federal penetration of the North Carolina sounds by the capture of Fort Hatteras in August.[81] For nearly six months the routine of drill and training went on amid sickness, boredom, and frequent rumors of enemy invasion.[82] The fall of Roanoke Island in February, 1862, caused the withdrawal of the Twenty-Sixth to New Bern,[83] where it joined six other regiments under the command of Brigadier General L. O'B. Branch, a former colleague of Vance in Congress, though a Democrat and an original secessionist.

The battle of New Bern,[84] fought on March 14, 1862, was Vance's first experience in ordeal by combat. Along the Neuse River for ten miles below the town, Branch had begun fortifications to protect the town from an assault from the River, and had also begun two defense lines from which to meet any land attack from troops landed below the forts. But the Federal commander, Brigadier General Ambrose E. Burnside, outflanked the first line by landing about 11,000 men between the two lines, thus forcing Branch to abandon the first and stronger defensive position. In the battle that followed at the second line Vance's regiment occupied the extreme right flank of the Confederate position, between the railroad and the swamp and just behind Bullen's Branch and about 150 yards to the rear of the Confederate left wing between the River and the railroad.

The battle began with an assault by five Federal regiments against the main Confederate line between the River and the railroad, and this was soon followed by the attacks of four Federal regiments upon Vance's right wing. By 8:30 A.M. his front was engaged all along his line. During the next four hours every Federal attempt to pierce his works was repulsed, but the Fed-

[81] Daniel Harvey Hill, *Bethel to Sharpsburg*, 2 vols. (Raleigh, 1926), I, chaps. VI and VII give adequate descriptions of the military situation in North Carolina (cited hereafter as Hill, *Bethel to Sharpsburg*).

[82] Z. B. Vance to Mrs. Z. B. Vance, September 15, October 13, 17, 1861, Z. B. Vance Papers.

[83] Z. B. Vance to Allen T. Davidson, March 4, 1862, War Department Collection of Confederate Records, National Archives, Washington D. C.; Hill, *Bethel to Sharpsburg*, I, 217-235.

[84] In addition to the general account of the battle in Hill, *Bethel to Sharpsburg*, I, 217-235, this account is taken from primary sources which include, Z. B. Vance to Mrs. Z. B. Vance, March 20, 1862, Z. B. Vance Papers and Vance's official report, dated March 17, 1862, in *The War of the Rebellion: A Complilation of the Official Records of the Union and Confederate Armies* (128 vols., Washington, 1880-1901), Ser. I, Vol. IX, 254-257 (cited hereafter as *O. R.*, with serial and volume numbers). The official reports of General Branch and other Confederate and Union officers are in the same volume.

erals found a weakness in the unprotected center, where the
line dropped back 150 yards along the railroad and where Branch
had put only untrained militia, and by 11:00 A.M. Union forces
had penetrated this gap and split the Confederate line. Unaware
of this disaster for more than an hour after it had occurred,
Vance's wing fought on until noon. He received no order to retreat and only when he learned that the entire Confederate left
wing had collapsed and was in full retreat toward the town did
he order his men out of the works and begin the five-mile retreat
to the bridges over the Trent. But the bridges were in flames.
Vance struck left up the Trent and managed to get most of his
men to safety by crossing Bryce's Creek and marching them on
to Kinston.

Unquestionably Vance and his regiment had behaved well.
With some help from the Thirty-Third, his regiment had fought
four Federal regiments to a standstill for more than four hours,
and had been forced to retreat only when another section of the
line had collapsed. It had inflicted more casualties upon the enemy
than had any other unit, and was the last unit of Confederate
troops to leave the field. He became something of a hero throughout the State, especially in Conservative newspapers, and recruits
flocked to his unit.[85]

During the spring at Kinston his regiment re-enlisted for the
War and he was re-elected colonel. He tried to raise a legion,
thinking this would make him a general, but he had trouble
getting leave to recruit the troops and claimed that Confederate
authorities in Raleigh and Richmond blocked his efforts because
they did not desire a popular general whose politics differed from
their own.[86] Certainly Vance himself did not forget politics in
the excitement of war.

Out of the confusion in Kinston a reorganization was soon
affected and Vance's regiment was placed in a new brigade under
Brigadier General Robert Ransom, a strict disciplinarian, under
whom the Twenty-Sixth served so long as Vance was connected
with it. The brigade was ordered to Richmond on June 20 and
reported to Major General Benjamin Huger on the Williamsburg
Road on June 25, as the Seven Days' Battles were about to open.
Picket duty and light skirmishing were its lot for a few days, but

---

[85] Z. B. Vance to Mrs. Z. B. Vance, March 23, 1862, Z. B. Vance Papers.

[86] Z. B. Vance to the Secretary of War, April 3, May 2, 17, 1862, War Department Collection of Confederate Records, National Archives, Washington, D. C.;
J. G. Martin to Z. B. Vance, April 23, May 5, 1862, Adjutant General's Department, Letter Book, N. C. Troops, 1862-1864, State Department of Archives and
History, Raleigh, N. C.

the climax of the campaign, and of Vance's military career, came late on the hot afternoon of July 1 at Malvern Hill, where George B. McClellan seemed about to escape Lee. As General John Magruder sought to drive the Yankees from their strong position he called on Ransom's brigade. With Huger's approval, the brigade swung into line as the last of five regiments on the right and "pushed forward under as fearful fire as mind can conceive." Brought into line under fire, the brigade advanced to within 100 yards of the Federal batteries when the enemy wheeled and, as Ransom reported, "opened upon us a perfect sheet of fire from musketry and the batteries. We steadily advanced to within 20 yards of the guns. The enemy had concentrated his force to meet us. Our onward movement was checked, the line wavered, and fell back before a fire the intensity of which is beyond description. . . . The behavior of all was highly creditable. I believe we failed to take the batteries from two causes—want of support and darkness." The loss to the brigade was extremely heavy—499 men—but Vance came through it all without a scratch.[87]

The balance sheet on Vance as a military leader has definite entries on each side. Among the debits are his restlessness and impetuosity, as well as his obvious ignorance of military affairs. More serious was his insatiable proclivity for mixing politics and war, which embarrassed the military and offended the politicians. He criticized political leaders and encouraged his friends to do the same. His patriotism could not be doubted, but he was discouraged and disappointed because he was convinced that his political enemies were getting all the good offices and that Old Union men were discriminated against continually. On the credit side of the ledger should be cited Vance's contagious good humor, a keen and sincere sympathy with his men, and an ability to inspire them with the belief that he had confidence in them. He was a cool and courageous leader. Most important of all, Vance learned that effective war is made not by brave men and grand charges alone, but by food, medicine, clothes, arms, and supplies of all sorts. He learned how necessary co-operation is to achievement. He was a better war governor for having been a soldier.

Even the realities of war never took Vance's mind far from politics or from his dissatisfaction with public affairs. The anti-administration party, now calling itself Conservative, had been greatly strengthened by the course of public events in North Carolina. The defeat at New Bern, coming after the loss of Hatteras and Roanoke Island, caused widespread criticism of the conduct of the War. The Confederates, stirring uneasily under attacks, sought some way to perpetuate their control in the State

[87] *O. R.*, Ser. I, Vol. XIII, 794-795.

elections scheduled for August, 1862. In the early spring the Democratic press began to suggest that the State be spared partisan strife by electing a convention which would nominate a candidate for governor, who would, in turn, agree to resolutions supporting the central government until independence was won, and who would then be unanimously elected, thus avoiding a state-wide contest.[88] Most secessionist papers accordingly decided to agree upon a candidate among themselves and eventually settled upon William Johnston, of Mecklenburg, whose election by acclamation began to be urged.[89]

The choice of Johnston was a calculated political move of great shrewdness. He had long been a Whig, but had been among the first to advocate secession after the election of Lincoln. He was politically obscure, and so had few enemies. He had shown business ability, financial acumen, and administrative skill as a railroad president and as State commissary general. By agreeing upon such a man the Confederates could thus support Johnston for what he was and hope the Conservatives would support him for what he had been.[90]

That these tactics did not succeed was due primarily to William W. Holden and the Raleigh *Weekly Standard*. This veteran journalist had been a constant and severe critic of both State and Confederate administrations for many months, and had thereby begun to organize the new Conservative Party as an instrument to win control from the Democrats, with whom for many years he formerly had been associated. His political acumen enabled Holden to see the Johnston nomination as a transparent plan to perpetuate power under the pretense of nonpartisan patriotism.[91] He attacked the Democratic plan with bold bluntness and made clear his advocacy of an anti-administration party, suggesting through public meetings at grass roots level the name of William A. Graham for governor. But Graham refused and eventually Holden came to the name of Vance, already prominent in political circles, extremely popular in the army, and already endorsed in several public meetings. Vance was really picked to oppose Johnston by a group of Conservative members of the State Convention just before it adjourned in May. A timely visit by Augustus S. Merrimon to Edward J. Hale, powerful editor of the *Fayetteville Observer*, secured the latter's support.[92] On June 4 Holden put Vance's name on the masthead of the *Standard* as

[88] Raleigh *State Journal*, February 12, 26, March 5, 1862.
[89] Charlotte *Western Democrat*, February 4, March 25, 1862.
[90] Raleigh *State Journal*, June 4, 1862.
[91] Raleigh *North Carolina Standard*, April 2, 1862.
[92] William Kenneth Boyd, (ed.), *Memoirs of W. W. Holden* (The John Lawson Monographs of the Trinity College Historical Society, Vol. II, Durham, 1911), pp. 18-20 (cited hereafter as Holden, *Memoirs*).

the Conservative candidate, and on June 16 from his army post, Vance wrote what amounted to a letter of acceptance,[93] carefully avoiding commitments of any kind beyond a promise to prosecute the War. Since the Democrats certainly supported the idea of independence, on the surface there appeared to be no difference between the parties.

But on one important point there was a crucial difference. The Democrats approved extreme centralization of governmental power and the exercise of extensive prerogatives of control by the Confederate government; the Conservatives, pointing to the letter of the Constitution and the logic of secession, insisted on limiting central power by means of states' rights. Yet Vance, in his letter of acceptance, made no reference to this crucial difference.

The campaign was conducted chiefly in the press, which was about equally divided. Johnston remained with his railroad and Vance remained with his regiment. The Confederate press criticized Vance for his youth and his lack of administrative experience, for his reputation as a joke teller, and for his record of bitter partisanship. Above all, they attacked him for his obvious identification with Holden, and claimed that the issue was between Union and secession.[94] Claiming that Vance opposed conscription, they insisted that Vance's election would be received in the North "as an indubitable sign that the Union sentiment is in the ascendancy in the heart of the Southern Confederacy." [95] The Conservative press did not attack Johnston personally, except to criticize his advocacy of original secession, but did continuously criticize his party associates in Richmond and Raleigh for their alleged partisan conduct of the War, neglect of the soldiers, high prices, military defeats, and conscription.[96]

The result was that Vance was elected Governor by the most overwhelming margin in the history of the State, receiving 52,833 votes to 20,174 for Johnston, and thus having a majority greater than Johnston's total vote. Vance won a majority of the army vote and carried every county except twelve. The legislature was also safely Conservative.[97]

The Confederate Party was repudiated not merely because Holden was an astute political leader or because Vance had a

[93] Z. B. Vance to the Editors of the Observer, June 16, 1862, Fayetteville Observer, June 23, 1862.

[94] Raleigh State Journal, June 25, 1862; Charlotte Western Democrat, June 10, July 29, 1862; Wilmington Journal, June 26, July 17, 1862.

[95] Raleigh Register, July 23, 30, 1862; Charlotte Western Democrat, July 29, 1862.

[96] Raleigh North Carolina Standard, quoted in the Raleigh State Journal, June 25, July 23, 1862.

[97] Governor Henry T. Clark Letter Book, p. 406, State Department of Archives and History, Raleigh, N. C.; Raleigh North Carolina Standard, August 20, 1862.

contagious appeal to soldiers and civilians. While the result of the election was certainly not a verdict for reunion, it was just as certainly an expression of dissatifaction with timid leadership, bad war conditions, military invasion, and the centralizing pretensions of Confederate consolidation. North Carolinians had come to be afraid of their own government, and they voted not so much for Vance as against the *status quo.*

On August 15 Vance left the army to prepare for his inauguration, set for September 8 by special action of the Convention. In Raleigh, on his way home to Asheville, he urged the people to allay partisan strife and to co-operate in a rigorous prosecution of the war.[98] Neither then nor later did he give any encouragement to those who identified his candidacy with reunion. In Asheville he asserted that conscripton was a matter of necessity and should be supported.[99] In pledging himself to its enforcement he was careful to correct northern interpretations of his victory. These sentiments anticipated the theme of his inaugural address in which he repeated his pledge to prosecute the War with full and renewed vigor, accepted secession as the "deliberate judgment of our people," and endorsed conscription even though "it *may have been* unconstitutional, though many of our ablest statesmen thought not." Earnestly and sincerely he appealed for harmony, admonishing the people to forget party and to unite to win independence.

His inaugural address, applauded by the press of both parties, revealed not only Vance's sincerity, but his acute awareness of his political position.[100] Instead of making commitments during the campaign he had shrewdly gauged the intensity of the dissatisfaction with the incumbents and had realized that he could be elected without specific promises on his part. Accordingly he allowed his supporters to gather votes for him as they could, neither agreeing with nor objecting to their claims made in his name. Then, after his victory, he assembled from the arguments of both parties a statement of policy which won well-nigh universal approval. He won enthusiastic support not because he represented reconstruction, as mistakenly charged, but rather because a partisan politician had made a nonpartisan inaugural and an Old-Line Union Whig had pledged a vigorous prosecution of a war the secessionist Democrats had claimed as their own. It was not the ends, but the means, of the Confederate Party which had been repudiated.

---

[98] Raleigh *Register,* August 20, 1862.

[99] *Asheville News,* August 28, 1862, as quoted in the Raleigh *Register,* September 10, 1862.

[100] Winston *Western Sentinel,* September 17, 1862; Charlotte *Western Democrat,* September 16, 1862; Raleigh *Register,* September 10, 1862; *Wilmington Journal,* September 18, 1862; Raleigh *State Journal,* September 17, 1862.

Thus Vance, despite any questions he may have had as to its constitutionality, took over the governorship publicly committed to the full enforcement of the unpopular conscription act. Many voices in North Carolina had been raised against the policy of conscription, among which Holden's was the strongest, but Vance began to enforce it by ordering the State militia to enroll conscripts,[101] boldly proclaiming that resistance to the law was treason.

But this policy of support did not mean there was to be no conflict between the State and the Confederacy over conscription. The exigencies of war caused the Confederacy to change practices and renege on guarantees which Vance, upon the assurance of the War Department, had made to the men. The first trouble grew out of the failure of the Confederacy to allow the conscript to choose his regiment if he enrolled willingly, though Vance had such a promise from Davis both orally and in writing. This change led to an exchange of bitter correspondence in which Vance virtually accused both Secretary George Wythe Randolph and President Davis of bad faith, but it did not change the policy.[102] Vance always afterwards felt that what appeared a callous disregard of promises given was a basic cause of evasion and desertions.

In other matters relating to the execution of the conscript laws Vance maintained a heavy and often acrimonious correspondence with Richmond throughout the War, frequently lecturing the administration on the realities of politics among the loyal opposition and strenuously complaining when he felt, as he usually did, that the rights of North Carolina men were violated or ignored. He was especially insistent that men should be enrolled only by proper officers and according to prescribed forms of law, that legal exemptions should be scrupulously respected, and that due regard be paid to the sensibilities of North Carolina with regard to appointments in the conscript bureau. On the whole, Vance enforced the conscription laws with great energy and resourcefulness, continuing to use both the militia and his personal influence until the end.[103] Although accurate statistics on the number of conscripts and the number of troops furnished the Confederacy are not available, it appears certain that North Carolina furnished about one-fourth of all the conscripts and

---

[101] Z. B. Vance to Peter Mallett, September 11, 1862, Vance Letter Book, 1862-1863, State Department of Archives and History, Raleigh, N. C. (cited hereafter as Vance Letter Book). This directive was embodied in General Order, No. 7, issued in Vance's name from the adjutant general's office in Raleigh, dated September 13, 1862. The order is printed in the Raleigh *North Carolina Standard*, September 17, 1862.

[102] See *O. R.*, Ser. IV, Vol. II, 114-115, 146-147, 154.

[103] Z. B. Vance to W. A. Graham, January 14, 1864, Vance Letter Book.

about one-sixth of all the troops in the Confederate service.[104] For this achievement the energy of Governor Vance was largely responsible.

Vance's great energies were expended not only in getting the soldier into the army but in keeping him there. By 1863 desertion had become serious; by 1864 it became fatal. North Carolina soldiers were probably the most numerous offenders. With their dissatisfactions brought on by suffering both in the army and at home, and by spectacles of speculation and mismanagement, the men were technically deserters "but really they were fathers gone mad."[105]

As a father, a family man, and a former soldier, Vance understood the causes and sympathized with the deserter in many instances, but he saw that the practice could not be condoned. He ordered the State militia to arrest deserters, but Chief Justice Richmond M. Pearson discharged prisoners on the ground that Vance had no authority to enforce Confederate legislation.[106] There followed a tortuous duel between the executive and judicial authority in North Carolina, in which Vance sought to find legal ways of helping the Confederacy keep the troops.[107] But he bowed to judicial authority and insisted to Secretary James A. Seddon that judicial consciences ought to be respected. He persisted in his maneuvers, however, and finally managed to obtain from a reluctant legislature authority for the State forces to arrest deserters.[108] In this manner the decision of the Chief Justice was legally set aside. No governor could have tried harder to co-operate with the Confederate policy. More effective than militia or Home Guard was Vance's personal influence and eloquent pen. Although Vance, with his humane nature and his scorn of military etiquette, had little patience with the rigors and senseless red tape of military law, there is abundant evidence that his stirring proclamations and his frequent personal intervention undoubtedly helped to keep the army in being, and he always deeply resented any implication that North Carolina, the only State to use militia to arrest conscripts and deserters, had neglected her duty in this matter.[109]

[104] O. R., Ser. IV, Vol. III, 1101.

[105] Quoted in Robert Digges Wimberly Connor, North Carolina, Rebuilding an Ancient Commonwealth, 1584-1925, 4 vols. (Chicago and New York, 1929), II, 187.

[106] O. R., Ser. I, Vol. LI, Pt. II, 709; Daniel G. Fowle in Raleigh Register, II, 709.

[107] Z. B. Vance to Jefferson Davis, May 13, 1863, O. R., Ser. I, Vol. LI, Pt. II, 709.

[108] Legislative and Executive Documents, Extra Session, 1863-'64 (Raleigh, 1864), Documents Nos. 1 and 2, November 23, 1863 (cited hereafter as Legislative Documents); James A. Seddon to Z. B. Vance, May 23, 1863, O. R., Ser. I, Vol. LI, Pt. II, 714.

[109] Z. B. Vance to James A. Seddon, May 25, 1863, O. R., Ser. I, Vol. LI, Pt. II, 714.

General resentment against Richmond's policies was not confined to conscription and desertion. Occasionally Richmond officials named to positions in North Carolina citizens of some other State, and frequently "foreign" officers were placed in command of North Carolina regiments. Criticism throughout the State was very strong, and Vance vigorously assailed President Davis and Secretary Seddon for allegedly ignoring the claims of North Carolina. He asserted his rights as to the appointment of officers in certain North Carolina regiments raised before the first conscription law was passed, causing confusion and endless quarrels before he was forced to yield in 1864. Even so, it was a rare thing for Vance to seek the appointment of any one of his political partisans, for the records reveal neither obvious political motive nor any special crony for whom he sought office. Once, when Secretary Seddon yielded and agreed to remove a Virginian who had been appointed a tax collector in North Carolina and asked Vance to name a successor, the Governor replied with great delicacy that, "having anxiously sought to remove Major Bradford for reasons purely prudential, I would not desire to run the risk of having them impugned by recommending anyone for his successor." [110] Complaints and resentment persisted in North Carolina throughout the War, and Vance sent steady and stinging rebukes at each slight or discourtesy. He always felt that Davis never understood, nor cared to understand, his political position in North Carolina.

During the War Vance was never able to concentrate on one problem at a time to the exclusion of all others. When he became Governor it was not only conscription and the hardships it brought to the soldier which troubled him, but the hardships of war had already begun to press heavily upon the people themselves.

Shortages in the essentials of life had begun to become acute, and suffering and complaints increased, especially among the families of soldiers. Scarcity of goods, high prices, the blockade, and depreciation of the currency had their effects upon politics as well as upon war.

Of such suffering and want Governor Vance took a serious view from the start, and insisted that relief was a proper function of government. He believed that speculation in the necessities of life was the major cause of suffering, and that hoarding had gone beyond the activities of individuals and become an organized business immensely profitable to the speculators and equally ruinous to the poor, especially in the cities. Currency was un-

---

[110] Z. B. Vance to James A. Seddon, August 1, 1863, Vance Letter Book.

acceptable to many when it became virtually worthless. Those with money found nothing that money would buy.

Soon after he became Governor, and long before the worst abuses had matured, Vance recommended measures to curb these evil practices.[111] These measures were confined principally to embargoes on exports from the State and were inadequate to meet the evils of the situation. Conscious of the laws of supply and demand, Vance thought in terms of standard laissez-faire economics, stopping far short of recommending price controls. His embargo measures were fairly successful until the late summer of 1863 in temporarily lowering some prices, but the permanent evils of speculation remained. Some proposals were made to "regulate the prices of all articles produced, manufactured, or sold in this State,"[112] but this was more radical than the legislature would support and neither this measure nor the proposal to limit the production of money crops was ever adopted. Instead of specific price fixing, only a general prohibition against speculation could be obtained, and this was inadequate to control the evil. In the last analysis Vance's main weapon lay in his eloquent appeals to public patriotism, but the effect of these was never more than temporary.

Economic distress in North Carolina was increased by Confederate impressment policies. Beginning in March of 1863 the Confederate Congress allowed the Confederate quartermaster and commissary officers to impress supplies of food and other produce at prices below the market value. This practice, intensified by the 10 per cent tax in kind which soon followed, fell with crushing severity on the small farmer, depriving him of the only commodity he had with which to obtain other necessities. Partiality and abuses resulted, and complaints were numerous.[113]

Unable to reform the situation, Vance turned to relief. His first concern was salt, in which speculation was particularly grievous. State salt works were established on the coast, financed by legislative subsidy, and by the end of 1862, in spite of numerous difficulties, 20,000 bushels had been produced from sea water and distributed to the people at one-third the market price. In addition, before Vance became Governor, the State had made a contract with Stuart-Buchanan Company, of Saltville, Virginia, for 300,000 bushels a year, to be sold to the counties at cost and resold by them to the people without profit. As a result of these practices, salt became plentiful for a time in 1863, but by the end of the War Federal interference with the coastal works, and

[111] Message to Legislature, November 17, 1862, in *Legislative Documents, 1862-1863*, Document No. 1.
[112] *Senate Journal, Adjourned Session, 1863*, p. 49.
[113] *Fayetteville Observer*, October 12, 1863.

transportation problems in Virginia, had again produced short-ages. But on the whole the policy was a great success.[114]

Vance moved with equal success to provide relief to the families of soldiers. In 1862 be began the purchase of certain necessities, such as corn and salt, by the State, and sold them to the soldiers' families at cost through the county agents at the local level.[115] Later direct gifts were provided to widows, wives, and children of soldiers to the extent of $6,000,000, in addition to aid from many of the counties. Since county aid was uneven, Vance appealed to the legislature to assume the whole burden of relief, but it refused to assume the entire obligation.[116]

The need for clothing was only a little less desperate than for food, and direct State aid was inaugurated by Vance in this area also. In homespun manufacture cotton or wool cards were essential to straighten out the fiber for spinning. Since these cards were scarce and exhorbitantly high, Vance imported some through the blockade and, what was more important, a number of machines to make them. In this manner soldiers' families were provided the essential cards at $5 instead of the market price of $75, and other families bought them for less than a third of the market price.[117]

With what money and legislative co-operation he had, Vance performed wonders for the relief of the people. Organizing a corps of provision agents in the productive regions, he gathered large stores of supplies, selling the surplus to the Confederacy when it was not required by the counties.[118] Despite individual complaints, relief was efficiently conducted and food was available to the poor throughout the War. The policy of dealing directly with the sufferings and hardships caused by the War did more than any other one thing to gain for Vance the lasting affection of his people and to give him the unique title "War Governor of the South."

Economic disasters were accompanied by military disasters throughout the War, and Federal invasions, or the threats of them, caused many bitter conflicts with the Confederate govern-

---

[114] Numerous reports from J. M. Worth, who was in charge of the coastal works, and from N. W. Woodfin, the N. C. Agent at Saltville, Virginia, are in the Governors' Papers (Vance), State Department of Archives and History, Raleigh, N. C. (cited hereafter as Governors' Papers Vance).

[115] Message to Legislature, November 17, 1862, *Legislative Documents, 1862-1863,* Document No. 1; *Laws of N. C. Adjourned Session, 1862-'63,* pp. 63-64; *Laws of N. C., 1863,* pp. 26-27; *Laws of N. C., 1864,* pp. 16-18; *Laws of N. C., 1864-'65,* pp. 66-68.

[116] Winston *Western Sentinel,* December 4, 1864.

[117] *Fayetteville Observer,* June 6, 1864; Charlotte *Western Democrat,* February 16, 1864.

[118] Message to Legislature, November, 1863, *Legislative Documents, 1863,* pp. 4-5; Z. B. Vance to J. A. Seddon, April 27, 1863, *O. R.,* Ser., I. Vol. XVIII, 1026.

ment. When Vance became Governor, Federal occupation extended from Fort Macon to the Virginia line, but it was not confined to the coastline, frequently penetrating inland to threaten the resources of the agriculturally rich eastern counties and the vital Wilmington and Weldon Railroad, which was the lifeline of the Virginia front. Since military defense was now a Confederate responsibility, any Federal threat led to petitions to Richmond to defend the State. When Richmond thought the threats were major in their nature, troops were provided to defend the railroad and the port of Wilmington, but Federal raids were often successful and most of them remained unchallenged by Confederate forces. As the War progressed and Vance came to realize that Confederate military success depended on Lee, he ceased his petitions for aid, but he could not ignore the profound apprehension produced in North Carolina by Federal invasions of the State.

As a consequence of repeated threats to the security of the State, Vance, in November, 1862, recommended to the legislature that the State raise at least ten regiments of reserves, composed of men over conscription age, to be used exclusively in the defense of North Carolina.[119] His proposal was vague as to details, but it is certain that Vance intended no conflict with the Confederate government and the conscription act. But when successful Federal invasions occurred in late November and December the House altered the original proposal and provided for the creation of a special army for local defense, not to exceed 10,000 men, to be armed and equipped by the Confederate government but to be under the control of the Governor for use in North Carolina alone. Such a bill passed the House in December, but was defeated in the Senate after the holidays. Although Holden insisted that he spoke for Vance when he supported the bill, it is more likely that Vance opposed it on the clear ground that it would either destroy the Confederate government or else bring a collision between it and the State. Although Vance made no public statement with regard to the House measure, it is probable that he used his influence in the holiday recess to defeat the bill. Certainly the stanch Vance Conservatives in the Senate voted against it.[120] Vance had asked for limited forces for a limited time and there is no evidence that he wished a law that would nullify a conscription bill he was trying to enforce. It is likely that he was publicly silent in the hope that the extreme discontent reflected in the House measure would produce more effective military aid from the Confederate government.

[119] Message to Legislature, November 17, 1862, *Legislative Documents, 1862-1863*, Document No. 1.
[120] *Senate Journal, 2 Session, 1863*, pp. 12-13, 37-38.

Other military crises followed periodically throughout the war and produced new appeals and complaints to Richmond. By 1863 Vance had learned that Richmond could not, or would not, detach large contingents of troops from Lee to protect North Carolina, so he turned to other measures to defend the State. His ultimate policy, as enacted by the legislature, abolished the unsatisfactory militia system and established the Guard for Home Defense, to consist of all whites between the ages of eighteen and fifty who were not liable to Confederate service and not exempt by State laws.[121] During 1864 about 25,000 men were enrolled in the Home Guards and placed under the authority of Vance for State defense. Although the Home Guard was frequently useful in arresting deserters and quelling disturbances, it was never as formidable a force as it appeared on paper. After exemptions were deducted, and after about 6,000 senior reserves were taken into the Confederate forces, only about 5,000 were present when it was called out late in 1864 to take part in the closing scenes of the War.

Zealous aid in the conscription of troops and tireless efforts to limit and prevent their desertion did not exhaust Vance's activities on behalf of the army. The troops must also be equipped and supplied. Under an arrangement made by his predecessor in office North Carolina had agreed to clothe its own troops in return for commutation of $50 per year from the Confederacy for each soldier.[122] In order to supply this clothing the State made contracts with local factories and so monopolized their product as to induce the Confederate quartermaster to look with longing eyes on the products of the thirty-nine cotton and seven woolen mills in North Carolina, which were almost one-half of the total number in the Confederacy. Hardly had Vance been inaugurated when the Confederacy requested the Governor to turn over the State contracts to the Confederacy, who would then assume the burden of clothing the North Carolina troops. Vance replied that he must consult the legislature, but before that body could meet commutation was abolished. Nevertheless Vance refused to turn over the contracts and ultimately made a new arrangement whereby North Carolina was to continue to clothe her troops and was to receive payment from the Confederacy.[123] But in the autumn of 1862 confusion and depression prevailed and as winter approached the condition of the troops was little short of desperate.[124] Vance tried a number of temporary expedients to get through the first winter. New contracts were negotiated,

[121] *Senate Journal, Extra Session, 1863*, pp. 19, 31.
[122] *Public Laws of N. C., 2 Extra Session, 1861*, chap. 21, September 20, 1861.
[123] A. R. Lawton to Z. B. Vance, September 28, 1864, *O. R.*, Ser. IV, III, 691.
[124] Charlotte *Western Democrat*, October 28, 1862.

appeals were made for contributions directly from the people which militia officers were ordered to collect and transport. Gratifying as the results of these measures were, Vance realized that such appeals could hardly be successfully repeated and that a more permanent solution must be found. It was in these circumstances that Vance turned to the most celebrated device of the War, the idea of running the blockade.

The idea did not originate with the Governor and had already been once rejected, but Vance seized upon it and began to implement it with remarkable results. The operation was conducted by John White of Warrenton, a merchant of wide experience and dependable character, with whom Vance, for the State, proposed a contract which provided that White should go to England as State agent and purchase such articles as Vance directed.[125] The legislature, in secret session, provided $2,000,000 and ratified the contracts.[126] With the appropriation Vance bought cotton and stored it. On the basis of the cotton, warrants were issued which entitled the purchaser to have cotton delivered to any port of the Confederacy east of the Mississippi upon sixty days' notice, with interest at 7 per cent until delivery. The responsibility of getting the cotton abroad thus rested with the purchaser of the warrants. With the money from the sales of the warrants, White purchased a steamer and supplies and paid expenses. When a blockade-runner unloaded supplies at Wilmington it was to take on more cotton to finance additional purchases by the State. Only the Federal blockade threatened the success of the enterprise and the irregular patrol of the coast gave promise that this could be eluded.

White's performance was a remarkable one. Arriving in England at the end of 1862 with neither business connections nor official influence, he won the confidence of a reputable firm, Alexander Collie and Company of London and Manchester, and from it obtained a loan of £100,000 with which he purchased the steamer "Clyde," christened by Captain Thomas M. Crossan the "Ad-Vance," and about 250 tons of assorted merchandise such as blankets, shoes, leather, and especially clothing. During the next year Vance supplied White with further State funds, including $1,000,000 in State bonds, which were deposited as collateral. Later still Collie extended credit when White's funds temporarily ran out.[127] By these means extensive supplies were

---

[125] Vance Letter Book, November 1, 1862.

[126] *House Journal, 1862-1863,* p. 15; *Acts of the General Assembly of the State of North Carolina, Passed in Secret Session, 1862,* pp. 71-72.

[127] W. K. Boyd, "Fiscal and Economic Conditions in North Carolina During the Civil War," *The North Carolina Booklet* (Raleigh, 1901-1926), vol. XIV, no. 4, (April, 1915), p. 209 (cited hereafter as Boyd, "Fiscal and Economic Conditions," *N. C. Booklet);* John White to Z. B. Vance, August 7, 1863, Vance Letter Book.

shipped to Bermuda, from which the "Ad-Vance" made regular trips to bring them into Wilmington. By October, 1863, Vance could boast that he could insure clothing for the North Carolina troops, shoes and blankets excepted, until 1865, and the next month reported to the legislature that the venture was a "complete success."[128] It was no idle boast.

The enthusiasm generated by this success caused Vance to attempt to enlarge the operation. With the consent of the legislature, a part interest was acquired in three other vessels so that by the summer of 1864 large surpluses had been built up in some items.[129] The sharing of cargo space with private owners brought some complications but Collie, who undoubtedly made money on the venture, became sincerely attached to the Southern cause and donated, through Vance, $20,000 for the relief of the North Carolina poor. Subsequently the State sold one-half interest in the "Ad-Vance" to Power, Lowe and Company of Wilmington, who remodeled the vessel to enable it to carry larger cargoes. But with the State having one-half interest in the "Ad-Vance," and one-fourth in the "Don," the "Hansa," and the "Annie," Vance was in an excellent position to ship out cotton and run in supplies, both in large quantities.[130]

The smoothness of these operations was marred by another acrimonious conflict with the Confederate government. Lacking sufficient cargo space in its own blockade-running enterprises, in the fall of 1863 it began to require that one-third of cargo space in all private ships be reserved for the Confederacy, at reasonable rates. Vance and Collie assumed that their vessels were not "private" but the Confederacy, far from agreeing, upped its claim to one-half in the spring of 1864. Once again bitter exchanges ensued between Vance and Davis.[131] As a last resort Vance, claiming that the "port of Wilmington is now more effectively blockaded *from within* than without," turned to the Confederate Congress, which was usually ready to pass resolutions against the central government.[132] But Davis vetoed the modifications

---

[128] Z. B. Vance to E. J. Hale, October 26, 1863, Edward Jones Hale Papers, State Department of Archives and History, Raleigh, N. C. (cited hereafter as Hale Papers); *Legislative Documents, 1864-65,* Document No. 1, pp. 5-6.

[129] The contract with Collie is in the Vance Letter Book, October 27, 1863; Reports of White to Vance, Nov.-Dec., 1863, in Governors' Papers, Vance; Z. B. Vance to E. J. Hale, February 11, 1864, Hale Papers.

[130] Z. B. Vance to A. Collie, February 1, 18, 1864, Vance Letter Book.

[131] Z. B. Vance to James A. Seddon, January 7, 1864, *O. R.,* Ser. IV, Vol. III, 10-11; Z. B. Vance to Jefferson Davis, March 17, 1864, *O. R.,* Ser. I, Vol. LI, Pt. II, 837-839; Z. B. Vance to C. G. Memminger, July 4, 1864, Vance Letter Book; Frank L. Owsley, *State Rights in the Confederacy* (Chicago, 1925), pp. 128-132.

[132] *Legislative Documents, 1864,* Document No. 1, pp. 1-2.

the Congress was willing to make and later ones obtained in 1865 were, by then, idle gestures.[133]

But long before this the "Ad-Vance," on her twelfth voyage in September, 1864, had been captured by a Federal steamer. During the life of the "Ad-Vance"—that is between June of 1863 and August of 1864—the State had exported more than 4,100 bales of cotton to finance her operations in England.[134] Before the port of Wilmington was closed in January of 1865 the State had imported enormous quantities of supplies, including 250,000 pairs of shoes, 50,000 blankets, wool for 250,000 uniforms, 100,000 pounds of bacon, overcoats, rifles, medicine, and many other vital commodities largely unavailable at home.[135]

It is impossible to compute profit and loss on a venture of this sort because no audit was ever made to furnish official figures. Vance and his friends claimed that great profits were made for the State by purchasing cotton with inflated Confederate currency and selling it for English gold;[136] Jonathan Worth, State Treasurer, thought that North Carolina suffered financially from blockade-running, but his statement, if true, is irrelevant. It is irrelevant because the purpose of the operations was not profits but produce, not balances but blankets. A State which is fighting for its life can afford to lose money, largely worthless anyway, if it gets the supplies.

North Carolina got the supplies. The very success of the venture brought efforts on the part of the Confederacy to secure a share. Though Vance was extraordinarily generous in some matters— for example he gave the Confederacy all the bacon stored in Bermuda and one-half of that already in North Carolina in December, 1864, and sold them 20,000 uniforms—yet he hoarded other materials, especially uniforms, of which he had nearly 100,000 which Lee desperately needed before he surrendered.[137] Vance had made agreements to sell the surplus to the Confederacy but that body could not afford to buy even with its own inflated paper. Throughout the War the Confederacy owed large balances to North Carolina, a debt which was never discharged.[138]

Throughout the war, as necessity seemed to dictate, the Confederate government tried to expand its powers and to use its

---

[133] *Journal of the Congress of the Confederate States of America, 1861-1865*, 7 vols. (Washington, 1905), IV, 167; VII, 693, 694, 720.

[134] Z. B. Vance to A. Collie, August 5, 1864, Vance Letter Book.

[135] Specified in Dowd, *Life of Vance*, pp. 70-71.

[136] See Z. B. Vance to the Legislature, *Legislative Documents, 1865-'66*, November, 1864; Raleigh *Conservative*, June 22, 1864; Boyd, "Fiscal and Economic Conditions," *N. C. Booklet*, 208-209.

[137] James A. Seddon to Z. B. Vance, December 31, 1864, Vance Letter Book; *O. R.*, Ser. IV, Vol. II, 183.

[138] Z. B. Vance to J. C. Breckinridge, April 22, 1865, Z. B. Vance Papers.

military authority wherever civil authority seemed to hamper the war effort. The nature of the governmental structure and the exigencies of the times thus combined to produce one of the fundamental and persistent themes over which the State and nation clashed during the war years. But every such effort to brush aside the civil law in North Carolina met the determined opposition of Governor Vance. Ceaselessly, and usually successfully, he fought against the illegal actions of the military, prevailed upon the Confederate government to respect the rights of North Carolina, upheld the decisions of State judges, and in numerous other ways asserted the sovereignty of North Carolina. Long after the War was over the War Governor's proudest boast became that in North Carolina "the laws *were* heard amidst the roar of cannon" and the "old legal maxim *inter arma silent leges* was expunged, and in its place was written *inter arma leges audiebantur,*"[139] despite temptations and pressures to ignore constitutional guarantees. But to maintain civil law in the midst of war was to insist on a course of action which many believed would hamper the bid for independence. This was a dilemma never solved by the South, where the rights of the States, ceaselessly asserted, contributed to the failure to make a nation.

For this failure Vance has been assigned a large share of the blame. Yet there was a political logic in Vance's position. Realizing that the Confederacy had been founded squarely on the doctrine of states' rights, Vance abandoned his Whig nationalism and vigorously opposed the consolidation tendencies of the central government. That such a course was politically expedient the election of 1862 had proved. Further, it is important to realize that Vance understood, at least afterwards, that this was no way to win a war.[140] But he truly represented the southern people when he fought both for independence *and* for constitutionalism. And he was correct in his analysis of public sentiment when he concluded that if the realization of the former required an executive or military dictatorship at the sacrifice of the latter, then even such an end did not justify such means.

The first clashes on civil rights involved the abuse of Confederate military power in North Carolina, where armed cavalry bands seized provisions and persons upon several celebrated occasions. Repeatedly Vance appealed to Richmond to respect the civil rights of persons and usually Davis or Seddon complied, at least for the moment.[141]

But a much more serious problem arose when Richmond began

---

[139] Vance, *Political and Social South*, quoted in Dowd, *Life of Vance*, p. 453.
[140] Dowd, *Life of Vance*, pp. 451-452.
[141] For example, see his letter to Jefferson Davis in *O. R.*, Ser. IV, Vol. II, 1061; Dowd, *Life of Vance*, p. 453.

a policy of ignoring adverse decisions of State judges. The Chief Justice of the North Carolina Supreme Court, Richmond M. Pearson, in April, 1863, maintained that the Conscription Act of September, 1862, did not apply to substitutes, though the War Department, on the very day that Vance became Governor, had ruled that "A substitute becoming liable to conscription, renders his principal also liable, unless exempt on other ground."[142] Already annoyed with Pearson for decisions which denied Vance authority to arrest conscripts and deserters, the Confederate government decided to pay no attention to Pearson's decision, and accordingly issued such instructions to its enrolling officers. This policy brought the State and the Confederacy to the verge of a showdown.

It also brought Governor Vance directly into the controversy. Though he sought to avoid a quarrel with Richmond, it was clear that public sentiment in North Carolina agreed that it was Vance's duty to prevent the substitution of military force for civil law.[143] Accordingly, Vance made it plain to Seddon that the decisions of North Carolina judges must be respected by Confederate authorities in North Carolina until overruled by higher judicial authority (of course there was none). He reminded the Secretary that "although the War Department may not be bound by the decisions of the state courts yet the Executive of that State is," having sworn to execute the laws.[144] Seddon denied the authority of the State courts to   accept jurisdiction in such matters.[145] Vance replied with a celebrated order to the militia not only to refrain from arresting those who had been dismissed but "to resist any such arrest upon the part of any person, not authorized by the legal order or process of a Court or Judge having jurisdiction in such cases."[146]

An open clash never matured because both sides sincerely sought a way out of the stalemate. Vance never tried to free an individual by force, and the Confederacy created no more such incidents. Vance met Seddon's gesture by expressing his sincere regrets at the impasse, but repeated that he had no option to the course he must adopt, as he considered himself absolutely bound by the decisions of a court he was not competent to review.[147] North Carolina judges continued to issue writs of habeas corpus and Seddon kept on arresting principals, arguing that decisions of courts applied only to the particular individual

[142] J. A. Campbell to Peter Mallett, a copy, May 11, 1863, Vance Letter Book.
[143] Fayetteville Observer, June 1, 1863.
[144] Z. B. Vance to James A. Seddon, May 22, 1863, Vance Letter Book.
[145] James A. Seddon to Z. B. Vance, May 23, 1863, Vance Letter Book.
[146] Dated May 26, 1863, in the Raleigh Register, June 3, 1863.
[147] Z. B. Vance to James A. Seddon, June 8, 1863, Vance Letter Book.

involved in each case. And Chief Justice Pearson kept on releasing them, inquiring caustically, "Who made the Secretary of War a judge?"[148]

In December, 1863, the Confederacy answered by abolishing substitution. Many argued that this was an act of bad faith, but Vance boldly defended it in his first major speech of the 1864 campaign,[149] although he promised that no principals of substitutes would be taken from North Carolina if the Supreme Court of the State held the law unconstitutional. The final Confederate answer was the suspension of the writ, to which position President Davis and the Congress reluctantly came in February, 1864.[150] Vance was critical of this action and deplored the withdrawal of "this time-honored and blood-bought guard of personal freedom," knowing that such a law could not be executed in many parts of North Carolina without great bitterness and possible conflict.[151]

Bitterness certainly followed, but conflict was confined to the judicial level. Pearson continued to discharge soldiers, contending that the suspension of the writ did not apply to principals of substitutes and insisting that it was never legally proper for a government to violate its own contract, as he charged the Confederacy with having done when it abolished substitution. Thus in the spring of 1864 a clash appeared imminent, but eventually Seddon agreed that the particular men discharged by Pearson would not be further molested until the full Court could decide the question, but he refused to apply the principle to principals in general.[152] When the full Court, in June, reversed Pearson the immediate crisis was passed.[153]

Vance had accomplished his two main objectives in this long and involved controversy: He had avoided an open clash between State and Confederate authority, and he had asserted the majesty of civil rights as he upheld and executed the judicial decisions of State judges. He had also, without doubt, helped deprive the Confederate army of the services of about eighty men.

Civil rights furnished hardly a more constant source of friction

[148] J. G. deR. Hamilton, "The North Carolina Courts and the Confederacy," *North Carolina Historical Review*, Vol. IV, No. 4 (October, 1927), pp. 370-375 (cited hereafter as Hamilton, "N. C. Courts and Confederacy," *N. C. Hist. Rev.*); 60 *N. C. Reports*, p. 61.

[149] At Wilkesboro, February 22, 1864.

[150] *O. R.*, Ser. IV, Vol. III, 69, 203-204.

[151] Message to Legislature, May 17, 1864, *Legislative Documents, Adjourned Session, 1864*, Document No 1, pp. 5-13.

[152] James A. Seddon to Z. B. Vance, March 5, 1863, *O. R.*, Ser. IV, Vol. III, 197-198.

[153] Hamilton, "N. C. Courts and Confederacy," *N. C. Hist. Rev.*, p. 399.

over the rights of the States than did the exemption of State personnel. Vance, from the beginning, insisted that "all State officers and employees necessary to the operation of this government—of which necessity I must judge—shall not be interferred with by the enrolling officers, and any attempt to arrest such men will be resisted." Assuring the bureau that it could "calculate with perfect confidence" upon his co-operation in enforcing conscription, he nevertheless claimed it "due to the rights and dignity of the sovereign State over whose destinies I have the honor to preside" that North Carolina officials be exempted.[154]

But it was not as simple as this. The law exempted judicial and executive officers of the State governments, "except those liable to militia duty."[155] But in North Carolina law everyone was liable to militia duty. As the conscription bureau began to enroll magistrates, constables, and other officers, including the Mayor of Raleigh itself, Vance turned once more to Davis.[156] Failing to get more than temporary concessions from the harassed President, Vance had more success with the North Carolina delegation in Congress, for on May 1, 1863, Congress passed such a law as Vance himself might have written, a law which provided for the exemption of all officers whom the governor claimed necessary for the due administration of the laws of the State, provided the legislature confirmed the list.[157] Whereupon Vance prepared an elaborate list of exemptions, later expanded, and the legislature agreeably made it permanent in December, 1863.[158] In February, 1864, Congress repealed all exemption laws and control was vested in the hands of the President and the governors.[159] These measures diminished, though they did not quite end, friction between the State and the Confederacy over exemptions. There were afterwards several celebrated incidents over which quarrels arose, particularly the case involving the army status of future Governor of North Carolina, Daniel L. Russell, Jr.

Inevitably there were charges of politics in the whole business of exemptions. The hostile press claimed that Vance protected his political friends, especially during the campaign of 1864, but direct evidence of personal favoritism does not exist. Although

[154] Z. B. Vance to T. P. August, March 20, 1863, Vance Letter Book; Z. B. Vance to J. G. Rains, March 31, 1863, O. R., Ser. IV, Vol. II, 465-466.

[155] J. G. Rains to Z. B. Vance, March 25, 1864, O. R., Ser. IV, Vol. III, 458.

[156] Z. B. Vance to Jefferson Davis, March 31, 1863, O. R., Ser. IV, Vol. II, 464-465.

[157] Clarence D. Douglas, "Conscription and the Writ of Habeas Corpus in North Carolina During the Civil War," Historical Papers Published by Trinity College Historical Society, XIV, 8 (cited hereafter as Douglas, "Conscription," Trinity College Society).

[158] Z. B. Vance to Peter Mallett, March 3, 1864, Vance Letter Book.

[159] O. R., Ser. IV, Vol. III, 179.

Vance admitted that many had been exempted in order to emphasize the rights of the States to withhold them, he did, in the fall of 1864, suggest to his fellow executives that all unnecessary State officers be turned over to the armies.[160] But he found his own legislature unwilling to co-operate.[161]

It is not possible to assert with complete accuracy the number of State officials exempted by the persistent efforts of Vance and the North Carolina legislature. The four principal reports vary widely in their figures, but perhaps the most authoritative and the most reasonable—but neither the lowest nor the highest—is the final report of the Superintendent of Conscription in February, 1865, which placed the North Carolina figure at 5,589, an estimate not so high as that of Georgia but higher than for most of the other southern States.[162] There can be little claim that all exemptions were strictly necessary. Although in the latter stages of the War Vance was accused of favoring consolidation, he had nevertheless gone so far, in the matter of exemptions, in maintaining the sovereignty of his State as to contribute to the ultimate loss of such sovereignty as it had.

By September of 1863, when Vance had been Governor just a year, the Confederate government was under constant criticism and attack in North Carolina. Scarcities of food and clothing had produced discontent. Inflation, exhorbitant prices, and embargoes had produced frustration. Conscription and impressment had produced alarm. Alleged neglect of North Carolina had produced resentment. Violations of civil rights and the ignoring of the judiciary had produced dismay. Military invasion and military disaster had produced defeatism. Discontent, frustration, alarm, resentment, dismay, and defeatism produced the peace movement, which was the crucial public issue for Vance and for the State for more than a year before the election of August, 1864.

Vance was never permitted to deal with one crisis at a time, but all of them seemed to coalesce into one gigantic crisis as the movement for peace gained momentum after the military defeats of the summer of 1863. From the beginning of the War politicians had cultivated the growing discontent of the people and had used it with telling effect. The leader in this movement was Holden and his *Standard,* whose incessant complaints of the Confederate government and adroit cultivation of discontent led

---

[160] Z. B. Vance to M. L. Bonham, September 23, 1864, in *O. R.*, Ser. IV, Vol. III, 684-685; Z. B. Vance to E. J. Hale, October 11, 1864, Hale Papers.

[161] *Legislative Documents, 1865-1866*, Document No. 1, pp. 12-13.

[162] Douglas, "Conscription," *Trinity College Society*, XIV, pp. 27-28; *O. R.*, Ser. IV, Vol. III, 98-99, 866-868; and Reports of November 20, and December 1, 1864, in Governors' Papers, Vance, and in the Vance Letter Book.

some to think that he was preparing the way for a return to the Union. Having been thrown overboard by the Democratic Party in the past, he seemed now to relish every chance to damage it. The records do not reveal his precise motives or ultimate aims, but his conduct was that of a political opportunist who would use any device to elevate himself to power.

Shortly after the election of Vance, for which he was more responsible than any other one man—including Vance—Holden began to hint that the War was a failure and that independence might not be won.[163] Until the summer of 1863 he contented himself with attacks on the weak points of Confederate administration: conscription, impressment, and the like. But in June, 1863, Holden, for the first time, openly threatened to take North Carolina out of the Confederacy,[164] though he modified this suggestion through the rest of the summer and talked instead of an "honorable" peace. This he never defined, but many observers, not without reason, thought he was preparing the way for reunion.[165]

By August, 1863, more than twenty counties had held public meetings and adopted peace resolutions of remarkable similarity, published regularly in the Standard. To some "it looks very like Mr. Holden has a party, and that he is putting it to work for his especial benefit." While only two other newspapers in the State and only a handful of politicians of any prominence came to his support, Holden increased his caustic criticism and agitation and with masterly pen exacerbated the fears and discontent of the people.[166]

Vance's first steps to meet this challenge were cautious and exploratory, seeking an amicable accommodation. At the suggestion of the President, he went to Richmond in August to discuss the problem there, but no record of their conversation is extant. He talked also with many other leaders, including Hale and Graham.[167] Finally, he talked with Holden himself, but with no effect except that Holden promised to say that he did not speak for the Governor.[168] But the effect was vitiated when he added that he and Vance were still on good terms. By August Vance

[163] E. J. Hale to W. A. Graham, December 5, 1862, Graham Papers, Raleigh.
[164] Raleigh North Carolina Standard, June 3, 1863.
[165] Raleigh North Carolina Standard, June 24, July 29, August 12, 1863; Jonathan Worth to J. M. Worth, August 9, 1863, Joseph Gregoire deRoulhac Hamilton, (ed.), The Correspondence of Jonathan Worth, 2 vols. (Raleigh, 1909), I, 253-255 (cited hereafter as Hamilton, Worth Correspondence).
[166] Raleigh Register, August 5, 12, 1863; Raleigh North Carolina Standard, August 12, 1863; Raleigh State Journal, August 5, 1863.
[167] Z. B. Vance to E. J. Hale, June 10, August 11, 1863, Hale Papers.
[168] Raleigh North Carolina Standard, July 29, 1863; Z. B. Vance to E. J. Hale, July 26, 1863, Hale Papers.

was persuaded that a break must come, but he was still unwilling to precipitate it. He went so far as to write an open letter to John H. Haughton[169] of Chatham County, where discontent was especially rife, which, in seventeen pages of rhetoric, drew the line sharply between Holden and himself and presented a bold and unequivocal statement of opposition to the peace movement. Then he did a strange thing: He showed the letter to Holden and asked his opinion of it. Naturally Holden thought it "very extreme and violent," an "ultra war letter," and advised against its publication.[170] The same advice came from Graham, but on the ground that Vance's position was already well known.[171] Vance's brother advised him "to kill him off by letting him alone." [172] But Hale, and many others, pleaded with the Governor to disabuse the people of any idea that he and Holden thought alike on this vital question. "Cut loose from Holden. He is trading on your capital, and every day strengthening himself by the idea that you and he agree except upon a point of minor importance." [173]

Puzzled by conflicting advice, and enmeshed in a complicated political situation which would have taxed the judgment of even a more mature politician, Vance was on the verge of despair. For the moment he continued the Fabian policy of letting each day take care of itself, and suspended the publication of the Haughton letter. This policy was little more than a refusal to meet the issue; when September came he had made no public move to arrest the growing peace movement and the increasing influence of Holden.

In fear of making a mistake, Vance called another conference. Hale, whose sentiments were already known, could not come, but on September 2 Vance met with Graham and other Whig leaders opposed to the peace movement. They sent for Holden and for three hours Graham pleaded with him earnestly and eloquently, urging him to withdraw his agitation of the peace movement, but all in vain.[174] It was finally agreed that Vance should issue a proclamation warning of the consequences of resistance to Confederate laws—even bad ones—and urging discontinuance of the peace meetings. But Graham's insistence that the proclamation should be mild and cautious was obeyed, so that when it appeared on September 8 it scarcely seemed to mention the subject it was aimed to combat. On the surface Vance appeared

---

[169] August 17, 1863, and revision of August 21, 1863, in Z. B. Vance Papers.
[170] Holden, *Memoirs*, pp. 23-24.
[171] W. A. Graham to Z. B. Vance, August 21, 1863, Z. B. Vance Papers.
[172] R. B. Vance to Z. B. Vance, August 24, 1863, Z. B. Vance Papers.
[173] E. J. Hale to Z. B. Vance, September 2, 1863, Z. B. Vance Papers.
[174] Z. B. Vance to E. J. Hale, September 2, 1863, Hale Papers.

in the proclamation to be ignorant of the peace meetings, for he made only a veiled reference to "assemblying together for the purpose of denouncing each other. . . . Surely, my countrymen, you will not seek to curb the evils of one revolution by plunging the country into another. . . ." Certainly the proclamation drew no clear line between Vance and Holden, nor did it afford any hint that the erstwhile allies had gone their separate ways.[175]

But some others did not practice the restraint that Graham and Vance had adopted. On the evening of September 9 a mob of about seventy-five soldiers from Benning's Georgia brigade, incensed by what they called Holden's "treason," marched from the depot to Holden's office, where they wrecked his equipment and threw the type into the street. Holden took refuge in the Governor's Palace. When Vance arrived on the scene much damage had already been done. The mob listened attentively while Vance told them bluntly that they had insulted the State and the Confederacy even though their motives were patriotic. Insisting that he would be the first to punish treason, he also emphasized that he would be the last to infringe upon the freedom of the press. The soldiers gave three cheers for Vance and marched off to their quarters near the depot.[176]

But the action of one mob led to that of another. The next morning about one hundred of Holden's friends advanced on the offices of the *Weekly State Journal* whose absent editor had continually called for Holden's repression, broke his furniture, scattered his type, destroyed his papers, and smashed his press with sledge hammers. As Editor John Spelman said, everything was destroyed except the spirit of the Editor. Once more Vance rode his horse to the scene of the riot and, this time with more difficulty, dispersed the mob. [177] He then telegraphed Davis an account of the two riots and asked him to "order immediately that troops passing through here shall not enter the city. If this is not done the most frightful consequences may ensue." The President complied, but it was almost a week, and many letters later—letters which threatened to call North Carolina troops home to preserve order—before Raleigh appeared safe from infuriated soldiers and citizens.[178]

---

[175] Proclamation of September 8, 1863, in Vance Letter Book.

[176] Raleigh *Progress*, September 18, 1863; George Little to E. J. Hale. September 21, 1863, Hale Papers; Raleigh *North Carolina Standard*, May 18, 1864.

[177] *Wilmington Journal*, September 17, 1863.

[178] Z. B. Vance to Jefferson Davis, September 10, 1863, *O. R.*, Ser. I, Vol. LI, Pt. II, 763-764; Z. B. Vance to Jefferson Davis, September 11, 1863, *O. R.*, Ser. I, Vol. LI, Pt. II, 764-765.

Holden gained sympathy by the attack[179] and resumed publication a month later, in plenty of time to concentrate on the congressional elections of November, which would provide the first test of strength for the new peace party. Ten congressional candidates, calling themselves both Conservatives and peace men, but running on maddeningly vague definitions of peace, entered the lists. Holden, though chastened by the memory of the mob, gave all of them powerful support. Of the ten elected at least seven were peace men.[180]

Shortly after the elections the legislature met in extra session, where the peace men were given an opportunity to test their strength. Though Vance, in his message, sought to decrease peace strength by informing the legislators that negotiations with the North would be futile and dangerous, the House passed a resolution calling for "formal negotiations for an amicable and honorable settlement . . . upon the basis of separation."[181] The Vance men, led by Graham in the Senate, managed to have the resolutions laid on the table.[182]

By the end of the year Holden had grown bolder and had begun the effective device of appealing for a convention. Arguing that the only power which can close the War is the power that began it, he proposed, in effect, that the authority to negotiate peace be taken from the hands of the general government and confided to the separate States.

Demands for a convention and separate State action convinced Vance that the Confederate government should show the people it was trying to obtain peace. If rebuffed by the North, the rebuff would serve to strengthen the determination of the southern people. Though statesmen might regard this as useless, the people would not. Davis explained that negotiations were impractical and that, having made three efforts already, it was impossible to obtain an audience with Lincoln. Further, the President used this occasion to urge upon Vance the same advice Hale had given him months before, to "cut loose from Holden" and "abandon a policy of conciliation and set them at defiance." [183]

During the closing days of 1863 Vance learned from private sources that Holden had decided to make his re-election turn on the question of calling a convention. If Vance opposed the

---

[179] Jonathan Worth to Archibald McLean, September 10, 1863, Hamilton, *Worth Correspondence*, I, 261.

[180] Raleigh *North Carolina Standard*, October 4, 1863, February 4, 1864; Raleigh *Progress*, September 23, 1863; Raleigh *Register*, November 27, 1863.

[181] *House Journal, Adjourned Session, 1863*, pp. 17-19.

[182] W. A. Huske to E. J. Hale, December 1, 1863, Hale Papers.

[183] Z. B. Vance to Jefferson Davis, December 30, 1863, *O. R.*, Ser. I, Vol. LI, Pt. II, 87; Jefferson Davis to Z. B. Vance, January 8, 1864, *O. R.*, Ser. I, Vol. LI, Pt. II, 808-810.

convention he would be opposed for re-election. Thus all the efforts of the Governor to maintain the harmony of the State and the unity of the party which had elected him to office were frustrated. On three successive days Vance wrote candid letters to his three most trusted advisers, and in them he revealed that he had at last made up his mind as to the stand he must take on the peace question. To Hale he wrote: "The convention question is to be my test and I am to be beaten if I oppose it."[184] To Graham, the next day: "I can not of course favor such a thing for any existing cause. I will see the Conservative party blown into a thousand atoms . . . before I will consent to a course which I think will bring dishonor and ruin upon both State & Confederacy! . . . Is Holden the leader of the Conservative party? If so I dont belong to it."[185] And to Swain he wrote, on January 2, the most revealing letter of all: "The final plunge which I have been dreading and avoiding, that is to separate me from a large number of my political friends, is about to be made . . . . There is something to be said on both sides. . . . As God liveth, there is nothing I would not do or dare for the people who, so far beyond my merits, have honored me. But in resisting this attempt to lead them back . . . I feel that I am serving them truly, worthily."[186]

So the new year opened with Vance having at last made the decision that the peace movement was to be opposed with all his power, even at the cost of a party split and at the risk of political defeat. But because it was strategically too early to open the campaign Vance did not announce publicly the decision that he had reached privately. His delay allowed the convention movement to attain dangerous proportions, demanding more vigorous efforts to defeat it, for Holden was still free of any open denunciation by Vance. By the middle of January Holden had served public notice on Vance that he must approve the convention idea or be defeated. With great skill and with equally great vagueness Holden presented arguments to the people in issue after issue of the *Standard*. He claimed to be greatly encouraged by the response of the people. Through the medium of petitions to the Governor and of resolutions adopted in public meetings, pressure began to be put upon Vance, who had as yet made no announcement of his opposition, to support the movement.[187]

But if Vance was embarrassed by these petitions and resolutions, he was embarrassed even further by the Confederate government.

[184] Z. B. Vance to E. J. Hale, December 30, 1863, Hale Papers.
[185] Z. B. Vance to W. A. Graham, January 1, 1864, Graham Papers, Raleigh.
[186] Z. B. Vance to David L. Swain, January 2, 1864, Z. B. Vance Papers.
[187] See Raleigh *State Journal*, quoting Raleigh *North Carolina Standard*, January 19, January 20, February 3, 1864; Raleigh *North Carolina Standard*, January 1. 1864.

Through letters and interviews President Davis had continually kept himself informed about the peace movement in North Carolina, but, though he was clearly alarmed, he had refrained from intervention. His alarm increased at the turn of affairs early in 1864, when he was advised that a majority of 30,000 would favor a convention. It was only a few days later that Davis asked Congress to suspend the writ of habeas corpus and Congress, on February 15, approved.[188] It could hardly be doubted that of the thirteen specified cases in which suspension was to apply, number eleven was proposed with North Carolina in mind: "Of persons advising or inciting others to abandon the Confederate cause, or to resist the Confederate States, or to adhere to the enemy."[189]

Thus the delicate political situation with which Vance was faced was made far worse by the very cause he was trying to sustain. It was obvious that Vance's opponent must be a radical peace man, and it was politically inevitable that as Vance opposed the peace movement he would necessarily support the Confederacy. Yet this act, universally interpreted as heavy-handed repression, compromised his position and made his task incalculably more difficult than he thought it had to be.

His immediate protest to Davis was so impassioned that Davis called it "discourteous and untrue." It was certainly discourteous, but Davis never appeared to realize that Vance was really asking for aid in order that he might help Davis himself. None of the voluminous war correspondence between President and Governor was conducted with more acrimony or less profit. Davis refused to say whether or not he would use force against the peace movement, and by this decision he refused to strengthen Vance's hand.[190]

He strengthened Holden's instead, for the peace movement was intensified as a result of martial law. On February 24 Holden suspended the *Standard,* saying by way of explanation: "I felt that if I could not print as a freeman I would not print at all, and I could not bear the idea of lowering or changing my tone." [191] Although Davis used his great power sparingly and very few arrests were made in North Carolina, the suspension of the writ spread something akin to terror over the State. When the legislature met in May it passed a strongly worded resolution against suspension

[188] Davis' Message to Congress February 3, 1864, is in *O. R.,* Ser. IV, Vol. III, 67-70.

[189] The law of February 15, 1864, is in *O. R.,* Ser. IV, Vol. III, 203-204.

[190] Jefferson Davis to Z. B. Vance, February 29, 1864, *O. R.,* Ser. I. Vol. LI, Pt. II, 824-827; Z. B. Vance to Jefferson Davis, *O. R.,* Ser. I, Vol. LI, Pt. II, 830-833; Jefferson Davis to Z. B. Vance, *O. R.,* Ser. I, Vol. LI, Pt. II, 844-846.

[191] W. W. Holden to Calvin J. Cowles, March 18, 1864, William Woods Holden Papers, State Department of Archives and History, Raleigh, N. C.

and defied the Confederacy by approving a bill making it a high misdemeanor to ignore a writ issued by a judge of the State.[192]

In the midst of controversy over the peace movement and martial law Vance began his campaign for re-election. From the time of his decision at the first of the year he had been planning an imaginative and dramatic way to begin his public denunciation of the man who had made him governor. Audaciously, he wangled an invitaton to speak at Wilkesboro—in the heart of the disaffected country—and on February 22 all doubts and uncertainties as to his position were swept away. In the midst of jokes, jibes, denunciations, and impassioned assertions of ultimate Confederate victory there was a quiet, sober discussion of the peace movement and the dangers of convention, which spread his fame all over the South. The address was repeated in several towns on the way back to Raleigh and was published in numerous newspapers amidst a flood of congratulations, even from Richmond. North Carolina papers were almost unanimous in their praise.[193]

The Wilkesboro speech clarified the political atmosphere for Holden as well as for Vance. Resuming publication of the *Standard* early in March with a special edition, Holden announced his candidacy for the governorship and promised the voters to obtain an honorable peace. To many the goals of the peace movement were now certain; it seemed a plan to lead a disappointed editor to the governor's chair. But if Vance's old ally was now against him, his old enemies must now be for him. His problem was not to alienate the stanch conservatives of his own party, whose votes he needed and to whom Holden was appealing. As he put it to Hale, as the campaign was about to begin: The secessionists "will be obliged to vote for me, and the danger is in pushing off too big a slice of the old union men with Holden. . . . I do not intend to allow him to read me out of the party if I can help it, for this would be ruinous. . . . Let them [the extreme Conservatives] abuse Jeff Davis and the Secessionists to their hearts content so they but oppose this convention movement and keep to their duty on the war question. . . ." [194]

The strategy decided upon, Vance began the first of his magnificent speaking tours of the State which left Holden—too wise to try to match it—all but helpless. Vance did not hesitate to criticize and ridicule Holden and seemed to relish his opportunities to review the Editor's checkered political career as being that of an

---

[192] *House Journal, Adjourned Session, 1864,* pp. 44-45; *Public Laws of N. C., Adjourned Session, 1864,* pp. 10-11.

[193] The new administration paper, the Raleigh *Conservative* began its career with the issue of April 20, 1864, in which it printed Vance's speech of February 22, 1864, at Wilkesboro.

[194] Z. B. Vance to E. J. Hale, February 11, 1864, Hale Papers.

opportunist trying to be all things to all men. He gave the Conservatives comfort by condemning the suspension of the writ, and pleased the Confederates by insisting that the War must be fought to a finish. Constantly attacking Holden with vigor and effect, he took pains to show the people what secession from the Confederacy would mean. With a mixture of contagious humor and sober reasoning he endeared himself to the people in a degree unmatched in the history of the State.[195]

Meanwhile Holden's campaign, ignoring the Confederate administration, concentrated on Vance in the columns of the *Standard*. He charged venality, waste, and corruption. "It is the opinion of many intelligent Conservatives, who have good opportunity to observe and ascertain the facts, that the administration of Governor Vance is the most corrupt and extravagant in the Confederate States. For our part, we fear there is much ground for this opinion. There is certainly much room for the hand of reform."[196] Direct charges were made about blockade-running for private profit, as Vance had admitted at Fayetteville that he had shipped out five bales of cotton. He also attacked Vance for his propensity to joke in such serious times, and for his vulgarity. "No decent gentleman can canvass with Governor Vance."[197]

To these personal charges were added sober condemnations of Vance's attitude toward the peace movement and the convention platform. Holden was the peace candidate; Vance was the war candidate and had gone over to the secessionists, since he had told the soldiers he wanted them to "fight till h-ll froze over, and then fight upon the ice." Denying that he intended to take North Carolina out of the Confederacy by making a separate peace, he nevertheless continued to be vague as to just what his proposed convention could do to secure peace. With support from only three papers which had opposed Vance in 1862, and only five members of the legislature, Holden labored under great handicaps in trying to organize his campaign on a state-wide basis.[198]

In addition to support from most of the former secessionist press, Vance's friends contributed funds to establish a paper of their own, which they boldly called *The Conservative*. Failing to persuade Hale to come from Fayetteville to edit it for him, Vance secured his former journalistic associate from Asheville, John D. Hyman, who came to Raleigh and began publication with the

[195] *Wilmington Journal*, May 5, August 4, 1864; Raleigh *Conservative*, May 4, 18, June 1, 1864; Raleigh *Confederate*, May 25, June 8, July 6, 1864; *Fayetteville Observer*, May 2, 1864.

[196] Raleigh *North Carolina Standard*, June 22, and July 6, 20, 1864.

[197] Raleigh *North Carolina Standard*, July 13, 1864.

[198] Raleigh *Progress*, March 3, 8, April 18, 1864.

issue of April 20, 1864. The daily and weekly issues came to match Holden's *Standard* by the end of the campaign.[199]

The policy of *The Conservative* was to attract the Secessionists but to hold the Conservatives. On April 27 Hyman published Vance's platform which amounted to a clever appeal to both parties.

> "The supremacy of the civil over military law.
> "A speedy repeal of the act suspending the writ of *habeas corpus*.
> "A quiet submission to all laws, whether good or bad, while they remain upon our statute books.
> "No reconstruction, or submission, but perpetual independence.
> "An unbroken front to the common enemy; but timely and repeated negotiations for *peace* by the proper authorities.
> "No separate State action through a Convention; no counter revolution; no combined resistance to the government.
> "Opposition to despotism in every form, and the preservation of our Republican institutions in all their purity." [200]

Of the seven planks, three appealed to Secessionists and four to Conservatives whom Holden was trying to attract. Instead of standing in the middle and being crushed by two extremes Vance intended to walk down the middle and draw from both sides. Since the Secessionists were compelled to support him, he paid them little notice and concentrated on winning the bulk of his own party. So Hyman emphasized that though Holden talked peace his policy would really bring civil war.[201] *The Conservative* published the least acrimonious of Vance's correspondence with Davis, in which the President was urged to attempt peace negotiations. Readers could see, therefore, that Vance had lent his moral influence for peace, had protested vigorously and endlessly against arbitrary acts of the central government, and had repeatedly defended the rights of the State. When the legislature met in May it helped the cause of Vance with resolutions on peace and civil rights which conformed to his platform statements about them and endorsed his course with almost unanimous majorities. In these ways much of Holden's thunder was stolen, with telling effect.[202]

For the most part Holden was kept on the defensive, especially during the last few weeks of the campaign when the Heroes of America were discovered in North Carolina and efforts were made to link him with that treasonable organization's attempts to protect those who favored a return to the Union. Though it was never proven that Holden held membership in the organiza-

---

[199] John D. Hyman to Z. B. Vance, January 12, 1864, Z. B. Vance Papers.
[200] Raleigh *Conservative*, April 27, 1864.
[201] Raleigh *Conservative*, June 8, July 6, 20, 1864.
[202] *Senate Journal, Adjourned Session, 1864*, p. 11; *House Journal, Adjourned Session, 1864*, p. 31.

tion, it was shown that its members were instructed to vote for him, and this fact greatly embarrassed his candidacy.[203]

When the soldiers voted on July 28 Holden received the first intimation of the crushing defeat he was to endure, for Vance won 13,209 of the 15,033 votes cast in the army. On August 4 the people added their verdict: Vance's total vote was 57,873 to Holden's 14,432. Vance thus had a majority three times the number of Holden's total vote. Holden carried only three counties, and these by small majorities. The legislature elected at the same time was safely in the Vance column.[204]

Holden charged that force and fraud defeated him. It is true that in the army some officers used pressure and intimidation to prevent votes for Holden, but there is no evidence of fraud, either there or in the State elections. There was some trickery over special yellow paper ballots for the Vance men, but Holden duplicated this to the best of his ability.[205]

Holden was crushed by more than pressure and trickery. He was defeated in part because he had too many obstacles in his own career to overcome. But most of all he was defeated because of Vance's magnificent campaign. Conducted with great skill and consummate diplomacy, it established once and for all Vance's matchless popularity among the people of North Carolina. Probably few among them realized the irony inherent in his 1864 victory: His election in 1862 seemed to many to prove the disloyalty of North Carolina, yet the re-election of the same man in 1864 proved its loyalty.

But if the re-election of Vance strengthened the Confederate cause in North Carolina it had little immediate effect upon the cause in the field. Lee was barely holding Grant, and Sherman was not being held at all. And it was not only the Confederate armies which were being inexorably subjugated; it was the Confederate spirit as well. If death, disease, and desertion were depleting the armies, resentment toward the Richmond government dampened the enthusiasm for the struggle.

From the moment of his re-election until the final surrender the next spring, Vance worked heroically for the cause he had come to embrace with enthusiasm and sincerity. In the fall of 1864 he was especially active in his appeal to deserters to return and in his efforts to arrest them when they ignored his appeals.[206] He talked of calling the legislature into special session in the

---

[203] Raleigh *Conservative*, July 6, 1864; Raleigh *North Carolina Standard*, July 13, 1864.
[204] The official vote is in the *Senate Journal, 1864-1865*, p. 75.
[205] Raleigh *North Carolina Standard*, August 3, 1864; Raleigh *Conservative*, August 3, 1864.
[206] Proclamation of August 24, 1864, Z. B. Vance Papers.

hopes that it would authorize sending some State officers and the Home Guard to help Lee, but the Council of State would not agree.[207] When the regular session convened in November Vance recommended that the military age be extended to fifty-five but the lawmakers, showing no interest in Lee's plight, again refused to adopt his recommendation. In December resolutions introduced by Senator Pool called for the appointment of commissioners to negotitate for peace through the States, and the resolutions were barely defeated.[208] Although the legislature did not call a convention, as many feared it would, it took no vigorous action for the prosecution of the War and denied firmly the right of the central government to impress or arm the slaves. "They not only did no good, but they passed every possible exemption to keep men out of the service, the purpose being openly announced."[209] This was the judgment of a Democrat and a secessionist, but Vance's verdict hardly disagreed: "The impression here seems to have taken hold of everybody that the fighting is over and the Legislature seems disposed to omit every proposition for the public defense. Never was there a greater error."[210] In his second inaugural address,[211] in December, Vance tried vainly to lift again the waning spirits, but the gloom of the people had spread to the armies and desertion, long serious, now became fatal.

Another vigorous proclamation in February,[212] which even the *Standard* admitted was "not destitute of a certain species of rude eloquence," implored the masses not to submit voluntarily to their own degradation and brought congratulations from the long-alienated Davis, but it brought little else. As the *Standard* commented further, if proclamations could have won the War victory would have come long ago.[213]

No number of earnest and eloquent appeals could counteract the loss of Fort Fisher and the capture of Wilmington, both of which had fallen to the Federals by the end of January, 1865. The waves of despondency mounted higher and, though no new formal peace movement was agitated, perhaps it was because it appeared that shortly none would be necessary. Holden advocated that the State open separate negotiations for peace: "We would

[207] Z. B. Vance to E. J. Hale, October 11, 13, 1864, Hale Papers.

[208] *Senate Journal, 1864-1865*, pp. 66-67, 87-88.

[209] D. K. McRae to J. Taylor Wood, February 7, 1865, *O. R.*, Ser. I, Vol. XLVII, Pt. II, 1250-1251.

[210] Z. B. Vance to David L. Swain, January 31, 1865, Z. B. Vance Papers.

[211] Inaugural address, December 22, 1864, Z. B. Vance Papers.

[212] Proclamation of February 14, 1865, Vance Letter Book.

[213] Raleigh *North Carolina Standard*, February 22, 1865.

negotiate with the government of the United States and we would obtain the best terms we could for North Carolina."[214]

In many of his energetic attempts to save a cause now beyond saving Vance was whistling in the dark. He had always believed that the "great *popular heart* is not now & never has been in this war. It was a revolution of the *politicians* not the people . . ." but he believed also that it was his duty to "hold the demoralized and trembling fragments of society and law together and prevent them from dropping to pieces until the rapidly hastening end of our struggle shall be developed."[215]

In the midst of these final traumatic events a serious peace movement developed in Richmond. After the abortive Fortress Monroe conference a committee of senators was appointed to consult with the President and learn what steps he proposed to take, and it was suggested to him that a proposal to return to the Union might be an acceptable basis of negotiation. Davis replied that he had no constitutional authority for such a proposal and that only the States, each acting for itself in its sovereign capacity, could negotiate for peace upon the basis of reunion. Accordingly, after failure to get this proposal before the Confederate Senate, some individuals persuaded Senator Graham to go to Raleigh and inform Vance that many representatives and senators, including some from North Carolina, had recently held a conference and had concluded that steps should be taken to end the War. They thought that North Carolina was in a position to lead the way to peace by an order from Vance bringing the North Carolina troops home. In great excitement Vance refused the invitation. "Were I to do that, the last of it would not be heard for generations to come. It would be charged that the Confederacy might have succeeded but for the treachery of North Carolina. So far as the honor of the State is in my keeping it shall be untarnished. She must stand or fall with her sisters." [216]

There can be no doubt but that his political instinct was sound on this proposition, though extreme Conservatives in his own party were critical of it. ". . . while we had the very wisest Senator in the Confederacy [Graham] . . . we had also a Governor who knew when to 'not to do it,' and who in an important crisis did *nothing* so effectually and efficiently, that he saved the State from a useless humiliation, and an infamous reputation." [217] Later Graham urged that the legislature be called into extra session to deal with the crisis. Once more Vance called the Council of

[214] Raleigh *North Carolina Standard,* January 18, 1865.
[215] Z. B. Vance to David L. Swain, September 22, 1864, Z. B. Vance Papers.
[216] Battle, Address, p. 31.
[217] Cornelia P. Spencer to Z. B. Vance, May 10, 1866, Z. B. Vance Papers.

State and on March 28 asked its advice on the question of the extra legislative session. But the Council was equally divided, and so the session was not called.[218] Jonathan Worth had felt sure the Council would call the session and the legislature would call a convention. "This is the only hope of saving anything from the wreck." [219]

So as Richmond was about to be captured and as Sherman approached Raleigh, Vance was left to handle the crises as best he could. He tried to call out the Home Guard but he could never get enough of them together. "We have nothing to rely upon but a miracle," wrote Worth, "and our statesmen exhibit their natural sagacity in relying on one."[220]

No miracle came, but Sherman did. Notified by General Joseph Johnston on April 10 of the necessity of uncovering Raleigh, Vance began the transfer of records and military supplies to the west.[221] Two days later, having been advised by Johnston to get the best terms he could, Vance, with Graham and Swain to advise him, composed a letter to Sherman requesting an interview and authorizing the two ex-governors to treat with Sherman for the protection of Raleigh.[222] When they had left on their mission Vance waited all day in his office at the Capitol and advised the many anxious visitors to remain quietly in their homes.[223] When the two commissioners had not returned by the expected hour, when Vance learned that they had been captured, and when he was advised that the city would be evacuated by the Confederates that night, he left Raleigh at midnight and rode on horseback eight miles west, where he spent the remainder of the night at a Confederate camp. The next day he went to Graham's home in Hillsboro, where he learned of the surrender of General Lee, the fall of Raleigh, and the desire of President Davis to talk with him in Greensboro. Declining the safe conduct which Sherman had sent for his return to Raleigh, Vance followed Davis to Charlotte, where he talked with the President and some of his cabinet members and decided that his duty was to return to Raleigh and do what he could to maintain law and provide security.[224] But he was not permitted to pass through military lines during the extensive surrender negotiations, and upon the final surrender of

[218] P. H. Winston to Z. B. Vance, March 28, 1865, Governors' Papers, Vance.

[219] Jonathan Worth to J. J. Jackson, March 22, 1865, Hamilton, *Worth Correspondence,* I, 373.

[220] Jonathan Worth to J. J. Jackson, March 31, 1865, Hamilton, *Worth Correspondence,* I, 374.

[221] Cornelia Phillips Spencer, *The Last Ninety Days of the War in North Carolina* (New York, 1866), p. 146 (cited hereafter as Spencer, *Ninety Days*).

[222] Z. B. Vance in Dowd, *Life of Vance,* p. 483.

[223] Spencer, *Ninety Days,* p. 147.

[224] Dowd, *Life of Vance,* pp. 485, 486; Spencer, *Ninety Days,* pp. 142-163, 183-185.

Johnston to Sherman he issued his last proclamation[225] and offered
to surrender himself to General John M. Schofield, who declined
to accept it and informed him that he was at liberty to go home.

On May 4 Vance joined his wife and four sons in Statesville,
where they had sought safety, and awaited the future. On May 11
General Grant telegraphed General Schofield: "By direction of
the President you will at once arrest Zebulon B. Vance, late
Rebel Governor of North Carolina, and send him to Washington
under close guard, and acknowledge receipt."[226]

Early on the morning of May 13, his thirty-fifth birthday,
Vance's home in Statesville was surrounded by 300 cavalry under
the command of Major Porter. On May 20, exactly four years
after the formal secession of North Carolina, Vance was placed in
the Old Capitol Prison in Washington where he remained until
his release on parole on July 6, 1865.[227] No reasons were ever
given for his arrest, and no charges were ever made against him.

His career as War Governor is more responsible than any other
thing for the fact that North Carolina has loved, idolized, and
rewarded no other man in her history as she has Zebulon Baird
Vance. During the hard years of the conflict he exhibited the
qualities of popular leadership; he knew the way to the hearts
of the people. He sounded all their depths, interpreted their feelings, took their part, sympathized with their wants, and they
showered upon him the rich plenitude of their affection. He
emerged from the ruin encircled with the halo of renown, and it
remained untarnished for the rest of his life.

His governorship was characterized by an executive versatility
combining courage, energy, boldness, and vision beyond the expectations of his most enthusiastic supporters. His capacity for the
routine of administration surprised everyone. In public he rarely
joked any more. He captured the imagination and admiration of
North Carolina by his successful blockade-running operations
whereby the troops were supplied with shoes, blankets, and
medicines and their families with many needed articles of
subsistence. The affections of the common people, heretofore
alienated by the legal exemptions of large slaveowners and to
whom the War had already begun to appear to be primarily one
for the protection of slavery—"a rich man's war and a poor man's
fight"—were regained not only by denouncing and curbing pro-
fiteers and speculators, or at least attempting to curb them, but by
the establishment of depots of provisions for the subsistence of the
people, and by organizing in every county relief agencies to save

[225] Proclamation, April 28, 1865, Z. B. Vance Papers.
[226] Dowd, *Life of Vance*, p. 99.
[227] Dowd, *Life of Vance*, p. 100.

them from starvation. The crowning glory of his administration remains the untiring care and the unstinted labor he devoted to the provision of every possible comfort for the soldiers and for their families. The weeping gratitude of hundreds of humble people, eloquently if often ungrammatically expressed, increased the burden of his labors, but he always saw that their letters were answered. He was their martyr and had suffered for their acts. He was their shield and had defended them from peril. He had protected them against their own government. He had been with them in the burning light of battle. They remembered the gray uniforms, the warm blankets, the good shoes, the blessed medicines which his energy and his sympathy had provided amidst the famine and pestilence of evil days. He had defended their liberties and preserved their priceless honor. These things were the solid foundations of his place in their minds and hearts, and of his place in history.

THE PAPERS OF ZEBULON B. VANCE

VOLUME I

JUNE, 1843—DECEMBER, 1862

CHAPTER I

JUNE, 1843—AUGUST, 1862

From M. M. Vance [1]

Lapland, [2] N⁰. C. June 11th 1843

We received your letter last Sabbath was a week ago and was
very glad to hear that you was well and that you was learning so
fast we hope that you will improve your time so as to make a
great & good man. I have nothing Knew to relate, but I returned
from Burnsville [3] last week and they was all sick with the Scarlet
fever and we herd last Knight that Lucias [4] was dead but we

---

[1] Mira Margaret (Baird) Vance (1802-1878), mother of Zebulon Baird Vance. She
was a daughter of Zebulon Baird (1764-1827), Scottish settler from New Jersey and
one of the pioneers in the settlement of Buncombe County, and of Hannah Erwin,
of a numerous and influential family of Burke County. Mira Margaret Baird married David Vance in 1825 and bore him eight children, of which number Zebulon
Baird Vance, born May 13, 1830, was the third. *Memoir of Mrs. Margaret M.
Vance, and Mrs. Harriette Espy Vance* (Raleigh, 1878); C. P. S. (Cornelia Phillips
Spencer) "Our Mothers," *North Carolina Presbyterian* (Old Series, Vol. XXI, no.
1184), October 30, 1878, p. 2. Her will is on record in the Madison County courthouse, Marshall, N. C.

[2] On the French Broad River, now Marshall, the county seat of Madison County,
but then a part of Buncombe County. The members of the David Vance family
moved from Reems Creek, about fourteen miles north of Asheville, where they lived
when Zebulon Baird Vance was born, to Lapland before 1836 and acquired about
1,500 acres of land. There they remained until about 1850 when, David Vance
having died, Mira Margaret Vance and her seven children moved to Asheville.

[3] About fifty acres of land at Lapland were given by Zebulon B. Vance to Madison
County by deed of April 20, 1853, "for the purpose of locating thereon the town of
Marshall." John Preston Arthur in his *Western North Carolina*, p. 195, erroneously
states that the county seat was located on lands of T. B. Vance and that said land
was deeded by David Vance. But David Vance had died in 1844. See Records,
Madison County, Land Deeds, Book G, pp. 138-139, in Madison County court-
house, Marshall, N. C.; David Vance to Jane Davidson, February 3, 1836, Z. B. Vance
Papers, State Department of Archives and History, Raleigh, N. C.; (cited hereafter
as Z. B. Vance Papers). John Preston Arthur, *Western North Carolina; A History*,
(From 1730 to 1913) (Raleigh, 1914). pp. 194-195, (cited hereafter as Arthur,
Western North Carolina).

[4] Lucius H. Smith (1841-1904), a son of Bacchus J. Smith (1804-1886) of Burnsville, who was later a mercantile partner of Robert B. Vance, brother of Zebulon B.
Vance, in Asheville, and of Sarah Ann (Baird) Smith (1816-1881), a younger sister
of Mira Margaret (Baird) Vance. P. A. Cummings, "Early Reminiscence of Asheville," *Asheville Citizen*, March 20, 1923, (cited hereafter as Cumming, "Reminiscence"); Albert S. McLean, "Notebooks," MS. accounts of western North Carolina
families compiled from cemetery records and other local sources, and in possession
of the author, 206 Aurora Drive, Asheville, N. C. (cited hereafter as McLean, "Notebooks").

hope the report is not true. I often think of you and would be very glad to see you. You must continue to write to us every week & some of us will answer it &c.
Washington College[5]

From Robt. B. Vance [6]

I now take the opportunity to address you a few lines we are all well at present without it is Aunt Lauretta [7] she is sick at M[r]. Barnards. I am very glad that you are pleased with your boarding [8] at M[r]. Grimes'. I would be very glad that you Could come home in September as we will have Fruit & Water mellons plenty. as the prospect is very fine the people in this Country is about to starve for want of Something to eate the Cry is Corn Corn. &c. there is a very distressing accident happened at M[r]. Brankses on Reams [9] Creek. Miss Rebeca [10] has a baby, it would have been better for her if she had been in her grave but I must

[5] Located near Jonesboro, Washington County, Tennessee. The school was founded by Rev. Samuel Doak in 1780 and became Washington College by charter from the Tennessee legislature in 1795. It was known as "the first institution of learning west of the mountains" but was hardly more than an academy when Vance was a student. For an account of its history see Howard Ernest Carr, *Washington College. A Study of an Attempt to Provide Higher Education in Eastern Tennessee* (Knoxville, 1935).

[6] Robert Brank Vance (1828-1899), brother of Zebulon B. Vance. He was named for his father's brother, a physician and congressman who was killed in a duel with Samuel P. Carson in 1827. Robert Brank Vance was a merchant in Asheville in the fifties, a farmer, clerk of court in Madison and Buncombe counties and became colonel of the Twenty-ninth North Carolina Regiment and brigadier general, C. S. A. during the Civil War. After the war he was a member of Congress (Dem.), 1873-1885; member of the State House of Representatives from Buncombe County, 1894-1896; and Assistant United States Commissioner of Patents, 1885-1889. R. D. W. Connor (comp. & ed.). *A Manual of North Carolina Issued by the North Carolina Historical Commission for the Use of Members of the General Assembly Session 1913* (Raleigh, 1913), pp. 518, 939-942 (cited hereafter as Connor, *Manual*; *Biographical Directory of American Congress 1774-1927* (Washington, 1928), p. 1,642 (cited hereafter as *Biog. Dir. of Am. Cong.*).

[7] Loretta T. Baird (1823-1905), a native of Tennessee. She was the wife of Adolphus Erwin Baird (1819-1878), a younger brother of Mira Margaret (Baird) Vance. He later became a merchant in Asheville in partnership with Bacchus J. Smith, his brother-in-law, and Robert Brank Vance, his nephew. McLean, "Notebooks."

[8] Each student at Washington College was responsible for securing his own room and board.

[9] The spelling varies. David Vance I, who was clerk of court and lived in that region, spelled the name "Rims," but "Reams," "Rheims," and "Reems" are common. The last spelling is the most usual one in the nineteenth century. Foster Alexander Sondley, *A History of Buncombe County North Carolina*, 2 vols. (Asheville, 1930), II, 463 (cited hereafter as Sondley, *Buncombe County*).

[10] Rebecca Brank of Reems Creek is listed in the *Census*, Buncombe County, 1850, as a daughter of Elizabeth Brank, age sixty-two. Just under Rebecca's name is listed that of Eliza J., age six, probably the child to whom reference is made. Rebecca Brank was about thirty-five in 1843. The Vance and Brank families were connected by the marriage of Zebulon B. Vance's grandfather, David Vance I, to Priscilla Brank, daughter of Peter Brank, of Morganton.

stop Chain sends her love to you & all send howdy, as you sent
a specimen of your hand write I send one in return
my respects to Robt. Brittian. [11]

From D. Vance [12]

I write you a line saying that we are all well your Mother and
Robert have written on the outside of this sheet [13] but so long
ago– that I thought I would give you the news up to this date.
Nothing new to tell you, we are getting on tolerably well with
our crop our Wheat looks well but we, are very fearful of the
rust as we have a great-deal of Wet Weather do mind your Books
and be careful of giving offense to your School Mates, we start
in a few moments to Church. So farewell.
Sunday Morning June 18 1843
[A. L. S. [14] Z. B. Vance Papers, State Department of Archives and
History, Raleigh.]

To Cousin Matt [15]

University of N [16] C Aug. 12 [1851]
I have been promising myself to write to you for some time
but have never found the proper time until this evening. You

---

[11] The Brittain family was related to the Vance family through the marriage of
Celia Vance (d. 1876) to Benjamin S. Brittain. Celia Vance was a sister of David
Vance II, Zebulon B. Vance's father, and after her marriage lived in Haywood,
Macon, and Cherokee counties. No reference to Robert Brittain has been found.
Robert B. Vance to Theodore F. Davidson, June 29, 1891, quoting family Bible,
Colonel Allen T. Davidson and General Theodore F. Davidson Papers, State
Department of Archives and History, Raleigh, N. C. (cited hereafter as Davidson
Papers).

[12] David Vance (1792-1844), the father of Zebulon B. Vance. He was a son of David
Vance (1745-1813), who was a captain in the Revolution, one of the pioneer settlers
of Buncombe County, large landowner, member of the legislature, clerk of superior
court; and of Priscilla Brank (1756-1836) of Burke County. David Vance II was a
farmer and merchant in Buncombe County and in what was later Madison County.
He left no will.

[13] The three letters are on the same folded sheet addressed on the outside in the
handwriting of David Vance to "Mr. Zebulon B. Vance, Washington College,
E. Tennessee, from D. Vance P. M., Lapland N C, June 18th."

[14] The handwriting of the first and second letter is the same. It does not appear
to be the same as other letters signed by Mira Margaret (Baird) Vance, and is much
more similar to later samples of the writing of Robert Brank Vance. He probably
wrote both of them. The third letter is unquestionably in the handwriting of
David Vance.

[15] Martha E. Weaver, at that time eighteen years of age, was the daughter of
Montraville Michael Weaver (1808-1882) and Jane Eliza Baird (1810-1899), who
was a daughter of Bedent Baird, brother of Zebulon Baird, Vance's maternal
grandfather. M. M. Weaver was a farmer, Methodist clergyman, and owner of
eighteen slaves in 1860. He lived at Reems Creek, a few miles north of Asheville.
Martha E. Weaver married, in 1853, John W. Vandiver (1821-1893), a Methodist
preacher, and they moved to Tennessee. *Census,* Buncombe County, 1850 and 1860;
James Samuel Tazewell Baird, "Historical Sketches of the Early Days," *Asheville
Saturday Register,* January, February, March, 1905 (clipping in University of
North Carolina Library, Chapel Hill, N. C.; cited hereafter as Baird, "Historical
Sketches").

[16] In the summer of 1851 Vance enrolled in the University of North Carolina as a

must excuse me for not fulfilling my promise to you sooner– I have so many to write to that I can hardly spare time to attend to them, and besides so few write to me in return, that I allmost feel like dropping them alltogether– It is indeed so vexatious to run to the post office in hot haste and impatience to receive letters from *home* & *friends* who are far away from you, to be disappointed– You have doubtless learned from Mental Philosophy what power association has in calling distant scenes and images with vividness back to the mind– There is nothing can do this so effectually and powerfully as the reception of a letter, from those we love, while away from home– You have never experienced it, but you will some day learn its truth. For all you know Cousin Matt this *may be a hint* for you not to be *allways* in replying to this letter!

I suppose you have heard from Mother all the particulars of my getting down here, my situation here and other things of like import, so I will not detail them to you again. This is a beautiful place indeed. The main college buildings are 3 in number each 3 story high coulored yellow and surrounded with neat terraces of earth thrown up and platted with grass. They are very large buildings. In addition to these are 3 other buildings, the ball room, Chapel and recitation hall large and tasty. They are all situated in a beautiful oak & popular grove, checkered off with splendid white gravel walks, set out in shrubbery, and the whole, I suppose about 20 or more acres surrounded with a stone wall neatly put up. The elevation is likewise high and I presume healthy, tho' one of our fellow students named Watters [17] is laying near unto death at this time. The weather has been warmer here than ever I felt it in my life before. The thermometer has been up to 102°F. If I thought it would'nt plague you I would tell you that I am writing this letter to you in my shirt-tail now– Dont blush at my folly Cousin Matt.

I am studying Botany, the science of flowers, among other things. It is a Ladies' science in particular, and if I learn enough about it I will teach you and Sister Ann [18] when I get home– It would interest you extremely I am sure– I am getting on very well in everything I have taken up– Indeed you would hardly believe that I had taken to tremendous hard study would you?

special student, remaining one year. The arrangement was made through the interest and influence of David L. Swain, president of the University and a close friend and neighbor of Vance's father and, more especially, of his uncle, Dr. Robert Brank Vance.

[17] Samuel Paxon Watters (1833-1912), of Wilmington, who graduated in 1855. He became a lieutenant in the Confederate army, a planter, and an Episcopal minister in 1879. Daniel Lindsey Grant (ed.), *Alumni History of the University of North Carolina* (Durham, 1924), p. 650 (cited hereafter as Grant, *Alumni History*).

[18] Mary Ann Weaver (1830-1890), a sister of Martha E. Weaver. *Census*, Buncombe County, 1860; McLean, "Notebooks."

Its the fact notwithstanding. I rise at 5 and go to bed at 10 and I give you my word, I dont lose more than 2 hours during that time, and that is necessary for recreation– I think I am establishing the character of a well-behaved student, in the eyes of the Faculty– I trust I may do so– I have heard of the duel, [19] fights &c but not the results of the election [20] yet. I am quite anxious. How are you doing at school? How many young ladies are there? and especially how are they? How is Miss Jane? [21] Give my compliments to her and Miss Tim Siler. [22] Her brother [23] is quite well say to her. Also say to Miss L. Johnston [24] that her brother [25] is well. He is rooming with me– I should like to hear

---

[19] Probably the duel fought at Saluda Gap between Marcus Erwin, brilliant editor of the Democratic *Asheville News* and ardent advocate of secession, then representing Buncombe County in the House of Commons, and John Baxter, then of Hendersonville and a strong Union man. According to Judge A. C. Avery, the duel was the result of political quarrels. Baxter was wounded in the hand. Arthur, *Western North Carolina*, pp. 157, 368-369.

[20] Congressional elections were then held in August of the odd-numbered years. In the early 1850's the Western Congressional District was tending toward secession in its sentiment. In deference to this trend Thomas L. Clingman, the incumbent, sought a return to Congress in 1851 as a "Southern Rights Whig." He was opposed by Burgess S. Gaither, of Morganton, who was persuaded by the Old Line Union Whigs to run against Clingman. Clingman won by a large majority and the next year left the Whig party for the Democratic, carrying his district with him. William Kenneth Boyd, "Thomas Lanier Clingman," Allen Johnson, and Dumas Malone, and Harris E. Starr (eds.), *Dictionary of American Biography*, 21 vols. and index (New York, 1943-1944), IV, 220-221 (cited hereafter as *Dict. of Am. Biog.*); Arthur, *Western North Carolina*, pp. 644-645; Samuel A'Court Ashe, "Burgess S. Gaither," Samuel A'Court Ashe (ed.), *Biographical History of North Carolina*, 8 vols. (Greensboro, 1905), II, 93-99 (cited hereafter as Ashe, *Biog. Hist. of N. C.*); "Burgess S. Gaither," (a typed summary of his career loaned to the editor by United States Senator Samuel J. Ervin, Jr., of Morganton, N. C.); Clarence Newell Gilbert, "The Public Career of Thomas L. Clingman," (unpublished M. A. thesis, University of North Carolina, 1947).

[21] Probably Jane R. Fagg, then seventeen, a daughter of John A. Fagg (1807-1888), prominent farmer and politician, member of the House of Commons from Buncombe County in 1844, 1846, 1852, and from Madison County in 1858 and 1860. He was postmaster at Asheville from 1873 to 1879. *Census*, Buncombe County, 1860; Connor, *Manual*, pp. 517, 689; E. J. Aston to Samuel McDowell Tate, December 6, 1873, Samuel McDowell Tate Papers, Southern Historical Collection, University of North Carolina, Chapel Hill, N. C. (cited hereafter as Tate Papers).

[22] Harriet Timoxena Siler (1835-1900), of Franklin, Macon County, who later married William Sloan. All these girls were probably students at Holston Conference Female College in Asheville.

[23] Leonidas Fidelis Siler (1830-1870), valedictorian of the class of 1852 at the University of North Carolina. He became a lawyer, journalist, teacher, and Methodist minister. Grant, *Alumni History*, p. 563; Kemp Plummer Battle, *History of the University of North Carolina*, 2 vols. (Raleigh, 1907-1912), I, 628-633 (cited hereafter as Battle, *History of U. of N. C.*).

[24] Louisa J. Johnston (1836-1867), a daughter of William Johnston of Haywood County, a wealthy farmer and merchant who had emigrated from Ireland, and of Lucinda Gudger. The Johnston family moved to Asheville in the fifties. *Census*, Haywood County, 1850; *Census*, Buncombe County, 1860; McLean, "Notebooks."

[25] Robert Bruce Johnston (1832-1896), who graduated in 1854. He became a farmer and a lawyer, but he practiced very little as he was independently wealthy. During the war he was sergeant in the Sixteenth North Carolina Regiment and captain in the Sixty-second North Carolina Regiment. Grant, *Alumni History*, p. 325; Lawrence Pulliam in *Asheville Times*, February 10, 1929.

how my fair Cousin M. J. B.[26] is getting along with Branch.[27]. I spent a part of a day very agreeable in Morganton as I came on. I saw Miss Harriett Espy [28] and several other young ladies of my acquaintance. Cousin Celia Tate also but did not get to speak to her. Have you seen John Wilsons wife yet? For justifiable reasons I did not stay to see him married. What young gentleman is boarding at Mothers? I dont expect I can go home until next June, as I will have to go to Raleigh in vacation to get license if they dont reject me as they have Sam McDowell [29] and others. Cousin M. I am sorry I undertook to write you on this small sheet, but next time I will take a larger one. Kiss all the girls for me at Mothers. bless their sweet souls! Kiss Ann,[30] Sarah, [31] & Hannah [32] for me, also, and all the other girls that would accept it. I have not written half I wanted to. Please write soon and tell all about the girls &c. Everything you can think of will interest me, so dont hunt up nice words &c to write to me– Tell Ann [33] its her time next.

[Asheville]

---

[26] Margaret Jane Baird (1836-1907), a daughter of Israel and Mary (Tate) Baird and granddaughter of Bedent Baird. Her kinship to Vance stemmed from the fact that their grandfathers were brothers. At this time she lived in Asheville. In 1852 she married Augustus Summerfield Merrimon. McLean, "Notebooks."

[27] Probably Branch Hamlin Merrimon, Jr. (1836-1883), who was a son of Branch Hamlin Merrimon (1802-1881) and Mary Evelyn (Paxton) Merrimon and a brother of Augustus Summerfield Merrimon. At this time the Merrimon family lived about fourteen miles from Asheville, where the father carried on his varied businesses as merchant, farmer, and Methodist minister. *A Memoir: Augustus Summerfield Merrimon* (n. d., n. p.).

[28] Harriett Newell Espy (1832-1878), a daughter of Thomas Espy (1800-1833), a Presbyterian minister, and of Sarah Louisa (Tate) Espy. She married Zebulon B. Vance in 1853, but at this time she lived with her kinsman Charles McDowell (1786-1859) at Quaker Meadows near Morganton, by whom she was reared after the death of her parents. *Memoir of Mrs. Margarett M. Vance, and Mrs. Harriette Espy Vance.* See p. 16, 81n.

[29] Samuel Moffett McDowell (1825-1853), a son of Charles McDowell of Quaker Meadows. He had lived and studied law with his two brothers-in-law, N. W. and J. W. Woodfin, in Asheville. In 1851 he went to California in search of gold and returned to Asheville in 1853 without it. He became an attorney in Asheville, Diary of Augustus Summerfield Merrimon, Southern Historical Collection, University of North Carolina, Chapel Hill, N. C. (cited hereafter as Merrimon, "Diary").

[30] Annie Edgeworth Vance, a sister of Zebulon B. Vance. She was born in 1836 and in 1855 married Rev. Richard N. Price, a Methodist minister and educator. They moved to Tennessee the same year. *Census,* Buncombe County, 1860; *Asheville News,* May 8, and November 29, 1855.

[31] Sarah Priscilla Vance, another sister of Zebulon B. Vance. She was born in 1838. She later married Douglas Holt and they moved to Tennessee. *Census,* Buncombe County, 1860; McLean, "Notebooks."

[32] Hannah Moore Vance, youngest sister of Zebulon B. Vance. She was born in 1842 and afterwards married Edmund W. Herndon (1839-1883). They lived in Asheville. *Census,* Buncombe County, 1860; McLean, "Notebooks."

[33] See p. 4, 18n.

State Department of Archives and History

The restored Vance birthplace, located on Reems Creek near Weaverville and Asheville, is administered as a Historic Site by the State Department of Archives and History. The upper view shows the log house, the plan of which is fairly typical of the larger plantation houses of the period, with one of the outbuildings. The lower interior view represents the Vance sitting room. Some of the woodwork has incorporated wood from the original structure.

[on front]

Give love to sister Harrit [34] why dont she write? Write, write, write, write, write—

[A. L. S. Zebulon B. Vance Papers, State Department of Archives and History, Raleigh.]

To Cousin John [35]

University of N. Ca. Sep 14 [1851]

I do not know when I have been more gratified than I was in receiving your letter the other day. I did not know that you thought so much of me as to write to me, but I was agreeably disappointed in finding that according to the motto on the seal of your letter that I was "absent but not forgotten," by you. It gives one great pleasure to receive letters from his friends when he is away from home and among strangers, so thank you!

Well John as you know all the news about Asheville better than I do, I have nothing much to tell you about, but myself, my situation and prospects here, &c.

I am studying the studies of the Senior Class [36] entire, except, French & Greek, which keep me very busy, besides I am reading law [37] as hard as ever. That will serve to show the value of time

[34] Harriett N. Baird, a daughter of Israel Baird, and Margaret Jane Baird's sister. She later married Captain Natt Atkinson of Asheville, who was a real estate dealer, attorney, proprietor of the *North Carolina Citizen,* and a member of the legislature. Tate Papers, *passim;* McLean, "Notebooks."

[35] John Mitchell Davidson (1829-1917). His mother was Elizabeth Vance (1787-1861), a sister of Zebulon B. Vance's father. In 1804 she married William Mitchell Davidson (1780-1846), and they moved from Asheville to Duck River, Tennessee. Later the family moved back to Haywood County, N. C., and in 1844 to Texas, where William Mitchell Davidson died in 1846. John Mitchell Davidson went to Texas also, but returned with his mother in 1847. Elizabeth Vance Davidson then married her first husband's brother, Samuel Winslow Davidson, who was a leader in local politics in Buncombe County in the fifties. From 1847 to 1855 John Mitchell Davidson worked as a clerk in the mercantile house of his cousin, James M. Smith and his sons, in Asheville. From 1855 to 1862 he was in the mercantile business with his step-father (and uncle) in Ducktown, Tennessee. In 1862 he entered the Confederate army, where he served in the Thirty-ninth North Carolina Regiment, of which his brother, Hugh Harvey Davidson (1814-1889) was lieutenant colonel. After the war John Mitchell Davidson moved to Calhoun, Adairsville, and Kingston, Ga., where he was agent for the Western and Atlantic Railroad until his retirement in 1901. He was married in Calhoun, Ga., November 1, 1855, to Julia A. Dunn, formerly of Asheville. Their youngest son, born in 1876, was named Zebulon Vance Davidson. Davidson Papers, *passim;* Theodore H. Morrison Papers, Asheville, N. C.; *Census,* Buncombe County, 1850; *Asheville News,* November 22, 1855 and June 26, 1856.

[36] At the University during his year of study Vance was classed as an "irregular" or "partial course" student. The senior course of study for 1851-52 was as follows: first term, chemistry and mineralogy, political economy, moral philosophy, Greek, and French; second term, national and constitutional law, chemistry and geology, Cicero, and French. *Catalogue of the Trustees, Faculty, and Students of the University of North Carolina, 1851-'2,* p. 20 (cited hereafter as *University Catalogue).*

[37] The law course consisted of *Blackstone's Commentaries, Kent's Commentaries, Stephen on Pleading, Greenleaf on Evidence, Chitty on Contracts, Cruise's Digest of Real Property, Williams on Executors,* and lectures on the municipal laws of the state as modified by acts of the legislature and decisions of the state courts. *University Catalogue, 1851-'2,* pp. 30-31.

and the many things we can do in a given amount of time if we will but make the proper effort. I am taking a severe course of studies in college which occupy more than half my time from Law, and yet I am reading Law faster and learning more than when I was reading at home [38] with nothing else to do. You know I had to loaf with Jim McDowell, [39] and play marbles with Jesse [40] & Jeptha [41] (that man of family). But the scales have fallen from my eyes John, and I have taken to real hard confinement & study. I am going down to Raleigh this winter in vacation to get license; the Judge [42] says I shall have them like a deer in a walk. I am really in hopes I'll not meet with the fate of Sam McDowell [43] & others. I reckon you saw my preceptor-in-law [44] (not my dady-in-law) up the country. I like him extremely well. He is much of a gentleman. * * * * * Old Buncombe has been playing the devil I suppose in the way of *Bloomer's* fancy

---

[38] Vance began the study of law by reading with John W. Woodfin in Asheville in 1850. He continued this study until he went to the University in the summer of 1851. His fellow student with Woodfin was Augustus Summerfield Merrimon, later the Chief Justice of the Supreme Court of North Carolina. Merrimon, "Diary," December 5, 1850 through July 27, 1851.

[39] James C. S. McDowell, a son of Charles McDowell of Quaker Meadows, who often visited his sisters, Mrs. J. W. Woodfin and Mrs. N. W. Woodfin, in Asheville. He was afterwards colonel of the Fifty-fourth North Carolina Regiment and was mortally wounded at Marye's Heights, near Fredericksburg, during the battle of Chancellorsville. He died on May 8, 1863. He married Julia Manly, a daughter of Governor Charles Manly. Walter Clark (ed.), *Histories of the Several Regiments and Battalions from North Carolina in the Great War 1861-'65.* Written by Members of the Respective Commands. 5 vols. (Goldsboro, 1901), III, 269 (cited hereafter as Clark, *N. C. Regts.*); McLean, "Notebooks."

[40] Jesse Siler Smith. His father was James M. Smith, known as "the first white child born west of the Blue Ridge," and who was at this time a prominent merchant in Asheville. John Mitchell Davidson clerked in his store. Jesse Siler Smith was born in 1832. *Census,* Buncombe County, 1850.

[41] Jeptha M. Israel (1820-1896). He was born on Avery's Creek in Buncombe County, worked in James M. Smith's store, and served in the War with Mexico. He was instrumental in getting the old Asheville Female College and served as the first steward of the college. He was very active in local politics and during the war, after Vance became governor, Major Israel was the main assistant of Nicholas W. Woodfin of Asheville as agent for North Carolina at the salt works in Saltville, Va. The reference to his being a "man of family" is related to the fact that he had just been married to Susan Ellen Hastings, a native of Massachusetts. *Census,* Buncombe County, 1850 and 1860; McLean, "Notebooks."

[42] Judge William Horn Battle (1802-1879), a native of Edgecombe County, graduate of the University of North Carolina in 1820, member of House of Commons from Franklin County in 1833 and 1834, co-reporter for the Supreme Court, 1834-1839, and active Whig. He became a superior court judge in 1840 and served until 1852, when he was elected to the Supreme Court, where he remained until 1868. In 1843 he moved to Chapel Hill and in 1845 became professor of law in the University of North Carolina. Samuel A'Court Ashe, "William Horn Battle," Ashe, *Biog. Hist. of N. C.,* VI, 20-24; Connor, *Manual,* pp. 446, 449, 609-610.

[43] See p. 6, 29n.

[44] Judge Battle was his preceptor. As a superior court judge he rode the circuit and often held court in the western district. For an account of one of his visits to Asheville see Kemp Plummer Battle, *Memories of an Old-Time Tar Heel.* Edited by William James Battle (Chapel Hill, 1945), chap. 10 (cited hereafter as Battle, *Memories*).

Balls, Duels, fighting, elections, Camp Meetings, Southern Company, weddings &c, &c. I have never heard the like in my life. I thought for a while that everybody was killed, everybody married, everybody elected, * * * * * and everybody converted at C. Meetings. I am missing all the fun. I reckon tho' I am doing most as well down here. There is a great chance of mischief down here which does me to laugh at, every night in the week allmost. Gov. Swain [45] & Dr. Mitchell [46] slept in the College last night with spies on the lookout for the enemy. I aint with them John. Your Sincere friend & Cousin

[Asheville]

[Copy of A. L. S. Zebulon B. Vance Papers, State Department of Archives and History, Raleigh. Original in possession of John M. Davidson, Kingston, Ga.]

To Cousin Matt [47]

University of North Carolina
Sep. 24th [1851]

I sit down with pleasure this evening to answer your letter which I was so happy as to receive in due time.

I was not disappointed in my expectations concerning your punctuality, for I knew that you would not be *allways* in answering my letter, like *some folks* I could mention if I felt disposed to do so— I thank you for it— Well Cousin, I suppose by the time this will reach you, that your excitement will be all passed: the folks all married, the Camp-Meeting all over and the examination too. I do hope you enjoyed yourself so much amid all this life

---

[45] David Lowry Swain (1801-1868), a native of Buncombe County, who was President of the University of North Carolina when Vance was a student. He was a neighbor and friend of Vance's father and, more especially, of his uncle, Dr. Robert Brank Vance. Swain was educated by the Rev. George Newton at Asheville, spent a few days at the University of North Carolina, and read law under Chief Justice Taylor at Raleigh. He began the practice of law in Asheville in 1822. He represented Buncombe County in the House of Commons in 1824, 1826, 1828, and 1829; was a judge of the superior court, 1830-1832; was three times elected governor, 1832-1835; and was president of the University of North Carolina, 1835-1868. It was Swain, who was called "Governor" by his friends as long as he lived, who arranged for Vance to spend a year at the University. Samuel A'Court Ashe, "David Lowry Swain," Ashe, *Biog. Hist. of N. C.,* I, 447-457; Connor, *Manual,* pp. 418, 448, 516, 869.

[46] Elisha Mitchell (1793-1857) was a native of Connecticut who had come to the University of North Carolina as professor of mathematics, and was afterwards professor of chemistry, mineralogy and geology. He was a graduate of Yale and had been ordained by Orange Presbytery in Hillsboro in 1821 as a Presbyterian minister, but he spent his life teaching at Chapel Hill and exploring the mountain section of North Carolina until his death. Samuel A'Court Ashe, "Elisha Mitchell," Ashe, *Biog. Hist. of N. C.,* I, 384-391; *A Memoir of Rev. Elisha Mitchell, D. D.* (Chapel Hill, 1858), pp. 5-12. For Mitchell's habit of sleeping in the dormitories see Battle, *History of U. of N. C.,* I, 538.

[47] See p. 3, 15n.

and stir. I hope Cousin Mary Ann *Reagan*[48] is happy, where are they? Have they gone to Tennessee? Do tell me all about the wedding, C. Meeting and everything else that's been happening in Buncombe since I left. Where is Maj Israel[49] & lady? and what about them? I too have been having a little fun down here among the ladies. I made a start last week visiting, and in company with a friend, called on some very pretty ladies. I have just attended another large party at Gov. Swains[50] (on Thursday night) when I saw more ladies than I have seen since I left home before– I saw two nieces of Mr. Norwood[51] of our town, then, and all that kept me from falling desperately in love was because I couldn't for my life make a choice between them. They were so pretty! No that wasn't all that kept me out either Cousin Matt. I *thought of somebody's bright eyes,* way up in the mountains, and that kept me away from danger. I thought of making no lady friends here at all, when I first came, but the temptation is too strong. I cant help it. However, I have set myself bounds, as to how often I shall go visiting and I am determined not to exceed them on any pretence whatever. There is not a great many ladies here, but they are very select, and the most intelligent ones I have ever met with in my life. It allmost scares me to venture into conversation with them. There are some here on a visit all the time, from every direction, but principally from St. Marys School[52] in Raleigh and the Edgeworth Seminary[53] at Greensboro. But my heart

[48] See p. 4, 18n. In 1851 Ann Weaver married James Americus Reagan (1824-1890), who came to live in Weaverville, just north of Asheville, in that same year. He was a Methodist circuit rider and a physician, and settled on Reems Creek in Buncombe County. He was known as a very scholarly physician and was appointed to the State Board of Medical Examiners in 1884. He was a native of Tennessee. Gaillard S. Tennent, "Medicine in Buncombe County Down to 1885; Historical and Biographical Sketches," reprinted from *Charlotte Medical Journal,* May 1906, pp. 18-19 (cited hereafter as Tennent, "Medicine in Buncombe County"); *Census* Buncombe County, 1860.

[49] See p. 8, 41n.

[50] See p. 9, 45n.

[51] James Hogg Norwood (1804-1852), a native of Hillsboro who graduated from the University of North Carolina in 1824. He became a lawyer, but conducted a classical school in Buncombe County with Stephen Lee. Lee moved his school to Chunn's Cove and Norwood went to Haywood County. Norwood was a bald man who wore a wig and was generally accounted a failure at disciplinary work in his schools. He became an agent of the Sioux Indians and was murdered at Sargent's Bluff on the Missouri River in 1852. Grant, *Alumni History,* p. 461; Arthur, *Western North Carolina,* p. 397; Baird, "Historical Sketches"; *Census,* Buncombe County, 1850.

[52] St. Mary's was begun in 1824 by the Episcopalians as a school for boys and, after some interruptions, became in the 1840's a female seminary directed, as a private venture, by Dr. Albert Smedes and his son. In 1897 it was bought for the Episcopal diocese, and the Diocese of South Carolina later joined in the enterprise. Samuel A'Court Ashe, *History of North Carolina,* 2 vols. (Raleigh, 1925), II, 410, 1346-1347 (cited hereafter as Ashe, *History of N. C.*)

[53] Edgeworth Female Seminary was founded in Greensboro in 1840 by John Motley Morehead. Unlike most female schools it was not supported by a denomination or a muncipality, but was privately owned. C. Alphonso Smith, "John Motley Morehead," Ashe, *Biog. Hist. of N. C.,* II, 250-258.

is in the mountains without a doubt– I suppose the courting
still goes on at Asheville among the folks. Every letter I get is
giving me a hint to that effect. I am so much in hopes they will
all be married off and out of my way when I get back next summer. I know they would not ask me to the weddings no how. How
does Miss Jane [54] get on? Give her my kindest regards will you.
Will you not go to school any longer after this session. I really
do think Cousin Mont [55] should send you by all means. I believe they ought to turn him out of the church if he does'nt
send you longer. How is Cousin Jane's [56] school getting on? And
Kate Smith, [57] where is she and what is she doing? I have not
received a letter, except one today from Brother Robert, [58] from
Burnsville, in two weeks. I tell you I feel wrathy at the folks up
the country! Do make everybody *write* and then everybody will
do right. Aint that *rite* funny? *Write soon.*

I am still making fine progress in my studies. I feel that I
am doing myself more benefit than I ever have before, at least
as regards studying and improvement. The longer I try to study,
and the more I strive to resist habits of idleness & folly, the
easier I find it is to do right and attend to the business for which
I am here. I have received several marks of flattering consideration lately both from the Govr. and my fellow students, but fear
you would think me vain, I will not say what they were. My
health is excellent. My big sheet is most out and I am not half
done talking, but give my love to everybody that you see and
just consider that I said all the ballance that I had to say and
that will do until the next time. The front of this is a very good
picture [59] of the College buildings. The left hand building is
called East, right hand West, the large one with the lightning
rods the South the last one on the right of the South is the
Chapil, and the tall slim one in front the belfry. I room in the
West [60] building. Write to me there.

[Asheville]

[A. L. S. Zebulon B. Vance Papers, State Department of Archives
and History, Raleigh.]

---

[54] See p. 5, 21n.

[55] Martha E. Weaver's father, Montraville Michael Weaver. See p. 3, 15n.

[56] Jane L. Smith (1828-1910). She was a daughter of Margaret R. (Baird) Smith
and Samuel Smith, who was born in 1797 in Tennessee. They lived in Ashe and
Madison counties, but about 1850 moved to Asheville. Jane Smith married John
A. Fagg and died in Washington, D. C. The kinship with Vance stemmed from
the fact that their grandfathers were brothers. McLean, "Notebooks."

[57] Kate Erwin Smith, a daughter of Sarah Ann Baird, who was a younger sister
of Zebulon B. Vance's mother, Mira Margaret (Baird) Vance. Sarah Ann Baird
married Bacchus J. Smith, prominent merchant and landowner of Burnsville and
Asheville. Cumming, "Reminiscence"; McLean, "Notebooks"; *Asheville Citizen*,
March 20, 1923.

[58] See p. 2, 6n.

[59] The picture is the same as that in Battle, *History of U. of N. C.*, I, opposite
p. 632.

[60] Vance's room was #5 West. *University Catalogue, 1851-'2*, p. 17.

To Cousin Matt [61]

Chapel Hill Feb. 8th '52

I reckon you have begun to entertain the opinion that I had forgotten my cousin up in the mountains alltogether from my long silence, but this letter I hope will prove satisfactorily, the contrary. I am not the boy "what" forgets his kinfolks easily, and especially when those kinfolks are his *friends*, which is not allways necessarily the case. I have to write to so many and write so much besides letters that I get perfectly tired down at it; and so in order to gather material for a letter and to work myself up into the proper spirit for interesting anyone, I necessarily suffer some time to intervene between my attempts. Besides, if it would not seem a little revengeful I might say that you suffered *some little time* to pass by before you answered my last, also— But let that go, I was glad to receive it, late though it was, and hope you will do better in future.

Well Cousin, we are some four weeks advanced in the session, and the arduous duties of College life are upon us again. I am taking hold of my textbooks in good spirits and in good health, so I am hoping to derive a considerable amount of improvement this session also if I meet with no reverse of luck. The attendance is quite full, I believe some few more than last term. I spent the greater part of my vacation quite hard at work preparing to apply for license and after my return from Raleigh [62] I did nothing much except try enjoy myself with the Ladies here, reading &c. There are some very pleasant Ladies here indeed. I am quite pleased with some of them, but as for falling in love I must plead not guilty, for I assure you my heart is in the mountains, and you know its quite a hard matter for a man to "fall in" when he is already "in" heels over head. But I am afraid you would tell on me if I said too much, so I'll say no more. Well, what are you all doing up home? Has every body got married lately? I can scarcely take up a paper but what contains the notice of some friends or acquaintance's wedding. Sometime I am trembling all over for fear I shall hear of my own sweetheart getting married without asking me to the wedding! I should'nt be surprised at anything now-aday— I believe you last wrote me that you were still at school (*at College I* mean) are you? and how is the College getting along? I hear the attendance is rather slim, which I am sorry to hear, and hope it be larger next summer. Don't you reckon that the reason the young Ladies dont come

---

[61] See p. 3, 15n.

[62] Vance secured his license to practice in the county courts at the December, 1851 term of the Supreme Court.

in larger numbers is because they know *I aint at home?* I cant
see anything else!! How are your friends at Rims Creek? I want
to see Cousin Jane [63] and all of them out there very bad. The
fact is I want to see everybody, or in other words, Cousin Matt.
I want to see *home, home,* that sweetest of all places especially
when you are away from it. Home is like health, we never properly appreciate its blessings until we are far from it. I am going
to make tracks for that place about the first of May. I am going
to put my trunk in the stage and take it on foot in company with
Albert Siler, [64] (a kin folk of yours) all the way up if we dont
break down or get into too much of a hurry to get home. We
will take it slowly and expect to have a great chance of fun. I
hear that lawyer Merrimon [65] and Cousin M. J. B. [66] are *not*
engaged as formerly. How is that? Mr. Sullens and my friend

[63] See p. 11, 56n.

[64] Albert W. Siler (1829-1904), of Cherokee County. He, like Vance, was taking
only a "partial" course at the University, which he attended for one year. He was
later a planter in Macon and Buncombe counties. The kinship to which reference
is made was based on the marriage of Jacob Weaver, the uncle of Martha E.
Weaver, to Elizabeth Siler. Grant, *Alumni History,* p. 563; *Census,* Macon County,
1860.

[65] Augustus Summerfield Merrimon (1830-1892), who had read law with Vance
in the office of John W. Woodfin, in Asheville, in 1850 and 1851. He was a son of
Branch Hamlin Merrimon (1802-1881) and Mary Evelyn Paxton, whose mother
was a sister of Captain Charles McDowell, in whose home Vance's future wife
was reared. Augustus Merrimon was born at "Cherryfields" in what was then
Buncombe County, now Transylvania County, but the family lived on a farm at
Hooper's Creek, about fourteen miles from Asheville, during most of his boyhood.
He attended school in Asheville, studied law with J. W. Woodfin, who had married a daughter of Charles McDowell, became county attorney for Buncombe
County after Vance had served in that capacity, and represented her in the House
of Commons in 1860. When war came he volunteered in Vance's company, the
"Rough and Ready Guards," but soon transferred and became a captain in the
commissary department under Colonel William Johnston. From 1862 until the
end of the war he was solicitor for the Western District and was chosen by the
legislature, in December 1865, a judge of the superior court after he had been
defeated as a candidate for the Convention of 1865. He resigned the judgeship
because he was unwilling to obey military law during Reconstruction, moved to
Raleigh and established a law firm with Samuel F. Phillips, afterwards United
States Solicitor General. Merrimon declined the Democratic nomination for governor in 1868, but accepted in 1872, when he was narrowly defeated by Tod R.
Caldwell. That same year he was elected to the United States Senate over Vance
in a long and bitter struggle. He was defeated by Vance in 1879 for the same
office and returned to Raleigh where he established another law firm with Thomas
C. Fuller and Samuel A. Ashe. When Ashe withdrew in favor of journalism the firm
became Merrimon & Fuller. In 1883 he was appointed by Governor Jarvis to
the Supreme Court of North Carolina; in 1889 he was appointed Chief Justice,
in which position he served until his death. His relations with Vance were cordial
until the 1872 struggle; afterwards they were strained. For most of their careers,
beginning with the contest for county attorney in 1852, which Vance won, they
were rivals, regardless of the fact that during the same year Merrimon married
one of Vance's numerous cousins, Margaret Jane Baird (1836-1907). Merrimon,
"Diary"; Walter Clark, "Augustus Summerfield Merrimon," Ashe, *Biog. Hist. of
N. C.,* VIII, 334-341; Connor, *Manual,* pp. 446-447, 449, 517, 939-940.

[66] See above and p. 6, 6n.

Miss Teresa Shepherd [67] I hear are engaged, but dont think it true. You can tell I suppose better than I. The first no. of the University Magazine [68] will be out tomorrow and I should like to send you a copy, but I only take one and that I send home to Robert. [69] If you will read it you will find some of my composition[70] there. I allmost forgot to tell you what a fine time I have at my boarding house. I with some others eat at a private table with two of the finest young Ladies, O hush! Dear me how hard it is to be true to my mountain "surety" aint it? But I am glad my paper is out for I have nothing to write but foolishness. Bob Johnston [71] my chum, is writing a letter to his sweetheart & he is afraid I'll look at it, so I'll close my letter and get away from the candle. Write soon. Give my love to all my friends and believe me to be

[Asheville]

[A. L. S. Zebulon B. Vance Papers, State Department of Archives and History, Raleigh]

To Cousin Kate[72]

[University of North Carolina]
[1852?]

[fragment]

obtain since my first acquaintance with her. She will make some man a true hearted and affectionate wife, but whether she was ever destined to be mine or not is what the fates can alone reveal– Cousin Kate I will make a part of a confession to you under the seal of my honor and tell you that in my reflecting hours, and they are more frequent than of old, alas yes, I am the most miserable man alive I suppose– My confounded, excuse for saying my *accursed,* rash, headlong and inconsiderate folly has led me

---

[67] Theresa E. Shepherd (1833-1903), of Yancey County. She did not marry Mr. Sullens, but married Dr. John Daniel Reynolds (1832-1874) in 1854. They settled in Asheville at the corner of North Main and Woodfin streets. See Tennent, "Medicine in Buncombe County," p. 17, where the named is spelled Sheppard; *Asheville News,* May 18, 1854 and March 8, 1855.

[68] This was a revival of the magazine which had been issued for one year in 1844. Battle, in *History of U. of N. C.,* I, 632 says that "Zebulon B. Vance was an editor for a few months; resigned when he secured his law license." But the title page does not list him with the other editors and a notice in the March number, p. 80, comments: "one of the editorial corps having left college on account of his health, his place has been supplied by Mr. Z. B. Vance." This was several months after Vance had secured his law license.

[69] See p. 2, 6n.

[70] The articles are unsigned, but Vance is usually credited with having written the one in the February number entitled "Theorizing" and another in the March number entitled "Indian Legend." *North Carolina University Magazine,* vol. I, no. 1, pp. 9-12; vol. II, pp. 59-61, February and March, 1852.

[71] See p. 5, 25n.

[72] See p. 11, 57n. The Smith family had by this time moved from Burnsville to Asheville.

into more awkward difficulties and unhappy situations than you could well imagine— It seems that even to this day I never will learn wisdom from the aching teachings of experience, when tis said even fools can learn— My disposition you know is very elastic, all gaiety and life, and therefore I can in general put away from my mind allmost anything that I wish to by seeking company, books &c but there are times I can assure you when I feel most completely and thoroughly miserable— The why and the wherefore of this Kate I shall take the Liberty of withholding from you, hoping to rid myself of it before very long in some way or another. But remember me to Miss Sallie[73] when she comes up in the kindest manner, and dont say anything about this confession of mine to her or any body else, mind that—

Well the session has opened with a large number of students and I have gone to work again with might and main upon my college books and especially upon my lawbooks as they are my only hopes of giving starvation a wide berth— So Miss Eliza Jane has taken a husband I suppose and Mr Tim Harrison at that. Well hurra for her, Shes gone to Tennissee where she will never want for fat pork and corn bread I I am in hopes at least— It seems that several of my acquaintances have done "that same" of late of which I was duly informed before it took place by some friends of mine who are a little more punctual than Cousin Kate. I wish them all happiness and prosperity— When is your time coming? Who is that beau of yours that that only staid *one week?* Poor fellow! He must have come after fire, he was in such a hurry! Why in the world didnt you ask him to stay all night? Tell Jane[74] its her time next and she may look for a long one before long; I mean a letter, not a beau. Make Hale[75] write to me and dont burn up his letters as fast as he writes them: any of them will do for me; for "gracious sakes" I dont reckon he's writing to Fillmore[76] that he should be so particular— You see Kate I received yours & Jane's letter this evening and set down the same day to answer it— now if you cant take a hint how I want mine answered I dont know what you can do— Thunderation! its most one o'clk and Johnston[77] my *Chum* is nearly frozen in bed and grumbling for me to get in to keep him warm, the scoundrel! so I'll have to quit you for the present— Do write soon and write a great long letter, I do despise *notes* when I am so far off from

[73] Probably Catherine Smith, born in 1831, daughter of Margaret R. (Baird) Smith and Samuel Smith. She was thus a first cousin of Kate Erwin Smith. They lived in Ashe County. McLean, "Notebooks."

[74] See p. 11, 56n.

[75] Hale Smith, born in 1824, brother of Catherine and Jane Smith. McLean, "Notebooks."

[76] Millard Fillmore (1800-1874), a New York Whig, had succeeded to the Presidency of the United States upon the death of President Zachary Taylor, July 9, 1850.

[77] See p. 5, 25n.

home– My love to all the family and all others who may enquire after me and believe me to be as the words import.
[Asheville]
[P.S.]   I hear from D[r]. John Reynolds[78] every week or so in Charleston. I reckon he wont look at you when he gets back– "poor gal"–
[A. L. S. Z. B. Vance Papers, State Department of Archives and History, Raleigh.]

From Chs. McDowell [79]

[Quaker Meadows,[80] Burke]
[April 25, 1852]
Some time Sins I Receivered a letter from you asking from me a precious favor in the person of my niecs.[81] I have Raised her

---

[78] See p. 14, 67n. John Daniel Reynolds (1832-1874) was not yet a doctor, but was studying medicine in Charleston. He graduated in medicine at Nashville in 1854 and settled in Asheville. Tennent, "Medicine in Buncombe County," p. 17.
[79] Captain Charles McDowell (1786-1859) of Quaker Meadows, Burke County, N. C. He was the son of General Charles McDowell (1743-1815), and married Annie McDowell, the daughter of his father's brother, Major Joseph McDowell. Captain Charles McDowell was a soldier in the War of 1812 and a prominent farmer and citizen of Burke County. McLean, "Notebooks."
[80] About two miles from Morganton, on the Catawba River. It was formerly a famous outpost against the Indians, so named because a Quaker trader camped where the Indians had cleared the bottom lands into meadows.
[81] Harriett Newell Espy (1832-1878), who married Zebulon Baird Vance at Quaker Meadows, August 3, 1853. The relationship of Harriett Espy to Captain Charles McDowell was involved, but understandable, he being the half-brother of her maternal grandmother. James Greenlee, born in 1707, married Mary Elizabeth McDowell, born in 1711. Their daughter Grace (or Grizel) Greenlee married Captain John Bowman, who was killed at Ramsaurs Mill during the Revolution. Then she married, secondly, her cousin, General Charles McDowell, and they became the parents of Captain Charles McDowell. By her first marriage Grace Greenlee Bowman had a daughter, Mary Bowman, who married William Allison Tate. Their daughter, Sarah Louisa, married Thomas Espy, and they were the parents of Harriett Newell Espy. Thomas Espy (1800-1833) was born in Cumberland County, Pennsylvania, graduated at Washington College, Pennsylvania, and at Princeton Theological Seminary and went, in 1828, to Burke County as a Presbyterian minister. There he met Sarah Louisa Tate and after their marriage they settled in Salisbury, N. C. where Harriett Newell Espy, named after a prominent missionary of that name, was born on July 11, 1832. Later Thomas Espy served Bethel and Centre churches in Mecklenburg and Iredell counties, but he was of a sickly constitution and died at Beattie's Ford, on the Catawba River, in April 1833, leaving a young widow and a baby daughter not yet a year old. Sarah Louisa (Tate) Espy died soon afterwards and the child Hattie was adopted by Captain Charles McDowell, who already had six children of his own. Harriett Newell Espy had known, therefore, no other home than that at Quaker Meadows. Alphonso C. Avery, "Historic Homes of North Carolina - Pleasant Gardens and Quaker Meadows, in Burke County," *The North Carolina Booklet* (Raleigh, 1901-1926), vol. IV, no. 3 (July, 1904), pp. 5-24; Franklin Brevard McDowell, *(The) Broad Axe and the Forge; or, A Narrative of Unity Church Neighborhood, From Colonial Times Until the Close of the Confederate War* (Charlotte, 1897), p. 5 (cited hereafter as McDowell, *Broad Axe and Forge*); William Henry Foote, *Sketches of North Carolina* (New York, 1846), pp. 363-366 (cited hereafter as Foote, *Sketches of N. C.*); William Carson Erwin, "Grace Greenlee, a Revolutionary Heroine," *The North Carolina Booklet*, vol. XV, no. 1 (July, 1915), pp. 12-27.

and I think a greate dale of her Had your Character not been Represented to me in the light it has I might have held my Consent you say your patrimony is all gon to Secure you an education poverty under Sutch Circumstances is I think a blessing it shows that you are determined to Relye on your Resorses for a living may you be sucessfull is my Cincear wish you have been represented to me as an ennerJetick Sober young man I have a high Regard for your family there four I give my Consent and trust you and my Nice may live hapily and long in the enjoyment of all nesary Earthly Blessings.
April the 25th 1852
[Chapel Hill?]
[A. L. S. Z. B. Vance Papers, State Department of Archives and History, Raleigh.]

From H. R. Dickson[82]

Charleston S. C. Oct 26th 1852
I fully appreciate, I do assure you, the kindness of your effert to give me pleasure. I do not understand precisely the bearing of so much apology, either for your conduct or your letter,– which does not deserve in my humble judgment the abuse and obloquy which your outbursting modesty has bestowed upon it.– By the way, in the outset, Zeb, you will let me say one thing, in the introduction of our (as I most truly hope) long and continuous correspondence, I must protest against criticism of composition, wit &c being made a part of it. For my humble self it is my way in epistolary scribblings, to send my notations to my correspondent, whoever the misfortunate being be, in a wild & careless manner, as a matter of purpose, desiring that he do the same. If I have any notion of letter-writing at all, it is that it, is conversation in ink, on paper,– as when a couple of good fellows meet and tell each other of matters and things, as they interest or amuse each party. You Know, my dear fellow, what a humbug the conversation of friends would soon become, if two men were to carry into each others company, when they met, note-books to take down each others sayings to *criticise* them. But I grow

---

[82] Henry Robertson Dickson was born in Charleston in 1833. He was a son of Dr. John Dickson (1795-1847) who, with his brother, Dr. Samuel Henry Dickson (1798-1872), came to Asheville before 1836 for reasons of health. The former was a graduate of Yale in 1814, studied medicine and divinity, and was pastor of the Presbyterian Church in Asheville from 1843 to 1845. The latter built Swannanoa Hill and later Forest Hill, which were notable centers of social life. Henry R. Dickson graduated from the College of Charleston and from Columbia Theological Seminary. As a Presbyterian minister he served pastorates in South Carolina and New York. *Census*, Buncombe County, 1850; Tennent, "Medicine in Buncombe County," p. 10; George Howe, *History of the Presbyterian Church in South Carolina*. Prepared by order of the Synod of South Carolina. 2 vols (Columbia, 1870, 1883), II, 770; John A. Dickson Papers, Southern Historical Collection, Chapel Hill.

prosy, with my moralizing, and shall plunge in medias *res,* which
is more *reas*onable, Eh! I have been reading "Hoggs Tales," by
way of a lark, since I came down, until I've got a stye on my eye,
so that I shall not probably with this lamplight see these lines
very straight. I am looking over my paper with one eye, and so
look out for some original views of things generally! My journey
down was not one of any striking adventure by "flood or field",
nothing like our call on Gen. Burgin,[83] which ride is I suppose
still wet in your memory. We had not even a turnover by way
of breaking into the monotoy of Stage and railroad travel. Do
tell anybody whom you you may Know to be coming down in
this direction by all means to take the Rutherfordton and Chester
route, unless the object be expedition and in that case I suppose
via Greenville &c will be fond a rapid and directer route. But
you are so well treated at the Inns and the Outs, and the scenery
villages &c &c are all so delightful that I would protest against
any friend of mine coming any other way. Since I came down
I have been perfectly miserable. Nostalgia-home-sickness- hank-
ering after the hills and their dear blue scenery,— my sunny home
among the sparkling water and all that sort of thing— it would
seem that I'd die of thirst, and panting to be with you in that
Switzerland of America. The doctors say, that to an absent Moun-
taineer in this sort of Indian Summer weather, it is the most
common and natural thing in the world. And then, drat it, to
add to my misery, I was Chucked into Quarantine as soon as I
got into the City, the condition of my remaining for a time longer, in the land of the living being, that I should not go into the
City lower than the old Boundary of the town, and that I should
never be seen out of doors after Sunset. Was that not enough
to Kill me with *room*atism? I could know of Nothing that was
going on so that when I wrote a letter for Mr. Atkin[84] last week,
I could not for the life of me make up any news for him. I hope
that it has pleased him, to wipe himself with it, as I do not think
it worthy of publication. I'm much obliged to you for Newtons[85]

[83] General Alney Burgin (c. 1773-1840) had lived near Old Fort, formerly in
Burke County but in 1852 in McDowell County. He was a social and political
leader of Burke County and represented Burke in the House of Commons in 1824,
1830, 1831, 1832, and 1833; he was a member of the State Senate from Burke in
1842, when McDowell County was formed. He was a colleague of Samuel P. Carson in the legislature of 1824 and his second in the duel with Dr. Robert Brank
Vance in 1827. Arthur, *Western North Carolina,* p. 360; Connor, *Manual,* pp. 521-
522; McLean, "Notebooks."

[84] Rev. Thomas W. Atkin. He was born in Tennessee in 1823 and came to Asheville from Knoxville about 1848, where he became founder and editor of the Dem-
cratic *Asheville News.* He represented Buncombe County in the House of Commons in 1848. Arthur, *Western North Carolina,* p. 449; Connor, *Manual,* p. 517;
Census, Buncombe County, 1850.

[85] Newton Coleman, who was an ardent Democrat and who, with Thomas W.
Atkin, represented Buncombe County in the House of Commons in 1848. Connor,
Manual, p. 517.

astonishing effusion. Give my love to him. He's brilliant. Hurrah for Pierce.[86] What do you blue Whigs, over the Blue Ridge, think of the way the sovereigns of Pennsylvania & Ohio and other sensible republican States are rolling up whopping Democratic majorities? Believe me, dear Zeb, that Scott expedition, right straight to Washington has killed old Fuss & Feathers[87] this lick. Eh.' and Jim Patton[88] has gone off to Pearsons, Eh, (I like to hear of a young Scott sub-Elector going to Piercing) Pardon me dear fellow for all this stuff. Tell me in your next about Brownlow[89] and his behavior in Asheville? And so Miss Mag[90] has faded away into Burke again? Did she make a Mag-pie of any unfortunate amorous youth about your parts. But my paper has come to an end. Do give especial love to Mr D. Coleman.[91] I hear of his accomplishing wonderful exploits, in the way of stumps. Give me a eulogy on Webster[92] in your next? Let it be *anno concilli*

---

[86] Franklin Pierce (1804-1869), of New Hampshire, Democratic candidate for President of the United States in 1852. He carried every state but four.

[87] The nickname of General Winfield Scott (1786-1866), Whig candidate for President of the United States in 1852. The nickname was given because of his punctiliousness in dress and decorum.

[88] James Alfred Patton (1830-1864), a son of James W. Patton (1803-1861), wealthy merchant and farmer of Asheville. James Alfred Patton was valedictorian of the class of 1851 at the University of North Carolina, became a lawyer, merchant, and farmer, a lieutenant in the Bethel Regiment, C. S. A., and a member of the Council of State in 1862, when Vance was governor. *Census*, Buncombe County, 1860; Connor, *Manual*, p. 439; Battle, *History of U. of N. C.*, I, 625.

[89] William Gannaway (Parson) Brownlow (1805-1877), a Methodist preacher and politician who at that time was the editor of the *Knoxville Whig*.

[90] Margaret C. McDowell (1830-1860), of Morganton, who often visited her relatives in Asheville. In 1854 she married Marcus Erwin, one of the editors of the *Asheville News*. See below, p. 65, 240n. Matilda Abernathy to Thomas Dickson, June 12, 1854, William Dickson Papers, Southern Historical Collection, University of North Carolina, Chapel Hill, N. C. (cited hereafter as Dickson Papers).

[91] David Coleman (1824-1883) was a son of William Coleman, a hatter of Buncombe County, and of Cynthia Swain, a sister of David L. Swain. He was educated at Newton Academy in Asheville, graduated at the University of North Carolina in 1842, and at the United States Naval Academy. In the navy he served in the African, Mediterranean, and South American Squadrons and in the siege of Vera Cruz. About 1850 he resigned from the navy, returned to Asheville, was admitted to the bar, and developed a large practice in Asheville and in Yancey County. In 1852 he ran as a Democrat for the State Senate against Nicholas W. Woodfin, the incumbent, and was defeated, but Coleman defeated Woodfin in 1854 and Vance in 1856. In 1859 Vance and Coleman were rival candidates for Congress, Vance winning. During the war Coleman was colonel of the Thirty ninth North Carolina Regiment and served throughout the war in the western theatre, part of the time in the brigade of Vance's brother, Brigadier General Robert B. Vance. After the war Coleman resumed the practice of law in Asheville, was solicitor for the western circuit, and represented Buncombe County in the Convention of 1875. He never married. See an article by Lawrence Pulliam (undated) in the Pack Memorial Library, Asheville, N. C.; Clark, *N. C. Regts.*, II, 722-723; Arthur, *Western North Carolina*, p. 403; Sondley, *Buncombe County*, II, 768-769.

[92] Daniel Webster (1782-1852), great Whig leader in Senate and cabinet, had died two days before.

very soon. My love to Marc Erwin,[93] when you see him to all who care for Dickson.

Did you get a pamphlet I sent to Marc and you and D. Coleman? P.S. I have been making inquiries about Bob Murdoch,[94] but cannot hear of him. Have his relations heard of him yet? *Do write soon* HRD

P.S. I forgot to mention that I have had Fever (not Yellow Fever) for two weeks. Please tell Dr. Hardy[95] that it has kept me from writing to him.

[Asheville]

[A. L. S. Z. B. Vance Papers, State Department of Archives and History, Raleigh.]

From David Rankin[96]

Asheville July 30th 1853

I have just returned from my campaign through the sleepy hollows & over the backbone ridge of East Ten. I was sorry not

[93] Marcus Erwin (1826-1881), a son of Leander Erwin of Burke County. Marcus Erwin graduated with honors at Transylvania University, Lexington, Kentucky, and studied law in New Orleans, whence his father had moved. He settled in Asheville about 1849, where he was a lawyer and editor of the *Asheville News* after 1854. He represented Buncombe County in the House of Commons in 1850 and 1856, and in the State Senate in 1860. He was a strong Democratic leader and an early and ardent advocate of secession. During the war he was major of the second battalion; after the war he was United States assistant district attorney. Sondley, *Buncombe County*, II, 775-776; Connor, *Manual*, p. 517; *Asheville News*, May 11, 1854; Clark, *N. C. Regts.*, IV, 245; obituary in *Asheville Citizen*, July 21, 1881.

[94] Robert J. Murdoch, age nineteen, was born in Ireland, the son of William and Margaret Murdoch. He and his parents were farmers in Buncombe County. *Census*, Buncombe County, 1850; McLean, "Notebooks."

[95] Dr. James F. E. Hardy (1802-1882) was the most prominent physician in Asheville. He was born in the Newberry district of South Carolina and came to Asheville about 1821 for reasons of health. In 1824 he married Jane Patton (1808-1834), of a very prominent Asheville family, and soon thereafter went to Charleston for his medical training. In 1840 he married, secondly, Cordelia Erwin of Morganton, and soon thereafter moved to Swannanoa Hill, where he lived until 1860, when he sold this fine estate and moved to Belleview, on South Main Street, which had been built as a summer home by his son-in-law, Gilbert Tennent. Soon after the Civil War he withdrew from practice and built a brick house on the Hendersonville road, beyond Biltmore. Here, in the midst of financial adversity, he died at the age of eighty. For many years he was cashier of the Asheville branch of the Bank of Cape Fear. Though a strong Democrat he had little to do with public service and nothing to do with public office. In spite of political differences he was often the Vance family physician while they lived in Asheville. He was a universally beloved and popular man, socially engaging and an acknowledged leader in his profession. He was the only Asheville physician who was not in the war at some time. Tennent, "Medicine in Buncombe County," pp. 8-10; Arthur, *Western North Carolina*, pp. 504-505.

[96] David Rankin, age 20, was a son of William David Rankin, a native of Cocke County, Tennessee who had established a large mercantile house in Asheville in partnership with R. W. Pulliam. David Rankin was associated in business with his father after the partnership with Pulliam was dissolved in 1857. Still later he

to find you at home when I reached here, as it becomes necessary for me to offer you an apology which I Should like to have done in propia persona.

I am unexpectedly Called upon to go to New York & Boston and will leave in the next Stage. Consequently I must of necessity forego the pleasure I anticipated in attending your wedding.[97] Disappointment seems to meet me every time I attempt a visit to Morganton. I hope that you may find some young man equally as good looking, and that will discharge the duties of groomsman with as much *grace* & *dignity* as I could *possibly* do it.

In conclusion 'old fellow', allow me to return you my sincere thanks for the distinction you have conferred upon me in selecting me to stand by you in that *trying* hour;– and to express the wish that all the happiness you anticipate may be abundantly realized, that all your *responsibilities* may be *"little ones"*— that plenty & prosperity may be your fortune,– and in a word that every earthly good may be yours & your dear little wife's forever–

I saw Alf Taylor alias "Clabber" at Elizabethton, he begs to be remembered to you– & says to be sure to write to him as soon as you are married– & also to recommend him to some fair one in Burke Please to present my kindest regards to Mrs. Vance– Should you feel disposed, you can address me to the care of J & J Stuart New York.

[Morganton]
[A. L. S. Z. B. Vance Papers, State Department of Archives and History, Raleigh.]

To Cousin Kate[98]

Asheville N. C.
6th Sepr. 1854.

Here I am again! You thought I had given you up entirely this time, didnt you? Yes but you are entirely mistaken if you think I am going to let you slip in that way, for altho' business, trouble, absence from home and a thousand other annoying things should render me silent for a long time, yet I will drop in upon you every now & then with a long letter informing you of all that is going on here among our kindred and friends, changes sickness, removals, &c. &c. On the present occasion I have a great many things to relate which I hope may compensate to some

became cashier of the Bank of the Republic in New York. *Census*, Buncombe County, 1850; *Asheville Spectator*, September 3, 1858; Lawrence Pulliam in *Asheville Times*, February 10, 1929; Merrimon, "Diary"; Diary of John Evans Brown, March 16, 1891, W. Vance Brown Papers, State Department of Archives and History, Raleigh, N. C. (cited hereafter as Brown, "Diary").

[97] Zebulon B. Vance and Harriett N. Espy were married August 3, 1853, at Quaker Meadows, Morganton.

[98] Probably Kate Erwin Smith. See p. 11, 57n.

extent for my long delay; and should any apology be necessary I hope you will be able to perceive an ample one in the many vexations and exciting scenes I have gone through since I last wrote.

I forget when I *did* write last, but I have an idea it was in April; or at any rate "long, long ago"– Since that time however, I became seized with a hungering and thirsting after the equivocal honors of politics, and in due time yielded to the solicitations of a few (yes very few) friends, and became a Candidate for a seat in the house of Commons. The canvass lasted three months and was warm in a great many respects besides the weather I can tell you. I run as a regular built, old fashioned Whig[99] (Frank would say an *old fogy Fed*) and had to run against the Democratic party and the Southern Rights party too,[100] who combined, as they always do in this county, have a majority of six hundred voters– That prospect was rather "blue" was'nt it? But I put in with unparalleled impudence, fought the race through, and beat my competitor (Col Reynolds)[101] one hundred and ten votes–[102] I hope you will not think me vain for saying that my friends all agree in saying it was greatest triumph that has been accomplished in this country for many years– Consequently I am something

---

[99] His candidacy was announced in the *Asheville News,* April 27, 1854.

[100] This was true only in the sense that Democrats and Southern Rights men, whether Whigs or Democrats, were more apt to vote against Vance than for him. The Democrats put up no candidate of their own, but they supported Reynolds, who was technically a Whig. Reynolds and Vance were in accord in supporting the state policies to which their party was committed, but on the slavery question they were wide apart. Vance stood with his party in accepting the Compromise of 1850 as a "final settlement in principle and in substance" of that question; Reynolds stood with the Democrats in advocating the Kansas-Nebraska Bill, which allowed for the possible expansion of slavery through the exercise of popular sovereignty. This difference between them was doubly important in view of the fact that the legislature to which they sought a seat would elect two United States Senators. Prominent among the candidates was their fellow Buncombe citizen, Thomas L. Clingman, who hoped to draw support from the pro-slavery Whigs, of whom Reynolds was an example, as well as from his new Democratic associates who, he felt, owed him the election as a reward for his recent abandonment of the old Whig associates. Reynolds came out for the election of Clingman and thus drew to himself the support of the Democrats. Vance disliked Clingman personally and distrusted him politically; he simply announced, therefore, as a good party man, that if elected to the legislature he would support the regular nominee of the Whig caucus. *Asheville News,* August 10, 1854.

[101] Daniel Reynolds (1809-1878). He was born on Bent Creek in Buncombe County and married one of Vance's numerous Baird cousins, Susan A. Baird (1826-1915), a daughter of Israel and Mary (Tate) Baird and a sister of Mrs. Augustus Summerfield Merrimon and of Mrs. Natt Atkinson. His title of "colonel" implied no military rank; most public figures were either "esquire" or "colonel"; they were what were later called "courtesy colonels," or "Yarborough House" colonels. Reynolds was a hotel owner and Methodist minister and the grandfather of a future Senator from North Carolina, Robert Rice Reynolds. Baird, "Historical Sketches."

[102] The *Asheville News,* August 10, 1854, gives the vote as Vance 688 and Reynolds 579.

Mira Margaret (Baird) Vance, mother of Zebulon B. Vance

of a *lion* at present, among grocery men and Cross-roads politicians in particular. To crown my success more completely, a few days before the election came off, a merciful God gave Hattie[103] and me a large hale, blue-eyed little boy,[104] who weighed ten pounds at his birth! He is one of the brightest, sweetest little fellows that you ever beheld in the world— Oh Cousin Kate, he is such a little darling! We do nothing scarcely but sit by his little crib and watch with a perfectly unspeakable delight his infantine gambols and emotions. What a comfort to his Mother and me he is— How I begin to build on him already, and devise plans never to be realized, perhaps! I can now walk around my *extensive plantation* consisting of a *five acre lot* [105] and have the consolation of knowing that if the Sherriff doesnt get hold of all those vast possessions, I have a son and *heir* that will! Oh comforting thought!! So you see my crop of earthly happiness is as full as I could expect— I saw Mr. J. H. Coleman[106] from near Abingdon the other day, and in return for the many kind enquiries he brought me from my friends in Va, I told him to give my love to all of them, and to say to them that I was emphatically a *rising* young man— a lawyer (not much practice tho') a married man, a member elect to the next legislature, and the *dady* of a *ten pound*-boy! That will do for the present, wont it?

For fear now that I speak too much of myself (you know there *can* be too much of a good thing) I shall try to refer briefly to something else. As to our friends in this country, I am happy to [be] able to state that they are all in good health as when I last wrote. I might except my third Sister, Sallie,[107] who lives with me. She is recovering from quite a severe spell of fever, and we trust will be well again in a few days— Our Cousin

---

[103] Harriett Newell Espy Vance was always called "Hattie" by her family and friends.

[104] Robert Espy Vance, called Espy. The card file of cemetery records in the State Department of Archives and History, Raleigh, N. C. lists Robert E. Vance as "Infant son of Z. B. & H. N. Vance. Age 4 yrs." but his mother wrote that "he died at the age of one year." Years afterwards Hattie Vance described him as "a most lovely little creature - better fitted to dwell with the Angels, around the throne of God in Heaven than with us, on earth. 'Twas an afflicting wound, but sent by Him who alone can heal & who is too wise to be mistaken & too good to be unkind." Harriett N. E. Vance to Thomas Espy, March 5, 1869, Zebulon B. Vance Papers, State Department of Archives and History, Raleigh, N. C. (cited hereafter as Zebulon B. Vance Papers).

[105] The lot was at the corner of College and Spruce Streets in the heart of Asheville. Vance purchased it from Alexander D. Smith, of Charleston, S. C., who had bought it from Montraville Patton in 1849. The Vances paid $2300, the money having been "received with my first wife in Marriage." Record of Deeds, Buncombe County, Book 29, pp. 257-258; Book 33, pp. 127-129.

[106] John H. Coleman, a son of William Coleman and Cynthia Swain and a brother of Newton Coleman and David Coleman. Baird, "Historical Sketches."

[107] See p. 6, 31n.

Allen Davidson[108] in Cherokee, the lawyer, was also a candidate for the Commons this summer, but I am sorry to state was defeated in consequence of the unpopularity of the Temperance movements, in which he has been an active and praiseworthy participator– I shall see him next week at Court. He is already acquainted with you through my representations– Has my Sister Ann[109] ever written to you? I am afraid she has not. She promised she would, but she is quite a timid creature and perhaps is waiting for you to open the ball. I wish you would, I wish very much for you to become acquainted with her.

Well are you still in Tazewell [110] teaching? I am thinking perhaps you will have left that place and gone home to Virginia before this reaches you– Where is Cousin Frank and how is he? Tell him I intend writing to him shortly to get a copy of the Charter for our Cumberland Gap rail road and also the report of the Engineer, as I shall need both this winter. I will start to Raleigh about the 15th November and expect to be there about four months– I should be delighted to receive a letter at that place from you, and would also take pleasure in informing you of whatever takes place then, that might interest you.

Please write soon. Remember me kindly to all my relations whom you may see. Hattie sends love, and a kiss from the little boy–

[Copy of A. L. S. Zebulon B. Vance Papers, State Department of Archives and History, Raleigh. Original in possession of Major W. G. Vance, Morristown, New Jersey, a grandson of Governor Vance.]

---

[108] Allen Turner Davidson (1819-1905), of Cherokee County, His father was William Mitchell Davidson (1780-1846) and his mother was Elizabeth Vance (1787-1861), a sister of Zebulon B. Vance's father. For other family details see p. 7, 35n. Allen T. Davidson was born in Haywood County and worked, as a boy, in his father's store in Waynesville. In 1845 he was admitted to the bar, and in 1846 moved to Murphy, where he became a leader of the bar and, in 1860, president of the Merchant's and Miner's Bank. In 1865 he moved to Franklin, in Macon County, and in 1869 to Asheville. In politics he was a Whig, being defeated in the 1854 campaign by John Roland. He was elected to represent Cherokee County in the Convention of 1861 and was chosen by that convention a delegate to the Provisional Congress of the Confederate States. He was re-elected to the Confederate Congress in 1862, but in 1864 he was defeated by George W. Logan, of Rutherford County. That same year he was elected by the legislature a member of the Council of State. In 1885 he retired from active legal work and died in Asheville in 1905, the last surviving member of the Confederate Congress. John Gilchrist McCormick, *Personnel of the Convention of 1861* (James Sprunt Historical Monographs No. 1, Chapel Hill, 1900), p. 29 (cited hereafter as McCormick, *Personnel*); Arthur, *Western North Carolina*, pp. 400-403; Connor, *Manual*, p. 439; Kemp Plummer Battle, *Legislation of the Convention of 1861* (James Sprunt Historical Monographs No. 1, Chapel Hill, 1900), p. 126 (cited as Battle, *Legislation*); Davidson Papers.

[109] See p. 6, 30n.

[110] Tazewell, Tennessee, thirty-five miles north of Knoxville and the county seat of Clairborne County.

To the Editor[111] *of the Raleigh Register.*

House of Commons,[112] Dec. 15, 1854.

The Committee on Education,[113] to whom was referred a bill [114] to distribute the school fund [115] among the several Counties of the State, according to white population,[116] having agreed to report unfavorably on the same, I, as the only dissenting

---

[111] Seaton Gales (1828-1878), first honor graduate of the University of North Carolina in 1848, had edited the *Raleigh Register*, the leading Whig paper in the state, since the death of his father, Weston Gales, in the same year. He continued as its editor until 1858 when he sold the paper to John W. Syme. *A Tribute to Major Seaton Gales,* University of North Carolina Library, Chapel Hill, N. C.; Grant, *Alumni History,* p. 212.

[112] In August of 1854 Vance was elected as a Whig to represent Buncombe County in the House of Commons. Connor, *Manual,* p. 517.

[113] The Democrats were in the majority in the legislature and dominated the committees of both the house and the senate. The speaker of the house was Samuel P. Hill, of Caswell County, a Democrat, and he appointed the members of the committee on education. They were: T. H. Williams of New Hanover, Jesse R. Stubbs of Beaufort, William Black of Mecklenburg, J. H. Headen of Chatham, William A. Jenkins of Warren, Lotte W. Humphrey of Onslow, Milton Selby of Hyde, W. K. Martin of Franklin, W. W. Wilkins of Anson, Gaston Meares of Brunswick, and Z. B. Vance of Buncombe. Stubbs, Headen, Wilkins, and Vance were Whigs; the others Democrats. But, what was more significant, every member except Vance was from a large slaveholding county. *Journals of the Senate and House of Commons of the General Assembly of the State of North Carolina, at its Session of 1854-'55* (Raleigh, 1855), p. 43 (cited hereafter as *Senate Journal* and *House Journal,* with appropriate dates).

[114] The bill was introduced by Leander Bryan Carmichael (1823-1862), a Whig of Wilkes County, on November 28, 1854, and on his motion referred to the Committee on Education. On December 15, 1854, Chairman T. H. Williams reported the bill back to the house and recommended that it not pass. *House Journal, 1854-'55,* pp. 60, 126; Thomas Felix Hickerson, *Happy Valley: History and Genealogy* (Chapel Hill, 1940), pp. 49-50 (cited hereafter as Hickerson, *Happy Valley*).

[115] The school fund had been authorized by a law of January 4, 1826, and took the form of a permanent endowment, the interest from which could be used for common school purposes. This plan reflected the general aversion to taxation for educational purposes, and was used by all southern states, except South Carolina, to begin their public school systems. Before 1836 the income had come from dividends to the state arising from stock held by the state in the Bank of New Bern and the Bank of Cape Fear (except what was already pledged to internal improvements), from dividends from certain navigation companies, from the tax imposed on retailers of spirituous liquors and on auctioneers, from the unexpired balance of the agricultural fund, from all monies paid to the state for the entries of vacant lands (except the Cherokee lands), and from all of the vacant and unappropriated swamp lands in the state, plus about $21,000 owed by the United States to the State of North Carolina for advances to the Cherokee Indians. The fund thus provided was to be administered by a corporate body called the President and Directors of the Literary Fund, consisting of the Governor, the Chief Justice, the Treasurer, the Speaker of the Senate, and the Speaker of the House. This body was allowed considerable freedom in the investment of the money. Charles L. Coon, *The Beginnings of Public Education in North Carolina: A Documentary History, 1790-1840.* 2 vols. (Raleigh, 1908), I, 280-282 (cited hereafter as Coon, *Public Ed. in N. C.*); *Laws of North Carolina, 1825-1826* (Raleigh, 1826), chap. I (cited hereafter as *Laws of N. C.,* or as *Public Laws of N. C.* and *Private Laws of N. C.,* with appropriate dates).

[116] The original law of 1826 provided that the fund be distributed to the counties on the basis of white population, but this law had been changed by an act of January 11, 1841 to provide, among other things, for distribution on the basis of federal population, i. e., white population plus three-fifths of the negro population. *Public and Private Laws of N. C., 1840-'41,* chap. VII.

member of your said committee have deemed it my duty to the three thousand poor white children whom I represent to make a contrary report. A brief statement of the considerations upon which I have arrived at a different opinion from all my fellow committee men will, I hope, be indulged me by the House. I submit for your consideration the following facts:

It is a fact that this fund, intended for the education of the poor children of the State, was principally derived from the General Government [117] as our portion of the proceeds of the public lands and from various sources other than taxation.

It is a fact, that if ever there should be a call from the General Government upon us to refund the principal sum of this fund, that no resort to taxation would be necessary– a simple transfer of the stocks in which this fund is vested being all that would be required to be done.

It is a fact that we have a statute law forbidding under fines and penalties the education of slaves and colored persons beyond the use of figures,[118] the public safety making such a law absolutely necessary.

It is also a fact, and a very singular one too, that in the distribution of this fund for the education of whites, that particular county which shows the largest number of slaves and free negroes should get the greatest amount of money.[119]

Now, it is a fact, a great, undying & eternal fact, that public education, the enlightening of the masses, is of the most vital,

---

[117] The United States had provided for the distribution of the surplus revenue by act of Congress in 1836. North Carolina's share was $1,433,757.39, of which sum all but about $100,000 ultimately went to the cause of public schools. Coon, *Public Ed. in N. C.,* II, 802.

[118] Such a law was passed at the session of 1830-1831. *House Journal, 1830-1831,* p. 231; *Laws of N. C., 1830-1831,* chap. VI.

[119] An illustration of the manner in which the distribution of the educational fund militated against the western counties may be afforded by using the first distribution of 1854. Buncombe County received $1,480.56; New Hanover County, in which there were more negroes than whites, received $1,708.32. For both counties this was twelve cents per capita on the basis of federal population. But on the basis of white school population Buncombe's share amounted to about thirty-five cents per capita, and New Hanover's share, on the same basis, to about sixty-six cents per capita. Thus, although each county received the same amount based on per capita of federal population, yet New Hanover received for each white child of school age (and it was illegal to educate negroes) for whose benefit the fund was created, nearly twice as much as Buncombe. It was this condition which the west sought to remedy by this bill. But the principle was too closely involved in the political predominance of the slaveholding counties for it to receive much support, for such a change in the basis of distribution of the school fund would be an entering wedge for a similar change in the basis of representation in the legislature demanded by the west, to which Democrats and eastern Whigs alike were unalterably opposed. As a result, a motion by one of Vance's western colleagues to print his minority report was promptly tabled. *Report of Comptroller of Public Accounts* (Raleigh, 1854), p. 7 (cited hereafter as *Report of Comptroller,* with appropriate dates); Calvin H. Wiley Papers, Southern Historical Collection, University of North Carolina, Chapel Hill, N. C. (cited hereafter as Wiley Papers CH).

1854

paramount importance to all well-ordered governments, and to none so much as ours, where the *people* are sovereign, judge, priest, and law; where the existence of all our blessings, "life, liberty & the pursuit of happiness," depend upon their virtue and intelligence: and this we must suppose was the design of our predecessors in setting apart this fund.

It is certainly a fact, that the giving of this money to the few and withholding it from the many, does not effect this most desirable object, and is agreeable to neither fairness, justice, good economy, nor what old fashioned people would teach us to regard as common honesty.

It is equally a fact that this fund was intended as a great public charity, a boon which the generosity of a great State would confer upon its poor children— those who, being unable to educate themselves, have yet to fill the earth that we may eat bread and live, to fight the battles and sustain the safety and honor of our country, and to tread the ceaseless round of toil that our comforts may be complied with; and that the dispensing of this money among those who in the number of negroes they list upon the tax rolls show *prima facie* that they are rich enough to do without it, is not a charity, nor a boon from the government to its citizens, but a gross, monstrous and wholesale injustice.

It is also a fact, a small fact, it is true,— in fact rather an insignificant fact, that every member of your Committee on Education, the undersigned alone excepted, hails from eastern and large slave-holding counties, and as a necessary incident to which fact they are against changing the present mode of distribution.

And lastly, it is a fact, and a lamentable one, too, that the undersigned entertains no hope of being able to influence in the least degree the opinions of this House, or that the supplication of three thousand poor children in his county praying for means of education, will be heard and answered, when there is nothing but right and justice to put in the scales against the weight of dollars and cents.

All of which is respectfully submitted,[120]
[Raleigh]
[From *Raleigh Register,* Dec. 20, 1854.]

To the Editor of the Raleigh Register[121]

House of Commons
Feb. 2nd 1855.

I observe this morning in the "Newbern Journal", an attack

---

[120] The signature in the *Register* is "W. B. Vance," but it is manifestly an error.
[121] See p. 25, 111n.

upon the Greenville and French Broad Rail Road,[122] a bill for the incorporation of which passed this House[123] sometime since, and is now before the Senate. This article is based upon such gross ignorance of the provisions of the bill and the geography of the country, and, above all, is conceived in such a spirit of unfairness towards that project, as to demand a refutation at the hands of the friends of that Road. This road does not run "from Charlotte, N. C., to Sparta, S. C." and would not "make Charleston more accessible to the west than any of our sea-port towns." It runs from the Paint Rock, on the Tennessee line, through the Valley of the French Broad, in the direction of Greenville and Spartanburgh, S. C., and connects with the Central Road at the mouth of the Swannanoa. The gage[124] of this road is to correspond with that of the Central Road, and gives it a connection with the East Tennessee and Virginia Road, and reaches out an arm toward Cincinnati and Chicago, thereby giving the North Carolina roads a chance for that immense trade which they *never* could otherwise have. In fact, the provisions of the bill were so carefully prepared, that the warmest friends of the great Central project are perfectly satisfied,[125] not only with its non-

---

[122] The Greenville and French Broad Railroad proposed to build a line from one of the South Carolina roads along the French Broad Valley to a connection with the East Tennessee and Virginia Railroad beyond Paint Rock. It expressed the desire of the mountain section for a railroad of some sort, though it connected the area with South Carolina towns, and came at a time when debate on the Western North Carolina Railroad was being held in the legislature. Cecil Kenneth Brown, *A State Movement in Railroad Development. The Story of North Carolina's First Effort to Establish an East and West Trunk Line Railroad* (Chapel Hill, 1928), p. 131 (cited hereafter as Brown, *Railroad Development*).

[123] The bill to charter the Greenville and French Broad Railroad was introduced into the House of Commons by John Baxter of Henderson County, who had been speaker of the house at its previous session. It passed the house on January 15, 1855 by a vote of 69 to 27. It asked no financial aid from the state. *House Journal 1854-'55*, pp. 263-264.

[124] The gauge on the North Carolina lines was 4 feet, 8½ inches, while the gauge on the South Carolina and Tennessee roads with which it was intended to connect was 5 feet. In 1856 the charter of the Greenville and French Broad was so amended as to allow the use of the 5 foot gauge between Paint Rock and Asheville. The idea of the lawmakers was that of preventing the uninterrupted flow of goods from Tennessee via Asheville into South Carolina. In 1859 a proposed bill to grant the right to use the wider gauge south of Asheville as well was defeated in the legislature by a vote of 43 to 46. *Private Laws of N. C., 1854-'55*, chap. 229; *Private Laws of N. C., 1856-'57*, chap. 77; Raleigh *North Carolina Standard*, February 16, 1859; Brown, *Railroad Development*, p. 137.

[125] Nevertheless opposition had been strong in the House of Commons on the ground that the proposed Greenville and French Broad Railroad would injure the North Carolina Railroad, often referred to as the "Central project" and then under construction, and in which the state was a large stockholder. The opposition was led by John Gray Bynum of Rutherford County, a western rival of Buncombe, and by Samuel F. Phillips of Orange and Ralph Gorrell of Guilford, who contended that the new road would divert business from the "Central" road to the railroads of South Carolina and build up Charleston at the expense of Wilmington and Beaufort. The earliest speech of which we have record made by Vance in a legislative body was delivered on this subject, January 13, 1855. In this speech Vance argued that the proposed road would help rather than hurt

interference with that cherished work, but that its operation will
be decidedly advantageous to it.

Permit me to regret sincerely, that the Editor of the Journal
has not been personally present to exercise a paternal and superintending care over the well-meaning but misguided members
of the Legislature. If our "journals should be stained with a
charter for this South Carolina Road," he must certainly blame
himself for it, as his advice did not reach us in time. I would
suggest that an examination of Colton's[126] Map of N. C., would
doubtless show the gentleman the relative positions of Charlotte
and *Sparta.*
[Raleigh]
[From *Raleigh Register,* Feb. 7, 1855.]

From J. S. T. Baird [127]

[Asheville, N. C.]
[July 9, 1855]

The last two numbers of your paper[128] contain matter of an
extremely denunciatory & offensive character aimed at me. I
understand that you have avowed the authorship of one at least

the North Carolina Railroad by giving it connections with the Mississippi Valley beyond the mountains. The charter was granted, and afterwards amended,
but the road was never built. Many years later the Asheville and Spartanburg
Railroad was built along almost this same route and fully justified the expectations and predictions of the advocates of the Greenville and French Broad road.
House Journal, 1854-'55, pp. 263-264; *Raleigh Register,* January 17, 1855; *Private
Laws of N. C., 1854-'55,* chap. 229; *Asheville News,* January 25, February 8, 1855.

[126] The 1855 edition was published by Joseph Hutchins Colton, of J. H. Colton
& Co., 172 William Street, New York. Many later editions were published.

[127] James Samuel Tazewell Baird (1831-1913), a son of Israel Baird and grandson
of Bedent Baird, who was a brother of Zebulon B. Vance's grandfather. James
S. T. Baird was born in 1831 at Beaver Dam Creek, just north of Asheville, attended medical lectures at Charleston and graduated from Jefferson Medical College in Philadelphia in 1851. He practiced medicine in Asheville for a short time
before moving to Tennessee, but he returned to Asheville in the middle fifties,
where he continued to practice medicine until 1887. He represented Buncombe
County in the House of Commons in 1858 and in the House of Representatives
in 1889. Tennent, "Medicine in Buncombe County," p. 15; Baird, "Historical
Sketches"; Connor, *Manual,* pp. 517, 518; McLean, "Notebooks."

[128] In March of 1855, shortly after his return from the legislature, Vance purchased
a half interest in the *Asheville Spectator,* the leading Whig paper of western North
Carolina. The *Spectator* grew out of the old *Highland Messenger* which had been
founded in Asheville in 1840. The name was changed in 1853 when John D.
Hyman became the editor under the control of James M. Edney. Vance was associated with Hyman in the editorial direction of the paper for about eighteen
months. Only one issue of the *Spectator* during Vance's connection with it is known
to exist; it is in the University of North Carolina Library. There are scattered
issues in the Duke University Library and among other personal collections, such
as the W. Vance Brown Papers in the State Department of Archives and History,
but all of these are from the period before Vance's association with the paper, or
after his connection with it had been severed. What we know of its policies and
editorials during his association with it we learn from the columns of its chief
rival, the Democratic *Asheville News. Asheville News,* March 15, 1855.

of these offensive articles.[129] In addition to this I am informed by several Gentlemen who were present that you denounced me before a large assemblage of Ladies and Gentlemen on Saturday last at Fair View [130] as *"a dammed liar"* For these unprovoked assaults upon my character I demand of you personal satisfaction—

The bearer of this note Mr M Erwin [131] is authorized to act for me in this matter & will arrange with any Gentleman you may Select.— all the Preliminaries for a meeting[132]
Asheville

[A. L. S. Z. B. Vance Papers, State Department of Archives and History, Raleigh.]

To David L. Swain[133]

Asheville N. C.
6 July 1857.

I have a most melancholy and unfortunate piece of information to communicate, and think it best to do so at once before rumor

---

[129] The quarrel grew out of Dr. Baird's resignation from the Know-Nothing, or American, party with which Vance had become associated upon the collapse of the Whig party in 1854-1855. Dr. Baird announced his resignation in a public letter of June 11, 1855, in which he said that the principles of the new party were simply old Whiggery, and that its profession and practice did not agree. Since he had formerly been a Democrat, he announced his return to that fold. The *Spectator* charged that Baird's withdrawal had been motivated by nothing higher than his disappointment over his failure to have been appointed a delegate to the Know-Nothing convention which had met in May, and his hopes that the Democrats would now send him to the legislature. These charges Dr. Baird called "false" and "lies" and asserted that the main object of the Know-Nothing order was to defeat Clingman for Congress. Furthermore, he explained his withdrawal on the ground of his conviction that "this association is dangerous to the public liberty, and destructive of the very foundations of peace and prosperity, and calculated in the end to place all political power in the hands of a few designing demagogues, and to overturn our Republican system of government. . . ." It was "full of evil and disaster to the country." Calling the charges of the *Spectator* false, he challenged the editor to publish the constitution and laws of the order, in spite of their secret character, and continued: "The conscience of the *Spectator* is sufficiently elastic to do this, for it has not scrupled to publish whatever might benefit the order, despite of his obligations to keep it secret." The *Spectator*, as reported in the *News*, told the doctor to "take care, we are loading our old American musket that played the very devil with the Hessians. . . ." Dr. Baird referred to the *Spectator* editors as "fools" and "bullying blackguards" and suggested that if they wished to avoid discussion and "make it a personal quarrel, I would just say to them that we can settle the matter in a different way beside through the columns of a newspaper; and if they or any of their crew wish anything from me, they can have satisfaction at any time and in any way they may desire." *Asheville News*, May 2, June 14, 28, July 5, 1855.

[130] In Buncombe County.

[131] Marcus Erwin, one of the editors of the rival paper, the *Asheville News*. See p. 20, 93n.

[132] Vance's reply is not preserved, but Theodore F. Davidson, who said that he got the facts from Dr. Baird himself, told Dr. R. D. W. Connor in 1915 that Vance accepted the challenge but that, being cousins, members of their families intervened and patched up the quarrel. R. D. W. Connor to the editor, July 12, 1947.

[133] See p. 9, 45n.

renders it more unpleasant, if that were possible, than the sad reality.

Our dear old friend Dr. Mitchell [134] is no more. He is lost among the mountains and the utmost search we have been able to make has as yet proved unavailing. He left his work [135] on the Swannanoa side of the Black Mountain on Saturday the 26 ult. to go across to Caney River, and has not been heard of yet. I left the mountain this morning at 4½ oclk, & up to the time I left, the only trace we could discover was a slight trail along which we traced him for some three miles, when that became undistinguishable. It seems that he left the path which leads through the mountains and undertook to go a straight course through the woods, and the general opinion is that he has met with an accident and perished— miserably perished in the mountain solitudes! That he is still alive there is hardly a possibility much less a probability.

The whole country is deeply concerned and numbers of mountaineers and towns-people are out searching[136] in all directions. My wife is up at the mountain with Miss Margaret,[137] and I am going back again this evening although our court is going on here.

I do not know what course you should take in regard to breaking the news to his family, perhaps you had best keep it secret until next mail by which time I will write again and give further news, if by that time the body or our dear friend should be found.   In great haste

[Chapel Hill]

[A. L. S. David Lowry Swain Papers, Southern Historical Collection, Chapel Hill.]

---

[134] See p. 9, 46n. Dr. Mitchell had first explored what came to be known as the Mt. Mitchell area in 1835, and had made other trips in 1838, 1844, and 1856, as well as the last one in 1857. Mitchell had been one of Vance's teachers when he was at the University. *Memoir of Mitchell,* pp. 5-12.

[135] Because of a controversy with Thomas L. Clingman as to which had visited the highest peak, and after an extensive discussion of the question in the newspapers, Dr. Mitchell proceeded in the summer of 1857 to make an instrumental survey and obtain the testimony of those who had assisted him in his former barometrical measurement. He had been at work about two weeks when he undertook alone to journey over the mountain to reach the settlements on Caney River. During the course of the journey he slipped over a precipice forty feet high into a deep pool of the Sugar-camp branch of the Cat-tail Fork of the Caney River, and was killed. Z. B. Vance, "The Search for Professor Mitchell's Body," *Memoir of Mitchell,* pp. 13-19. This account by Vance was first published in the *Asheville Spectator* and subsequently reprinted, together with other tributes and addresses, in the *Memoir* cited above.

[136] There were two principal search parties organized, comprising altogether more than a hundred men. One party searched from the Yancey side and the other from the Buncombe side. Dr. Mitchell's body was found by the Yancey party on July 8, 1857, eleven days after his death. Vance was with the Buncombe party.

[137] Margaret Elliott Mitchell (1825-1905), a daughter of Elisha Mitchell, who had accompanied her father to the mountains.

To D. F. Caldwell [137a]
Asheville, N. C.
19 Feb. 1858.

Your friendly letter touching on matters of political interest, was duly rec^d, and ought to have been answered sooner. I was however in the midst of my county courts when it reached me, and since their conclusion I have had much to do, and have been quite unwell a great part of the time. This I hope will serve to excuse me from any seeming neglect.

You say you hardly "know how I stand", and appear to evince some hesitation in expressing yourself, fully and fairly to me. You are excusable for that suspicion, (if indeed it amounted to a suspicion) as I am not so prominent a politician as that the public listen to my opinions and watch my motions. Besides this, I have been purposely quiet, attending closely to my profession, and endeavoring to make bread for my family, which is encreasing in a truly *mountain ratio*. But for your information, and of any-one who might care to know, I will tell you how I stand, poli-tically, and this definition, unlike an almanac, will not need to be changed with the incoming year, but would answer as well for my grave stone as it does now—I learned the alphabet at my Father's knee, from the old dutch head-letters of the National Intelligencer [137b] and Raleigh Register, with the old motto,

---

[137a] David Franklin Caldwell (1814-1898), active Union Whig leader of Guilford County, who was born in Greensboro and lived there his entire life. He was at first a merchant and throughout his life was actively engaged in many and various business and banking enterprises. He was one of the prime movers in the North Carolina Railroad, the Greensboro and Cheraw, and the Cape Fear and Yadkin Valley; he organized the Bank of Greensboro, was its president and largest stock-holder; and in 1860 began the study of law. He was admitted to the bar in 1861 and practiced for a few years with James A. Long. He represented Guilford County in the House of Commons from 1848 to 1858, and again in 1864; he was a member of the Convention of 1865 and of the State Senate in 1879. Neither law nor politics ever made him lose his interest in railroad, industrial, and banking affairs. During Reconstruction he was nominated for Congress and claimed that he was counted out by General Canby. In 1879 he was a member of the committee to compromise the state debt, and his knowledge of finance aided in that difficult enterprise. His relations with Vance varied; they served together as Whigs in the legislature of 1854 and they zealously advocated the Union in the crisis of 1860. Tradition says that Vance refused Caldwell a commission in the Senior Reserves in 1864 and that he was thus forced to serve as a private when nearly fifty years of age. Whatever the reason, Caldwell opposed Vance's senatorial ambitions in 1872 and was an active supporter of Merrimon both then and again in 1879, when Caldwell was a member of the legislature. Caldwell never married. Connor, *N. C. Manual*, pp. 634-635, 882; David Franklin Caldwell Papers, Southern Historical Collection, University of North Carolina, Chapel Hill, N. C. (cited hereafter as Caldwell Papers); Jerome Dowd, *Sketches of Prominent Living North Carolinians* (Raleigh, 1888), pp. 308-312 (cited hereafter as Dowd, *Sketches*); obituary in Greensboro *Patriot*, January 4, 1899.

[137b] *The National Intelligencer* was a well-known conservative paper published in Washington, D. C. A daily since 1813, it was usually the "recognized organ" of the Whig administrations. Its editors for almost fifty years were Joseph Gales, Jr., and William Winston Seaton. These brothers-in-law edited the paper jointly until Gales' death in 1860; Seaton continued as editor until his retirement in 1864. W. E. Smith, "Joseph Gales," and "William Winston Seaton," *Dict. of Am. Biog.*, VII, 100-101, XVI, 541-542; Charles Lanman, "The National Intelligencer and Its Editors," *Atlantic Monthly*, VI (October, 1860), pp. 470-481.

"Ours are the plans of fair delightful peace
Unwarp't by party rage, to live like brothers." [137c]

And from their pages I drank in an early and an earnest love for
the *conservative,* a sincere admiration for our state and federal
constitutions, and a lasting veneration for the wise and true men
who formed them. I thus learned to oppose *democracy,* ever the
antipodes of conservatism, which from its very nature drew into
its embrace, the factions, the fragments, the odds & ends of every
ism in the land. And from that day to the present, the sectionalism which it has engendered & fostered with paternal care,
the wild, reckless, lawless, violent & dangerous spirit which
characterizes it, and the reeking, loathsome corruption which has
made it smell to high heaven, & a stench among the nations, has
but day by day, confirmed me in the opinion that I was doing God
a service in opposing it to the full extent of my abilities! I think
so yet. I believe most firmly, that the Democratic party, with
some of good, combines so many of the elements of death & destruction, that it has not only already brought us to our present
dangerous pass, but will eventually overthrow us entirely &
irredeemably. The many facts upon which this opinion is based,
I need not recite to you. I need not show you that in every state
where Democracy has obtained the power, the last one of the great
and conservative statesmen whose talents and patriotism, whose
prayers and tears, have held the Union together thus far, over so
many difficulties, has been swept away, and replaced by half-
brained fire-eaters who had *served the party.* I need not tell you
how Badger,[137d] Mangum[137e] & Graham[137f] fell in our own state,

---

[137c] The Raleigh *Register* (1799-1863) was for many years of Vance's boyhood the
chief Whig voice in North Carolina. It had been edited principally by Joseph Gales,
Weston Raleigh Gales, and Seaton Gales, but in December 1856 came under the
direction of John W. Syme. It was principally a weekly paper, though it did attempt
a daily for a few weeks in 1850-1851. The quotation cited by Vance was used for
many years just under the masthead of the *Register.* Robert Neal Elliott, Jr., *The
Raleigh Register, 1799-1863* (Chapel Hill, 1955) cited hereafter as Elliott, *Raleigh
Register.*

[137d] George Edmund Badger (1795-1866), United States Senator from North
Carolina (1848-1855), who incurred the wrath of Democrats because he refused
to agree with the Democratic position that Congress had no power to legislate
about slavery in the territories. He was defeated for re-election by the Democrats,
who were in control of the North Carolina legislature in 1854.

[137e] Willie Person Mangum (1792-1861), United States Senator from North Carolina
(1830-1836, 1840-1853), who was forced into resignation in 1836 by the Democrats
when he refused to vote for expunging the resolution of censure which the Whigs
had adopted against President Jackson. In 1852 Mangum failed to be re-elected
because the legislature of North Carolina was Democratic.

[137f] William Alexander Graham (1804-1875), also a Whig Senator from North
Carolina (1840-1843), who was defeated for re-election by the dominant Democratic
legislature. See below, p. 155, 634n.

how Crittenden,[137g] Bell,[137h] Everett [137i] & Choate[137j] went down
for their conservatism, how Webster,[137k] though he "still lives," yet
was dead before he died—physically, nor how the great and glorious Fillmore[137l] was brought low before his relentless foes, who
to *serve the party* (God save the mark) covered him with slanderous and blackguardish vituperation. "I stand" *therefore,* opposed
to Democracy, & shall so stand till democracy amends or I grow
corrupt—And though I am completely shut off from advancement,
by these opinions, which to a young man endowed with considerable ambition, is a gloomy enough prospect, yet I can say it
with a clear conscience before God & man, that the very fact of my
standing almost alone in defense of what I believe to be the
right, in the face of overwhelming odds, affords me a gratification
—an internal feeling of moral rectitude—that I would not surrender for a seat in the senate of the United States, were I old enough
to be allowed one! And when I meet with the many, many young
men of my acquaintance, who, unable to withstand this mighty
current, have apostatised & joined the democracy against their
convictions, I can not look on them as my equals: I can not but
feel that they have done themselves & their country a wrong. I
joined the American party, but because I believed its principles
were correct, and that without surrendering a single *iota* of Whiggery. The overthrow of this party furnishes no argument to me,
though it has to many, against the rectitude of its motives and
principles. I sustain them yet, every one of them, and ever shall—
I hope you know by this time "where I stand", and that my
friends may always know where to find me. As to state politics,

---

[137g] John Jordan Crittenden (1787-1863), of Kentucky. He was forced out of the
cabinet in 1841 when President Tyler began his evolution toward Democratic policies. Crittenden was United States Senator from Kentucky for twenty years, and
was noted as a leader of conservative Whiggery. See below, p. 76, 288n.

[137h] John Bell (1797-1869), Whig leader from Tennessee who had, as United
States Senator (1847-1859) defied the instructions of the Tennessee Democratic legislature and refused to vote for the admission of Kansas to the Union under the
pro-slavery Lecompton Constitution. He had also been forced from Tyler's cabinet
in 1841, along with Crittenden and Badger. See below, p. 69, 259n.

[137i] Edward Everett (1794-1865), conservative Whig congressman from Massachusetts and Secretary of State, who had resigned from the United States Senate
in 1854, because of public pressure, at the time of the Kansas-Nebraska Bill. He
was a moderate Whig and ardent Union man. See below, p. 69, 259n.

[137j] Rufus Choate (1799-1859), an anti-Jackson Whig who had served in both
houses of Congress and who was often attacked in the North for his conservative
attitude toward the sectional issues of the fifties.

[137k] Daniel Webster (1782-1852), Senator from Massachusetts, who had forfeited
much of his influence in Massachusetts by his moderate and "conservative" position
during the debates on the Compromise of 1850.

[137l] Millard Fillmore (1800-1874) of New York, the last Whig President. Because
of his advocacy of conciliation rather than coercion he had generally received the
support of the Southern Whigs, but he was defeated by the more extreme Northern
Whigs for the nomination of the party in 1852. He became the nominee of the
Know-Nothing party in 1856.

I hardly know what to say to you. I sympathize with most of your notions in regard to the banks, and all of your views in regard to Western Rights. We up here have always looked to the true men about Greensboro' as our friends and champions, and have a warm side for you & your town. But I am fearful, that no question we could present would have power enough to draw the attention of the people away from the hue and cry against Know Nothingism, or break the strong party drill under which they work. I felt at first inclined to fall into the McRae[137m] movement, as our only means of breaking & disorganizing the Democratic party, but when I learned from your letter & other sources, his probable position on internal improvements, I felt smartly cooled off. I could not possibly put myself in the position of antagonism to the Western Extension[137n], to gain any possible advantage over the party dominant, & this is the feeling I believe of all our people, though our hopes for aid from the next Legislature are small no matter how the thing goes. I wrote Syme[137o] inquiring after McRae's position, and received a very cautious and unsatisfactory reply. I think I see how the thing is going, but cant see that we are to better our condition by anything we can do. It is quite out of the question in my opinion to attempt running a man of our own, for beside that we cannot expect success, by our organizing and making a regular fight we cause them to organize and solidify their ranks, which are not the most compact in the world at this time, and are daily growing more loose. If we could fix upon a less exceptionable Democrat in favor of distribution[137p], and who had at the same time, some weight and influence with his own party, I would advise going for him. But I know of none

[137m] Duncan Kirkland McRae (1820-1888), Democrat from Cumberland and Wake counties, who had announced himself as an independent candidate for governor in opposition to the regular nominee of the Democratic party. The old Whigs made no separate nomination, but Whig papers usually advised support for McRae. For further details on McRae see below, p. 163, 2n. When McRae announced himself an independent candidate he went on record as opposed to state aid to internal improvements, in direct contrast to his party's platform.

[137n] The Western Extension was the name in general use for the Western North Carolina Railroad Company, which had been chartered February 15, 1855, during Vance's term in the legislature. The charter provided for an extension of the North Carolina Railroad from Salisbury "to some point on the French Broad River, beyond the Blue Ridge. . . ." Four years later the route of the proposed line was more definitely fixed, though the road never quite reached Morganton before the outbreak of the war. *Laws of N. C. 1854-'55*, chap. 228; *Private Laws of N. C. 1858-'59*, chap. 170.

[137o] John W. Syme, editor of the Raleigh *Register*. Formerly the owner and editor of the Petersburg (Va.) *Intelligencer*, he had purchased the *Register* in December 1856, and operated it until he moved the paper to Petersburg in 1863. Syme had come out for McRae in his issue of February 3, 1858. Elliott, *Raleigh Register*, pp. 102-103.

[137p] The State Democratic Convention in 1858 had denounced the distribution of the proceeds of the sale of public lands as "unconstitutional, anti-democratic, and impolitic." McRae came out in favor of distribution, which he had been publicly supporting ever since his campaign for Congress in 1851.

such. Leak[137q] & McRae are the only ones in market and I dont feel like bidding for either. What then are we to do? I do not feel capable of advising; but will only say that I will abide by anything that my brother Whigs will say is best. I must bring this to a close, as some gentlemen are coming in on business and once laid down I might not resume it again in a week. I would like to hear from you again, as I like to hear often from those "few names in Sardis that have not defiled their garments." A better day will surely come. Let us patiently bide our time & await its coming, strong in the rectitude of our intentions & firm and steadfast in the upholding of the right.

May God bless you.

[Greensboro]

[A. L. S. Zebulon Baird Vance Papers, Duke Manuscript Collection, Duke University Library, Durham.]

To R. B. Davidson [138]

Asheville N C
2 April 1858

The gentleman from whom I rec[d] the bad bill was not at home when yours was rec[d]. As soon as he returned I presented the bill which was promptly redeemed, he professing to be "an honest man"—I herewith enclose two Georgia bills for $10 each which are at par here, and I hope they may be equally good in your place. Please acknowledge reception.

There is no copy of the Christian Observer[139] taken in this place. Please [one word torn] me a copy when Aunts [several words torn]

All are well.

[Shelbyville, Tenn.]

[A. L. S. Colonel Allen T. Davidson and General Theodore F. Davidson Papers, State Department of Archives and History, Raleigh.]

[137q] Walter F. Leak, of Richmond County, who had been a member of the House of Commons in 1831 and of the State Senate in 1832. Connor, *N. C. Manual,* p. 776.

[138] Robert Brank Davidson, born in 1817, was the son of Hugh Davidson (1768-1841) and Jane (Vance) Davidson (1777-1858). Robert B. Davidson was a lawyer and lived in Shelbyville, Tennessee. Davidson Papers.

[139] *The Christian Observer* was a Presbyterian weekly then published in Philadelphia. The issue of March 25, 1858, contained an obituary of Jane Vance Davidson, aunt of Zebulon B. Vance. She had died at her home in Coffee County, Tennessee on January 12, 1858. She was a staunch Presbyterian. A copy of the paper may be found in the Historical Foundation of the Presbyterian and Reformed Churches, Montreat, N. C.

To Miss Margaret Mitchell [140]

Asheville N. C.
25th May 1858.

I gladly embrace the permission given me in your last letter to Mrs. Vance, to direct my letters to you in future. Without intending to drop my friend Charlie,[141] I shall take pleasure in writing to you also.

I yesterday wrote to Mr. Phillips,[142] informing him that I had succeeded at last in finishing the arrangements for the removal of your Fathers remains to their last wild, and sublime resting place.

Mr. Stepp[143] wrote me on Saturday, that the road was finished, leading from the mountain house[144] to the top of Mt. Mitchell.[145] I have appointed the 16th proximo. as the day for the removal, and advertise it in this weeks paper, to give notice to those many noble men of the mountains who desire to attend. Mr. Stepp

---

[140] See p. 31, 137n. Many incidents of her life are given in Hope Summerell Chamberlain, *Old Days in Chapel Hill* (Chapel Hill, 1926). (cited hereafter as Chamberlain, *Chapel Hill*).

[141] Charles Andrews Mitchell (1838-1868), a son of Elisha Mitchell and brother of Margaret Mitchell. He had just graduated from the University of North Carolina and had become a tutor there. During the war he was assistant surgeon to the Fortieth North Carolina Regiment (artillery). John W. Moore, *Roster of North Carolina Troops in the War Between the States*, 4 vols. (Raleigh, 1882), III, 113 (cited hereafter as Moore, *N. C. Roster*); Grant, *Alumni History*, p. 432.

[142] James Phillips (1792-1867), who was born in England and came to Chapel Hill in 1826, where he took over Dr. Mitchell's duties in mathematics. He was also a Presbyterian minister and delivered a funeral discourse on Dr. Mitchell in Chapel Hill. Phillips Russell. *The Woman Who Rang the Bell: The Story of Cornelia Phillips Spencer* (Chapel Hill, 1949), pp. 7-13 (cited hereafter as Russell, *The Woman Who Rang the Bell*).

[143] Jesse Stepp, who was born in 1811, was a farmer who lived at the foot of the Black Mountain on the Buncombe side. He owned considerable real estate along what is now the Asheville watershed on the north fork of the Swannanoa River. It was at his house that Dr. Mitchell established his headquarters in June, 1857. After the tragedy Stepp wrote to Miss Margaret Mitchell and offered to donate to the family fifty or a hundred acres of land "on the top of Black Mountain" if Dr. Mitchell could be buried on the peak. David Lowry Swain Papers, July 23, 1857, Southern Historical Collection, University of North Carolina, Chapel Hill, N. C. (cited hereafter as Swain Papers CH); *Census*, Buncombe County, 1850; McLean, "Notebooks."

[144] The "Mountain House," or "Halfway House," was built in the early fifties by William Patton of Charleston, S. C. partly for his own accommodation and partly to attract attention and visitors to the mountains. It was about four miles up the ascent on the Buncombe side. William Patton died in 1858 and was buried in the grave where Dr. Mitchell's body had lain for nearly a year. Sondley, *Buncombe County*, II, 532-533.

[145] Dr. Mitchell had been buried first in Asheville by the desire of his family, but on June 16, 1858, in compliance with the general opinion of its fitness, his body was removed and reinterred on the summit of Mt. Mitchell. Vance led a movement in the columns of the *Spectator* for contributions for the erection of a granite monument, but only a small portion of the required $5,000 was pledged and the effort came to nothing. Circular in Z. B. Vance Papers, dated 1857.

will make preparations to furnish food, and *quasi* shelter at least, to all the ladies and strangers who may attend, and we look for many. He is going to build an additional cabin on the mountain, and will send up provisions in abundance. The road will permit a lady to ride, comfortably, to the very spot.

Do you think of coming up? Hattie is very anxious that you & Mrs. Mitchell [146] and all the family should come, and expects you, of course, to come to our house.

We are hoping to see many of your citizens up here on that occasion.

We all continue in pretty good health. Our dear little boys[147] are quite hardy and stout, and are to us a source, at once of unbounded pleasure & delight, amusement, anxiety and annoyance— You would be much pleased to see them I know— my leisure hours are very pleasantly spent with them, when the weather is fine.

Hoping to hear from you soon, and that many of you will be prepared to come up in June, and tendering my kindest regards & Mrs. V's to you & yours, I remain

[Chapel Hill]

[A. L. S. J. H. Summerell Papers, Southern Historical Collection, Chapel Hill.]

To D. L. Swain[148]

Asheville N. C.
30 Augst 1858.

I have just returned from a visit of some 10 days to Morganton, and find your letter enclosing Mss.[149] I have looked over it as requested, and find nothing that I think needs correction. I think the statements plain, simple and to the point, and think it will have the desired effect.[150] In one place you say Rev. D. R. Mc-

---

[146] Maria S. (North) Mitchell, daughter of a physician of New London, Connecticut. She married Elisha Mitchell in 1819. In addition to Charlie and Margaret, already mentioned, the family consisted of Mary and Ellen, elder sisters of Margaret. Battle, *History of U. of N. C.*, I, 251; Chamberlain, *Chapel Hill*, p. 28.

[147] The Vances then had two sons living: Charles Noel, who was born March 27, 1856, and David Mitchell, who was born December 8, 1857. David's middle name was given him to honor Dr. Mitchell, who had been killed a few months before David was born.

[148] See p. 9, 45n.

[149] When Dr. Mitchell's body was reinterred on the top of Mt. Mitchell, June 16, 1858, President Swain delivered an address which he was later asked to write out for publication. It was this manuscript that he sent to Vance for his corrections. It is published, along with other proceedings of that occasion, in the *Memoir of Mitchell*, already cited, pp. 79-88.

[150] The "desired effect" was to substantiate Dr. Mitchell's claim to have first visited the highest peak over the claim of Hon. Thomas L. Clingman, whose name had been given to the mountain on a map published by William D. Cooke in 1847. Swain says that Cooke made no effort to obtain the best private materials. Swain

Zebulon Baird Vance at twenty-eight years of age

Anally[151] was Editor of the Highland Messenger. You will remember that he was associated with Joshua Roberts[152] in the conduct of that paper, and it would perhaps be respectful to mention his name also.

I am quite unwell today, so much so, that I am not able to give your paper so thorough an examination as I would like, and fear to delay answering lest it be too late. But if I were well, I dont think I could make any further valuable suggestion. I send you herewith the statement of R. V. Blackstock,[153] and also a paper containing my sketch [154] of the search for Dr. Mitchell's body. You will observe a few typographical errors in it, which the proof reader can easily correct.

My head is aching so that I can hardly see the lines on the paper. You will therefore excuse me from further writing. I

sent a copy of his address to William A. Graham, who advised him not to mention Clingman by name. W. A. Graham to D. L. Swain, August 17, 1858, Swain Papers CH. For Mitchell's controversy with Clingman see the detailed account in Sondley, *Buncombe County*, II, 527-577.

[151] Rev. David Rice McAnnally. He was born in Tennessee in 1810, graduated from Emory & Henry College and became a Methodist minister in 1831. Together with John A. Christie and Joshua Roberts, he established the *Highland Messenger* in June, 1840; it was the first newspaper ever printed in Asheville. Christie married, in 1842, Sarah, a daughter of Roberts, and moved to Athens, Georgia, where he edited the *Southern Watchman.* In 1851 McAnnally moved to St. Louis, where he edited the *St. Louis Christian Advocate,* a Methodist journal. He was also for a time president of the Female Institute in Knoxville. In a letter to Swain he agreed that Mitchell measured the highest peak in 1835, as he claimed, and that it was reported in the *Highland Messenger* of June 19, 1840. McAnnally to Swain, August 19, 1858, Swain Papers CH; Arthur, *Western North Carolina,* p. 449. For an account of McAnnally's suffering during the Civil War because of his southern sympathies see John A. Marshall, *American Bastile. A History of the Illegal Arrests and Imprisonment of American Citizens During the Late Civil War* (Philadelphia, 1869), pp. 487-500 (cited hereafter as Marshall, *American Bastile*); Sondley, *Buncombe County,* II, 777-780.

[152] Joshua Roberts (1795-1865) was a lawyer and merchant of Asheville who was born in Lincoln (now Cleveland) County and who married Lucinda Patton (1802-1869) of Asheville. Roberts was better known for his social graces and his pleasant home on the French Broad River than for his legal practice. Arthur, *Western North Carolina,* p. 449; Baird, "Historical Sketches"; McLean, "Notebooks."

[153] Robert Vance Blackstock (1824-1906) was born on Big Ivy Creek in Buncombe County, the son of Nehemiah Blackstock, in whose home Zebulon B. Vance lived when he first went to school at Flat Creek. Robert Vance Blackstock married into the Weaver family, his wife being Mary C. Weaver, and during a long life was actively identified with local politics in Buncombe County. He, like his father before him, was county surveyor and remained a great friend of the Vance family. He sent to Swain, by way of Vance's letter, a statement, quoting from a memorandum made on May 28, 1845, that he and his father, Nehemiah Blackstock, made a survey of the area and that this survey substantiated the claim made by Dr. Mitchell. Robert Vance Blackstock was at that time the chain bearer for his father. The map, drawn by R. V. Blackstock, is in the Swain papers. R. V. Blackstock to D. L. Swain, August 12, 1858, Swain Papers CH; McLean, "Notebooks."

[154] The sketch by Vance was entitled "The Search for Professor Mitchell's Body," and is printed in *Memoir of Mitchell,* pp. 13-19.

start to Cherokee Court on Thursday. Richard [155] (your son) is here, and is looking very well.
[Chapel Hill]
[A. L. S. David Lowry Swain Papers, Southern Historical Collection, Chapel Hill.]

To Cousin Jane[156]

Ho. of Rep's,[157] Washington City
10 Feb 1859.

Your letter was rec'd tonight just after dinner (I dine at the fashionable hour of 5. P. M.) and I sit down to answer it immediately, for I get so many letters, that if I lay one aside for future attention it loses its chance and I can never catch up. I have just come in from visiting some very pleasant ladies, where I spend whatever time I have for recreation. This is an invariable rule with me, and one I should recommend to all young men—spend as much of your leisure as possible with ladies. When I am with them, I feel that I am not only out of harm, but out of *temptation* to a great extent. And though I neither drink, gamble, nor do anything else *very* bad, yet a young man is always in danger when amid temptations, and I really believe, in point of wickedness and vice, that the cities at the bottom of the Dead Sea were holy places, compared to this. But I did not start out to moralize. I will send on Jimmie's[158] warrant as soon as it is sent me from the Navy Office, with instructions &c. I fear you over-estimate what I have done, and that you may think there is something of the *politician* in it, but I beg you not to think so. When your Father came to me last summer voluntarily, and to my perfect surprise told me that he & all the family would support me; and

---

[155] Richard Caswell Swain (1836-1872), familiarly known as "Bunk." He became a physician after his graduation from the University of North Carolina in 1858, and was later killed in a railroad accident. Grant, *Alumni History*, p. 604; Russell, *The Woman Who Rang the Bell*, p. 24.

[156] Jane L. Smith. See p. 11, 56n.

[157] In 1858 Asa Biggs resigned his place in the United States Senate in order to accept appointment as federal district judge in North Carolina. Congressman Thomas L. Clingman, of Vance's district, was appointed to the Senate in Biggs' place and, in December 1858, was elected by the legislature to serve out the remaining two years of Biggs' term. Vance was a candidate for Clingman's place in the United States House of Representatives and defeated William W. Avery, of Burke County, in a special election in 1858.

[158] James M. Smith, brother of Jane Smith and son of Samuel Smith, who had supported Vance in his recent race for Congress. Vance nominated James M. Smith, who was seventeen at the time, as a candidate for a midshipman's warrant at the Naval Academy. When he failed his examination in September 1859, Vance again nominated him, but he did not qualify a year later when he tried the second time. Z. B. Vance to Samuel Smith, January 29, 1859; Z. B. Vance to Isaac Toucy, Secretary of the Navy, February 8, 1859, Z. B. Vance Papers.

when I saw him stand firm to his promise despite of all that was brought to bear on his feelings as a democrat, I determined to repay him if in my power. What I have done has only been the payment of a just debt– nothing else influenced me. When I found the appointment vacant, I wrote to Brother Robert,[159] suggesting Jimmies name & in case he refused, little Bob Wells's and requesting him to Keep the matter a Secret, as if the vacancy had been generally Known, I would have been besieged with applications and would have made enemies by taking one & refusing the balance.

I would go into a description of men and things here, manners, parties, balls, &c., but I have not time tonight. Two or three letters are at my elbow to be answered, and it is getting late. I have had the honor of dining with the President and Swinging the accomplished Miss Lane[160] to my arm; and of supping with Judge Douglas[161] & his magnificent wife.[162] But all this when I see you.

Say to Kate[163] that she is not smart for sending me such a message– if she has left my friend David [164] for one bunch of seeds, that its not worth my while to send her anything else! She ought to have held out for Coleman until I had sent her every thing I had– Dont you see how much she missed? My kind regards to all. Good night.

[A. L. S. Z. B. Vance Papers, State Department of Archives and History, Raleigh.]

---

[159] See p. 2, 6n.

[160] Harriet Lane (1830-1903) was a niece of President James Buchanan, who was a bachelor, and served as hostess of the White House during her uncle's incumbency. She was known for her beauty and gaiety and largely because of her social graces the Buchanan administration is sometimes called the "Gay Administration." In 1866 Harriet Lane married Henry E. Johnston, of Baltimore. Mary Ormsbee Whitton, *First First Ladies, 1789-1865. A Study of the Wives of the Early Presidents* (New York, 1948), pp. 266-283.

[161] Stephen Arnold Douglas (1813-1861), Democratic Senator from Illinois, was earlier in his carrer a judge of the Supreme Court of Illinois and, in spite of greater political honors thereafter, was known as "Judge Douglas" to the end of his life. Allen Johnson, "Stephen Arnold Douglas," *Dict. of Am. Biog.*, V, 397.

[162] Douglas' second wife, whom he married November 20, 1856, was Adele Cutts, daughter of J. Madison Cutts of Washington. She was a great-niece of Dolly Madison, whom she is said to have resembled in beauty and charm of manner. George Fort Milton, *The Eve of Conflict. Stephen A. Douglas and the Needless War* (Boston and New York, 1934), pp. 4, 255-258.

[163] Probably Kate Erwin Smith, a cousin of Jane Smith. See p. 11, 57n. When Vance speaks of her having "left" David Coleman he is using the word in the political, not the amorous, sense.

[164] See p. 19, 91n. Coleman had been a candidate for the seat in Congress in the 1858 contest, but had withdrawn in favor of Avery in an effort to unite the Democrats. He was Vance's opponent in the 1859 race.

From D. Coleman[165]

Asheville 15th Aug. 1859

In our discussion at Waynesville, at more than one period, you *questioned* me, in an extremely offensive manner; declaring, as regarded one particular question, before that crowded audience, that you were asking it me, in order to pronounce my answer *false,* in the contingency of my replying in a certain way.

You may enquire why I bring this up at this late day. I treated the indignity in the calm and jesting mode then pursued by me, *because,* I *then* was resolved that, while the canvass should not be interrupted nor I compromised by personal conflicts, if possible, I designed calling on you, *after its conclusion,* for reparation, not only for *that,* but the other grievances of the same nature, which your then manner and conduct led me to expect in subsequent discussions.

The length of time that has elapsed, our courteous relations since, and my consciousness that my motives, in this particular instance, are liable to the greatest misconstruction from the public, had lately caused me to doubt the propriety of reviving my original intention; but very deliberate reflection convinces me that I cannot, consistently either with duty or self respect, suffer the indignity so to go by.

The necessities of my late position, which restrained me, having passed away with the canvass, I have now the honor to insist, to Mr. Vance, on my right to reparation as public as was the affront.

I take the occasion to add— I found it publicly current in Caldwell county, on election day, (at Lenoir), that you had given countenance to a report that I was intoxicated, on the occasion of our stay at a Mr Suddereth's,[166] at the head of the Yadkin: that is; that Mr. Vance would say, when questioned about the report, (in substance), "that he (Mr. V.), was a candidate, and had nothing to say about it."

I am happy to afford Mr Vance the opportunity to give the

---

[165] See p. 19, 91n. The quarrel related in the letters which follow grew out of the campaign for Congress between Vance and Coleman in 1859, a race which Vance won. While always opposed politically before the war, Vance and Coleman were never personal enemies. Each had respect for the other, but they were bitter political rivals for most of the decade. Coleman was a tall, slenderly built man of great native ability, of fine presence and courtly bearing, and held a high place in his profession and in public esteem. He took his Democracy and his championship of secession with great seriousness and was crushed when the Confederacy failed. After the war he would often walk alone about the country for hours at a time with his hands folded behind him, always dressed in clothes of homespun make, and always of a gray color. Sondley, *Buncombe County,* II, 768-769.

[166] The Sudderth family was a prominent family of Caldwell County. They lived north of Lenoir, near the present suburb of Valmead. W. W. Scott, *Annals of Caldwell County* (Lenoir, 1930), p. 34 (cited hereafter as Scott, *Caldwell County*).

lie to these calumniators, alike of him, (as I assure), and of me. Asheville.
[A. L. S. Z. B. Vance Papers, State Department of Archives and History, Raleigh.]

To D. Coleman[167]

Asheville, Augst 16 [1859]

Youre note of the 15th inst, was handed me this morning by Col Hardy.[168]

After what had passed between us since the discussion you allude to at Waynesville I must confess to some surprise at the purport of your note, as you seem very reasonably to anticipate. I must say that I am at a loss how to answer the first matter contained in yours, for if my recollection is right of that part of the discussion to which I suppose you refer an ample and satisfactory explanation was made then & there. The general language of your note does not permit me to Know specifically wherein my offense consists, and I would respectfully suggest that you point out more definitely what conduct I observed toward you on that occasion that was offensive.

The latter part of your note I have no dfficulty in answering. I positively deny having by insinuation or otherwise "given countenance" to a report that you were intoxicated during our stay at the Sudreth, last spring, but on the contrary have contradicted it often in private conversations, and as you know did so publicly and without solicitation at Burnsville. Knowing this as you do, I am at a loss to Know why you ask me again publicly to refute that which you know has already been publicly denied.
Asheville
[A. L. S. Z. B. Vance Papers, State Department of Archives and History, Raleigh]

---

[167] See p. 19, 91n and p. 42, 165n.
[168] Washington Morrison Hardy, a son of Dr. James F. E. Hardy, was born in 1835. He was a lawyer who was acting as Coleman's second in the affair. His title of colonel arose from the fact that he was colonel of the Eighty-third Regiment of North Carolina Militia. During the war he was first lieutenant of company E of the Bethel regiment and, on June 10, 1863, became colonel of the Sixteenth North Carolina Regiment. He was assistant secretary of the Convention of 1875, and several times a candidate for minor offices. All his life he was, like his father, a Democrat, though he came to be considered a drone on the party and was accused of spending his time in Raleigh in drunkenness and never having enough money to get home at the end of a session. Moore, *N. C. Roster,* I, 419, III, 674; Clark, *N. C. Regts.,* III, 483, IV, 334, 440; *Census,* Buncombe County, 1860; Natt Atkinson to Samuel McDowell Tate, August 18, 1874, Tate Papers; McLean, "Notebooks."

From D. Coleman[169]

Asheville 3 P. M.
Tuesday Aug. 16th [1859]

Your note of this morning has just been handed to me by my friend Col. Hardy.

I must confess that I am at a loss to see how I can, for all practicable purposes, more fully specify "in what your offence consists—" (on the occasion at Waynesville, referred to.) Let me recall to you as if you were a stranger, who had never even heard of the incidents of that discussion, the definitive "offence."

I was speaking—charging that the *object* of Mr "Grow's[170] Resolution," Resepcting the Post Office appropriation bill,[171] *intended* by him and his friends, was, by defeating that bill to force the calling an extra session of Congress, by means of the hasty assemblage of which, to have Mr Grow elected speaker of the House of

---

[169] See p. 19, 91n and p. 42, 165n.

[170] Galusha Aaron Grow (1822-1907) was born in Connecticut and graduated from Amherst College in 1844. He studied law and became a partner of David Wilmot at Towanda, Pa. In the Thirty-second Congress, of which he was the youngest member, he became a strong advocate of homestead legislation and a conspicuous figure in the alignments that produced the new Republican party. To southern politicians Grow was among the most aggravating of Republicans; he was one who could, and did, goad impulsive southerners to desperation, in which he took delight. He was elected speaker of the special session of Congress in July 1861, but was defeated for re-election in 1862. Beginning in 1893, he again served through four congresses as a picturesque veteran. James T. DuBois and Gertrude S. Mathews, *Galusha A. Grow: Father of the Homestead Law* (New York and Boston, 1917), *passim* (cited hereafter as DuBois and Mathews, *Galusha A. Grow*); Roy F. Nichols, "Galusha Aaron Grow," *Dict. of Am. Biog.*, VIII, 30-31.

[171] Grow's Resolution on the Post Office Appropriation Bill was the object of house debate on March 3, 1859, as the second session of the Thirty-fifth Congress was about to adjourn. The resolution reads as follows: "*Resolved*, That House bill No. 872, making appropriations for defraying the expenses of the Post Office Department for the year ending 30th June, 1860, with the Senate amendments thereto, be returned to the Senate, as section thirteen of said amendments is in the nature of a revenue bill." Grow contended that the House bill was simply an appropriation measure and that the Senate, by raising certain postal rates in section thirteen, was initiating a revenue measure and had thereby breached the privileges of the House. The House sustained Grow by a vote of 117 to 76, Vance voting for the resolution. The vote in favor included twenty-nine Democrats, nine "South Americans," and every Republican who voted. Thus Vance was found voting with such notorious "Black Republicans" as Grow and Sherman. Many Democrats charged Grow with a political manoeuvre by which he hoped to force an extra session of Congress because appropriation bills had failed to pass. The dispute continued into the next session, at which Lawrence O'Bryan Branch, a Democrat, a colleague of Vance from North Carolina, and an ardent secessionist whose antagonism to Grow had long been unconcealed, challenged Grow to a duel as a result of this quarrel. Grow declined the challenge and the atmosphere soon cleared. *Congressional Globe*, 35 Congress, 2 session, pp. 1599-1600, 1666-1667 (March 3, 1859), (cited hereafter as *Cong. Globe*, with appropriate dates); DuBois and Mathews, *Galusha A. Grow*, pp. 231-235; "Responsibility for Organizing the House, and for the Defeat of the Post Office Appropriation Bill," (pamphlet, 8 pp., n. d.; two speeches of Grow and one of Branch). The challenge from Branch, together with Grow's reply, is in the Mrs. Lawrence O'Bryan Branch Papers, December 29, 30, 1859, State Department of Archives and History, Raleigh, N. C. (cited hereafter as Mrs. Branch Papers).

Representatives, before Some of the Western democratic members could arrive; and I censured you for having voted for the Resolution. You, very peremptorily, demanded to know, if I charged *you* with wishing the election of Mr Grow.

I offered immediately to explain—You would not wait for an "explanation," but repeatedly and most offensively and even threateningly, demanded an instant answer in the simple affirmative or negative, (Springing to your feet if I remember aright, and standing, during this strange scene), and before I could, as I did, "make haste" to explain, declared that you wished an answer, in order, if it was affirmative, to pronounce my charge *false.*

It required all the tact and calmness I can muster to quiet you —I did so because I believed a conflict then would seriously damage my prospects as a candidate; because it has been an axiom of mine that rather than stop all discussion in public, candidates had better, if possible, postpone the adjustment of all quarrels until after the election; and because I had the deliberate intention *then* to bring the matter to your attention again, at a time and under circumstances, when it could be more decorously adjusted.

Your "offence" then, Sir, is—you threatened me—and who threatens insults me; you wantonly and without excuse, (for I had not made the suppostious charge referred to), gave notice of a *contingent* intention to give me the *lie*—the lie itself is about as well,—and you heightened your threatening and offensive *words,* by your threatening and offensive *manner.*

The "explanation" you gave "then and there," as well as I can remember, was merely to the purport that *you* were satisfied—

After I seemed "backed out," you may have been gracious enough to have signified that fact with, what you considered, graciousness—This however I well remember, that I was perfectly conscious that to prevent the discussion being broken up, I placed myself in the false position before the audience, of quietly submitting to insult—putting to the severest test my observance of the rule, that a gentleman must, on all such occasions, be his own judge of when such matters can "keep cool" until the proper time.

I do not mean to say, Sir, that I regard this as the only exceptionable portion of your bearing toward me, during the canvass, but it is that (as being the most palpable), on which I chose to base my note of yesterday.

This, Sir, being the "definite offense," I leave it to you to evince what atonement you think proper to make, to place me *in statu quo* before the public, and before myself. I trust this note is sufficiently explicit, to leave you no difficulty in making up your decision.

Permit me to express myself satisfied and gratified with respect to your explanation of the Caldwell Slander. I brought it to your attention, because your supporters there were giving you as authority in the way I have mentioned.

Asheville

[A. L. S. Z. B. Vance Papers, State Department of Archives and History, Raleigh]

To D. Coleman[172]

Asheville August 17 [1859]

Your note dated 3 P. M. yesterday was handed me too late for a reply.

Your last is sufficiently explicit, and enables me to make you an answer. I find Sir, that we differ materially as to the parts connected with the discussion at Waynesville. You say that you charged that the object of Grow[173] "& his friends" in supporting said resolution was to defeat the P. O. Bill &c. &c. Now Sir, I did not so understand you, for I could not have felt myself included in the number of Grow's "friends," but I understood you to include in your charge *all who supported the resolution,*[174] which of course comprehended myself as you had often done before. Stinging under what I thought from it being so often repeated was a deliberate insult, I rose to my feet and asked if you charged that I voted for the resolution with a view to the election of Grow as Speaker. If my manner was offensive, I certainly did not so intend it, but I was very much excited. In regard to what followed we differ still more materially; you say "I offered immediately to explain—you would not wait for an explanation"—Now my distinct recollection is that you *hesitated* to explain—turned and looked at me offensively—took out your watch and noted the time, saying this interruption must be allowed you &c, leaving myself and the audience to infer that you included me on the charge as I thought. There it was that I made the remark of which you complain. If you had "made haste to explain," I certainly should have given you time, but as I thought, you were using every effort to avoid an explanation. After some further remarks you stated that you would show my vote and probable effect of it, and would draw no inference whatever as to my motives, and asked me if that was satisfactory. I said you had a right to do that, and I was entirely satisfied. You then went further and said that since I had expressed myself satisfied, you would entirely disclaim im-

---

[172] See p. 19, 91n and p. 42, 165n.

[173] See p. 44, 170n.

[174] See p. 44, 171n.

parting any such motives to me whatever, as desiring the election of Grow.

This is my recollection of the occurence and taking it to be substantially correct it would place me in quite a different light in the matter. Had I Known or thought Sir, that you were going to explain and do me justice, then my language & conduct might have been justly regarded as offensive. In a heated debate it is I assure, somewhat difficult to agree upon precisely what did occur in a particular part of the discussion but a proper recognition on your part of the position I occupied, and the view I took of your hesitation when asked the question about your charge upon the supporting of Grows resolution, together with the candor you exhibited immediately afterwards in disavowing the imputation which I supposed you had made, would enable me no doubt to give an answer amply satisfactory

Asheville

[on reverse]

Reply No 2, to Mr C's 2nd note

[A. L. S. Z. B. Vance Papers, State Department of Archives and History, Raleigh.]

From D. Coleman[175]

Asheville 17th Aug. 1859.

In reply to your note of to day — I consider it altogether immaterial whether, or not, I used the expression "Grow[176] and his friends" (respecting "said resolution") [177] or merely charged that the object of the resolution was, to have Grow elected Speaker.

I distinctly recalled that I never charged you with wishing his election, for I did not know what was your wish—that was between you and Divine Providence; but censured you, because, *that* being the object of his resolution, you voted for it. The journal shows, and you admit, you *did* vote for it. I had a right to state the truth, and you had no right, admitting your vote, to insult me for *telling the truth,* when, at that very time, I left the audience to draw their own inference, not drawing any myself.

You say "my (your) distinct recollection is that you" (I) "hesitated to explain."

In the first place, you had no right to any explanation at all. It was a political, and not a personal charge: but if you *had* had such a right, I might have very properly, "*hesitated,*" as to what conciliatory reply I should make to *keep the peace,* to one who was on his feet, in a threatening attitude, excitedly and peremptorily demanding of me an instant answer.

---

[175] See p. 19, 91n and p. 42, 165n.
[176] See p. 44, 170n.
[177] See p. 44, 171n.

But I think even then, (being a man of peace, and anxious to keep the peace), I did *not* "hesitate" to intimate to you, that if you would "keep cool," and give me moderately reasonable time, I would explain; (when I knew you had no right to such explanation.)

You say that I "turned and looked at you very offensively." I think it very probable I looked at you, Sir, It is said, " a cat may look at a king," and I might venture to look at a man who has sprung to his feet, and showed strong signs of a readiness to attack me. I *generally* look at such people—and *right in the eye*—and have no doubt I looked at you on that occasion.

You say, I, "took out my watch and noted the time, saying, this must be allowed me &c"—(that is, must be deducted from my time for argument) .

Certainly I did—I was very deliberate—But I would beg to know what in all this justifies your inference, that I thereby, included you in the charge &c. " (See your note to day.)

Now, Sir, to "pan out" the whole matter — from your own note of to day, it is "eliminated," that, to quote your own words, "your language and conduct might have been justly regarded as offensive"—(but for the excuse, you give, and I leave all men to judge of the justness of that excuse.)

You stand before me, then, by your own note, as an insulter. You make a *lawyerlike* argument to convince me, that I should submit to that insult—as a *politician,* I *did, temporarily,* submit to it—for supposed prudential "cause."

But permit me to say, that, under insult, on the final settlement, the lawyer and the politician sink, and the gentleman reasserts his province. I have not only to assert the ordinary rights of a gentleman, in such cases, but to vindicate—a very important *"franchise,"* —freedom of discussion between candidates.

I will never consent, that, through me, and especially in this, my native district, the rule shall be established, that *any* language can be used "on the Stump" with impunity, and that candidates must either stop the canvass, or submit to it, or be without remedy afterwards.

I have, therefore, Sir, the honor, (having failed to draw from you any reparatory explanation, or any expression of intention to explain on proper terms, and having exhausted all the arts of conciliatory diplomacy, to request you to name the time, place, weapons and terms, (such as you have a right to make), under which we can bring this controversy to a finally satisfactory termination.

Asheville

[A. L. S. Z. B. Vance Papers, State Department of Archives and History, Raleigh.]

To D. Coleman[178]

Asheville Augst 18, 59

Sir, your note of the 17th is rec[d]

The extraordinary tenor of that note makes me regret the conciliatory tone of the two I have heretofore addressed you. Rest assured Sir, that they were dictated under the impression that you were really desirous of an amicable adjustment of matters between us. But now when by your last it becomes so apparent that your object is simply to seek a dificulty, in order perhaps to take away some of the sting of the late defeat, I beg leave to recall anything of a conciliatory character which they may contain.

I shall have to ask a brief delay before naming the final particulars, as I desire to see a friend, who is not now present, and there are no suitable weapons in this place that I could command.

As soon as these matters can be adjusted you shall hear from me Sir again
Asheville
[on reverse]
3[d] Note in reply to Colemans 3[d]
[A. L. S. Z. B. Vance Papers, State Department of Archives and History, Raleigh.]

From D. Coleman[179]

Asheville 18th Aug. 1859.

In accepting your note of this morning, it gives me pain to have to make my earnest protest against the *tone* of that communication.

It is my understanding, that courtesy and respect toward an opponent are as essential requisites of a note of acceptance, as of one in challenge.

I, therefore, protest against your imputation, therein contained, that I am actuated, in this controversy, by unworthy motives—which I emphatically disclaim.

For myself, while recognising firmly the relation of mortal hostility in which we stand, I beg to say, that there is not a Single "conciliatory" or respectful expression I have used, in our correspondence or elsewhere, that I either "regret," or "recall."

Of course, for purposes of this quarrel, I waive all objection, and receive your note.

Any accommodation you may need as to time, &c, it will be my pleasure cheerfully to acquiesce in. I remain,
Asheville.
[A. L. S. Z. B. Vance Papers, State Department of Archives and History, Raleigh.]

---

[178] See p. 19, 91n and p. 42, 165n.
[179] See p. 19, 91n and p. 42, 165n.

To D. Coleman[180]

Asheville N. C. 19th August '59

I have the honor to refer you to my friend John D. Hyman[181] Esq who will confer with any gentleman you may designate in arrangeing a meeting between us.

Asheville

[A. L. S. Z. B. Vance Papers, State Department of Archives and History, Raleigh.]

From Jno. D. Hyman[182]

[Aug. 22, 1859]

The parties will meet at Waddell's cabin, Cocke County, Tennessee, near the North Carolina line, on Tuesday, 30th August, instant, at 8 o'clock, A. M.

Each party may be accompanied by not more than two friends[183] and a Surgeon. The ordinary smooth-bored duelling pistol shall be used—each to be loaded on the ground in the presence of the parties. Distance twelve paces. The choice of position and the giving of the word shall be determined by lot.

The parties shall stand with their shoulders in a line and facing in opposite directions, each with the muzzle of his pistol downward

---

[180] See p. 19, 91n and p. 42, 165n.

[181] John Durante Hyman, who was a student at the University of North Carolina in 1848-1849, and came to Asheville about 1850 from Edgecombe County. In Asheville he became associated with Vance and they edited the *Asheville Spectator* together for a year and a half in that decade. Hyman, though a lawyer, never practiced law very much until he moved to Hendersonville after the *Spectator* failed. But he was the journalistic champion of the Whig cause and, after the demise of that party, of the Know-Nothing or American party. During the war he went to eastern Carolina and volunteered for military service, becoming a captain in the commissary in the Fourth North Carolina Regiment and an aide to Colonel George Burgwyn Anderson. He was permanently disabled early in the war and forced to return home, but in 1864 he came to Raleigh to edit an administrative organ for Governor Vance, known as the *Conservative*. Hyman had political aspirations which were never realized, but he was always a faithful and devoted friend of Vance. He had already acquired some experience in affairs of honor. He was very probably a second in the duel between Marcus Erwin and John J. Baxter and in 1855 had himself fought a duel, also in Cocke County, Tennessee, with Dr. W. L. Hilliard, a physician of Asheville who was postmaster and who challenged Hyman because Hyman had written in the *Spectator* that the mail service was not as efficiently conducted as when it had been under Whig control. Hyman lived in Hendersonville the remainder of his life, and is buried there. Arthur, *Western North Carolina*, pp. 369-371, 449; Clark, *N. C. Regts.*, I, 230, 268-269; *Asheville News*, July 10, 1856; *Census*, Buncombe County, 1860; Battle, *Hist. of U. of N. C.*, I, 804; Grant, *Alumni History*, p. 312; Sadie Smathers Patton, *The Story of Henderson County* (Asheville, 1947), pp. 124-125 (cited hereafter as Patton, *Henderson County*).

[182] See above, 181n.

[183] In addition to Hyman, the other friend of Vance was Samuel Brown, a brother of Vance's law partner, William Caleb Brown. Vance's brother, Robert B. Vance, said that Samuel Brown was to have been Vance's second, and that he practiced Zebulon in the woods near Arden, in Buncombe County. Clement Dowd, *Life of Zebulon B. Vance* (Charlotte, 1897), pp. 37-38 (cited hereafter as Dowd, *Life of Vance*).

in a perpendicular position, the arm and pistol being parallel with his body.

After the parties shall have taken their places, the second of the party winning the word shall take his position equidistant from each, and give the word as follows: "Gentlemen, are you ready?" and being distinctly answered by each, *I am ready"* then he shall say "fire—one—two—three". The interval shall be about one second of time between the different words above given. In order that there may be no mistake or misunderstanding, the word shall be distinctly rehearsed by the winning second after the parties have taken their position and before it is finally given. The pistol of each shall remain directly muzzle downward till the word "fire."

These terms shall be rigidly enforced upon the ground by the friends of the parties.

[Asheville]

[A. L. S. Z. B. Vance Papers, State Department of Archives and History, Raleigh.]

From J. F. E. Hardy[184] and J. W. Woodfin [185]

Asheville Augst 22ᵈ/59.

The undersigned having heard that a difficulty is likely to occur between you and D. Coleman[186] Esq, and being honestly desirous of seeing the same honorably adjusted between you; we beg leave to ask you to allow the whole corespondence, to be at least, temporarily, and for purposes of adjustment, withdrawn.

Asheville

A duplicate of this also sent Mr Coleman

[This appears to be a copy, in the handwriting of Z. B. Vance, Z. B. Vance Papers, State Department of Archives and History, Raleigh.]

To Messrs. J. F. E. Hardy[187] and J. W. Woodfin [188]

Asheville, Augst 22ᵈ 59

Your note of today has just been handed me. In it you state that as mutual friends you are honestly desirous of settling ami-

---

[184] See p. 20, 95n.

[185] John W. Woodfin (1818-1863) was a wealthy lawyer and farmer of Buncombe County, having been born in what is now Henderson County and coming to the Asheville bar about 1845. He was of a genial and sunny disposition, but a master of sarcasm and invective. He married Maria McDowell of Quaker Meadows, a daughter of Captain Charles McDowell, in whose home Vance's wife had been reared. The friendship of Vance and Woodfin had been strengthened by the fact that Vance had begun his reading of law under Woodfin in 1850-1851. Woodfin was killed by Kirk's men at Hot Springs in 1863. Arthur, *Western North Carolina,* pp. 385, 392; Merrimon, "Diary," for 1850 and 1851.

[186] See p. 19, 91n and p. 42, 165n.

[187] See p. 20, 95n.

[188] See above, 185n.

cably a pending difficulty between Mr D. Coleman[189] and myself, and ask me for that purpose to permit temporarily, a withdrawal of the correspondence that has taken place between us.

I have no objection to the proposition provided of course, that it is preceded by a similar intimation on the part of Mr Coleman. My notes being based upon and in reply to his addressed to me, the withdrawal of mine could of course only properly follow the withdrawal of his.

Asheville
[A. L. S. Z. B. Vance Papers, State Department of Archives and History, Raleigh.]

From D. Coleman[190] to Messrs. J. F. E. Hardy[191] and J. W. Woodfin[192]

Asheville 22.[d] Aug. 1859.

I have the honor to acknowledge the receipt of your joint note, of this date.

While I highly appreciate the friendly and laudable motives which dictated that note, permit me to suggest, that I do not see how I, after my challenge and its acceptance, can now "allow the whole correspondence to be, at least temporarily, and for the purposes of adjustment, withdrawn," without some authorized intimation that this proposition has the sanction of Mr Vance.

Having, from the first wished nor demanded nothing more, nor less, than a just and honorable settlement of the matter in controversy, I shall, in that event (of Such intimation on the part of Mr Vance) be willing to accede to your proposition—and to make such adjustment on the basis of my former notes.

Asheville
[A. L. S. Z. B. Vance Papers, State Department of Archives and History, Raleigh.]

From D. Coleman[193] to J. W. Woodfin[194]

[August 22, 1859]

I think it due Mr Woodfin to assign my reasons for still thinking it best to assume in my note the fact of a former correspondence.

1st.   To ignore it would be a studied suppression of a train of fact material to the case, which could scarcely otherwise than place Mr V. and me both in false positions—

2[d]   If I recited in lieu of that such expression as "reasons known to Mr V. and myself," those who became cognizant of my note

---

[189] See p. 19, 91n and p. 42, 165n.
[190] See p. 19, 91n and p. 42, 165n.
[191] See p. 20, 95n.
[192] See p. 51, 185n.
[193] See p. 19, 91n and p. 42, 165n.
[194] See p. 51, 185n.

would wonder what reasons could account for such lukewarm and vaccilating delay—

The only reason they could think a good one would be that Some earnest correspondence *had* taken place—which it would be the very object of the omission to conceal.

3ᵈ   So enveloping the matter in (as I think) unnecessary mystery, would have greater room for misconstructions of the conduct of both, than any other course—and we perhaps could not justly complain, when we had the means of preventing it—

4ᵗʰ   Recognition of the fact of the correspondence, its withdrawal while it has the good effect which such a frank statement always has, could not operate to the disadvantage of Mr V. more than myself—On the contrary I being the "actor", the inference from withdrawal would be, that if I had been too aggressive I had been obliged to *back* from that position; and no proposition came from Mr V. for withdrawal or compromise.

Asheville

[A. L. S. Z. B. Vance Papers, State Department of Archives and History, Raleigh.]

To "My Dear John" [195]

Asheville N. C. 22d August 1859

It has been so long since I wrote you that I am almost ashamed to do so now—but better late than not at all. I have a letter in Paris, with the U. S. Consul waiting your arrival at that place, it

---

[195] John Evans Brown (1827-1895), a son of William John Brown (1803-1884) and Ann Marshall (Evans) Brown (1803-1858), was born in Lewiston, Pa., and went to school in Wilmington, Delaware, and at Dickinson College. He studied medicine and law until ill health led him out of doors to Ohio and North Carolina, where he became a surveyor. He came to Buncombe County with his father about 1843 but left in 1849 to join the gold rush to California. He returned to Asheville for a brief period in the fifties, but in 1856 he sailed from San Francisco for Australia, where he became a gold miner, sheep rancher, and business man. In 1864 he removed to Canterbury, New Zealand and repeated his successful business enteprises there and at Christchurch, where he later settled. He was a member of the New Zealand General Assembly and Minister of Education, in which position he did much to establish a system of free, compulsory education. He was a strong advocate of provincial federation, and actively interested in railroads. In 1858 he married Theresa Australia Peacock, an Australian by birth, but the daughter of an English merchant and shipper of Sydney. She died in 1880 and in 1883 he married a Mrs. Martin of Wellington, New Zealand. In 1884 he returned to North Carolina and in 1889 built "Zealandia," a miniature of Moro Castle at Havana, on the mountain crest east of Asheville, where he resided until his death in 1895. He owned many thousands of acres of land in the mountains of western North Carolina and Tennessee and Vance was his legal agent for the sale of about 50,000 acres. "Memoirs of an American Gold Seeker," *Journal of American History*, vol. II, no. 2 (1908), pp. 129-154; J. N. Ingram, "New Zealand's Early Destiny Directed by North Carolinian," *Uncle Remus Magazine*, December 1911, p. 20; Records of Deeds, Buncombe County, Book 35, pp. 73-74; John Evans Brown Letter Book (1878-1887), W. Vance Brown Papers, State Department of Archives and History, Raleigh, N. C. (cited hereafter as Brown Papers); *Asheville Daily Citizen*, July 9, 1895; *Asheville Citizen*, December 17, 1884; W. J. Brown to John Evans Brown, March 21, 1861, Brown Papers; *Asheville Spectator*, September 3, 1858.

being written some 18 mos ago under the silly impression that it would meet you there on your way home.

Since you left California, many important events have taken place in this end of the old North State, most of which I suppose have been given you by your Father[196] and the others. I scarcely therefore know what to say without inflicting some old news upon you. I will begin with your own family—In passing, they are in tolerable health: your Father tho' is not very stout neither is Samuel[197]—but as much so as usual. William[198] is now in the mountains of Watauga—has been practicing law in partnership with me in the County Courts for twelve months past, and got his superior court license the 5th of this inst: As I am now in other business I expect to turn all my practice in both courts over to him, which gives him at once a fair start in his profession. I have

---

[196] William John Brown (1803-1884), a son of John Brown (1772-1845) and Ann Brown (1777-1848) of Lewiston, Pa. He was a lawyer who came to Buncombe County about 1843, having claims to great tracts of land in western counties concerning which there was dispute and litigation for many years. These claims were known as the "Brown Speculation" and were said to comprise about a million acres in Haywood, Buncombe, and Mitchell counties. He married Ann Marshall Evans in 1826, by whom there were three sons and two daughters, all born before the family came to North Carolina. After her death in 1858 he married, at the Governor's Mansion in Raleigh, April 7, 1864, Mrs. Mary Taylor of Richmond, Va., who was twenty-six years younger than he. William John Brown was an ardent Christian and sincere Presbyterian, and counted the Vance family his dearest friends among all his new-found neighbors. He lived about nine miles south of Asheville, at Cabin Home. W. J. Brown to Major James Wilson, May 27, 1879, W. J. Brown to Samuel McDowell Tate, March 17, 1881, Tate Papers; W. J. Brown to John Evans Brown, April 15, 1861, Brown Papers; obituaries in *Asheville Daily Advance*, December 7, 1884 and *Asheville Citizen*, December 17, 1884.

[197] Samuel Smith Brown (1837-1862), youngest son of William John Brown, and brother of John Evans Brown. He was born in Dayton, Ohio, and became a surveyor when the family moved to North Carolina, though he was frequently confined at home because of erysipelas. In May 1861 he became second lieutenant in Vance's company "The Rough and Ready Guards," which afterwards became company F of the Fourteenth North Carolina Regiment. He died in camp at Smithfield, Va., February 28, 1862, and was buried in Asheville on March 8, 1862, "greatly esteemed for his many good qualities of head and heart." *Asheville News*, March 13, 1862; William Caleb Brown to John Evans Brown, March 22, 1861; John Evans Brown Letter Book, Brown Papers, showing the certificate of Colonel Risdon Tyler Bennett, August 8, 1862; Moore, *N. C. Roster*, I, 527.

[198] William Caleb Brown (1832-1862), second son of William John Brown, and brother of Samuel Smith Brown and John Evans Brown. He accompanied John Evans Brown to California but returned to Asheville in 1855, where he became a surveyor and a lawyer. He and Vance formed a law partnership together in 1858 and this relationship continued until the war, when William Caleb Brown became a first lieutenant in Vance's company and was afterwards captain and quartermaster in the Fourteenth North Carolina Regiment. In the summer of 1862, during the midst of the gubernatorial campaign, Vance said that he intended giving William Brown a private position if he himself were elected governor. But William Brown died of a fever in Richmond on July 6, 1862, a month before Vance was chosen governor. He had never married. John Evans Brown Letter Book, Brown "Diary," April 4, 1888, Mrs. Mary Taylor Brown to John Evans Brown, June 20, 1865, Brown Papers; obituaries in Raleigh *North Carolina Standard*, December 3, 1862, *Asheville News*, July 16, 1862. The William Caleb Brown Notebooks and Diaries in the W. Vance Brown Papers give many items in regard to the relationship of Vance to the entire family, but especially concerning the law partnership.

Dowd, *Life of Vance*

The first law office of Zeb Vance was located in Asheville. Vance was admitted to the bar in 1852 and was elected solicitor for Buncombe County that same year, when he was twenty-one years old.

no doubt but he will hold all his business and get more rapidly, as he evinces much tact, talent and industry. Health and strength permiting, you need have no fears about William, *he is bound to go through certain.*

My own family now consists of Mrs Vance & two little boys[199]— the youngest nearly 2 years old. They are fine hearty fellows and great pets with your father. Mrs. V. is still in delicate health. She desires many kind messages to you and advises you to come home.

In 1858, Clingman[200] was appointed to the Senate leaving a vacancy in this District. Avery[201] & Coleman[202] came out and be-

---

[199] See p. 38, 147n.

[200] Thomas Lanier Clingman (1812-1897) was born in Huntsville in Surry, later Yadkin, County, N. C. He graduated from the University of North Carolina in 1832, leading his class, and studied law under William A. Graham at Hillsboro. He represented Surry County in the House of Commons in 1835; moved to Asheville in 1836 and was elected state senator in 1840. In 1843 he represented the mountain district in the Twenty-eighth Congress, was defeated in the next election, but from 1847 to 1858 he continuously represented his district in the United States House of Representatives. When he resigned in 1858 he was appointed by Governor Thomas Bragg to fill the unexpired term of Asa Biggs in the United States Senate. Clingman was subsequently elected Senator and served until he withdrew on January 21, 1861; he was formally expelled on July 8, 1861. Until 1852 he was a Whig but, becoming distrustful of the attitude of the Northern Whigs toward the slavery question, he left that party for the Democrats, carrying his district with him. In 1861 he was a delegate from North Carolina to the Confederate States Convention at Montgomery, Ala. In August 1861 he became colonel of the Twenty-fifth North Carolina Regiment, and on May 17, 1862, was made a brigadier general. His political career after the war was undistinguished; he was a delegate to the Democratic National Convention in 1868 and to the State Constitutional Convention of 1875. Clingman never married; he lived after the war at the old Swannanoa Hotel in Asheville and, somewhat in his dotage, would talk endlessly with anyone who would listen; when there was no one else he would talk to himself. He has been described by Foster A. Sondley as "an intrepid man of the most arrogant and aggressive character, greatest self-confidence, unlimited assurance, prodigious conceit, stupendous aspiration, immense claims, more than common ability, no considerable attainments or culture, great boastfulness, and much curiosity." Both before and after the war he devoted much time to the exploration and development of the resources of western North Carolina. William Kenneth Boyd, "Thomas Lanier Clingman," *Dict. of Am. Biog.,* IV, 220-221; Connor, *N. C. Manual,* pp. 517, 816, 869, 931-936; Arthur, *Western North Carolina,* pp. 644-645; Sondley, *Buncombe County,* II, 535; A. W. Long in *Asheville Citizen-Times,* April 14, 1937; Clarence Newell Gilbert, "The Public Career of Thomas L. Clingman" (unpublished M. A. thesis, University of North Carolina, 1947).

[201] William Waightstill Avery (1816-1864), of a prominent family of Burke County, who was first honor graduate of the University of North Carolina in 1837, studied law with William Gaston, and became an ardent and active leader of the states' rights wing of the Democratic party. He represented Burke County in the House of Commons in 1842, 1850, and 1852, and in the Senate in 1856 and 1860, being speaker in 1856. He was chairman of the North Carolina delegations to the Democratic National Conventions of 1856 and 1860, where he led the secession sentiment. He was elected by the North Carolina Convention of 1861 a member of the Provisional Congress of the Confederate States, where he was chairman of the Committee on Military Affairs. He was mortally wounded in militia action against unionists from Tennessee and died at his Morganton home July 3, 1864. He had married, in 1846, Corrinna, daughter of Governor John M. Morehead. Alphonso C. Avery, "William Waightstill Avery," Ashe, *Biog Hist. of N. C.,* VIII, 9-11; Z. V. Walser, "Colonel W. W. Avery," *Greensboro Daily News,* July 18, 1926; *Asheville News,* April 6, 1854.

[202] See p. 19, 91n and p. 42, 165n.

gan the contest as if the district was Ten thousand strong democratic. I pitched out between them. Coleman drew off leaving Avery & myself to run through, which we did, and I beat him by 2049 majority. They all apologised for his defeat by saying it was the Flemming[203] matter, & that I could not do it again. So this Spring when I returned from Washington they put Coleman after me early in March, and we had a hot and furious canvass, twice over the district, every stone was turned, & heaven & earth moved against me, but it wouldnot do: at the election just past I beat him 1695 majority, and but for over confidence in my friends my vote would have been largely increased. We only got 59 votes more than Avery got, while in my strongest counties I could not get up excitement enough to get them to the polls. This will do. You may rest assured that when I get back to Washington I will use whatever of influence I can command in procuring you the consulship at Sidney.[204] You know that I am not of the right politics to have influence with the present administration.

You have waited too long John, Miss Lou Patton[205] will be mar-

[203] Samuel Flemming represented Yancey County in the House of Commons in 1840, 1844, 1846, 1848, and 1850. Kemp P. Battle describes the affair to which Vance makes reference. He depicts Flemming as a man of rough tastes and temper who campaigned with a tin quart-pot of whiskey in his right hand while he made his speeches. He was principally engaged in buying horses and selling them south. He got into a quarrel with Avery and struck him with a horsewhip. For three weeks Avery brooded over the indignity and disgrace of having been horsewhipped. Then, as he was sitting in the courtroom Flemming came in to speak to his lawyer and ostentatiously passed in front of Avery; whereupon Avery shot him dead. Judge Battle was on the bench and witnessed the tragedy and the next day Avery was tried; acquittal on the ground of emotional insanity was prompt. Kemp Battle says that his father, the judge, told him that the jury would have found him and every member of the bar guilty before they convicted Avery. "Public opinion in that day was clear that any man subjected to the ignominy of being horsewhipped would be *ipso facto* rendered insane and the death of the assailant would be righteous retribution." Battle added that Avery's popularity was increased by the act, which seems to be contrary to what Vance suggests in this letter. Battle, *Memories,* p. 91-92; Connor, *N. C. Manual,* p. 859.

[204] J. N. Ingram, in "New Zealand's Early Destiny Directed by North Carolinian," *Uncle Remus Magazine,* December 1911, p. 20, says that John Evans Brown was consul at Sydney for four years, and that his commission was signed by Daniel Webster as secretary of state. This is obviously incorrect, as Brown did not go to Australia until 1856, four years after Webster's death. Actually, Vance was never able to secure the consulship for him. William Caleb Brown wrote to his brother in Australia, on March 22, 1861: "You write very urgently about the Consulship. I saw Mr. Vance and he said he moved in the matter last winter at Washington, but that the President was so much engaged about the affairs, and the Secession of some of the Southern States that nothing could be done. If by the time Mr. Vance goes back to Washington things get settled down we will make another effort to have you appointed Consul under Old Abe provided you will consent to hold office under him." William Caleb Brown to John Evans Brown, March 22, 1861, Brown Papers.

[205] Louisa Patton (1836-1915), a daughter of Thomas Taylor Patton and Louise (Walton) Patton, who lived on the Swannanoa. Louisa's father was a brother of John E. Patton, long the owner and operator of the famous Warm Springs Hotel, thirty-seven miles northwest of Asheville on the French Broad River, for whom Vance clerked as a young boy just out of Washington College. Baird, "Historical Sketches"; Arthur, *Western North Carolina,* p. 492; McLean, "Notebooks."

ried in a few days to a Mr. Cheessboro[206] of Charleston former son-in-law of Wm Patton[207] (now dead) a widower *with five children!* Jehoshaphat! See what you have lost. Is there any gem in all the mines of Australia that can compensate you?

Things are moving along here pretty much in their accustomed channel. Our town still grows and improves, and each successive assessment shows that the prices of lands in the county is rapidly increasing. The Western Extension[208] of the Central Rail-Road will reach Morganton in about 12 months, and the prospects of our French Broad Road [209] are infinitely better than ever. The counties of Polk, Henderson, Buncombe & Madison have taken $500.000 stock and S. C. promises to help. Depend upon it an old country can improve as well as a new one, and I think by the time you get back to Buncombe you will see a change for the better.

When will you get back? My own notion is you ought to close out there and come home. You have enough I take it to live comfortably here, and *(with a wife)* enjoy some of the sweets of life after so many of its hardships—Write me often & I promise you to do better in future.

Accept my Kindest wishes for your success and for your soon & safe return to your friends—

[A. L. S. Zebulon B. Vance Papers, State Department of Archives and History, Raleigh.]

From W. M. Hardy[210] and Jno. D. Hyman[211]

Asheville N. C.
Augst 25th/59

Dr. J. F. E. Hardy[212] & J. W. Woodfin[213] Esq[s] having taken the Responsibility as the Mutual friends of the parties of acting as

---

[206] John Cheeseborough (1817-1903).

[207] William D. Patton, a native of Charleston, S. C. and who built the "Mountain House," had died in 1858. See p. 37, 144n.

[208] See p. 35, 137n.

[209] For the early legislative history of this railroad see p. 28, 122n, 123n, 124n. The legislature had amended the charter during the session of 1858-1859 to allow counties to subscribe whatever sum was approved by a majority of the county justices and ratified by the voters. If the money was voted, the county was authorized to issue bonds and to levy the necessary taxes to meet the interest payments and to liquidate the principal as due. On June 2, 1859, the voters of Buncombe decided by a vote of 955 to 158 that the county should take $125,000 worth of its stock. Other counties soon followed with similar actions. The presidents and directors of several South Carolina roads, including the Greenville and French Broad and the Spartanburg and Union, met in Hendersonville, N. C. on July 28, 1859, for the purpose of discussing plans for a railroad through the mountains. *Private Laws of N. C. 1858-'59*, chap. 166; Brown, *Railroad Development*, p. 142; *Asheville News*, June 9, August 4, 11, 1859.

[210] See p. 13, 168n.

[211] See p. 50, 181n.

[212] See p. 20, 95n.

[213] See p. 51, 185n.

Mediators in the affair of Honor between Messrs Coleman[214] & Vance And they having obtained the Consent of the principals thereto, We as the friends of Messrs Coleman & Vance do hereby Mutually & Simultaneously Withdraw the Whole Correspondence between the parties & Surrender up the same to their Said Mutual friends It being distinctly agreed that the Same is not to prejudice either party, but to place both on the grounds which they occupied before Mr Colemans first note to Mr Vance

[Asheville]

[A. L. S. Z. B. Vance Papers, State Department of Archives and History, Raleigh.]

From D. Coleman[215]

Asheville Aug. 27th 1859

The correspondence between us, commencing on the 15th, instant, having been, through the mediation of mutual friends, by an agreement simultaneously executed by the immediate friends of you and of me, respectively, with a view of leaving the fullest opportunity for further and satisfactory adjustment; I have the honor again to address you, to say: that, while I consider your language and bearing on various occasions, during the discussions in our late canvass to be such as a gentleman should not submit to from another gentleman, I hold myself particularly aggrieved by your words and manner toward me in the discussion at Waynesville. I allude specially to your declaration, and the manner in which it was made, regarding one particular question, that you were asking it me, in order to pronounce my answer *false,* in the contingency of my replying in a certain way. I need not, here, repeat, at length, my views of the conduct a candidate should pursue under such circumstances of provocation. It is sufficient to say, with regard to the occurance at Waynesville, (that being the principal occasion, and I having, heretofore, in effect, waived all others) , that I treated it in the calm and bland mode then pursued by me, *because* I *then* was resolved that, while the canvass should not be interrupted nor I compromised if possible by personal conflicts, I designed to bring the matter to your attention again, *after* the close of the canvass.

The necessities of my then position having passed away with the election, it devolves on me to present to you, Sir, my claim of right, (as I consider it), to such appropriate reparation as will right me before my own self respect, and before the public.

To this original cause of grievance, I am under the necessity of adding the imputation, in your note of the 18th instant, of the

214 See p. 19, 91n and p. 42, 165n.
215 See p. 19, 91n and p. 42, 165n.

unworthy motive on my part, that my "object is simply to seek a difficulty, in order perhaps to take away Some of the Sting of your " (my)" late defeat,—a communication which yet, under the circumstances, I could not decline to accept, and did accept, under protest against that expression.
Asheville

[A. L. S. Z. B. Vance Papers, State Department of Archives and History, Raleigh.]

To D. Coleman[216]

Asheville Aug^st 29th [1859]
Your note of the 27th instant was not received until last evening too late for me to reply.

You say that "while I consider your language and bearing on various occasions during the discussions in our late canvass to be such as a gentleman should not submit to from another gentleman, I hold myself particularly aggrieved by your words and manner towards me in the discussion at Waynesville."

As to my general manner toward you during the canvass, I can say with entire sincerety that it was not my purpose to be offensive. I have as you Know, a manner in debate that is peculiar to myself as you have likewise, that is perhaps liable to be misunderstood. And though many things said and done by you during the canvass might have with equal justice been regarded as designedly offensive yet, judging from the relations that had hitherto existed between us and the latitude generally allowed to political discussions, I did not feel at liberty to see any intended affront.

As to the particular grievance occurring at Waynesville I can only say that my language and conduct there was called forth by the impression that you had charged me or were endeavering to leave the impression on the audience, with a design to elect Grow,[217] a Black Republican, Speaker of the next House, and by your hesitation to explain when asked if such was your intention. Being fully under that impression *at the time,* I can not but consider that my language and manner was proper to the occasion, but since you, in your note of the 18th inst. disavow having made such a charge or intending to make it it becomes evident I misunderstood you of course Sir, I can but regret and withdraw any offensive expression used toward you whilst under *that false impression.* This would have been done in reply to yours of the 18th had not the character of that note in which your disavowal was made precluded any but the one answer which I did make.

---

216 See p. 19, 91n and p. 42, 165n.
217 See p. 44, 170n.

The latter part of your note also complains of the tenor of my note of the 19th, & in other notes you complain of it as being unusual and improper to the situation in which we were placed at the time of its date. As to this Sir, I can say that I was inexperienced in affairs of this Kind and when your note protesting against my reply was received I submitted the matter to those in whose judgment I had confidence. They without exception say, that in imputing to you motives of any Kind in my note accepting your challenge I overstepped the bounds of what was proper and usual in such cases. It remains therefore for me to frankly own it & to say it was not intentionally done, as it certainly was my wish to be governed by what is usual among gentlemen.

Confident that I have answered your note fully and with sincerety,

Asheville

[A. L. S. Z. B. Vance Papers, State Department of Archives and History, Raleigh.]

From D. Coleman[218]

Asheville Aug. 29th 1859.

Your note of to day, in reply to mine of the 29th instant, is full, frank, and satisfactory.

Permit me, in this, the conclusion of this correspondence,[219] to join you in the expression of my regret that anything should have occurred to give rise to this unpleasant controversy.

Asheville

[A. L. S. Z. B. Vance Papers, State Department of Archives and History, Raleigh.]

From W. Caleb Brown[220]

Asheville N. Ca.
Dec. 24th 1859

I have waited thus long in expectation of hearing from you but as I receive no letters or anything from you, I am constrained to write. Mrs Vance I suppose Keeps you advised of everything concerning the family, so I will not say a word on that subject.

Some of our very wise friends are acting very strangly, to say the least of it, they are perfectly indignant and wild on the subject

---

[218] See p. 19, 91n and p. 42, 165n.
[219] Vance made complete copies, in his own hand, of the entire correspondence concerning the quarrel with Coleman. They may be found in the Zebulon B. Vance Papers.
[220] See p. 54, 198n.

of the Speakership.[221] They appear to think that you should go
or have gone over to the Democracy[222] and elected Bocock,[223] not

[221] The House of Representatives was locked in the famous struggle over the
speakership, which required forty-four ballots and lasted from December 5, 1859,
to February 1, 1860. The composition of the House was one hundred and nine
Republicans, eighty-eight administration Democrats, thirteen anti-Lecompton Democrats, and twenty-seven Americans, all but four of whom were from the South.
Since no one party had a majority a contest was certain, and in it the twenty-three
South Americans, of whom Vance was one, held the balance of power. No Democrat could possibly win, even if the two factions of that disrupted party were
united, without support from the South Americans. On the first day the inevitable
conflict was made more bitter by a resolution introduced by John B. Clark,
Democrat of Missouri: "*Resolved,* That the doctrines and sentiments of a certain
book, called "The Impending Crisis of the South - How to meet it," purporting
to have been written by one Hinton R. Helper, are insurrectionary and hostile
to the domestic peace and tranquility of the country, and that no member of
this House who has indorsed and recommended it, or the compend from it, is
fit to be Speaker of this House." This resolution struck at many Republicans, but
especially at John Sherman, of Ohio, and Galusha A. Grow, of Pennsylvania, for
whom Republicans had voted for the speakership on the first ballot. Grow withdrew
after one ballot and Republicans concentrated on Sherman for thirty-nine ballots,
but without success, for they could not elect him without votes from the South
Americans. The Clark resolution never came to a vote, but it was endlessly and
bitterly debated for eight weeks. On February 1, 1860, the choice finally fell on
William Pennington, of New Jersey, who had become the Republican nominee
after the withdrawal of Sherman following the thirty-ninth ballot. A former Whig,
he was said not to believe slavery wrong in itself, and to be in favor of the fugitive
slave law. Two Americans made his election possible by voting for him on the crucial
forty-fourth ballot; one was from New York and the other from Maryland. *Cong.
Globe,* 36 Congress, 1 session, part 1, *passim,* especially pp. 1-3,, 269, 644, 654.

[222] During the long contest Vance voted for twelve different individuals: six
Americans and six Democrats, but thirty-six of his forty-four votes were for Americans. Of the thirty-six votes cast for an American, eleven times his vote went to
Alexander R. Boteler of Virginia, eleven times to William N. H. Smith of North
Carolina, and ten times to John A. Gilmer, also of North Carolina. The Democrats
for whom he occasionally voted were all conservative — by which he meant anti-
secession — or anti-Lecompton Democrats. Similar voting patterns were characteristic of all the South Americans. Only once, on the twenty-seventh ballot, did
Vance vote for Thomas S. Bocock, the caucus nominee of the administration
Democrats, and it was manifest by that time that he could not win. On December
27, 1859, Vance himself received seven votes for speaker during the twenty-second
ballot; he also received Smith's vote during the thirty-ninth ballot on January
27, 1860, when Smith came within three votes of election. Twice Vance made
brief speeches to explain his vote, once on December 29, 1859 and again on
January 31, 1860, as he voted for Democrats. Friendly papers in North Carolina
praised Vance for his "liberality" in voting for Democrats, but the *Asheville News*
thought Vance deserved no credit for it since he usually threw his vote away on
Democrats who were not the regular nominees of the party. "We object to this
effort on the part of Mr. V. and his friends to manufacture for him a bogus
Democratic record. He belongs to the "straightest sect" of the opposition, and
let him be content to stand on his own proper foundation." "Mr. Vance hates
Democracy with a cordial hatred, and his friends need not try to make a Democrat of him." Charging that Vance was trying to ride both parties because he
felt insecure in his district and that some of his votes did not "suit his latitude,"
the *News* called his actions "nauseating" and added: "We do not doubt Mr. Vance
is ready to desert every odious non-paying principle that he loves, to cheat and
break down Democracy that he hates, as fast as his supporters will let him — no
doubt of it. But when it is attempted to pull the wool over our eyes and gouge it
in, we protest." *Cong. Globe,* 36 Congress, 1 session, part 1, *passim,* especially pp.
1-3, 269, 286, 348, 611, 644, 654; *Asheville News,* January 26, February 16, 1860.

[223] Thomas Stanley Bocock (1815-1891), congressman from Virginia and nominee

only to have spited the Republicans, but to have shown an un-
broken front to them and a determination of supporting the
South and in the very next breath admit that the South Americans
are true to the South, a few of them excepting Gilmer[224] & Ether-

---

of the administration Democrats for the speakership. He was first honor graduate
of Hampden-Sydney College in 1838; member of the general assembly, 1842-1845,
1869-1870; member of Congress, 1847-1861; delegate to the Democratic National
Conventions of 1868, 1876, and 1880. After the war he was known mainly for his
activities as a railroad attorney, as a collector of fine books, and as a benefactor
of Hampden-Sydney College. On the first ballot for speaker in 1859 Bocock led
the field with eighty-six votes; he never got more than eighty-eight on any subsequent ballot, and withdrew. He was known as a skillful parliamentarian and
was by unanimous vote chosen Speaker of the Confederate House of Representatives in both the First and Second Congresses. The story used to be told after
the war that members of the House sometimes absent-mindedly voted "Bocock"
or "Sherman" instead of "Yes" or "No." Early Lee Fox, "Thomas Stanley Bocock,"
Dict. of Am. Biog., II, 402; clippings in Z. V. Walser Papers, Southern Historical
Collection, University of North Carolina, Chapel Hill, N. C. (cited hereafter as
Walser Papers); Biog. Dir. of Am. Cong., p. 863 where, incidentally, the middle
name is Stanhope.

[224] John Adams Gilmer (1805-1868) of Guilford County, congressman from the
fifth North Carolina district. He had studied law under Archibald D. Murphey,
served as county solicitor, and represented for ten years (1846-1856) his district
in the State Senate. In 1856 he was the candidate of the Know-Nothing party
for the governorship, but was defeated. He served in Congress for two terms
(1857-1861). He was a member of the North Carolina Secession Convention in 1861,
and of the Confederate Congress in 1864-1865. After the war he supported President Johnson's policies and was a delegate to the National Union Convention of
1866. Gilmer's course in Congress was criticized by many southerners because
he, as one of the outstanding Southern Unionists, had won some Northern support by his opposition to the admission of Kansas under the pro-slavery Lecompton Constitution, and had worked actively to prevent the injection of the slavery
issue into the struggle over the speakership. Indeed, he had gone so far as to
offer an amendment to the explosive Clark resolution: "Resolved, That . . . it is
the duty of every good citizen of this Union to resist all attempts at renewing,
in Congress or out of it, the slavery agitation, under whatever shape and color
the attempt may be made." Although Gilmer was the owner of nearly 100
slaves, he was bitterly criticized by many Democrats and many southerners for his
compromise attitude and his opposition to secession. This criticism reached its
peak in Congress on December 12, 1859, when John W. Noel, Democrat of Missouri, charged him with attempting to aid the Republicans. In spite of Gilmer's
willingness to revise his resolution to make it more acceptable to all parties it
was never allowed to come to a vote. During much of the struggle over the
speakership he was the nominee of his party; Vance voted for him ten times.
But he never got more than thirty-six votes, since the southern Democrats would
not support him. Because Gilmer once voted for Henry Winter Davis of Maryland, who was technically an American but who was charged by the southern
press with being an abolitionist, and because Vance voted for Gilmer on the
same ballot, Vance was charged with aiding and abetting and approving the
abolitionists themselves. Joseph Gregoire deRoulhac Hamilton, "John Adams
Gilmer," Dict. of Am. Biog., VII, 307-308; Connor, N. C. Manual, p. 634; Gerald
W. Johnson, "John Adams Gilmer," Founders and Builders of Greensboro 1808-
1908 (Greensboro, 1925), pp. 95-102 (cited hereafter as Founders of Greensboro);
Cong. Globe, 36 Congress, 1 session, part 1, pp. 18, 20, 117, 170 (December 6, 12,
16, 1859); Biog. Dir. of Am. Cong., p. 1213; Asheville News, February 16, 1860.

ridge.[225] What surprises me is that Hyman[226] & Chunn[227] are such hotheaded fire-eaters as they profess to be. They are almost rampant. I cannot understand the move and have heard it suggested that Hyman was thinking of running for the Commons if he found his present position would do to stand on. I have not heard him say a single word on the subject

They had a meeting a short time ago and formed a Vigilant Com and ran your first man out of town. They have also formed a Military Company and are determined to have blood from some source it appears

W. W. McDowell [228] Capt—Hyman,[229] Wash Hardy[230] & J. M. Israel [231] Lieuts — &c D[rs] Hardy[232] Summey,[233] Bob,[234] J. N. Os-

[225] Emerson Etheridge (1819-1902), who was born in Currituck, N. C. but moved to Tennessee in 1831. He was a member of the State House of Representatives 1845-1847; elected as a Whig to the Thirty-third and Thirty-fourth Congresses 1853-1857; failed of re-election to the Thirty-fifth but won election to the Thirty-sixth Congress 1859-1861. When Tennessee seceded he did not follow his state out of the Union, but became clerk of the House of Representatives in Washington, 1861-1863. He was a member of the State Senate in 1869 and 1870; unsuccessful candidate for governor in 1867; and surveyor of customs in Memphis, 1891-1894. During the session of 1859-1860 he joined and supported Gilmer in his efforts to advance compromise. Though listed in the Congressional Globe as the lone Whig member of the Thirty-sixth Congress, he was in all essentials the same as the other South Americans. He offended many southerners when he referred to the Lecompton Constitution as a "despotism," and when he consistently opposed all secessionists efforts. Cong. Globe, 36 Congress, 1 session, part 1, pp. 2, 206 (December 5, 12, 1859); Biog. Dir. of Am. Cong., p. 1137.

[226] See p. 50, 181n. Hyman never adopted the secessionist platform for in December 1860 he was still a strong and active Union man. Raleigh North Carolina Standard, January 5, 1861.

[227] Probably A. B. Chunn, forty-seven year old, wealthy farmer of Buncombe County. Census, Buncombe County, 1860.

[228] William Wallis McDowell (1823-1893), ardent Democrat and secessionist. He raised the first company from Buncombe for the Civil War and led the "Buncombe Rifles" into the first battle of the war at Bethel as captain of company E. He was later promoted to major of the Sixtieth North Carolina Regiment. Tennent, "Medicine in Buncombe County," p. 20; Clark, N. C. Regts., I, 78, 90; Moore, N. C. Roster, I, 419; Raleigh North Carolina Standard, June 15, 1861.

[229] See p. 50, 181n.

[230] See p. 43, 168n.

[231] See p. 8, 41n.

[232] John Geddings Hardy (1829-1885) was a son of Dr. J. F. E. Hardy. He was born in Asheville, where he spent his youth, but he went to Charleston for the study of medicine, where he graduated in 1851 and then moved to Georgia. He returned to Asheville before the war, in which he was first sergeant of company E in the Bethel Regiment, became assistant surgeon of the same unit and, on August 1, 1862, was commissioned surgeon in the Sixty-fourth North Carolina Regiment. He fell heir to much of his father's practice in Asheville. Tennent, "Medicine in Buncombe County," p. 16; Moore, N. C. Roster, 1, 419, IV, 50; Asheville News, June 15, 1854.

[233] Daniel F. Summey, about twenty-nine years old, was a native of Lincoln County who studied medicine under Dr. J. F. E. Hardy in Asheville, and who graduated in medicine from the University of the City of New York. Before he practiced medicine in Asheville he operated an icehouse and a drugstore. During the war he was quartermaster of the Sixteenth North Carolina Regiment, and became an army surgeon by commission of February 26, 1863. After the war he practiced medicine in Asheville until 1885, when he retired to Leicester in Buncombe County. Tennent, "Medicine in Buncombe County," pp. 19-20; Clark, N. C. Regts., I, 751, IV, 629; Moore, N. C. Roster, II, 2.

[234] Robert B. Vance. See p. 2, 6n.

born[235] &c being high privates. I returned from Jackson Thursday evening.

Everything comparatively quiet in that direction. The most fuss is in and around this little burg and even your best friends think there is danger that unless some favorable issue comes from the present contest there is trouble ahead as no doubt whoever runs against you two years hence will take advantage of it to charge Black Republicanism on you and no doubt but the course taken by some of the aforementioned men in their rampant talking will aid the Democrats very materially.

The S.C. Legislature have as good as Killed the Raburn Gap Road[236] and voted down ours once to be consistent but at last advises there was a prospect of our getting some aid.

The Western Extention[237] is under as far as the Western portal of the tunnel.

Look sharp and make a clean record as you will have the mischief to meet when you run again

We have but little news here that would interest you had better not write anything to M[rs] Vance about what is going on among persons as she is a good deal excited and it would only be adding fuel to the flame by writting names to her Let me hear from you soon

[A. L. S. Z. B. Vance Papers, State Department of Archives and History, Raleigh.]

---

[235] John N. Osborn was in the mercantile business with James W. Patton in Asheville. Baird, "Historical Sketches."

[236] The Rabun Gap Road was a local name given to the Blue Ridge Railroad Company, a South Carolina project to link Charleston with the Ohio River, and which was in essence a revival of Robert Y. Hayne's celebrated Cincinnati project of two decades earlier. The new project planned a connection between Anderson, S. C., one of the western terminals of the Columbia and Greenville Railroad, and Knoxville, Tenn., but through Rabun Gap, Ga. instead of down the French Broad River through Asheville. To some in western North Carolina the Rabun Gap road was a rival of the Greenville and French Broad project; to others, because of restrictions and delays to the building of the Western North Carolina Railroad, it gave expression to the belief that it might be best to build west from Asheville through Haywood County to Ducktown, Tenn., a mining town just over the state line, to a connection with the Blue Ridge Railroad. The Blue Ridge Railroad had received some qualified state aid in South Carolina as early as 1852, and the contract was let and the grading begun in 1854. But the road became involved in both financial and political difficulties and a move to have the South Carolina legislature subscribe an additional $1,000,000 to its capital stock was defeated in 1858. In 1859 another effort was made to obtain further state aid necessary to completion of the project, but the bill was defeated in the lower house in December 1859 by a vote of 55 to 64. Work was suspended and Asheville papers spoke of the project as dead. Eventually enough support was obtained to provide for building the road to Walhalla, S. C. John G. Van Deusen, *Economic Bases of Disunion in South Carolina* (New York, 1928), pp. 248-253; Brown, *Railroad Development*, pp. 131-132, 138-139; *Asheville News*, February 25, September 9, December 16, 1858, January 6, 1859.

[237] See p. 35, 137n.

From Hattie Vance[238]

Asheville
March 6th, 1860

I am truly thankful to be able to tell you tonight that our sick are all better. Isaac is able to sit up and I trust, with care, will be able to go to work next week. I do hope so for the garden &c is needing him very much. I want potatoes planted, but will have to wait until he is able to do it—indeed there are various things needing his attention—the weather is so beautiful and warm that it puts me quite in the notion of having many things put in the ground, tho' I am not able to attend to it much, consequently I fear we will have a late garden. I am quite unable to get about much, at times I am very helpless—tho' it won't be a great while now until all will be well with me. Now it cheers me to think of so soon having you with us, and the dear children are also delighted at the thought—one week from day after tomorrow. What a disappointment it would be, not to see you then—how long to be separated from one another my dear—three months and a half—I try to be submissive tho' and trust I am willing to make any sacrifice that we may get out of debt—having almost abandoned the idea of going to Washington at all. I guess you will be willing. I couldn't I suppose go before the first of May and if Congress adjourns as early as you hope for now it will hardly be worthwhile to go—tho' I must confess I dislike to think of your going back without me—but this is not right—we should enjoy the present and trust Our Heavenly Father for the future.

There has been so many passing from here through Washington, that I guess you know how pretty well all that is going on among us. Mr. Hyman[239] I guess will give you all the news especially political for I think he has, from all I can hear, abandoned matrimony for politics and is quite an aspirant for political honors—at least this is the opinion of some.

Poor Mark Erwin[240] arrived yesterday with his poor little children and his wife's body—they go on with it tomorrow, I believe, to Burke. What a sad, sad, occurance. Not being able to go out I know but little of his state and other particulars about it.

It is late my dear so I must hasten to close my letter. All about the house I think, are asleep, and it is time I was too. Sister

---

[238] See p. 16, 81n.
[239] See p. 50, 181n.
[240] For Marcus Erwin see p. 20, 93n. His wife was a girlhood friend of Hattie Vance in Morganton, Margaret C. McDowell (1830-1860). She married Marcus Erwin in 1854, and she died, January 7, 1860, in a fire in New Orleans, where her father-in-law lived and where her husband had studied law. There were two children. She was buried in the Erwin family cemetery in Morganton. Matilda Abernathy to Thomas Dickson, June 12, 1854, Dickson Papers; Sondley, *Buncombe County*, II, 775; *Census*, Buncombe County, 1860.

Hannah[241] is with us tonight. Some of them come almost every night. I don't think Cousin Elvira[242] can make up her mind to stay with me any more. I haven't yet heard from old Mrs. Magie (?)—hope I can get her, if I cant, I will try Mrs. Franks which is a most excellent person you know.

The friends are all pretty well—Sister Lauras[243] babe has been quite sick, but is getting better. Mother[244] was to stay with me tonight but is suffering with pain in her eye. I hardly need write you more than once or twice more I guess. I was quite disappointed not to have a letter from you darling, hope certainly for one by mornings mail. There came one by this mornings mail for William Brown.[245] He is now staying up at his Fathers—much to my satisfaction. I am so delighted to hear how pleased you are with your new lodgings and also to hear is such a saving to you, for dear we should try to economise, we already have a family and prospect of a large one if we should live. Good night my darling— Heaven bless you. I could write much more, but it is too late, and then I hope soon to see you face to face. God grant us this blessing is the sincere prayer of

> Your own devoted *Hattie*

[Washington]
[A. L. S. Zebulon B. Vance Papers, State Department of Archives and History, Raleigh.]

From Robert B. Vance[246]

Asheville N° Ca April 16th 1860

I leave in a few moments for Madison Court, and hasten to drop you a line. Hattie has been quite sick. She has had what is called

---

[241] See p. 6, 32n.

[242] Elvira Jane Holt Erwin (1824-1903), of Morganton, another girlhood friend of Hattie Vance. She often stayed with Mrs. Vance when her husband was away from home for extended periods of time. The relationship was through the Erwin family, Vance's grandmother having been Hannah Erwin of Burke County. McLean, "Notebooks."

[243] Laura Henrietta (Vance) Neilson, Zebulon B. Vance's oldest sister. She was born in 1826 and in 1844 married Dr. Morgan Lines Neilson (1822-1894), a native of Tennessee who came to Asheville in 1839 and, after he became a doctor, practiced there for most of his life. Tennent, "Medicine in Buncombe County," pp. 12-13. The baby's name was Sarah, who was born in 1859. *Census,* Buncombe County, 1860.

[244] i. e. Vance's mother, Mira Margaret (Baird) Vance. See p. 1, 1n. She usually lived with her daughter Ann, who was Mrs. Richard N. Price.

[245] William Caleb Brown, Vance's law partner. See p. 54, 198n. He boarded, beginning on August 31, 1857, from time to time at the Vance house. The rate was $9 a month and "he to furnish everything lost time deducted." His father was William John Brown, see p. 54, 196n, who lived at Limestone in Buncombe County. William Caleb Brown Memorandum Book, *passim,* Brown Papers.

[246] See p. 2, 6n.

weed.[247] She is much better now, but not able to write. You need not feel special uneasiness, as it is not a dangerous disease, but I suppose painful and unpleasant while it lasts.

I find since I wrote you that the democratic Leaders have succeeded in pulling the wool over the eyes of many in regard to equal Taxation,[248] and accordingly things will be nearer on a party line than *I anticipated;* though they cannot *all* be whipped in. They say "this is not the time"—"it is done to break down demic party" &c—"Only an electioneering hobby & that the oppositionists don't want it— only want the offices. This goes down with many. Buncombe, it appears, is one of the hardest counties. Bill Thomas[249] will scare off hundreds out west by making them believe it will Kill off the R. R. So goes the World. I hear you go to Baltimore to make a Union Speech.[250] You will have to be

[247] A sudden illness or relapse, often attended with fever, especially apt to attack mothers who are nursing young children. The Vance's fourth son, Zebulon Baird Vance, Jr., had been born on March 22, 1860.

[248] In 1835 the slave interests wrote into the Constitution of North Carolina a provision that exempted property in slaves from all taxation except a poll tax, and even this poll tax was applicable only to slaves between the ages of twelve and fifty. Slaves under twelve and over fifty were thus exempt from all taxation. The result was a glaring inequality in favor of the slaveholders. Land bore a disproportionate share of the tax load, and small farmers and laborers were critical of the system. They demanded a constitutional amendment providing for *ad valorem* taxation of slave property. Since the Democratic party was, by the fifties, the acknowledged political haven of the slaveholding vested interests, the Know-Nothings, now calling themselves Whigs once again, took up the cry for equal taxation and endorsed the *ad valorem* amendment in their state party convention in February, 1860. The Democratic party, in March, 1860, denounced *ad valorem* as "premature, impolitic, dangerous, and unjust" and claimed that it would interfere with "southern rights." In this fashion the issue became a bitter one in the campaign of 1860. Robert Diggs Wimberly Connor, *North Carolina, Rebuilding an Ancient Commonwealth, 1584-1925,* 4 vols. (Chicago and New York, 1929), II, 83-88 (cited hereafter as Connor, *North Carolina*); Kenneth Rayner to Thomas Ruffin, February 24, 1860, Joseph Gregoire deRoulhac Hamilton (ed.), *The Papers of Thomas Ruffin,* 4 vols. (Raleigh, 1920), III, 70 (cited hereafter as Hamilton, *Ruffin Papers*).

[249] William Holland Thomas (1805-1893), often called the "Father of the Western North Carolina Railroad." He was born on Pigeon River in Haywood County and as a young boy clerked in Felix Walker's store at Qualla Town in the Cherokee settlement. At the age of seventeen he went into business with John B. Love at the site of Webster and by the time he entered politics in the forties had acquired a comfortable fortune. He espoused the Cherokee cause and represented their claims in Washington for a quarter of a century. He represented his district in the State Senate in 1842 and from 1848 to 1860, and in the Secession Convention in 1861. When the war came he raised and equipped several companies and commanded Thomas' Legion, and in September of 1862 became colonel of the Sixtieth North Carolina Regiment. Soon after the war his health failed and from 1867 to his death in 1893 he was but a wreck of his former self. He was a staunch Democrat during all of his political career. McCormick, *Personnel,* pp. 83-84; Connor, *N. C. Manual,* pp. 554, 647, 665, 885; Clark, *N. C. Regts.,* III, 732.

[250] Vance spoke at Carroll Hall in Baltimore on April 12, 1860. The occasion was a meeting of the friends of a new political organization subsequently known as the Constitutional Union party. The object of the meeting was to organize the new party and to find a platform on which all Whigs and Americans could meet in unity. Vance also made an address that evening in Monument Square in Baltimore, along with several other prominent leaders of the movement. Baltimore *Sun,* April 13, 1860, which refers to him as Zebulon D. Vance.

careful of such men as Cousin Sam Smith,[251] as he still sticks closely to the party & against advalorem.

I think I would have as little to do with parties as I could, as parties are so torn about now no one can scarcely see his own standing place. The only thing on which they hope to beat you is your acting with the *opposition*. Dave Coleman[252] never can make half a run for Congress. The whole Western delegation to the Convention here, Bill Thomas in particular, fell out with him.[253] *He defeated Thomas for delegate to Charleston Convention.*[254] Old Bill Welch cursed him all over town. Will write from Bairds[255]

[Washington.]

[A. L. S. Z. B. Vance Papers, State Department of Archives and History, Raleigh.]

From W. J. Brown[256]

Limestone May 17th 1860

I resume my prolific pen to address you another note (if not to inflict on) to you, being prompted to do so from seeing Mrs. V. on yesterday morning just as she had your letter of the 12th informing her of the attack of sickness you were labouring under, I found her fretting and tryd to console her as to the probable danger saying I hoped the disease would most probably pass off in a few days, trusting that such may have proven to have been the case at this time of writing, be careful of your diet & of exposure to cold from damp feet & *cold*. Those inflamations of the bowels have been in two long & marked attacks came near ending my unprofitable days on earth, the effects of which I still feel frequently to this day. *My dear Sir,* you cant be too *carefull of* your diet for at such times as you least anticipate, it will turn on you, it requires great caution to avoid it. I fear my epistle will be more enoying to you than entertaining but as I promised Mrs. Vance to write to you I do so fulfilling my promise. It was the week of Examination and the H. F. College.[257] I had gone in to see them, & must say was much pleased & entertained the scholars done exceedingly well all performing their parts well & acquitting

---

[251] Samuel Smith was the father of Jane Smith and a staunch Democrat except when Vance was a candidate. See p. 11, 56n; p. 40, 158n and Z. B. Vance to Cousin Jane, February 10, 1859, above, p. 40.

[252] See p. 19, 91n and p. 42, 165n.

[253] Thomas, though always a staunch Democrat, was not a secessionist, and so broke with Coleman.

[254] The Democratic National Convention met in Charleston, S. C. on April 21, 1860.

[255] Adolphus Erwin Baird (1819-1878), an uncle of Vance, who then lived at Marshall, in Madison County. McLean, "Notebooks."

[256] See p. 54, 196n.

[257] The Holston Conference Female College, in Asheville.

themselves with much credit, the graduating class particularly, the compositions showed their hearts & minds had both been cultivated, so to speak, the valedictory as read by Miss *Price* was highly creditable & effecting. Some 21 graduate I believe, much to the credit of the school teachers. Mr. Price[258] delivered the address & I say done it well, both very appropriate & instructive & much to his credit; there was not so many in attendance as heretofore but all were pleased & all went off satisfactory. I see the Balt. Conv.[259] have made a good ticket & as I think in the proper manner, both as to time, place & platform, & if its *Providence's will,* hope we shall be able to elect it, & thereby calm down the troubled waters & drive all factiousists & commorants out of place & power & give a quietus to the disorganizer of all sections. I dont like the complexion of Territorial Act just passed by the house in regard to the New Mexico territory,[260] & all as *Grow*[261] said the other incoming territories, I presume it was all you could do as the vote was close 92 to 90. I presume we shall learn the proceedings of the Chicago Convn.[262] in a few days I think it will be possibly Bates or Seward with a conservative man.[263] I would like to see Cor-

[258] Richard Nye Price, a Methodist preacher and educator, who had married Vance's sister, Annie Edgeworth Vance, in 1855. Price was the same age as Vance, had been born in Virginia and preached in Tennessee. He was the principal of the Burnsville High School before his marriage and professor of mathematics at the American Temperance University at Harriman, Tennessee in the nineties. *Census,* Buncombe County, 1860; *Asheville News,* March 30, 1854, May 10, November 29, 1855.

[259] The national convention of the Constitutional Union party met in Baltimore on May 9, 1860, and nominated John Bell of Tennessee for the presidency and Edward Everett of Massachusetts for the vice-presidency. Both were former Whigs, and conservatives. The platform was a brief two paragraphs emphasizing devotion to the Union, but ignoring most of the divisive sectional questions of the moment.

[260] This was H. R. No. 64, a bill "to disapprove and declare null and void all territorial acts and parts of acts heretofore passed by the Legislative Assembly of New Mexico which establish, protect, or legalize involuntary servitude or slavery within said Territory, except as punishment for crime upon due conviction." On May 10, 1860, the bill was voted on and passed 97 to 90. Vance voted against it, and after the vote made a statement to the House in which he complained of the discourtesy shown by the majority in forcing a vote at a time when many members were absent at the Baltimore convention of the Constitutional Union party. *Cong. Globe,* 36 Congress, 1 session (May 10, 1860), pp. 2045-2046.

[261] For Galusha Aaron Grow see p. 44, 170n. In the debate on the bill to provide a temporary government for Idaho Territory Grow remarked that "All these bills for the organization of Territories are alike, except as to the names. I propose to take one of them as a test, and let whatever course the House shall take in regard to it apply to all the others." *Cong. Globe,* 36 Congress, 1 session (May 10, 1860), p. 2048.

[262] The national convention of the Republican party met in Chicago on May 16, 1860.

[263] William Henry Seward (1801-1872), former Whig Governor of New York, and currently Republican Senator from New York was the favorite against the field, but among those often mentioned for the nomination was Edward Bates (1793-1869), formerly a Free-Soil Whig from Missouri, whose nomination by the Republican party some thought might avert secession. Seward led on the first ballot and Bates received only forty-eight votes.

win,[264] & Ellott [265] speaches recently made in the house as I see them spoken of in the paper as being able arguments pro. & con. We have fine growing weather which was much needed, the small grain looks unpromising for a good crop. it has been too dry & cold. the oats bid fair to make a partial failure, corn is too small as yet to judge of the prospects. Will,[266] or I expect to be along in the course of two weeks. It would afford me some consolation to be there at this time if I could be of use to you in your sickness. however I trust you are on the mend or will be by the time this reaches you. I *repeat,* be *care*full *of* yourself & abstain from heating stimulants on account of the irritation of your bowels. use good olive oil freely in broken doses with occasionaly divers powder & Blue pill. At night, to stimulate the free action of the liver, avoid preparation with *aloes.* Knowing your predisposition to piles I recently got an almost infalible cure for the piles & one that Dr. H. Dickson[267] of Charleston invariably uses with great success. If you require it I will send the Recipe to you & you can try it. I go into town today & will mail this letter there. I hope you will accept this with all allowance, with Drs. & my kindest regards,

---

[264] Thomas Corwin (1794-1865), then a Republican congressman from Ohio, but formerly a Whig who had been congressman, 1831-1840, governor of Ohio, 1840-1842, Senator from Ohio, 1845-1850, Secretary of the Treasury, 1850-1853, and who became, during the war, United States Minister to Mexico, 1861-1864. On sectional questions Corwin was outspoken; he advocated the abolition of slavery in the territories but upheld the right of each new state to decide the slavery question for itself. After Lincoln's election he sought means of allaying sectional fears and served as chairman of the House Committee of Thirty-three. In Corwin's answer to Eliot he defended the fugitive slave law. His speech was returned to him for revision and never submitted for publication, but points made in debate by his opponents reveal the general temper of Corwin's remarks. *Cong. Globe,* 36 Congress, 1 session (April 26, 1860), p. 1859; Thomas Cary Hockett, "Thomas Corwin," *Dict. of Am. Biog.,* IV, 457-458; *Biog. Dir. of Am. Cong.,* p. 1021.

[265] Thomas Dawes Eliot (1808-1870), of Massachusetts. He was a member of the House of Representatives in 1854-1855 as a Whig, and from 1859 to 1869 as a Republican. On April 25, 1860, he made a long speech in which he attacked the administration's territorial policy in orthodox Republican language. *Cong. Globe,* 36 Congress, 1 session, appendix, pp. 255-260; *Biog. Dir. of Am. Cong.,* p. 1124.

[266] William Caleb Brown, Vance's law partner. See p. 54, 198n. He or his father went north to Philadelphia and New York several times while Vance was in Washington. The journeys were made in the interest of the extensive land claims of the Brown family in western North Carolina. William Caleb Brown Memorandum Book, *passim,* Brown Papers.

[267] Dr. Samuel Henry Dickson (1798-1872) Professor of the Institutes and Practice of Medicine in the Medical College of the State of South Carolina, author of *Essays on Pathology and Therapeutics,* 2 vols. (New York, 1845). He was a brother of Dr. John Dickson, who had been the pastor of the Presbyterian Church in Asheville. Dr. Henry Dickson often came to Asheville in the summers, where he built Swannanoa Hill and Forest Hill. Tennent, "Medicine in Buncombe County," p. 11; Edgar Erskine Hume, "Samuel Henry Dickson," *Dict. of Am. Biog.,* V, 305-306. See also p. 17, 82n.

from Asheville N B. Mr. Shipp.[268] Hyman & Lady[269] arrived in the stage this morning, glad to hear you are so much better be carefull of your self, diet &c
[Washington City]
[A. L. S. Zebulon B. Vance Papers, State Department of Archives and History, Raleigh.]

To William Dickson[270]

Ho of Reps
Washington City
Dec. 11, 1860

I replied to your dispatch rec[d] tonight, but thought it best to write also. I wish I could see you, as it is almost impossible to give you a fair idea of things here in the compass of a letter.

Since receiving your dispatch I have had a conference with Mr. Crittenden[271] & other friends. He is of opinion that the only earthly chance to save the Union is to *gain time*. This is the general opinion of our friends here. The whole southern mind is inflamed to the highest pitch and the leaders in the disunion move are scorning every suggestion of compromise and rushing everything with ruinous and indecent haste that would seem to imply that they were absolute fools—Yet they are acting wisely for their ends - they are "precipitating" the people into a revolution without giving them time to think - *They fear lest the people shall think;* hence the hasty action of S. Carolina, Georgia & the other States in call-

---

[268] William Marcus Shipp (1819-1890), who was born in Lincoln County, graduated at the University of North Carolina in 1840 and was admitted to the bar in 1842. Before the war he practiced law in Rutherfordton and Hendersonville, and afterwards in Charlotte. He was a member of the House of Commons, with Vance, in 1854, of the State Senate in 1862, and of the Secession Convention of 1861. After the war he was attorney general of North Carolina, 1871-1873, and judge of the superior court, 1863-1868 and 1881-1890. He was also the chairman of what came to be known as the Shipp Commission and distinguished himself by the able manner in which he conducted the investigation of the Swepson-Littlefield frauds of 1868-1869. During the war he was briefly captain of company I in the Sixteenth North Carolina Regiment. McCormick, *Personnel*, pp. 74-75; William L. Sherrill, *Annals of Lincoln County North Carolina*. Containing Interesting and Authentic Facts of Lincoln County History Through the Years 1749 to 1937 (Charlotte, 1937), pp. 254-255 (cited hereafter as Sherrill, *Lincoln County*).

[269] For Hyman see p. 50, 181n. He had just married, within the year, Ellen Patton, who was twenty years of age. *Census*, Buncombe County, 1860.

[270] William W. Dickson, member of the House of Commons from Caldwell County. His father, William Dickson had been a prominent local politician in Burke County and in Caldwell County when it was formed in 1841. He was a lawyer and a business man. The son was later a second lieutenant in company A of the Twenty-second North Carolina Regiment until he was captured and imprisoned. General information concerning the Dickson family is in the Dickson Papers. See also Scott, *Caldwell County*, p. 92; Moore, *N. C. Roster*, II, 209; Clark, *N. C. Regts.*, IV, 706; and Connor, *N. C. Manual*, pp. 521, 529.

[271] John Jordan Crittenden (1787-1863), United States Senator from Kentucky. Crittenden had supported the Constitutional Union ticket in the election of 1860 and was the acknowledged leader in Congress of efforts to effect a sectional compromise.

ing conventions[272] & giving so short a time for the election of delegates - But the people *must* think, and when they do begin to think and hear the matter properly discussed they will consider long and soberly before they tear down this noble fabric and invite anarchy and confusion, carnage, civil war, and financial ruin with the breathless hurry of men flying from a pestilence—If we can gain time we get the advantage of this sober second thought, and no people on Gods earth have this in a greater degree than ours, and we also get the advantage of the developments in Congress which I hope may be favorable. Eminent and patriotic men of all parties here are maturing plans of compromise which will be offered soon, and I will not allow myself to believe that *all* of them will fail. But if they do, and we should be forced to go out at last, what difference in the name of common sense could a few months make? Fear of Lincoln when he comes into office is perfect humbuggery, and those that urge it know it to be so. If we go out now we cant take the army and the navy with us, and Lincoln could as easily employ them to force us *back* as he could to *prevent* our going out; and the Yankees would as readily fight to whip us back as they would to keep us in! Its all stuff. I tell you this great rashness that burns the public mind *must and will burn out,* and cooler councils rule the day; but it must have *time*—"Make haste slowly" is the maxim—We have everything to gain and nothing on earth to lose by delay, but by too hasty action we may take a fatal step that we *never* can retrace—may lose a heritage that we can never recover "though we seek it earnestly and with tears."

I am not only reconciled to the idea of a Convention[273] but think it the proper course, if you can put it off as long as possible, and give ample time for the candidates for seats to canvass. I think our friends ought to lead in the Convention movement, in order that they may as far as possible control it, and that its being called may not seem a disunion victory. Say that we *confide* in the *people:* are willing to trust them with their own rights and liberties;

---

[272] The bill authorizing a convention passed the South Carolina legislature on November 10, 1860; election of delegates was scheduled for December 6 and the convention was to assemble on December 17, 1860. In Georgia the bill authorizing a convention passed the legislature on November 18, 1860; elections were to be held on January 2, 1861; the convention was to convene on January 16, 1861. By the date of this letter seven states had passed convention bills. A convenient summary of these actions is in Dwight Lowell Dumond, *The Secession Movement 1860-1861* (New York, 1931), p. 148 (cited hereafter as Dumond, *Secession Movement*).

[273] The North Carolina legislature had met on November 19, 1860 and Governor John W. Ellis, an avowed secessionist, had recommended that a convention of the people be called to consider the question of secession. A convention bill was introduced on December 2, 1860, and, after many changes, received the support of many conservative unionists. It was adopted January 29, 1861. *House Journal 1860-61,* pp. 163-164; *Senate Journal 1860-61,* p. 245; Joseph Carlyle Sitterson, *The Secession Movement in North Carolina* (Chapel Hill, 1939), pp. 181-208 (cited hereafter as Sitterson, *N. C. Secession).*

and if, after full and fair discussion, after hearing what our Northern bretheren have to offer us, and after such mature and *decent* deliberation as becomes a great people about to do a great act, if *they* choose to undo the work of their wise and heroic ancestors, if *they* choose to invite carnage to saturate their soil and desolation to waste their fields, they can not say their public servants *precipitated* them into it! The people must and should rule, but we must see to it that we do our duty in warning, instructing, and advising them, as they have made us their servants for guarding their rights.

A Convention would also have a good effect in hastening the North into such action, if any, as it intends ultimately adopting for a settlement. For when North Carolina gives away, they in the North almost look upon the sheet-anchor of conservatism as gone. But I have not time tonight to say more. Show this to Merrimon,[274] Cowles,[275] Martin[276] & such others you think proper— I cant you know write to all I wish to address—Let me hear from you—

[Raleigh]
A. L. S. Wm. Dickson Papers, Southern Historical Collection, Chapel Hill.]

From B. F. Eller[277]

Wilk's County, N. C.
December the 17th A D 1860

Never haveing any personal acquaintance with you I propose to pick up correspondence with one who I think is a friend.

[274] For Merrimon see p. 13, 65n. He was then a member of the House of Commons from Buncombe who, though a staunch Union Whig, favored the calling of a convention on much the same grounds that Vance argues for it in this letter. Connor, *N. C. Manual*, p. 517.

[275] Calvin Josiah Cowles (1821-1907), Wilkes County merchant. He operated a store at Elks Mouth before moving to Wilkesboro in 1858. At this period he was an ardent Union man and openly advocated the perpetuation of the Union at a public meeting in Wilkes County on December 22, 1860, at which secession was denounced and a convention was opposed. During the war Cowles was a Union sympathizer, though he held the postmastership at Wilkesboro under the Confederate government until he was arrested in 1863. He married a daughter of W. W. Holden and after the war was president of the Convention of 1868 and a leader in Republican party councils. He was superintendent of the United States Assay Office at Charlotte, 1874-1884. Calvin J. Cowles Papers, State Department of Archives and History, Raleigh, N. C. (cited hereafter as Cowles Papers); Hickerson, *Happy Valley*, p. 53; Connor, *N. C. Manual*, pp. 864-865; Raleigh *North Carolina Standard*, January 5, 1861. For Cowles' own interpretation of the postmastership controversy see an interesting letter of B. S. Hedrick to K. P. Battle, July 23, 1867, William Alexander Graham Papers, State Department of Archives and History, Raleigh, N. C. (cited hereafter as Graham Papers R).

[276] Augustus H. Martin, who represented Wilkes County in the House of Commons in 1856, 1858, and 1860. He was another active opponent of secession. During the war he was captain of company G of the Fifty-fourth North Carolina Regiment and was killed in action while acting as commander of the regiment on the retreat to Appomattox, April 5, 1865. Connor, *N. C. Manual*, p. 855; Moore, *N. C. Roster*, III, 543; Clark, *N. C. Regts.*, III, 283.

[277] B. F. Eller (1835-1909) was a member of a prominent political family of Wilkes County which led the Union Sentiment of the region during the secession crisis. Raleigh, *North Carolina Standard*, January 5, 1861.

Dear Sir as the topic of the day has risen so high and to such a growing Evil That our country seem to be in a unprospering condition, Which Have Sprung from the Evil womb of democracy and
republicans of the North.

I see Mr Clingman has made a disunion speech [278] at first page
and seems to add That a Majority of old N. C. is in favor of secession I believe That Nearly all the democrats is for it, It is thought
That our Legislature will put some conservative Man in Mr T. L.
Clingmans place, I recon he thinks That if he can succeede in geting a Southern Confederacy that he will Mount the presidents
Chair, it'S True anough I suppose That South Carolina has gone
so fare as to declare her Self out of the Union[279] I would like to
know What The president will do. With her, it appears from his
Message[280] that it would not do to try to bring her to subjection by
force, Our Governor[281] is one of These out braking Secessionist
to bring the people to Shame and Suffering, it is True it would be
a shame to our grand and glowing Nation Which will prove its
down fall. Mr Vance Stand up to Mr Clingman and let him know
that all the good old State is not Such a turncoat as he is, Nor
neither are we all willing to unfurl the great Flag of our Country
for for the Cause of Lincons Election until We have seen his Ways
& does require such an act to be don. I will stop for fear of tire-
ing your patience.

Would like to Read a few lines from your hand,

Washington.

[A. L. S. Z. B. Vance Papers, State Department of Archives and
    History, Raleigh.]

To W. W. Lenoir[282]

Ho of Reps
Dec. 26, 1860.

Your acceptable and interesting letter was rec^d some time ago.

278 See p. 55, 200n. Senator Clingman made a disunion speech on December 4, 1860,
the day after Congress opened. *Cong. Globe*, 36 Congress, 2 session, pp. 3-5.

279 South Carolina did not actually secede until December 20, 1860.

280 In his message to Congress, December 3, 1860, President Buchanan took the
ground that secession was not legal, but that making war upon a state was not a
valid federal power. Thus he denied the validity of both secession and coercion.
James D. Richardson (ed.), *A Compilation of the Messages and Papers of the
President*, 20 vols. (New York, 1896-1916), VII, 3157-3184 (cited hereafter as
Richardson, *Messages*).

281 The governor of North Carolina was John Willis Ellis (1820-1861), Democrat,
of Rowan County. He was a secessionist leader and in his message to the legislature
concluded that the rights of the South were seriously threatened by the election of
Lincoln, and recommended military preparation and the calling of a convention.
Senate Journal 1860-61, pp. 11-43. The message was prepared in consultation with
leading Democrats, including Senator Clingman. Diary of John W. Ellis, November
17, 1860, John W. Ellis Papers, Southern Historical Collection, University of North
Carolina, Chapel Hill, N. C. (hereafter cited as Ellis Diary and Ellis Papers).

282 Walter Waightstill Lenoir (1823-1890), lawyer and planter, was a son of

Hurry, excitement, and the dislike of sending you disponding news have all operated to delay my answer; but today, our House not being in session, I undertake a hasty response.

The crisis here is rapidly approaching its denouement. The Administration is literally dropping to "smash".[283] The timidity, vascilation and corruption of the President; the recent discovery of astounding and enormous frauds and defalcations,[284] and the known and acknowledged complicity of the Executive with all the plans and schemes of disunion,[285] make every honest man damn the day that placed Buchannan in office. So there is no help but con-

---

Thomas Lenoir, and a grandson of both General William Lenoir and Colonel Waightstill Avery. He was valedictorian in 1843 at the University of North Carolina, and always a man of large public spirit, maintaining a deep interest in the social, industrial, political, and economic questions of the day. In 1860 he lived in Caldwell County, but later lived in Haywood and Watauga, and was a member of the North Carolina House of Representatives from the latter in 1883. During the war he joined Vance's "Legion," but when that body failed to materialize he became captain of company A in the Thirty-seventh North Carolina Regiment, was wounded in September 1862 and resigned, December 18, 1862. In 1860 he was a Douglas Democrat. Grant, *Alumni History,* p. 362; Clark, *N. C. Regts.,* III, 433; Moore, *N. C. Roster,* III, 3; Connor, *N. C. Manual,* p. 844; *North Carolina University Magazine,* Old Series vol. XXI, no. 5, New Series vol. X, pp. 245-248; J. A. Weston, *Funeral Sermon of Walter Waightstill Lenoir* (New York, 1890); Walter Waightstill Lenoir to Rufus T. Lenoir, October 27, 1860, Lenoir Family Papers, Southern Historical Collection, University of North Carolina, Chapel Hill, N. C. (cited hereafter as Lenoir Papers).

[283] Buchanan's administration had begun to fall to pieces early in December. On December 2, 1860, Howell Cobb of Georgia resigned as Secretary of the Treasury because of the president's denial of the right of secession; on December 12, 1860, Secretary of State Lewis Cass of Michigan resigned on the ground that the Charleston forts should be reinforced. On December 29, 1860, Secretary of War John B. Floyd of Virginia resigned, though the reasons are disputed, to be followed by Jacob Thompson of Mississippi as Secretary of the Interior on January 8, 1861, and by Philip F. Thomas of Maryland on January 11, 1861, as Secretary of the Treasury.

[284] This is probably a reference to an apparent defalcation, just then brought to light, of $870,000. of Indian trust bonds in the Department of the Interior for which acceptances given by Secretary Floyd in the War Department to army contractors had been substituted. On December 24 Representative Isaac N. Morris, of Illinois, introduced a resolution providing for the appointment of a special committee of the House to investigate the matter. The committee was appointed, with Morris as its chairman and, on February 12, 1861, made a unanimous report which declared the issue of the acceptances "unauthorized by law and deceptive and fraudulent in character" and irreconcilable with "purity of private motives and faithfulness to public trusts," though it did not hold Floyd directly responsible in the matter. In 1868 the Supreme Court held the issue of acceptances in violation of the law. The whole complicated business, in which partisan politics doubtless played a large part, may best be followed in James Ford Rhodes, *History of the United States From the Compromise of 1850,* 7 vols. (New York, 1893-1896), III, 236-241 (cited hereafter as Rhodes, *History*); *Cong. Globe,* 36 Congress, 2 session, part 1 (December 24, 1860, February 12, 1861), pp. 190-191, 207, 218; *House Report No. 78,* 36 Congress, 2 session, pp. 19-20; 7 *Wallace,* 666.

[285] Vance's indictment of Buchanan's administration is typical for the time from one who belonged to another political party. Buchanan's policies are still characterized by some historians as timid and vascillating, but it is hardly correct to charge him with corruption, or with complicity with "all the plans and schemes of disunion."

stant harm from that quarter. The House crisis Committee[286] is a complete failure, is virtually dissolved now and will go to pieces tomorrow when it undertakes to report. The Senate Committee[287] was then our hope but it too has failed. Mr. Crittenden's propositions[288] (some of them in substance what you suggested) were refuted by a decided vote, as usual the extremes meeting. Jeff

[286] This committee was set up on motion of Alexander R. Boteler, American of Virgina, on December 4, 1860. After the reading of Buchanan's message to Congress Boteler moved "that so much of the President's message as relates to the present perilous condition of the country, be referred to a special committee of one from each State." The motion was put to a vote without debate and was carried 145 to 38. The committee, known generally as the House Committee of Thirty-three, was composed of sixteen Republicans, fourteen Democrats, and three South Americans. None of the proposals considered by this committee in the following weeks ever came close to solving the sectional crisis. *Cong. Globe*, 36 Congress, 2 session, part 1 (December 4, 1860), p. 6; *Journal of the Committee of Thirty-three, in Report of the Select Committee of Thirty-three on the Disturbed Condition of the Country, in Reports of Committees of the House of Representatives*, 36 Congress, 2 session, vol. I, No. 31, pp. 3-11 (cited hereafter as *Journal of Com. of Thirty-three*).

[287] The Senate Committee of Thirteen was proposed by Senator Lazarus W. Powell, of Kentucky, on December 6, 1860, to consider "so much of the President's message as relates to the present . . . distracted condition of the country, and the grievances between the slaveholding and the non-slaveholding States . . . to a special committee of thirteen members." After nearly two weeks the committee was authorized on December 18 without a record vote, and with some modification of the resolution. The committee was appointed on December 20, but it never reported any resolutions with regard to the sectional crisis, though it was composed of far abler men than the House committee. Its membership had two cotton states men, three border state men, three Northern Democrats, and five Republicans. *Cong. Globe*, 36 Congress, 2 session, part 1 (December 4, 10, 1860), pp. 5, 28, 32; *Journal of the Committee of Thirteen, in Reports of Select Committee of Thirteen on the Disturbed Conditions of the Country, in Reports of Committees of the Senate*, 36 Congress, 2 session, vol. I, No. 288 (cited hereafter as *Journal of Com. of Thirteen*). On December 28, 1860 the committee adopted a resolution that it "had not been able to agree upon any general plan of adjustment," and so reported to the Senate. *Journal of Com. of Thirteen*, p. 18; *Cong. Globe*, 36 Congress, 2 session, part 1 (December 28, 1860), p. 211.

[288] The proposal of Senator Crittenden, the most notable of the compromise plans presented in Congress, was concerned primarily with slavery in the territories. It did not concern itself with the slavery issue as such so much as it treated the issue of the impingement of federal jurisdiction upon slavery. To remove the question of slavery from the realm of federal activity, therefore, it was necessary to deal with it in limited and specific areas, such as territories, arsenals, and forts. On some of the minor aspects of the slavery question statuatory action was deemed sufficient: among his resolutions were those which called for the faithful execution of the Fugitive Slave Law, the repeal of the Personal Liberty Acts, and the enforcement of the laws prohibiting the foreign slave trade. But the heart of Crittenden's proposition had to do with the territorial question, where the success of compromise depended upon comprehensiveness. Accordingly, Crittenden proposed to make his compromise irrevocable by embodying the major part of it in a series of unalterable Constitutional amendments which "no future amendment of the Constitution shall affect." He proposed amendments to the Constitution to provide that the territories be divided along the line of thirty-six degrees and thirty minutes; that slavery be forever prohibited in the territory north of that line; that it be allowed to go into the region south of that line and receive congressional protection there so long as the area remained under territorial governments; that when a state should be organized in the southern area the people thereof could exclude or maintain slavery as they desired; that the United States guarantee payment for escaped slaves; that slavery be protected in the states in which it was

Davis & Toombs voting with Seward & Wade! [289] It is further understood that the North will offer *no terms*[290] whatever. Now what? The Union is dissolved of course. S. C. is already gone and I make not a doubt but every Gulf State will be with her by the 4th March. Must N. C. and the border states go with them is our question? We are not compelled to do so. Many think we could do better, and the method is to form a great middle confederacy, composed of the border slave and border free states.[291] In this way

---

legal; and that Congress should not interfere with the interstate slave trade. Crittenden introduced his resolutions on December 18, 1860; on December 22 they were defeated in committee; in the last hours of the session they were allowed to come to a vote in Congress and were defeated: in the Senate 20 to 19; in the House of Representatives 113 to 80. In the Senate not one affirmative vote was Republican, but every negative vote was Republican. In the House of Representatives the minority of 80 contained not one Republican, and 110 of the 113 negative votes were cast by Republicans. *Cong. Globe,* 36 Congress, 2 session, part 1 (December 18, 1860, February 27, March 2, 1861), pp. 112-114, 1261, 1405; *Journal of the Com. of Thirteen,* pp. 5, 8.

[289] Jefferson Davis (1808-1889), at this time Senator from Mississippi, and Robert Toombs (1810-1885), Senator from Georgia, were the cotton states representatives in the Senate Committee of Thirteen, and reflected the extreme southern view of the sectional crisis. William H. Seward (1801-1872), Senator from New York, and Benjamin F. Wade (1800-1878), Senator from Ohio, were Republican members of the same committee. Wade was a known and blatant opponent of compromise and Seward, though he may have personally favored the Crittenden measures, was by this time the spokesman of president-elect Lincoln, who did not favor the main proposition of Crittenden. At the outset the committee adopted a rule that no motion could be carried except by dual majorities of the Republicans on the committee and of the other members as well. This meant that any measure to be reported to the Senate must be adopted by a majority containing at least three Republicans and five other members; this rule was adopted for the very sound reason that no measure of compromise, and certainly no Constitutional amendment, could be finally adopted unless it were supported by a large proportion of the Republican party. This rule explains the phenomenon of the extremes voting together, for when the Republican members of the committee voted against all compromise measures Davis and Toombs also opposed them in the conviction that they could never be affected without Republican support. So, in a vote on the vital first resolution to revise and extend the Missouri Compromise line, the five Republican members were joined in opposition by Davis and Toombs to defeat the measure in committee by a vote of seven to six. Seward was not present on December 22 when the vote was taken, but when he returnd to Washington on December 24 he asked that his vote be recorded, and he joined his Republican colleagues in voting against every important feature of the proposed Crittenden Compromise. *Journal of the Com. of Thirteen,* pp. 5, 8; David Morris Potter, Jr., *Lincoln and His Party in the Secession Crisis* (New Haven, 1942), pp. 170-173 (cited hereafter as Potter, *Secession Crisis*).

[290] Republicans in both houses were frequently criticized for their refusal to accept any terms offered by others, or to suggest any of their own. So they were made to appear responsible for the failure to solve the crisis. On December 28, 1860, certain suggestions, or "terms," were offered in the Committee of Thirty-three by Charles Francis Adams of Massachusetts, though he was not the author of them. Their subsequent history suggests that the purpose of this offer was not to settle the crisis so much as to divide the southerners; they were directed not to the secessionists but to the southern Whigs of the border states. When, on March 1, 1861, the resolutions had served their purpose Adams himself voted against them and helped bring about their defeat. Potter, *Secession Crisis,* pp. 290-303.

[291] This idea of a Central Confederacy is given expression from time to time in the private writings of moderates during the crisis period. Vance did not publicly disclose this view because he feared that every admission of the improbability of compromise would increase the trend toward secession. Sitterson, *N. C. Secession,* pp. 199-200.

we preserve this Capitol, the public lands, the form and prestige of
of the old government, secure greater homogeniousness, and finally
re-organize and reconstruct the whole Union around this grand
and over-shadowing neuclus! It is the policy of the cotton states as
disclosed here by their commissioners and leading men, to keep
out the border states from joining them until they can confederate and form a constitution embodying their own peculiar dogmas
and Rhett-Yancey policy.[292] The leading ideas of this policy is the
reopening the African slave traffic and free trade and direct taxation. The voice of the great border states is against this of course;
hence their hasty action. Their confederacy once formed, we go
into it acceding to their policy or we stay out and be their border
guard against abolitionism—*They don't care which!* Thats the
present state of the case. I confess I am *not willing to do either.*
And I think the only way that the Union can be reconstructed and
these cotton states be brought to treat us with proper respect, is
this idea of a great Central Confederation. It could dictate terms
of compromise which Georgia would be compelled to accept, and
the withdrawal of Georgia would break the back bone of the
whole seceding Kingdom. As for New England, we would *kick*
it out if it refused to secede, and would never let it back unless
as the single state of New England with only two Sumners[293] in
the Senate to play the blackguard. What do you think of it? Medi-
tate upon it and write me. I have not space to iluminate, but will
send you a pamphlet prepared by an eminent citizen of Maryland.[294] It is too the only way to prevent civil war I fear.

I guess you keep posted as to our doings here. Great excitement
pervades all ranks and classes, though little will be done till after
the holidays. Then I think ten days will bring things to a head.

My family are quite well, though if the excitement increases I
shall send them home. Coercion will not be popular with any
party, and is scarcely threatened here.

Fort Defiance

[A. L. S. Lenoir Family Papers, Southern Historical Collection,
Chapel Hill.]

---

[292] Robert Barnwell Rhett (1800-1876), former Senator from South Carolina, and
William Lowndes Yancey (1814-1863), former member of the House of Representatives from Alabama, personified, and had for a decade, the southern group which
sought, not to compromise and reconstruct the Union, but to further the cause of
secession and of southern independence.

[293] Charles Sumner (1811-1874), Senator from Massachusetts (1851-1874), though
nominally a Republican, had long personified the anti-southern, abolitionist sentiment prevalent among New Englanders.

[294] Probably Henry Winter Davis (1817-1865), a former Whig and Know-Nothing
and a member of the House of Representatives from Maryland. He had supported
the Bell and Everett ticket in the 1860 campaign and was a vigorous and
courageous leader of Union forces by means of both tongue and pen.

From W. W. Lenoir

Ft Defiance,[295] N. C. Jan 7th 1861

I received on yesterday your favor of the 26th, ult. and read it
with the interest which it was calculated to inspire, relating as it
does, to the present all absorbing crisis in our political affairs. I
agree with you entirely in believing that the salvation of the constitution laws treaties and flag of the United States can now no
longer be hoped for except by the formation of a central government, embracing those who are still loyal to them, and desire to
maintain them and obey them. You have probably before this
time received a copy of the resolutions passed at Lenoir[296] on
the 22d ult. which were prepared by myself, and which you will
see at a glance embrace that as the plan of action. They were
cordially received by the meeting, and, I think express the almost
unanimous sentiment of the county. I sent a copy of them, with
a short communication advocating a central government, for publication in the New York Journal of commerce. As I do not take
the paper, I do not know whether the communication has appeared. If so, it may have caught your eye.

It is not for me to say what ought to be the policy of a state
which believes our constitution to be a bad form of government,
and our union a clog upon her material prosperity. The events of
the day prove that such is the creed of the leading politicians of
the States south of us, and that the masses in those states, if they
think otherwise, are, for the present at least, lulled or cowed into
silence. I can only say that in my humble way of thinking a grave
error seems to underlie their theories, that they will find that the
laws of commerce have for their ministers the currents of the sea
and air, the winds, the tides, and the seasons; and that those mighty
agencies will not obey the pigmy voices that echo from the halls
of human legislation. But they have made their choice.

What shall we do, who are still loyal to the constitution, the
union, the laws, the treaties and the flag of our country, who still
look upon them as the polladium of our political safety, who still
true to our first love? For the States that are still loyal and obedient
to the constitution, it would be a feeble policy, it would be an unsafe policy, nay, it would be a policy that would leave a soil on
their honor, to abandon to men wrong doers our vast and increasing national wealth, our magnificent capitol and public buildings,
our archives, our soul stirring national traditions, our army, our
navy, and our proud flag, now known and honored in every land.

---

[295] See pp. 74-75, 282n. Fort Defiance was in Happy Valley, Caldwell County, and
was the Lenoir home.

[296] Between the secession of South Carolina on December 20, 1860, and the end
of the following January, Union meetings were held in at least twenty North
Carolina counties, including that in Lenoir, Caldwell County, on December 22.
Raleigh *North Carolina Standard,* December 26, 1860, January 2, 9, 16, 23, 1861.

Let us rather rend it in twain and tramp the fragments in the dust, than desert it to be waived in defiance and insult over the hosts of a mad fanatacism. If such sentiments shall find a ready echo in the hearts of the people of the border slave states, why may they not write and form the nucleus of a great central conservative party which will isolate the advocates of New England nullification and disobedience, on the one hand, and of South Carolina secession on the other? Such a policy would save the mighty fabric of liberty and free institutions founded upon the constitution laws and treaties of the United States, for those at least who were loyal to them; and would lay the best foundation for the ultimate reconstruction of the union in its present integrity of territory, when the madness of the hour has passed away.

Events are hastening with such speed to the vortex, that government may be a wreck before this reaches your eye. I believe that in this part of North Carolina, at least, the idea of a central government upon the plan I have indicated is the one that alone is viewed with favor, as an escape from the wreck of the present, and that any means which may be prudent and necessary to inaugurate it will be sustained with enthusiasm. For my own part, I am willing if Congress dispenses, so as to leave less than a quorum, and thus virtually dissolves the government, to see the public property placed under a sufficient police or other guard, and a provisional president and congress provided for and chosen immediately by the central States, New England, at least, being shaken off, and thus a new status peacefully inaugurated before the fourth of March. I am afraid that New England will be, like Lucio in the play, something of a bur,[297] and will try to stick; but if she wont drop off she must be shaken off; she must leave her country for her country's good. It is to be hoped that some less revolutionary plan than the one I have suggested will be found, to save the country from the ruin that seems to impend. We must trust that for the present, in great degree to our faithful watchmen at the seat of government.

Our resolutions show that I stand out as stoutly as any southern man ought for full justice from the north as an indispensible condition to union with the north, or any part of it. But if we are to have an entire separation from the north, I am opposed to joining our state with the schemes and politics of the cotton states, and prefer a union with Virginia Kentucky and Tennessee, with Maryland Delaware and Missouri if they would join; or even our separate independence. I am utterly opposed to reopening the slave trade, have no faith in the new political dogmas which I

---

[297] Lucio was a minor character in Shakespeare's *Measure for Measure* who, at the close of Scene III in Act IV remarks: "By my troth, I'll go with thee to the lane's end: . . . I am a kind of burr; I shall stick."

believe they will engraft in their constitution, and have no desire to engage in the silly project of trying in vain to carry slavery into Mexico and Central America, two old long inhabited countries, which have rejected slavery once, and wont receive it again, even if the north remain quiet. Nor do I wish to take part in a civil war between the North and the South, for the possession of those God forsaken regions, which will be sure to come about unless we have a central government to keep the peace. Please let me hear from you again on the progress of this most important movement. Washington.

[A. L. S. Z. B. Vance Papers, State Department of Archives and History, Raleigh.]

To G. N. Folk[298]

House of Representatives
Washington City, Jan. 9, 1861

The rapidity and magnitude of passing events, pregnant with the issues of revolution and civil war, make me, of course, painfully interested in the action of your body. Such has been my devotion to the Union and so deep my appreciation of the blessings it has showered upon the American people, that I cannot bring myself to look upon the possibility of its destruction without the extremist sorrow. But we are swallowed up and hurried along the rushing tides of time, and, having reached a point where we can no longer steer it, it now becomes us to prepare, if possible, for our safety and honor, by steering with, and not against the rushing volume. Unable to do as we wish, we must do as we can. Whether wisely or unwisely, our Southern neighbors are everywhere in motion, taking such steps as our safety and interests seem to require in the fearful condition of the times. Ought North Carolina alone to stand still? Whether she decides to remain in the Union, to join a Southern Confederacy, a Central Confederacy, or set up for her-

---

[298] George N. Folk was a native of Virginia who came to Watauga County, N. C. just after having been admitted to the bar. He became an outstanding lawyer, though his reputation was more that of a student than of advocate. He lived at "Gable Ends" across the Yadkin from Riverside, in Happy Valley, where for a time he taught a law school. He represented Watauga County in the House of Commons in 1856 and 1860, and Caldwell County in the Senate in 1876. He resigned from the commons in 1861 when the war came and was appointed a captain in the Ninth North Carolina Regiment (cavalry). Here he served until he resigned on May 5, 1862, when he raised six companies of troops and eventually became colonel of the Sixty-fifth North Carolina Regiment (cavalry) on August 3, 1863. He was captured at Heath's Mills in June of 1864 and for several months was a prisoner at Fort Delaware, resuming command of his regiment upon his release. After the war he moved to Caldwell County and resumed the practice of law. In the session of 1860-1861 he was one of the Whig leaders who early favored the calling of a convention and made a notable speech on the subject on January 11, 1861, shortly after receiving this letter from Vance. Winston *Western Sentinel*, February 8, 1861; Clark, *N. C. Regts.*, I, 418, 485, III, 673, 680-683; Connor, *N. C. Manual*, pp. 521, 844; Bettie A. Folk to Samuel McDowell Tate, January 13, 1881, Tate Papers.

self, involves a great and perilous responsibility. And I hold that issues such as these, embracing such extraordinary and fundamental changes in her national condition should be committed directly to the people, in whom all political power is vested. As they, after mature deliberation, see proper to make their political bed, so they must lie upon it; if they see fit and think it best to destroy our present forms and substitute others, battling in the meantime with all the stern and desolating consequences attendant on such change, then the responsibility rests, as does the suffrage, with the people.

I do not regard the call of a Convention[299] as a disunion movement; I regard it rather as the conducting steel to the lightning freighted cloud. Firm, temperate and decided action may save our rights and the Union, too; non-action will precipitate us into disunion. We want a Convention for other purposes than secession alone, though others, I know, desire it for no other object. We want it for the purpose of demanding terms of the Northern people; if they are refused, then for making our voice heard with the Southern States which are rapidly inoculating the people with many dogmas, of which North Carolina does not approve. Above all, we want a Convention for the purpose of consultation concerning the common good. Though some of our Southern sisters have contemptuously refused to consult the wishes of 180,000 fighting men, over whose dead bodies an invading host, treading through the ashes of their homes, must reach them, yet there are others who anxiously seek general and fraternal counsel, and their desire we should regard.

In short, in my opinion, no better method could be devised to promote the peace, the material interest and the honor of our State, than the calling of an open and unrestricted [300] Convention of the people to consider our national affairs, giving as much time as the urgency of the case will permit. The whole Southern people, assembled, through their freshly elected delegates unitedly and simultaneously demanding a moderate and reasonable ultimatum of the North, would in my opinion, get it; and those States that desired to remain in the Union upon honorable terms could do so whilst those that think it accursed and damnable, and prefer

---

[299] The convention movement, when it began in December of 1860, was primarily a move of the secessionists, since they could not succeed without it, but a small number of Unionists had favored it from the beginning, especially in the hope that it might prove to be a means of obtaining guarantees for the rights of the south which would preserve the Union. By the middle of January most of the press and most of the local meetings favored the calling of a convention, the conservatives arguing that the convention would check secession and serve to calm the public mind. A convention bill passed the legislature on January 29, 1861, calling for elections on February 28. Sitterson, *N. C. Secession,* pp. 192-200.

[300] The Convention Act, as finally adopted, restricted action to federal affairs and required that its action be submitted to the people. *Laws of N. C. 1860-61,* pp. 27-31.

to go out rather than to stay in on any terms could depart in peace.

I should be glad to hear from you, and to interchange advice often.

[Raleigh]

[From Winston *Western Sentinel*, Feb. 1, 1861.]

From Jno. Baxter[301]

Knoxville, Tenn.
Jany 13th, '61

Please buy and send me by The Express a Pistol of the Kind which you described to me while I was in Washington. Notify me of its Cost, and I will remit immediately.

Reflection Satisfies me that rebellion ought to be arrested by *force,* and I hope the Government will apply this remedy at once and efficiently.

Washington.

[A. L. S. Z. B. Vance Papers, State Department of Archives and History, Raleigh.]

From D. F. Caldwell [302]

Greensboro N C Jan 13 1861

I have a small favor I wish to ask of you; and that is, that you get the editors of the National Inteligencer,[303] if you can, to pub-

---

[301] John J. Baxter (1819-1886) was a native of Rutherford County, but lived in Hendersonville and in Asheville until 1857, when he moved to Knoxville. He began his career as a merchant, but soon took up law and was admitted to the bar in 1841. He was a member of the House of Commons from Rutherford County in 1842, and from Henderson County in 1846, 1852, and 1856, being chosen speaker in the extra session of 1852. In politics Baxter was a strong Whig and, as a result of a political quarrel, fought a duel with Marcus Erwin in the early fifties. In the crisis of 1860-1861 he was an ardent Union advocate and he remained one all during the Civil War, being arrested in the spring of 1862 "upon frequent representations of suspicions of his loyalty." After the war he became a very prominent lawyer in Knoxville in partnership with Thomas E. Champion and A. E. Ricks. He was a member from Knox County of the Tennessee Constitutional Convention of 1870 and was chairman of its Judiciary Committee. He was appointed United States Circuit Court Judge by President Rutherford B. Hayes in 1877 and held this position until his death at Hot Springs, Arkansas. Connor, *N. C. Manual,* pp. 472, 648, 798; Arthur, *Western North Carolina,* p. 397; Clarence W. Griffin, *History of Old Tryon and Rutherford Counties North Carolina 1730-1936* (Asheville, 1937), p. 228 (cited hereafter as Griffin, *Old Tryon and Rutherford*).

[302] See p. 32, 137a.

[303] See p. 32, 137b.

lish Daniel Webster's first speech, delivered at the capon Springs in Va.[304] It was delivered in the summer of 185 or 51 It is quite short and quite pithy It rests on secession, if remember aright, in the way I like to see men take hold of a matter. The only draw back to having it published is the comfort the abolitionist might derive from it at the present, but as well as I remember, it gives it to the *higher* laws gen ly as strongly as it does the secessionist if not more vigorously and with a keener lash.

P. S.

The Union forces are gaining strength every hour or I am greatly deceived and all that is now wanting to give us a brilliant triump in this State — is for the Black Republicans to give us some assurance that they intend to act upon liberal and National principals But the fact that they persisted in organizing a Sectional party and keeping it in the field, so soon as they obtained the power to elect their candidates, by a sectional vote—the character of their platform — circulating the helper book [305] — giving away all the

---

[304] Capon Springs, sometimes written Caphon Springs, was in Fredrick County, Virginia, twenty-one miles southwest of Winchester. Webster, defending his support of the compromise measures of 1850, made two speeches here on the same day, June 25, 1851. In the first speech he ridiculed secession, saying: "I have little patience with those who talk flippantly of secession and disunion; they do not appear to me to understand of what they speak, nor to have the least idea of its consequences. . . . But secession and disunion are a region of gloom, and morass, and swamp; no cheerful breezes fan it; no spirit of health visits it; it is all malaria; it is all fever and ague. . . But one thing, gentlemen, be assured of, the first step taken in the programme of secession, which shall be an actual infringement of the Constitution or the laws, will be promptly met." Then, turning on the "higher law" concept and attacking its invocation of religion to justify its ways, he added: "No common vision can discern it; no conscience, not transcendental and ecstatic, can feel it; the hearing of common men never listens to its high behests; and therefore one should think it is not a safe law to be acted on, in matters of the highest practical moment. It is the code, however, of the fanatical and factious abolitionists of the North." In the second speech he attacked fanatics at the North and secessionists at the South as equally dangerous to the welfare of the Union. He admitted that it was absurd for either party to a compact to disregard any one provision and expect the other party to observe the rest. "I have not hesitated to say, and I repeat, that if the Northern States refuse, wilfully and deliberately, to carry into effect that part of the Constitution which respects the restoration of fugitive slaves, and Congress provides no remedy, the South would no longer be bound to observe the compact. (Immense applause.) A bargain cannot be broken on one side, and still bind the other side." The speeches are given in full in George Ticknor Curtis, *Life of Daniel Webster*, 2 vols. (New York, 1893), II, 511-520.

[305] In 1857 Hinton Rowan Helper (1829-1909), a middle-class nonslaveholder of North Carolina, published in New York *The Impending Crisis of the South: How to Meet It*. By selecting and twisting and misinterpreting figures from the census of 1790 and 1850 it presented slavery as an economic fallacy and bitterly attacked the slaveholder as the cause of the South's economic backwardness. Thirteen thousand copies had been sold by the end of 1857 and 142,000 by 1860. *A Compendium*, published in 1859, amounting to 100,000 copies, was circulated by the Republicans as a campaign document in the election of 1860. Though Lincoln did not endorse it other prominent Republicans did, including John Sherman and Galusha A. Grow. The South was infuriated by the book, though few read it. Joseph Gregoire de Roulhac Hamilton, "Hinton Rowan Helper," *Dict. of Am. Biog.*, VII, 517-518.

public lands[306] — Creating a large National debt to build the Pacific Rail Road [307] Their personal liberty laws[308] Their refusing to return fugitive slaves &c &c &c is hard to overcome very hard — And had the South not departed from the principal laid down in the ordinance of 1787 [309] by all the slave states when the constitution was framed repealed the Missouri Compromise[310] and filabusters reopened the slave trade we could not tollerate their conduct even in N C

Washington.

[A. L. S. Z. B. Vance Papers, State Department of Archives and History, Raleigh.]

From J. M. Hamilton[311]

Columbus N. C.

Jan 14th 1861

I hope you will do me the favor to Send me a Good newes paper from the City weekly as we onley have Weekly mails and what it will Cost & I will forward you the Money forthe with.

You will pleas Give me the prospects of the union I deSire your final Opinion uppon the State of the political State of things we have much exsitement on the State of things hear now it seames

[306] The Republican platform included a plank which advocated a homestead bill with regard to the public lands. Galusha A. Grow had long labored for such a bill, which in 1860 passed both houses of Congress; but Buchanan vetoed it. Another bill of like nature was adopted in 1862.

[307] The Pacific Railroad Bill, which called for large federal subsidies, was likewise a part of the Republican platform. Sectional differences as to route caused the defeat of all such measures until 1862.

[308] Personal liberty laws were state enactments, mainly after 1840, ostensibly to establish and safeguard traditional rights in all questions involving "personal liberty," but actually to prevent the rendition of fugitive slaves. In the case of Prigg v. Penn. (16 Peters 539) the Supreme Court declared unconstitutional a Pennsylvania statute which made it a felony to remove a Negro by force for the purpose of slavery, on the ground that federal power in the matter of fugitive slaves was exclusive. This seemed to mean to southerners that state officials could not be required to execute a constitutional provision, but that performance was required by national authorities, and by them alone. In 1860 South Carolina named thirteen states in the north whose laws "nullify or render useless" any attempt to carry out the guarantees under which the slaveholding states had accepted the Constitution.

[309] The Ordinance of 1787 set limits upon the expansion of slavery into the territories and this principle had since been vigorously attacked by southerners who argued that slavery followed the flag.

[310] The Missouri Compromise of 1820 had been repealed implicitly by the Compromise of 1850, and explicitly by the Kansas Nebraska Act of 1854, in which slavery was allowed to advance into regions formerly prohibited to it, if the people of the territory so desired. The repeal was not the work of southerners alone, though most of the southern members of Congress were in favor of the measure, for it was sponsored by Senator Stephen A. Douglas of Illinois and made an administration measure by President Franklin Pierce of New Hampshire.

[311] Colonel J. M. Hamilton (1816-1894), a planter of Polk County. He was born and reared on the Old Hamilton place on White Oak Creek, became a colonel in the state militia, or home guard, during the war, and represented Polk and Rutherford counties in the House of Commons in 1865. Connor, N. C. Manual, p. 799; Griffin, Old Tryon and Rutherford, p. 320.

to me that the Dinocrats ar making their last effort as a party I think we have a cleare majority in Polk for the Union Some prominint Democrats are now strong for the Union tho many of them are Saying their is no union you have been denounced as a "Abolilionest by many of the Dems & many other hard Sayings Call a Nashionial Convention & Save the Union if posable Washington.

P. O. I rec^d a coppy of the Covode[312] committee & my Brother a Pat office report from your for which favors you have our best respect & will for any other favor

[A. L. S. Z. B. Vance Papers, State Department of Archives and History, Raleigh.]

From G. W. Logan[313]

Rutherfordton N. C.
15 Jany 1861 —

Enclosed is $2— from T. B. Justice[314] Esqr of this place, he wishes you to have him sent the National Intelligencer[315] so long as the pay will justify —

There was attempt to have a Secession Meeting here yesterday, headed by Dr C. Mills[316] of Polk, but was a most signal failure, the

---

[312] John Covode (1808-1871) was a Whig and Republican congressman from Pennsylvania, 1855-1863, 1867-1871. During the Thirty-sixth Congress Covode was chairman of a partisan committee to investigate President Buchanan's use of money and patronage to influence congressmen. Interpreting its powers broadly, the committee uncovered a few sinecures and some irregularities in printing contracts. The major purpose of obtaining campaign material for the 1860 elections was realized in the publication of a voluminous report denouncing the Democratic administration. It is known as *House Report* No. 648, 36 Congress, 1 session, and contains both majority and minority reports. The House took no action on either report. Robert S. Cotterill, "John Covode," *Dict. of Am. Biog.*, IV, 470.

[313] George Washington Logan (1815-1899) was born in Rutherfordton; studied law and was admitted to the bar; was clerk of the county court, 1841-1849; county solicitor, 1855-1856; and brigadier general of the State Militia in the forties. He kept a tavern, and prospered greatly in his numerous business enterprises. Before the war he was an Old Line Union Whig, during it he was a Unionist, and afterwards a Republican. In 1863 he was elected to the Confederate Congress as a peace advocate, and as judge of the superior court, 1868-1874, he became a notorious figure during the Ku Klux disturbances of the Reconstruction period. He was a member of the House of Commons from Rutherford in 1866 and of the Convention of 1865 from Rutherford and Polk counties. His post-war conduct made him a highly controversial local figure, but in 1861 he was a staunch Unionist and an uncompromising opponent of secession before Lincoln's call for troops. Connor, *N. C. Manual*, pp. 449, 799, 895; Griffin, *Old Tryon and Rutherford*, p. 227; Arthur, *Western North Carolina*, p. 404; clippings in Walser Papers.

[314] Thomas Butler Justice (1813-1892), Baptist preacher of Rutherfordton and agent for the Speculation Land Company. He was elected county treasurer in 1884 as a Democrat; was mayor of Rutherfordton, 1887-1888; and was the father of Michael Hoke Justice (1844-1919), state senator and superior court judge. Griffin, *Old Tryon and Rutherford*, pp. 254, 345, 532, 601.

[315] See p. 32, 137b.

[316] Dr. Columbus Mills (1802-1882), a prominent physician and planter of Polk County who took an active part in politics. He was state senator in 1846, 1854, and

Meeting adjourned without attempting a vote or *any thing*. Write me — hold on to the vessel
Washington.
[A. L. S.   Z. B. Vance Papers, State Department of Archives and History, Raleigh.]

From Robert G. Twitty[317]

Rutherfordton N C. Jany 16 1860 [1861]
I ride to the Village often to hear the news The times are Exciting I think that South Carolina has done wrong in being too hasty but the act is done and I think the best way is to let them alone the abolitionist is to blame for the situation the Country is in If the General Government undertakes to force South Carolina It will be the cause of all the Slave holding. States to secede at once and prevent any settlement I see It States in the papers that Gen¹ Wool [318] says he would raise 200 000 at short notice such statement has a bad effect for the south can raise some men and If they come here they may not all get Back I do not wish to influence you for you are as strong for the South as I am I am a union Man but when they send men South It will change my Notion I can do nothing against my own people we are looking to see what will be done. I am not fearful of Lincoln he can do but little we are as a community very much Excited Its said by some of your enemies that you go for coercing South Carolina I do not believe It for we are differently situated from 32 when Jacksons[319] time was there It was a question of Tariff but Critenton[320] plan I think would satisfy the South and I am willing they have time to study & If on reflection we cannot stay together let us part and do the best we can for the South will be a slave Country or a Negro Country that I think is a settled question. What Providence intends the

---

1856, and was the moving spirit in the creation of Polk County in 1855. The county seat was named Columbus in his honor. In 1861 he was an active secessionist; during the war he was surgeon of the Sixteenth North Carolina Regiment until his resignation in March, 1863; after the war Dr. Mills left Polk County and lived on a farm near Concord, N. C. until his death. Griffin, *Old Tryon and Rutherford*, p. 229; Connor, *N. C. Manual*, p. 799; Moore, *N. C. Roster*, II, 2, 31.

[317] Robert G. Twitty was a large landowner and slaveholder who lived in the Broad River section of Rutherford County. He held several minor county offices from time to time. Griffin, *Old Tryon and Rutherford*, pp. 176, 183, 221, 222, 234, 304, 553, 555.

[318] John Ellis Wool (1784-1869) of New York, veteran of the War of 1812 and of the Mexican War, at that time in command of the Department of the East with the brevet rank of major general. William A. Ganoe, "John Ellis Wool," *Dict. of Am. Biog.*, XX, 513-514.

[319] In 1832 South Carolina had called a convention which had nullified the tariff acts of Congress and forbade the collection of duties within the state. Jackson countered with a proclamation threatening to use force if necessary in the execution of the law. In this proclamation he assumed the right to coerce a state.

[320] See p. 76, 288n.

Result to be but we hope and wait to what is to be the result My Family are all well & Hope you are
Washington.
[A. L. S. Z. B. Vance Papers, filed under 1860, State Department of Archives and History, Raleigh.]

To T. G. Walton[321]

Ho. Reps
Washington City Jan. 19, 1861.

Have you an Agricultural Society in Burke, & if so who is the President? There are books and seeds at the Patent Office for distribution to Societies but I do not know the name of the Presidents thereof in my district. Please write me as to your own county, and also Caldwell & McDowell if you know whether or not they have societies.

I guess you see all of our doings in the papers. My hopes and fears alternate in almost equal proportions. The Report of the Committee of Thirty three[322] gives us very little, Crittendens Compromise[323] the fairest and best of any, were defeated in the Senate[324] and then reconsidered.[325] There is a faint hope of their passage, they gain popularity every day.

The general opinion seems to be that nothing practical or definite will be done until all the Gulf States are out — there will then be a temporary lull in the storm and if the North are going to do anything they will do it then. In the mean time we stand up for the Union as square as possible.
Morganton.
[A. L. S. George T. Walton Papers, Southern Historical Collection, Chapel Hill.]

---

[321] Thomas George Walton (1815-1905), of Morganton. With W. M. Walton he operated the Walton House as a hotel in Morganton. During the war he was captain of company F in the Forty-first North Carolina Regiment, but resigned upon its reorganization, May 3, 1862. Afterwards he was state agent in Burke County for the distribution of the salt supply and later became colonel of the Eighth Regiment of Home Guards where, in a skirmish with Stoneman's cavalry in 1865 he was furnished a cannon by Governor Vance. George T. Walton Papers, Southern Historical Collection, University of North Carolina, Chapel Hill, N. C. (cited hereafter as Walton Papers); Moore, N. C. Roster, III, 159; Clark, N. C. Regts., V. 635-636.

[322] See p. 76, 286n.

[323] See p. 76, 288n.

[324] On January 16, 1861, by a vote of 25 to 23, the Senate adopted a substitute resolution which prevented the main Crittenden resolutions from being brought to a vote on the Senate floor. On this resolution six Southern Democrats declined to vote, and every affirmative vote was Republican. Cong. Globe, 36 Congress, 2 session, part 1 (January 16, 1861), p. 409.

[325] The motion to reconsider was made by Senator Cameron of Pennsylvania and was adopted on January 18, 1861, by a vote of 27 to 24, Cameron voting against his own motion. Cong. Globe, 36 Congress, 2 session, part 1 (January 18, 1861), p. 443.

From Robert B. Vance[326]

Asheville Jany 21/61

This leaves us pretty well except Hattie,[327] who is still in bed, but recovering slowly. Your folks are doing well enough. The great Municipal election came off to day, as follows

I. B. Sawyer[328]   Mayor

R. B. Vance

G. W. Shackelford [329]

W D Rankin[330]   Aldermen

P. W. Roberts[331]

Dʳ J. F. E. Hardy[332]

Your bro is at last in Office!

Byers publishes your votes on the Maj Anderson subject[333] & your Letter to Folk[334] this week. You would be astonished at the activity of *one horse politicians* here in circulating that you voted to coerce SᵒCᵃ. I don't regard it of course, only I hate to see people lie so.

---

[326] See p. 2, 6n.

[327] See p. 16, 81n.

[328] Isaac B. Sawyer (1810-1880), magistrate of the county court and first mayor of Asheville. He was born in Macon County, now Swain, and was an engineer who was several times elected mayor. *Census,* Buncombe County, 1860; Arthur, *Western North Carolina,* p. 152; Sondley, *Buncombe County,* II, 663.

[329] George W. Shackleford (1818-1881), a brickmason, was a native of Tennessee. *Census,* Buncombe County, 1860.

[330] William David Rankin (1804-1879), also a native of Tennessee, was a partner of R. W. Pulliam in the mercantile business in Asheville. They brought their goods by wagon from Charleston and Baltimore. Sondley, *Buncombe County,* II, 710; Baird, "Historical Sketches."

[331] Philetus W. Roberts (1825-1862), formerly clerk of court and an able lawyer of Asheville. He was born in Macon County, attended Emory & Henry College and, when the war came, became first lieutenant in Vance's company. He was later colonel of the Fourteenth North Carolina Regiment and died of fever in Richmond on July 5, 1862. See letter of A. W. Cummings in *Asheville News,* July 24, 1862, and the editorial of the same paper in the issue of July 17, 1862; Moore, *N. C. Roster,* I, 527; Baird, "Historical Sketches."

[332] See p. 20, 95n.

[333] Major Robert Anderson (1805-1871), of Kentucky, who was in command of the forts in Charleston Harbor, S. C. On December 26, 1860 without orders, he shifted the garrison from Fort Moultrie to Fort Sumter, which, rising from a shoal in the harbor, could not be approached by land. On January 7, 1861 Representative Adrain, Democrat of New Jersey introduced into the House the following resolution: "*Resolved,* That we fully approve of the bold and patriotic act of Major Anderson in withdrawing from Fort Moultrie to Fort Sumter, and of the determination of the President to maintain that fearless officer in his present position; and that we will support the President in all constitutional measures to enforce the laws and preserve the Union." On the same day, the rules being suspended, the resolution was brought to a vote and was adopted 124 to 56. Vance voted against the resolution. By many persons this vote of the House was taken to mean a determination to coerce South Carolina. *Cong. Globe,* 36 Congress, 2 session, part 1 (January 7, 1861), pp. 280-281.

[334] See letter on p. 81 and 298n.

I must close as it is late & the mail will soon lock up. No letter from you since 12th Rumored that Scott has Killed Toombs.[335]
Love to all
Washington.
[on reverse]
Col Howell[336] left to day Thankful & improving.
[A. L. S. Z. B. Vance Papers, State Department of Archives and History, Raleigh.]

From J. C. L. Gudger[337]

Hominy Creek[338] Jan 27th 1861

It seems that Pres. Buchanan's P. M[s]. in and around this part of North Carolina are determined to keep the people in the dark as regards the state of affairs at present existing at Washington & elsewhere for we can get no papers at all till they are two or three weeks old &c &c.

I will therefore trespass so far on your kindness & time as to request you to give me a statement of affairs generally as regards the present existing state of things at Washington &c.

Now we hear any amount of reports but the words are scarcely uttered until we hear them contradicted. I would therefore be glad to get something reliable & I know of no one better prepared to give me such information than yourself.

Crittendens propositions[339] were endorsed by us at a meeting of our citizens during Court week; but I am sorry to learn they were voted down in the House and that *Six* Southern members refused to vote on them[340]
I learn subsequently that they are to be reconsidered and that they may possibly be passed. I hope to God that some measures of compromise will be adopted.

---

[335] Winfield Scott (1786-1866), lieutenant general and general-in-chief of the army, who had just moved his headquarters from New York to Washington. Robert Toombs (1810-1885), formerly Senator from Georgia, had made his farewell speech to the Senate on January 7, 1861, and had departed to work for secession in the Georgia convention. The rumor was, of course, a false one.

[336] George W. Howell, of Buncombe County, who was later captain of company I in the Twenty-fifth North Carolina Regiment, of which Thomas L. Clingman was colonel. Moore, *N. C. Roster*, II, 354.

[337] James Cassius Lowery Gudger (1837-1913), son of Samuel Bell Gudger and Elizabeth Siler Lowery, was born in Buncombe County, educated at Reems Creek High School, later known as Weaverville College, and was admitted to the bar in 1860. After the war he moved to Waynesville, in Haywood County. During the war, in which he served throughout, he was first lieutenant and adjutant of the Twenty-fifth North Carolina Regiment. After the war he became judge of the superior court, 1879-1886, and for many years thereafter held a position in the United States Treasury. Connor, *N. C. Manual*, p. 450; Arthur, *Western North Carolina*, p. 397; Clark, *N. C. Regts.*, II, 292, 301; Moore, *N. C. Roster*, II, 354 which lists him as second sergeant of company I.

[338] Hominy Creek was south west of Asheville, on the west side of the French Broad River.

[339] See p. 76, 288n.

[340] See p. 88, 324n and 325n. The vote was not in the House but in the Senate.

We learn also that Sen. Tooms & Gen Scott have a duel [341] and by first report Scott was killed by Second that Scott killed Tooms I mention this to show you the number of reports afloat for mind you I've had no papers for eight or ten days & I find contradictory reports in them also.

I would mention something of the state of affairs here if I thought I could make it interesting & that you had been written by others more able to post you than myself

However I would say that in the counties at which I attended the courts I think the *people,* mind you the *people* are in favor of the Union for a while yet & in Madison I found some in favor of the Union any how, under all circumstances. I am confident that if our Legislature has given us a convention that your district will almost unamimously vote against immediate secession

I hope Mr. Vance that you will do the best that can be done for us and that you will exhaust all Measures of compromise before you cease fighting in behalf of the Constitution, the Union, & the Enforcement of the laws.

I would remark here that some of the *great unterified* (!!!) are circulating the report that *Zeb Vance is a dead dog, he's gone in for coercian,*[342] while one half of the *cussed devils* don't Know what coercian means.

But pardon this long letter & I will not weary your patience further. Please remember me in distributing documents & if you have the leisure I shall be much obliged for any information you may be pleased to give me. I am
Washington.
[A. L. S. Z. B. Vance Papers, State Department of Archives and History, Raleigh.]

From S. O. Deaver[343]

[Ivy P.O] [344]
January the 28th 1861

I have been Requested by Several to write to you asking you to give your Views in a few words Concerning this Secession Movement Madison County is three fourths Union but Still they will have a good Union of it Yancey is Union by More than Three

---

[341] See p. 90, 335n.

[342] This is doubtless a reference to the rumor which is explained on p. 89, 333n.

[343] Samuel O. Deaver, of Madison County, who was born in 1834, lived in Madison County until the war, when he helped operate the firm of Gaines, Deaver & Company, manufacturers of leather, in Asheville. An extensive account of the Deaver family, which is very numerous in western North Carolina, may be found in W. C. Allen, *The Annals of Haywood County North Carolina: Historical, Sociological, Biographical, and Genealogical* (n. p., 1935), pp. 371-376 (cited hereafter as Allen, *Annals of Haywood*); see also Raleigh *North Carolina Standard*, January 25, 1862, quoting *Asheville News.*

[344] Ivy River flowed west into the French Broad River in Madison County, just north of the Buncombe County line.

fourths I Saw a Man from Cherokee to day and he Says they are all Union or about it in his country the people here are all waiting to Know what is right it has Split Whig & Democracy all into h___l in this County Edney[345] Coleman[346] & N W Woodfin[347] are all in the field for Secession but Woodfin is the only man that is doing any thing they threatened to tar and Feather Coleman at Ivy the other day, we have a hot time. They hung you in Burnsville Court week it tuck place after night But the Man cannot be found Sum large Sums of Money were offered to any Man who own it, but oh! *allas!!* and wo be unto him one man (*M Broyles*) [348] has been suspicioned but it is not certain he denies it write Zeb to me at Ivy P O and give me Sum news from yourself

Excuse Errors

Washington.

yours Truly for the union

[A. L. S. Z. B. Vance Papers, State Department of Archives and History, Raleigh.]

---

[345] Bayles M. Edney was a lawyer, known best for his sparkling wit, his forthright manner, and his passion before juries. He was, likewise, a man of fine physique and commanding appearance, who always kept his whiskers trimmed "*a la mode.*" He was a general in the militia and had represented the Buncombe district in the State Senate in 1858. *Asheville News,* April 6, 1854; Arthur, *Western North Carolina,* pp. 390-391; Connor, *N. C. Manual,* p. 517.

[346] See p. 19, 91n.

[347] Nicholas Washington Woodfin (1819-1875), a son of John Woodfin and Mary (Grady) Woodfin, was born in the Mills River section of Buncombe County (now Henderson), attended the neighborhood schools when they were in session, and read law with Michael Francis and David L. Swain. He was admitted to the bar in 1831 and, about that time, moved to Asheville. In 1840 he married Eliza Grace McDowell, a daughter of Captain Charles McDowell of Quaker Meadows, in whose home Vance's wife had been reared. He attained great distinction at the bar in western North Carolina, and also as a farmer and an exponent of intensive agriculture. In politics he was a Whig until 1860, representing the Buncombe and Henderson district in the State Senate for ten years (1844-1855). He was a member of the Convention of 1861, by which time he had become an advocate of secession, and was named by that body as chairman of a committee on salt supply for the state, and acted during the war as agent for North Carolina at the salt works at Saltville, Va. He was defeated for membership in the Confederate Congress by Allen T. Davidson. Before the war Woodfin accumulated a considerable fortune, but he lost most of it during and after that conflict. Samuel A'Court Ashe, "Nicholas Washington Woodfin," Ashe, *Biog. Hist. of N. C.,* II, 481-486; McCormick, *Personnel,* p. 90. Both of these accounts claim that Woodfin was opposed to seccession until Lincoln's call for troops on April 15, 1861. This is an error, as he was certainly favorable to secession as early as December 22, 1860, when he addressed a public meeting in Asheville and spoke in favor of resolutions which supported the action of South Carolina in having seceded two days earlier. In the February 28, 1861, election for delegates to a state convention to consider the question of secession Woodfin was the secession candidate in Buncombe and was defeated by Montraville Patton by the decisive margin of several hundred votes. After the election Vance's law partner wrote: "Nick is angry with everyone who did not vote for him, indeed he and I do not speak, and I have heard of some who he insulted when they offered to speak to him." William Caleb Brown to John Evans Brown, March 22, 1861, Brown Papers. The newspapers listed him as an original secessionist, and so does Battle. See Raleigh *North Carolina Standard,* January 5, March 13, 1861; Battle, *Legislation,* p. 126.

[348] Possibly J. M. Broyles, who was postmaster at Burnsville. *U. S. Official Register 1859,* p. 260.

From J. P. Eller[349]

Ivy Bend Madison Co N C
Jan 28 1861

Dear Sir it is with *pleasure* & Regret that I take this opertunity to Drop you A line in the first place I Am glad to let you no that the majority of the people in this country is for the union All the Countys West of the Blue Ridge is union By a large majority & my opinion is the state is from the Part information that I can gether it is set Down that North Carolina is ceessian But if it is left to the people to say they will say Difernt Demagogs is a trying to so the seed of Discord thruout this Country But they have faild As yet Secondly I Regret that I'm under the necessity of inquiring of you if nothing can Bedone to settle this Momentus question that is convulsing the Country from center to circumference and threating our pece & hapiness Do all you can if Acomplished it you Will do a Greate Work As A National Body if not All is lost if Divison is the Result And the South has to set up for itself this people is As true to the south As Any people that ever trod the Soil But let it Be The Last Resort I would like to hear from you ocasionaly Rite soon the people Wants to hear your opinion As to the Probability of compromise if not the chanc of Arms for protection this Country is in A Defencless Condition Provided War is the Result I want to no Who is to Blame the south or the North It is Argued in the Country By the leaders that it is the North Country by the for the Dificulty But I Am of A Deferent opinion I Believe that Boath Sections is to Blame your enemies in the County is trying to make Capital of your Being A union man I hope you Are At Burnsville last Weeke throu the influence General Edney[350] & others they hung you in Efigy & if the thing had Been got Hold of rite thir lives Would A paid the forfeit I Dont rite those things to Agetate you But to let you no What are Going on here keepe it rite on & take care of our interest & We Will take Care of you Pardon the length of my leter I must come to a close By subscribing my Self your Friend
Washington.

[A. L. S. Z. B. Vance Papers, State Department of Archives and History, Raleigh.]

[349] Joseph P. Eller (1820-1892), who was born on Flat Creek in Buncombe County, married Susan Anderson (1828-1880), and became a Baptist minister. He was a strong Union advocate and in a public meeting held in Madison County on January 24, 1861 was a member of a committee which drafted very strong anti-secession resolutions. Raleigh *North Carolina Standard*, February 14, 1861; McLean, "Notebooks."
[350] See p. 92, 345n.

From Wm. L. Love[351]

Webster No. Ca.

Feb. 1st 1861

Menny of your former political supporters are secessionists. I still stand firm for the Union and find many Dems as I am— But the leaders of Dem. in Jackson— such as Fisher[352] Dills[353] Allison[354] & c are Dimunionists. "Thad" [355] is sound.

On the 16th or 17 ult sen. Simmons[356] made a Speech in the U. S. Senate in which he said the *first* "Liberty Law" was enacted by a Dem. Legislature signed by a Dem. Gov.[357] &c. This is a

---

[351] William L. Love was born in 1830 and had become a prominent farmer and union leader in Jackson County. At a public meeting in Webster, the county seat, on December 22, 1860, Love debated L. C. Bryan, Love being for union and Bryan for disunion for existing causes. "The discussion continued between them until nearly sundown, when the resolutions were tabled, and when Gabriel sounds his trump he will find them 'thar." Love was instrumental in Vance's defeat for United States Senator in 1872. Raleigh *Daily Sentinel,* December 20, 1872; Raleigh *North Carolina Standard,* January 8, 1861; McLean, "Notebooks."

[352] Allen Fisher (1812-1869), who had succeeded James R. Love in the House of Commons from Jackson County when Love resigned in 1860. Connor, *N. C. Manual,* p. 665.

[353] John Ramsay Dills (1830-1875), member of the House of Commons from Jackson County in 1856. During the war he became captain in the Sixty-second Regiment of North Carolina volunteers and was captured and imprisoned on Johnson's Island until the close of the war. Clark, *N. C. Regts.,* III, 516, IV, 706; Moore, *N. C. Roster,* III, 733; Connor, *N. C. Manual,* p. 665.

[354] John B. Allison (1807-1886), of Jackson County.

[355] Thaddeus Dillard Bryson (1829-1890), a prominent political leader of Jackson and Swain counties. He represented Jackson County in the House of Commons in 1854, 1858, 1865, and 1866 and in the House of Representatives in 1870. He also represented Swain County in the House of Representatives from 1872 to 1881. In 1854 he became colonel of the Jackson militia, and during the war was captain in the Twenty-fifth North Carolina Regiment. Connor, *N. C. Manual,* pp. 665-666, 817-818; Arthur, *Western North Carolina,* p. 210; Moore, *N. C. Roster,* II, 328.

[356] James Fowler Simmons (1795-1864), Republican Senator from Rhode Island. He was a manufacturer; a member of the State House of Representatives, 1828-1841; United States Senator, 1841-1847 and 1857-1862, when he resigned. *Biog. Dir. of Am. Cong.,* p. 1525.

[357] Senator Simmons' speech was delivered on January 6, 1861. In the course of his remarks he attempted to defend the Republican party from the charge that it was responsible for the sectional crisis and said, among other things, that "The first personal liberty bill . . . was passed when both houses of the Massachusetts Legislature were Democratic, with a Democratic Governor approving of it; and the negro equality law passed the same month. . . . And that same Governor who signed this personal liberty bill and the negro equality bill, was sent into the Senate for the best office in New England, nominated by Mr. Polk, and every Democratic Senator voted for him . . ." *Cong. Globe,* 36 Congress, 2 session, part 1 (January 16, 1861), p. 407. The Massachusetts liberty law, entitled "An Act further to Protect Personal Liberty Approved by Governor . . ." of March 25, 1843, is printed in *The Norfolk Democrat* (Dedham, Massachusetts), April 21, 1843. As to the complexion of the legislature there is some question. The Democrats were in power except in the house, where they had the speaker and the standing committees against them. In the house of 357 members there were 177 Democrats, 175 Whigs and five Liberty party members, who held the balance of power. But during the last week of the session, some "illegal" members having been eliminated, and with one or two members deserting party, the bill was passed. *The Norfolk Democrat* (Dedham, Massachusetts), March 31, 1843; Arthur B. Darling, *Political Changes in Massachusetts 1824-1848. A Study of Liberal Movements in Politics* (New Haven, 1925), chaps. V, VI. For personal liberty laws in the north see above p. 85, 308n.

sweet *morsel*. I *relish* any thing that makes Dem. *look damnable.* Who was this Dem. Gov.[358] What appointments did "Polk" give him? I would very much like to know what was the political character of "The" several Leg's that passed these Laws— who was then Gov &c. that is if they were Dem.
Let me hear from you—
Washington.
[A. L. S. Z. B. Vance Papers, State Department of Archives and History, Raleigh.]

From C. C. Jones.[359]

Lenoir   Feby 4th 1861
I hope you will pardon the liberty I take in addressing you the following lines and if convenient let me hear from you in response at an early day —.
You are aware that we have a convention in N. C. and it would aid our Cause (The Union) if indications of a settlement of this unfortunate difficulty are of such a character as we can claim them with Confidence & promise the masses of the people that this question is really to be settled on the Crittenden proposition or plan— he is a great favorite with all the Union men in N. C. Will the Free States accept them? If so in this great emergency why do they hesitate longer? Will they wickedly persist in straining the Conservative element, until its cords are snap't asunder — I hope not! You know the nature of the southern people is impulsive and sectional feeling contagious! North Carolina and especially Caldwell and Wilkes are deeply attached to the Union, as well as the larger section of the State I hope — as for my self I cant contemplate a disolution of this government without horror and indignation — and it is deeply humiliating (or ought to be) to any citizen of a Border State if they will allow these arrogant Cotton Obligarchys South of them to dragoon them into their service After all the Action of Virginia[360] will decide the fate of North Carolina if she (Va) goes out of the Union I fear N C must follow her very soon, therefore we look to the course and action of Va

---

[358] The Governor was Marcus Morton (1784-1864), lawyer and jurist, who for sixteen successive years (1828-1843) was the Democratic nominee for governor of Massachusetts. Only twice was he successful, in 1839 and in 1842. In 1845 President James K. Polk appointed him collector of the port of Boston, which position he held for four years. Scott H. Paradise, "Marcus Morton," *Dict. of Am. Biog.* XIII, 259-260.

[359] Calvin C. Jones (1813-1896), of Caldwell County, was a political leader who was a candidate for the House of Commons in 1862, but withdrew in favor of S. P. Dula before the election. Jones was later a member of the Convention of 1868. Raleigh *North Carolina Standard,* July 26, 1862; Connor, *N. C. Manual,* p. 865.

[360] The election of delegates to the Virginia convention occurred on February 4, 1861, the day this letter was written. The Virginia convention convened on February 14, with a clear majority for Union for existing causes. As late as April 4, 1861 a motion to draw up an ordinance of secession was voted down, 88 to 45.

with great interest, and as far as I am Concerned with serious misgivings — much very much depends upon the Republicans at this moment — if they are fatally bent upon mischief it must come and that soon.

Excuse his hastily written Scroll and accept the best wishes of your Cincere friend
Washington.
[A. L. S. Z. B. Vance Papers, State Department of Archives and History, Raleigh.]

From J. W. McElroy[361]

Jacks Creek Yancy Co N Ca
February 5th 1861

Yours of the 23d ult from Washington was Received last mail and I was pleased to hear from you as it was the first thing I had Received from you Since you Returned there last fall. As to my papers I would like to continue it until I see how Maters will terminate Relative to this Union, I see we are to have a Convention the Election to come off 21st Instant.[362] I do not know who will Run as a candidate in this County but I suppose. Pearson,[363] Broyles[364] or old Sam Byrd,[365] as I understand thay all want to be Elected to that body. I Suppose a disunion Man will be Elected.[366] I have no time my self to attend any Maters of the kind I am engaged in an other Mans business and my whole time and attention is Required in his business. If you Renew my Subscription for the Intellengencer[367] I will pay you the Money on your Return and also for last year.

Give my best Respects to your Lady & Children.
Washington.
[A. L. S. Z. B. Vance Papers, State Department of Archives and History, Raleigh.]

---

[361] John W. McElroy (1808-1886), a prominent merchant and farmer of Yancey County, was the father-in-law of Vance's brother, Robert B. Vance, and colonel of the Yancey Militia. In September of 1863 he was appointed a brigadier general in the Home Guards by Governor Vance. Asheville Spectator, May 11, 1853, Asheville News, November 8, 1855; Clark, N. C. Regts., IV, 651, V, 7.

[362] The election of delegates was scheduled for February 28, 1861.

[363] Probably Isaac A. Pearson.

[364] Probably J. M. Broyles, postmaster at Burnsville.

[365] Samuel D. Byrd, of Burnsville, who became lieutenant colonel of the Seventy-second Battalion of Home Guards in 1863. Clark, N. C. Regts., IV, 650.

[366] The delegate from Yancey to the Convention of 1861 was Milton Pinkney Penland (1813-1880), a merchant who usually refused political preferment, who was known as a conservative man in politics, but who was a pronounced secessionist after the election of Lincoln. McCormick, Personnel, pp. 66-67. In the election of February 28, 1861, the people voted down a convention, and Penland was elected later to represent Yancey County.

[367] See p. 32, 137b.

From W. W. Lenoir[368]

Lenoir N. C. Feb. 5th 1860 [1861]

Please excuse me for troubling you again with a letter on politics. I shall write in great haste, as the mail will soon be closed. Events are hurrying to their consummation with fearful rapidity. It has become apparent that the border Slave States, including North Carolina and Tennessee, are willing to accept the Crittenden Compromise.[369] It has also become apparent that the North are willing to grant it, that a little delay is all that is needed in order that the awakened people of the North may oust the political leaders who have so grossly deceived them, and give them sanction at the ballot box to that just and honorable compromise. But the country has scarcely time to begin to breathe easily in the dawn of returning peaceful counsels, when hope is again obscured by another dark cloud rising in the seceded States. In the consummation of this compromise which would keep the border Slave States in the Union, the seceded States see the commerce of St. Louis and Louisville and Memphis, and Nashville Slipping from their grasp to enrich the seaports of the Union. If they can make the sea ports of the Union foreign ports to those four great western cities, they will have secured for their own ports a prize of inestimable value. For this brilliant prize they are willing to play the perilous game of war. They know that war will defeat the compromise. They know that if they can inaugurate a state of War with the North that the border Slave States cannot stand on the side of the North in that war. Of this the gallant devotion of those states to southern interests gives confirmation strong as holy writ. War then *must* separate us from the north. The Seceeding States know and safely calculate upon that. What will we do when we have separated from the north? The seceded States have many chances in their favor, that we will join them, and gallantly take the brunt of the war upon ourselves. In the madness of the hour we will be almost compelled to do so. Yet there is a wiser course for us, if some skillful pilot could sieze the helm, and guide us into it. Why should we take upon us a war waged in defiance of our wishes, our counsels our policy and our interests, to forward the interests and selfish ambition of the states which wage it, and which in doing so treat us not as equals, but as dependants? I believe that our best interests would be more truly consulted, if, in the event of war we withdrew from the north and constituted ourselves an armed neutrality. I believe that if we did so the great northwest which is so closely

---

[368] See pp. 74-75, 282n. Lenoir had just returned, in the fall of 1860, from a trip throughout the middle west, and his letters reflect his realization of the importance of the commerce of that section to the South. Lenoir Papers, *passim*.

[369] See p. 76, 288n.

allied to the border slave states in every great interest, would join them in the attitude of neutrality instead of seeking to fight them across the Ohio. The fight would thus whittle down to a broil between New England and South Carolina and such of their excited neighbors as were mad enough to join in with them. It would then soon become apparent to those engaged in the fight that it was not a respectable fight, and they would get ashamed and quit. If the war is once commenced I believe that the course I have indicated would be the wisest way to smother it out, and for the best treatment of it that could be adopted by the border slave states. I have only a faint hope that such a plan could be carried in to effect.

The war might be entirely prevented and the secessionists thoroughly whipped, by the immediate withdrawal of the troops from the Southern forts. I have but little hope that the administration can be induced to take this course; yet how obvious it is that it would achieve for it a brilliant and bloodless victory! Perhaps if the compromise convention now in session in Washington[370] would urge this course upon the President he might be induced to adopt it. Is it not worth their attention? Perhaps if that convention finds that there is no way to prevent the seceded states from playing their last great card of War, they will do well to devise a plan of trumping that card with the armed neutrality of the border states. Perhaps the suggestions which I have thrown out so hurriedly have occurred to a thousand minds and been thrown out from a thousand other pens and tongues, but you will doubtless be pleased to hear the view of one of your constituents though they may present nothing new. If you think it worth while, please show this to Governor Morehead,[371] if the convention of which he is a member is still in session. I will be pleased to hear from you, if you find a spare moment to devote to me.
Washington.

[A. L. S. Z. B. Vance Papers, State Department of Archives and History, Raleigh.]

---

[370] The Peace Convention, a conference of twenty-one states which assembled in Washington on February 4, 1861, at the call of the Virginia Legislature. On February 27 it presented a plan of conciliation to Congress, but it received negligible support in the Senate, and all that the convention accomplished was to demonstrate the strength of Unionism in the upper south. *Cong. Globe*, 36 Congress, 2 session, part 2 (March 2, 1861), pp. 1254-1255.

[371] John Motley Morehead (1796-1866), a member of the Peace Convention from North Carolina. His political career had been a distinguished one. He was a member of the House of Commons from Guilford County in 1826 and 1827; a member of the State Senate from Guilford in 1860; a member of the Convention of 1835; Governor of North Carolina, 1841-1845; father and first president of the North Carolina Railroad; and leader of the Whig party. Connor, *N. C. Manual*, pp. 418, 633-634; C. Alphonso Smith, "John Motley Morehead," Ashe, *Biog. Hist. of N. C.*, II, 250-258.

From W. N. H. Smith [372]

Murfreesboro N.C.

April 26 1861

I write a line to give you some idea of the conditions of public opinion in this part of the State, looking for a reciprocation from you. The Union feeling *was strong* up to the recent proclamation.[373] This War Manifesto Extinguishes it, and resistance is now on every mans lips and throbs in every bosom. We regard the government as over-thrown—a military usurpation in its place—and a sense of common danger unites us in a common cause. I learn that Dr Speed [374] and other Union men are now such no longer. What think you of our future? The North is mustering its legions — to intimidate, and we see with pain the defection of professed friends — but our security is to be found in the Concentration of our Entire strength to repel the first invasion — There will be I suppose, no Cong. Elections in the States.[375] Will you go to the Convention? [376] Living near the Scene of

---

[372] William Nathan Harrell Smith (1812-1889), of Hertford County. He graduated from Yale College in 1834 and took his law degree at the same institution in 1836. He was a member of the House of Commons in 1840, 1858, and 1865; of the State Senate in 1848; solicitor of the first judicial circuit, 1849-1858; member of Congress (American) 1859-1861, in which he failed by only one vote to be elected speaker; member of the Confederate Congress 1861-1865, where he was the only member who served during its entire existence; in 1878 he was appointed by Governor Vance to be the Chief Justice of the Supreme Court of North Carolina, in which office he continued until his death. In politics Smith was an Old Line Union Whig and American before the war, and a Democrat after the war. He was chief counsel in the defense of Governor W. W. Holden in the impeachment trial of 1871, and was long recognized as one of the very ablest lawyers in the state. Vance once referred to Smith as his "beau ideal of a statesman." Samuel A'Court Ashe, "William Nathan Harrell Smith," Ashe, *Biog. Hist. of N. C.*, VII, 429-436; *Biog. Dir. of Am. Cong.*, p. 1544; Connor, *N. C. Manual*, pp. 446, 653, 936; Benjamin B. Winborne, *The Colonial and State Political History of Hertford County, N. C.* (Raleigh, 1906), pp. 165-166 (cited hereafter as Winborne, *Hertford County*); clippings in Walser Papers.

[373] On April 15, 1861, after the firing on Fort Sumter, President Lincoln issued a proclamation calling forth the militia to suppress "combinations . . . too powerful to be suppressed by the ordinary course of judicial proceedings," and soon afterwards launched other war measures.

[374] Dr. Rufus King Speed (1810-1897), of Pasquotank County. He was a native of Mecklenburg County, Va., a doctor, and a politician. He represented Chowan and Gates counties in the State Senate in 1838 and 1840, and the first senatorial district in 1866 and 1870. In 1860 he was an elector on the Bell and Everett ticket, and was chosen a delegate to the February, 1861 convention, which was not voted. He was known as a strong union man until Lincoln's proclamation. In 1862 he was a candidate for the State Senate from Perquimans and Pasquotank counties. Raleigh *North Carolina Standard*, July 30, 1862; Connor, *N. C. Manual*, pp. 560, 748; McCormick, *Personnel*, p. 77.

[375] Delegates to represent the state in the Provisional Congress of the Confederacy were elected by members of the convention on June 18, 1861. Party lines between former unionists and original secessionists were sharply drawn. Battle, *Legislation*, p. 126.

[376] A convention had been voted down by the people in the February 28, 1861 election, but it was now, after the events of mid-April, assumed that such a meeting was necessary. Governor Ellis had issued a proclamation calling the legislature into special session, but it was May 1, before a convention was actually authorized in North Carolina.

active operations, we are in a feverish Excitement — kept so by constant intelligence — In haste but yours truly
Asheville.
[A. L. S. Z. B. Vance Papers, State Department of Archives and History, Raleigh.]

To Mrs. Z. B. Vance[377]

In Camp[378] Near
Statesville May 18th [1861]

We start in the morning for Weldon— and I sit down tonight tired & chilled with the night dew to write you my last letter from the Camp. I am still quite well but in rather low spirits at the way things are managed at Raleigh.[379] I see a pretty determined purpose there to carry on affairs under a strict party regimen; none but Locos[380] and Secessionists will be appointed to the Offices: the old Union Men will be made to take back Seats and do most of the hard work and make bricks without straw. So be it. I am prepared to serve my country in spite of the small men who control its destinies— But many persons are disgusted. Companies are disbanding and I fear the result unless a different policy is adopted.— My uniform has been Completed and the men look splendid in it— We receive the praise every where; many persons

[377] See p. 16, 81n.
[378] Upon Lincoln's call for troops, April 15, 1861, Vance and most of the other North Carolina Unionists were persuaded that secession was assured. Accordingly, they cooperated in measures to prepare for war and, on May 4, 1861, in Asheville, Vance raised and organized a military company called "The Rough and Ready Guards," of which he became the captain. It was composed almost entirely of men from Buncombe County, and was the second company raised from that county.
[379] On April 17, 1861, a proclamation by Governor Ellis had called for an extra session of the legislature to meet on May 1. Since this was the legislature chosen in 1860 it was dominated by Democrats, most of whom had been secessionists before Lincoln's call for troops. The special session lasted from May 1 to May 13 and was concerned principally with preparations for war. Among other measures, it authorized the governor to enlist and organize ten regiments of state troops for the duration of the war, and 50,000 volunteers for twelve months. All officers of the state troops, and general officers of the twelve-months volunteers, were to be appointed by the governor; but the volunteers were to elect their own company officers, by whom the field officers were to be chosen. Because Governor Ellis' health was precarious, the legislature authorized him to appoint a military board to advise him with regard to military appointments. This board was dominated by Democrats, and the numerous appointments that became necessary under these acts were the occasions of many criticisms from men of the old Whig party, such as Vance, who charged partisanship in the appointments. Ashe, *History of N. C.,* II, 603.
[380] "Locos" was a familiar label designating, originally, a radical faction of the Democratic party in New York allied with Jacksonian Democracy. When, in 1835, this faction wrested control of the city caucus from the conservatives by producing candles and lighting them with loco foco matches and continuing the meeting, when their opponents turned off the gas, newspapers derisively called them the "Loco Foco Party." From about 1837 until the war the term was applied to the National Democratic party by its opponents, such as Vance.

pronounce us the finest company in the state— The people of
Statesville have been Kind to us beyond description— My camp
chest has been filled with cake & all sorts of good things ever since
I came, and such piles of flowers, you never saw as grace my tent.
I have a trunk full of bouquets to send home to you when I get
an opportunity From the appearance of things I guess we will
be sent on to Norfolk very soon — an attack is expected there
momentarily and the sooner the better as we would be enabled
to get away from them before the sickly months of August and
September. Do not feel uneasy about our stay at Weldon — it is
not at all a sickly place till later in the season and then not much
so. I will write from every point.

I did not get your letter today and was greatly disappointed —
I am always so anxious to hear from you my dear wife and children — you seem more dear to me than ever since I have been
called to peril my life for your defense May God protect us all
and restore us to peace and happiness once more I saw Mr
Woodfin,[381] Shipp[982] and various others going on to Raleigh
today— they brought me no special news from home however —
The election did not surprise me. I had a hope that the Convention
would be of such a Complexion[383] as to change the face of affairs,
but I suppose not. Let it go.

I am sitting in my tent now listening to the whip-poor-wills —
I guess you and the dear babies are all asleep — I trust in God
you may ever be allowed to sleep in peace — that no foe shall ever
come near our sacred precincts — I think so much of you and all
the dear pleasures & sweets of home — our children, our garden,
our flowers, &c. And my dear old Mother,[384] how does she do?
And Sister Ann,[385] Laura,[386] Hannah[387] and all the rest — God
bless and preserve them all. Tell them to write me when ever they

---

[381] See p. 92, 347n. Woodfin had been chosen Buncombe County's delegate to
the convention in the election held on May 13. He was on his way to Raleigh for
the meeting of the convention on May 20.

[982] See p. 71, 268n. Shipp was delegate-elect from Henderson County to the convention and, with Woodfin, was on his way to Raleigh.

[383] It is difficult to determine just what Vance means by this reference. There
was no issue in the campaign for delegates to the convention; all were agreed
upon the necessity of separation and all were conscious that separation meant
war. Perhaps there was a question as to whether separation should be accomplished
by secession or revolution, and whether North Carolina would join the Confederacy, but these matters could hardly have caused this comment two days
before the convention met and was organized. Actually, former Whigs and Unionists
were in the majority in the convention, though the original secessionists succeeded in organizing it and in electing the president. Evidently the people were
determined to accomplish separation through the agency of Union men. Joseph
Gregoire de Roulhac Hamilton in Daniel Harvey Hill *Bethel to Sharpsburg,* 2 vols.
(Raleigh, 1926), I, 39 (cited hereafter as Hill, *Bethel to Sharpsburg.*).

[384] See p. 1, 1n.

[385] See p. 6, 30n.

[386] See p. 66, 243n.

[387] See p. 6, 32n.

can. It is so late I must go to my *straw*. I need several things and when I get to a camp where I am likely to stay any time I will send you to get them made & you can send them to me by Express. No more tonight. Kiss my dear *War like* boys & accept assurance of my undying love and affection —
[Asheville]
[A. L. S. Z. B. Vance Papers, State Department of Archives and History, Raleigh.]

From Robert B. Vance[388]

Asheville N°Ca, May 28th 1861
I wrote you Sunday to Weldon & directed Hattie's[389] letter there also. If you wish those letters you can direct PM at Weldon to return them to Raleigh. We did not Know that you were to remain in Raleigh any length of time. But now we hear thro' Dr Hilliard [390] that you, Love[391] Peek,[392] Shipp[393] & McElroy[394] await

---

[388] See p. 2, 6n.

[389] See p. 16, 81n.

[390] William Lewis Hilliard (1823-1890), a physician of Asheville. He was born in Hall County, Ga., grew up in Spartanburg, S. C., studied medicine in Asheville under Dr. Thomas C. Lester, and graduated from Philadelphia Medical College in 1850. He then settled in Asheville, where he was a doctor and druggist for forty years, and where he came to be known as the perfect type of family physician. In politics he was an ardent Democrat and opponent of Vance: in the fifties he was a Clingman lieutenant and was postmaster in Asheville; in 1860 he was an original secessionist and was elected a member of the Council of State. On July 16, 1861, he was commissioned as surgeon in the Ninth North Carolina Regiment (cavalry). He took politics seriously: in 1855 he fought a duel with Vance's friend, John D. Hyman, who had charged in the *Asheville Spectator* that the mail service under Hilliard's direction was not as efficient as it had been under Whig control. Connor, *N. C. Manual*, p. 439; Arthur, *Western North Carolina*, pp. 369-371; Tennent, "Medicine in Buncombe County," pp. 13-15.

[391] Robert Gustavus Adolphus Love (1827-1880), of Haywood County, who was prominent in political affairs, having been representative from Haywood in the House of Commons from 1848 to 1854, serving with Vance in the last term. In 1858 he became colonel of the militia in Haywood County; in May 1861, he raised a company which became company L of the Sixteenth North Carolina Regiment when it was organized on June 17 in Raleigh, and on that date Love became lieutenant colonel of the regiment. In July 1862, he was promoted to colonel of the Sixty-second North Carolina Regiment, but resigned in 1864 because of ill health. General John W. Frazer, of the Union army, charged that upon Love's resignation he became an open advocate of reunion in his home county, but there appears to be no substantiation. Clark, *N. C. Regts.*, I, 751, III, 515-516, 524-525; W. C. Allen, *Centennial of Haywood County* (Waynesville, n. d.), pp. 68-69 (cited hereafter as Allen, *Centennial of Haywood*); Connor, *N. C. Manual*, p. 647.

[392] John Peek, of Madison County, whose company became company B of the Sixteenth North Carolina Regiment. Clark, *N. C. Regts.*, I, 751; Moore, *N. C. Roster*, II, 2.

[393] See p. 71, 268n. Shipp's company of Henderson men became company I of the Sixteeenth North Carolina Regiment. Moore, *N. C. Roster*, II, 25.

[394] John S. McElroy, of Yancey County, whose company became company C of the Sixteenth North Carolina Regiment. Upon the reorganization of the regiment in April of 1862 McElroy was elected lieutenant colonel; he became colonel later in the same year, and was wounded severely at Chancellorsville in May 1863. He was universally trusted by his men and esteemed as a brave and chivalric gentleman, and

the arrival of the troops here, including the McDowell & Polk Co's[395] to form a Regiment. I suppose this is all correct. D^r H said you were urgent for the companies to go on for the purpose named. Hyman[396] & Hilliard do not agree in their statements. Hilliard says Hyman made the impression along the route that no more Volunteers would be accepted — that men must now join the State troops of N. C. or be drafted.

Hilliard says they still take them for 12 months. Who is right? [397] We learn here that Harkins[398] declined to join your company, and to day it is reported that he was *trying secretly to raise a mutiny in your camp*. Is this all so? I trust not for decency's sake, and for the honor of old Buncombe!

The Mail has come and brought your letter. There never was a baser falsehood than that Jos Randall's[399] wife has nothing to eat. She has shoes 2 or 3 dresses and plenty to eat and so with every man's wife left behind. Charge the men to believe no lie, for I am here and I say that none shall suffer. Newton Pattons[400] wife was here to day. I gave her Bacon & flour. I particularly *now* want you to send to Weldon for the letter I wrote you. That has details

---

some thought that he deserved promotion to brigadier general. After the war he represented the fortieth district in the State Senate in 1874. Clark, *N. C. Regts.*, I, 751-763, V, xii, 677; Connor, *N. C. Manual*, p. 517.

[395] The Polk County company, of which J. C. Camp was the captain, became company K of the Sixteenth North Carolina Regiment, but no company from McDowell County was in the regiment, nor was that of Vance. The regiment was first commanded by Colonel Stephen Lee, of Buncombe County. Moore, *N. C. Roster*, II, 1, 29; Sadie Smathers Patton, *Sketches of Polk County History* (Asheville, 1950), p. 48 (cited hereafter as Patton, *Sketches of Polk*).

[396] See p. 50, 181n.

[397] The confusion arose over the terms of the transfer of the North Carolina troops to the Confederacy. On May 27, 1861, Governor Ellis reported that there were 10,717 volunteers already accepted, but the legislature had provided for the possibility of 50,000 and a minimum of 20,000. At the same time the governor reported that the 10,000 state troops, enlisted for the war, had been entirely raised. On June 27, 1861, an ordinance for the transfer of North Carolina troops to the Confederacy was ratified by the convention. The ten regiments of state troops, enlisted for the war, were to be turned over by regiments, and recruitment for them to cease on August 20. Also, President Davis indicated in the agreement that he would accept 2,000 volunteers for twelve months in addition to the four twelve months regiments already in service. All other volunteers who, by August 20, were not accepted by the Confederacy, were to be discharged. Some volunteers were actually discharged because of these terms, and such terms were necessary on the part of the Confederacy as she had little with which to arm troops when they were raised. August 20 was the date set for the transfer. Battle, *Legislation*, pp. 106, 109; *Ordinances and Resolutions Passed by the State Convention of North Carolina 1861-1862* (Raleigh, 1852), pp. 37-40 (cited hereafter as *Convention Ordinances*).

[398] No soldier by the name of Harkins appears on the roster of the company when regimental organization took place in June. Harkins left the company in Raleigh. See Z. B. Vance to Mrs. Vance, June 19, 1861, Z. B. Vance Papers.

[399] Joseph Randle, a private who enlisted May 4, 1861, and was discharged in November of the same year. Moore, *N. C. Roster*, I, 530.

[400] George Newton Patton, another Buncombe County private, who enlisted with Vance on May 4, but was later discharged. Moore, *N. C. Roster*, I, 530.

in full about these matters & that before I knew of Harkins miserable conduct. He is an ass and a scoundrel and if I were you he should not disgrace my company.

I will try and write often. Wm Brown[401] will leave in a few days and I will send you the recruits.

Raleigh.

[A. L. S. Z. B. Vance Papers, State Department of Archives and History, Raleigh.]

From J. A. Reagan[402]

Reems Creek
June 9th '61

John Garrison[403] felt his inability to remain in service, & *unfortunately* left without a proper discharge. He states that he was sick when your company was sworn in, and hence he never was regularly mustered into service. He intended returning to your company this week with Dr. Neilson,[404] but is not able. My object in writing at this time is simply to state what I know in regard to John Garrison's disease. He has been laboring under *Fistula In Ano,* for some years. Under treatment it healed for a time, but exercise — walking & hard labor — causes it to return. He is now suffering from it owing to his fatigue in getting home. If there is any way for him, under the circumstances, to be honorably discharged without the labor of a trip to your company I

---

[401] See p. 54, 198n. Brown had been left in charge of the business of Vance and Brown when Vance left for the war, but he became assistant quartermaster of the Fourteenth North Carolina Regiment on September 8, 1861. This was just after Vance had left the regiment for other duty. Moore, *N. C. Roster,* I, 509.

[402] James Americus Reagan (1824-1910), a physician who was born in Tennessee and moved to Weaverville, just north of Asheville, in 1851. He was a circuit rider of the Methodist church, but he studied medicine and began its practice in 1859. He married one of Vance's cousins, Mary Ann Weaver (see above p. 10, 48n. and p. 4, 18n.), and practiced medicine in Yancey, Madison, and Buncombe counties. In 1867-1868 Dr. Reagan was vice-president of the first Buncombe County Medical Society, and was later its president. In 1884 he was appointed to the State Board of Medical Examiners. Tennent, "Medicine in Buncombe County," pp. 18-19.

[403] There is no John Garrison on the roll of the company at the time of regimental organization early in June. Moore, *N. C. Roster,* I, 527-530. He left the company at Raleigh. See Z. B. Vance to Mrs. Vance, June 19, 1861, Z. B. Vance Papers.

[404] Morgan Lines Neilson (1822-1894), a physician who was born in Tennessee, educated at Tusculum College, and came to Asheville in 1839. He spent two years in the California gold fields, four years in the army during the Civil War, and six

would much prefer it. He left, not understanding matters as he ought, and feeling that he was not able to stand the labor of a campaign. I give it as my honest opinion that John Garrison is far from being able for services. No surgeon will be willing to pass him as a healthy man, who understands his case. Respectfully [A. L. S. Zebulon B. Vance Papers, State Department of Archives and History, Raleigh.]

From A. S. Merrimon[405]

Raleigh N. C.
June 13[t]. 1861

Your letter of the 6[t] inst. was received yesterday evening on my return from the Sea-board & hence the delay of my reply.—I have been absent for a week and while my trip was not pleasant on several accounts, it was nevertheless interesting and instructive. Our coast is very much exposed and if the enemy does not come upon our soil it will be because he does not wish to do so. Ft. Macon[406] is strongly fortified and its strength will be rapidly increased. But the Fort only commands Beaufort-Harbor and the Inlet, while troops may be landed North or South of the Fort within five or six miles of it. Indeed, the enemy Might surround the Fort, unless some additional force is sent to the coast. The Fort at Beacon Island [407] is not complete by a great deal. There are four guns Mounted & others will be as soon as the Carriages can be had This fortification is far from being a strong one compared with Fort Macon. There are several points within a few

---

[405] See p. 13, 65n. Merrimon, from May 16 to August 24, 1861, held the rank of captain in the North Carolina commissary general's department. He served until just after the transfer to Confederate control was made on August 20, 1861. Moore, *N. C. Roster,* IV,14.

[406] Fort Macon controlled the harbor of Beaufort, one of the best on the North Carolina coast. The fort was situated on the eastern extremity of Bogue Banks, a narrow strip of wind-driven sand, with the ocean on one side and Bogue Sound on the other. It had been built originally by the United States government between 1826 and 1834 at an initial cost of about $350,000, and was a strong old-fashioned, case-mated structure with two tiers of guns—the one below in casemated bombproofs, the one above in barbette. In 1860 it was in very poor condition because of neglect and disuse. The exposed condition of the fort is described by Brigadier General Walter Gwynn in a letter to Governor John W. Ellis, May 27, 1861 in *The War of the Rebellion: A Compilation of the Official Records of the Union and Confederate Armies* (128 vols., Washington, 1880-1901), Ser. I, Vol. LI, Pt. II. 116-117 (cited hereafter as *O. R.,* with serial and volume numbers); Richard Schriver Barry, "Fort Macon: Its History," *North Carolina Historical Review* (1924-   ), Vol. XXVII, No. 2 (April, 1950), pp. 163-177.

[407] Beacon Island was at Ocracoke Inlet and the battery there formed a part of the coastal defense of Pamlico Sound. On May 30 Gwynn reported that "probably five guns are mounted, and in a few days twelve more will be mounted." *O. R.,* Ser. I, Vol. LI, Pt. II, 120-121.

miles south of this at which troops might land.—Ft. Hatteras[408] is not completed and will not be soon. Four guns are mounted there and others will be soon. North of this, there are several very exposed points totally unprotected. Our authorities are neglecting the coast defence most criminally. Gen'l Gwynn[409] has made a requisition for 6000 troops[401] and he declares that he must have them. Our coast is the key to our State and to Southern Virginia. Some very decided action will be taken soon touching this matter. The Six Regiment Bill [411] passed its third reading, but there is a motion pending to reconsider.[412]

---

[408] Fort Hatteras was about six miles from Cape Hatteras and about thirty miles north of the defenses at Ocracoke. Though only two guns were mounted there on May 30 Gwynn expected a total of eighteen shortly thereafter. O. R., Ser. I, Vol. LI, Pt. II, 121.

[409] Walter Gwynn (1802-1882) was a Virginian and a graduate of the United States Military Academy in the class of 1822. After he resigned from the army in 1832 he became chief engineer of several Virginia and North Carolina railroads during the next twenty-five years, including the Wilmington and Raleigh Railroad (1836-1840) and the North Carolina Railroad (1850-1856). He was also consulting engineer for various public works between 1837 and 1861. From 1836 to 1841 he served as aide-de-camp, with the rank of major, to Major General McRae of the North Carolina Militia; he was a captain in the Virginia Militia, 1842-1849, and a colonel, 1851-1853. On April 26, 1861 he was assigned to the command of the Virginia forces in and about Norfolk, with the rank of major general, which position he held until he was relieved on May 23, 1861. On May 27, he became commander of the Northern Department of the coastal defenses of the State of North Carolina, with the rank of brigadier general. This department consisted of the coastal area east of the Wilmington and Weldon Railroad between New River, in Onslow County, and the Virginia line. Gwynn made his headquarters at New Bern. North Carolina papers referred to Gwynn at the time of his appointment as an "able engineer" and "superior commander of troops," and identified him with the disunion and original secessionist group in politics. In August 1861, when the transfer of state troops to the Confederacy took place, Gwynn was relieved of his North Carolina command, as President Davis considered it necessary to appoint some native North Carolinian. But in October of 1862 he was called back to North Carolina and, as an agent of the War Department, given charge of an examination of the navigable rivers of eastern North Carolina with a view to their defense against naval and land attack. Gwynn died in Baltimore in 1882. George W. Cullum *Biographical Register of the Officers and Graduates of the U. S. Military Academy*, 6 vols. (Boston and New York, 1891-1920), I, 180-281 (cited hereafter as Cullum, *Biog. Register); O. R., Ser. I, Vol. II, 783, 867; Vol. LI, Pt. II, 116, Vol. XVIII, 754; Raleigh *North Carolina Standard*, May 29, June 12, 1861 and September 4, 1861, quoting the *Petersburg Express.*

[410] After a tour of inspection upon his appointment to command, Gwynn asked for 5000 troops of all arms and for a more effective organization of auxiliary services. Walter Gwynn to Governor John W. Ellis, May 30, 1861, O. R., Ser. I, Vol. LI, Pt. II, 120-121.

[411] On May 28, Richard Henry Smith, of Halifax County, introduced a measure into the convention to authorize the governor to raise seven regiments of volunteers from the counties lying on the east of the Wilmington and Weldon and the Seaboard and Roanoke Railroads, for the exclusive defense of the seaboard counties of the state. The ordinance was adopted on June 7 by a vote of fifty-eight to thirty-six. *Journal of the Convention of the People of North Carolina, Held on the 20th Day of May, A. D., 1861* (Raleigh, 1862), pp. 44, 81-82 (cited hereafter as *Convention Journal*).

[412] On June 8, the day after the ordinance had been adopted, John Powell Fuller, of Robeson County, who had voted for the measure, moved to reconsider. The

But enough of this. I regret to learn that the Quartermaster is so negligent about the troops.[413] I have complained to day about the matter and I learn that a Paymaster has gone to Va. If you do not get money, I need hardly say that I will cheerfully give you any aid in my power to get it. Advise me any time touching the matter.

I fear nothing can be done for Price.[414] I do not think there would be any difficulty or impropriety under the circumstances, in his returning home. But if nothing better can be done, let the Co elect him their Chaplain. I will do anything for him in my power and I beg you to assure him of this.

I heard from him last night. My wife[415] is sad indeed, and I learn that Mrs. V. spent last saturday or friday nite there and that she is greatly sad. Mrs. M. speaks of joining me a week or two hence. I shall encourage her to do so & I would be happy indeed to have Mrs. V. join her. She could visit you without much trouble & much to your & her gratification I have no doubt. What do you think of this suggestion? See Roberts[416] about the matter

motion to reconsider was adopted on June 14 by a vote of fifty-five to forty-eight, and the ordinance was rescinded the same day by a vote of fifty-five to fifty. The reasons for rescinding the ordinance appear to have been three: the optimistic assurance of Governor Ellis that the defensive power of the state's forts was sufficient; the opposition of the Military Board; and a fear that the enlistment of these regiments might interfere with the prompt meeting of the state's quota of Confederate troops. Others explained the reversal more bluntly: Holden declared that the supreme authority of the people in convention had yielded to one-man power, as the only argument against it was that it interfered with Governor Ellis and his authority. The ordinance was reconsidered and defeated "by exercise of the strickest party drill, and by the agency of the immense patronage of the government. . . ." Raleigh *North Carolina Standard,* June 19, 1861.

[413] The quartermaster and paymaster general of North Carolina from May until September was Lawrence O'Bryan Branch, an able lawyer who had resigned the presidency of the Raleigh and Gaston Railroad to enter Congress, where he served three terms (1855-1861). He was a Democrat and a secessionist. Raleigh *State Journal,* October 1, 1862.

[414] Richard Nye Price a Methodist teacher and preacher who was born in Virginia in 1830. He was a brother-in-law of Vance, having married Annie Edgeworth Vance in Asheville in 1855. He is not listed in Moore, *N. C. Roster,* but in 1897 he wrote an account of his relationship with Vance, and said that "he spent a year with him in the war of the States, a large part of the time as tentmate and mess-mate." Dowd, *Life of* Vance, p. 136. In Clark, *N. C. Regts.,* II, 396 he is listed as chaplain of the Twenty-sixth North Carolina Regiment, of which Vance was colonel for almost a year. Vance himself wrote that Price had been appointed chaplain "by the President." Vance to Secretary of War, November 30, 1861, War Department Collection of Confederate Records, Office of the Secretary of War, Letters Received, 1861, War Records Division, National Archives, Washington, D. C. (cited hereafter as Confederate War Department Records). See also p. 69, 258n.

[415] Mrs. Merrimon was the former Margaret Jane Baird, a cousin of Vance. See p. 6, 26n.

[416] For Roberts see p. 89, 331n. He was first lieutenant in Vance's company at this time. His wife's name was Salena M. Roberts (1832-1911).

too. I found that Capt. Sparrow[417] & Capt. Gilliam[418] at Ocracocke are takeing their wives with them and I learn that Mrs. Burton[419] is at Norfolk in Camp. Think of this suggestion and write me. The ladies might stay a week or two and return home or go to some safe & healthful locality.

I have not yet been able to get all the facts about the Bread. I enclose to you Mr. Simpson's statement and I will get the statement of the number of lbs. of flour you got. I hope in a day or two. Everything at the Camp store-house is so confused that I could not get your requisitions with all the passes I could make.

I intend to visit your Camp as soon as I can get a little leisure. I am anxious indeed, to see you all & would feel more comfortable in feeling if I were with the Co. all the time. Remember me most cordially to all the Officers and the Whole Company. Heaven bless all of you.

A Camp has been established at *Asheville*[420] & I may be sent there a day or two to give directions touching provisions & supplys. —Write me.

Suffolk.

[A. L. S. Z. B. Vance Papers, State Department of Archives and History, Raleigh.]

---

[417] Thomas Sparrow (1819-1884), of Beaufort County, captain of the "Washington Grays" in the Seventeenth North Carolina Regiment. He was born in New Bern, graduated with first honor at Princeton in 1842, read law with William Gaston, and took a masters degree, also at Princeton. He began practice in Washington, N. C. in 1847 in partnership with Edward Stanly and served in the House of Commons in 1858. The next year he moved to Arcola, Ill., but upon the election of Lincoln he returned to North Carolina. He was captured at the fall of Hatteras, August 28, 1861, and was imprisoned for about six months in Fort Columbus and Fort Warren. He later served as major of the Tenth North Carolina Regiment. After the war he resumed his legal practice and his political career, representing Beaufort County in the House of Representatives in 1870 and 1880, and was the House manager in the celebrated impeachment trial of Governor William W. Holden in 1871. His wife was Annie Blackwell, whom he married in 1844. Lindsay C. Warren, *Beaufort County's Contribution to a Notable Era of North Carolina History* (Washington, 1930), *passim* (cited hereafter as Warren, *Beaufort County History*); Clement Anselm Evans, (ed.), *Confederate Military History*, 12 vols. (Atlanta, 1899), IV, 752-753 (cited hereafter as Evans, *Conf. Mil. Hist.*); Connor, *N. C. Manual,* pp. 498-499; Clark, *N. C. Regts.,* V, 35-54, 680.

[418] Thomas H. Gilliam (1830-1893), of Perquimans County, who was first lieutenant of company L in the Seventeenth North Carolina Regiment, of which he was later captain. He was also captured at the fall of Hatteras on August 28, 1861. Moore, *N. C. Roster,* II, 69.

[419] Mrs. Julia L. Burton, wife of Augustus W. Burton (1825-1877), of Cleveland County. He was captain of company E of the Seventeenth North Carolina Regiment, and later its major. Some description of the gay life, the lack of discipline, and the emphasis given to social affairs is presented in Clark, *N. C. Regts.,* I, 607.

[420] The camp at Asheville was named Camp Patton.

To Mrs. Z. B. Vance[421]

Suffolk [422] V^a. June 19th ['61]

I was much distressed last night at the gloomy tone of your letter just received, and I am very sorry that you felt hurt at my not writing you by Brother. I wrote immediately by the mail telling you how it happened and I hope before this you have received my letter. I try hard Darling to write you regularly and let you Know my fate as we advance, as it is all that I can do now, and it would grieve me to have you think I neglected you.

My health continues good since my last spell of diahrea, and I intend to be more careful in future of what I eat. Alexander[423] improves, as does all the rest. I fear though I will have to send Frank Harris[424] home— I am looking for William[425] every day, as I suppose he started on Monday I need a few recruits, as two of my men left me at Raleigh (Harkins[426] & Garrison) [427] and two have been detailed by the Colonel [428] for regimental duty. I have written Garrison's father about him. I have no power to do anything with him as he had not been sworn in when he left. I see that Cousin Allen[429] has been elected by the Convention a delegate to Richmond. I am glad of it, as he is a worthy and a true man. I think however that my friends might have tendered

---

[421] See p. 16, 81n.

[422] Early in June, Vance's company was sent to the Department of Norfolk, where it became company F of the Fourteenth North Carolina Regiment. Most of the two and a half months that Vance was in this regiment was spent near Suffolk, at several different camps. A good description of Suffolk as a military post at the time Vance's company was stationed there is in Raleigh *North Carolina Standard,* July 17, 1861.

[423] James M. Alexander (1841-1908), of Buncombe County, a private in Vance's company. He later transferred to the Sixtieth North Carolina Regiment in the Army of Tennessee and was wounded in the battle of Bentonville in 1865. Moore, *N. C. Roster,* I, 528; Clark, *N. C. Regts.,* III, 496.

[424] A. Frank Harris, of Buncombe County, third corporal in Vance's company. He was discharged. Moore, *N. C. Roster,* I, 528.

[425] William Caleb Brown. See p. 54, 198n.

[426] See p. 103, 398n.

[427] See p. 104, 403n.

[428] The colonel of the Fourteenth North Carolina Regiment at this time was Junius Daniel (1828-1864), who was known as a good organizer and a strict disciplinarian. He was born in Halifax County, N. C., graduated at West Point in 1851, and resigned from the service in 1858 when he became a planter in Louisiana. In September of 1862 he was promoted brigadier general and died on May 13, 1864, of wounds received in the battle of Spottsylvania. W. C. Allen, *History of Halifax County* (Boston, 1918), pp. 196-201 (cited hereafter as Allen, *Halifax County*); Cullum, *Biog. Register,* II, 466.

[429] See p. 24, 108n. In the convention Davidson was nominated by Dr. James Calloway, of Wilkes County, who, like Davidson, was a Whig and had been opposed to secession until Lincoln's call for troops. Dr. Joseph A. McDowell, of Madison County, nominated Nicholas W. Woodfin, of Buncombe County to oppose Davidson from the eighth district. Both McDowell and Woodfin had originally been Whigs but they had become advocates of secession in the February 1861 elections. Davidson therefore had the endorsement of the old Union Whigs and the original secessionists had agreed to vote for Woodfin. Davidson won by a vote of fifty-five to forty-seven, and resigned from the convention to take his seat in Congress. McCormick, *Personnel,* p. 29; Battle *Legislation,* p. 126.

it to me, though I told them expressly when in Raleigh that I
could not accept it, and for that reason they left my name out.
But I thought the tender of it due me as a matter of courtesy,
though I dont attach any importance to the matter anyway.
You ask me to give you a description of Suffolk. We are two miles
from it, and would gladly be further still. It is a straggling, ragged,
old fashioned town about the size of Asheville. I have only been
there once and did not see much of it. I took dinner by invitation
with a gentleman by name of Norfleet. We are Sixteen miles from
Yorktown, 18 from Norfolk and about 26 from Newport News
where the enemy have landed a large force. Our position here
commands the junction of the Petersburg & Norfolk & Roanoke
& Seabord rail roads, quite an important post. for should the
enemy strike across the country and sieze our position no more
troops north or south could be thrown in to the relief of Norfolk.
We do not anticipate any attack here though for the present, as
everything seems tending toward Manassas Junction and Alexandria and we look for a tremendous fight there in the course of ten
days. Our time may come sooner though than we expect— I hope
we will be ready to give them a warm reception— We sleep with
our arms at hand, and have picket guards thrown out one mile
& a half every night— I am writing amid many interruptions and
my ideas are scattering. I hope you will have an abundance of
every thing to eat— Every one tells me crops are fine and I hope
we may be blessed with an abundant harvest. I hope you will
have my horse taken care of— Make Isaac Keep him in good order
and *please* dont loan him. I have not yet had time to answer my
dear Mothers[430] letter but will write her tomorrow or next day—
Tell Charlie & David [431] that Pa will bring them "Swords from
the War" when he comes home. How I do long to see the dear
little fellows! Dear little Zebbie[432] I reckon is growing so much
and beginning to talk — Bless my darlings, shall I ever see them
again? May God bless and preserve them and restore us to our
dear home once again in peace for His names sake!
I have much more to write but it is nearly midnight and I am
officer of the day tomorrow & must up at 4½ oclk — So Good
night Darling— As ever yours devotedly
Asheville.
[On attached paper]
Camp Bragg June 12, 61
Countersign for to-night
    Buncombe
[A. L. S. Z. B. Vance Papers, State Department of Archives and
  History, Raleigh.]

To Mrs. Z. B. Vance[433]

Camp Bragg,[434] Near
Suffolk Vª. June 29 1861

Again— I hasten to write you a short note, merely to let you Know that I continue quite well. Your letter was recᵈ. yesterday and I was exceedingly pained to learn that you were so unwell as to be in bed. I fear your debility and loss of appetite will make you quite poor and feeble. I hope you will take the bitters as you suggest and will ride about all you can.— You can have little idea of the distress it would give me to hear of your continued sickness when not able to get to see you. Orders now are very strict against absences, no one allowed to leave the State except by order of Gen. Hugher[435] at Norfolk. Poor little Zebbie[436] how it pains to hear of his suffering too! I rather feared from your letter darling, that he was worse off than you would say. I hope you will not Keep anything back dear, let me Know the worst bad as it may hurt me. Kiss the dear little cherub for his Father and may God spare him to us. Jo Randle has just called in and says for Robert to get a house for his wife to live in[437]—she writes him that she is going to be turned out of her present place—in fact she writes him all sorts of things, that she is not half provided for, gets nothing but *meat & bread* "while others get lots of things;" another time that she is dying & he must come home &c. Tell Bob to write me all about her situation—

We have no news of importance at all—Everything is quiet here though there is no doubt but Gen Beauregard [438] is marching upon Alexandria and we listen every moment to hear of a great battle there. I have sent you the daily Richmond Dispatch [439] which I hope you receive—

---

[433] See p. 16, 81n.

[434] Camp Bragg, named for Thomas Bragg, was at the Blackwater, a railway crossing 2½ miles from Suffolk.

[435] Benjamin Huger (1805-1877), of South Carolina, who graduated from West Point in 1825 and had served continuously in the army since. On May 23, 1861, as a brigadier general of the volunteer forces of Virginia, he was assigned to the command of the troops in and about Norfolk, relieving Walter Gwynn. The Department of Norfolk was subsequently enlarged to include the North Carolina counties around Albemarle Sound. *O. R.*, Ser. I, Vol. II, 867; Hill, *Bethel to Sharpsburg*, I, 192-193; Cullum, *Biog. Register*, I, 343-344.

[436] See p. 110, 432n.

[437] See letter of R. B. Vance to Z. B. Vance, May 28, 1861, p. 103, 399n.

[438] Pierre Gustave Toutant Beauregard (1818-1893), of Louisiana, who graduated from West Point in 1838. He had become commander, near Manassas, Va., on June 1, of one of the two Confederate armies which were being assembled near the Potomac. At the moment he had a high reputation as a soldier and great popularity because of the reduction of Fort Sumter. Cullum, *Biog. Register*, I, 697-698.

[439] The Richmond *Dispatch* (1850-1903) was a daily and weekly published by James A. Cowardin & Co., editors and proprietors, at the corner of Main and 13th Streets. It was usually moderate in tone and sympathetic to the administration.

In great haste darling your devoted husband
Asheville.
[A. L. S. Z. B. Vance Papers, State Department of Archives and
History, Raleigh.]

To Mrs. Z. B. Vance[440]

Camp Ellis[441] V[a]
Near Suffolk
July 21st 1861

I write you a line again this evening to inform you of my continued good health. Things have not changed here since my last—
No fighting yet and no telling when we will have any. Today
every body thinks the Yankees are certainly going to land at Smithfield and take Norfolk in the rear through our Camp, and tomorrow we think we will be here all summer & fall without
smelling a Yankee—So it goes—We really dont know any thing
about it, and must just wait.

I am sorry to say that David Gudger[442] has typhoid fever, and
from the manner in which he has been taken I fear he will have
a serious time of it. We have him in good quarters and will give
him every attention in our power, but I would greatly prefer
some of his family would come and see to him— It would relieve
me of a very great weight of responsibility. Tell Brother to inform
them immediately—Lt Roberts[443] has written them also, but
perhaps his letter may be delayed. David is a great favorite with
us all and his friends may rest assured he will be attended to in
every respect.—

I am almost afraid to hear from you again, but trust in God you
may be better. Your last letter affected me almost to distraction.
Almost everybody I see from home tells me you are so lonely &
low spirited, that I fear Darling you are worse off than you will
confess. Do my dear wife write me the worst, it is better than
suspense. Dear Zebbie[444] too. I have not forgotten him. I trust he
will survive his teething. I think you ought to have sent for a

---

[440] See p. 16 81n.

[441] About July 4, 1861 the Fourteenth Regiment moved from Camp Bragg to Camp
Ellis, named for Governor John W. Ellis, which was just beyond the suburbs of
Suffolk. In August another move was made to Camp Bee, at Burwells' Bay, about
twenty-three miles from Suffolk.

[442] David M. Gudger, of Buncombe County, who was fourth corporal in Vance's
company. He recovered from the typhoid fever but was severely wounded at
Malvern Hill, July 1, 1862, and discharged from the service. After the war he
studied medicine and graduated at Philadelphia in 1868; he settled at the old
Gudger place in the lower Hominy valley, where he practiced medicine for many
years. Moore, *N. C. Roster,* I, 528; Tennent, "Medicine in Buncombe County,"
pp. 20-21.

[443] See p. 89, 331n.

[444] See p. 110, 432n.

physician before this and I hope you will hesitate no longer about it. Send for Dr Hardy[445] by all means.

Mr Merrimon[446] is here again, has returned from a visit to York-town and tells us the troops have suffered hardships there—He will return home in two weeks. I am again officer of the day and shall have to tramp all night around our lines and pickets—The moon is at full though and the nights are beautiful—I shall cast many a thought tonight toward my dear home and many a prayer for my lonely wife & sweet children! Dear little children! Of such indeed, must be the Kingdom of God. Purity and love! Good night my darling—Kiss my little ones and believe me as ever your own devoted husband
Asheville.
[A. L. S. Z. B. Vance Papers, State Department of Archives and History, Raleigh.]

From J. G. Martin[447]

Headquarters N. C. Troops,
Adjutant General's Office,
Raleigh, August 27th 1861

Official information has received at this office that you are elected Colonel of the 26 Regiment N. C. Troops[448] Will you accept? if so report here in person without delay.
Asheville
[A. L. S. War Department Collection of Confederate Records, Office of Secretary of War, Letters Received, National Archives, Washington.]

---

[445] See p. 20, 95n.
[446] See p. 13, 65n and p. 105, 405n.
[447] James Green Martin (1819-1878). He was born in Elizabeth City N. C., graduated from West Point in 1840 and served in the Mexican War, where he lost an arm at Churubusco. When the Civil War came he was with the expedition of Albert Sidney Johnston in Utah, and when Martin returned to North Carolina and resigned from the United States army, June 14, 1861, he was appointed adjutant general of the North Carolina State Troops consisting of the first ten regiments which had enlisted for the war. When the legislature met later, in September, Martin was elected adjutant general of all North Carolina troops, in which position he did a great deal to raise, equip, and put into the field most of the North Carolina soldiers. The entire supervision of the defense of the state was turned over to him. On June 1, 1862, Martin was appointed brigadier general in the Confederate army and given command of a brigade in Holmes' department. He did not then resign his commission from the state as adjutant and inspector general, and some controversy ensued from this double office holding. In 1863, after he had retired from this state office, he commanded troops in Virginia, around Kinston, N. C. and, in July 1864, in western North Carolina with head-quarters at Asheville. After the war he studied law and practiced it in Asheville. Walter Clark, *Memorial Address upon the Life of General James Green Martin* (Raleigh, 1916); Cullum, *Biog. Register*, II, 41.
[448] The Twenty-sixth North Carolina Regiment was organized at the Camp of Instruction near Raleigh on August 27, 1861. It consisted of ten companies from central and western counties which had largely opposed secession until Lincoln's call for troops.

To Mrs. Z. B. Vance[449]

Camp Burgwyn[450] near Morehead City
Sep. 15—1861

Two weeks this morning since I left you and yet not a word or line from you or any one else—What on earth is the matter? I am getting quite anxious about you. You certainly have written & so has Brother, where did you Direct your letters? I feel sometimes quite hurt about it, but I Know that something has happened to delay your letters. We are still here on the sand banks, see the Yankee vessels every day, but still they dont attack us though they could lay off out of range of our guns and throw shells into our camp easily—They are evidently preparing for a grand demonstration against our coast somewhere. This point is so strongly fortified however that I dont now believe they will attempt a landing here—We have altogether in this vicinity at least 2000 troops including the men in the Fort (Macon) [451] and have tolerable batteries besides. Wilmington or some of the inlets towards Virginia will most likely be assailed. Rumors are afloat here to the effect that Gen Butler[452] has a large force at Hateras has been landing troops in Hyde County and compelling many citizens to take the oath of allegiance.[453] If so, we may soon be ordered up there to stop his incursions—

---

[449] See p. 16, 81n.

[450] The Twenty-sixth Regiment left its Raleigh camp of instruction on September 2, 1861 for Fort Macon, but Vance was on furlough in Asheville and joined the regiment later that month. In the meantime it was commanded by the lieutenant colonel, Harry King Burgwyn, for whom its first camp was named. Clark, *N. C. Regts.*, II, 303-306; Moore, *N. C. Roster*, II, 362.

[451] For Fort Macon see p. 105, 406n. Accounts of the number of guns at Fort Macon vary widely, but Colonel J. A. J. Bradford, reporting to the Military Board of North Carolina, of which he was a member, the result of an official inspection of the fort, said that there were twenty-one guns mounted on August 21, 1861, and that the number would soon be increased to forty-two. Papers of the Military Board, State Department of Archives and History, Raleigh, N. C. (cited hereafter as Military Board Papers); Hill, *Bethel to Sharpsburg*, I, 247.

[452] Benjamin Franklin Butler (1818-1893), then a major general in the Union army who had been in command at Fort Monroe from May 23 to August 18, 1861, when he was succeeded by Major General John E. Wool. After August 17 Butler was in command of troops exclusive of those in Fort Monroe and so was in charge of the infantry which, with the aid of Union naval forces, captured Fort Hatteras on August 28, 1861. Butler had been a member of the Massachusetts House of Representatives in 1853 and of the Massachusetts Senate in 1859, as a Democrat. In the election of 1860 he supported Breckinridge. During the war he was always a controversial figure, especially because of his decrees declaring slaves coming into Union lines to be "contraband," and his orders concerning the status of ladies in New Orleans. After the war he became a Radical Republican and served in Congress (1867-1875, 1877-1879); was elected governor of Massachusetts in 1882; and afterwards ran for the presidency on independent tickets. He was associated with the Greenback movement in several campaigns. Carl Russell Fish, "Benjamin Franklin Butler," *Dict. of Am. Biog.*, III, 357-359; *Biog. Dir. of Am. Cong.*, pp.768-769; *O. R.*, Ser. I, Vol. II, 640-641, Vol. IV, 580, 601-602.

[453] Colonel Rush C. Hawkins of the Ninth New York Regiment was assigned to take command of the captured territory around Hatteras after its fall. He offered to allow the people, largely cut off and destitute, to remain in their homes

A great many sick in the Regiment, measles & mumps. I want to go up to Richmond as soon as I can leave here with safety & make arrangements for getting my Company into this Regiment—I had a letter lately from Lt. Roberts[454] on the Subject—I have the Governors word that it shall be done. I shall then be able I hope to run up home again & see you a short time. If I am not to be moved from the State we can be together most of the time this fall & winter—How are the Children doing? Bless their dear hearts, I hope they keep well! I was so sorry to hear of the death of poor Greene;[455] he was one of the best men in the Company, kind, generous & brave. Peace to his memory. I hope the citizens will be kind to his family—Do write me often darling, I am so anxious about everything at home—I still keep quite well & strong, have fine eating with figs and scuppernongs grapes—wish I could send you a basket of them. God bless you & my little Children—As ever Yours
Asheville.
[A. L. S. Z. B. Vance Papers, State Department of Archives and History, Raleigh.]

To N. G. Allman[456]

Headquarters Twenty-Sixth Regiment N. C. Troops,
Camp Burgwyn, Near Morehead City, Sept. 18th, 1861.
Your letter of the 2d inst., addressed to my brother, was forwarded by him, and received this day. In it you ask, first, if I will be a candidate for Congress, and second, if not a candidate, will I consent for my name to be run? To both questions I answer in the negative. To this course I am impelled by what I consider the most conclusive reasons.

You remember well the position I occupied upon the great question which so lately divided the people of the South. Ardently

if they would take an oath of allegiance to the United States government. He reported that about 250 took such an oath on his verbal assurance that he would give them whatever protection they might need. He later claimed that many others took the loyalty oath. O. R., Ser. I, Vol. IV, 606-609. On October 3, 1861, Judge Asa Biggs reported to General Gatlin that while only a few of the inhabitants were disloyal, the sentiment in Washington, Tyrell, and Beaufort counties gave uneasiness, and Hyde was even more amenable to Union persuasion than these. O. R., Ser. I, Vol. IV, 671-672.

[454] See p. 89, 331n. Upon Vance's election as colonel of the Twenty-sixth Regiment Roberts succeeded him as captain of "The Rough and Ready Guards." Roberts was commissioned September 20, 1861. The company never joined the Twenty-sixth Regiment, but remained in the Fourteenth. Moore, N. C. Roster, I, 527.

[455] A. J. Greene, Sr., of Buncombe County, who had enlisted in Vance's company upon its organization, May 4, 1861. He died on August 25, 1861, while Vance was away on furlough and while the company was still stationed at Suffolk. Moore, N. C. Roster, I, 529.

[456] N. G. Allman, of Franklin, in Macon County, operated a hotel later known as Junaluska Inn. He was later agent of the Western Turnpike Road. G. L. Houk, "History of Macon County," in the Franklin Press, June 19, 26, 1925; Vance Letter Book, May 1863.

devoted to the old Union, and the forms which the Federal fathers established, I clung to it so long as I thought there was a shadow of hope for preserving, purifying or reconstructing it. And you will also remember that in the last official communication I had the honor to make to my constituents as their Representative I pledged myself in case all our efforts for peace and justice at the hands of the North should fail, that their cause was mine, their destiny was my destiny, and that all I had and was should be spent in their service. Those hopes did fail, as you know, signally and miserably fail; civil war was thrust upon the country, and the strong arm of Northern despotism was stretched out to crush and subdue the Southern people. I immediately volunteered for their defense, in obedience, not only to this promise, but also, as I trust, to patriotic instincts; and I should hold this promise but poorly fulfilled, should I now, after having acquired sufficient knowledge of military affairs to begin to be useful to my country, escape its obligation by seeking, or even accepting a civil appointment.

Certainly, if there lives a man in North Carolina who ought to do all and suffer all for his country, I am that man. Since the time of my entering upon man's estate the people have heaped promotion and honors, all undeserved, upon my head. In everything I have sought, their generous confidence, their unfailing kindness have sustained me. Whilst I can never sufficiently repay it, I am determined, God helping me, to show them I was not altogether unworthy of their regard. I am, therefore, not a candidate for Congress, nor will I consent for my name to be run. I am perfectly satisfied to be represented again by the sound sense and sober judgment of the gentleman who has so lately represented us at Richmond,[457] or by a dozen gentlemen who live in our district not connected with the army, some of whom I hope the common peril and the common cause will induce our people to elect, without bickering and strife.

I cannot close this hasty letter without assuring you that I am not insensible to the compliment conveyed by your own and a hundred other similar interrogations, which have reached me from different parts of the district. No man can feel prouder or more grateful at such manifestations. Surely God has never blessed a man with more sterling and devoted friends than I can number in the mountain district.

May my name perish from the memory of my wife and children when I cease to remember these friends with gratitude.

Among the many who have adhered so faithfully to my poor fortune through good and through evil report, I am always proud to remember you, unfalteringly and unmistakably.

---

[457] Allen Turner Davidson. See p. 24, 108n and p. 109, 429n.

Please to accept, in conclusion, every assurance of my regards and good wishes to you and yours.

Most truly yours

Franklin, N. C.

[From Clement Dowd, *Life of Zebulon B. Vance,* pp. 68-69.]

To Mrs. Z. B. Vance[458]

Head Qrs 26 N. C. V.
Camp Burgwyn
near Carolina City
October 13 1861.

I wrote you a short note yesterday and must write you another tonight. I was then rather unwell am now quite restored again except the piles, which you Know can scarcely ever be permanently cured. Mrs Steven's medicine has proved very good indeed and I have to thank her for relieving me of much pain. I rec^d. your second letter since you got home this morning, with a great long one from Mr Brown[459]—how pleased I was to hear of our dear child's improving health—Have you money enough? I have none now to send you, but the paymaster will be here in five or six days and there is about 300 dollars due me. I shall then be able to send you some. I want to send you enough to buy another horse; I shall write tonight to some friend to buy you one, a good gentle family horse—I wish much you would come down to Newbern to Synod,[460] it would be the very thing. I dont think it exactly safe for you to come here now—Since I wrote yesterday we have news that the Yankees have landed at Bogue Inlet near Swansboro[461] and were marching across the country to sieze & destroy the Road between this & Newbern. Co^l Campbell,[462] who is located on the

---

[458] See p. 16, 81n.

[459] William John Brown. See p. 54, 196n.

[460] The Synod of North Carolina, of what came to be called the Presbyterian Church in the Confederate States, did not meet in New Bern in 1861, but in Raleigh, October 30-November 2. Vance's reference is probably to a conference of elders and deacons of the Synod of North Carolina, which was scheduled to meet in New Bern in the autumn of 1861. Deacons were never members of synod, which was composed exclusively of elders, both teaching and ruling. Mrs. Vance was an earnest and ardent Presbyterian; Vance himself belonged to no church until 1878, when he became a Presbyterian. *Minutes of the Forty-Eighth Sessions of the Synod of North Carolina, Held in the Church of Raleigh,* October, 1861 (Fayetteville, 1862); *Minutes of the Convention of Elders and Deacons of the Synod of North Carolina at Fayetteville, March 6th and 7th, 1861* (Fayetteville, 1861), pp. 8-10, where the 1861 meeting is scheduled for New Bern. Apparently it was not held because of the military situation in the eastern counties.

[461] General Daniel H. Hill believed that the Yankee activity near Swansborough was explained by the presence of a large amount of cotton in the neighborhood, which he directed should be moved to the interior. D. H. Hill to R. C. Gatlin, October 27, 1861, *O. R.,* Ser. I. Vol. IV, 694.

[462] Reuben P. Campbell (1818-1862), of Iredell County, colonel of the Seventh North Carolina Regiment. He graduated from West Point in the class of 1840, was appointed colonel of the Seventh on May 16, 1861, and was killed in action at

mainland, has sent a portion of his Regiment up—and we expect the balance will leave tonight if the news should prove Serious. Every thing begins to look Seriously like an attack soon—The ocean is smooth & a great many ships are seen every day cruising around. But you might safely come to Newbern, I could run up to see you there & you could come down here if things were fair.

I must close for this time, I am gratified at your taking such a share in the work for the soldiers—Let me again beg you to learn patience & contempt for our enemies who are slandering Brother & myself—envy should receive some compassion—and they are dying with it. Kiss my little darlings, and accept my dear wife the love and blessings of your devoted husband
Asheville.
[On the side of the page]
I have written uncle Dolph [463] to get you a horse—write him & urge him up to get it soon—
[A. L. S. Z. B. Vance Papers, State Department of Archives and History, Raleigh.]

To Mrs. Z. B. Vance[464]

Camp Wilks near Fort Macon
Oct 17 1861—

Your long letter was rec[d]. yesterday and I was deeply grieved at its contents in more respects than one—My poor child it seems gets no better but rather worse. Dear little fellow how my heart bleeds for him—I will try to get permission to visit you by the 1st November at least, but it is very uncertain as to my getting permission—We are in constant doubt here, immense naval preparations have certainly been made by the Yankees for attacking the Southern Coast, but where they will strike no one can say—We may be here till Spring without being molested, and then a days carelessness might see us surprised and ruined—We have to watch & be patient. I regret exceedingly Mothers conduct towards you about Herndon,[465] she is certainly very inconsistent—Whilst

---

Gaines' Mill, June 27, 1862. Many leaders, among them General Gatlin and W. W. Holden, believed that he deserved promotion. *O. R.*, Ser. I, Vol. IV, 705; Raleigh *North Carolina Standard*, April 9, 1862; Moore, *N. C. Roster*, I, 237; Cullum, *Biog. Register*, II, 50.

[463] Adolphus Erwin Baird, a younger brother of Vance's mother. Formerly a proprietor of an Asheville hotel and a prominent merchant, he now lived at Marshall, in Madison County. See p. 68, 255n.

[464] See p. 16, 81n.

[465] Edmund W. Herndon (1839-1883), who had married Vance's youngest sister. He had enlisted in Vance's company as a private; later he was promoted lieutenant and subsequently became a major on the staff of General Robert B. Vance. In 1864 he served in the quartermaster department of General Lane's brigade. After the war he was for a time clerk of the superior court and probate judge in Buncombe County. Moore, *N. C. Roster*, I, 527, 529; Edmund W. Herndon to Z. B. Vance, October 22, 1864, Zebulon B. Vance Papers.

Harriette Espy Vance, wife of Zebulon B. Vance

in my company I paid every attention to Herndon and tried to
wear off every thing unpleasant between us. But he would not
reciprocate any of my advances—the truth is he is a low bred fellow and cant apreciate what is genteel & becoming & I soon gave
up all attempts to put us on a brotherly footing. I should regret
bitterly to see that Mother was determined to trample on the
feelings of the whole family for the sake of a fellow who clearly
proves his unworthiness— But it is often so—Hannah [466] has more
complete control of Mother than all the balance of the family; she,
that has been most undutiful and brought most distress upon her
Mothers grey hairs, is not only forgiven, which was right enough,
but is made to control all the rest! It is very hard for any shadow
to come between me & my mothers love, but I never can &
never will sacrifice my self respect for a dirty pupy as I believe
Herndon to be, nor do I want you to do it. This is all private
darling, you must not let any of them see this letter, it would do
no good; I write my sentiment to you that you may Know how I
wish you to do in the matter. Of course I desire you to treat my
Mother with all Kindness, but let Herndon & his wife be a forbidden subject between you—In fact dont talk about them to
anybody, not your best friends—
    Kiss my darling Children & receive my blessing upon you all
    In haste most truly your husband
Can you spare me a pair of good bed blankets? I begin to need
them now—
Asheville.
[A. L. S. Z. B. Vance Papers, State Department of Archives and
    History, Raleigh.]

To Allen[467]

H'd Qrs 26N.C.V.[468]

Near NewBern Mar 4th [1862]
My regiment is going in for the war,[469] and I have the offer of
some new companies from the mountains. In thirty days, I could

---

[466] Hannah Moore Vance, the wife of Edmund W. Herndon. See p. 6, 32n.

[467] Allen Turner Davidson, member of the Confederate Congress. See p. 24, 108n.

[468] Vance's regiment was sent to New Bern after the fall of Roanoke Island, February 10, 1862, opened up the sounds to the invading Federal forces. In view of the
threatened attack on New Bern by General Burnside, Vance's regiment was assigned
to the command of Brigadier General Branch which, as then constituted, was
composed of the Seventh, Twenty-sixth, Twenty-seventh, Thirty-third, Thirty-fifth,
and Thirty-seventh North Carolina Infantry Regiments, and Latham's and Brem's
batteries of artillery, Colonel Spruill's Second Cavalry (the Nineteenth North
Carolina Regiment), a battalion of militia under Colonel H. J. B. Clark, and a
few detached companies. Brigadier General R. C. Gatlin, commanding the Department of North Carolina and coast defenses, with headquarters at Goldsboro, was
in supreme command. General Branch commanded the district of Pamlico, having
succeeded Daniel H. Hill. Clark, *N. C. Regts.,* II, 308.

[469] On February 19, 1862 the Convention adopted an ordinance to raise North
Carolina's quota of Confederate troops. It provided that the governor should con-

raise another regiment for the war, two companies of cavalry & one of artillery. This would make a handsome brigade with which I would like to take the field on active service. Do you suppose the President would give me the authority to raise it? If so, I would pledge myself to raise it in 30 days. Cant you feel of the authorities for me? I think they might commission the men who can raise the troops. Try it & write me. If you think it probable, I would run up to Richmond for a "few days" — I am exceedingly tired of watching and waiting behind ditches; and really believe I could better serve my country now by using my influence in the mountains to raise troops than in any other way— Besides, our men deserve *something* at the hands of the administration— In haste yrs

[on reverse] Authority to raise the troops but can't promise he shall be General— send through Mr Davidson
[Richmond]
[A. L. S. War Department Collection of Confederate Records, Letters Received, 1862. National Archives, Washington.]

To L. O'B. Branch[470]

Hdqrs, Twenty-Sixth Regt.
North Carolina Vols.
Kinston, N. C., March 17, 1862.
I have the honor to report, in accordance with military usage,

---

tinue to call upon the counties for troops and encouraged the re-enlistment of those already in service, especially the twelve months volunteers, many of whose terms of enlistment were about to expire in the next few months. In section 4 of the ordinance it was provided "That the governor shall call upon the several captains of volunteer companies from North Carolina in the field for twelve months, . . . to muster their companies for re-enlistment, and shall make known to them the earnest desire of this Convention and the people of North Carolina, that they shall enlist for three years or the war, . . ." In order to forward this purpose the ordinance set forth ways and means by which captains should re-enlist their men individually, permitted companies to retain their organization or to reorganize, as they chose, and provided for recruiting and the payment of bounties. It was under this law that Vance's regiment had re-enlisted for the war, and he sought official encouragement of proposed recruiting activities with the view that he might become thereby a brigadier general. *Convention Ordinances*, No. 23, February 19, 1862.

[470] Lawrence O'Bryan Branch (1820-1862), of Halifax County, in command of the District of Pamlico in the Department of North Carolina. Upon being left an orphan he was reared by his uncle, John Branch, who was governor of North Carolina, congressman, Senator, Secretary of the Navy in Jackson's cabinet, and prominent Democrat. The nephew was first honor graduate at Princeton in 1838, studied law and practiced it in Florida, where his uncle was territorial governor from 1843 to 1845, when it became a state. In 1844 he married Nancy Haywood Blount, only daughter of General William Augustus Blount. They moved to Raleigh, where he became a member of the Literary Board, a director of the Bank of the State, presidential elector on the Pierce ticket in 1852, and president of the Raleigh and Gaston Railway. In 1855 he was elected to Congress as a Democrat, where he served three terms, faithfully supported the party and President Buchanan, 'in whose cabinet he was offered two posts, both of which he declined. In the crisis of 1860-1861 he counseled moderation, but became an active secessionist when he was persuaded that coercion would be employed against the southern states. When

the share of my command in the operations of last Friday.[471]

While in temporary command of the post of New Berne, on Thursday, my regiment was ordered to Croatan works,[472] under command of Lieutenant-Colonel Burgwyn,[473] to assist Colonel Sinclair's[474] regiment should the enemy land below those works.

war came he volunteered as a private, but was soon commissioned by Governor Ellis as quartermaster and paymaster general of the state troops, with the rank of colonel. He resigned this post in September, 1861, when he was elected colonel of the Thirty-third North Carolina Regiment. On January 17, 1862, he was commissioned brigadier general by President Davis and assigned to command in the District of Pamlico. He was killed in the battle of Antietam, September 17, 1862. Richmond *Southern Illustrated News*, Vol. I, No. 39, June 7, 1863, p. 7 in L.O'B. Branch Papers, State Department of Archives and History Raleigh, N. C. (cited hereafter as Branch Papers); Raleigh *State Journal*, October 1, 1862; Marshall De-Lancey Haywood, "Lawrence O'Bryan Branch," Ashe, *Biog. Hist. of N. C.*, VII, 55-59; obituary in Raleigh *North Carolina Standard*, October 1, 1862; Allen, *Halifax County*, 192-194.

[471] The battle of New Bern was fought just below the town on Friday, March 14, 1862, between the forces of Brigadier General Ambrose E. Burnside, the Federal commander, and those of Brigadier General Lawrence O'B. Branch, the Confederate commander. The Federals won the victory, driving the Confederates from their defences and capturing the town of New Bern.

[472] The Croatan works were the first of the defence lines of the Confederates, and were located about ten miles below the town of New Bern. Part of a total defence line, the works ran from a point on the Neuse River, about a mile above the mouth of Otter Creek, to the creek and an impassable swamp on the right, along the Atlantic and North Carolina railroad, which ran from New Bern to Morehead City. The whole Croatan line was not quite a mile in length; Branch pronounced it "a well-planned and well-constructed work, which 2000 men and two field batteries could hold against a very large force." *O. R.*, Ser. I, Vol. IX, 241.

[473] Henry King Burgwyn, Jr., (1841-1863), who was born in Massachusetts, but whose paternal ancestors came from Northampton County, N. C. where they resided at the time of the war. Young Burgwyn attended the University of North Carolina and Virginia Military Institute, from which he was graduated in the spring of 1861. He was appointed commandant of the Camp of Instruction at Crabtree, near Raleigh, July 5, 1861 and was elected lieutenant colonel of the Twenty-sixth North Carolina Regiment upon its organization, August 27, 1861. When Vance was elected governor of North Carolina, Burgwyn became colonel of the Twenty-sixth. He was killed on the first day of Gettysburg, July 1, 1863. William H. S. Burgwyn, "Harry King Burgwyn, Jr." Ashe, *Biog. Hist. of N. C.*, VIII, 67-72.

[474] Rev. James Sinclair, a Presbyterian minister of Robeson County, who was colonel of the Thirty-fifth North Carolina Regiment. He was formerly a chaplain in the Fifth North Carolina Regiment and had acquired a reputation for bravery at the battle of First Manassas. It is contended by the historian of the Thirty-fifth that these rumors were false ones, but that they had influence in gaining him the colonelcy of the Thirty-fifth, which he got by trading votes. He was not re-elected upon the reorganization of the regiment on April 10, 1862, but Sinclair later claimed that he was not a candidate. A court of inquiry was held after the battle of New Bern concerning the conduct of the Thirty-fifth Regiment in that battle, but the charges of "unsoldierly conduct" were dropped. In 1861 Sinclair had been an ardent secessionist; after the war he became a Republican and represented Robeson County in the State House of Representatives in 1868. For Vance's opinion of Sinclair's military conduct see Vance to James Sinclair, February 17, 1863, Governors' Papers (Vance), State Department of Archives and History, Raleigh, N. C. (cited hereafter as Governors' Papers (Vance); see also Connor, *N. C. Manual*, p. 781; Clark, *N. C. Regts.*, II, 592-595; James Sinclair to T. D. McDowell, March 17, 1863, T. D. McDowell Papers, Southern Historical Collection, University of North Carolina, Chapel Hill, N. C. (cited hereafter as McDowell Papers); James Sinclair to Daniel L. Russell, Jr., May 11, 23, 1874, Daniel L. Russell Papers Southern Historical Collection, University of North Carolina, Chapel Hill, N. C. (cited hereafter as Russell Papers).

Learning soon after that Colonel Campbell [475] was at his post, I instantly transferred to him my temporary command and proceeded to Croatan to assume command of my regiment. When near there I met Colonel Sinclair retreating, who informed me that the enemy were landing in force at Fisher's Landing,[476] and nearer still to the works I met Colonel Campbell, who had just ordered my regiment to take the cars and return to Fort Thompson.[477] Before my return they had been posted by Lieutenant-Colonel Burgwyn in the series of redans constructed by me,[478] on the right of the railroad, in the rear of Bullen's Branch,[479] extending from the railroad to the swamp, about 500 yards from the road, by Weathersby's.[480]

At this road, as you will remember, I had constructed the night before a breastwork commanding the passage of the swamp, with the assistance of Mr. _____ Hawks,[481] a gentleman whose skill

---

[475] Reuben P. Campbell, colonel of the Seventh North Carolina Regiment. See pp. 117-118, 462n.

[476] Fisher's Landing was the point at which the Croatan line anchored on the river, being just above the mouth of Otter Creek between the Croatan line and New Bern. Hence Federal troops landing at Fisher's outflanked the defence line at the Croatan works. Federal gunboats drove Sinclair's men from Fisher's landing, the Thirty-fifth sustaining the loss of one killed and two wounded, all on the retreat. Colonel Campbell, seeing that the breastwork was turned, ordered the Confederate units of Vance and Sinclair to retreat to the next line of defence. O. R., Ser. I, Vol. IX, 243.

[477] Fort Thompson was the anchor on the river for the second line of defence, which was about six miles above the Croatan line, and hence about four miles from New Bern. Fort Thompson, with thirteen guns, was the largest of the seven forts along the river, but ten of its thirteen guns were trained on the river and were useless in an attack by land, such as Burnside made. The fort was erected by, and named for, Major W. Beverhout Thompson, who was state engineer and who defended himself vigorously from subsequent attacks upon his handiwork by the *Raleigh Register* and the *Wilmington Journal*. The *Goldsboro Tribune* called him "incompetent" and added: "This Engineer has long been an incubus on our military operations. He ought to be removed forthwith, and an abler man put in his place." Quoted in Raleigh *North Carolina Standard,* March 19, 1862. Thompson's defence is in the *North Carolina Standard* of September 3, 1862. He had been in favor of disunion and a strong secessionist. O. R. Ser. I, Vol. IX, 242-243; Raleigh *North Carolina Standard,* June 12, 1861.

[478] The Fort Thompson line, as the second line of defence was called, consisted of a continuous line of breastworks made of earth and logs, and provided with rifle pits, from Fort Thompson to the railroad—a distance of about one mile. Originally the line had been planned to extend beyond the railroad to an impenetrable swamp at Bryce's Creek. But because of insufficient men to man so long a line, and because of insufficient time in which to construct it, Branch dropped the line back about 150 yards at the railroad and ordered Vance to construct on the right of the railroad, not a continuous breastwork, but a series of redans, or unjoined pillboxes, moderns would say, conforming to the features of the ground. See map of the field in O. R., Ser. I, Vol. IX, 248.

[479] Bullen's Branch, labeled Bullen's Creek on the map, rises near the railroad and flows into Bryce's Creek about a mile and a half west of the railroad.

[480] The Weathersby Road left the Old Beaufort Road just east of the railroad and south of the town of New Bern, crossed the railroad and bent around to the rear and right of Vance's redans, crossing Bullen's Branch about a mile west of the railroad and crossing Bryce's Creek about a mile and a half south of Bullen's Branch. It was the road to Pollocksville.

[481] Probably Francis L. Hawks, Jr., of Beaufort County, who was commissioned in 1862 as a captain in the department of engineers. Moore, *N. C. Roster,* IV, 17.

in engineering, untiring energy, and zeal I take pleasure in
noticing favorably; and there was placed a section of Brem's[482]
artillery, lieutenant Williams[483] commanding, and Captain Mc-
Rae's[484] company of infantry, with a portion of the companies
of Captains Hays[485] and Thomas,[486] Second North Carolina Cavalry, dismounted.

About 2 o'clock Friday morning, in compliance with orders
received, I pushed companies B, E, and K of my right wing across
the small swamp alluded to, so as to make my extreme right rest
on the battery at the Weathersby road.

This was our position on Friday morning, which remained unchanged during the day, except that two companies of the Thirty-
third Regiment, under Lieutenant-Colonel Hoke,[487] came to my
assistance about 9 o'clock, which were placed in the redans vacated
by my right companies which were thrown beyond the swamp.
You will perceive that my forces covered almost as much ground
as all the rest of our troops together. Taking my own position near
the center, a little nearer to the right, under Lieutenant-Colonel

---

[482] Thomas H. Brem, captain of artillery. His battery had but six guns, only two
of which were with Vance's flank protection. Hill, *Bethel to Sharpsburg*, I, 223.

[483] Arthur B. Williams, of Cumberland County, who was later captain of company
C in the Tenth North Carolina Regiment (artillery). Moore, *N. C. Roster*, I, 350;
Hill, *Bethel to Sharpsburg*, I, 223.

[484] Probably Walter G. MacRae, who was born in Wilmington in 1841, studied at
Harvard until the outbreak of hostilities, and later joined the Eighteenth North
Carolina Regiment. He was wounded at Gettysburg and captured at the Wilderness.
After the war he resided in Wilmington, where he was general freight agent of
the Atlantic Coast Line Railroad, and later superintendent of a cotton print mill.
He was also a successful civil engineer. At the time of the battle of New Bern his
was an independent company, not attached to any regiment. Evans, *Conf. Mil.
Hist.*, IV, 629-630.

[485] George W. Hayes (1804-1864), of Cherokee County, captain of company A in
the Nineteenth North Carolina Regiment (second cavalry). He resigned April 30,
1862. Clark, *N. C. Regts.*, II, 79; Moore, *N. C. Roster*, II, 174.

[486] Columbus A. Thomas, of Wilson County, captain of company E, Nineteenth
North Carolina Regiment (second cavalry). These two companies, together with
company K, of which Josiah Turner, Jr. of Orange County was captain, fought
dismounted under the command of Vance. Thomas resigned April 1, 1862. Clark,
N. C. Regts., II, 324; Moore, *N. C. Roster*, II, 127.

[487] Robert Frederick Hoke (1837-1912), of Lincoln County, a son of Michael Hoke
and Frances Burton Hoke. His father was a lawyer and orator of note, and was
Democratic candidate for governor in 1844. Robert F. Hoke attended school in
Lincolnton and at the Kentucky Military Institute, but at the age of seventeen
began the management of the iron and textile interests of the family. He enlisted
in the Bethel Regiment, and became lieutenant colonel of the Thirty-third North
Carolina Regiment on January 17, 1862. On August 5, 1862, he was made colonel
of the Twenty-first North Carolina Regiment; was promoted brigadier general
January 17, 1863 and major general April 20, 1864. He served in North Carolina
in late 1863 and early 1864 in both the piedmont and tidewater sections, and
surrendered with Johnston to Sherman, April 26, 1865. After the war he declined
all public honors except when Governor Vance made him a State Director of the
North Carolina Railroad Company in 1877. Samuel A'Court Ashe, "Robert
Frederick Hoke," Ashe, *Biog. Hist. of N. C.*, I, 320; C. C. Pearson, "Robert Frederick Hoke," *Dict. of Am. Biog.*, IX 126-127, *North Carolina Review*, February
2, 1913.

Burgwyn, about whose position I was considerably uneasy, owing to the unfinished state of our works there, I placed the left under the command of Major Carmichael [488] and awaited the engagement. It began on my left wing about 7.50 o'clock, extending toward my right by degrees until about 8.30 o'clock, when all the troops in my command were engaged so far as the swamp referred to. The severest fighting was on my extreme left, the enemy advancing under shelter of the woods to within easy range of our lines. Whenever they left the woods and entered among the fallen timber of the swamp in our front they were driven back in confusion by the most deadly and well-directed fire from our lines who, with the greatest coolness, watched for their appearance.

The fight was kept up until about 12 'clock, when information was brought to me by Capt. J. J. Young,[489] my quartermaster, who barely escaped with life in getting to me, that the enemy in great force had turned my left by the railroad track at Wood's brick-yard, had pillaged my camp, were firing in reverse on my left wing, and were several hundred yards up the railroad between me and New Berne; also that all the troops on the field were in full retreat, except my command. This being so, there was no alternative left me but to order an immediate retreat or be completely surrounded by an overwhelming force. Without hesitation I gave the order. My men jumped out of the trenches, rallied, and formed in the woods without panic or confusion, and, having first sent a messenger with an order to Lieutenant-Colonel Burgwyn to follow with the forces on the right, we struck across the Weathersby road for Bryce's Creek, with the intention of getting into the Pollocksville road. On arriving at the creek we found only one small boat, capable of carrying only three men, in which to pass over. The creek here is too deep to ford and about 75 yards wide. Some plunged in and swam over, and, swimming over myself, I rode down to Captain Whitford's[490] house, on the Trent,[491] and through

[488] Abner Bynum Carmichael (1830-1862), of Wilkes County. He was a son of Abner Carmichael of Stokes County, who had moved to Wilkes as a young man, and was for several years sheriff of Wilkes County. He was also a brother of Leander Bryan Carmichael, who was Vance's Whig associate in the House of Commons in 1854. Hickerson, *Happy Valley*, pp 49, 50; Moore, *N. C. Roster*, II, 362.

[489] Joseph J. Young, of Wake County. He was born in 1832 and joined company D of the Twenty-sixth Regiment when it was organized August 27, 1861. He was appointed quarter master of the regiment by Vance and remained in that position throughout the war. After the war he moved to Johnston County with his brother, B. W. Young, who was a school teacher. Clark, *N. C. Regts.*, II, 414; Moore, *N. C. Roster*, II, 362; W. M. Saunders in *Smithfield Herald*, March 25, 1914, clipping in Walser Papers.

[490] Probably John N. Whitford, of New Bern, who lived about half a mile from the creek. He had a company in the Tenth North Carolina Regiment before he became colonel of the Sixty-seventh North Carolina Regiment, January 18, 1864. Clark, *N. C. Regts.*, I, 14, III, 708.

[491] The Trent River flows into the Neuse River at New Bern. Bryce's Creek flows into the Trent shortly before it reaches the Neuse.

the kindness of Mr. Kit Foy,[492] a citizen, procured three more small boats, carrying one on our shoulders from the Trent, with which we hurried up to the crossing. In the meantime Lieutenant-Colonel Burgwyn arrived with the forces of the right wing in excellent condition, and assisted me with the greatest coolness and efficiency in getting the troops across, which after four hours of hard labor and the greatest anxiety we succeeded in doing. Lieutenant-Colonel Burgwyn saw the last man over before he entered the boat. I regret to say that three men were drowned in crossing.

I must here mention favorably the good conduct of the troops under these trying circumstances, a large Yankee force being drawn up in view of our scouts about 1 mile away and their skirmishers appearing just as the rear got over.

Musician B. F. Johnson,[493] Company B, deserves particular mention for his exertion, having ferried over the greater portion of the troops himself, assisted by a negro boy.

Once over, we were joined by Lieutenant-Colonel Hoke, Thirty-third Regiment, with a large portion of his command, and took the road for Trenton. We marched night and day stopping at no time for rest or sleep more than four hours.

We arrived at this place safely at noon on the 16th. The loyalty and hospitality of the citizens greatly facilitated our march, furnishing us cheerfully with provisions, wagons, shelter, and guides.

I regret to say that many of our men, despairing of the boats at the creek and determined not to be taken, threw away their guns to swim over; a serious loss to our Government, but scarcely blamable under the circumstances.

This concludes the narration of the principal matters connected with my command during the engagement and retreat. The number of my killed and wounded has not yet been ascertained. Our baggage, of course, was lost, but our sick were safely brought away.

It remains for me to speak of the noble dead we left upon the field. Maj. A. B. Carmichael fell about 11 a. m., by a shot through the head, while gallantly holding his position on the left under a most galling fire. A braver, nobler soldier never fell on field of battle. Generous and open-hearted as he was brave and chivalrous,

---

[492] Christopher D. Foy, a giant of a man nearly sixty years of age, who often did picket and scouting duty between New Bern and Washington, N. C. According to William A. Graham, Jr., first lieutenant in company K of the Nineteenth North Carolina Regiment, it was a negro belonging to Mr. Foy who helped them find the boats. William A. Graham, Jr. to Hillsborough *Recorder*, March 29, 1862, quoted in Raleigh *North Carolina Standard*, April 16, 1862; Clark, *N. C. Regts.*, III, 704.

[493] Brazel B. Johnson, of Union County, was a musician in company B of the Twenty-sixth; B. F. Johnson, of Iredell County, was a private in company A of the Thirty-third Regiment, which crossed with the Twenty-sixth on the retreat. Vance confused either the initials or the individuals. Moore, *N. C. Roster*, II, 367, 604.

he was endeared to the whole regiment. Honored be his memory. Soon after Capt. W. P. Martin,[494] of Company H, also fell near the regimental colors. Highly respected as a man, brave and determined as a soldier, he was equally regretted by his command and all who knew him. The Twenty-sixth Regiment are justly proud of their glorious fall. The fate of Captain Rand,[495] of Company D, is yet unknown. When last seen he was almost surrounded by a large force; but, disdaining to fly or surrender, he was fighting desperately with Lieutenant Vinson[496] and a large portion of his company, who refused to leave him. Lieutenant Porter,[497] of Company A, was also left behind wounded. Capt. A. N. Mc-Millan[498] was badly wounded, but got away safely.

In regard to the behavior of my regiment generally, I am scarcely willing to mention particular instances of gallantry where all did their duty. Observing a large portion of the regiment myself, and making diligent inquiry as to the rest, I could learn of but one man in all my command who remembered that he had legs until after the command to retreat was given. They were the last of our troops to leave the field.

I cannot conclude this report without mentioning in terms of the highest praise the spirit of determination and power of endurance evinced by the troops during the hardships and sufferings of our march. Drenched with rain, blistered feet, without sleep, many sick and wounded, and almost naked, they toiled on through the day and all the weary watches of the night without murmuring, cheerfully and with subordination, evincing most thoroughly those high qualities in adversity which miltary men learn to value still more than courage upon the field.

I have the honor to be, most respectfully, your obedient servant, [Printed in *The War of the Rebellion: A Compilation of the Official Records of the Union and Confederate Armies.* Series I, Vol. IX, pp. 254-257.]

---

[494] William Pinckney Martin (1817-1862), of Moore County, captain of the first company to volunteer from his county. Martin was a local political leader who had been elected to represent his county in the proposed convention of February 1861. He was succeeded as captain by Clement Dowd, also of Moore County, who was a future law partner of Vance in Charlotte. Clark, *N. C. Regts.*, II, 418.

[495] Oscar R. Rand, of Wake County. His company had been part of the force with which Major Carmichael had attempted to check the Federal breakthrough at the railroad. Rand was captured and later exchanged. Moore, *N. C. Roster*, II, 376.

[496] In Moore, *N. C. Roster*, II, 376 there is no lieutenant named Vinson in company D, but James W. Vincent, of Wake County, was second lieutenant of that company.

[497] James Porter, of Ashe County, who was second lieutenant of company A. Moore, *N. C. Roster*, II, 363.

[498] Andrew N. McMillan, of Ashe County, was captain of company A. Moore, *N. C. Roster*, II, 363.

To Editor of Standard [499]

Head Quarters 26th Regiment,)
Kinston, March 17, 1862.   )

Will you please announce to the good people of the State, that my regiment is here in a most destitute condition. Any persons that will send a coarse cotton shirt, drawers, or socks, will be doing us a great kindness,[500] as it will be weeks before the State can supply us.

[Raleigh]
[The *North Carolina Standard*, Raleigh, March 22, 1862.]

[499] William Woods Holden (1818-1892), who had edited the Raleigh *North Carolina Standard* since 1843. He was born in Orange County, N. C., educated in the "old field schools", and while very young entered the employment of Dennis Heartt in his printing establishment in Hillsboro. In 1836 he went to Raleigh and became a typesetter for Thomas J. Lemay on the *Raleigh Star*, which was a Whig journal. In his spare time he studied law and was admitted to the bar in 1841. In 1843 he became owner and editor of the *Standard*, the chief organ of the Democratic party in the state, and within ten years was an undisputed power in the councils of the party. As an editor he showed enthusiasm, aggressiveness, business acumen, style, knowledge of human nature, and ready political sense. In large measure he was responsible for the rejuvenation of the Democratic party; in all but the titular sense he led it to victory in the fifties and his office was sometimes dubbed "the Vatican on Hargett Street." When, in 1858, Holden was denied the nomination of his party for governor and was defeated for the United States Senate he began that slow departure from the Democrats which characterized his politics during the next few years. By 1860 Holden was a supporter of Stephen A. Douglas and had lost the lucrative position of public printer, being repudiated by Governor Ellis and the titular leaders of the party in North Carolina. For years Holden had expounded the right of peaceable secession for just cause, but in 1860-1861 he fought secession, plead for the Union, and helped defeat the call for a convention. He was a member of the Convention of 1861, in which he aligned himself with Graham and other anti-Democratic leaders and helped them found the Conservative party which elected Vance to the governorship in 1862. There is no doubt but that Vance was supported by Holden and that the *Standard* had much to do with his election. Thus Holden became a power in the party which overthrew the Democrats, he was restored as public printer, and was one of Governor Vance's chief advisors for about a year. He broke with Vance by 1864, led the peace movement and opposed Vance as a candidate for governor in 1864, winning only two counties. After the war he was made provisional governor of North Carolina by President Andrew Johnson (May-December, 1865), was defeated by Jonathan Worth in the election of 1865, was elected governor as a Republican in 1868, and was impeached and dismissed from office when the Democrats regained control of the legislature in 1870. He did newspaper work in Washington for a time thereafter, but later returned to Raleigh, where he was postmaster, and where he lived for the remainder of his life. Thomas M. Pittman, "William Woods Holden," Ashe, *Biog. Hist. of N. C.,* III, 184-206; McCormick, *Personnel,* pp. 45-46; Edgar Estes Folk, *W. W. Holden, Political Journalist* (Nashville, 1934); William Kenneth Boyd, (ed.), *Memoirs of W. W. Holden* (The John Lawson Monographs of the Trinity College Historical Society, Vol. II, Durham, 1911), especially chap. II, (cited hereafter as Holden, *Memoirs*).

[500] The *Fayetteville Observer* also appealed for aid for the troops and copied this letter. In Fayetteville there was collected a total of sixty-four shirts, ninety-eight pairs of socks, forty yards of carpeting, three pairs of pants, one coat, some tobacco, and $98.70 in cash for one company alone. The *Standard* asked other papers to copy this letter of Vance's, especially papers in the western part of the state. Kemp Plummer Battle gave to Sheriff High, of Wake County, $114, which was the amount of his pay as a member of the convention in its last session, to be applied to the purchase of clothing for Vance's regiment, and for the Wake County destitute at Kinston. *Fayetteville Observer,* March 24, 1862; Raleigh *North Carolina Standard,* March 26, April 9, 1862.

To Mrs. Z. B. Vance[501]

Kinston N. C. March 20th [1862]

Again I try to write you a note— My finger is much better[502] & I can now write without so much pain—You will see an account of the fight in the papers. It began about 7 Oclk on Friday morning and lasted till 12 M. I was stationed on the right wing with a swamp in front. By 11 Oclk every one of our regiments had left except mine, the enemy had crossed the trenches on my left gone through my camp and got half a mile in my rear toward NewBern before I was aware of it— They had Killed Major Carmichael,[503] Capt Rand [504] & various others and were marching right down the works to take me in the rear when my QuarterMaster Capt Young[505] came to me & told me of my danger. Gen Branch had left without giving me any orders[506] and when I finally started and got in sight of the River I saw the bridge[507] in flames! After getting all the troops over but my regiment they deliberately left me to my fate! [508] Fortunately, I knew something of the country, and striking to the left up the Trent I came to a large creek called Briers Creek, almost as big as the Trent, in fact navigable for steam boats, and there we found only one small boat that would carry three men at once. The Yankees by this time drawn up just one mile away! I jumped my horse in to swim him over but when a little way he refused to swim, sank two or three times with me, and I had to jump off and swim across with my sword, pistols and cartridges box on. Once over I rode about half a mile to a house & got three boats which we carried on our shoulders to the creek

---

[501] See p. 16, 81n.

[502] Vance's hand had been hurt by a fall on the logs of the breastworks built below New Bern. See Vance to Mrs. Vance, March 23, 1862, p. 130.

[503] See p. 124, 488n.

[504] See p. 126, 495n. Captain Rand was not killed, but captured.

[505] See p. 124, 489n.

[506] In his official report General Branch wrote that he "dispatched two couriers to Colonel Avery and two to Colonel Vance with orders for them to fall back to the bridges." *O. R.*, Ser. I, Vol. IX, 245.

[507] There were two bridges over the Trent River: one about 1840 feet long upon which the railroad entered the town of New Bern; the other, described by Branch as "an indifferent private bridge" about a mile and a half above New Bern. The railroad bridge is the one referred to; it was also the one which, just one week before, had mysteriously caught fire between three and four o'clock in the morning of March 7. Unknown persons had approached the bridge in a boat. Some believed them to have been "real live Yankees" from Burnside's fleet; others thought them Lincoln sympathizers among themselves. The fire was discovered by a military guard and the bridge saved from destruction. John D. Whitford to Governor Henry T. Clark, March 7, 1862, Governors' Papers (Clark), State Department of Archives and History, Raleigh, N. C. (cited hereafter as Governors' Papers (Clark); *O. R.*, Ser. I, Vol. IX, 245.

[508] This was another mistake of Vance's, as Branch wrote in his official report: "Proceeding to the Trent Bridge, I placed Colonel Campbell in command of all the forces there, with instructions to hold the bridge as long as possible for the passage of Avery and Vance. . . ." *O. R.*, Ser. I, Vol. IX, 245.

and after four hours of hard labour got them all over but three poor fellows who were drowned—I cannot now speak of the thousand dangers which I passed through— Balls struck all around me, men were hit right at my feet— My men fought gloriously— the first fire was especially magnificent — It was a dark foggy morning and the men were situated in small half moon redans, they fired by company beginning on the left, and the blaze at the muzzle of the guns was bright and glorious— Many of the Yankees tumbled over & the rest toddled back into the woods— For five hours the roar of the small arms was uninterrupted, fierce and deafening. Thirty old pieces of artillery (field) were in constant play, whilst the great guns of our batteries and the enemys ships made the earth tremble. I was surprised at my feelings, excitement and pleasure removed every other feeling and I could not resist cheering with might and main. Our total loss so far as I can learn is 5 Killed, 10 wounded & 72 missing—[509] of the missing I suppose one half are killed— having to leave the field as we did it was impossible to tell our dead — Numbers were sure to fall as we left the trenches— My loss was greater I suppose than any other regiment—[510] We feel quite proud of the good name we have obtained [511] and are determined to maintain it— It is not known yet if the enemy are going to follow us to this place. Troops are gathering here rapidly, we will soon be able for a stand.

I have been almost as anxious about you my dear as you have about me. The first news that went up the country was that I was Killed or taken.[512] Such was the natural conclusion, after their leaving me on the field and burning the bridge before me, but thank God I am full of expedients & use to hard times. I warned you darling against first rumors, and I hope you did not put any confidence in them. I rec^d. two letters from you yesterday, written the 9th & 11th

---

[509] These are the losses given for the Twenty-sixth Regiment in the return of casualties in *O. R.*, Ser. I, Vol. IX, 247.

[510] This is incorrect. The Thirty-third Regiment reported thirty-two killed, twenty-eight wounded, and 144 missing. *O. R.*, Ser. I, Vol. IX, 247.

[511] While Branch especially commended the Seventh and the Thirty-third regiments he added: "No troops could have behaved better than the Twenty-sixth, Twenty-seventh, and Thirty-seventh." *O. R.* Ser. I, Vol. IX, 246. Branch gave more candid expression of his sentiments regarding the battle in two private letters to Governor Clark, one written before and one after his official report was prepared on March 26. He wrote the governor that Colonel Sinclair's report was "a tissue of misrepresentations," and declared his purpose to "expose and punish those who had acted badly on the field." Further: "I regret that a desire to disgrace me on the part of personal and political enemies should have caused the troops at New Bern to be deprived of all credit for the fighting they did. It is always so in No Ca." There is no criticism of Vance in either letter. L. O'B. Branch to Henry T. Clark, March 23, April 2, 1862, Governors' Papers (Clark).

[512] For example, a letter from Goldsboro written on the day of the battle announcing the fall of New Bern added that "Col. Vance with a good many of his men were captured." R. D. Graham to Mrs. Joseph Graham, March 14, 1862, William Alexander Graham Papers, Southern Historical Collection, University of North Carolina, Chapel Hill, N. C. (cited hereafter as Graham Papers CH).

and was glad to hear you were mending though so slowly — God grant that the excitement and suspense may not have injured you seriously. I want to hear from you so much— Do write, to this place at once. I should like to dwell upon the many instances of love and affection exhibited by the regiment toward me during the fight & the retreat — I believe they would every one follow me into the jaws of certain death if I lead the way. I dont believe any man could have got them through such a dreary march, 48 miles in 40 hours! Look on the map & see Pollocksville, Trenton, & Kinston, you will see our march—
My hand is hurting me again—Good night darling—Kiss my dear, dear children, who have got a father alive preserved to them through a thousand dangers—My Kindest love to my dear Mother, & Sisters, and may God bless you & preserve you all with His great right arm which has been over me is my prayer—

As ever devotedly yours

This is a pretty long letter isn't it?

Poor Sam Brown![513] I was so sorry to hear from him, carried home dead. His old Father[514] is almost alone now— God be with him. A nobler boy was not alive than Samuel, and as true a friend as I had in this world Peace to his memory— it shall live long and green in my heart—
Asheville.

[A. L. S. Z. B. Vance Papers, State Department of Archives and History, Raleigh.]

To Mrs. Z. B. Vance[515]

Camp 7 miles from Kinston[516]
March 23ᵈ 1862

Since my last we have moved up here and struck up camp— large reinforcements are daily coming in and we begin to feel able to give the Yankees another fight. I was most Kindly treated in Kinston indeed stopt with a Mr Peebles[517] whose Kind wife overloaded

---

[513] See p. 54, 197n.

[514] The father was William John Brown, who was even more alone a little later in the year. One son, John Evans Brown, was in Australia; another, William Caleb Brown, died July 6, 1862 in Richmond; his daughter, Elizabeth, married W. B. Carter, a Union sympathizer, and they lived in Elizabethton, Tennessee. Brown Papers. See p. 54, 196n, 198n.

[515] See p. 16, 81n.

[516] The camp was seven miles from Kinston out toward Goldsboro. Major General Holmes, on March 27, 1862, wrote that he would ". . . order General Ransom, with his brigade, to advance 5 or 6 miles beyond Kinston to some point from whence he can more closely watch the enemy." O. R. Ser. I, Vol. IX, 453.

[517] John Henry Peebles (1813-1864), a Virginian who had come to Kinston in 1834, where for thirty years he was a prominent merchant. His wife was Harriett E. A. Cobb (1822-1898), a native of Kinston, who, after the death of her husband, for many years ran a boarding house across King Street from the courthouse. The Peebles had nine children, all of whom died in infancy or earliest childhood. Information from Charles R. Holloman, Box 70, Raleigh, N. C.

me with attentions— My Regiment is now in Gen. Ransoms[518] brigade[519]— Clingman[520] is with us— My Regiment is now much cut down by sickness and loss in battle, but they are all gay & in good spirits[521]— You will see by the papers that the 26th has made a name — I am pretty well, my hand which was hurt by a fall on the logs of my breastworks, is getting better. My trouble is not being able to hear from you — Not a word since yours of the 11th inst, and my anxiety is very great indeed —

I am great haste this evening darling, so you must excuse this brief note God bless you & my dear Children—
Asheville.
[A. L. S. Z. B. Vance Papers, State Department of Archives and History, Raleigh.]

---

[518] Robert Ransom (1828-1892), of Warren County, who graduated from West Point in 1850, became a lieutenant of dragoons, and after several years of hard campaigning on the border became an instructor in cavalry at West Point in 1854, while General Lee was superintendent of the academy. He later served in Indian campaigns and was among the troops sent to quell the disturbances in Kansas. At the outbreak of the war he was chosen colonel of the First North Carolina Cavalry; in March of 1862 he was appointed a brigadier general and sent to North Carolina. General Ransom was known as a very strict disciplinarian, attained a reputation for tyranny, and found it difficult to get along with his associates. Perhaps these qualities explained the fact that he never remained very long at any one assignment. He was a brother of General Matt W. Ransom. John A. McDowell to T. D. McDowell, March 11, 1863, McDowell Papers; Cullum, *Biog. Register,* II, 418-419.

[519] On March 15, 1862, the day after the defeat at New Bern, Brigadier General Richard C. Gatlin was relieved of command at his own request and Brigadier General Joseph R. Anderson, commanding at Wilmington, was named his successor in the Department of North Carolina. One week later President Davis appointed Major General Theophilus H. Holmes to command the Department of North Carolina. Brigadier General Samuel G. French, who on March 13 had been called to Richmond and ordered to relieve Branch at New Bern but who did not reach North Carolina until the defeated troops were assembling at Kinston, was assigned first to the Pamlico District, formerly comanded by Branch, but five days later to the Wilmington District. It was at this time that Ransom was detached from his command in Virginia and ordered to report to General Holmes, who now proceeded to organize his troops into four brigades. Ransom was put in charge of the first brigade, which was the largest, and which was composed of the Twenty-fifth, Twenty-sixth, Twenty-seventh, and Thirty-fifth North Carolina Regiments of infantry, plus several units of cavalry and artillery. The brigades of Branch and Ransom constituted a division, of which Branch was the commander. *O. R.,* Ser. I, Vol. IX, 445, 450, 453, 460.

[520] See p. 55, 200n. Clingman's regiment, the Twenty-fifth, had been stationed at Wilmington from September to November, 1861, when it was sent to the coast defence of South Carolina and camped near Grahamville most of the winter. On March 14, 1862, the regiment left Grahamville for New Bern, but it was too late to be of aid in the battle and met the retreating troops at Kinston. Clark, *N. C. Regts.,* II, 293-294.

[521] The good spirits of Branch's troops is a matter of record. Holmes wrote that he "was assured by the colonels that there was no demoralization, and that the men were . . . most anxious to advance." General French declared, after an official inspection, that the men were "cheerful and seemingly not at all discouraged by their defeat." *O. R.,* Ser. I, Vol. IX, 453; Hill, *Bethel to Sharpsburg,* I, 305

From A. Carmichael [522]

Briar Creek[523]
March 25 [1862]

For the sake of myself and afflicted family I hope you will use every endeavor to recover the remains of my noble, though fallen son Bynum which I learn the enemy has refused to give up. My only and youthful son, William, went down immediately after the battle and I suppose has not succeeded in getting his brothers body, he is inexperienced, and I have been indisposed for some time and unable to travel consequently we beg of you to use every exertion in our behalf. My dear son must be brought home for internment

[Kinston]

[A. L. S. Zebulon B. Vance Papers, Undated. State Department of Archives and History, Raleigh.]

To the Secretary of War [524]

Hd Qrs 26 Regt N.C.T.
near Kinston N.C. April 3[d], 62

I write for the purpose of getting the authority to raise a legion[525] for the war, two regiments of infantry, two companies of cavalry and one of artillery. Should the authority be given me

---

[522] Abner Carmichael (1788-1866) was born in Stokes County but moved to Wilkes County as a young man, where he became sheriff for a number of years. His oldest son, Leander Bryan Carmichael, Vance's colleague in the assembly of 1854, died in Wilkesboro on March 13, the day before his brother Abner Bynum was killed at New Bern. Three grown brothers of this family died within twelve months. Hickerson, *Happy Valley*, pp. 49-50; Raleigh *North Carolina Standard*, April 5, 1862. The remains of Major Carmichael were sent up from New Bern in February 1863 to Raleigh, where Governor Vance took charge of them to send on to Wilkes County. See telegram of Wm. H. Harvey to Governor Vance, from Goldsboro, February 23, 1863, Governors' Papers (Vance).

[523] In Wilkes County.

[524] The Secretary of War was George Wythe Randolph (1818-1867), of Virginia, a grandson of Thomas Jefferson. He served as secretary from March 22 to November 15, 1862. Randolph was educated in Massachusetts, served for six years as midshipman in the navy, and at the age of nineteen entered the University of Virginia where he remained for two years. He then resigned from the navy and studied law, practicing it in Albemarle County and, after 1850, in Richmond. In 1860 he organized the Richmond Howitzers, served as one of the peace commissioners from Virginia to the United States government early in 1861, and attended the Virginia State Convention as a secessionist. He was one of the first advocates of a stringent conscription law for the Confederacy. Early in the war he commanded the Howitzers, was promoted colonel and then brigadier general, and served in Southeastern Virginia. After his resignation as Secretary of War Randolph asked for a field assignment, but soon resigned. He was found to have pulmonary tuberculosis and went to France for his health. After the war he returned to Virginia and died at the family estate at "Edgehill." Robert Douthat Meade, "George Wythe Randolph," *Dict. of Am. Biog.*, XV, 358-359.

[525] A legion required about thirty companies, counting the ten already in the regiment, with the complement of cavalry and artillery usually attached to a brigade. Those who commanded such forces were ordinarily brigadier generals.

I will guarantee the requisite number of men within thirty days—
[Richmond]
[A. L. S. War Department Collection of Confederate Records,
Office of the Secretary of War, Letters Received, 1862. War
Records Division, National Archives, Washington.]

To North Carolina Newspapers

Kinston, N. C.
April 18, 1862

I AM AUTHORIZED BY THE SECT'Y OF WAR TO raise
a LEGION for the war. I want an additional regiment of Infantry,
two Companies of Cavalry, and one company of Artillery.[526] A
bounty of ONE HUNDRED DOLLARS [527] will be paid to each
soldier upon his enlistment. Cavalry are required to furnish their
own horses, for which the government will pay them forty cents
per day, and their full value if killed in battle. The best arms and
equipments to be had in the Confederacy will be furnished. Recruits will be received singly or by companies. Turn out, and
let's make short work with Abe.

Address me for the present at Kinston, N. C.
Fayetteville Observer, Greensboro Patriot, Charlotte Bulletin,
Salem Press and Asheville News, please copy four times.
[The North Carolina Standard, Raleigh, Ap. 19, 1862]

From J. G. Martin[528]

Executive Department of North Carolina
Adjutant-General's Office
Raleigh, North Carolina
April 23, 1862

Your letter of the 20th inst. has been received and submitted to
the Governor.[529] He declined to give any instructions in regard to
your legion, as the law of this State does not recognize such an

[526] By the terms of the Conscription Act of April 16, 1862 the complement of
troops required in each unit had been raised as follows: an infantry company 125
men, each company of field artillery 150 men, and each cavalry company eighty men.
Section 12 of Conscription Act, O. R., Ser. IV, Vol. I, 1096.

[527] The Confederate States, in section 7 of the Conscription Act, offered fifty
dollars bounty, and the State of North Carolina offered fifty dollars by the terms
of ordinances of the convention, adopted February 10, 1862. O. R., Ser. IV, Vol. 1,
1096; Convention Ordinances, No. 16.

[528] See p. 113, 447n.

[529] Henry Toole Clark (1808-1874), of Edgecombe County, had become governor
on July 7, 1861, upon the death of Governor John W. Ellis. Clark was a planter who
had been State Senator from Edgecombe County from 1850 to 1860, being Speaker of
the Senate in 1858 and 1860 and succeeding to the governorship by virtue of that
office. He was a Democrat and a secessionist. Connor, N. C. Manual, pp. 419, 437, 603;
Grant, Alumni History, p. 111.

organization. And as it is raised by authority of the Confederate States, he thinks the instructions should be given by them.
[Kinston]
[Adjutant-General's Department, Letter Book, N. C. Troops, 1862-1864, State Department of Archives and History, Raleigh.]

From J. G. Martin[530]

Executive Department of North Carolina
Adjutant-General's Office
Raleigh, North Carolina
April 26, 1862

Your letter of the 24th inst. has been received. The Governor directs me to say that he has uniformly encouraged voluntary enlistments, and has sought to keep in the field the full quota[531] required from North Carolina. As a result of these efforts there are now already transferred the full number required by the President. In addition there is now at Camp Mangum[532] the number authorized by law to be raised as a reserve.[533] For these reasons he is not inclined to encourage further the formation of new Companies, considering it better policy to fill up those already in service, if an increase of force be necessary.

I am glad to hear of your reelection under the reorganization[534] of your Regiment, and especially that it has been conferred by a unanimous vote.

I am having a copy of all the Muster Rolls of your Regt. made, will forward them in a few days.

Very respectfully your obt. servant
Kinston   -
[Adjutant-General's Department, Letter Book, N. C. Troops, 1862-1864, State Department of Archives and History, Raleigh.]

---

[530] See p. 113, 447n.

[531] Before the passage of the Conscription Act of April 16, 1862 the usual quota of troops was 6% of the white population. In the case of North Carolina this meant 6% of 631,480, or just under 38,000 troops. The adoption of conscription abolished the quota system, it being assumed that men between the ages of eighteen and thirty-five would be of the same proportion in all the states. See Governor Henry T. Clark to Jefferson Davis, April 23, 1862 and Clark to Secretary Randolph, April 24, 1862, Governor Henry T. Clark Letter Book, State Department of Archives and History, Raleigh, N. C. (cited hereafter as Clark Letter Book).

[532] Camp Mangum was near Raleigh.

[533] Section 6 of the Conscription Act provided that when a state did not have sufficient units in the army to absorb all men subject to conscription from that state they should be kept as a reserve under rules and regulations laid down by the Secretary of War. The reserve was to be called at stated periods to fill up regiments which needed troops, or the entire reserve could be called out by the President if, in his judgment, the public service required it. O. R. Ser. IV, Vol. I, 1096.

[534] The Twenty-sixth Regiment was a twelve-months regiment and under the terms of the Conscription Act could reorganize within thirty days after the passage of the act. The men in the ranks were given the right to elect their company officers, and the company officers the right to elect field officers. There were a few changes made in the regiment as a result of these elections. Clark, N. C. Regts., II, 328-330.

Zebulon B. Vance was the first colonel of the Twenty-Sixth North Carolina Regiment. Harry K. Burgwyn, who was later killed at the Battle of Gettysburg, was the second and youngest colonel. The third was John R. Lane, who served throughout the War. The painting was done in 1897 by W. G. Randall.

To W. W. Holden[535]

Headquarters 26th Regiment,
Near Kinston, April 28 [1862]

I learn that the impression prevails that I cannot organize the troops I have advertised for, since the act of conscription. This is a mistake. The act allows me thirty days from its passage, to enrol my men,[536] which I shall be able to do, beyond a doubt. Persons, therefore, wishing to join my command, may rest assured they will be received until my number is filled. Notice will be given in a few days of the place of rendezvous.

[Raleigh]

[The *North Carolina Standard*, Raleigh, May 3, 1862]

To the North Carolina Standard

Near Kinston, (N.C.)
April 29, 1862

THE RECENT ACT OF CONGRESS REQUIRES each Company to be raised to 125 rank and file. Company E, of my regiment requires 28 men, (from Chatham county) Company G, from Chatham, 20 men; Company B; from Union county, 28 men; Company C, from Wilkes, 50 men; Company D, from Wake, wants 70 men; Company K, from Anson, wants 51 men; Company H, from Moore county, wants 16 men; Company A, from Ashe county, wants 23 men. Men liable to draft in those counties had better come along at once and fill up their companies like white men, and not wait for the sheriff to bring them to me.

[Raleigh]

[The *North Carolina Standard*, Raleigh, April 30, 1862.]

To the Secretary of War[537]

Hd Qrs 26 Regt. N.C.T.
May 2ᵈ, 1862

Sir, Your letter[538] of the 29th ult is before me, in which you refer my "application for leave of absence made through Hon Mr.

---

[535] See p. 127, 499n.

[536] This provision is section 2 of the Conscription Act and provided that all organizations in process of being set up by authority of the Secretary of War were given thirty days from the passage of the act to complete their organization, after which they would be in Confederate service with the right to elect company, battalion, and regimental officers. *O. R.,* Ser. IV, Vol. I, 1095.

[537] See p. 132, 524n.

[538] No letter from the secretary is found among the Vance papers, but the substance of it may be obtained from Gaither's letter to the Secretary of War, which is found in the National Archives in Washington, D. C., and quoted, in part below, in 540n.

Gaither[539] to the General Commanding" &c. If the Hon Mr
Gaither made any application for a *leave of absence* for me, he did
so without my authority.[540] The late Secretary Mr. Benjamin,[541]
authorized me to raise a certain number of troops for the Confederate Service, and to receive & muster them. Gen Holmes[542] refuses

---

[539] Burgess Sidney Gaither (1807-1891), of Burke County, a member of the Confederate Congress. He was born in Iredell County, but moved to Morganton at an
early age. Educated at Dr. Hall's famous school in Iredell, at Morganton Academy,
and at the University of Georgia for a time, he studied law under his brother,
Alfred Moore Gaither and upon his brother's death with Judge David F. Caldwell of
Salisbury. He was clerk of the superior court of Burke County, 1830-1837; a member of the Constitutional Convention of 1835; a delegate to the Whig National Convention of 1839; superintendent of the United States Mint in Charlotte, 1841-1843;
and solicitor of the seventh judicial district, 1844-1852. In state politics he was
a prominent leader of the Whig party in the west; he was a member of the State
Senate in 1840 and 1844, being speaker the second time, but was defeated for the
State Senate in 1838 and 1860; he was twice defeated by Clingman for Congress,
in 1851 and 1853; he was a member of the First and Second Confederate Congresses,
1862-1865, being chairman of the congressional committee to investigate the
Roanoke Island disaster. After the war he was first a Conservative and later a
Democrat; by whatever party label he remained a bitter opponent of Radical
Reconstruction. Samuel A'Court Ashe, "Burgess Sidney Gaither," Ashe, *Biog. Hist
of N. C.*, II, 93-99;" "Burgess S. Gaither," (a typed summary of his career loaned to
the editor by United States Senator Samuel J. Ervin, Jr., of Morganton, N. C.);
Connor, *N. C. Manual*, pp. 471, 522, 869; Clark, *N. C. Regts.*, V. 57-62.

[540] On April 21, 1862, from the House of Representatives, Gaither wrote to the
Secretary of War that he had that day received a letter from Colonel Vance in
regard to his proposed legion. In the letter Gaither said that Vance had "only
received the Secretary's permission in the last few days in consequence of some delay
of the mail or other causes, that he immediately commenced recruiting and enlisting and says he will have no difficulty in raising a Legion forthwith, but the
conscription law requires that it be done within thirty days from the date thereof
and unless he can get a short furlough to leave his regiment and go into the
country he fears the project will fail." He went on to say that Vance had applied
to Generals Holmes and Ransom for a furlough, which had been refused, and
had requested Gaither to apply to the secretary for permission to leave his regiment
for the purpose stated. Gaither called on the secretary, found that he was in a
cabinet meeting, and, being forced to leave town the next morning, wrote the letter
making the request. Of Vance he said: "He is a gallant officer, and greatly distin-
quished himself at the battle of New Bern—a great favorite with the people of my
state and will have no diffculty in raising any reasonable number of troops, provided he can get permission to go among our people." Burgess S. Gaither to the
Secretary of War, April 21, 1862, Confederate War Department Records.

[541] Judah Philip Benjamin (1811-1884), who had been Secretary of War from
September 17, 1861 until March 22, 1862, when he became Secretary of State (1862-
1865). He had also been a distinguished lawyer, United States Senator from Louisiana (1852-1861), and Attorney General of the Confederacy. After the war he
enjoyed an eminent legal career in England. Nathaniel Wright Stephenson and H.
W. Howard Knott, "Judah Philip Benjamin," *Dict. of Am. Biog.*, II, 181-186.

[542] Theophilus Hunter Holmes (1804-1880). He was born in Sampson County
and educated at West Point, where he graduated in 1829 as a classmate of Jefferson
Davis. His military service afterwards included Indian warfare in Florida and participation in the Mexican War, and routine service at various military posts. In
June 1861, his friend Jefferson Davis appointed him a brigadier general; subsequently he became a major general and was assigned to the command of the
Department of North Carolina on March 23, 1862, just after Branch's defeat at
New Bern. In October 1862 Davis made him a lieutenant general and placed him
in command of the Trans-Mississippi Department. Holmes did not wish either

to permit me to leave camp for that purpose, though the troops are ready to be mustered into service and twice as many more as I called for. I know not what to do with them, and asked Mr Gaither to consult you in regard to the matter. That was all. But it makes no sort of difference. I suppose it to be an indirect method of repealing the authority granted me by Mr Benjamin.

As this letter does not go up officially through my superior it is discretionary with the Honorable Secretary whether or not it is answered.[543]

[Richmond]

[A. L. S. War Department Collection of Confederate Records, Office of the Secretary of War, Letters Received, 1862, War Records Division, National Archives, Washington.]

From J. G. Martin[544]

Executive Department of North Carolina
Adjutant-General's Department
Raleigh, North Carolina
May 5, 1862

Your letter of the 1st inst. is received. The Camps are not established as yet in this State, and it is not known at what point the War Department will locate them.

Under the "Conscription law" the Camp near this city established by the State will cease on the 17th, as no more companies can be taken by the State under that law, after that date. I am therefore unable to give you the information you want as the War Department has the entire control of the matter after the 17th.

[Kinston]

[Adjutant-General's Department, Letter Book, N. C. Troops, 1862-1864, State Department of Archives and History, Raleigh.]

---

promotion or command and served reluctantly until he was relieved by E. Kirby-Smith in 1864. Holmes returned to North Carolina, where he was in charge of the reserves until the end of the war. After the war he lived in Cumberland County. Holmes' attitude toward command is illustrated by a letter he wrote to General Lee, April 15, 1862, from Goldsboro. He insisted that some other general must be sent to command in his stead, saying: "Believe me, my dear General, this is not false modesty on my part; I know my deficiencies, and I love the cause too much to permit its vital interests to be intrusted to my management. All my life has been passed in executing the orders of others; send therefore a superior to me, or else change me for another who is capable, or who has his own as well as your confidence.

Do not ascribe this to a want of ambition or to diffidence, but rather believe that I know myself and have the honesty to sacrifice my vanity to the interest of my country. I can execute, but I cannot originate." O. R., Ser. I, Vol. IX, 459; C. C. Pearson, "Theophilus Hunter Holmes," Dict. of Am. Biog., IX, 176; Cullum, Biog. Register, I, 446-447.

[543] The letter has on the reverse the endorsement "Rec'd May 8th," but, unlike most of them in the collection, there is no date of answer. Because of the irregular procedure by which it was sent, probably none was made. Also on the reverse is the notation "no furlough are granted here. Rec'd Ap. 22, 1862 Answ'd Ap. 28, '62."

[544] See p. 113, 447n.

To G. W. Randolph[545]

Hd Qrs 26 Regt. N.C.T.
near Kinston N. C. May 17th (1862)

Learning from you on my late visit to Richmond that the *muster rolls* of the troops I was authorized to raise must be sent you this day, I hurried home and attempted to get them prepared. But inasmuch as they were scattered over different portions of the State, in counties remote from the Telegraph & daily mails I have found it impossible to get them. I have only the rolls of four Companies & they are not in form. Supposing from the terms of the law,[546] that you would only require to be assured of the completion of the companies, I have not provided for this contingency. The scheme is therefore a failure unless you will have the kindness to allow me a week or two[547] to get in my rolls & return them to your office.

[Richmond]
P. S. Please telegraph me—[548]

Z.B.V.

[A. L. S. War Department Collection of Confederate Records, Office of the Secretary of War, Letters Received, 1862, War Records Division, National Archives, Washington.]

To Mrs. Z. B. Vance[549]

Kinston, May 25 [1862]

I rec^d. yours yesterday & was sorry to see you sad, though I fear I am greatly to blame for it. I ought not to write you such fretful & often gloomy letters. But somehow I cant help it; when anything troubles me badly, it relieves me to let it all out to you. I

[545] See p. 132, 524n.

[546] The terms of the law were specific on this point. Section 2 of the Conscription Act provided that only such organizations as were "so far completed as to have the whole number of men requisite for organization actually enrolled, . . . " within thirty days after the passage of the bill, could be mustered into Confederate service with the privileges which accompanied success. *O. R.,* Ser. IV, Vol. I, 1095.

[547] The request for extension of time was taken to General Lee, on behalf of Vance, by D. W. Barringer, who requested a "reasonable prolongation." "I have every reason to believe," he wrote, "that the force to constitute this Legion is already enlisted and tendered to Colonel Vance—but the troops are not yet ready for the camp. Public service will be promoted and public wishes gratified if this postponement can be allowed by the War Department." Lee referred the letter to the Secretary of War for his opinion and action, but the secretary claimed that he had no power to extend the time fixed by law. D. W. Barringer to R. E. Lee, May 17, 1862 (with endorsements), Confederate War Department Records.

[548] The Secretary of War, on May 19 and May 21, sent telegrams to Vance on the subject of his legion. They are as follows: "If you had the whole number requisite for organization actually enrolled on the 17th inst. they will be received." "Send in your muster rolls as speedily as possible. It is necessary that the number necessary for organization shall have been enrolled on the 16th ult." War Department Collection of Confederate Records, Telegrams Sent, Chap. 9, Vol. 34, pp. 234, 238, National Archives, Washington, D. C.

[549] See p. 16, 81n.

am happy that it is in my power to write more cheerfully Though the news we have is not of much importance the aspect of things is decidedly better than they have been for some time past. It is pretty certainly ascertained that the enemys gun boats can not get up the James River to Richmond,[550] there are over 20.000 troops at Petersburg[551] to prevent them operating on the south side of the James, whilst McLellan[552] is almost certain of being whipt if he attacks Richmond by land & without his boats. In the West, the whole country relies with implicit confidence in the glorious Beauregard [553] who has 100.000 of the bravest men on the continent under his Command — He is gathering strength every day, & the impression begins to prevail that he will annihilate Hallecks[554] whole army— Gen Banks[555] has retired across the Blue Ridge to Fredericksburg, leaving the road open for old "Stonewall" Jackson[556] into Maryland & Penn^a. He is going certain, & it is said he will be joined by 30.000 Marylanders with arms in their hands. God grant it.

My Legion is thriving and will yet be a success I think— (I had

[550] After the Confederates withdrew from the Yorktown line and evacuated Norfolk, May 9, 1862, the James River was clear for the Union fleet to a point about seven miles from Richmond. There, at Drewrys Bluff on the right bank, there was a Confederate fort which withstood an attempt by the Union fleet, under Commodore Rodgers, to reduce the fort and pass it. In a four hour action on May 15 the Federal fleet was defeated and Richmond was saved from the naval threat.

[551] No exact returns are available for Petersburg on the date of this letter. In April 1862, there were about 22,000 in the Department of North Carolina, which was extended on June 21, 1862, to include Petersburg and Drewrys Bluff. with headquarters at the former. On July 15, 1862 there were only 3,000 at Petersburg itself, but 26,000 in the Department. O. R., Ser. I, Vol. IX, 469, 475, 476.

[552] George Brinton McClellan (1862-1885), commander of the Army of the Potomac, had begun his movement up the peninsula between the York and James Rivers toward Richmond early in April 1862. By the time of this letter, May 25, the advance of his forces had crossed the Chickahominy River and were within ten or twelve miles of the city.

[553] See p. 111, 438n. After the death of General Albert Sidney Johnston at Shiloh, April 6, 1862, Beauregard had succeeded to the command of the Army of Tennessee, had withdrawn from the battlefield to Corinth, Mississippi, and on the day of this letter made the decision to withdraw further south to Tupelo, Mississippi, and thereby abandon Corinth to the Federals. He did not have 100,000 men, but rather about 50,000. Stanley F. Horn, The Army of Tennessee. A Military History (New York, 1941), pp. 45-50 (cited hereafter as Horn, Army of Tennessee).

[554] Henry Wager Halleck (1815-1872), a graduate of West Point in 1839, and a major general in the Union Army in command of the Department of Mississippi. After Shiloh he took the field in person and assumed active command of the army before Corinth. He had about 125,000 men. Cullum, Biog. Register, I, 733-740.

[555] Nathaniel Prentiss Banks (1816-1894), five times congressman from Massachusetts, governor of Massachusetts, 1858-1860, former speaker of the House of Representatives, and major general in the Union Army assigned to the fifth corps in the Department of the Shenandoah. Banks did not "retire across the Blue Ridge to Fredericksburg," but Shields' division of Banks' army was moved to Fredericksburg on May 1, 1862.

[556] Thomas Jonathan Jackson (1824-1863), Confederate major general in command of the Shenandoah Valley, a district of the Department of Northern Virginia. As Vance wrote this letter Jackson was driving Banks through Winchester in part of his celebrated "Valley Campaign."

a desperate spell of cholic night before last, from eating green peas but am well again. I had yesterday another letter from Brother,[557] and also a long and very affectionate one from Sister Laura,[558] the first I have had from her since the war began. I do wish darling you & she could become reconciled again for my sake.) Col Burgwyn[559] has gone to Raleigh and I shall be very busy this week, but I feel better when I have so much to do, and am able to do it. We dont leave this place I learn— some of the troops at Goldsboro will go to Richmond or Petersburg soon but our Brigade will remain here I fear. Davids[560] friend M[r] Kendall [561] is now our Major. I enclose a letter for Charlie,[562] which I hope will please him— Give my love to Mother[563] & all— Keep Cousin Ann Lizzie[564] with you as long as you can— Kiss my namesake[565] & the other dear boys & Cousin too! *I would if there.* God bless you all. As ever darling your affectionate husband
Asheville.
[A. L. S. Z. B. Vance Papers, State Department of Archives and History, Raleigh.]

To Editor of the Standard [566]

Hdqs. 26th Regt.
Kinston, 28 May 1862

With the many lies, whether official or simply officious, that have appeared in the papers in regard to my share in the Battle of Newbern, I have not seen proper to interfere, being content to rest my course in the hands of my companions in arms, *who were in the fight.*[567] But, Sir, in the case of a gallant officer and chivalrous gentleman who yielded up his life on that unfortunate field, I feel it due the noble dead that I should speak. I allude to

---

[557] See p. 2, 6n.

[558] See p. 66, 243n.

[559] Lieutenant Colonel Burgwyn. See p. 126, 473n.

[560] See p. 38, 147n.

[561] James S. Kendall, of Anson County, formerly first lieutenant of company K, was elected major of the Twenty-sixth Regiment upon the reorganization in April, 1862. Moore, *N. C. Roster,* II, 402; Clark, *N. C. Regts.,* II, 330.

[562] See p. 38, 147n. The letter is in the Z. B. Vance Papers, under date of [May 25, 1862].

[563] See p. 1, 1n.

[564] Ann Elizabeth McCall Pearson (1835-1906), of Morganton, who was a girlhood friend of Harriett Espy and who often visited Mrs. Vance after she moved to Asheville.

[565] The namesake was Zebulon Baird Vance, Jr. See p. 110, 432n.

[566] See p. 127, 499n.

[567] After the battle of New Bern, and especially after Vance's name was frequently mentioned for governor, the press of the state carried on a lively controversy over the part that Vance's regiment had played in the battle of March 14. Papers which were Democratic and which opposed Vance's nomination usually belittled his part in the battle, and the Charlotte *Western Democrat* touched off much of the dispute by saying that "Colonel Vance was not in the fight at Newbern." It later explained that "In saying that Colonel Vance was not in the fight, we meant . . . that he

Major Abner B. Carmichael,[568] 26th Regiment of N. C. Troops. In the official report [569] of General Branch his name is *not mentioned*. Surely, surely, when so much fulsome adulation is lavished upon those who fought and escaped, the aged parents and numerous friends of a brave and intrepid soldier might have expected at least to hear from his commander a mention of his fate, if not his heroism. I wish them to know at least that his immediate commander was not indifferent to his merits, either as a man or as a soldier, and that his memory is cherished, fresh and green, in the hearts of the entire regiment.

The same remarks are applicable to the brave Capt. W. P. Martin,[570] Co. H., these two officers being the highest in rank who fell that day.

[Raleigh]

[From *Fayetteville Observer*, June 5, 1862. Copied from *North Carolina Standard*.[571]]

From A. M. Erwin[572]

Kittrell [573]

June 4th 1862—

I arrived here safely yesterday & found four or five men of

---

was not under fire—that the position *he* occupied was out of danger." The Raleigh *State Journal* wrote that "Colonel Vance neither fired a gun himself nor commanded a gun to be fired by others." The *Raleigh Register* claimed that Vance and his regiment were only "technically" and not really in the fight at New Bern, and that although the regiment itself was in the battle "Colonel Vance himself was not where the actual fighting was carried on." These papers were joined by the *Wilmington Journal* and the *Asheville News* in similar statements. The arguments increased as the campaign for governor neared its August climax, but most of the charges made were printed before official reports of the participants had been published. The Raleigh *North Carolina Standard* and the *Fayetteville Observer* were the principal defenders of Vance, the former saying that "The truth is, *he fought the enemy for one hour and a half after General Branch had left the field.*" The Charlotte *Western Democrat* charged that the political friends of Vance were trying to create a faction against the Democratic administrations at Raleigh and Richmond, and it vigorously objected to "the *Standard's* cococting stories about Col. Vance and the battle of Newbern for party purposes." The Charlotte *Western Democrat*, April 1, June 10, 1862; *Asheville News*, March 27, 1862; Raleigh *North Carolina Standard*, June 12, July 26, 30, 1862; *Fayetteville Observer*, June 12, 1862.

[568] See p. 124, 488n.

[569] General Branch's report is dated March 26, 1862, but it was not published until almost two months later *O. R.*, Ser. I, Vol. IX, 241-247.

[570] See p. 126, 494n.

[571] Editor Holden remarked that this letter "speaks for itself." The *Fayetteville Observer* added that friends, army, and people generally will thank Vance for his "timely and eloquent allusion" to these brave men. *Fayetteville Observer*, June 5, 1862.

[572] Alpheus M. Erwin, who was authorized by Vance to act as commissary agent for the proposed legion.

[573] Kittrell's Springs was in Granville County (now in Vance County), near the Raleigh and Gaston railroad. The resort was operated by G. W. Blacknall, later proprietor of the Atlantic House in Morehead, N. C. and of the Yarborough House in Raleigh. He began operations at Kittrell's on May 15, 1862. Charlotte *Western Democrat*, January 7, May 6, 1862.

Cavalry Co from Anson (Capt Johnsons),[574] come on to make preparation for the Cᵒ & see if all things were ready—looking every hour for the Cᵒ—I saw Maj Morrison[575] in Goldsboro he couldn't do any thing for me but gave me a good deal of information as soon as the Coˢ mustered in he would issue, he told me I couldn't muster in the men as I was not a Confederate Officer until I recᵈ. a commission, but said if Capt Dula[576] had been mustered in any Commissioned officer in that Co could muster in the balance & I will have it done; Capt Pierce[577] told me after the Coˢ were accepted he would furnish every thing but clothing upon my requisition— Genl Martin[578] says you never *consulted he* or the *Gov* about your Legion & he would not do any thing for you, but tried to persuade Capt Dula to go & he could get him in Col Radcliffe[579] Regmt at Wilmington, so you

---

[574] A. L. Johnson, of Anson County, who had just enlisted on May 10, 1862. His company was later assigned to the Fifty-ninth North Carolina Regiment (fourth cavalry) as company A. Moore, *N. C. Roster*, III, 654; Clark, *N. C. Regts.*, III, 457.

[575] William W. Morrison, late of the Bureau of Construction, Equipment and Repairs, United States Department of the Navy. Upon Lincoln's proclamation he left Washington and returned to his native North Carolina. He was captain, then major, in the Commissary General's Department of North Carolina until his resignation. Moore, *N. C. Roster*, IV, 14; Raleigh *North Carolina Standard*, May 4, 1861.

[576] Thomas J. Dula, of Caldwell County. His company was raised for Vance's legion and went into camp at Kittrell's in May of 1862. When the legion failed it was assigned to the Fifty-eighth North Carolina Regiment as company H, and joined that regiment at Johnson City, Tennessee in August of 1862. Upon the transfer Dula was promoted major and later became lieutenant colonel. He was wounded at Chickamauga, September 20, 1863, and resigned from the service August 29, 1864. Dula was born in Caldwell County, attended Emory and Henry College, studied law under Judge A. Mitchell and, in 1871, moved to Wilkesboro. He represented Caldwell County in the House of Representatives in 1872, 1873, and 1901. He was also a member of the Convention of 1875 from Wilkes County. Hickerson, *Happy Valley*, p. 57; Moore, *N. C. Roster*, III, 633; Clark, *N. C. Regts.*, III, 433; Connor, *N. C. Manual*, pp. 529, 855, 905; W. W. Lenoir to his brother, May 25, 1862, Lenoir Papers.

[577] W. W. Peirce, formerly of the Ordnance Department, now captain in the Quarter-Master General's Department of North Carolina. He was later a major. Moore, *N. C. Roster*, IV, 14-15.

[578] See p. 113, 447n. On June 1, 1862, Martin had been appointed a brigadier general in the Confederate army and given command of a brigade in Holmes' department. On May 1, 1862, he had written General Lee and asked to be made a major general and on May 8 Lee replied and explained why the president could not make him a major general. Martin was thus Adjutant and Inspector General of North Carolina and a brigadier general in the Confederate army at the same time. *O. R.*, Ser. I, Vol. IX, 471, 473.

[579] James D. Radcliffe (1839-1878), of New Hanover County. He had been principal of a military school in Wilmington for several years before the war and became colonel of the Eighteenth North Carolina Regiment. Upon the reorganization he was defeated for re-election and later was transferred to the colonelcy of the Sixty-first North Carolina Regiment in August 1862. General Branch called Radcliffe's regiment the best drilled one he had seen in the army and referred to Radcliffe as "a gentleman, a thoroughly educated soldier, and a most faithful and attentive officer" who had been defeated for doing his duty. "If such men are to be put out of service, we may as well give up the contest." L. O'B. Branch to Governor Clark, April 29, 1862, Governors' Papers (Clark); Moore, *N. C. Roster*, II, 72; Clark, *N. C. Regts.*, II, 17, III, 503.

see how things are working— Did you see Capt Clarke[580] (I believe his name is) went to Kinston on Sunday last, from Halifax, he was uneasy about his Co as it was already in a Regmt I have been looking for it daily— Col Clarkes[581] Regmt it was attached to— I hope you could get it out Capt Dula lost a man yesterday, & more sick, they need a Surgion, they have employed one here for awhile— I wish you could come up but I guess no chance now— I am buying what provisions I need for the men—
It is reported here Col Davis (Champ) [582] is Killed, also Capt A Simonton[583] of Iredell is certainly Killed— Col Christie[584]

---

[580] David C. Clark, of Halifax and Bertie counties. He was a student at the University of North Carolina with Vance, was later a physician and a planter, and a member of the House of Commons from Halifax in 1866. His company was company D of the Twenty-fourth North Carolina Regiment. He died in 1886. The name is spelled Clarke in Connor, *N. C. Manual*, p. 642, but not in Grant, *Alumni History*, p. 111, or in Moore, *N. C. Roster*, II, 299.

[581] William John Clarke, of Raleigh and New Bern, a graduate of the University of North Carolina in 1841 (A. B.) and 1844 (M. A.). He became a lawyer and business man who was connected with numerous railroad interests, lumber mills, and iron works between 1850 and 1880. During the War with Mexico he was a captain, and became colonel of the Twenty-fourth North Carolina Regiment upon its organization in July 1861. When the regiment was reorganized Clarke was re-elected colonel and served in Huger's division in eastern North Carolina and tidewater Virginia during 1861 and early 1862. In politics Clarke was a Democrat and had served as Comptroller of Public Accounts, 1851-1855; after the war he became a Republican, supported the Fourteenth Amendment and the Radical Constitution, was State Senator in 1870, a judge of the superior court, 1871-1874, and an elector on the state Republican ticket in 1876. About 1880 he launched, in Raleigh, the *Signal* as a journalistic organ of the Republican party. Many people, including his wife, believed that his propensity for drink destroyed his efficiency and regarded this enterprise as "his last chance." "His success is certain if he will only let whiskey alone." He died shortly thereafter, in 1886. Mrs. Clarke to Clarke, no date (folder #26), William J. Clarke Papers, Southern Historical Collection, University of North Carolina, Chapel Hill, N. C. (cited hereafter as Clarke Papers); Grant, *Alumni History*, p. 113; Moore, *N. C. Roster*, II, 288; Clark, *N. C. Regts.*, II, 271; William J. Clarke to John F. Hoke, May 17, 1857, William Alexander Hoke Papers, Southern Historical Collection, University of North Carolina, Chapel Hill, N. C. (cited hereafter as Hoke Papers); Benjamin Huger to William J. Clarke, December 3, 1862, Clarke Papers.

[582] Champion Talleyrand Napoleon Davis (1826-1862), a lawyer of Rutherford County. He was a member of the House of Commons from Rutherford in 1860, and of the State Senate from McDowell and Burke counties in 1854. In politics he was a Whig, with southern rights leanings, then a Democrat, then a Know-Nothing, over whose convention in Raleigh he presided in 1856. When war came he raised, equipped, and commanded company G of the Sixteenth North Carolina Regiment. In April 1862, when the regiment was reorganized, he became its colonel, and was killed in action at the battle of Seven Pines, May 31, 1862. Connor, *N. C. Manual*, pp. 523, 799; *Asheville News*, April 24, June 29, 1854, August 10, 1856; Griffin, *Old Tryon and Rutherford*, pp. 244-245; Clark, *N. C. Regts.*, I, 755.

[583] A. K. Simonton (1835-1862), of Iredell County, who had been captain of company A in the Fourth North Carolina Regiment, but was elected major on May 1, 1862. He was described as "a prominent figure in the regiment, and gave promise of a most brilliant career. He was a soldier by nature, and a gentleman in every sense of the word." He was killed in action at Seven Pines, May 31, 1862, where all but one of the twenty-five officers of the regiment were killed or wounded. Moore, *N. C. Roster*, I ,122; Clark, *N. C. Regts.*, I, 239, 267.

[584] Daniel Harvey Christie (1833-1863), of Granville County. The report was false, as Christie was only wounded at Seven Pines. A native of Virginia, he became a

killed all the field officers in the 23ᵈ Regmt were either Killed or badly wounded, & the Sr Capt [585] was killed, the rest wounded— Kinston.

[A. L. S. Z. B. Vance Papers, State Department of Archives and and History, Raleigh.]

To George W. Randolph[586]

Hdqrs. Twenty-sixth North Carolina Troops,
Kinston, N. C., June 15, 1862.

(Through Brigadier-General Martin,[587] commanding First Brigade.)

Sir: Pardon me for troubling you once more and for the last time about the troops I have been endeavoring to raise. Several companies are now in camp, and others are drilling at home, and some have been taken from me, and put into another regiment. I learn that both General Holmes[588] and the State authorities have advised the War Department to disband my troops on the ground that when our present regiments are filled to the maximum, North Carolina will have more than her quota in the field, and I find it impossible to raise and organize troops with both State and Confederate authorities against me,[589] and have there-

citizen of Henderson, then in Granville County, in 1857, where he established the Henderson Military Institute. He was subsequently wounded at Cold Harbor and at Gettysburg, from which wounds he died in Winchester, Virginia in August of 1863. He was commissioned colonel of the Twenty-third North Carolina Regiment on May 10, 1862. Moore, *N. C. Roster*, II, 252; Clark, *N. C. Regts.*, II, 238-239.

[585] The senior captain was Ambrose F. Scarborough, of Montgomery County. He was captain of company C and was killed while in command of four companies reconnoitering. Moore, *N. C. Roster*, II, 260; Clark, *N. C. Regts.*, II, 203, 205.

[586] See p. 132, 524n.

[587] See p. 113, 447n and p. 142, 578n.

[588] See p. 136, 542n.

[589] The press discussed the alleged opposition of the administrations at Raleigh and Richmond to Vance's legion. Opposition papers regarded the discussion as a manoeuvre to make votes for Vance by charging interference from state authorities. "The fact is, Colonel Vance got up the noise about a legion for the purpose of helping elect him Governor," and others believed that it was designed largely to obtain a promotion to brigadier general. The degree to which authorities may have interferred is difficult to determine. Vance claimed that General Holmes would not grant him a furlough in order that he might leave camp to raise the troops. This seems to be true. On the other hand, Holmes endorsed Vance's letter to the Secretary of War with the remark that "no obstacle has been interposed by me to Colonel Vance raising his legion." Holmes' friends claimed that Vance wished the general to receive his troops company by company as they were raised; Holmes claimed that he had authority to receive all thirty companies at one time, but in no other way. Also, Holmes is reported to have advised Vance, as an individual and not officially, that the project was expensive and that he had grave doubts as to the advisability of mixing raw troops with a good regiment and possibly thereby ruining the whole, and that "he was opposed to losing any more time about the legion, and would recommend the Secretary of War to disband what had been raised." While Governor Clark was said to have avoided all connection with it, the letter to Vance of April 26, printed on p. 134, was certainly discouraging to the project. Holden wrote that when the adjutant of Vance's regiment applied at Raleigh for tents and other needed equipment for the camp at Kittrell Springs the "request was granted, and the Adjutant left the office and had reached the northern gate of the Capitol, when

fore quit trying to get my companies together. I hope that you will issue an order in the matter at once, that I may know what to do with those in camp. Supposing of course that General Holmes and Governor Clarke's[590] advice will be followed, I have been waiting some ten days for your orders.[591]

[Richmond]   [*Official Records,* Ser. I, Vol. LI, Part II, 571.]

To the Editors of the Observer[592]

Headquarters Twenty-Sixth Regiment N. C. Troops,
Kinston, N. C. June 16th, 1862.

A number of primary meetings of the people and a respectable portion of the newspapers of the State having put forward my name for the office of Governor,[593] to which I may also add the

---

he was called back by an officer and the order taken away and refused. The question occurs again and again, why was Vance not made a brigadier by the powers at Richmond?" *O. R.,* Ser. I, Vol. LI, Part II, 571; Charlotte *Western Democrat,* July 1, August 5, 1862; Raleigh *North Carolina Standard,* May 7, 21, 1862; Holden, *Memoirs,* p. 23.

[590] See p. 133, 529n. Governor Clark's position on the matter of the legion is explained in the letter on p. 134.

[591] Randolph wrote as an endorsement on this letter: "Inform him that no advice has been received from Governor Clark and that the Department is not informed of any obstacle imposed by General Holmes, but considering the attempt as abandoned order already received. Order General Holmes to disband such companies as cannot be made efficient by discharging all not liable to conscription and by transferring the conscripts to the old regiments. Such companies as promise well he may attach to regiments needing companies to complete them or many organize a battalion." *O. R.,* Ser. I, Vol. LI, Part II, 571-572.

[592] The editors of the *Fayetteville Observer* were Edward Jones Hale (1802-1883) and his sons, Peter Mallett Hale (1829-1887) and Edward Joseph Hale (1839-1922). The father acquired the paper in 1825, when it was known as the *Carolina Observer,* and continued its publication under the name of the *Fayetteville Observer* until it was destroyed by Sherman's troops, March 12, 1865. Samuel A'Court Ashe, "Edward Jones Hale," Ellen Hale Wilson, "Peter Mallett Hale," Walter Clark, "Edward Joseph Hale," Ashe, *Biog. Hist. of N. C.,* VIII, 179-199. The paper was a strong Whig journal throughout the editorship of the elder Hale.

[593] No party conventions were held for the nomination of candidates in the elections of 1862. Nominations were made by the party newspaper organs and by meetings of groups in local areas who endorsed certain names already in the public discussion, or suggested new names. Vance's name had been put forward by numerous meetings by this date and the Conservative party needed to settle on one man for the position. After William A. Graham declined all overtures from party leaders Holden wrote "I then determined to fix on Z. B. Vance for Governor." Holden believed that some Whig paper ought make more properly to hoist Vance's name on its masthead, so he arranged for A. S. Merrimon to go to Fayetteville and interview Hale, and then to go by Kinston, where Vance was with his regiment, and obtain Vance's acceptance letter. This having been done, Holden began to back Vance early in June and this letter to the *Observer* followed when the trial balloons appeared to be successfully received by the public. Undoubtedly Vance was Holden's choice at this time, but Holden wished Vance to avoid the implications of the association with a former Democrat, and so engineered the cooperation of the *Fayetteville Observer.* The Confederate press, as the Democratic papers which had supported the original secessionists were called, early settled on William Johnston, a railway executive of Mecklenburg County, a former Whig who had become a Democrat because of his secession and pro-administration views. The newspapers of the state were about evenly divided between the two in their support, eleven being for Johnston and ten for Vance. Holden, *Memoirs,* pp. 18-20; Ashe, *History of N. C.,* II, 712-715.

reception of numerous letters to the same purport, I deem it proper that I should make some response to these flattering indications of confidence and regard.

Believing that the only hope of the South depended upon the prosecution of the war at all hazards and to the utmost extremity so long as the foot of an invader pressed Southern soil, I took the field at an early day, with the determination to remain there until our independence was achieved. My convictions in this regard remain unchanged. In accordance therewith I have steadily and sincerely declined all promotion save that which placed me at the head of the gallant men whom I now command. A true man should, however, be willing to serve wherever the public voice may assign him. If, therefore, my fellow-citizens believe that I could serve the great cause better as Governor than I am now doing, and should see proper to confer this great responsibility upon me without solicitation on my part, I should not feel at liberty to decline it, however conscious of my own unworthiness.

In thus frankly avowing my willingness to labor in any position which may be thought best for the public good I do not wish to be considered guilty of the affectation of indifference to the great honor which my fellow-citizens thus propose to bestow upon me. On the contrary, I should consider it the crowning glory of my life to be placed in a position where I could most advance the interests and honor of North Carolina, and if necessary lead her gallant sons against her foes. But I shall be content with the people's will. Let them speak.

Sincerely deprecating the growing tendency towards party strife amongst our people, which every patriot should shun in the presence of the common danger, I earnestly pray for that unity of sentiment and fraternity of feeling which alone, with the favor of God, can enable us to prosecute this war for liberty and independence against all odds and under every adversity, to a glorious and triumphant issue.

[Fayetteville]

[*Fayetteville Observer,* June 23, 1862.]

To Mrs. Z. B. Vance[594]

Camp Johnston near
Kinston June 18th

I rec[d]. yours last night of the 10th & was sorry to learn that you had suffered so much uneasiness on my account. I read the state-

---

[594] See p. 16, 81n.

ment in the newspapers that I had gone to Richmond [595] & thought it would make you uneasy but supposed of course that my letters would remove it. But you did not get them. The mails are very provoking, but I suppose it is hardly to be expected what they should run with regularity when everything else is so out of joint in the country. I was greatly pleased however to learn that you were better; I hope you will continue to improve now that the weather is fine. You have written me a time or two before to ask what you should do for a physician & I forgot to reply sooner. You will have to employ Dr Hardy,[596] he is a good physician & I have no doubt will be Kind to you, notwithstanding his political prejudices At all events darling it is the only chance unless Dr Stevens[597] were in reach of you. He is a very fair young physician Dr Reynolds[598] is out of the question & I know of nobody else there..

What has become of Cousin Elvira[599] and the suit of jeans she was to make for me? I should like very much to have a piece of nice country Jeans. I would have it made up and trimed elegantly, Confederate style, and if elected Governor I would be inaugurated in it. If she cant make it I wish you would get some celebrated Jeans maker to make me the best piece that can be put up without saying what it is for except that it is for me a sort of uniform.

I enclose you herewith a fifty dollar bill to pay our taxes &c. It is all I have now, I will send you some more at next pay day which will be the 30th—inst. or soon after. Please let me Know if rec^d.

---

[595] The *Fayetteville Observer* of June 5, 1862, quoted reports that the Twenty-sixth Regiment had left on June 2 for the Richmond front. Actually the regiment was ordered to Richmond on June 20 and arrived in Petersburg on June 24; the next night, as part of Ransom's brigade, it reported to General Huger on the Williamsburg road and took its place on picket duty in front of the enemy. Its principal activity during the Seven Days campaign was at Malvern Hill, July 1, 1862. S. P. Dula to Editor of *Standard*, July 3, 1862, quoted in the *Fayetteville Observer*, July 21, 1862; Clark, *N. C. Regts.*, II, 331.

[596] See p. 20, 95n. Dr. Hardy had always been a staunch Democrat. Tennent says that "During the four years of the war Dr. J. F. E. Hardy was the only physician who practiced uninterruptedly in Asheville, all the others being in some way or at some time connected with the army." Tennent, "Medicine in Buncombe County," p. 20.

[597] James Mitchell Stevens, of Buncombe County, then about thirty-five years of age. He was born on the Swannanoa near Asheville, and studied medicine in Asheville and in Charleston. He practiced in Asheville from 1853 to 1859 when he removed to Leiscester, a settlement west of Asheville but still in the county. During the war he was for a time captain and assistant surgeon in the Sixtieth North Carolina Regiment, until he resigned at Tullahoma, Tennessee early in 1863. Tennent, "Medicine in Buncombe County," pp. 16-17; Clark, *N. C. Regts.*, III, 474-475.

[598] John Daniel Reynolds (1832-1874) who lived only about one block from Vance's home in Asheville. Tennent says that he was surgeon of the Twenty-ninth North Carolina Regiment, of which Robert B. Vance was colonel, but he is not listed in either Moore, *N. C. Roster* or in Clark *N. C. Regts.* See p. 16, 78n and p. 14, 67n.

[599] See p. 66, 242n.

I did not get your letter written by Mr Merrimon[600] or Major Israel,[601] dont Know what became of them You speak of your Despatch[602] having stopt & the train being out, do you want it sent again? If so I will send it at once. Let me Know. When will Cousin Ann Lizzie[603] leave you. I hope not soon darling, for I Know she has been a great comfort to you in your lonliness. Keep her as long as you can. My love to every body. I keep quite well. Kiss my Children for me and God bless you all and protect you is the prayer of your ever faithful & devoted husband Asheville.

[A. L. S.   Z. B. Vance Papers, State Department of Archives and and History, Raleigh.]

From H. W. Miller[604]

Raleigh June 18. 1862

It will never do in the world for you to withhold your name from the People as a Candidate for Governor—You can do more for the Cause—and for the State—in the Executive Office than you can in the field—Your election is certain—There is great enthusiasm for you. The secesionists are endeavoring to make the impression that you will not serve if elected[605]—This should

---

[600] See p. 13, 65n. Merrimon had now resigned from the commissary general's department, where he had held the rank of captain, and was serving as solicitor of the western judicial district, to which he had been appointed by Judge French. He was subsequently elected by the legislature to the same post.

[601] See p. 8, 41n. He was at this time in the commissary department of the Sixteenth North Carolina Regiment, from which he resigned on July 8, 1862. Moore, N. C. Roster, II, 2.

[602] See p. 111, 439n.

[603] See p. 140, 564n. She left Asheville about this time. See letter of Ann Lizzie Pearson to Mrs. Z. B. Vance, from Morganton, July 7, 1862, Zebulon B. Vance Papers.

[604] Henry Watkins Miller (1814-1862), of Raleigh. He was a native of Virginia but moved to Raleigh when twelve years of age. He graduated from the University of North Carolina in 1834 and was thereafter a lawyer in Raleigh until his death. He was long a Whig but cooperated with the Democratic party in the 1850's because he thought it might be able to save the Union. But in the spring of 1861 he was an ardent Union leader in Wake County, often speaking at Union meetings, and was nominated a member of the proposed convention, but failed of election. At a Union meeting at Cedar Fork, in Wake County, on March 20, 1861 he was nominated as a candidate for Congress to oppose Lawrence O'Bryan Branch, the Democratic incumbent. Miller was described at this meeting as "a man who never wanted office, never had office, and never was fed from the Federal crib." After Lincoln's call for troops he withdrew as a candidate for Congress in a public letter, and urged southern unity. He was clerk of the State Senate for the two sessions of 1846-1847 and 1848-1849, and was member-elect of the House of Commons from Wake County in 1862, but he stumbled down his own stairs and was killed in September before the legislature convened. Connor, N. C. Manual, p. 471; Raleigh North Carolina Standard, February 12, 21, March 23, April 3, 24, 1861, September 24, 1862; Battle, History of U. of N. C., I, 674. For his Democratic leanings see letter of John Pool to David F. Caldwell, March 30, 1858, Caldwell Papers.

[605] In September 1861, Vance had declined to allow his name to be put forward for the Confederate Congress (see p. 115) and when he was mentioned for governor many papers, such as the Raleigh Register, for example, expressed the belief that

be put to rest—All your friends wish you to say is—"I am no Candidate of my own seeking—I am honored by & satisfied with my present position—But if the people of Old North Carolina elect me their Governor, I cannot refuse to serve them. I shall never shrink from my duty to my State and her people. Come weal or come woe, I am *with* them & *for* them forever."

Say something like this & you will carry everything like a whirlwind.

Kinston.

[A. L. S.   Z. B. Vance Papers, State Department of Archives and and History, Raleigh.]

To Gen. G. W. Randolph[606]

Hd Qrs 26 Redg N C T
In the field near Richmond
July 4th (1862)

Permit me again to trouble you in regard to my legion. Having failed to organize it, for reasons explained in a former note, I am anxious to know what to do with those companies I had rec[d] and accepted into the service. I have made three or four inquiries of you and received no answer—They are exceedingly anxious to be put into service and expressed to me their choice as to what corps they desire to be attached—It is impossible for me to leave my post to see you, and some disposition must be made of them—would it therefore please you to say to Lt. Lenoir[607] who bears this, if they can have permission to enter the corps which he will designate, or whether I have power to dispose of them myself—The muster rolls are with my baggage at Petersburg & can be forwarded at any time—

[Richmond]

[A. L. S. War Department Collection of Confederate Records, Office of the Secretary of War, Letters Received, 1862, War Records Division, National Archives, Washington.]

---

the same principles which made him decline one civil office would make him decline the other. The *Register* professed to believe that Holden, having brought out William A. Graham, who declined, and now Vance, was bringing out men who would not accept and so would pave the way for his own candidacy. Ashe, *History of N. C.*, II, 715.

[606] See p. 132, 524n.

[607] See pp. 74-75, 282n. Lenoir had helped raise the troops for Vance's proposed legion. On April 24, 1862 S. P. Dula wrote Lenoir that Vance was "anxious for you to join the company" and that he "doubtless can get an office." Lenoir was elected lieutenant without opposition. Upon the failure of the legion the unit was assigned to the Fifty-eighth North Carolina Regiment. In July of 1862 Lenoir became a captain in the Thirty-seventh North Carolina Regiment. Lenoir Papers; Clark, *N. C. Regts.*, III, 433.

To Sec'y of War[608]

Hd Qrs 26th N. C. T.
Drurys Bluff Va July 26th (1862)

You will doubtless remember that you authorized me verbally to establish a camp of instruction for the troops I was assembling to form my Legion—since abandoned. I did so, and appointed A. M. Erwin[609] A.Q.M. & W. A. Pearson[610] A.C.S. for the Post, intending to ask for their appointment & have them bonded. The Legion failing, I applied to & obtained from the Q.M. & Commissary General an order for the settlement of expenses incurred by the troops in camp preparatory to their being sent forward into the service as you suggested. Nothing remains unsettled except the pay of those gentlemen—which Col Myers[611] said I must present to you. Will you please to order Maj. Cameron[612] A.Q.M. Dept. of N. C. to pay them, or intimate how they must proceed to obtain compensation for their services?
[Richmond]
[A. L. S. War Department Collection of Confederate Records, Office of the Secretary of War, Letters Received, 1862, War Records Division, National Archives, Washington.]

From the Secretary of War[613]

Confederate States of America,
War Department, Richmond, Aug 1, 1862

I have received your letter of the 26th ult.

---

[608] See p. 132, 524n.

[609] See p. 141, 572n. Erwin served as acting quartermaster from May 21 to August 13, 1862.

[610] William A. Pearson, of Halifax County, was formerly lieutenant in company A of the Fourteenth North Carolina Regiment, Vance's old unit. He was afterwards major in the Second Regiment of Home Guards, organized at Goldsboro on October 19, 1864. He served as acting commissary for the proposed Vance legion from June 1 to August 13, 1862. Since the legion was abandoned Pearson was not commissioned at that time. Moore, *N. C. Roster*, I, 510; Clark, *N. C. Regts.*, IV, 653.

[611] Abraham Charles Myers (1811-1889), first quartermaster general of the Confederate army, was born in South Carolina, graduated from West Point in 1833, and served principally in the quartermaster service until he resigned from the old army on January 28, 1861. On March 16, 1861, he was appointed lieutenant colonel in the quartmaster general's department of the Confederate States army. In December he became quartermaster general and was raised to the rank of colonel on February 15, 1862. He served in this post until dismissed by President Davis on August 7, 1863, for alleged inefficiency, though the Confederate Senate resolved that, since his successor had not been nominated to that body, Myers was still quartermaster general until the confirmation of Brigadier General Alexander R. Lawton on February 17, 1864. Myers refused to serve under Lawton and lived the remainder of the war in Georgia. He was never reconciled with Davis. After the war little is known of his life except that he died in Washington, D. C. Charles W. Ramsdell, "Abraham Charles Myers," *Dict. of Am. Biog.*, XIII, 375-376; *O. R.*, Ser. IV, Vol. III, 318-320; Cullum, *Biog. Register*, I, 562.

[612] John W. Cameron, of Cumberland County.

[613] See p. 132, 524n. The signature is torn off, but the letter is endorsed on the reverse as being from the Secretary of War.

The Legion was entitled to its own Staff, and the law not authorizing the appointment of a Quarter Master and Commissary to temporary Camps of Instruction, the Department supposed that the duties of those offices would be discharged by the Quarter Master and Commissary of the Legion.[614] If however the gentlemen mentioned will make out their accounts, and have them certified by yourself,[615] the Department will compensate them, if possible.

Drewrys Bluff, Va.

[A. L. S. War Department Collection of Confederate Records, Office of the Secretary of War, Letters Received, 1862, War Records Division, National Archives, Washington.]

To Mrs. Z. B. Vance[616]

Near Petersburg
Aug[st] 8th [1862]

The election is all over and if I only Knew what was the result I could tell whether or not I would be with you soon.[617] I have every assurance that I will be governor by a large majority, but it is not certain—From 38 Regiments in the army I have rec[d] more than two to one.[618] But enough—I will be satisfied anyway.

[614] Colonel Myers, the quartermaster general, ruled that "Commandants of regiments have no authority to appoint acting Quartermasters. A subaltern of the line may be designated to act as A. Q. M. and will receive extra pay as such; but there is no authority for paying this claim—as the power of appointing staff officers only belongs to the President. The Legion having been disbanded, no subsequent commission could be given to the A. A. Q. M. so as to assure him pay for the service, as in the case of an officer who is commissioned after having commenced to perform the service under a temporary assignment." Endorsement of Colonel A. C. Myers, August 14, 1862, Confederate War Department Records.

[615] The accounts were made out and certified by Vance. Erwin served two months and twenty-three days @ $140 per month, a total of $387.33. Pearson served two months and thirteen days @ $140 per month, totaling $340.66. The statements "Examined and approved" by Vance were taken to Richmond by Pearson with a note from Vance dated August 13, 1862. Confederate War Department Records.

[616] See p. 16, 81n.

[617] The constitutional status of Clark as governor had been debated by the Convention ever since the death of Governor Ellis in July 1861. During its fourth session, on May 2, 1862, the Convention adopted an ordinance which expressed the ruling that a proper interpretation of the Constitution made a vacancy in the office of governor after the expiration of Clark's term as senator from Edgecombe and as speaker of the senate. After the August elections, therefore, there would be no governor until inauguration day, Jan. 1, 1863. The ordinance provided for the election of a governor, and a legislature, on the first Thursday in August, and for his inauguration on the second Monday in September, to serve until his successor should qualify. Clark was to continue to be governor until his successor qualified. *Convention Ordinances*, 4 session, No. 6, pp. 141-142.

[618] The Convention had provided for the vote in the army to be taken on July 31, one week before the election in the state itself. The returns of the soldier vote were to be made to the respective counties within twenty days. The elections in the army were conducted by three freeholders in each company under the direction of officers who certified the returns. The army vote is given in the *Fayetteville Observer* of August 4, 11, and 18, 1862. In the issue of September 1, 1862 the

We have been in a constant state of excitement here by the Yankees landing on this side—We have prepared for battle every day, marched, counter-marched &c. and finally found out that the Yanks were only plundering along the coast under cover of their gun boats, & were not advancing as we at first supposed. Major Kendall[619] has resigned & Col Burgwyn[620] gone home sick so I have it all to do—I think I shall be with you by Saturday the 17th [621] if all things go right, or a few days further, at least not beyond the 20th—God grant it—I continue quite well but fearful that a return to an indoor life will give me fever—I hope to find you and the children quite well & I know you will be happy—I got your letter of the 31st, am glad to hear my likeness gave you such a pleasant surprise it is not a good one but I thought you would like it—I hope to show you the *original* soon— Kiss my brave boys, love to Mother & God bless you all—As ever yrs
Asheville.
[A. L. S. Z. B. Vance Papers, State Department of Archives and and History, Raleigh.]

From D. L. Swain[622]

Chapel Hill, 15 Aug. 1862

You and I are the sons of old friends, natives of the same county, born under the shadows of the same mountain and nurtured under similar influences, physical, intellectual and moral. I suppose you are about 32—I was but a month short of that age, when elected Governor, 30 years ago. The same causes that transferred me from the judicial, to the executive department of the government,[623] have operated to withdraw you from the army and place you in the chair of the state. There are other

---

"official" vote for the whole election is given, but the figures given there vary by several hundreds of votes from the official lists in the office of the Secretary of State, as quoted in the Clark Letter Book. The ordinance provided that the Governor should proclaim the results when examined and certified by the Secretary of State, the Treasurer, and the Comptroller on August 28. The official figures as found by them gave Vance 52,833 and Johnston 20,174. Clark Letter Book, p. 408.

[619] See p. 140, 561n. Since his election as major in May, Kendall had been ill with yellow fever contracted at Wilmington while on furlough. He died shortly after his resignation, in August 1862. Clark, *N. C. Regts.*, II, 330.

[620] See p. 121, 473n.

[621] August 17, 1862, was a Sunday. Vance arrived in Raleigh on Saturday, August 16, spent one night there and left by train for Asheville on Sunday. His resignation from the army was accepted on August 19, 1862, in Special Orders, No. 193. *Fayetteville Observer*, August 25, 1862; *Special Orders of Adjutant and Inspector General's Office, Confederate States, 1862*, p. 355.

[622] See p. 9, 45n.

[623] In 1830 Swain was elected a judge of the superior court by the legislature. He retained this position until elected governor in 1832, also by the legislature.

coincidences in our personal history, not less striking and of deeper interest which may supply topics of conversation, when we meet.

I was elected governor by a respectable legislative majority over candidates greatly my senior, and of established reputation,[624]—you have been called to office by a spontaneous expression of public sentiment an almost universal uprising of the people, without a paralel in our history. No more unwelcome intelligence ever reached me, than the annunciator of my election; I thank God, that the difficulties to be encountered were not so great as I feared, and that I was enabled so to discharge my duties, as to satisfy the most of my friends and escape to some extent bitter animosities from enemies. The same inspiring circumstances which herald your advent will involve you in greater difficulties,—more is expected and more will be required at your hands than was called for, in the boisterous, but *comparatively quiet sea,* on which my fortunes were embarked. The greater the difficulty, the greater the triumph in surmounting it. I trust you will meet it cheerfully, courageously and successfully.

The ordinance of the Convention requires that you shall take the oath of office before a Judge of the Superior or Supreme Court.[625] I think that the citizens of Raleigh who gave you such an overwhelming vote,[626] have a right to expect that the ceremony shall take place in the Commons Hall, under as inspiring circumstances as the importance of the occasion requires. I take it for granted that Gov. Clark[627] and other public officers, will spare all pains, to render the exit of the retiring and the advent of the succeeding chief graceful to say the least. If he does not I am certain the citizens of Raleigh will. Gov. Clark was Chairman of the Committee at the inauguration of Gov. Ellis[628] and I know from personal experience, understands what ought to be done, and am satisfied that he will take pride and pleasure in

[624] The principal candidates in 1832 were Richard D. Spaight, Thomas G. Polk, and John Branch. Governor Montford Stokes, though eligible for another term, announced that he had accepted an appointment from President Jackson to make treaties with the Indians, and therefore was not a candidate. Ashe, *History of N. C.,* II, 350.

[625] This was section 4 of the ordinance adopted May 2, 1862, and provided that the Governor-elect "on the second Monday of September . . . appear before some Judge of the Supreme Court, or some one of the Judges of the Superior Courts of Law. . . ." and take the oath prescribed by law. *Convention Ordinances,* 4 session, No. 6, p. 142.

[626] The Raleigh vote was Vance 794, Johnston 143. Will Dickson to his sister, August 8, 1862, Dickson Papers.

[627] See p. 133, 529n.

[628] See p. 74, 281n.

doing it, and having it done.[629] This will afford you an opportunity to define your views, in an inaugural address, in advance of the meeting of the General Assembly. Your overwhelming majority, will render this a most important document at home and abroad. Your note to the newspapers was well written,[630] and in the proper spirit. Your inaugural will of course be well considered, more extended and more elaborate, but brief nevertheless and to the point. You entered the conflict determined never to cease your efforts in behalf of your country, until every invader was driven or withdrawn from her borders. You will probably not be expected to go beyond a general and decisive expression of your views on this subject. It is important that with respect to this question your opponents at the South, and our public enemies at the North, should have not have it in their power to misrepresent you. Minor matters may be deferred, for your first message.

Your election by the people [illegible] to party will afford you an opportunity to discard party and the selfish tools of party. Beware of hasty committals to applicants for office. Gov. Clark has taken sides with high soldiers. Will not one able and trusty friend suffice? Your Private Secretary, will be a most important adjunct and should be most carefully selected. Learning, talent and integrity are indispensable. I may write you again on this head and suggest a name.[631]

Writing with no other view, than to serve a friend and the country, I know I need make no apology for intrusion of this note.

For haste and all defects I have a most melancholy apology. I write early in the morning after four anxious days and nights passed under the apprehension, that before the close of each, a daughter (our first born)[632] will have cleared a scene of suffering mental and physical, which I pray God to sanctify to her parents, her brother and sister, and to grant that the parallels presented

---

[629] Swain's letter to Vance was doubtless inspired by a letter he received from former Governor Charles Manly of Raleigh, who wrote him and suggested some of the advice Swain was now giving Vance with regard to his inauguration. Manly believed that "The authorities were, here, I suppose, opposed to Vance and will take no steps to give prominence and dignity to his instalment into office and I intend to disappoint them. I mean to kick up a mighty fuss, 'anyhow.'" He added: "If you approve of my sugestion write to Col. Vance that he may prepare himself." Charles Manly to David L. Swain, August 14, 1862, Swain Papers CH.

[630] This doubtless refers to Vance's letter of June 16 to the *Fayetteville Observer.* See p. 145.

[631] Swain subsequently recommended Edward J. Hale, a son of the editor of the *Fayetteville Observer,* who declined. He then recommended Richard H. Battle, who accepted the post. See below, p. 167.

[632] Anne Swain, who died in 1867. Of her Mrs. Cornelia Spencer wrote; "Sometimes partially, sometimes wholly deranged, and sometimes brighter than the best of us, yet suffering the agony of knowing that she was smitten; always affectionate, generous, charitable, humble. . . ." Quoted in Russell, *The Woman Who Rang the Bell,* p. 24.

in *our* personal history, may not extend. I have never known a greater sufferer.
[Raleigh][633]
[A. L. S.   Z. B. Vance Papers, State Department of Archives and and History, Raleigh.]

To W. A. Graham[634]

Raleigh, Aug[st] 17th [1862]

The state of my health renders it absolutely necessary that I should rest at home as long as possible before the inauguration. Every one I meet seems to think my address should be prepared with some care, in view of the impression my election is likely to have upon the North aided by the slanders of our opponents.[635] As I shall have to prepare it at home without the presence of many with whom I should like to consult, I should be greatly

---

[633] Charles Manly wrote from Raleigh on August 18, to Swain, that he "had the pleasure of handing your letter to *Gov. Vance* myself" as he came through Raleigh on his way from Petersburg to Asheville. Swain Papers CH.

[634] William Alexander Graham (1804-1875), son of General Joseph Graham, of Lincoln County. He was educated in the private schools of Lincoln County, at Dr. Muchat's Classical Academy at Statesville, at the Hillsboro Academy, and at the University of North Carolina, from which he graduated with high honor in 1824. He studied law under Chief Justice Thomas Ruffin at Hillsboro, where he settled and was soon a recognized leader of the North Carolina bar. His public career began in 1833 when he was elected a member of the House of Commons to represent Hillsboro. He was continuously in the House of Commons, and was twice speaker, until 1840, when he was elected United States Senator, his term expiring on March 4, 1843. He was governor of North Carolina, 1845-1849; a member of the State Senate from Orange County, 1854, 1862, and 1865; Confederate States Senator, 1864-1865; a member of the Conventions of 1861 and 1875 (he died before the latter convened); Secretary of the Navy under Fillmore, 1850-1852; and nominee for vice-president on the Whig ticket in 1852. He was also elected United States Senator in 1866, but was not allowed to take his seat. He was a trustee of the Peabody Fund at the time of his death, and for thirty-four years had served as a trustee of the University of North Carolina, from which he received in LL.D. in 1849. He died at Saratoga Springs, New York, while acting as an arbitrator in the dispute as to the dividing line between the states of Maryland and Virginia. Politically Graham was a conservative Whig and one of the outstanding leaders of moderate opinion in North Carolina. He was probably the choice of most of the leaders of the Old Line Union Whigs for the governorship in 1862, but he declined the nomination which Vance later received. Graham, Swain and Edward J. Hale were the advisers on whom Vance leaned most heavily throughout his governorship, especially after the break with Holden. Montford McGehee, *Life and Character of the Hon. William A. Graham* (Raleigh, 1877); McCormick, *Personnel*, pp. 38-39; Frank Nash, "William Alexander Graham," *Dict. of Am. Biog.*, VI, 480-481.

[635] Both northern papers and Democratic papers in North Carolina commented frequently on the meaning of Vance's nomination and election. He was often referred to as the "Federal candidate," "Union candidate," "Lincoln candidate," or even "abolition candidate," and as an "old Union man who will oppose Jefferson Davis and his corrupt cliques at Richmond." These labels were given currency throughout the North Carolina press and northern papers picked them up and used them to speculate on the meaning of the contest in North Carolina. The week before the election the *Raleigh Register* made a late appeal by saying "remember that if Zebulon Vance shall be elected Governor the Yankees will claim it as an indisputable sign that the Union sentiment is in the ascendancy in the heart of the Southern Confederacy." Some Yankee papers went that far: the Philadelphia *Inquirer,* asking the question as to whether the election of Vance meant peace,

obliged for, and most thankfully receive any suggestions from yourself, as to the character of the address it would be proper for me to deliver &c.

I shall leave for home this afternoon, feeling quite unwell; but hope and believe that two weeks in our mountain air will restore me. Write me at Asheville.

Hillsboro

[A. L. S. William A. Graham Papers,
Southern Historical Collection, Chapel Hill.]

To D. L. Swain[636]

Asheville N C
Aug 25th [1862]

Your letters were both rec.ᵈ I am so unwell today that I can hardly hold the pen—I write brieffy to acknowledge your favors, and to say that I entirely concur with you in regard both to the character of my address and the qualifications of my Private Secretary. My first thought was of Capt John D. Hyman[637] who is now lying here wounded & will not I learn be able to stand on his feet for many months But he is poor and the inadequacy of the salary[638] will prevent his acceptance I shall be only too happy to secure the services of Capt Battle[639] if he will make the sacri-

concluded that his victory "can hardly be expected to bear *immediately* upon the restoration of North Carolina to the Union" but that "when Richmond falls, the lines of the restored Union will, through the influence of the election on Thursday last, be extended at one sweep clear to the northern boundary of South Carolina. Then what a signal triumph will that be that carries the Union flag to the dome of the Rebel Capital, and liberates the 'Old North State'." The New York *Herald*, quoting North Carolina sources, considered the election a great test of Union and thought conservatives "united by the common tie of reconstruction." "Govs. Stanly and Vance, and a "conservative" Legislature will put you back under the Lincoln government, . . . Holden is striving for this and poor Colonel Vance is too infatuated to see the use which is to be made of him, . . ." "The election of Colonel Vance would indicate the popular will of the people of North Carolina to re-enter the old Union, . . ." The *Herald* also quoted the Washington (N. C.) *New Era* as hoping for the "election of conservative men, who yielded for a time from the pressure of necessity, to rebel force; but who still look forward to the restoration of the Union. The duty of the loyal electors under the circumstances is plain. Let them choose from the candidates placed before them those whose antecedents give token that they were, and still may be, friends to the Union." Since Vance did not campaign during the election, except for a few speeches to the army, there was no iota of justification by any words from him for associating him with sentiments such as those quoted above. Northern papers took the charges of the papers opposing Vance more seriously and more literally than there was any justification for doing. Philadelphia *Inquirer*, August 14, 1862, p. 4; New York *Herald*, August 7, 29, 1862, p. 2; Raleigh *North Carolina Standard*, July 30, 1862; Ashe, *History of N. C.*, II, 738.

⁶³⁶ See p. 9, 45n.

⁶³⁷ See p. 50, 181n.

⁶³⁸ The salary of the private secretary to the governor was $300 a year.

⁶³⁹ Richard Henry Battle (1835-1912), a son of William H. Battle, Vance's law professor at the University of North Carolina. Swain had known Richard Battle while he was a student at the University with Vance. Battle was born in Franklin County and lived as a boy in Raleigh and Chapel Hill, graduating from the University in 1854 with first honor, and for four years thereafter was a tutor in Greek and mathe-

fice—for such I would regard it—If you have his address you would greatly oblige me by writing him for me. I wish I felt able to write you more at length.

Accept my sincerest sympathies in your family affliction,[640] and believe me, my Dear Sir, Most truly yours
Chapel Hill.
[A. L. S. Z. B. Vance Papers,
State Department of Archives and History, Raleigh.]

From O. F. Manson[641]

Moore Hospital,[642]
Richmond, Va.,
Aug 27 1862

[Private & Confidential]
Having learned that there will probably be a change in the

---

matics. In 1858 he opened a law office in Wadesboro, but in February 1862, he joined the army as a first lieutenant in company I of the Forty-second North Carolina Regiment and served until he became Vance's private secretary. He remained secretary until August 1864, when he became state auditor. After the war he formed a law partnership in Raleigh with Samuel F. Phillips, but the firm was dissolved in 1868, when he became a member with his father and brother, Kemp Plummer Battle, of the firm of W. H. Battle & Sons. In 1876 he formed a new partnership with Samuel F. Mordecai, also in Raleigh. In politics Richard H. Battle was, in 1860, a Constitutional Union man and after the war became a Democrat, serving as chairman of the State Democratic Executive Committee from 1884 to 1888. Though always interested in politics, he rarely held office. He was nominated by his party for a seat in the Convention of 1875, but was defeated. He was a member of the House of Representatives from Wake County in 1911. During the last thirty years of his life he was a leader in Raleigh of many civic enterprises, and assisted in organizing many industrial and corporative ventures in the state. On August 22, 1900, he delivered the memorial address at the unveiling of the Vance statue on capitol square in Raleigh which was published in *Literary and Historical Activities in North Carolina, 1900-1905* (Raleigh, 1907), pp. 74 (cited hereafter as Battle, *Vance*); Samuel A'Court Ashe, "Richard H. Battle," Ashe, *Biog. Hist. of N. C.,* VI, 39-43. Swain wrote to Battle on behalf of Vance, as requested. See R. H. Battle to Z. B. Vance, p. 167.

[640] See p. 154, 632n.

[641] Otis Frederick Manson, M. D. (1822-1888) was born in Richmond, graduated from the medical department of Hampden-Sydney College in 1840, and moved to North Carolina in 1841, settling in Granville County where he practiced his profession with distinction until the advent of the war. He published many medical papers, pioneered in the use of quinine, and came to be known as an authority on smallpox and malaria. During the war he was medical agent for North Carolina in Richmond, looking after the medical needs of the state's soldiers at that center. After the war he was professor at the Medical College of Virginia from 1869 to 1882. Vance wrote of him: "I regard Dr. Manson a very superior man intellectually and professionally. As a high-toned gentleman, and a man of profound learning, and great kindness of heart, he endeared himself to me greatly during the war. He endeared himself not only to me but to every man, woman and child in North Carolina." Thomas F. Wood, *Memoir of Prof. Otis Frederick Manson, M. D.* (Raleigh, 1888), *passim* (cited hereafter as Wood, *Memoir of Manson*); S. S. Satchwell, *Memorial of Prof. Otis Frederick Manson* (Raleigh, 1888), *passim.*

[642] In May of 1862, Manson was put in charge of the North Carolina Hospital in Richmond, which he named Moore Hospital in honor of Dr. S. P. Moore, Surgeon General of the Confederacy. It was a three-story brick tobacco warehouse on Main Street, abundantly lighted with windows, and capable of caring for about 150 patients. Wood, *Memoir of Manson*, p. 8.

Medical Department of the Gov. of N. C. I have taken the liberty of addressing you a line upon the subject.

When the office of Surgeon General of N. C. was created at least two thirds of the Members of the State Convention then in Session recommended me to the Governor for the appointment, To these were added the principal members of the State Legislature and many other prominent citizens of our State. Besides these all of members of the Board of Medical Examiners[643] of the State except two urged the Governor to confer the appointment upon me. The two exceptions in the Board were D[r]. Johnson[644] the present incumbent and his intimate friend D[r]. McKee[645] of Raleigh. The friends of Gov[r]. Ellis [646] informed me afterwards that I would have received the place if the Governor had not promised the place to D[r]. Johnson then in professional attendance upon him.

I believe Sir I am but echoeing the public and professional view in declaring that the appointment was a very unfortunate one. Although a man of Some talent yet the present Surgeon General from his want of business capacity, energy & withal his posession of an unamiable disposition has proven himself unequal to the task before him. Need I point in proof of this to the fact that until I took charge of this Hospital in May our Noble old State had not a Single hospital in this place whilst every other State had prepared numerous places of refuge for her defenders here.

If I know my own heart Co[l]. my first wish is that the Surgeon Gen.[l] of our State should be a man of such capacity and zeal that

---

[643] The Board of Medical Examiners was created in 1859. The members were: J. H. Dickson, President, Charles E. Johnson, William H. McKee, Otis F. Manson, Christopher Happoldt, J. Graham Tull, and Caleb Winslow. *Transactions of the Medical Society of the State of North Carolina* (Raleigh, 1859), p. 15 (cited hereafter as *Medical Transactions*).

[644] Dr. Charles Earl Johnson (1812-1876), of Raleigh, a graduate of the University of Virginia and the University of Pennsylvania in medicine. He was president of the North Carolina Medical Society in 1856 and 1857 and was appointed surgeon general of North Carolina by Governor Ellis on May 16, 1861, with the rank of colonel. In his early professional career he had been a partner of Edward Warren's father, Dr. William Christian Warren, and so was acquainted with his successor in the office of surgeon general. Johnson was always interested in politics and wrote many political articles for the *Raleigh Register* after he moved to Raleigh in 1845. *Medical Transactions*, 1876, pp. 9-18; 1917, pp. 342-343; Clark, *N. C. Regts.*, IV, 623-624, 628. Johnson resigned as surgeon general on September 4, 1862, writing Governor Clark that there was nothing left to do in the office as the North Carolina hospitals were being turned over to the Confederacy by Clark's order. Governors' Papers (Clark).

[645] Dr. William H. McKee (1814-1875), also of Raleigh and also a graduate in medicine of the University of Pennsylvania, who had been secretary and president of the medical society, succeeding Johnson for two years in the latter office. John Wesley Long, *Early History of the North Carolina Medical Society*, p. 13 (An address before the 64th annual meeting of the North Carolina Medical Society at Asheville, April, 1917); *Medical Transactions*, 1875, pp. 9-20; 1917, p. 343.

[646] See p. 74, 281n.

he would be enabled to adopt and execute every practicable measure for the relief of our Suffering Soldiers I trust Sir as I believe that in making this appointment that the good of the Soldier will be the paramount consideration over-riding all others. Should you deem me worthy of the position I can only promise that every power of my mind and body shall be dedicated to the duties of the office, and it shall be my highest boast if at the termination of my career I shall be able to receive your commendation.

There is only one consideration which makes me hesitate in asking this position at your hands. I met D^r. Warren[647] yesterday who told me that you had already promised the position to him. If this is the case do not let my claims be an embarrassment to your decision. D^r. Warren is an educated gentleman and of acknowledged talents. It gives me pleasure to say this. Of his business Capacity my slight acquaintance with him does not permit me to speak.

Select an able man dear Co^l., one who will do everything possible to ameliarate the condition of our Soldiers and I shall be content.
[Raleigh.]

---

[647] Edward Warren (1828-1893) was the son of Dr. William Christian Warren, a native of Virginia who moved to Tyrell County, N. C., where Edward was born, and then to Edenton where the boy lived from the age of four to sixteen. He attended school at Fairfax Institute, near Alexandria, Va., the University of Virginia, and Jefferson Medical College in Philadelphia, from which he graduated in 1851. He studied medicine further in Paris, 1854-1855, and upon his return settled in Edenton. He became the first editor of *The Medical Journal of North Carolina,* 1857-1860; professor of materia medica and therapeutics at the University of Maryland, 1860-1861, where he was known as a graceful, fluent, and able lecturer; and surgeon general of North Carolina, 1862-1865. During the war he wrote a treatise on *Surgery for Field and Hospital,* which passed through two editions. In the summer of 1865 he returned to Baltimore, ruined by the war, and was refused his old chair at the University of Maryland. He undertook legal proceedings to secure it again, but abandoned the attempt because of his ruined financial condition and because of hostile faculty opinion. In 1868 he held the chair of surgery in Washington College and established the *Medical Bulletin,* a journal of extensive circulation. About 1872 he left Baltimore—the reasons were varied—and became the chief surgeon of the general staff of the Khedive of Egypt and surgeon-in-chief of the Egyptian army, being recommended by Vance, among others. In 1875 he began the practice of medicine in Paris and won many professional honors abroad. Warren was always interested in politics and had hoped to study law, but gave up the idea out of deference to his father's wish that he should be a doctor. He was an Old Line Union Whig before the war and tried to gain a seat in the Confederate Congress as a Conservative, but was defeated in 1863. At the time of the battle of New Bern Warren was on duty in Goldsboro as a member of the Board of Medical Examiners, but he volunteered for duty and remained under fire. This experience, together with his natural Whig proclivities in politics, brought him into association with Vance, and their relationship ripened into an enduring and affectionate friendship. *Biographical Sketch of Dr. Edward Warren (Bey)* (Paris, 1882), republished from *The Medical Journal of North Carolina; The Confederate Veteran,* vol. 34, no. 5 (May, 1926), pp. 172-173. Warren's own account of his life, which includes many intimate glimpses and opinions of Vance, is *A Doctor's Experiences in Three Continents* (Baltimore, 1885).

P.S. I enclose to you a few of the recommendations I previously rec^d. which were all I could obtain from Govr. Ellis, another was given by Mr. Holden his friend.

[A. L. S.   Z. B. Vance Papers,
State Department of Archives and History, Raleigh.]

From J. G. Shepherd[648]

Fayetteville
August 28. 1862.

I regret that by reason of my absence from home, I did not receive your letter in time for answering previous to this date. I should feel embarrassed in giving this reply, if you had not known me personally in our service together in 1854—when without reference to the political differences that divided us— we labored faithfully and pleasantly together in the cause of internal improvement for our state. I shall go the General Assembly with the feeling that it is my high duty to aid you in every measure proposed, which commands itself to my approbation and be assured that I shall earnestly support whatever you may recommend for our consideration—where I would give my support in the case of any other high officer or any other Executive in the State. I shall feel this to be a high and I may say a Christian duty. I respect you as a patriotic and gallant man—I have never had any other feeling towards you and to me it was a matter of mortification and shame that things were done in the late canvass[649]—which in cooler moments I hope that all will condemn.

I took no part in the late election—was not brought forward by any particular influence—and while I have said this much—I

---

[648] Jesse George Shepherd (1821-1869), a lawyer of Cumberland County was graduated from the University of North Carolina in 1841, studied law and became county attorney. He served in the House of Commons in 1854, 1856, 1862, and 1864, being speaker in 1856; was a judge of the superior court, 1859-1860; and a member of the Council of State, 1866. He married Catherine Isabella Dobbin, a sister of James C. Dobbin, Democratic leader and Secretary of the Navy in the Pierce administration. Shepherd was also a Democrat, being chairman of the Democratic State Committee in 1855, but in the crisis of 1861 he refused to follow the ardent secessionists of his party, though he was not so avowed a Unionist as his fellow Democrat, Bedford Brown, the leader of the Union Democrats. Grant, *Alumni History*, p. 558; Connor, *N. C. Manual*, pp. 440, 449, 473, 578; *Raleigh Register*, September 13, 1854; Raleigh *North Carolina Standard*, October 9, 1861; *Asheville News*, December 6, 1855.

[649] Shepherd doubtless refers to two lines of attack made on Vance by the press during the campaign. The first was the attack on his military record, particularly the charge that he was not "in the fight at Newbern." See p. 140, 567n. The second point of attack was the general charge that Vance and the Old Line Union Whigs were still Union men and at heart submissionists. They were often charged with infidelity to the southern cause and marked as traitors. The principal papers which took these lines of attack were the *Wilmington Journal*, the Charlotte *Western Democrat*, and, especially, the *Raleigh Register*. See p. 155, 635n.

must tell you candidly and truthfully—that I did not vote for yourself—for reasons in no manner relating to your virtue—your capacity—your honor and character—for all of which be assured that I have always commended and do now fully commend you. I feel that I owe it to this degree of respect in which I hold you— to speak this with outrightness. If then with this statement— you are willing to receive a suggestion from me—I would appeal to you to elaborate the views so well uttered in your Raleigh speech[650] avowing the most determined opposition to a reconstruction of the old Union—insisting that as North Carolina was *deliberate* in her severance from that Union and as all the history of this cruel and bloody war has served to show her wisdom in the separation and to teach her people that liberty and honor are to be found only in another government—it is madness—to suppose that any people moved by high and noble feelings as we have been—would turn back to a condition which to us would be full of humiliation and debasement. Is our whole struggle a mockery? Are lives lost—desolation and ruin around us witnessed in our fair land with no purpose—no motive—but the base looking thought that we shall kiss the hand that smites and submit to the imperious and despotic rule of cruel masters? All of our people say No—No! Let not the Lincoln government— let not extreme men among ourselves—be so misguided from passion or from any cause as for one moment to suppose that the late elections in this State look to reconstruction. We repudiate it as foul slander—we appeal to our own history in this struggle for our liberty to mark it as false—as a libel on us— we appeal to our common sufferings—to our common dangers— to our sacrifices—we appeal to reason itself—to the judgment by which men are governed—to declare it before the world as shameless *slander*.

If you are willing—let me suggest that you express your purpose to cooperate with the Confederate Government fully and freely in reference to the war. This is a question about which many feel *sensitively* concerned. You have read the admirable letter of Senator Hill[651] of Georgia. It is a platform in itself.

---

[650] The Raleigh speech was made on August 16, 1862, when Vance came through the capital city on his way to Asheville. In a twenty minute speech he made it plain that he was for the prosecution of the war until independence was achieved. He asked that the passions and the charges of the late campaign be forgotten and that the people absorb themselves in the task of winning independence. The Union charge he denounced as monstrous and he pledged that he would show no party spirit during the war. The speech was universally praised by the press of the entire state, especially by the former opposition papers. Raleigh *North Carolina Standard*, August 20, 1862; Raleigh *State Journal*, August 20, 1862.

[651] Benjamin Harvey Hill (1823-1882), Confederate Senator from Georgia, whose father had migrated to Georgia from North Carolina. Hill graduated from the University of Georgia in 1843 and established himself as a lawyer in western Georgia. His public career began as a Whig in 1851 when he was elected to the

I am glad that your majority is large—for it shows the turning of the popular heart *towards you* and puts you *above cliques* and *intrigues.* Allude to this in such way that the North & South may say that our people were in earnest in their movement.

To disabuse the public mind every where and to show *factious* and *malignant* men among ourselves upon what high ground you and your constituents stand—you will discuss in your address as you have done in the *field*—the Holy cause of our liberty and the prosecution of the war until peace is conquered.

My dear Sir—You are in a proud position where the highest good may be done to your State and the most ample political future made for yourself. Be independent—you are able to be-be yourself—you have a right to be—and may God bless—guide and inspire you with the wisdom that shall lead you to the best results. I renew my promise to support you as freely and I hope as faithfully as I have power—in all things where I would support any man.

[Asheville]

[A. L. S. Governors' Papers (Vance),
State Department of Archives and History, Raleigh.]

---

lower house of the Georgia legislature, where he helped promote the acceptance of the Compromise of 1850 by the people of Georgia. When the Whig party collapsed Hill became a Know-Nothing and, like Vance, supported Fillmore in 1856 and Bell in 1860. In 1857 Hill ran for governor of Georgia against the Democratic nominee, Joseph E. Brown, who was elected. Hill opposed secession in the Georgia Convention of 1861, but accepted the verdict of the body when he was outvoted. He was elected Conferedate States Senator in 1861 and remained a member of that body throughout its existence. Here he became the recognized spokesman and champion of Jefferson Davis and of the Confederate administration, not only in Richmond but against the formidable opposition of Brown, Toombs, and Stephens in Georgia. After the war he was a member of the United States House of Representatives, 1875-1877, and of the United States Senate, 1877-1882.

Hill's letter, to which Shepherd refers, was written from LaGrange, Ga., to the Atlanta *Confederacy* in reply to that paper's request for his views on conscription, taxation, states' rights, and other such public issues of the time. Hill took the ground that states' rights were to be saved, if saved at all, by soldiers, and so he would not enter the conscription controversy. He said that it was now the duty of everyone to unite and obey, not to criticize and argue, and that "The Administration ought to be supported cheerfully and without misgiving. No good can, but much harm will, come of opposition. . . . Above all, let us preserve our unity—obey the laws and help, not abuse, each other. . . . Let us be true to our only friends —ourselves."

Hill's letter was widely published over the south and appeared in many Old Whig papers, one such being the *Fayetteville Observer,* in Shepherd's home town. In his editorial comment on Hill's letter editor Hale pointed out that Hill was an Old Whig and Union man now supporting a Democratic administration which was opposed by Democrats such as Joseph E. Brown and his kind, who had been secessionists but were now fighting their own president. To Hale this fact illustrated how much of the administration's support came from former political opponents of the people who composed that administration, and how much opposition came from its former friends. The moral for Vance was plain. Haywood J. Pearce, Jr., "Benjamin Harvey Hill," *Dict. of Am. Biog.,* IX, 25-27; *Fayetteville Observer,* July 14, 1862.

CHAPTER II

SEPTEMBER—OCTOBER, 1862

From Thos. M. Garrett[1]

Richmond Va. Sept. 1st. 1862.

I fear you will be troubled with a great many such letters as the following, but if I am remembered by you as an old collegemate, at Chapel-Hill nothing upon the subject of my letters will appear improper to you—I am a Captain in the 5th Regt. State Troops I had the misfortune to be wounded in the desperate engagement of my regt with the enemy at Williamsburg and was taken prisoner—I was released on 5th August, Since which time I have been to my house in Bertie Co. giving time for my wounds to heal entirely, before joining my regiment— When I returned I heard that Col. McRae[2] has spoken very high-

---

[1] Thomas Miles Garrett (1830-1864), a lawyer of Bertie County who graduated from the University of North Carolina in 1851 and, in July 1861, became captain of company F in the Fifth North Carolina Regiment. He was wounded at the battle of Williamsburg and taken prisoner; he was exchanged and afterwards became colonel of the Fifth and was killed at Spottsylvania, May 12, 1864. The lieutenant colonelcy was the position at issue at the time of this letter. "Colonel Garrett was a gallant soldier and won for himself an enviable record for conspicuous personal courage and capacity for commanding troops." Many thought he should have been promoted to brigadier general. Clark, *N. C. Regts.*, I, 281, 284-285, 288-289, IV, xii; Connor, *N. C. Manual*, p. 504; Moore, *N. C. Roster*, I, 156, 177.

[2] Duncan Kirkland McRae (1820-1888), then colonel of the Fifth North Carolina Regiment. He was born in Fayetteville, a son of John McRae who was postmaster there from 1818 to 1853, and a brother of James C. McRae, afterwards an associate justice of the North Carolina Supreme Court and Dean of the Law School at the University of North Carolina. Duncan McRae was a lawyer of great ability with a consummate interest in politics. But he was of an independent character and chafed at the political discipline of party faithfulness. He represented Cumberland County in the House of Commons as a Democrat in 1842. Soon afterwards he moved to Raleigh, where he developed a lucrative practice; then to Wilmington in 1851, where he became an independent candidate for Congress, defending the distribution of the proceeds of the sale of public lands in his campaign. In the midst of the canvass he was appointed consul at Paris, where he served until 1857; upon his return he resumed the practice of law, this time in New Bern. In 1858 he was an independent candidate for governor against John W. Ellis, the regular Democratic nominee, by whom he was soundly defeated. In the campaign of 1860 McRae was a Douglas Democrat, but he favored secession in the spring of 1861, spoke at the "disunion convention" at Goldsboro on March 22 and 23, 1861, and was rewarded by the administration Democrats with the colonelcy of the Fifth North Carolina Troops, one of the original ten regiments whose officers were appointed by the Governor and the Military Board. The *Standard* quoted a typical comment from the press of the State at the time McRae became a secessionist: "Mr. McRae was a Democrat, then a Distributionist, then a Consul, then a Douglas Democrat, and is now a disunionist, having marked all the phases through which he has passed by a candidacy for something, without a solitary election that we recollect of." Quoted from *Ad Valorem Banner* in Raleigh *North Carolina Standard*, April 3, 1861. McRae remained colonel of the Fifth North Carolina Regiment until near the end of 1862, when he resigned, being most of the time engaged in military, political, and journalistic controversy. In 1863 he was sent by Governor Vance to Halifax (though he went to Europe

ly of me in his report,[3] and that he had recommended my promotion. I did not hear the particulars until a few days ago, when I met here several officers of my regiment who informed me, that a few days before the battles of Richmond, Col. McRae tendered his resignation[4] as Col. of the regt. and immediately after called a meeting of all the officers of the regt. and informed them of his purpose to resign, and said to them that there was no officer in the regt. into whose hands he would see it placed with entire Confidence except myself— and suggested that I should be recommended in a body for promotion to the place of Lt. Col. of the regt. then vacant. This proposal was sanctioned by every officer in the regt. but one and I understand that Col. McRae embodied this action of the officers in a letter to the Gov. of North Carolina, and urged strenuously that this appointment should then be made and thus place me in the line of promotion above Maj: Sinclair.[5] This endorsement was prompted I understand by the conviction among the officers of Maj: Sinclair's entire unfitness for the place of Col. of the Regt. A circumstance most flatering and

instead) as an agent of the state for the purchase of war supplies, over which mission there was a great controversy the rest of his life. In the spring of 1864 he became editor of the Raleigh *Confederate*, a journal which strongly supported the Richmond administration. After the war McRae resumed the practice of law in Memphis, Chicago, and finally in Wilmington, N. C., where he strengthened his already great reputation for ability, brilliance, and controversy. Evans, *Conf. Mil. Hist.*, IV, 626-628, John MacRae Papers, Southern Historical Collection, University of North Carolina, Chapel Hill, N. C. (cited hereafter as MacRae Papers).

[3] In his report of the battle of Williamsburg Colonel McRae did not specifically compliment individuals, but remarked: "All of my officers and men behaved with equal courage, and no discrimination can be made among them." The report is dated May 10, 1862. *O. R.* Ser. I. Vol. XI, Pt. I, 611.

[4] McRae's health was poor and he often considered resignation, but he did not actually resign until November 14, 1862, and then for other reasons. See below, p. 355.

[5] Peter J. Sinclair (1837-1914), who was born in the highlands of Scotland and came with his father, an eminent Presbyterian minister, to Pennsylvania, where the son was educated and studied law. In 1858 he came to Fayetteville, was admitted to the bar, and began to edit the Fayetteville *North Carolinian*, a strongly Democratic paper which advocated secession. When the war came he stopped the paper "because I deemed my duty as an advocate of secession to be in the fight," volunteered with the Lafayette light infantry in company F of the First North Carolina Volunteers, but soon after raised a company in Cumberland County, of which he became captain, and was assigned as company A to the Fifth North Carolina Regiment. He was promoted major on March 6, 1862 and when Lieutenant Colonel John C. Badham was killed at the battle of Williamsburg, May 5, 1862, the controversy between Sinclair and Garrett arose, involving not only personal differences between them but the authority of appointment in the state troops as well. When McRae resigned as colonel and Garrett was promoted Sinclair refused to serve under him and himself resigned in January 1863. Later that year he sought from the Secretary of War a pass for his family to return to the north, but he remained and indicated his willingness to serve again as a private. After the war he resumed the practice of law at Marion, in McDowell County, became counsel for the Ohio River and Charleston Railroad Company, for William John Brown and John Evans Brown, Vance's friends, and gained distinction at the bar. Clark, *N. C. Regts.*, I, 286-287; Moore, *N. C. Roster*, I, 156; Evans, *Conf. Mil. Hist.*, IV, 743-744; P. J. Sinclair to Secretary of War, October 26, 1863, Confederate War Department Records; Brown Papers.

gratifying of all connected with this matter is that there are two Captains in the Regt who outrank me both of whom[6] yielded their claims and joined in this recommendation— Notwithstanding this strong recommendation I understand that Gov. Clark[7] has appointed Maj. Sinclair Lt. Col. and my appointment as Major (which was urged in case of the promotion of Sinclair) has been held back and it is still doubtful whether the Gov. will make the appointment as asked for by the officers of the regt.— I think Gov. Clark has had his attention directed to me as a whig politician of decided opinions & feelings, and the withholding this tribute to me, which my companions in arms were willing to see accorded to me, has been actuated by the same spirit of proscription which has governed his whole administration— I hope you will do justice to one who has labored zealously for the old whig cause and one whose friends in Bertie Co. in the late election were your friends— Maj: Sinclair, you will remember previously to the war, was the editor of the Fayetteville North-Carolinian— I understand that Col. McRae has again tendered his resignation, and that the officers of the regt. in a body will recommend me for promotion over Sinclair— Should this happen and their wishes are disregarded, they express a determination to resign and refuse to serve under him— I hope you will not regard what I have written as immodest— I preferred to state the facts in regard to this matter myself, and with the spirit of frankness in which I know this will be received— If you see any gentleman from Bertie Co. at the Inaugural ceremony or at any time soon, enquire of them about me— I refer you to Lewis Thompson[8] Esq. Col. S. B. Spruill,[9] Mr. Bond [10] or any one whom you may see from this region—

In regard to the election in Bertie I was informed that a vote among the Conscripts at Raleigh elects Col. Outlaw[11] to the

---

[6] The captains who outranked Garrett were Norman A. H. Godkin, of Wilson County, who was commissioned May 9, 1861, captain of company G, and Solomon B. Doudge, of Gates County, commissioned May 6, 1861, captain of company H. Garrett was commissioned captain on May 16, 1861. Moore, *N. C. Roster,* I, 181, 185.

[7] See p. 133, 529n.

[8] Lewis Thompson (1808-1867), planter, was an Old Line Union Whig from Bertie County, having been a member of the House of Commons in 1831, 1832, and 1840, and of the State Senate in 1844, 1848, and 1852. He was nominated by the Raleigh *North Carolina Standard* as a presidential elector in 1861. Connor, *N. C. Manual,* p. 503; Raleigh *North Carolina Standard,* October 9, 1861.

[9] S. B. Spruill represented Bertie County in the House of Commons in 1852. Connor, *N. C. Manual,* p. 503.

[10] James Bond (1831-1903) was a Vance candidate for the House of Commons from Bertie County in the election of 1862. He was a member of the Commons in 1862 and 1864. Raleigh *North Carolina Standard,* July 26, 1862; Connor, *N. C. Manual,* p. 504.

[11] David Outlaw (1806-1868), a veteran political figure from Bertie County. He was a member of the House of Commons in 1831, 1832, 1834, 1854, 1856, and 1858, and of the State Senate in 1860, 1862, and 1866. He is not listed for 1862 in Connor, *N. C. Manual,* pp. 503-504, but he appears in *Senate Journal, 1862-'63.*

Senate by 4 maj: but it was not returned to the Sheriff nor counted It would be necessary therefore for Col. Outlaw to bring forward the matter in a contest for the seat before the Senate— This he will scarcely do, if I conclude to go to the Legislature— This I certainly shall not do if I am promoted— and I shall leave it for you to decide upon the legality of my election or rather the legality of the vote of the conscripts by resigning all claim to the place, and allow Outlaw to take it if you shall not see fit to order a new election— If there should arise any embarrassment to you in connection with the matter, I could relieve you by assuming to be elected and resign[12] my place and let the contest be between Col. Outlaw and some new party with whom he would certainly have to contend— I am disposed however to yield to him if you hold the opinion that the vote of the conscripts was legal and authorized—

There seems to be some conflict between the Confederate and State Authorities, as to who has the power to fill vacancies in the offices in the State Troops[13]— Mr. Smith[14] will write to you and

[12] In October 1862, Garrett wrote a public letter to the people of Bertie County resigning his seat in the State Senate to which he had been elected while a prisoner of war. Declaring that his health had been restored, he thought his usefulness would be greater in the army than in the legislature. Outlaw became senator from the seventh district. The letter is printed in the Raleigh *North Carolina Standard,* November 7, 1862.

[13] This question was long a matter of acute controversy. The claim of the state to appoint officers went far beyond the assertion of the right to officer the first ten regiments which had been raised for the war and which were usually referred to as "State Troops." Governor Clark claimed the right to determine the question not only in the first ten regiments but also in the following additional ones: regiments nineteen and thirty-three which had been raised for the war under state law, regiments eleven and seventeen and from forty-two to fifty-seven inclusive, as they were raised under state acts authorizing a reserve; regiment number forty, which was composed of ten artillery companies raised for the war; regiments twenty-eight and thirty-seven which, though twelve-months regiments, had been continued in service under state re-enlistment acts. There remained for the Confederacy to officer regiments twelve to forty-one inclusive, with the exceptions made above, as these had been continued in service under the conscription bill with the right to reorganize and elect their own officers within forty days of the passage of the act. In all regiments except the last group the Governor of North Carolina claimed the exclusive right to commission officers, fill vacancies, and make promotions according to the laws of the state. Governor Clark sent the North Carolina assistant adjutant general, William B. Gulick, to Richmond to make "arrangements with the War Department as to what Regiments under the conscript law are to receive the commissions of their officers from the Confederate Government and which are to be commissioned by the Governor of the State." Gulick had an interview with the Attorney General and with the Secretary of War, who told him that the department "was in the habit of issuing commissions to all the troops under its orders upon application" and suggested the possibility of a ruling by the Attorney General. When Vance became governor the question was by no means a settled one and remained to plague smooth relationships with the Richmond government. William B. Gulick to Governor Clark, September 4, 1862, Governor Clark to William B. Gulick, August 23, 1862, William B. Gulick to Secretary Randolph, August 27, 1862, Clark Letter Book, pp. 401, 416-418.

[14] See p. 99, 372n, and letter of Smith to Vance, September 5, 1862, below, p. 168.

give you all the points in regard to the matter—He has already introduced a bill [15] to settle the point in favor of the State authorities—

[Raleigh]

[on reverse]

Garrett has been appointed *No ans^r- req^d.*

[A. L. S. Governors' Papers (Vance), State Department of Archives and History, Raleigh.]

From R. H. Battle, Jr.[16]

Richmond— Sept. 2^d 1862

I was surprised & gratified yesterday by receiving the complimentary tender you have made me, through our mutual friend Gov. Swain,[17] of the position of private Secretary under you— I take pleasure in returning my thanks & signifying my acceptance of the place— conditioned of course upon my resignation of my commission in the army being accepted by the Secretary of War, of which I suppose there can be little doubt— Could I honestly regard my health, after consulting the surgeons of our regiment & my friends, sufficient to stand the exposure of camp life— I would have greater hesitation at leaving the service; but as it is I consider myself fortunate to have so good an excuse as the one you have afforded me for retiring before I am literally "a used up man."

I have tendered my resignation & I apprehend there will be no difficulty in the way of my joining you at an early day—

Hoping our intercourse will be as agreeable to you, as I have every reason to anticipate it will to me, & that you will not find the Gubernatorial Chair a more unpleasant seat than your saddle, while Col. on a March, I am—

[Raleigh]

[A. L. S. Governors' Papers (Vance), State Department of Archives and History, Raleigh.]

From David S. Reid [18]

Pleasantville, N. C.
Sept. 2, 1862

I have received yours of the 21 ultimo, and feel flattered by the compliment paid by asking me to Make suggestions in relation to

---

[15] On September 1, 1862, Congressman Smith introduced "A Bill in relation to the mode of filling vacancies in the offices of regiments organized under State authority; which was read the first and second times and referred to the Committee on Military Affairs." *Journal of the Congress of the Confederate States of America, 1861-1865,* 7 vols. (Washington, 1905), V, 332-333 (cited hereafter as *Journal of Conf. Cong.*).

[16] See p. 156, 639n.

[17] See p. 9, 45n and Swain's letter to Vance, p. 156.

[18] David Settle Reid (1813-1891), of Rockingham County, Democratic leader and

your Inaugural. I have no doubt however that your own judgment will readily prompt all that I can Suggest.

The present struggle for independence is paramount to all other questions— life, liberty, property, and all that is dear to freemen depend upon it— and party prejudices and all minor differences should be sacrificed upon the alter of the Common Cause. *We are right and the enemy wrong;* re-Union with the North by the Consent of the people is impossible. Urge the vigorous prosecution of the War, and invoke the fortitude and patriotism of the people to meet the crisis like freemen; Concert and harmony between the Confederate and State Governments and the endorsement of the action of both by the people should be urged as of the highest importance to the successful prosecution of the War, the taking of private property, *slaves* included, requires retaliatory measures to secure our citizens and if possible to deter the enemy from the exercise of their theivish propensities.

I suppose a general allusion to matters of State policy will be all that will be expected at this time.

I direct this to Raleigh, as owing to the present derangement of the mails it would probably not reach Asheville before you leave.

Altho' I did not vote for you yet I trust you will believe that I sincerely hope your Administration may be prosperous, and that all your public acts may tend to the promotion of the welfare of the Country. In haste
Raleigh.
[A. L. S.   Z. B. Vance Papers,
State Department of Archives and History, Raleigh.]

From W. N. H. Smith[19]

Richmond
Sept 5 1862

There seems to be no established rule with the authorities here for filling vacancies in the offices of such of our Regiments as enlisted for the war and retain their organization. It is not determined whether appointments to them are made in conformity with laws of the State, or by promotion as provided by the law of Congress. To settle the matter I have introduced a bill now

---

governor (1850-1854) when he was elected to the United States Senate by the legislature. He was a member of the State Senate in 1835, 1836, 1838, and 1840; a member of Congress, 1843-1847; and Democratic nominee for governor several times, 1848-1852, being elected the last two times. He was also a delegate to the Peace Conference in Washington in 1861, and held seats in the Conventions of 1861 and 1875. McCormick, *Personnel*, p. 69; Connor, *N. C. Manual*, pp. 419, 786, 897, 931-935.

19 See p. 99, 372n.

before the House Military Committee.[20] In the event of its devolving upon you to supply the vacancy in the 5th Regt. N. C. Troops Col. McCrae[21] created by the death of Lt. Col. Badham.[22] I beg strongly to recommend the claims of Capt. Thomas M. Garrett [23] of Bertie Co. commanding one of the companies comprising it. Capt. Garrett acquitted himself with great credit at the first important collision of our forces with those of McClellan[24] at Williamsburg, when he fell wounded and was taken prisoner. I refer you to the official report of Col McCrae, and to his recommendation which I suppose is on file in the Executive Department, for his promotion for good conduct and gallantry on that occasion, as the best proof of his appreciation of Capt Garretts merits as an officer.

I have heard also that the two company officers having precedence of position in the Regiment over Capt. Garrett, as most of the others, have expressed their willingness to see him appointed to a field office. If so I presume there is some evidence of this also in your office. Capt Garrett returned from his imprisonment some three weeks ago and after a short visit home has now gone on to rejoin his former comrades and take command of his company, in the important movements progressing near the Potomac.

It is proper I should state that while I should be gratified to see him appointed Lt. Colonel, and ask it, if the vacancy exists, I find on reference to the roles in the adjutant Generals office here that Major Sinclair[25] has been appointed or rather promoted to that office. This act depends for its validity of course upon the supposition that promotion & appointment in such regiments are controlled by the laws of Congress. Precisely the contrary was

---

[20] See p. 167, 15n.

[21] See p. 163, 2n.

[22] John C. Badham, of Chowan County, a lawyer and Democratic political leader who had been an ardent advocate of secession. He had represented Chowan County in the House of Commons with Vance in 1854, and again in 1856 and 1858, and was lieutenant colonel of the Fifth North Carolina Regiment when he was killed in action at the battle of Williamsburg, May 5, 1862. Badham had complained to R. H. Riddick, Confederate assistant adjutant general, who forwarded his letter to Governor Clark, that political enemies had slandered him in order to prevent his promotion, and that his sickness before the battle of Manassas was a coincidence. John C. Badham to R. H. Riddick, December 11, 1861, Governors' Papers (Clark); Connor, *N. C. Manual*, p. 560.

[23] See Garrett's letter to Vance, p. 163, and 1n.

[24] See p. 139, 552n.

[25] See p. 164, 5n. William B. Gulick reported to Governor Clark that, when on his visit to Richmond to try to reach agreement with the War Department with regard to the promotion of officers, he had seen Sinclair's commission as lieutenant colonel in the office of the adjutant general, issued by Confederate rather than by state authority. William B. Gulick to Governor Clark, July 23, 1862, Governors' Papers (Clark).

done, in the case of Col. now Brig. Gen. Pender,[26] who was assign-
ed by Gov. Clark[27] to the command of Fisher's[28] Regiment after
his fall. In my judgment the right of making these appointments
of which that case is a precedent fully in point, belongs to the
State of N. Carolina and is regulated by our laws.
Raleigh.
[A. L. S.   Z. B. Vance Papers,
State Department of Archives and History, Raleigh.]

From D. K. McRae[29]

Near Frederick M[d].
Sept 9th. 1862

I enclose a letter recd from the Adjt Gen[l]. Office[30] during the
term of your predecessor to which I have had no opportunity
of replying— Several of the promotions in this Regt have already
been made Some have been announced in the order of seniority—

---

[26] William Dorsey Pender (1834-1863), of Edgecombe County, who graduated
from West Point in 1854 and had been elected colonel of the Third North Carolina Volunteers in May of 1861, but had been transferred by Governor Clark to
command the Sixth North Carolina Regiment of State Troops on August 15,
1861. He was thus transferred from a twelve months regiment to one enlisted
for the war, whose officers were subject to appointment by the governor. Pender
was promoted brigadier general after the battle of Seven Pines and assigned to
command a North Carolina brigade in A. P. Hill's division. On May 27, 1863, he
was promoted major general at the age of twenty-nine. He died, July 18, 1863,
in Staunton, Va., of wounds received July 2, 1863, at Gettysburg. W. A. Montgomery, "William D. Pender," W. J. Peele, (comp.), *Lives of Distinguished North
Carolinians* (Raleigh, 1898), pp. 436-455 (cited hereafter as Peele, *N. C. Lives*);
Samuel J. Heidner, "William Dorsey Pender," *Dict. of Am. Biog.,* XIV, 416-417;
Cullum, *Biog. Register,* II, 586.
[27] See p. 133, 529n.
[28] Charles Frederick Fisher (1816-1861), of Rowan County, who had represented
that county in the State Senate in 1854 and was subsequently president of the
North Carolina Railroad. He was appointed colonel of the Sixth North Carolina
Regiment of State Troops by his fellow-townsman and fellow-Democrat, Governor John W. Ellis. Evans, *Conf. Mil. Hist.,* IV, 485. Fisher was killed at First
Manassas, July 21, 1861.
[29] See p. 163, 2n.
[30] The letter is not enclosed, but is found in Governors' Papers (Clark), dated
August 20, 1862. In it James G. Martin, Adjutant General of North Carolina,
wrote that with regard to promotions in McRae's regiment "I have to say that
the Governor makes the appointments and issues the commissions in all the
Regiments from North Carolina in the Confederate Service except those twelve
months volunteers continued in service by the Conscription Act. He is exercising
this power in all the Regiments raised for the war, and he is not advised that
any appointments or promotions in them have been made except through this
office. In pursuance of this right of the Governor you were requested to submit
the names of persons to fill vacancies, and he is desirous that you should do so
at the earliest moment practicable."

under Gen¹ orders No 43 ³¹ & 36 ³² and one that of Major P. J. Sinclair³³ to be Lt. Col has been recᵈ. direct from the office of the Adjt Genl Richmond ³⁴ My Regt is greatly disorganized for want of officers and if I shall be obliged to hold election for 2ⁿᵈ. Lt. its efficiency will be seriously impaired. I am anxiously desirous of avoiding this— and will be glad if some measure may be speedily adopted to avoid this evil I shall be glad to hear from you your views on the question raised in the enclosed communication The injustice³⁵ I have recᵈ. at the hands of the Govt. has long since determined me to surrender my commission— but I could not resign while disaster impended over the country and since we have been blessed with victory— I have not had a field officer present My health ³⁶ has suffered much and I am laboring under a local Malady which is threatening to become serious from the exposure to which I am subjected I deem it proper to notify you that I shall tender my resignation just as soon as the danger of battle shall be less imminent— and I trust the selection of a field officer may be made with reference to the vacancy then to occur. Raleigh

[A. L. S. Governors' Papers (Vance), State Department of Archives and History, Raleigh.]

---

³¹ General Orders, No. 43, issued by the adjutant and inspector-general's office at Richmond, dated June 13, 1862, stated that "When vacancies occur among the company officers of reorganized regiments the brigade commander will announce in orders the promotion of the officer next in rank in the company in which such vacancies exist, except in the cases covered by paragraph II of General Orders, No. 36, current series. A copy of the order will in all cases be furnished to this office for the approval of the Secretary of War." O. R., Ser. IV, Vol. I, 1151-1152.

³² The same source had issued General Orders, No. 36, on May 17, 1862, which stated in paragraph II that "In all cases where promotion is due from seniority, and the competency of the parties entitled by position to promotion is questionable, a board of examiners shall be convened by brigade commanders to determine the candidate's capabilities of instructing and controlling the commands commensurate with the grade to which promotion is expected, as also their efficiency and perfect sobriety. All newly elected officers will be examined before similar boards of examiners, to determine their competency and the confirmation of their election." O. R., Ser. IV, Vol. 1, 1122-1123.

³³ See p. 164, 5n and p. 169, 25n.

³⁴ The letters-sent books of the Confederate States War Department from May 23 to September 12, 1862, were never received by the United States, so details of Sinclair's promotion, which might be expected there, are missing from the records. O. R., Ser. IV, Vol. I, 1.

³⁵ McRae was criticized for the heavy losses his troops sustained in the battle of Williamsburg and often wrote, both publicly and privately, defending himself against all critics. Furthermore, he believed that he should have been made a brigadier general. On August 1, 1862, he wrote his father: "It is now ascertained that the Prest. did confer promotion on me and I was defeated by No Ca politicians of whom Mr. [George] Davis was conspicuous." D. K. McRae to John MacRae, August 1, 1862, MacRae Papers. See also letter of McRae to Clark about Williamsburg in Governors' Papers (Clark), May 12, 1862.

³⁶ McRae's health was never good; in Paris while a consul he was very ill, and throughout his army career maladies are frequently complained of. From several descriptions in family letters it sounds as if he had tuberculosis. MacRae Papers, passim.

From T. Ruffin, Jr.[37]

Camp near Frederick Town Md
Sept 9th 1862

I have purposly postponed writing, on the subject of this letter, until such time, as I knew you would occupy the chair of State—

It has so chanced that our regiment— the 13th N Ca Regt commanded by Col Scales[38]—has received no pay from the Confederate States for six months & our men are in great want: I believe too that ours is the only N Ca Regt. to whom the State bounty remains unpaid:

The confederate States is not to blame for the delay inasmuch as it has been our misfortune not to have been able to make our Muster-rolls for a long time, we being Either on the march or engaged in fighting on every muster day: But our State authorities are without excuse as the proper rolls for the bounty are made out & they paid us $10— on them:

May I not ask you to give this matter your attention? If you knew how much our men are suffering for the want of

[37] Thomas Ruffin, Jr. (1824-1889) was born in Hillsboro, the fourth son of Chief Justice Thomas Ruffin. After a preparatory education in local schools he attended the University of North Carolina, where he graduated with distinction in 1844. He then studied law and located in Rockingham County where, in 1848, he formed a partnership with John H. Dillard. In 1850 he represented Rockingham County in the House of Commons being, like his father, a Democrat. The legislature of 1844 elected him solicitor of his district; Vance voted against him, since Ruffin was a Democrat. In 1860 he supported Breckinridge for the presidency, though Ruffin was not so ardent a secessionists as some of Breckinridge's supporters. After Fort Sumter Ruffin raised a company in Alamance County and entered the war; in the fall of 1861 he was named a judge of the superior court, but he resigned to re-enter the army. On April 26, 1862, upon the reorganization of the volunteer regiments, he was elected lieutenant colonel of the Thirteenth North Carolina, which was soon afterwards placed in Garland's brigade. Here he served with distinction until a severe wound at the battle of South Mountain incapacitated him and he resigned from the service March 2, 1863, though later he became presiding judge of the military court in General E. Kirby-Smith's corps in the west, where he served until the end of the war. He resumed his partnership with John H. Dillard and, in 1875, formed one with John W. Graham. He was appointed an associate justice of the Supreme Court of North Carolina by Governor Jarvis in 1881, but he resigned for reasons of health in 1883. After the battle of Sharpsburg, where General Garland was killed, Colonel Duncan K. McRae commanded the brigade. He and Ruffin did not get along well, and the Thirteenth Regiment was transferred to Pender's brigade, where they were reunited with their first colonel, now a brigadier general. Clark, *N. C. Regts.*, I, 654, 663; Moore, *N. C. Roster*, I, 471; Samuel A'Court Ashe, "Thomas Ruffin, Jr.," Ashe, *Biog. Hist. of N. C.*, V, 360-366; Connor, *N. C. Manual*, pp. 447, 449, 786; John W. Graham, *Some Events of My Life* (n.p., 1918?), p. 13 (Reprinted From *Proceedings of the North Carolina Bar Association*, 1918).

[38] Alfred Moore Scales (1827-1892), of Rockingham County. He was a Democrat who was a member of the House of Commons in 1852 and 1856; a member of Congress, 1857-1859, 1875-1885; and governor of North Carolina, 1885-1889. When the war began he raised a company and became a captain in the Thirteenth North Carolina Regiment; was commissioned colonel on October 11, 1861 after being selected to replace William Dorsey Pender upon his transfer to the sixth regiment. Scales was made a brigadier general on January 13, 1863. Connor, *N. C. Manual*, pp. 419, 935, 940-942; Moore, *N. C. Roster*, I, 471.

money I am sure you would dispatch a paymaster for their relief.[39]—

Our men are without clothing & shoes as the government cannot furnish them their only Chance to get them is to buy them: Our other regiments are provided with money, While ours is destitute.

Even this does not make them murmur, but this adds to our regret on their account.—

Col Scales is absent sick, which accounts for my having the honor to address you.—

[Raleigh]

[A. L. S. Governors' Papers (Vance), State Department of Archives and History, Raleigh.]

From T. Davis[40]

Rutherford Cty N. C.
Sept. 11th. 1862

Although we have not agreed heretofore in Politicks, your speech at Raleigh[41] was all I could have desired, and I feel it my duty to give whatever Influence & Support to your administration my limited Influence will permit. I feel shure the state will have & energetic Administration, & one that will endeavor to do Justice to all. I am aware Your administration will be Closely Scrutinized, but I think there is one road Chalked out by you, that will make you everything that you can or may desire, that is the active prosecution of the war, in that you have the advantage of any of your predecessors, during the time you remain in office I have no doubt this terable war will be terminated, & you will have much to do in enforcing Military obedience as well as Civil— I am sorry to say there are Citizens of our country that say they will not sirve as Conscripts, there are others that have got little mail contracts & Schools to keep them out of the war,

---

[39] Vance replied, expressing sympathy for the neglected men and promising to send the paymaster. Vance to T. Ruffin, September 18, 1862, Zebulon B. Vance Letter Book, State Department of Archives and History, Raleigh, N. C. (cited hereafter as Vance Letter Book).

[40] Tolivar Davis (1810-1866) was a planter and slaveowner of the Cathey Creek section of Rutherford County. Though his education was limited he took a leading part in public affairs. He developed large realty holdings, owned a saw mill, wheat mill, and a corn mill, all of which he operated by water power. He represented Rutherford County in the House of Commons in 1844. He was a staunch Baptist and an equally staunch Democrat and secessionist, and he furnished three sons to the Confederacy. Griffin, *Old Tryon and Rutherford*, pp. 228-229; Connor, *N. C. Manual*, p. 798; *Asheville News*, January 9, 1861.

[41] Vance's Raleigh speech was delivered impromptu on August 16. In it he urged the people to forget the passions and the charges of the late political campaign and to concentrate on the task of winning independence. The charge that his candidacy advocated a return to the Union he classified as monstrous. He pledged himself to a prosecution of the war, and promised to show no party spirit during his governorship. Raleigh *North Carolina Standard*, August 20, 1862.

while brave boys are pouring out their blood like water on the battle field, this is certainly rong I think it is a common cause, and I think able bodeyd men ought to make common sacrifices, with out resorting to evry little means to evade the law, I am sory that the law made Such provision, I hope that it will yet be so amended as to Include every able bodeyd man in the Confederacy.[42] If men because they happen to be a postmaster or School master or mail contractor can be excused from serving their country, then I think it time that the common citizen should be excused— but while our sons that are Just as good as those are undergoing all the Labour & hazzard of war, it is nothing but right that all should bear their part, there is enough over forty five to do all the business that is wanting with those that are unable to go by Infirmity of body, the boys under 18 years & the old men & women of the country can with the help of Negroes make with ordinary Seasons enough to eat if salt can be got to Save it, & I think if our people can whip the next call of the North it will end the war, & that will depend uppon the energy & the Efficiency of the Confederate & State Governments, we must be as much united as possible, & we must expect to Suffer much before we get our Independence, hoping & praying that you may be Instrumental in assisting & carying out all the measures necessary under providence for our speedy deliverance from the grasp of the enemy and a safe return to piece, with this blessing we shall no doubt rejoice although a large a mount of our sons may find a premature grave far off from Home. Yours very Truly

PS Since writing the above I have read your Inaugural [43] it is all that could be desired, I think it will have a tendency to arouse some of your personal friends that have been lukewarm in the Cause & Make them active. I hope your Action will have the effect to unite us all as one. you may think this letter rather untimely from Me so soon but it breaths my best wishes for your welfare & that of the old North State, and may a kind providence

---

[42] The Exemption Act of April 21, 1862, specified numerous classes who were exempt from military service regardless of age, among which were those of which Davis speaks in this letter: "all engaged in carrying the mails"; "all ferrymen on post routes"; "all teachers having as many as twenty scholars"; postmasters who were "in the service or employ of the Confederate States." *O. R.*, Ser. IV, Vol. I, 1081.

[43] Vance's inaugural address was delivered on September 8, 1862 and sounded an optimistic note. Especially satisfactory to secessionists and ardent Confederates such as Tolivar Davis were his statements that separation was not a whim or a freak, but the deliberate judgment of the people; that the people should cease their arguments and debates over the responsibility for the war and unite in fighting it; that there was as much for the people to do at home as for the soldiers on the battlefield; and that there was no thought of reconstruction. Furthermore, he asserted that conscription might be harsh, but it was necesssary and probably constitutional, and that he favored its impartial execution. Raleigh *North Carolina Standard*, September 10, 1862.

smile on your Administration & make it Just what you may desire
[Raleigh]
[A. L. S. Governors' Papers (Vance), State Department of Archives and History, Raleigh.]

From Peter Mallett [44]

Headquarters, Camp of Instruction,[45]
Camp Holmes, September 11th, 1862
In conformity with my instructions from the Secretary of War, I most respectfully ask permission to employ the officers of the State (Militia) to enroll all persons between the ages of 18 and 35, liable to military duty under the law known as the "Conscript Act." [46]

---

[44] Peter Mallett (1824-1907) was a son of Charles P. Mallett, a banker and planter of Fayetteville. Before the war Peter Mallett was a wholesale merchant in New York City, but when war came he sacrificed his business interests there and returned to North Carolina, where he raised a company and became a captain in the Third North Carolina Regiment. At the urgent insistence of General Theophilus Holmes he was appointed assistant adjutant general by the Confederate government, with the rank of major, on May 23, 1862, to take charge of the drilling, subsistence, and distribution of the conscripts in North Carolina. He was generally known as Commandant of Conscripts. He was appointed colonel in November 1862, but the appointment was not confirmed by the Senate and Secretary of War James A. Seddon wrote that he must revert to the rank of major as of June 14, 1864. Seddon claimed that his predecessor had exceeded his powers of appointment in 1862, and that this demotion meant no dissatisfaction with Mallett's services. Thomas Bragg wrote to the Secretary of War urging his confirmation and asked for the intervention of the North Carolina congressional delegation. Mallett led a group of conscripts into battle at Kinston in December 1862, where he was wounded and disabled for several months. After the war Mallett returned to New York and became a commission merchant. *Fayetteville Observer*, May 26, 1862; Thomas Bragg to James A. Seddon, July 20, 1864, Confederate War Department Records; Moore, *N. C. Roster*, I, 88; Peter Mallett Papers, Southern Historical Collection, University of North Carolina, Chapel Hill, N. C. (cited hereafter as Mallett Papers).
[45] The camp of instruction for the training of conscripts was established near Raleigh in the early part of June 1862. It was named for General Holmes, who then commanded the Department of North Carolina. Peter Mallett to S. Cooper, June 10, 1862, *O. R.*, Ser. IV, Vol. I, 1148-1149.
[46] The instructions for the enrollment and disposition of recruits was a part of General Orders, No. 30, and, among other things, required that "Application will be made immediately to the Governors of the several States for permission to employ State officers for said enrollment. . . . Where State officers are employed the regulations of the respective States in regard to military enrollment will be observed as far as applicable." *O. R.*, Ser. IV, Vol. I, 1097. Until Vance became governor there was much confusion and a lack of cooperation between state and Confederate authority with regard to the enrollment of conscripts under General Orders, No. 30. Clark's assistant adjutant general, John C. Winder wrote, July 29, 1862 that Governor Clark never ordered, nor had any intention of ordering, the militia officers to enroll the conscripts, but that he had no objection to it. John C. Winder to Cyrus P. Mendenhall, July 29, 1862, Adjutant General's Department, Militia Book, State Department of Archives and History, Raleigh, N. C. (cited hereafter as Militia Book). Clark himself wrote to President Davis that "the Governor has not been asked for a State officer or even consulted about any Confederate Officer being sent. But finding an officer sent here I directed every facility afforded him." Clark to Davis, Clark Letter Book, pp.

I take pleasure in reporting that these officers thus far have voluntarily rendered efficient service (with few exceptions) in this capacity.

Under your orders & clothed with authority, the work can be done more effectually. I am authorized to allow these officers for enrolling conscripts such compensation as is allowed by the State for enrolling the Militia.

Being informed there has been no compensation allowed Militia Officers by the State, I reported the same to the Secretary of War, and requested that they be paid for this service.

I most respectfully ask your co-operation in the discharge of the duties pertaining to my office.
Raleigh.
[A. L. S. Governors' Papers (Vance), Vance Letter Book, 1862-1863, State Department of Archives and History, Raleigh.]

To Peter Mallett [47]

STATE OF NORTH CAROLINA
EXECUTIVE DEPARTMENT
Raleigh— Sept. 11th. 1862

In accordance with your request,[48] I have ordered the Militia Officers of the State to Enroll & bring in the Conscripts.[49]

When necessary they are instructed to apply to you for assistance, the troops furnished in such cases to be under the control of the officers applying[50]—
[Raleigh]
[Vance Letter Book, 1862-1863,
State Department of Archives and History, Raleigh.]

386-387, July 21, 1862. On August 22, 1862, Clark again wrote to Davis that no request had come to him to cooperate in enrolling the conscripts. He had called out the militia, furnished the rolls, and ordered them to receive the conscripts, but he had never ordered them to enroll them, and the militia officers, in the absence of such an order from the governor, had refused to enroll them on the orders of Mallett. Clark Letter Book, p. 402. So Mallett was now requesting Vance to give the order which Clark said he had never been requested to give. Sec *O. R.,* Ser. IV, Vol. II, 67-59.

[47] See p. 175, 44n.
[48] See above, Mallett to Vance, p. 175.
[49] This direction was embodied in General Orders, No. 7, issued in Vance's name from the adjutant general's office in Raleigh, dated September 13, 1862. It ordered the colonels of militia regiments to bring all men liable to conscription and all absent without leave to the camp of instruction in Raleigh, and granted all power necessary for the enforcement of the order. For failure to comply, officers were subject to courts martial and reduction in rank. The order explained that Vance was trying to get North Carolina officers to do this service so that Confederate officers would not be necessary. The order is printed in Raleigh *North Carolina Standard,* September 17, 1862.
[50] Instructions from the War Department provided that in case state officers were not assigned to the duty of enrolling the conscripts that officers of the Confederancy would be selected by the War Department for the duty. This happened, for example, in Alabama until the legislature decided to cooperate by an act of November 25, 1862. *O. R.,* Ser. IV, Vol. I, 1097, II, 87, 226.

To G. W. Randolph [51]

STATE OF NORTH CAROLINA
EXECUTIVE OFFICE
Raleigh Sept. 11th. 1862

I respectfully request that you will not in the future confer authority on persons to enlist soldiers within the limits of this State, unless the applicant be endorsed by this department. Allow me likewise to express the hope that it will not be deemed by you incompatible with the interests of the service to revoke all Such authority heretofore given to other than citizens of North Carolina.

Permit me to enquire whether late enlistments of citizens of this State, residing beyond the Blue Ridge Mountains,[52] made under the authority (as represented) of Gen. E. Kirby Smith,[53] commanding Department of East Tennessee &c. were authorized by you. If authorizied by you I request that such authority be revoked, if not that you cause such enlistments to be discontinued.[54]

I make the above request for the following reasons. Much confusion has been produced. Many soldiers have been Enlisted in the Confederate Service without this States being credited with the same in her quota of troops— The operation of the Act of Congress known as the Conscript Act is much hindered, & it will be difficult, if not impossible, for this State to fill up its thinned regiments already in Service.

[Richmond]
[Vance Letter Book, 1862-1863,
State Department of Archives and History, Raleigh.]

---

[51] See p. 132, 524n.

[52] By Special Orders, No. 127, dated June 3, 1862, "That part of North Carolina west of the Blue Ridge, and adjoining East Tennessee, will be embraced within the Department of East Tennessee, under Maj.-Gen. E. K. Smith." *O. R.*, Ser. I, Vol. IX, 473.

[53] Edmund Kirby-Smith (1824-1893), major general in command of the Department of East Tennessee. He was born in Florida, graduated at West Point in 1845, served in the War with Mexico, and entered the Confederate Army in the spring of 1861. He rose successively in rank from colonel to general. Early in 1862 he was sent to command the East Tennessee Department which embraced for a while parts of Kentucky, Georgia, and North Carolina as well. He served here until February 1863, when he became commander of the Trans-Mississippi Department until the close of the war. After the war he went to Mexico and to Cuba, but soon returned and was president of the University of Nashville, 1870-1875, and professor of mathematics at the University of the South, 1875-1893. Joseph Gregoire deRoulhac Hamilton, "Edmund Kirby-Smith," *Dict. of Am. Biog.*, X, 424-426.

[54] Throughout the fall of 1862 Smith complained that the Conscript Act could not be enforced in the region of his command without the use of troops under his command "owing to the disloyalty of the citizens." Eventually, in November 1862, the Secretary of War, upon the approval of the adjutant general, ordered all enrolling officers in Smith's department to report to the general commanding. *O. R.*, Ser. I, Vol. XX, 405, 406.

From Jno. R. Winston[55]

Camp Near Drewry's Bluff Va
Sept. 12th. 1862

I address you a note because I wish it to be of authority. So if you condescend to answer it, please direct to Petersburg V[a].

In case a Major in the service should resign,[56] will the senior Captain of that Regt. go up by promotion; or will there be an election for Major.[57] An early reply will very much oblige Your humble servt.

[Raleigh]
[on reverse]
The Senior Capt will go up unless objections be made to his competency. No election—

Z. B. V.

[A. L. S. Governors' Papers (Vance),
State Department of Archives and History, Raleigh.]

To G. W. Randolph [58]

STATE OF NORTH CAROLINA
EXECUTIVE DEPARTMENT
Raleigh— Sept. 13th. 1862

In order to facilitate the collection of the Conscripts in this State I have imposed that duty upon my Militia officers and hope and believe their action will be much more rapid & efficient.[59] Permit me to urge the propriety of compensating them. Your instructions to Major Mallett said they might be allowed the same pay they received from the State for enrolling the Militia, which is nothing.

[Ricmond]
[Vance Letter Book, 1862-1863,
State Department of Archives and History, Raleigh.]

---

[55] John R. Winston, of Rockingham County, was captain of company F in the Forty-fifth North Carolina Regiment. He was promoted major, lieutenant colonel, and colonel; was several times wounded during the war; was captured at Gettysburg and imprisoned on Johnson's Island, from which he escaped in January 1864 and returned to his regiment by way of Canada and the West Indies. He was known as a man of deep piety, stern integrity, and cool courage. Clark, *N. C. Regts*, III, 37; Moore, *N. C. Roster*, III, 258, 276.

[56] The major of the regiment was Andrew J. Boyd, also of Rockingham County. He was promoted to lieutenant colonel, but resigned in January 1863. Moore, *N. C. Roster*, III, 258.

[57] This matter is covered in General Orders, No. 36, and No. 43, the pertinent parts of which have been quoted on p. 171, 31n and 32n. Vance wrote Winston that there would be no election unless there was objection to the competency of the senior captain. Vance to Winston, September 16, 1862, Vance Letter Book.

[58] See p. 132, 524n.

[59] Vance's order was issued the same day and was published in the papers throughout the state. A copy is found in the Raleigh *North Carolina Standard*, September 17, 1862, and the order is summarized on p. 176, 49n.

From S. F. Patterson[60]

Palmyra Caldwell Co.
Septem[r] 13th 1862

I have just had the pleasure of reading your inaugural address,[61] and cannot withhold the expression of my most cordial approbation of every position taken, and every sentiment uttered in it— So long as you adhere firmly to the views therein contained, the people of our good old State will never I think have cause to regret the choice they have made with such remarkable unanimity of a Chief Magistrate to preside over them during the trying & difficult times in which we find ourselves involved.—

It would have afforded me much pleasure to have been present on the interesting occasion of the 8th. but my personal condition for the past two years has been such as to confine me almost entirely at home—

Wishing you as many of the enjoyments and as few of the cares and responsibilities of your position as is possible.

[Raleigh]
[A. L. S. Governors' Papers (Vance),
State Department of Archives and History, Raleigh.]

From Lotte W. Humphrey[62]

Camp near Swansboro.
Sep. 15th 1862.

The unattached Cavalry Companies in our State have been recently organized into a Regiment by the Secretary of War and

---

[60] Samuel Finley Patterson (1799-1874), a native of Rockbridge County, Va. who was a clerk in a store in Wilkesboro from 1814 to 1820, when he began a business of his own which he conducted for twenty years. After 1845 he was primarily a farmer. In 1821 he was elected engrossing clerk of the House of Commons, and for fourteen years held some clerkship in the legislature, being chief clerk of the Senate, 1829-1832. He was public treasurer of North Carolina, 1835-1837, president of the Raleigh and Gaston Railroad, 1840-1845, resigning upon the death of his father-in-law, General Edmund Jones, and retiring to his estate at Palmyra. He was chairman of the court of pleas and quarter sessions from 1845 until it was abolished in 1868; represented Caldwell County in the State Senate in 1846, 1848, and 1864; and was a colleague of Vance in the House of Commons of 1854. He also represented Caldwell County in the Convention of 1865 and was the Conservative candidate for Superintendent of Public Works in 1868, but suffered his only defeat. He was an active Whig, Episcopalian, and Mason, being Grand Master of North Carolina masons in 1833 and 1834. The legislature elected him a brigadier general, then a major general of the militia, a justice of the peace, and a trustee of the University of North Carolina. Connor, *N. C. Manual*, pp. 442, 468-469, 529, 870; Hickerson, *Happy Valley*, pp. 48-49.

[61] Vance's inaugural is summarized on p. 174, 43n.

[62] Lotte Williams Humphrey (1830-1891), of Onslow County. The same age as Vance, he went to the legislature the same year, but Humphrey was a Democrat and Vance a Whig. Humphrey was re-elected to the Commons in 1856, and to the Senate in 1858 and 1860, where he became chairman of the Committee on Corporations and began to show that interest in business matters which

the Senior Officer placed in command. The order of the Sec. of War says the Senior Officer will take Command *until Field Officers are appointed*. The Officers of many of the Companies composing the Regiment have suggested me to address your Excellency in their behalf. They ask to be allowed the privilege of having a voice in choosing officers to Command them, and in all respects to be organized and recognized as a Regiment of N. C. T. Although organized by the Confederate War Department they feel that they have the right of effecting a field organization by election— for, they represent to me, that many of the companies— being twelve months Companies— were reorganized for the War under the Conscript Laws which, they understand, gave the right of election. The other Companies, which were already organized for the War, were raised under the Authority direct from the Secretary of War and in that authority the right was expressed that whenever a sufficient number of Companies should be raised to form a Battalion or Regiment that they should be organized by electing Field Officers.[63] By order of Maj. Gen D. H.

characterized his later career. He studied law under Chief Justice Richmond M. Pearson and received his license in 1858. In the crisis of 1860-1861 Humphrey supported his party in its demand for a secession convention and, after the special legislative session of 1861, he raised a military unit known as the "Gatlin Dragoons," which for nearly a year served as an independent company. In the summer of 1862 Lieutenant Humphrey raised another company known as the "Humphrey Troops," of which he was captain, and which eventually became a part of the Forty-first North Carolina Regiment (third cavalry), though not with Humphrey as its captain. He resigned from the army in 1863 because of illness and, in December, was elected by the justices of Onslow as solicitor. During the occupation of eastern North Carolina by the Federals he removed his family and negroes to Davie County; after the war he moved to Goldsboro where he lived the remainder of his life, representing Wayne County in the State House of Representatives in 1872, in which session he opposed the election of Vance as United States Senator and was instrumental in electing Augustus S. Merrimon. Soon after this struggle Humphrey joined the Republican party and was rewarded with the presidency of the Atlantic and North Carolina Railroad, a position he held until Vance's re-election as governor in 1876, when Humphrey was replaced by a Vance Democrat. He remained influential in local political and business matters the remainder of his life. An item of interest is that he was the father-in-law of a future United States Senator from North Carolina, Furnifold M. Simmons. Connor, *N. C. Manual*, pp. 735, 849; Joseph Gregoire deRoulhac Hamilton et al, *History of North Carolina*, 6 vols. (Chicago and New York, 1919), VI, 149-151 (cited hereafter as Hamilton, *History of N. C.*); Frank Daniels, *History of Wayne County* (Address given November 30, 1914), pp. 39-40.

[63] There were ten unattached cavalry companies in eastern North Carolina in the summer of 1862 and that August they were formed into a regiment that came to be known as the Forty-first North Carolina (third cavalry). Ashe, in *History of N. C.*, II, 753 says that Humphrey was elected colonel and directed to report in Raleigh, but that when he came his commission could not at once be issued and that he was directed to proceed with the organization of the regiment; that when Vance became governor in September he ignored Humphrey's election and appointed John A. Baker of Wilmington, who had no connection with any company in the regiment, as the colonel. "Humphrey had been an original secessionist; that determined Vance." Humphrey's anonymous biographer claims that Humphrey's election as colonel "was fully recognized by Adjutant-General Martin, and he was officially recognized with that rank. However, a few

Hill [64] to Brig Gen- Clingman[65] the Officers of this Regiment were assembled in Goldsboro on the 25th ult. and had an election. Six Companies were there and voted. The absent Companies, with one exception, have either voted or acquiesced— all of which have been sent to Brig. Gen. Martin,[66] Raleigh, N. C. I was elected to the Command and that is the reason that I have been requested to address you for the officers. That election, I suppose, has been held to be illegal. I do not think that the election was fair and just to all the Companies and if they have the right then there should be a new election.

I am no applicant for a place in the field and address you in an unofficial capacity.

I have read your Inaugural [67] with a great deal of pleasure, and I congratulate you upon the universal and hearty endorsement it receives in this section, as I have not the slightest doubt it has in every section of the state. With great respect,

[Raleigh]

[A. L. S. Governors' Papers (Vance),
State Department of Archives and History, Raleigh.]

---

days later Colonel Z. B. Vance, on being inaugurated governor, chose to disregard this election and appointed a former whig as colonel of the Third Cavalry. He thus ignored the patent claims and merits of Colonel Humphrey, and his action was one that Colonel Humphrey resented all through his life." Hamilton *History of N. C.,* VI, 149. While the details of what occured remain obscure it is probable that Vance did not "choose to disregard this election" nor even appoint Baker as colonel. The Forty-first Regiment was not one which the Governor of North Carolina claimed the right to officer and by the admission of Governor Clark it came among those in which Confederate control was admitted. Furthermore, Baker was commissioned colonel on September 3, 1862, and Vance did not become governor until September 8. Regardless of who held the right of appointment, there was certainly no right to an election, as the Conscription Act extended this privilege to twelve months regiments but only within forty days of April 16, 1862. Baker was made colonel by Confederate authority and not by Vance's appointment. Moore, *N. C. Roster,* III, 146; Clark, *N. C. Regts.,* II, 769. For the regiments that Governor Clark claimed the right to officer see p. 166, 13n.

[64] Daniel Harvey Hill (1821-1889), a graduate of West Point in 1842, veteran of the War with Mexico, and former professor of mathematics at Washington College and at Davidson College. He resigned from the latter institution in 1859 to become Superintendent of the North Carolina Military Institute at Charlotte. He became colonel of the First North Carolina Regiment, led it into the Battle of Bethel in June of 1861 and was made a brigadier general in September 1861. He rose in rank until nominated as lieutenant general in July 1863, but President Davis withdrew his name from the Senate after Hill's quarrel with Braxton Bragg. He served briefly in North Carolina in 1861 and 1862, and for a longer period in 1863. After the war he edited *The Land We Love* and the *Southern Home* in Charlotte; he was president of the University of Arkansas, 1877-1884 and of Middle Georgia Military and Agricultural College, 1885-1889. Hill was a brother-in-law of "Stonewall" Jackson, they having married daughters of Robert Hall Morrison, former president of Davidson College. Francis P. Gaines, "Daniel Harvey Hill," *Dict. of Am. Biog.,* IX, 27-28.

[65] See p. 55, 200n.

[66] See p. 113, 447n. The results were sent to Martin as adjutant general of the state troops, not as brigadier general in the Confederate army.

[67] See p. 174, 43n.

From D. L. Swain[68]

Chapel Hill, 15 Sep. 1862

It seems to me that the best disposition, I can make of the enclosed letter[69] is to send it to you. You will treat it as confidential of course. Your opportunities while stationed in the neighborhood of Goldsboro, Kinston and New Bern to ascertain the true state of facts, will enable you to act upon your own judgment. I have heard occasional intimations that Gen[l]. Martin held a plurality of lucrative officers,[70] but have no personal knowledge upon the subject. Gov. Graham has had much better opportunities to learn the facts in relation to the claims of both these gentlemen to your consideration and his opinions are entitled to high respect. I have never exchanged a word with him, about either, and do not know what he would advise.

I was gratified by the remarks in your inaugural, of your desire to encourage retrenchment in public and private expenditures— A reference to our revolutionary history may serve to direct and encourage your efforts.

The Wilmington Committee in this State with Cornelius Harnett, at their head resolved on the 26. Nov. 1774, in the language of the Continental Congress "to discountenance and discourage every species of extravagance and dissipation, especially all horse racing and all kinds of gaming cock-fighting exhibitions, shows

---

[68] See p. 9, 45n.

[69] No enclosure is found with the letter.

[70] See p. 113, 447n. Martin was made adjutant general of the ten regiments of state troops on September 20, 1861, and on September 28 was commissioned major general of North Carolina Militia and given command of all the state forces and supervision of the entire defense of the state. In May of 1862, he was made a brigadier general in the Confederate army and on June 1, 1862, he was given command of the District of North Carolina, with headquarters at Kinston, but he did not resign his state position. There was some murmuring because he held two positions simultaneously. The *North Carolina Standard* remarked that anyone with such a penchant for feathering his own nest could hardly avoid popular indignation. While Holden admitted that Martin was a good bureaucrat and understood the details of his office, he charged that "the temper of the man and his old army regime, have made him the most unpopular officer with all classes of the community we have ever known in North Carolina. Whilst he has apologists, he had no admirers as an officer that we know of in or out of the army." On December 15, 1862 the House of Commons adopted a resolution, by a vote of 64-14, declaring the office of adjutant general vacant. But Martin did not resign even then, declaring that he wished the Supreme Court to settle the matter. He pointed out that he had never drawn salary from the Confederate government, as regulations did not permit it, but that regulations did not forbid the holding of two offices. Martin continued to hold the office until March 14, 1863, when Daniel G. Fowle, a member of the House from Wake County, was elected. Clark, *Memorial of Martin;* Raleigh *North Carolina Standard*, December 31, 1862, January 6, 1863; *House Journal, 1862-1863*, pp. 120-121; *O. R.*, Ser. I, Vol. IX, 471-473. For the part of the Supreme Court in the controversy see In the Matter of J. G. Martin 60 N. C. 153, 156 (1863), Governor's Request March 2 and Justices Reply, March 11, 1863; *Public Laws of N. C., 1862-1863*, p. 51; Preston W. Edsall, "The Advisory Opinion in North Carolina," *North Carolina Law Review* (Chapel Hill, 1927-   ), Vol. 27, No. 3 (April, 1949), pp. 297-344.

and plays and other expensive diversions and entertainments." [71]
On the 20. Jan. 1775, they proscribed Billiard Tables.[72] On the
1 March following a public ball was forbidden,[73] and on the 6th
they resolved "that all dances, public as well as private should be
discouraged and stigmatized." [74] The times were not more perilous
then, than now.

All distillation of drawn spirits during the present year, from
bread stuffs is prohibited by an Ordinance of the State Convention[75]. As M[rs] Vance will not take charge of the Palace[76] until
some weeks hence, she will have leisure to consider whether in
the face of the precedents, the introduction of spiritous liquors
and wines, shall be permitted at her reception.
Raleigh.
[A. L. S.   Z. B. Vance Papers,
State Department of Archives and History, Raleigh.]

From W. J. Yates[77]

Charlotte, Sept. 16th.
.62

Your letter, asking me to retain my post as a member of the

---

[71] The Wilmington Safety Committee quoted the ordinance of the Continental
Congress and sent letters to several gentlemen who were about to race horses.
William L. Saunders, (ed.), *The Colonial Records of North Carolina*, 10 vols.
(Raleigh, 1886-1890), IX, 1090-1091 (cited hereafter as *Colonial Records*).
[72] *Colonial Records*, IX, 1113 gives the date of this proscription as [Jan 27, 1775].
[73] *Colonial Records*, IX, 1136.
[74] *Colonial Records*, IX, 1150.
[75] This ordinance was adopted at the third session of the Convention and ratified
on February 21, 1862. It levied a tax of thirty cents a gallon on all spirituous
liquors manufactured in North Carolina out of corn, wheat, rye, or oats up to
April 15, 1862; it prohibited manufacture after April 15 and levied appropriate
penalties for violation; it also provided for a tax of one dollar a gallon on liquor
manufactured elsewhere but sold in North Carolina after March 1, 1862. The law
was to prevail until January 1, 1863. *Convention Ordinances*, 3 session, No. 24.
[76] The residence of the governor stood at the south end of Fayeteville Street in
Raleigh, with the State Capitol at the north end.
[77] William J. Yates (1827-1888), of Mecklenburg County, editor of the Charlotte
Western Democrat. Yates was born in Fayetteville and was educated as a journey-
man printer, never going to college. At the age of twenty-seven he purchasd the
Fayetteville *North Carolinian* and published it until he moved to Charlotte in
1856, when he took over the *Western Democrat*. In both instances his policies
were Democratic, and it was his journal which had first nominated William
Johnston, Vance's opponent, for the governorship. His issues were especially strong
on politics and in their support of the common schools. In 1858 Yates was elected
to the Council of State by the Democratic legislature; he was also a director of the
Charlotte Central and the Charlotte Airline Railroads, and of the Insane Asylum at
Morganton, as well as a trustee of the University of North Carolina. He retired
from the active management of his paper in 1881 upon its consolidation with the
Southern Home into the *Home-Democrat*, though he resumed the management
of it from time to time until his death. Yates was very pronounced in his opinions,
but was not so extreme in political denunciation as some other editors of his
time. Zeb F. Curtis, "William J. Yates," Trinity *Archives*, Series II (Durham, 1898),
pp. 21-28; J. B. Alexander, *The History of Mecklenburg County From 1740 to 1900*
(Charlotte, 1902), pp. 142-143 (cited hereafter as Alexander, *Mecklenburg County*).

Literary Board [78] until the expiration of my term of office, was received. I had determined to resign for the simple reason that I thought you ought to have the opportunity to select your own advisers and assistants; and as I was appointed by the old administration, I felt it a duty to resign so that the new one might have the privilege of selecting such persons as might be desired. But if I can be of the least service to you on the Literary Board (as your flattering note would indicate) I will remain a member until my successor is appointed, and will endeavor to be present at the next meeting.

If convenient to you, I would be pleased if the next meeting was appointed on some *Wednesday,* as I can attend on Wednesdays or Thursdays than any other days in the week.

The Common School matter is one of great importance, and one in which I have always felt much interest, as I doubt not you have. I hope we may be able to Keep the system in operation and revive feeling in its favor.

With sentiments of high regard, I am your obt. servt.
Raleigh
[A. L. S. Governors' Papers (Vance),
State Department of Archives and History, Raleigh.]

From Jonathan Worth [79]

Asheboro Sep 16/62

I See in The Fayetteville Observer, of the 15 inst.; an advertisement of Capt Murchison[80], notifying the conscripts of Cumber-

[78] See p. 25, 115n. Others than state officers had later been provided for the Board. A new board, without Yates as a member, was chosen by the Council of State on January 8, 1863. Raleigh *North Carolina Standard,* January 13, 1863.

[79] Jonathan Worth (1802-1869), of Randolph County, a former Whig of influence and ability, and member-elect to the House of Commons. He was born in Guilford County, attended the neighborhood schools and Caldwell Institute in Greensboro, and studied law under Archibald D. Murphey, whose niece he married in 1824. He moved to Asheboro the same year and began the practice of law. He represented Randolph County in the House of Commons in 1830, 1831, and again in 1862, until he resigned that office upon his election as state treasurer, 1863-1865. He also served in the State Senate in 1840; was an unsuccessful Whig candidate for Congress in 1841 and 1845, but in 1858 he returned to the legislature and represented his district in the State Senate, 1858-1860. In 1860 he was an uncompromising opponent of secession, voting against the bill to submit the question to the people, against all the bills for military preparation and, after the call for troops, against the call of a convention. He refused to be a candidate for that convention, but he supported the south when the war came, though his sentiments were for peace, and perhaps some of his deeds and letters brought him to the verge of disloyalty. He was elected governor in 1865 and again in 1866, serving until 1868 when he was removed, over his protest, by order of General Canby, commanding the second military district. Joseph Gregoire deRoulhac Hamilton, (ed.), *The Correspondence of Jonathan Worth,* 2 vols. (Raleigh, 1909), I, v-xiii (cited hereafter as Hamilton, *Worth Correspondence*); Joseph Gregoire deRoulhac Hamilton, "Jonathan Worth," Ashe, *Biog. Hist. of N. C.,* III, 435-453; Connor, *N. C. Manual,* pp. 419, 442, 770-771.

[80] John R. Murchison, of Cumberland County, then captain of company E in the Eighth North Carolina Regiment. He was later lieutenant colonel of the same regiment and was killed in action at Cold Harbor, June 1, 1864, while in command of the regiment. Moore, *N. C. Roster,* I, 273, 285; Clark, *N. C. Regts.,* I, 405.

land & Harnett, that: those of them who have failed to report themselves, will be received into his company[81]. I learn that there are many conscripts in this County who have not reported themselves, and I am sure nearly all them (excepting the Quakers) would immediately report, if allowed to join companies of their choice. If such assurance can be given, they can be speedily in the ranks, I am sure. A portion of those who went to the camp of instruction ran away, reporting that they were not properly cared for & not allowed to Select their companies[82]. This makes it difficult to get in others. I am ready to do anything I can to get our conscripts into the field and therefore make this communication. I know not whom I ought to address. An agent to arrest them has been sent here, who is exceedingly odious to them and in whom they have no confidence. Perhaps I ought to address Major Mallett. I am not acquainted with him. If you are not doing any thing in this matter, let this communication go for nothing. If Murchison be authorized to fill up his company with conscripts surely others should have the like privilege and as I know Capt Murchison to be a gentleman and a man of intelligence, I do not doubt but he has been so authorized.

This county has furnished some 8 or 9 companies—met the draft manfully and would have faced conscription, if the men had not been induced to believe that they would be allowed, as

---

[81] Captain Murchison claimed authority to receive into his company any persons in Cumberland or Harnett counties who were liable to conscription and to take charge of any who had failed to report themselves. He appealed to them to join now, or else the militia colonels would take them to camps of instruction. *Fayetteville Observer*, September 15, 1862. Authority for such details came from section 9 of the rules and regulations issued by the War Department when the Conscription Act was adopted. This section provided that recruiting officers might be detailed by generals commanding military departments, and by commandants of regiments and corps, to recruit from their respective states all volunteers desiring to join them. *O. R.*, Ser. IV, Vol. I, 1098. General Orders, No. 6, January 27, 1862, provided for recruiting officers from each county below maximum organizational strength "to proceed to the neighborhood where his company was raised, and there enlist recruits to raise the company to the maximum organization." *O. R.*, Ser. IV, Vol. I, 926.

[82] War Department regulations, based on the Conscription Act of April 16, 1862, provided that "persons liable to military service . . . wishing to volunteer in any particular company . . . may report themselves prior to their enrollment at a camp of instruction within their respective States, where they will be enrolled, prepared for the field, and sent to the said company until the same shall be filled up." Section 8, *O. R.*, Ser. IV, Vol. I, 1098. These provisions were modified by the new Conscription Act of September 27, 1862 and by the new Exemption Act of October 11, 1862. The Conscription Act of April 16, 1862 and the Exemption Act of April 21, 1862 may be found in James M. Matthews, (ed.), *Public Laws of the Confederate States of America Passed at the First Session of the First Congress; 1862* (Richmond, 1862). pp. 29-32, 51-52 (cited hereafter as Matthews, *Public Laws of Confederacy*, with appropriate designations); the Conscription Act of September 27, 1862, and the Exemption Act of October 11, 1862 may be found in James M. Matthews, (ed.), *Public Laws of the Confederate States of American Passed at the Second Session of the First Congress; 1862* (Richmond, 1862), pp. 61-62, 77-78 (cited hereafter as Matthews, *Public Laws of the Confederacy*, with appropriate designations).

far as possible to select the Companies in which they were to serve. As it is, I fear some will only be got by force, and this may be better effected by requiring the militia officers of each company to arrest their own conscripts, under such penalty for neglect as you may have power to impose. One great cause of the refusal of our conscripts to enrol themselves, is the exemption of their officers.

[Raleigh]

[on reverse]

Jonathan Worth ansed 21ˢᵗ Sept /62 enclosed copies of orders No 2⁸³ & No 7⁸⁴

[A. L. S. Governors' Papers (Vance), State Department of Archives and History, Raleigh.]

From I. M. St. John[85]

CONFEDERATE STATES OF AMERICA
WAR DEPARTMENT
NITRE & MINING BUREAU
Richmond Sept 16ᵗʰ 1862

I have the honor to state that the delivering of nitre under a

---

[83] General Orders, No. 2, dated Raleigh, September 9, 1862 and issued from the North Carolina adjutant general's department provided: "I. All persons liable to military duty under the Conscription law are hereby required to come to the Camp of Instruction, near this city, at once. Those doing so will be allowed to select the Infantry Regiments they wish to join, and unless full, they will be assigned accordingly. II. The Regiments of Infantry and Artillery on duty in this State are authorized to enlist Conscripts to increase each company of Infantry and Heavy Artillery to one hundred men, but not exceeding it; the Light Batteries to one hundred and fifty men." *Fayetteville Observer*, September 15, 1862; *O. R.*, Ser. I, Vol. XVIII, 754. The essence of the confusion arose from two facts: the numbers of the regiments as dictated in General Orders, No. 2, were in conflict with the requirements of the Conscription Act, as pointed out by Secretary Randolph in *O. R.*, Ser. I, Vol. XVIII, 753; and the right to select companies applied only to volunteers before enrollment. Conscripts who were enrolled without having volunteered had no right to select their units, but many of them did not understand this. Recruits who were enrolled without having volunteered were to be distributed to units as commandants of regiments or corps saw fit, in accordance with military needs. See *O. R.*, Ser. IV, Vol. I, 1097, and Randolph's endorsement on Martin's letter of October 5, 1862 in *O. R.*, Ser. I, Vol. XVIII, 752-753.

[84] General Orders, No. 7, dated Raleigh, September 13, 1862 read: "I. Colonels and other officers in command of the Militia of North Carolina are hereby ordered to bring all men liable to conscription in their commands and all soldiers absent from their regiments without leave to the camp of instruction at Raleigh. All power necessary for the enforcing of this order is hereby given them. II. A failure or refusal to comply with this order will subject the offender to the penalties of a court-martial and consequent reduction to the ranks. III. The executive, through its own officers, having thus undertaken to collect all persons liable to militia duty instead of allowing Confederate officers to do so, it is earnestly hoped that all will come up promptly to the performance of their duty. By order of Governor Vance." *O. R.*, Ser. I, Vol. XVIII, 753.

[85] Isaac Munroe St. John (1827-1880), superintendent of the Nitre and Mining Bureau of the Confederate States. He was born in Augusta, Georgia, where his

proposition from this Bureau accepted by Gov Clark[86] in his letters of August 13 and 18th will commence on Oct. 15th the day specified by Mr. Waterhouse[87]—but earlier if you desire.

For your information as to this agreement I quote from my letter of July 10th. to Gov Clarke—offering upon the part of the C. S. Government to assume the obligation of the State of N Carolina[88] to Waterhouse & Co—the "obligation" as you then

---

father was in business, but the family soon moved to New York City and Issac graduated from Yale College in 1845. He began the study of law in New York, but soon abandoned it to become assistant editor of the *Baltimore Patriot,* but he gave up journalism in 1848 to become a civil engineer. Until 1855 he was on the engineering staff of the Baltimore and Ohio Railroad and then moved to Georgia, where for five years he was in charge of construction divisions of the Blue Ridge Railroad. When the Civil War came he volunteered as a private but was soon transferred to engineering duty with Magruder's army, of which he became chief engineer. Here he attracted the attention of the War Department, was promoted to major on April 18, 1862, and made chief of the nitre and mining bureau. He was later promoted to colonel and, on February 16, 1865, was appointed commissary general of the Confederacy with the rank of brigadier general. After the war he returned to his profession of civil engineering, serving several railroads, and the city of Louisville, Kentucky. Samuel J. Heidner, "Isaac Munroe St. John," *Dict. of Am. Biog.,* XVI, 302-303.

[86] The letters between Governor Clark and the Bureau of Nitre and Mining, dated July 10, 25, August 13, 18, 23, 1862, are in Clark Letter Book, pp. 374-375, 396, 400, 407-408, and in Governors' Papers (Clark) under appropriate dates.

[87] George B. Waterhouse who, with Michael Bowes, formed the Raleigh Powder Mills known as Waterhouse, Bowes & Company and made contracts with the state for the manufacture of powder. Papers of the Quartermaster Department, Contracts and Bonds, Box 107, State Department of Archives and History, Raleigh, N. C. (cited hereafter as N. C. Quartermaster Contracts).

[88] The agreement with Waterhouse, Bowes Co. was entered into under the authority of a law passed during the second extra session of the legislature in 1861, in which the governor was authorized to subscribe for stock in or loan money to any company for making powder, or erecting a powder mill, or buying machinery, provided not more than four such companies were formed, or more than ten thousand dollars advanced to any factory. *Public Laws of N. C.,* 2 extra session, 1861, chap. 2. Under this act Governor Clark advanced ten thousand dollars to Messrs. Waterhouse & Bowes toward the erection of the Raleigh Powder Mills. The mill was erected but was afterwards destroyed by an explosion. At the solicitation of Governor Clark the Raleigh Paper Mills were purchased for the purpose of building another plant, and twelve thousand more was advanced to them. The original contract was made on September 4, 1861 and the amended contract on June 23, 1862. The mills contracted to make 700 pounds per day at a profit of fifteen cents per pound. When Vance became governor eight thousand dollars more was advanced and means were arranged by which the money was to be refunded to the state from the proceeds of operation through the security of a first mortgage. Of the venture Vance wrote: "The mill will be nearly enough completed by the 1st of December to commence operations and will yield weekly about four thousand pounds of powder. The Confederate States will furnish the mills with three thousand pounds of nitre per week." The enterprise proved to be a complete success as shown by the report of the adjutant general the following year, by which time the state had turned over to the Confederate government over half a million dollars' worth of powder, and had been repaid for the loans advanced to the company. N. C. Quartermaster Contracts, September 4, 1861, June 23, 1862; Report of Adjutant General James G. Martin to Governor Vance, October 1, 1861-September 30, 1862, *Legislative Documents, 1862-1863* (Raleigh, 1863), Document No. 1, pp. 28-29 (cited hereafter as *Legislative Documents*); Governor Vance's Message to the Legislature, November 17, 1862, *Legislative Documents, 1862-1863,* p. 8; *O. R.,* Ser. IV, Vol. II, 184-185; Clark, *N. C. Regts.,* I, 44.

indicated (or as I understood you) being to supply their powder mill with a working supply of 4000 lbs of saltpetre per week. Assuming this obligation the Nitre Bureau is to receive & to have the benefit of outstanding contracts made by the State of North Carolina or its Agents, with parties in the Confederate States, the State also withdrawing its purchasing agents.

To which Govr Clark replied Augt 13

"I have accepted your proposition in behalf of the Nitre & Mining Bureau, C. S. Ordnance Department, contained in your letter to me of the 10th July ult according to the terms therein stated." & Aug.st 18^h

"Your proposal to the State to accept our contract for Nitre & to assume for the Confederacy the entire business of making & collecting nitre; and in return to Supply the powder mill of Waterhouse & Bowes near Raleigh with a stipulated amount of nitre, has been duly accepted and answered—"

In arranging to day with Mr. Waterhouse the details of transportation and delivering, it was found necessary to substitute refined nitre from Lynchburg (Gov.^{t}) refinery for the "Grough" or crude saltpetre named by Gov Clark & myself in the correspondence quoted.[89]

The difference was equated by us at 25 per cent as an average percentage of loss in refining, that is to say, in place of 4000 lbs "Grough" 3000 lbs refined nitre are to be delivered by this Bureau.

This arrangement is respectfully submitted for your assent— To deliver Grough Grough saltpetre would require an expensive inspection & would probably lead to much difficulty in arranging final settlements with the Ordnance Dept.

I will further submit that this settlement be determined upon our own invoice verified by the Ordnance Officer designated to act for the State. And upon his receipts will be charged the Government price for nitre, 75 cts per lb of 90 per ct— and 83 1/3 cents per lb of absolute—together with the cost of transportation: and this charge to be credited to the C. S. Ordnance Department in their account with the Raleigh Powder Mills: upon which the requisitions of the Chief of Ordnance will be made as heretofore for all powder not wanted by the State, and upon the Same terms.

---

[89] The Nitre & Mining Bureau, through Richard Morton, requested Governor Clark to change the verbal agreement made between the parties on July 10, 1862 so that refined saltpeter instead of crude could be supplied, and that this be delivered at Lynchburg, Va. Clark agreed to accept the refined material, but not the inconvenience of the Lynchburg delivery. Richard Morton to Governor Clark, August 23, 1862, Governor Clark to Richard Morton, August 28, 1862, Clark Letter Book, pp. 407-408.

I now request that the Nitre Contracts referred to by Gov[r] Clarke be transferred to this Bureau.[90]
[Raleigh]
[Vance Letter Book, 1862-1863,
State Department of Archives and History, Raleigh.]

From S. P. Moore[91]

CONFEDERATE STATES OF AMERICA
SURGEON GENERAL'S OFFICE
Richmond Va. 17th. September 1862

Having been officially informed that SmallPox has made its appearance in several sections of the South, among the residents near the large cities, and throughout the Country along the lines of Rail Road: the interests of the Government suggest the propriety of my requesting that prompt and vigorous action be taken on your part for the thorough vaccination of the citizens of your State.

I have the honor to inform you that since the commencement of the War, no efforts to secure this protective influence to the military have been omitted by this Department, and that the measures adopted for the accomplishment of this purpose are Still in force.
[Raleigh]
[Vance Letter Book, 1862-1863,
State Department of Archives and History, Raleigh.]

From A. C. Myers[92]

Richmond, Sept. 17th. 1862

I find that the manufacture of Army Clothing in the State of North Carolina, is still carried on through State Agents.[93] I

---

[90] The original suggestion that the obligation to supply the mill with powder be transferred to the Confederacy was made in letters of Governor Clark to Josiah Gorgas, Chief of Ordnance, on January 15 and January 28,, 1862. Clark Letter Book.

[91] Samuel Preston Moore (1813-1889), surgeon general of the Confederate Army. He was born in Charleston, S. C. and graduated from the Medical College of South Carolina in 1834. The next year he entered the United States Army, served at many posts and in the War with Mexico, rising to the rank of major by 1861, when he resigned and began the practice of medicine in Little Rock, Arkansas. But trained military surgeons were few and in June 1861 he was made surgeon general of the Confederate forces, and retained this position throughout the war. In this office he was regarded as strict and exacting and as a severe disciplinarian. After the war he remained in Richmond, devoting his time to educational and agricultural matters, but he did not resume medical practice. Percy M. Ashburn, "Samuel Preston Moore," *Dict. of Am. Biog.*, XIII, 137-138.

[92] See p. 150, 611n.

[93] By a law of September 20, 1861, the governor of the state was required to furnish the North Carolina troops with suitable clothing, and to make arrangements with the Confederate States to receive commutation money for the clothing to be furnished by the state to what were by then Confederate troops. Governor

think it very desirable, with a view to Systematizing & Extending this branch of the service, that there should be a complete transfer to the Confederate authorities of all the Contracts & facilities held by North Carolina for the manufacture of Army Clothing. I was under the impression that Q. Master Genl. Martin[94] had directed this to be done; but finding my error, I have to request that you will sanction the transfer. Captains Sloan[95] & Garrett,[96] I understand have been employed by the State in superintending the manufacture of the clothing referred to: & I would wish to retain their Services by recommending their appointments as Ast. Q. Masters in this Department.[97]

Clark entered into an agreement with the Confederate Quartermaster Department with regard to the provision of clothing, shoes, and blankets, whereby North Carolina was to receive commutation money and be responsible for supplying her own soldiers. Confederate agents seeking supplies agreed to stay out of North Carolina if the state would agree to sell its surplus to the Confederacy. Myers grew to dislike the arrangement before a year was out and wrote Governor Clark, June 12, 1862, charging the state with falling down on its supply of the troops and claiming that since the Confederacy was having to clothe North Carolina troops anyway she ought to have the benefit of North Carolina production. But Vance charged just the contrary, saying that the state was, in spite of the agreement, swarming with Confederate agents who were stripping bare the markets and putting enormous prices upon the North Carolina agents, and that consequently North Carolina troops could not get supplies at home and nothing at all from the Confederate government, because of the agreement to furnish themselves. *Public Laws of N. C.,* 2 extra session, 1861, chap. 21; Report of Adjutant-General James G. Martin to Governor Vance, *Legislative Documents, 1862-1863,* p. 25; Governor Vance's Message to the Legislature, November 17, 1862, *Legislative Documents, 1862-1863,* Document No. 1; Clark, *N. C. Regts.,* I, 26; A. C. Myers to Governor Clark, June 12, 1862, Governors' Papers (Clark).

[94] See p. 113, 447n. Martin was quartermaster general of North Carolina only in the sense that the law of September 20, 1861, under which he was elected, made him chief of all war departments of the state. Major John Devereux was chief quartermaster.

[95] James Sloan was a former Whig of Guilford County. He was known as captain, but was never a staff officer but a state agent, in charge of locating, collecting, and buying supplies for the state throughout the central region. William H. Oliver was state agent for the eastern part. After the war Sloan was a merchant in Greensboro, but went into bankruptcy. Clark, *N. C. Regts.,* I, 24; Jesse H. Lindsay to William A. Graham, January 25, 1871, Graham Papers CH. Sloan was appointed by the Military Board on June 22, 1861. Minutes of Military Board, p. 42, State Department of Archives and History, Raleigh, N. C. (cited hereafter as Minutes of Military Board).

[96] Isaac W. Garrett, of Edgecombe County, was a commissioned first lieutenant in company I of the Fifteenth North Carolina Regiment, whose detail Governor Clark requested of General Cooper because of Garrett's "peculiar qualifications for clothing establishment work." He was selected by Martin to take charge of the manufacture of clothing for North Carolina troops. His report is in *Legislative Documents, 1862-1863,* p. 30 and shows operations for the year ending September 30, 1862 of more than a million and a quarter dollars. Moore, *N. C. Roster,* IV, 14; Clark, *N. C. Regts.,* I, 6, 24, 28. Clark's letter to Cooper, November 27, 1861, is in Clark Letter Book, p. 207. He is often confused with Charles W. Garrett, who also served in the clothing department with the quartermaster corps until the spring of 1863.

[97] Through an aide Vance replied to Myers that he was unwilling to make any transfer without consulting the General Assembly and that since it would meet shortly he would call the matter to its attention and then make known his decision. David A. Barnes to Col. A. C. Myers, October 14, 1862, Vance Letter Book.

[Raleigh]
[A. L. S. Governors' Papers (Vance),
Vance Letter Book, 1862-1863,
State Department of Archives and History, Raleigh.]

[Raleigh, N. C.]
[September 18, 1862]

A PROCLAMATION[98] BY Z. B. VANCE
GOVERNOR OF NORTH CAROLINA

WHEREAS information has reached me that certain persons, unmindful of the calls of patriotism & forgetful of the duties of good citizens, are using their influence to prevent obedience to the law of Congress, known as the Conscription Law, and that others are attempting to organize an open resistance to its execution: whereas, such conduct, being not only in direct violation of law, but also detrimental in the highest degree to the cause of our country, it becomes my sacred duty to prevent & repress the same by all the means in my power.

Now therefore, I, ZEBULON B. VANCE, Governor of North Carolina, do issue this my proclamation, warning all such persons to desist from such unpatriotic & criminal conduct: earnestly hoping that all, who are disinclined to defend their homes themselves, either by reason of age, infirmity or cowardice will cease to dissuade those, who are willing: and notifying positively all persons contemplating an armed resistance to the law, if there really be any such misguided & evil-disposed persons in our midst, that they will commit the crime of treason according to the laws of Congress, and must not expect to escape its penalties— Whilst thousands upon thousands of our best & bravest have obeyed the law & by their patriotic valor have driven the enemy back to the Potomac, it would be an intolerable outrage upon them, to permit others to shirk or evade the law, or worse still, to resist it by open violence. Let no one therefore be deceived, the law will be enforced, & I appeal to all loyal & patriotic citizens to sustain those who are charged with its execution.

Given under my hand and attested by the Great Seal of the State— Done at the City of Raleigh the 18th day of September 1862.

Zebulon B. Vance

By the Governor
R. H. Battle, Jr.
Private Secretary

[Vance Letter Book, 1862-1863,
State Department of Archives and History, Raleigh.]

---

[98] This proclamation is also found in O. R., Ser. I, Vol. XVIII, 753.

From J. D. McIver[99]

Hd. Qrs. 26" Regt N. C. T.
Sept 18th 1862

I have now been in active Service about fifteen months, and with what fidelity I have served my country during that time you can testify. I would like to remain, could I do so consistently, but my position, which hitherto was a Source of pleasure & pride, is now anything but pleasant & agreeable. Numerous causes, which I need not now enumerate, conspire to produce this state of things which I very much deplore but could not avoid. For the first time since I enlisted, I have concluded to retire from active service, should I be favored with an opportunity to do so. I could not have done so could I have remained in my present position, consistently with my sense of honor as a soldier or dignity as a man.

I will not ask for a civil position, as I conceive that my services in a different Capacity, are urgently demanded by my country. I should like to be an Instructor of some Camp[100] as I believe my experience & Knowledge of the duties of a soldier, qualifies me for that position. And if Maj Mallett[101] has an appointment, (provided he has that power) I should feel myself under lasting obligation to you if you can consistently recommend me to him. My health is declining, & I should ever esteem it as a great favor, especially as it is the first time I ever ventured to ask one of you.
[on reverse]
Ans.ʳ that I can do nothing for him at present Kind wishes &c
[Raleigh]
[A. L. S. Governors' Papers (Vance),
State Department of Archives and History, Raleigh.]

From A. S. Merrimon[102]

Asheville N. C.
Sept. 18th 1862

I have read with much satisfaction your excellent Inaugural

---

[99] James D. McIver (1833-1912), of Moore County. He graduated from Davidson College in 1859, volunteered in the first company raised in his county and was elected second lieutenant of what became company H of Vance's Twenty-sixth Regiment. Upon the resignation of Captain Clement Dowd, McIver became captain of the company and led it in all the battles except Gettysburg until the fall of 1863, when he left the regiment. After the war he was county solicitor, represented Moore County in the House of Representatives in 1876, was solicitor of his district from 1878 to 1886, and judge of the superior court, 1890-1898. Clark, *N. C. Regts.*, II, 418; Connor, N. C. *Manual*, p. 713; Moore, *N. C. Roster*, II, 394.

[100] War Department regulations for the drill and training of recruits at camps of instruction provided that "competent drill officers to instruct the recruits" were to be called for by commandants of camps from the general commanding the military department in which the camp was situated. *O. R.* Ser. IV, Vol. I, 1097.

[101] See p. 175, 44n.

[102] See p. 13, 65n. He was now solicitor pro-tem of the western district.

Address.[103] It is an able State-Paper, adapted to the exigencies of the time and more than this, it gives almost universal satisfaction, not only to our own people. but also, to the whole people of the Confederate States. Those who object to it, do so upon selfish and interested motives. I have heard of but one person in this section of the State, who expresses dissatisfaction, and his good will opinion is not worth attention. The people of this section of the State are delighted with it.— Allow me to offer you my most cordial congratulation upon so decided a success in the production of your first official State-paper. If you had matured your notions upon a system of Policy for the Confederate States,[104] I could have wished you to allude to this subject, but it is perhaps as well to delay any suggestions of this character until a future occasion that will be quite as appropriate for such a purpose. I beg to recommend to your most favorable consideration our mutual worthy friend, D. G. Fowle[105] Esq.—I have reason to fear that he has been defeated for the Colonelcy of the Reg. of which he was late Lt. Col. If so, he is left without any position and subject to be Conscripted. He is worthy and very capable and all of a gentleman.— He would like the appointment of Paymaster. That office, I learn is vacant. by the resignation of the late in-

---

[103] See p. 174, 43n.

[104] While Vance did not expound a general policy with regard to the relations of North Carolina with the Confederacy, he did touch upon the dangers of military rule and the exercise of arbitrary power and promised to regard it as his "sacred, paramount duty to protect the citizen in the enjoyment of all his rights and liberties." *Legislative Documents, 1862-1863,* Document No. 18, p. 8.

[105] Daniel Gould Fowle (1831-1891), then a resident of Raleigh. He was a lawyer who had served with Merrimon in the North Carolina commissary department under Colonel William Johnston early in the war. He held the rank of major, but was elected lieutenant colonel of the Thirty-first North Carolina Regiment when it was organized on September 19, 1861. He was captured at Roanoke Island, February 10, 1862, paroled and exchanged. When the reorganization of the Thirty-first took place September 18, 1862, Fowle was defeated for the colonelcy by John V. Jordan; Edward R. Liles was elected lieutenant colonel and Fowle resigned. He was then nominated by the Conservatives, as Vance's party was called, as a candidate for the House of Commons from Wake County to fill the vacancy caused by the death of the member-elect, Henry Watkins Miller. In the special election of October 23, 1862, Fowle defeated Oscar R. Rand, a secessionist Democrat who had been a captain in Vance's regiment until his capture at the battle of New Bern, by the vote of 824 to 259. Fowle served in the legislature until he was chosen adjutant general of North Carolina on March 12, 1863; he resigned on August 26, 1863, because of a number of disagreements with Vance over his conduct of the adjutant general's office, and over Vance's policies with regard to the war. He was elected to represent Wake County in the House of Commons in 1864. He married Ellen Brent Pearson, a daughter of Chief Justice Richmond M. Pearson, and practiced law in Raleigh after the war. He was subsequently a judge of the superior court, 1865-1867, and governor of North Carolina from 1889 until his death in office, April 8, 1891. Connor, *N. C. Manual,* pp. 419, 449, 831-832; Raleigh *North Carolina Standard,* October 1, 15, 17, 29, 1862; Moore, *N. C. Roster,* II, 540, 544, IV, 13; Clark, *N. C. Regts.,* I, 18, 37, 50, II 507 511.

cumbent.[106] Assign Fowle some genteel position,[107] if consistent with duty and the public good. Pardon this liberty.
[Raleigh]
P. S. Pardon me for adding that Judge Saunders[108] complimented you in almost every charge he has made from Clay to Jackson. He is emphatically a *Vance Man!*

A. S. M.

[A. L. S. Governors' Papers (Vance),
State Department of Archives and History, Raleigh.]

To D. K. McRae[109]

STATE OF NORTH CAROLINA
EXECUTIVE DEPARTMENT
Raleigh Sept. 18th. 1862

Yours of the 9th Inst.[110] is to hand & in reply I would say that

[106] Augustus M. Lewis, of Wake County, was paymaster. His office was a part of the quartermaster department, in which he held the rank of major. Minutes of the Military Board, p. 5; Clark, *N. C. Regts.*, I, 45.

[107] Merrimon was not the only Conservative using his influence to obtain some "genteel position" for Fowle. Bartholomew Figures Moore wrote William A. Graham asking his influence on Vance in behalf of Fowle for paymaster. He explained that "some matters have occured which would make it very unpleasant" for Fowle in the regiment, even if elected colonel. Believing that Fowle was in "every way qualified very highly for the office," he asked Graham to accompany Vance on the train from Hillsboro to Raleigh on the way to the inauguration, and so to make Fowle the earliest applicant for the position. Moore promised to see Vance about the same matter as soon as Vance arrived in Raleigh. Bartholomew Figures Moore to William A. Graham, September 2, 1862, Graham Papers CH. Holden also used his influence for Fowle in the columns of the *Standard,* and had used Fowle, along with Merrimon, to talk with Vance about the nomination for governor in the early summer of 1862. Holden, *Memoirs,* pp. 18-20. Holden further claimed that Fowle had been proscribed from the lieutenant colonelcy of another regiment for political reasons, and that the place had been given to a less competent original secessionist. Upon his defeat for the colonelcy of the Thirty-first Fowle, according to Holden, reported himself to Major Mallett as subject to conscription, but was told by Mallett not to bother about it until after the special election of October 23. Holden calls this a rare example. Raleigh *North Carolina Standard,* October 15, 17, 1862.

[108] Romulus Mitchell Saunders (1791-1867), judge of the superior court. He was born in Caswell County, studied at the University of North Carolina, read law with Hugh Lawson White, and began the practice of it in Caswell County in 1812. He was a member of the House of Commons from Caswell County in 1815, 1818, 1819, and 1820, being speaker in 1819 and 1820, and a member of the State Senate from Caswell in 1816. He moved to Raleigh in 1831 and represented Wake County in the House of Commons in 1850 and 1852. From 1821 to 1827 he was a member of Congress, and again from 1841 to 1845, resigning to become minister to Spain, 1845-1849. He was also attorney general of North Carolina, 1828-1833, resigning to accept the presidency of the Board of Commissioners on the French Indemnity, tendered him by President Andrew Jackson. He was judge of the superior court, 1835-1840, 1852-1867, and Democratic candidate for governor in 1840. In the National Democratic convention of 1844 he introduced the famous two-thirds rule. Samuel A'Court Ashe, "Romulus Mitchell Saunders," Ashe, *Biog. Hist. of N. C.,* III, 386-393; W. J. Saunders MS. on R. M. Saunders, Cornelia Phillips Spencer Papers, Southern Historical Collection, University of North Carolina, Chapel Hill, N. C. (cited hereafter as Spencer Papers CH); Connor, *N. C. Manual,* pp. 444, 448-449, 465-466, 543, 831, 923-924, 930-931.

[109] See p. 163, 2n.

[110] See p. 170.

I have determined to exercise the right of appointment, claimed by my predecessor in office, as set forth in the letter from the Adjt. Gen.¹ of the State to you ¹¹¹ & enclosed with yours to me. I have the right to fill vacancies in regiments raised in this State (as was yours) originally *for the War* & I will take pleasure in commissioning such officers as you may recommend as qualified for positions now vacant in your regiment—¹¹²
[Vance Letter Book, 1862-1863,
State Department of Archives and History, Raleigh.]

*To Weldon N. Edwards*¹¹³

NORTH CAROLINA
EXECUTIVE DEPARTMENT
Raleigh Sept. 18ᵗʰ.

I learn that an application¹¹⁴ has been made to you by several Delegates to call the Convention together¹¹⁵ again, for the purpose of rectifying some omission in the constitution.¹¹⁶ I have

---

¹¹¹ See p. 170, 30n.

¹¹² The circumstances and the controversy are explained in Thomas M. Garrett to Vance, September 1, 1862, p. 163 and p. 166, 13n; W. N. H. Smith to Vance, September 5, 1862, p. 168; and D. K. McRae to Vance, September 9, 1862, p. 170. In spite of the claim asserted by Vance in this letter, the question remained unsettled. The Confederacy claimed the right to officer all regiments raised after the Conscription Bill was passed. In October Vance went to Richmond and conferred with the president on the subject, and the president promised to take the opinion of the attorney general on the matter. See *O. R.*, Ser. IV, Vol. II, 188-189.

¹¹³ Weldon Nathaniel Edwards (1788-1873), president of the Convention of 1861-1862. He was born in Northampton County, but after obtaining his license to practice law he settled in Warren County, which he represented in the House of Commons in 1814 and 1815. A kinsman of Nathaniel Macon, he succeeded Macon in the United States House of Representatives when Macon became United States Senator. Edwards was congressman for eleven years (1816-1827); ten times elected state senator from Warren County (1833-1844, 1850, 1852), and was Speaker of the Senate his two last terms. He was a member of the Conventions of 1835 and 1861 and defeated William A. Graham for the presidency of the latter. Edwards was a stalwart Democrat and a leader of the secessionist element of the Democratic party in 1860 and 1861. Not so learned a man as some of his contemporaries, such as Ruffin or Graham, he nevertheless had integrity, comprehension, and practical wisdom. Samuel A'Court Ashe, "Weldon N. Edwards," Ashe, *Biog. Hist. of N. C.*, I, 263-269; Connor, *N. C. Manual*, pp. 472, 836-838, 864, 903, 920-924; McCormick, *Personnel*, p. 33.

¹¹⁴ The application was in the form of a memorial assembled and sent to Edwards by David A. Barnes, an aide of Governor Vance. Edwards later said that only eleven persons had signed the memorials. Weldon N. Edwards to David A. Barnes, October 4, 1862, Raleigh *North Carolina Standard*, October 15, 1862.

¹¹⁵ On April 30, 1862, the Convention, in its fourth session, adopted a resolution which provided for adjournment on May 13 subject to the call of the president and, in case of his death or resignation or inability, a committee of five, or the residue thereof, at any time until November 1, 1862; "and if not then called together by that time, that this Convention do stand dissolved." *Convention Journal*, 4 session, pp. 29-32. The vote on the resolution was 49 to 33.

¹¹⁶ During its four sessions the Convention frequently contemplated a revision of the State Constitution, and debated a number of proposals with regard to it, but they were never submitted to the people. *Convention Journal, passim.*

not investigated the subject sufficiently to judge of its necessity upon that ground, but I beg leave to join in the call for other reasons.

Extortion and speculation have attained such proportions that I find on investigation, it will be impossible to clothe & shoe our troops this winter without incurring a most enormous outlay & submitting to most outrageous prices.

The Cotton & Woolen factories have advanced their prices to an unheard extent & refuse to make contracts which would prevent them raising next week if they saw proper. The price of common shirting, for example, is fifty cents per yard. It requires one million yards to furnish each soldier two shirts & two prs. drawers, which is the winter allowance. This you will see amounts to 500,000 dollars, simply for under clothing. When you take in shoes & clothing (coats & pants) which have advanced in the same ratio, the sum will be almost incredible. By calculations submitted to me by intelligent gentlemen, it appears that 25^{cts} per y^d. for cotton cloth will actually pay the mill owners near 300 per cent.

The cry of distress comes up from the poor wives & children of our soldiers also, from all parts of the State. If these prices bear so hard upon the government, what will become of them, when in addition we consider the enormous rates at which provisions are selling? It is a subject that distresses me beyond measure, the more so as I feel powerless to remedy any of the evils. The Legislature if convened would be cramped & hampered by the forms of the constitution.[117] The Convention alone can

[117] The request of Vance that the Convention be reassembled greatly embarrassed Edwards and his fellow Democrats. Though at the beginning of the sessions the secessionists had been able to organize the convention they had lost that control by the spring of 1862 because of changes in both personnel and opinion. But while in control the Democrats had taken the high ground that the war might make certain legislation necessary that was beyond the powers of the legislature; that is, the convention had acted on the basis that it held power directly from the people in their sovereign capacity. It had passed ordinances which it had declared to be irrepealable and asserted its superior power over the legislature by changing the General Assembly's time of meeting and by repealing or modifying some of its acts. If the convention were to meet again, with Conservatives in control of it, it could, on the basis of precedents set by the Democrats, claim power to ignore the Constitution and enact whatever measures the Conservative majority might desire. Edwards, therefore, did not wish it to meet again and, as he wrote Thomas Ruffin, felt "much embarrassment" because of the memorials and the governor's letter. He realized, however, that "An appeal from such a high source cannot be treated slightly and must be responded to in a manner that will at least evince a proper respect for the Executive—and a due regard for the public Interests." Weldon N. Edwards to Thomas Ruffin, September 22, 1862, Hamilton, *Ruffin Papers*, III, 259. Edwards also wrote to William A. Graham and asked his advice with regard to calling the convention. Weldon N. Edwards to William A. Graham, September 20, 1862, Graham Papers CH.

Edwards never answered Vance's letter, so far as the records show. He did, however, reply to David A. Barnes, who had assembled the memorials and sent them to him. In explaining his refusal to reassemble the convention Edwards argued that

properly take the matter in hand and save our Country & Army from suffering & ruin, if indeed anything can rescue them from the ungodly — inhuman spirit of averice which is rampant in the land.

In view of these & many other suggestions which I can not elaborate in a brief letter, but which have no doubt been apparent to you for months past, I feel it my duty to urge it upon you to assemble that body together as soon as possible, to adopt such remedies as it may think best for the disorders of our country. Its business might be easily gotten through with before the Legislature assembles,[118] so that there would be no conflict between the two bodies.

Earnestly hoping Sir, that you may concur with me in the propriety of this course, as I know you do in the desire to relieve, if possible, the burdens of our people.

I remain with Sentiments of sincere regard

[Ridgeway, N. C.]

[Vance Letter Book, 1862-1863,

State Department of Archives and History, Raleigh.]

---

the convention had abandoned any idea of remodeling the constitution, else it would not have adjourned *sine die*; he asserted that the spirit of the resolution of April 30 was that only developments between that date and November 1 would justify calling it again, and that war developments in that interval did not justify the call; and he claimed that the legislature had ample power to deal with the needs of the state under the constitution. "To condense my views in very succinct form," he summarized, "I will say, that I cannot, according to my understanding of the true meaning of the purposes of the Convention, go in search of reasons for reassembling it, behind the date of adjournment, and that no event has since occured to require another session." Weldon N. Edwards to David A. Barnes, October 4, 1862, Raleigh *North Carolina Standard,* October 15, 1862. He declined therefore to call the convention and on the date fixed by itself it passed out of existence.

[118] After Edwards' refusal to reassemble the convention the only way to deal with speculation and extortion was through the legislature. The legislature which had been chosen when Vance was elected governor in August was safely Conservative, but it could not constitutionally meet in regular session until November 17, 1862. Any special session had to be called by the governor and the Council of State, according to the 26th section of the 52nd chapter of the *Revised Code,* and then only when absolutely necessary. The Council of State was composed of seven men chosen by the legislature, and so the Council of State in October 1862 was the one chosen by the legislature which had been elected in 1860, and which was Democratic. Every member of the Council of State was a secessionist except one, and he had replaced a secessionist who had resigned. Vance called a meeting of the Council of State for October 19, intending to ask it to join in a call for a special session of the legislature to deal with the acute problem of feeding and clothing the troops for which the state was responsible under its arrangement with the Confederacy, to attack the problem of speculation and extortion by a proposed embargo, and to defend the eastern part of the state from Federal invasion. But only three members appeared for the meeting while four were required by law for a quorum. Another call for an October 25 meeting yielded no better result. So Vance was prevented from convening the legislature at an earlier date than its regular meeting, having also been prevented from reassembling the convention. Both delays were blamed on the Democrats. Raleigh *North Carolina Standard,* October 21, 24, 29, 1862; Journal of Council of State, October 9-October 21, 1862, pp. 120-123, State Department of Archives and History, Raleigh, N. C.

From John Pool[189]

Colerain Sept. 18th. 1862

Some of the leading farmers and citizens of Bertie County had a consultation on the 15th Inst. in Windsor—it being Monday of Superior Court—for the purpose of making representations to your Excellency in regard to the condition of affairs in this County, & to ask some executive action in their behalf. Lewis Thompson[120] Esqr was appointed to visit Raleigh, & see you in person. But he is not able to go until about the 1st. Oct., I was requested, in the mean time, to lay before you, in writing the points agreed to be presented & the reasons which induced the gentlemen present to ask some action upon them

This county is almost entirely surrounded by the waters of the Albemarle Sound & the Roanoke & Chowan Rivers—all of which are navigable to the largest of the enemy's steamers— while the Caskie River and Salmon Creek, running into the very heart of the Country, are navigable to his steamers of highest draft. Upon these water courses lie the main body of the excellent farming lands of the county, & several thousand slaves are upon these lands. The gun boats of the enemy are traversing these waters almost daily. Occasionally the enemy lands a few troops at unexpected points—but so far, has committed very little depredation. The Military Post at Plymouth is upon the very border of the county & is accessible by the water courses above named. There is not a Confederate soldier here, & not the least show of protection extended to the citizens. They are completely at the mercy of the enemy—& nothing but his clemency prevents their total ruin. The people are, for the most part, loyal to the Confederacy & have acted with surprising prudence & faithfulness,

---

[119] John Pool (1826-1884) was for many years a resident of Pasquotank County, but moved to Bertie County during the war. He graduated from the University of North Carolina in 1847 and was soon admitted to the bar, but he never liked the legal profession. In 1856 and 1858 he was elected to the State Senate from Pasquotank County and made such a reputation for ability that he was nominated by the Whigs for governor in 1860. He made a brilliant campaign, but was barely defeated by John W. Ellis, the Democratic candidate. Pool was a strong Union man and took no part in the secession movement and determined to take none in the war. But in 1864, having moved to Bertie County, he was again elected to the State Senate, where he introduced peace resolutions which were defeated. He was a member of the Convention of 1865 and of the State Senate the same year, when he supported William W. Holden for governor. He was elected to the United States Senate after Worth's election as governor, but was denied his seat, whereupon he identified himself with the Radical Republicans and was again elected to the United States Senate in 1868, but failed of re-election in 1872. He remained in Washington, D. C. for most of the remainder of his life, and rejoined the Democratic party in 1880. He was a fine debater, and handsome in looks and suave in manner. Joseph Gregoire deRoulhac Hamilton, "John Pool," *Dict. of Am. Biog.*, XV, 64-65; Connor, *N. C. Manual*, pp. 504, 748, 686, 937-938; *Biog. Dir. of Am. Cong.*, p. 1692.

[120] See p. 165, 8n.

But how long long is it prudent to Suffer these people to depend entirely upon the enemy for safety, & feel that they are neglected if not abandoned by their own Government?

The greater part of the able bodied men of the county have volunteered in companies raised in this & the adjoining counties, & are now in the Army. Some have been taken out by the Conscript law— & the attempted execution of that law has driven many, of not very reliable character, to the enemy at Plymouth— & many more, of little better character, are in readiness to repair to Plymouth or to the gunboats, if its further execution is attempted. The loyal citizens have more to dread from these deserters than from the regular enemy.

By the Census of 1860, it appears that there are 8000 slaves in this County, & only 6000 whites. They have as yet, lost comparatively few slaves, but it is with great difficulty that the few men left here, unsupported by a show of military force, are able to guard the avenues of escape & keep up efficient police regulations. If they should attempt to remove the slaves, the most of them would run off, at once— & any general attempt to move them would produce an almost universal stampede, resulting in the loss of the negroes, & endangering the lives of the few citizens. But if the removal could be effected, how could so large a number be fed elsewhere, & what would become of the property necessarily left behind? But as Southern men, they take another view of the consequences of such a removal. If the Slave holders, being men of means, fly, upon the approach of the danger, & leave the poorer classes who are unable to move, & the families of soldiers in the Army, exposed not only to the enemy, but to the gangs of run away slaves, it will produce a state of things & of feeling much to be dreaded. Is it not the duty of the influential slaveholder to remain & exert himself to preserve social order, & prevent an entire disruption of Society? It is hoped that the enemy will soon be driven away, & these people are bearing up under their troubles sustained by that hope — feeling that they have been & still are neglected — but yet willing to believe that the best has been done that circumstances would allow. Several months spent in this state of constant danger & anxiety has enabled the thinking men of this county to see what is necessary to be done, more clearly perhaps, than can be seen by those at a distance, even in authority, who must judge from reports only.

They met in Windsor on the 15ᵗʰ. Inst. & agreed to ask the influence of your Excellency, with the Confederate Authorities, to adopt the following measures & such others as may be deemed most expedient.

First— That two companies of Cavalry be quartered in Bertie County, permanently— and they desire especially the two companies commanded by Capts. Randolph[121] & Eure,[122] which are now somewhere on the Seaboard & Roanoke R. R.[123]— They ask these two officers because they know them to be men of great discretion— having the entire confidence of the people of this section— They think a force under an indiscreet officer would be of more injury than benefit. For instance should an officer exhibit any troops upon water courses, in sight of the enemy, it would cause a shelling of the whole neighborhood — & if near any dwelling would insure its destruction— They deem the character of the officer sent in this emergency, of the greatest importance— & would prefer no force to one under an officer of doubtful judgment. With this Cavalry to back them, the citizens left could preserve order, and prevent any great number of slaves from escaping. The very presence of such a force would intimidate the enemy, & embolden the loyal citizens to speak & act with freedom & zeal. The loyal citizens of this county ought to have some support. The interest of the Confederacy in this section, requires it—

Secondly— That the President be requested by your Excellency to exercise the discretion vested in him by the late Act of Congress, to exempt this county from the further execution of the Conscript law[124] There are not now men enough in the County for efficient police duty— & any attempt at executing the law, instead of getting soldiers for our Army, would send recruits to the enemy — for the correct minded men, subject to the law, have already gone to Camp. The substantial men of the county dread to see the others made their enemies. If the Conscript law is ex-

---

[121] John Randolph, of Northampton County, captain of company H in the Nineteenth North Carolina Regiment (second cavalry). He was commissioned July 6, 1861 and resigned November 29, 1863. Moore, *N. C. Roster*, II, 134; Clark, *N. C. Regts.*, II, 80.

[122] Mills L. Eure, of Gates County, second lieutenant in company C of the Nineteenth North Carolina Regiment (second cavalry). He later became captain of company G in the same regiment, was captured at Gettysburg, and imprisoned at Johnson's Island. After the war he was a judge of the superior court, 1874-1883. Companies of this regiment were frequently separated and sent on detached duty; among them being these two who moved, in August 1862, to Hamilton, in Martin County, to picket the Roanoke River. Moore, *N. C. Roster*, II, 131; Clark, *N. C. Regts.*, II, 80, 87, IV, 704; Connor, *N. C. Manual*, p. 450.

[123] The Seaboard and Roanoke Railroad ran from the Roanoke River at Weldon to Norfolk, Va., giving the port of Norfolk access to the Roanoke River valley.

[124] The second Conscription Act, which gave this discretionary power to the President, was not actually adopted by this date, but its provisions had already been debated and were public knowledge. It was adopted in Congress on September 27, 1862 and among its provisions was one which authorized the President "to suspend the execution of this act in any locality where he may find it impracticable to execute the same. . . ." *O. R.*, Ser. IV, Vol. II, p. 160; Matthews, *Public Laws of the Confederacy*, 2 session, 1 Congress, pp. 61-62.

tended to 45 years,[125] its execution would complete the ruin of the County.

Thirdly— That no military order requiring slaves to work on fortifications, or serve in the Army, be sent to this county.[126] Its effect would be to make the slaves run off— & very few could be obtained under the order, for it would be idle to attempt to hunt negroes in this section, now. But another reason why such an order should not be sent here, & why the counties bordering on the enemy's lines should be specially exempted by name, is this— If the Confederate authorities commence taking these exposed slaves or any part of them, the enemy will then have a military excuse to take those that are left— & they will not be slow to do so— Mr Thompson will be in Raleigh about the 1st, of Oct. to communicate verbally with your Excellency upon this subject, & to make more full & specific statements than can be well done within the limits of a letter.

I have written under the instructions of the meeting of Bertie gentlemen, as mentioned above — but allow me to add that for the most part, I approve their recommendations, & think that it is the best that could be done under the circumstances. Perhaps, so small a force as two companies might be in danger of being cut off by the enemy— but I think— in an emergency, the citizens would rally, with such arms as they could get, to repel an attack. If the Confederate authorities are not able to do something, it might be well to authorize the raising of a state force to operate in this section.[127] It could be done without difficulty under a proper officer— & would be efficient after awhile— But something ought to be done for this section of the State, at once.

Allow me, personally, to assure you of my esteem & readiness to render you all the service in my power, in any measures deemed best for the interest of the State

Raleigh— N. C.

[Vance Letter Book, 1862-1863,
State Department of Archives and History, Raleigh.]

---

[125] The Conscription Act of September 27, 1862 also raised the age limit of those liable to conscription from thirty-five to forty-five. Matthews, *Public Laws of the Confederacy*, 2 session, 1 Congress, p. 62.

[126] The military forces were from time to time granted rights to impress slaves as laboring forces on fortifications. Various regulations were made governing compensation, treatment, and other items. *O. R.*, Ser. IV, Vol. 1, 767. No state law was passed authorizing the practice until December 20, 1862. See *Public Laws of N. C., 1862-'63*, chap. 16.

[127] Governor Vance recommended the formation of some such force as is here suggested in his message to the legislature, November 17, 1862, but the bill providing for the force failed of adoption. See *Legislative Documents, 1862-1863*, Document No. 1.

From Jno. A. Richardson[128]

Head Quarters, Fort S^t. Philip[129] N. C
Sept. 19. 1862.

Lieutenant Blount,[130] whom I had sent to Raleigh for the purpose of recruiting his Company, in a letter received on yesterday, informs me that in a Conversation had between your Excellency and Genl. Martin[131] relative to the Regiment Commanded by Col Lamb,[132] General Martin stated that the grounds of objection to this Organization was that it was formed by taking in Some Companies from the 36^t. & 40th. Regts. In this the Genl. is Mistaken so far as the 40th. Regt^t is Concerned. Not a Company, or a part of a Company, of that Regiment ever having formed part of ours.

Your Excellency will, I hope, pardon me in my zeal for establishing our Claim to be Commissioned at your hands, in stating a few facts relative to our Regiment. You will please bear in mind that I have stated that *No part* of the 40th. Regiment has been incorporated with ours. Now permit me to explain as to the 36th—

At the time, or up to the time of the order organizing my Regiment, No such Regiment as the 36th. existed, or ever had existed. Nor ever *has* existed since. In the published list of N. C. troops,

---

[128] John A. Richardson was from Bladen County and organized the "Bladen Artillery" which became company I of the Thirty-sixth North Carolina Regiment (artillery) upon its organization on May 14, 1862. Richardson was captain of this company until it joined the regiment, when he was elected lieutenant colonel, holding that post until he was dropped on January 23, 1864. After the war he represented Bladen County in the convention of 1865 and in the House of Commons in 1866. Clark, *N. C. Regts.*, II, 630; Connor, *N. C. Manual*, pp. 508, 868.

[129] Fort St. Philip was at Old Brunswick, and formed a part of the defense of the Cape Fear region. Colonel Lamb remained at Fort St. Philip until July 1862, when he was sent to Fort Fisher, near Wilmington, but parts of his command remained at Fort St. Philip. Later the fort was called Fort Anderson. Clark, *N. C. Regts.*, II, 631.

[130] John Gray Blount, of Beaufort County, first lieutenant in company C of what became the Fortieth North Carolina Regiment (heavy artillery). He was later promoted to captain and quartermaster. His company was organized in September 1861 at Washington, N. C., and did garrison and picket duty at Fort St. Philip from April of 1862 until December of 1863, when it became a part of the Fortieth Regiment. Clark, *N. C. Regts.*, II, 745, 749; Moore, *N. C. Roster*, III, 113, 120.

[131] See p. 113, 447n.

[132] William Lamb was a Virginian who was a major in the Confederate Army when chosen colonel of the Thirty-sixth North Carolina Regiment upon its organization, May 14, 1862. Transferred from Fort St. Philip to Fort Fisher in July 1862 he became known as "the man who built Fort Fisher" and as "the friend of the blockade runners." He greatly enlarged and strengthened this famous fort and was wounded and captured there in the great Federal assault of January 1865. After the war he returned to Norfolk where he became a general cotton agent; in 1866 he formed an association with John White, formerly of Warrenton, N. C., who became the agent for the firm in Liverpool. Clark, *N. C. Regts.*, II, 630, 651, 761, IV, 305, 344; Moore, *N. C. Roster*, II, 711; James Sprunt, *Chronicles of the Cape Fear River* (Raleigh, 1914), pp. 288-289 (cited hereafter as Sprunt, *Chronicles*).

(I forgot the title of the pamphlett) *Six* Companies are Named under the head "36th. Regiment," to wit— Captain Buntings,[133] Captain Hedricks,[134] Captain Purdie's[135] Captain Mayo's[136] (now Captain Hunter's) [137] Captain McNair's,[138] and Captain Richardson's (My own). Captain Purdie's, however, Six months before the organization of our Regt. was lopped away from these six, thus leaving but five in the 36th. No Colonel, Lieut Col, or Major had or ever has been elected therein. What became of these five? My Company, raised for 12 months only, having seen that by the law of Congress a Company enlisting for 3 years, or the war, would be permitted to *Select* the Regiment to which it would prefer to go, *or to form with others into a Regiment,* reenlisted upon that faith and for the purpose, and the purpose only, of going into Lamb's Regiment, then in contemplation. But for this clause in the Act to which I refer, I state, upon My honor, that not five Men of My Command would have reenlisted. We were tired, heartily sick and tired of the 36th., the fabled 36th. that Never had existed, save in name, and never would have existed. We Knew that there was no chance of promotion in such a Condition of things! We felt that we ought to be permitted to elect officers, &c.

The other four Companies of the 36th., except Hunter's, remain with the Skeleton still. Hunter's *was* incorporated in ours, but if that interfered with General Martin's arrangements, and your Excellency *will Commission us*, we will drop that and take in its

---

[133] Samuel R. Bunting, of New Hanover County, who was captain of a company of light artillery raised in Wilmington in May of 1861. It later became company I of the Tenth North Carolina Regiment (artillery) and served in many parts of eastern North Carolina. Clark, *N. C. Regts.*, I, 582, IV, 221.

[134] John J. Hedrick, of New Hanover County, who was a major of engineers and in command at Fort Fisher until relieved by Colonel William Lamb on July 4, 1862. He was elected colonel of the Fortieth North Carolina Regiment upon its organization, December 1, 1863. In February 1861 Hedrick had organized a company and helped occupy Fort Johnston at Smithville, having already in January led men in a private capacity to take over Fort Caswell, from which he withdrew upon the order of Governor Ellis. Clark, *N. C. Regts.*, II, 631, 745, 762; IV, 47, 342 361, 413 419; V, 24-26.

[135] Thomas J. Purdie, of Bladen County. He rose from first lieutenant to colonel of the Eighteenth North Carolina Regiment and was killed at Chancellorsville, May 3, 1863. Clark, *N. C. Regts.*, II, 20, 34-39; Moore, *N. C. Roster*, II, 72, 109.

[136] James M. Mayo, of Edgecombe County. This same month he had been transferred from the artillery to the cavalry and, on September 11, 1862, was commissioned major in the Fifty-ninth North Carolina Regiment (fourth cavalry). He was wounded and captured at Upperville, June 21, 1863 and imprisoned at Johnson's Island. Clark, *N. C. Regts.*, III, 456; Moore, *N. C. Roster*, III, 653.

[137] Sam B. Hunter, of Craven County, captain of "The Pamlico Artillery" which became company F of the Thirty-sixth North Carolina Regiment on May 1, 1862. Clark, *N. C. Regts.*, II, 630; Moore, *N. C. Roster*, II, 729.

[138] Malcolm McNair whose company was from Richmond and Robeson counties and later formed company E of the Fortieth North Carolina Regiment. Clark, *N. C. Regts.*, II, 746; Moore, *N. C. Roster*, III, 127.

stead Captain Tait's[139] Co of Artillery which is like our Regiment, *Nullius Filius* Surely Hunter's Company *Must* be the *only* "bone of Contention." My Company reenlisted under an Act of Congress giving it the liberty to go into such a Regiment as it desired. I assert that at the time when the Companies of our (Lamb's) Reg^t.—had united for the purpose of being organized, only *two* Companies had ever belonged to the 36th. and the 36th. had never had but Six, and had never been organized by the election of field officers, *one week after our election, under order, to hold it,* General Martin, Gov. Clark,[140] or some one else, sent me a list of *Ten* Companies[141] which had *just then* been organized as the 36th.! Among these ten were named, *for the first time,* Several Companies which we had!

Gov Clark, I understand, complains that our proceeding was "irregular." What difference can that make? Suppose that we had taken two-thirds of the 36th. then we deserve the Governor's thanks for adding the other third, and for Saving him the trouble of organizing it. We are told that you, Sir, will Commission us if we will drop such of the Co's as belong to the 36 & 40th. (we have none of the latter) and will take in New Companies, of which we are informed there are plenty, Now, Sir, our organizing did not disorganize either the 36th, 40th. or any other, but General Martin's, or Gov Clark's policy toward us is Calculated not only to disorganize us, but to *repudiate the Official* acts of the Confederate Officer whose order we obeyed. (Genl French) [142] and thus place

---

[139] George Tait, of Bladen County, who organized Tait's Battery of Bladen Artillery, unattached, which was afterward's known as Clarke's Battery. He was captain of what became company A of the Eighteenth North Carolina Regiment, and was elected major on June 15, 1861. In September 1861 he attempted to resign, but was persuaded to reconsider; in January 1862 he tendered his resignation to the adjutant general in Richmond, and to his colonel, James D. Radcliffe, because of the "entire lack of good feeling existing between myself and my superior officers, and probably the interests of the Regiment would be advanced and its harmony restored by my retirement from it." His resignation was accepted in March 1862; in December 1863 he became lieutenant colonel of the Fortieth North Carolina Regiment (third artillery). After the war he moved to Norfolk, Va., where he became a seedsman and a florist. *Confederate States of America War Department List of Artillery Officers* (Richmond, 1864), pp. 91, 129; Moore, *N. C. Roster,* II, 72, 109; Clark, *N. C. Regts.,* II, 16-20, 745, 759; George Tait to his congressman, Thomas D. McDowell, January 17, 1862, McDowell Papers.

[140] See p. 133, 529n.

[141] The ten companies are listed in Clark, *N. C. Regts.,* II, 630 and include only Hunter's and Richardson's of those mentioned in this letter.

[142] Samuel G. French, a native of New Jersey and a graduate of West Point in the class of 1843. As a young officer of the engineers he had served at Fort Macon in North Carolina and at many other southern posts; he was wounded in the Mexican War and in 1856 resigned from the army and became a planter near Vicksburg, Mississippi. He relieved General Branch in command of the District of Pamlico in the Department of North Carolina on March 16, 1862; in August he was put in command at Petersburg where Vance's regiment was stationed when he was elected governor; in December 1862 he became commander of the Department of North Carolina; and in May 1863, he was ordered to Mississippi to join

him before the Country as having been *censured* in his official
acts by the Governor. Further than this— It is calculated to weak-
en our attachment to the State, which, receiving our allegiance
and our first love, thus would "turn upon and rend us." So far as
the *Material* of our Regiment is concerned, had the Governor
and Genl. Martin selected from all of North Carolina's Soldiery,
they could not have formed a Regiment better chosen for the
defense of its sea-coast. We are Cape Fear Men, Sir, "Native, and
to the manner born." Our homes, and the blue waters that wash
their thresholds, are here, and by the Cradles, where, in our
infancy our free fathers housed us, we are ready to swear, if needs
be, to hand down to our posterity, with every mark of an honorable Conveyance, their free homes and these blue waters, as we
received them, uncontaminated by a despots heel, and undisturbed
by the presence of his warlike engines.— Excuse me, Sir, if I have
grown tedious, or speak with feeling. *We have not been treated
well.* We did not expect that for what has been done with a
view to the public good, our State, would "spew us out of her
mouth." We did not believe such a thing. Nor do we believe so
now. We feel that if the Scepter has fallen into New hands, it
will be wielded with new energy, new Zeal, and new Spirit for
the promotion of our Country's Cause and every interest that
would promote it.
[Raleigh]
[A. L. S. Governors' Papers (Vance),
State Department of Archives and History, Raleigh.]

From Henry B. Watson[143]

Smithfield N. C.
Sep^t. 19th. 1862

My great desire to render my State and Country all the service it is in my power to do, induces me to state my case in the
hopes that your Excellency may have it in your power to assign
me to some duty in the service of that State where I may be
useful.— I served in the old Service nineteen years, and was
Brevetted for gallant and meretorious service in the Battles of
San Gabriel and the Mesa in California in 1847, and I resigned
from the U. S. Marine Corps on the 1st. January 1855. On the

---

General Joseph E. Johnston's army. Clark, *N. C. Regts.*, II, 328, 334, 769; *O. R.*,
I, IX, 450, XVIII, 1077; Cullum, *Biog. Register*, II, 166-167; Raleigh *North Carolina
Standard*, April 19, 1862. The Thirty-sixth North Carolina Regiment was organized
under French's supervision at Fort Caswell on May 14, 1862. Clark, *N. C. Regts.*,
II, 629.

[143] Henry B. Watson assumed command of the camp of instruction just outside
Raleigh on May 21, 1862. The camp was abolished in August as it was a state
camp and with the introduction of conscription many state training camps were
closed. *Clark, N. C. Regts.*, III, 318.

breaking out of the present war, I exerted myself to induce the prompt volunteering among the men of my County. In February last, Gov. Clark was pleased to appoint me a Col. and assigned me to duty first at Camp of Instruction at Weldon and afterwards to the command of the Camp at Camp Mangum. These camps of Instruction were discontinued on the 1st. August and consequently my appointment ceased. With an experience of twenty years in the Military service I flatter myself that I can render my State some efficient service, and contribute though feebly some little towards the accomplishment of the great object which we are all so anxious shall be speedily done that of Independence and Peace.— My age is Forty nine, my constitution vigorous and my health excellent.— I can give your Excellency references if they are desired. I have my former commissions which will speak for themselves. And I do most earnestly and respectfully ask the governor to consider my case favorably and be so kind as to assign me to duty as early as possible.

[Raleigh]

[on reverse]

Ans⋅. that the Gov. will be pleased to put him on duty the first opportunity &c.

[A. L. S. Governors' Papers (Vance),
State Department of Archives and History, Raleigh.]

From J. M. Worth[144]

Wilmington Sept. 19th. 1862

An ordinance of the Convention passed about the 1st. Dec. last making an appropriation for the purpose of manufacturing salt makes it my duty to report to you monthly.[145] To enable you

---

[144] John Milton Worth (1811-1900), of Randolph County. He was born in Guilford County, studied medicine in Lexington, Kentucky, and engaged in farming, gold mining, and merchandising in Montgomery County, North Carolina. Later he moved to Asheboro and established a general store. He was, like his brother Jonathan, a Whig and as such represented the district of Montgomery and Moore counties in the State Senate in 1842, 1844, and 1848. In 1861 he was a Union man until Lincoln's call for troops, became salt commissioner for the state and, in 1864, colonel of the Seventy-sixth Regiment, then known as the sixth, or senior, re-serves. In 1870 he was again elected to the State Senate, this time from the district of Randolph and Moore counties, where he voted for the impeachment of Governor Holden. He was re-elected to the State Senate in 1872, and served as state treasurer, 1876-1885, where he took the lead in the settlement of the state debt and in revising tax measures. He became one of the wealthiest men of his section, being president of the Bank of Randolph and of the Southern Stock Mutual Fire Insurance Company, as well as of the Worth Manufacturing Company, which operated cotton mills. Samuel A'Court Ashe, "John Milton Worth," Ashe, *Biog. Hist of N. C.*, III, 454-460; Connor, *N. C. Manual*, pp. 442, 708, 771-772.

[145] The ordinance was ratified in the second session of the Convention, on December 6, 1861. It provided for the appointment of a commissioner by the convention to supervise and provide for the manufacture of salt for the use of the people of the state, gave to him large powers of employment and material, forbade

to understand the whole thing, I will go back to the beginning. Immediately after my appointment as Commissioner I visited the coast & found the most eligible places at Morehead City & Currituck Sound & was prepared to make one hundred Bu salt per day when Newbern fell. I had done nothing at Currituck Sound but bargained for Supplies. I lost all the pans I had & was thrown back to a ground start at Wilmington. Private individuals had already engaged in the manufacture of salt much more extensively here than at any other place in the State or on the Coast.[146] Prices of everything was already high & it was very difficult to get the pans & other material. The extreme high prices of Salt induced private parties to pay most extravagant prices & to step in when I had contracts for pans & other materials & bid two or three prices & get them away from me. With all these difficulties I have only been able to make up to this time a little over two hundred Bu Salt per day, which will be increased to two hundred & fifty Bu with what pans I now have. I am now paying from $1— to $1⁵⁰ pr cord for wood on the Stump two miles distant from the works & should be entirely unable to get the teaming done so as to sell the salt at any reasonable price but for the exemption from military duty of the hands.[147] I have furnished all the counties in the State with from two to four hundred Bu Salt (except about ten mostly in the hands of the enemy) at from 3 to 4 dollars per Bu—Private parties have gotten from 8 to 13 dollars for all the salt they have made. You can readily see the difficulties I have had to contend with. Although I condemn extortion I think it fortunate for the country that salt went so high early in the season, for there has been & con-

---

speculation, appropriated $100,000 for the purpose, and required a report to the governor on the first Monday in every month. *Convention Ordinances,* 2 session, No. 8, pp. 52-54. On May 9, 1862 another ordinance concerning salt was adopted vesting the commissioner with extraordinary powers about the condemnation of land needed for making salt, about the price thereof, and about labor. He was allowed to employ free negroes and if he was unable to obtain as many as he needed the governor was required to impress them. *Convention Ordinances,* 4 session, No. 18.

[146] The Committee on Salt of the Convention reported, through Nicholas W. Woodfin, its chairman, that 500,000 bushels for one year were required and that it was necessary to manufacture it on the sea coast out of sea water because there were no interior sources of supply in the state. Fortified by a letter from Dr. E. Emmons, the State Geologist, the opinion was expressed that salt could be made at the sea coast at not over two dollars a bushel. William A. Graham moved a substitute which would have encouraged, by a bounty, private production, but the original proposal was adopted with the amendment which allowed the commissioner to establish works elsewhere than on the sea coast. The measure was adopted by a vote of about four to one. Dr. Worth was elected commissioner by the Convention over four other nominees, Philemon B. Hawkins being the closest competitor. Most of the commissioner's activities were confined to the coastal areas, as described in this letter. Battle, *Legislation,* pp. 119-120; *Convention Journal,* 2 session, pp. 52-53.

[147] In section 4 of the ordinance of May 9, 1862 "all persons who are or may be employed in making salt, under contract with the salt commissioner, shall be exempt from military duty and militia service while so employed." *Convention Ordinances,* 4 session, No. 18.

tinues to be a perfect rush from all quarters to get into the business & the most extravagant prices paid for the necessary materials. There is now about 1800 Bu salt made per day here, which will be increased to 2500 by Oct. 15th. I understand Mr Woodfin[148] promises to make 200 Bu pr day for the State. If that be true & the Salt be kept in the State it will soon be abundant at far less prices— 4000 Bu pr day would in 100 days give every inhabitant in the state 20 lbs— We have just 100 days before the pork season is over. There has been made at this place an average of at least 800 Bu pr day since 1st. March last. There has been a great deal of Salt brought from Virginia & several small cargoes ran the blockade, all of which has gone to the country & there is a large number of persons supplied, yet the great fear of the article being short makes them (the supplied) very quiet on the subject & leaves it very difficult to tell who or how many are supplied. The difficulty & expense of making salt increases rapidly as the distance to team the wood increases. I am now trying to bring the water 2½ miles into the woods. If I succeed it will be a great advantage. I have many letters from county agents[149] saying the salt is doing great good for the soldiers families; but all speak of the quantity being insufficient. I have done much less than I hoped to do at the outset but have done all in my power & given it my entire attention. I have about 200 men that are liable to military duty who are exempt by an ordinance of the State Convention; one third of whom are quakers,[150] whom at my suggestion Gov Clark[151] directed me to take at the time of the draft, another third are all men of limited means, who furnish their own teams, the other third are men of weak constitution & men that are afraid of the board of surgeons & would be of no use in the Army & are but little use to me. If the teams were taken from me I would be helpless. The State appropriation would be hardly sufficient to buy the teams requisite for the present work. The teamsters work for 3⁵⁰ per day finding themselves & teams (2 Horse teams) while

[148] See p. 92, 347n for Woodfin, who was in charge of the North Carolina interests in the salt works at Saltville, Va. under an arrangement begun by Governor Clark in the summer of 1862, whereby a contract with Stuart, Buchanan & Co. called for 300,000 bushels per annum for the duration of the war. Woodfin sold only to counties, through authorized agents, and not to individuals. *Fayetteville Observer,* September 22, 1862. The contract, dated June 30, 1862 is in Governors' Papers (Clark).

[149] According to the ordinance of December 6, 1861 the justices of the peace of the several counties were responsible for the delivering, distribution, and purchasing of the salt for their county. They usually appointed a county agent to handle the business for them. *Convention Ordinances,* 2 session, No. 8.

[150] On May 12, 1862 the Convention adopted an ordinance which exempted members of the Society of Friends from military duty on payment of $100. Those unable to pay were authorized to be employed on salt works or in hospitals. Battle, *Legislation,* p. 121; *Convention Ordinances,* 4 session, No. 34, p. 164.

[151] See p. 133, 529n.

private parties pay $6— for the same Service, so that they are contributing more to the Country by far than could be got from them in the field. I shall increase the work as fast as possible, endeavouring at the same time to keep down the price. I could have been making more salt if I had been regardless of the cost of making it but could see no advantage in outbidding private parties thereby making the State salt cost the people as much as if they bought it from private individuals. I have sent 5000 Bu salt to the different counties within the last month at $4. pr Bu making it cost the people $20000— while it would readily have sold for $60000 I only mention it to show that as small as the amount is it is doing great good. I feel confident that if this place does not fall into the enemies hands we will have enough salt to squeeze through.

All of which is respectfully submitted.

[Raleigh]

[Vance Letter Book, 1862-1863,

State Department of Archives and History, Raleigh.]

From Jason H. Carson[152]

White Oak, Polk Co., N. C. Sep. 20th. 1862.

I deem it my duty to advertise you of the condition of affairs in this section of the State. I was in Rutherford, a few days since, & ascertained, upon good authority, that there are more than one hundred conscripts in that County, who positively refuse to perform the military service they owe to the country. There are also several men, returned from the army, who do not deny that they are absent without leave, & who are in point of facts deserters.

Another abuse is the purchase of petty mail contracts, by young able bodied men, sometimes two combining to get a single contract, & both claiming exemption under it.

I can also state from my own personal knowledge that there are a good many persons of both the classes mentioned above in this (Polk) County.

Now what is the remedy for the state of things? No effort is

---

[152] Jason Hazard Carson (1814-1865) was a farmer who was born in the Green River section of Rutherford County, later Polk County. He represented Rutherford and Polk in the Convention of 1861, though he resigned before the convention adjourned. An ardent secessionist, he had spoken at a number of public meetings throughout the spring of 1861 in favor of the dissolution of the Union. In 1856 Carson predicted a war between the states and said that the North would win and free the slaves. So firmly did he believe this that he sold his slaves and invested in lands, but he later became so enthusiastic a secessionist when the war seemed to go well that he sold the land and reinvested in slaves. Clipping from *Asheville News*, January 1861 in Z. B. Vance Papers, Vol. 17, McCormick, *Personnel*, p. 25; Griffin, *Old Tryon and Rutherford*, pp. 232-233, 249.

being made to correct it, and the Sheriff of Rutherford [153] positively refuses to apprehend any one.

If enrolling officers previously appointed have been charged with this duty I can only say that it has not been performed. The remedy that suggests itself to me is the appointments of an officer who shall be permanently located for the purpose of examining the papers of all persons returning from the army, and seeing that the conscript law is rigidly enforced.

If this state of things is permitted to continue there is no telling where it will end, inasmuch as both the above classes of delinquents, the deserters & the conscripts, are received by the community with as much favor as though they had been guilty of no dishonourable conduct.

[Raleigh]
[on reverse]
Ans. that the Cols of Militia are ordered to arrest all such & I would be obliged if he would report any Col refusing to do his duty[154]

Z. B. V.

[A. L. S. Governors' Papers (Vance),
State Department of Archives and History, Raleigh.]

From T. J. Corbett [155]

New Hanover County
N C Sept 20th 1862.

You are aware that there are 20 men in the upper part of this County authorized & paid $40 per month by the State whose duty it is to patrol that portion of this county.[156]

Now Sir I am going to make a complaint to your Excellency & as you know nothing about me you will not know whether it comes from a respectable source or not & I do not know as that will make much difference as you will See that it is at least the truth

---

[153] Martin Walker was Sheriff of Rutherford County from August of 1860 to September of 1872, when he was elected to the State Senate. He was re-elected in 1874. Griffin, *Essays in North Carolina History* (Forest City, 1951), pp. 102-103 (cited hereafter as Grffin, *Essays*); Connor, *N. C. Manual*, p. 799.

[154] Militia jurisdiction was divided in Rutherford County between the 103rd and 104th North Carolina regiments of militia. Vance's order to the colonels is summarized on p. 186, 84n.

[155] T. J. Corbett was a justice of the peace and postmaster at Canetuck, then in New Hanover County, but now in Pender County. Canetuck was between the Black River and the railroad line and was a rich region of farm land. Mattie Bloodworth, *History of Pender County* (Richmond, 1947), 86-87 (cited hereafter as Bloodworth, *Pender County*).

[156] The Twenty-third Regiment of North Carolina Militia, a part of the Sixth Brigade, patroled only that part of New Hanover County west of the Northeast River.

If you will examine the Map of N. C. you will See that the portion of New Hanover forming the 23rd Regimental District is not in the least exposed to the Enemy in any shape mannor or form Then why should that portion of the State be patroled at the expense of the State in preference of any other portion of the State Why should it be allowed $9600 a year in preference of other & more exposed portions Now suppose all other counties allowed it in the same proportion & it would cost over a Million for patrol purposes an outlay which I know your Excellency would not allow even if you had the constitutional authority besides there are 20 able bodied healthy men kept out of the Service of our common country for the purpose of patroling a portion of the State not in the least exposed & owning conparitively but few slaves

I can assure your Excellency that it is considered by a great many influential Citizens even of that portion of the county where it is in operation one of the most gigantic frauds ever perpetrated on the State

I am a citizen of the patroled portion of the county own a few Slaves which I can have Kept in there place without the aid of the State & I can ASSure you that nine tenths of our Citizens are of the same opinion I further Say if we are allowed 10 thousand a year for patrols allow all other counties the Same in proportion & bankrupt the State at once

Now I do not wish to be considered as inpugning the motives of our Militia Col [157] at whose request our county Court petitioned our former Governor The court Gov or even of the patrol themselves for who would not Stay out of the war at $40 per Mo rather than go in at $11 especially if backed up by the Col & Gov.

Again, I contend if we must have a patrol to ride out about once in 10 days why in the name of all thats reasonable should thay be allowed So much more than our brave Volunteers who in fighting for their country are risking their all. property health life itself I know your Excellency well enough to know that you will agree with me that if we have especial favors that they should be Lavish on our brave Volunteers or their orphan wives & children & not on a Set of lazy patrols

---

[157] The colonel of the Twenty-third Militia Regiment was John D. Powers, of Sills Creek, New Hanover County. On June 20, 1862, the assistant adjutant general of North Carolina John C. Winder, informed him that his patrol would be paid not more often than once in two months. Roster of North Carolina Militia, Adjutant-General's Department, State Department of Archives and History, Raleigh, N. C., pp. 482-483 (cited hereafter as Militia Roster); John C. Winder to John D. Powers, June 20, 1862, Militia Letter Book, Adjutant-General's Department, State Department of Archives and History, Raleigh, N. C., p. 148 (cited hereafter as Militia Letter Book).

Knowing your Excellency to be fair honest & upright the people expect you as our Governor to discontinue this unnecessary State expense at once

In conclusion I will State that I am 60 years of age have been an Acting Justice of the Peace for 25 years & Post Master at Cain Tuck & am known by our county officers &c
[Raleigh]
[A. L. S. Governors' Papers (Vance),
State Department of Archives and History, Raleigh.]

From M. A. Buie[158]

Edgefield C. H. S. C. Sept 21 1862

In the first place, I must introduce myself to you— and in the second place congratulate you, that the people of noble N. Carolina have been true to their trust in the election of Governor Vance a *true* and tried patriot a military man and statesman, in this hour of national birth— 1st. I am Miss M. A. Buie a native of the "Good old North State. I have been professionally engaged— teaching school in this State (S C) and in Augusta Geo— for the last eight years. I have written for the press several for years, wrote for amusement— The public have known me as "Viola," "Carolina," Justice "Independent Carolina" &c— I was pleasantly situated and I may add profitably, as I was principal of a female school receiving a stated salary of $800. for ten months. for 1 yr. I have a very high position in Society as I came to this section very highly recommended from N. C. by the very first from my section Richmond Co N. C. and the Pres. of the college where I graduated— Floral C[159]— The Pres. was much interested in my educated as he was a first cousin of my father. J. R. Buie who has many relations in Fayetteville N. C. I have been teaching for the most refined and wealthy in this State and Geo. and with much success and satisfaction to parent and pupil. I have the respect and confidence of the first citizens in this Section and have been intro-

---

[158] Mary Ann Buie, known as "The Soldier's Friend," was a daughter of J. R. Buie, of Richmond County. She died at Aiken, S. C., October 29, 1878. *Daily Charlotte Observer,* November 1, 1878.

[159] Floral College was located at the village of Shoeheel, in Robeson County, near the present town of Maxton, where a settlement dated from the time of the construction of the Wilmington, Charlotte and Rutherfordton Railroad (now the Seaboard) before the war. D. A. Buie taught at the college, and was possibly the president spoken of. Robert C. Lawrence, *The State of Robeson* (Lumberton, 1939), pp. 23, 27 (cited hereafter as Lawrence, *Robeson*); Charles Lee Smith, *History of Education in North Carolina* (Washington, 1888), pp. 117-118 (cited hereafter as Smith, *Education in N. C.*). The college closed during the early part of the war but the board unanimously resolved to reopen at the end of 1862, but the principal, Rev. Daniel Johnson, declined to accept the terms. *Fayetteville Observer,* November 26, 1862.

duced to many distinguished personages— I know Gov Brown[160]
of Geo personally as I was at the Atlanta Springs at the same time
he had the Trout House there for the Executive Department—
I presume you heard of the suspension of schools in this section—
not one in twenty have continued I am very fond of history and
have studied the best of Authors— Historians have paid a beautiful tribute to Woman's patriotism since War, *cruel War;* disturbed
the peace and happiness of man. and when disgrace and dishonor
threatened a nation and the men had to defend their rights or fight
out a quarrel. Woman has wielded a powful influence and in the
accomplishment of much which gave success to the efforts of *the*
Soldiers in all ages. When the startling realities of this terrible
Revolution burst forth in all its fury and desolation, and devasta-
tion threatened us on every side and the whole country was in
confusion and terror. The very   The cry of war was heard all
over the land every was a soldier — Revolution was on us &
we had prepare for it as the very earth seemed to tremble beneath
the tread of contending armies. The honor of the South was at
stake. Every one knew he was fighting in a good cause. Such scenes
and circumstances were eminently calculated to awaken the liveli-
est emotions of interest, and to kindle the flame of patriotism in
every Southern heart. Old *men* forgot their heavy hairs and
infirmities, boyhood its inexperience and want of physical *development,* even women, tender beautiful confiding women forgot
her weakness in natural *timidity* of her sex and *join* in the cry
for freedom, And were working for their soldier friends, making
flags & clothing them also To volunteer or to die in defence of
Southern liberty is the proudest boast of a Southern youth— I
resigned my school and imitated my grand mothers of N C 75
for in N. C. the first fires of patriotism blazed in the War of 76
with England I am proud of my native State, May I say proud of
my sex in this War— The fair creatures have resolved to weild their
potent influence which has spread like a gentle dew reviving the
spirit of thousand drooping heads. Women has nerved the arm of
the stalwart Soldier going forth to conquer or die. The records
of the past furnish no instance in which the success of arms have
been secured by the influence of Woman as in this War We do
not wish to detract from the heroism of southern men. The historians writing for the state of Ala. S. C. and Geo. are recording all
the events happening in their armies & states because the writers
are employed to write— N° Carolina is much neglected by the

---

[160] Joseph Emerson Brown (1821-1894), governor of Georgia, 1857-1865. He was
born in South Carolina, studied law at Yale, served in the State Senate in 1849,
became Chief Justice of the Supreme Court of Georgia in 1868, and United States
Senator, 1880-1891. He was also president of the Western and Atlantic Railroad and
a business man who dealt in coal and iron and Atlanta real estate. Robert Preston
Brooks, "Joseph Emerson Brown," *Dict. of Am. Biog.,* III, 141-143.

historian I have conversed with two historians who are writing by refering to News papers. I saw the description of several battles in manuscripts I read them with regret as N. C. had not the place she so richly deserves. It is not right it is not just that after all she has done that posterity will not know the place N. C. occupies in this War— I have read daily the Charleston & Augusta papers— I take two N. C. papers Fayetteville observer & *Wilmington Journal* the paper historians are recording events of N. C. during the War— I heard a brave S. C. Capt. say that Col Fisher[161] was certainly the first man at Manasas to take Sherman's battery but that as he was a N. C. Col— it would not be known I asked him to give me his statement in writing and he did. I sang Fisher's praise and wrote for history a description of his charge on the *Battery* We may read of Grecian and Roman heroism and Spartan patriotism, but if only deeds of N. C. Soldiers are correctly written (not the whole Southern States) in this war it would astonish the world— Every state has acted well its part— N. Carolina has been one of the most liberal states & her Soldiers will live on the green page of fame if only a part of her deeds are placed in history for posterity to admire and imitate. She was not *hasty* and *rash* nor carried away by the promptings of *mad ambition* but was willing to listen to the voice of reason to see if the sinking *Ship* of State sinking with its price freight could be saved, when our gallant good N. C. statesmen firmly stood, with burning tongue, for peace. Truth, justice, peace and freedom were the mottoes they held forth, till they saw war was inevitable Saw that those who long professed to be our brothers had proved themselves to be our bitterest enemies, and had forgotten the glories of the past. N. C. then nobly resolved not to submit to wrong, and by the army that volunteered shows her citizens were determined to uphold that resolution, I have seen a list of names to day in an Ala paper said to be fallen heroes. *Not one* North Carolinian is in the list I can say I know you will agree with me that Cols Fisher Mearse[162] and a host of N C heroes (superior to half the *heroes* made by the press, extolled to the skies by historians & Editors and poets in S. C.) been South Carolinians I do not hesitate to give my opinion that their people would be still singing their fame in beautiful sentences and studied periods. Do you read the papers of this section Ala Miss, Geo, S. C. and then N. C papers and see the difference. Braver men never lived

---

[161] See p. 170, 28n. The Raleigh *North Carolina Standard* of August 7, 1861 reprinted from the August 2 Richmond *Examiner* the story of Fisher's first charging Sherman's battery, and the story decried the lack of publicity about North Carolina heroism in Virginia and the South. The capture of the battery was a turning point in the battle. Raleigh *North Carolina Standard,* August 7, 1861.

[162] Gaston Meares, of Wilmington, colonel of the Third North Carolina Regiment. He was killed at Malvern Hill, July 1, 1862. Clark, *N. C. Regts.,* I, 178, 183.

than the sons of the North State & now her native sons in other
states are known as Louisianians Bragg,[163] & Polk [164] and Peti-
grue[165] of S. C. Zollicoffer[166] of Tenn. Ben. McCullouh [167]of Texas
Rangers, all are native born N. C. heroes. The three first were
bred & lived there till after manhood's prime. It is cruel as it is
unjust that a state whose grand army dots the Hillsides and valleys
of every invaded state, or at least form a gigantic *Legion* of Honor
where heroism is as widespread as sunshine and their liberality
universal. I say such *armies* as *hers* should not be neglected and
their histories written by *those* who are prejudiced to N. C. or
ignorant of the part she has performed Va writers and S. C.
writers expect to make their heroes to please their people— I do
nothing but read and make subscriptions for Soldiers and always
head my lists *liberally* with my own cash that I have earned in
the school room till it has cost me nearly $1500. (fifteen dollars) I
wish to ask you if you will sustain and aid me in writing history.
I think the patriotic people would not hesitate to erect a Monument at Raleigh to the gallant Dead of N. C. no matter where
they sleep or when they fell whether at picket post, on hospital
cot at the flaming battery or, on the gory fields or ploughed by
canon ball in victories or defeats altho— I have heard Hatteras
Roanoke & Newbern *cast* up to N C as cowardly as defeats no one

---

[163] Braxton Bragg (1817-1876), who was born in Warrenton, N. C. and who, when
he resigned from the United States Army in 1856 bought a plantation in Louisiana
and became commissioner of public works in his adopted state. He became a Confederate general on April 12, 1862. Conrad H. Lanza, "Braxton Bragg," *Dict. of Am.
Biog.,* II, 585-587.

[164] Leonidas Polk (1806-1864), who was born in Raleigh. In 1841 he became bishop
of Louisiana and never lived in North Carolina after graduating from West Point
in 1827. He became a Confederate lieutenant general on October 10, 1862. Robert
Douthat Meade, "Leonidas Polk," *Dict. of Am. Biog.,* XV, 39-40.

[165] James Johnston Pettigrew (1828-1863), who was born in Tyrell County, N. C.,
graduated from the University of North Carolina in 1847, but had practiced law
in Charleston for a decade before the war. During the war he became a brigadier
general, February 26, 1862, was distinguished at Seven Pines, and killed July 17,
1863 on the retreat from Gettysburg. He was usually counted as from North Carolina. Cornelia Phillips Spencer, "James Johnston Pettigrew," Peele, *N. C. Lives,*
pp. 412-435.

[166] Felix Kirk Zollicoffer (1812-1862), a brigadier general in the Confederate army
who was killed at the battle of Fishing Creek, January 19, 1862. In many newspaper
accounts thereafter it was claimed that he was born in Halifax County, N. C. and
emigrated to Tennessee as a boy, but all the main sources of his life place his birth
in Maury County, Tennessee. Among North Carolina newspapers claiming his
North Carolina birth were the Raleigh *North Carolina Standard,* February 1, 1862;
the Charlotte *Western Democrat,* January 28, 1862; and the *Asheville News,*
January 30, 1862. Placing his birth in Tennessee are *Biog. Dir. of Am. Cong.,*
p. 1740, and Edd Winfield Parks, "Felix Kirk Zollicoffer," *Dict of Am. Biog.,* XX,
659- 660.

[167] Ben McCulloch (1811-1862) was not born in North Carolina, but in Rutherford
County, Tennessee. He lived in Alabama, western Tennessee, and then Texas,
where he acquired great fame as a leader of rangers and for his part in the Mexican
War. He was killed in action early in the Civil War, at Elkhorn Tavern, March 7,
1862. Robert G. Caldwell, "Ben McCulloch," *Dict. of Am. Biog,.* XII, 5-6.

but cowardly Carolinians would permit— At the Trout House in Atlanta Geo— last year when Hatteras fell after brave men as the Spartan Martyrs of *Thermopylae*— were so situated by bad management of civil authorities they surrened as prisoners of war after they had evinced as much daring bravery under the concentrated fire of the enemies ships— In the history of this War there never has been a more striking indifference to death than that of the brave North Carolinians in every battle. At Newberne and Roanoke the few soldiers from Va claimed to have done all the fighting at Roanoke[168] & a Maryland Regiment at Newberne[169] & I have the Editorials & remarks in Geo & Ala papers speaking in the most slanderous terms of N. C. denouncing them as Union loving cowards & did not wish to defend their State as they wanted to return to the North. Now too since your election stupid ignorant people are casting at it me like they did Hatteras that N C has elected a *Union Gov*— I have insulted a boasting rich man that has never given over $5 all together since the War that was abusing N. C this week said they run in Va & S- C- Soldiers of S. C. Reg had to walk over N. C cowards to a battery I told him that a man like him who never done any thing for S- C- or his country could easily talk I told him he was no better than the tories of 76 & I all such were the Tories of this War and that I was glad he did not live in N- C as he said he would not live there— I have a state reccommendation from Gov. & many other recommendations which will show you that I am a lady of character if not of means. If you will write me word what you think of my efforts and promise to sustain me I will serve your State during the War. I can teach for $1000 yr—but I wish to work for N. C. in this Revolution

[Raleigh]

[A. L. S. Governors' Papers (Vance), State Department of Archives and History, Raleigh.]

From T. M. Shoffner[170]

Jamstown N. C.

September 21st 1862

Venerable Sir I desir to lay my former & present course befor you hopeing you will be so kind as to answer me and tell me what I may depend on in regard to the subject which I shal hear address you apon

---

[168] The principal forces at Roanoke Island on February 8, 1862, when the Federal attack was made, were North Carolina troops, but portions of two regiments of Virginia troops, the Forty-sixth and the Fifty-ninth, were ordered to reinforce the garrison, but arrived after the main fighting was over, though they sustained some casualties. *O. R.*, Ser. I, Vol. IX, 186.

[169] There was no Maryland regiment at the battle of New Bern, March 14, 1862.

[170] T. M. Shoffner does not appear on any of the muster rolls of the army as given in Moore, *N. C. Roster*. He was very probably never in the army.

Sir I am a native & a citizen of the county of Alamace & early last spring at the request of Mr. Jils Meaban[171] one of the representatives of our county I tooke stepes to rais a companey for sirvis & was joined in that efort by Mr. G. M. Albright [172] & had elisted men to the amount required to give me a commisheon but not a sufficient number for a ful company when I was sent for by Messrs Mendenhall Jones & Gardner[173] to worke for them in thear gun manafactoring esstablishnent near Jamstown N. C. I then had to give up my companey & Mr. Albright who assisted me in raising it becum the captain of the companey & is now in the armey & I have bin imployed by Messrs Mendenhall Jones & Gardner from that time on. It is sum distance from my place of imployment to my residence in the county of Alamance though I make it a rule to go home to my famely once a month & have never yet been malested on my way to or from home

But thear has bin men arrested on thear way to home & to this place & tooke to the army & put in sirvis. this has all occured since the inroleing of the conscrips.

I would have had no objection to going in the armey if I could have went last Spring when I had the chance of being capten of a companey but after having maid up a company I would be verry reluctan to have to go now as a privet when I had the chance of a more honorable persition which I would have held had it not have bin that I was put on another Duty

Now Sir as thear seams to be no bounds to the Milatary arthoroty I wish to know wheather or not I may Expect your protection if I should be arrested when on my way hone & back to this place

[171] Giles Mebane (1809-1899) was born in Orange County, afterwards Alamance. He studied at Bingham School, graduated at the University of North Carolina in 1831, taught for a brief time, but then studied law under Chief Justice Ruffin and was admitted to the bar, practicing until the close of the Civil War, when he moved to Caswell County and farmed. He represented Orange County in the House of Commons in 1844, 1846, and 1848, when he introduced the bill to create Alamance County. In 1858 and 1860 he represented Alamance County in the House of Commons; in 1862 and 1864 he was state senator from Alamance and Randolph, and was president of the Senate while Vance was governor. In 1865 he was a member of the convention and returned to the Senate in 1878. In politics he was a Whig, supported internal improvements and opposed secession until the crisis of 1861. After the war he became a Democrat. William P. McCorkle, "Giles Mebane," Ashe, *Biog. Hist. of N. C.*, VII, 335-338; Connor, *N. C. Manual*, pp. 482, 545, 741.

[172] G. M. G. Albright, of Alamance County, who became captain of company F in the Fifty-third North Carolina Regiment on May 5, 1862; he was killed at Gettysburg in July 1863. Clark, *N. C. Regts.*, III, 262; Moore, *N. C. Roster*, III, 517.

[173] The firm was composed of Cyrus P. Mendenhall, E. P. Jones, and Grafton Gardner. Their contract with the state called for 5,000 guns @ $21 each, of the Mississippi rifle pattern. They agreed to begin on November 1, 1862 with forty rifles, and to supply eighty per month thereafter, forfeiting $5 per rifle for any not delivered on time. Because of the rise in prices the contract underwent future adjustments, the state agreeing to pay a profit of $10 on each gun. The first contract bears no date; the adjustment was made in December 1862. N. C. Quartermaster Contracts, Box 107.

The time that I loose is but verry little as this esstablishment is near the N. C. Railroad and I can go the most of the way by railroad.

And as the arthoretys of the confederat stats has saw fit to exemp men from Milatary service who wear imployed in manafactoring fire arms for the goverment [174] I thearfore would prefur to remain at my present vocation as I was prevented from going in to the armey at the time hear to fore spokeing off and as we yet live in a free country I hope men may not be interrupted by unlawful arthorety.

[Raleigh]
[A. L. S. Governors' Papers (Vance),
State Department of Archives and History, Raleigh.]

From Nathaniel Boyden[175]

Salisbury Sept 22⁽ᵈ⁾ /62

I received your letter to my son[176] in relation to his engaging in the manufacture of Salt, & on reading, I discovered, that my son must have wholly failed in apprising you of his object. He did not wish to engage in the salt business on behalf of the State, nor at the expense of the state, but upon his own account & at his own risque.

You probably know, that my son married the sister of Mrs. A

---

[174] The first Exemption Act, April 21, 1862, did not specifically exempt those employed in manufacturing fire arms for the government, but it did relieve from military duty "superintendents and operatives in wool and cotton factories, who may be exempted by the Secretary of War." Matthews, *Public Laws of Confederacy*, 1 session, 1 Congress, chap. LXXIV. The Act of October 11, 1862, was more specific and provided for the exemption of "all artisans, mechanics, and employees in the establishments of such persons as are or may be engaged under contracts with the Government in furnishing arms . . . and other munitions of war" provided he was approved by the chief of the ordnance bureau or, in the case of state contracts, by the governor or the secretary of state. Matthews, *Public Laws of the Confederacy*, 2 session, 1 Congress, chap. XLV; Raleigh *North Carolina Standard*, April 30, October 15, 1862; *O. R.* Ser., IV, Vol. II, 162, 167. The law provided that such employees be enrolled and then detailed to their work for periods of sixty days at a time.

[175] Nathaniel Boyden (1796-1873) was a Massachusetts Yankee who came to North Carolina as a school teacher in 1822, but he read law and was licensed in 1823. He lived for a time in Guilford, Rockingham, Stokes, and Surry counties until 1842, when he moved to Salisbury. He represented Surry County in the House of Commons in 1838 and 1840 and Rowan County in the State Senate in 1844. Boyden was a strong Whig and Conservative until 1868, when he joined the Republican party. He was United States Congressman (Whig) from 1847 to 1849 and from 1867-1869 (Republican); a member of the State Convention of 1865; and from 1871 to 1873 was an associate justice of the North Carolina Supreme Court. Boyden was a man of some learning, having graduated from Union College at Schenectady, New York, and of decided opinions on almost every public question. Hamilton, *History of N. C.*, IV, 1-3; Connor, *N. C. Manual*, pp. 793, 816, 932; *Biog. Dir. of Am. Cong.*, p. 877.

[176] Nathaniel Boyden, Jr.

Stuart,[177] one of the principal owners of the salt works,[178] & on acount of this connection, he had given my son the privilege of manufacturing Salt to the amount of one, or two hundred thousand bushels, provided the governor of North Carolina would signifiy his willingness, that my son should engage in the business; it being especially understood, that my sons engaging in the business should in no way interfere with the right & privilege granted to the state.[179] Governor Clarke told him verbally he was willing but refused to say so in writing at first., but at length agreed to write him a letter giving his approbation but finally refused or rather he wrote a letter to Mr Woodfin[180] leaving the matter to him to decide the question; He declined giving his assent. This was no doubt on account of the political stripe[181] of myself and son as it is manifest that the more Salt could be manufactured there the better it would be for the people & the lower could be the price to consumers. Please talk with our friend B. F. Moore[182] Esqr., he can tell you all about the course of governor Clarke I cannot imagine any reason for the refusal of this assent so far as our citizens are concerned, the condition being, that it shall in no way enterfere with the right of the State to make salt.

Mr. Stuart desired this assent of the state, for his own satisfaction. Please have the goodness to talk with Mr Moore & write to my

---

[177] Mrs. Alexander Stuart, whose husband was a brother of General J. E. B. Stuart.

[178] The salt works were about sixteen miles northeast of Abingdon, Va., on the north bank of the Holston River, in Smyth County. The partnership of Stuart, Buchanan & Company was composed of William Alexander Stuart, Benjamin K. Buchanan, George W. Palmer, and George B. Parker. Walter H. Robertson, *Saltville* (Washington County Historical Society, Abingdon, 1943), p. 24. In 1880 Stuart bought the celebrated White Sulphur Springs in Greenbrier County, W. Va. Asheville *North Carolina Citizen*, April 8, 1880.

[179] The first contract, dated June 30, 1862, is in Governors' Papers (Clark). See p. 208, 148n. Woodfin was the state agent at Saltville.

[180] Clark's letter to Woodfin was written on July 24, 1862. He wrote: "Mr. Boyden made another application thru an attorney (B. F. Moore Esq) to get my sanction or written approval of any contract he may make with Stuart-Buchanan & Co for the manufacture of salt. I could not see the object or force of the application and therefore referred it to you. On the face of it, it merely professes to increase the manufactury of the Article which is entirely proper. But where is the necessity or object of my name to it?" Governor Clark to N. W. Woodfin, July 24, 1862, Clark Letter Book, p. 383.

[181] Boyden and Woodfin had both been Whigs until the secession crisis, when Woodfin had supported secession before Lincoln's call for troops. Boyden remained a strong advocate of Union and opposed secession.

[182] Bartholomew Figures Moore (1801-1878), a native of Halifax County who graduated from the University of North Carolina in 1820, read law, and practiced it in Nash and Halifax counties until 1848, when he moved to Raleigh, where he soon gained a reputation as a shrewd, learned, and profound lawyer, possessed of solid wisdom and moral power. He represented Halifax in the House of Commons from 1836 to 1844 except for 1838; in 1848 he became Attorney General of North Carolina and was the principal author of the *Revised Code*. He was a conservative even among Whigs, and opposed secession even after Lincoln's call for troops. Joseph Gregoire deRoulhac Hamilton, "Bartholomew Figures Moore," Ashe, *Biog. Hist. of N. C.*, V, 275-286; Allen, *Halifax County*, pp. 188-190.

son your determination He is at the salt works Saltville Virginia
Raleigh
[Vance Letter Book, 1862-1863,
State Department of Archives and History, Raleigh.]

From John H. Robeson[183]

Cottage Hill N C.
Sept. 22ᵈ. 1862

I am almost detered from writing you since seating myself for
that purpose: knowing that you are hindered with communica-
tions

And but for the redemption of a promise made to a friend I
should certainly not trouble you: pleasant as it always is to con-
verse with a *Special* friend.

I sometime ago promised J. W. Harbin to use my influence
(if I had any) with you to procure his appointment to the Super-
intendency of the Western Turnpike road from Asheville to the
Georgia line.[184] I know not fully the requirements of the position:
but presume that they are Such as *Wesley* would be able to meet.
The present Superintendent is said to be an *inefficient,* and I *know*
an *unworthy* man. You know him. The Rev. B. Turner of Haywood, who quit preaching—and declared that he was called of God
to make Political speeches for Democracy. I trust you know me
well enough to believe that I would not use my influence nor give
my consent for the appointment of *any* man, to *any* position, who
was in any way disqualified.

For that very error, for that very Sin, the county is now terribly
suffering. Let us beware I should have no scruples in appointing
Harbin, who tho, a rather obscure man is nevertheless a man of
good Sense of correct principle, and firm integrity— and I believe
would make a faithful and efficient agent. I am not dictating—
do what seemes best in your Judgement. While writing I would
mention another subject in which I am personally interested,

[183] John Hamel Robeson, of Sandy Mush, who was so disillusioned upon the defeat
of the Confederacy that in 1866 he sold his mountain lands because "carpet baggers
were rampant and taking control" and moved to Clear Creek, Texas. Richmond
Times-Dispatch, February 20, 1949.

[184] The Western Turnpike was the name by which the road from Salisbury to the
Georgia line was originally known. It was chartered by the legislature in 1849 and
amended in 1855 to make Asheville the eastern terminus and the Tennessee line
at Ducktown the western terminus, with the extension to the Georgia line only a
branch of the main road. In 1862 the control of the road was divided into two
sections; the first from Asheville to the Macon-Jackson line, and the second from
there to the state lines of Georgia and Tennessee. The governor was to appoint
two agents, one for each section, who were to supervise construction, repair, and
collection of tolls. In the original charter the agent was to receive $2 a day. *Public
Laws of N. C., 1848-'49,* chap. XC, pp. 193-195 (January 27, 1849); *Laws of N. C.,
1854-'55,* chap. 22 (February 15, 1855); *Private Laws of N. C., 1862-1863,* chap. 14,
pp. 20-22 (December 17, 1862); Arthur, *Western North Carolina,* pp. 239-240;
Sondley, *Buncombe County,* II, 624, 668.

because it is a most vital interest of the County. I mean the supply of Salt. There is great destitution here now, and I fear worse in the future

I fear the agent for the State[185] in Virginia is the *wrong* man. for good reasons the people have no confidence in his doing right You will look well to that matter— The prospect is alarming— and is creating much complaint— Something must be done and done speedily.

I will not allude to the troubles of the Country— You know them all— I sympathize with you in your Herculean labors— Yes! *Herculean* for you must clean out the "Augean Stables" at Raleigh preparatory to success May God give you strength of body and mind requisite to the task! I am much pleased with the *patriotic* spirit of your inaugural— that's right! Only let us seek earnestly to be guided by the light of truth and wisdom— do right under every circumstance— and have faith in God. and all will be well—

[Raleigh]

[on reverse]

Ans[r]— that I would take great pleasure in giving it to Harbin but that the Western counties have always claimed the agent, and would excite prejudice against Buncombe were I to depart from the custom.   Z. B. Vance

[A. L. S. Governors' Papers (Vance),
  State Department of Archives and History, Raleigh.]

From P. H. Roane[186]

Wainsville N. C. Sept. 23rd- 1862,

The object, of this letter is to obtain some information, concerning the extensive enforcement of the Conscript Law so as to include all men within certain ages, irrespective of regular and honorable discharges. — There seems, Gov, to be different and forced constructions placed, upon the *law* in its administration in the several States; and different interpretations given by the numerous diversified oracular exponents of Conscript Law,

I, myself, am a discharged soldier of the immortal 16th Regt, which I left July 2nd 62, after many months suffering and an ineffectual, attempt to serve my country,

I accepted a discharge on the ground of permanent, constitutional imbecility; returned home, and after some what recuperating, I embarked in the study of law in which I have persued with flattering progress, notwithstanding my feeble state of health; the

---

[185] The salt agent for North Carolina in Virginia was Nicholas W. Woodfin of Buncombe County. See p. 92, 347n and, for the contract, p. 208, 148n.

[186] P. H. Roane, of Macon County, was second corporal of company H of the Sixteenth North Carolina Regiment, enlisting on May 14, 1861. According to Moore, *N. C. Roster*, II, 23, he was discharged on June 12, 1862.

fact of which, will be affirmed by Gen. Henry,[187] Capt Ship,[188] Mr. Merriman,[189] and other cordial friends of short acquaintance,

Greatly to my supprise, while pursuring my studdy with a uncommon avidity and assiduity; my plans all concocted; my prospects of success encourageing to me at least, I am startled by an order from the Col, of the Macon militia,[190] prepare ye to dance to the music whether you like the tune or not,

What I now desire to know, is, whether the true intent of the law, is to nulify all discharges, as well subsequent, as antecedent to the passage of the law; [191] if so, if you in the plentitude of your primitive derivative powers, cant extend to me some merciful exoneration, so that I will not be deranged in my plans of studdy, or harrassed and driven off by the lash, which is essential, only to false and recreant, wretches, who for the sake of a little animal repose, would barter off their inherent rights and liberty, for down right chains and slavery; and if the prerogative and discretionary power des not reside in your hands, and if it des, and you cant make a compatible use of it; do pray tell me when the irreconsilable collision of authorities and a bare faced absurdity will cease; or is the regular authorized and necessary action of our army sergeons &c to be a prelude only, to that conceivedly odious thing, called conscription.

Any satisfactory information you will please to give me or favor bestow, will be gratefully received and long remembered. You will please address your unworthy and ever zealous supporter, at Franklin N C.

May you have signal success in the honest, thorough, and energetic administration of all laws and duties, incumbent on the discharge of your high official functions, is the desire of yours &c.
[Raleigh]
[A. L. S. Governors' Papers (Vance),
State Department of Archives and History, Raleigh.]

[187] Robert M. Henry, of Macon County, a lawyer and militia general who was captain of company D in the Sixty-second North Carolina Regiment. He was a strong opponent of secession in 1860 and a member of the Convention of 1865 from Macon County. From 1868 to 1876 he was solicitor of the western circuit. Arthur, *Western North Carolina*, p. 392; Connor, *N. C. Manual*, p. 887; Clark, *N. C. Regts.*, III, 515; Raleigh *North Carolina Standard*, January 8, 1861.

[188] William Marcus Shipp, Henderson County lawyer who was captain of company I in the Sixteenth North Carolina Regiment, in which Roane had served. See p. 71, 268n.

[189] See p. 13, 65n.

[190] The head of the Macon militia was LaFayette Howard of Franklin. In Militia Roster he is listed as a captain, no colonel being listed. Howard was commissioned March 1, 1862. The colonels of militia had been ordered by Vance to enroll the conscripts and to arrest deserters. See General Orders, No. 7, September 13, 1862, p. 186, 84n.

[191] The Conscription Act was vague on this point, but General Orders, No. 48, July 11, 1862, provided for "certificates of disability" for non-commissioned officers and soldiers when signed by the senior surgeon and the commanding officer, and when forwarded to the adjutant and inspector general. While the order does not specifically exempt the invalid from further liability to conscription, it does speak of the certificates as "final statements." O. R. Ser. IV, Vol. II, 3-4.

From H. A. Gilliam[192]

Smithfield, N. C.
Sept 23ᵈ 1862

I understand that the office of Adjutant General will, probably, soon be vacated—[193]

If it shall so transpire, I will be greatly obliged to you for the appointment— I am assured that my exchange[194] will be effected within a very few days and shall value the place the more because the reorganization of all the regiments from our state leaves me no chance for a place in the army.

I shall see you next week in Raleigh—

[Raleigh]

[A. L. S. Governors' Papers (Vance),
State Department of Archives and History, Raleigh.]

From Wm. S. Carter[195]

Fairfield Hyde Co N. C.
Sept 23ᵈ 1862

The pecular Situation of our people at this time—being entirely Surrounded by the Enemy— leads me to Seek your instructions as to the proper manner for us to govern ourselves in our intercourse with each other The Enemy have overrun and claim to hold in Their lines ten or eleven counties in eastern Carolina, with complete possesion of the Sounds and contiguous waters. Our County is included in this, number, Interspersed among our population is a class of men disloyal to the confederacy and the best interest of North Carolina, These men are constant spies on our actions,

[192] Henry A. Gilliam, who was a colleague of Vance in the House of Commons in 1854 and who represented Washington County again in 1856. He was likewise a Whig, interested in commercial conventions especially if they were concerned with the improvement of navigation in Albemarle and Pamlico Sounds. After the war he lived in Edenton and in Edgecombe County until 1878, when he moved to Raleigh and formed a law partnership with John Gatlin. In 1882-1883 he was a judge of the superior court. Connor, *N. C. Manual*, pp. 450, 843; *Raleigh Register*, November 8, 1854.

[193] For an explanation see p. 182, 70n.

[194] Gilliam was major of the Seventeenth North Carolina Regiment upon its organization and was captured with most of the regiment at the fall of Hatteras, August 28, 1861. Many were still prisoners when the reorganization of the troops took place in the spring of 1862. Clark, *N. C. Regts.*, II, 1; Moore, *N. C. Roster*, II, 39.

[195] William S. Carter, a prominent planter of Hyde County who represented his county in the House of Representatives in 1872 and 1876, and in the Convention of 1875. He was a brother of David M. Carter, a prominent lawyer and political associate of Vance, to whom William S. Carter wrote in 1863 urging him to use whatever influence he had with Vance to secure punishment to the buffaloes and looters in the occupied counties. At the time of this letter to Vance, Carter was colonel of the Thirteenth Militia Regiment, Connor, *N. C. Manual*, pp. 659, 884; William S. Carter to David M. Carter, June 1, 1863, David M. Carter Papers, Southern Historical Collection, University of North Carolina, Chapel Hill, N. C. (cited hereafter as Carter Papers).

are running off our property leading the Enemy to our doors and incourageing Him to commit all Manner of depredations upon us & ours If an outlet to this County could be opened we would soon rid ourselves of this Class and could give to the Confederacy Two hundred and fifty fighting men besides this our County alone Could and would send to the upcountry hundreds of thousands of pounds of Bacon and a Milion of Bushels of Corn, Our Graneries are full of the old crop and our prolific earth is groaning under the abundance of the New, Our intercourse with each other is very much restricted by the Strict police Sistem of the enemy The little commerce that we cary on with our neighboring counties is done by this disloyal Class of our citizens all ready spoken of I sugest, Would it not be better for the interest of our Confederacy our State and ourselves that our loyal Vessel owners & Sailors should engage in this internal trade— I mean with the citizens of other counties over run like ourselves— even if thay had to sail under Yankee papers than that It should be confined to a Class who profess to owe no allegiance to our government

I wrote some time since to Gov. Clark [196] for instructions upon this very point, He replyed by saying that he could afford us no protection and would not therefore give any positive instruction in the mater and refering the whole to my best Judgement I have not thought proper under these instructions to incourage the mater atall, I have no doubt but that 4/5 of the population in these over run counties are as loyal as any citizens of the State, in some parts of them I am creditably informed there is a scarcity of Substantial food, What I desire to know is, whether our citizens will be justifiable in sending provision to these men in vessels sailing under Yankee papers and wheather our Shipowners can be allowed to procure their papers

[Raleigh]

[A. L. S. Governors' Papers (Vance),
State Department of Archives and History, Raleigh.]

To S. P. Moore [197]

STATE OF NORTH CAROLINA
EXECUTIVE DEPARTMENT
Raleigh, Sept. 24th. 1862

Your letter to Gov Vance [198] recommending that measures should be taken for the thorough vaccination of the Citizens of

[196] See p. 133, 529n.

[197] See p. 189, 91n.

[198] This letter was signed by David Alexander Barnes (1819-1892), of Northampton County, who had been a member of the House of Commons in 1844, 1846, and 1850, and a member of the Convention of 1861. He was a graduate of the University of North Carolina, a lawyer, and a "gallant and gifted Whig" whom some preferred to describe as a "federalist of the old school." He became an aide to Vance,

this State has been received & been handed to our Surgeon General D[r] Edward Warren[199] who will doubtless give the matter that attention which its importance demands.

Your letter requesting two copies of the last Geological report of the State has also been received. D[r] Emmons[200] the State Geologist informs me that the copies of the last report have been misplaced. I send you by mail two copies of the only reports now in this office

[Richmond]
[Vance Letter Book, 1862-1863,
State Department of Archives and History, Raleigh.]

From Jno. M. Rose [201]

Fayetteville N. C.
Sept 24 1862

It is desirable to have a meeting of the Stockholders of the Fayetteville & Western Plank R[d] Co 2 or 3 weeks hence—the regular annual meeting *was to have* been held on *Apl last,* but the State did not appoint a proxy & no meeting Can be held for want of majority unless *the State* is represented—[202]

I write to ask when it will be Convenient for you to *appoint* a proxy— Some two or three *months Since* it was announced *in the papers that Geo M[c]Neill* [203] was appointed proxy in the *F&WPR Co* at its *next* meeting but I presume it was a *misprint* in the

---

probably through the suggestion of William A. Graham, to whom Barnes wrote that he wished some place under Vance because "my health is too delicate to endure the fatigue and exposure of camp life." After the war he was a judge of the superior court, 1865-1868, until he resigned upon the adoption of the Constitution of 1868. Thereafter he practiced law at his home at Jackson with much success. Connor, *N. C. Manual*, pp. 449, 729-730, 891; McCormick, *Personnel*, p. 16; *Raleigh Register, February* 7, 14, 1855; David A. Barnes to William A. Graham, August 26, 1862, John P. H. Russ to William A. Graham, August 20, 1862, Graham Papers CH.

[199] See p. 159, 647n.

[200] Ebenezer Emmons (1799-1863), state geologist since 1851. He was a native of Massachusetts, a graduate of Williams College, Rensselaer School, and the Berkshire Medical School. He was professor at Williams College for many years, assisted in the geological survey of New York State, wrote several books and many reports, and published, in 1860, an extensive report on North Carolina agriculture. He died in Brunswick County, N. C. "A Sketch of Ebenezer Emmons," *Appleton's Popular Science Monthly*, Vol. XLVIII, No. 3 (January 1896), pp. 406-411.

[201] John M. Rose was secretary of the Fayetteville and Western Plank Road Company.

[202] The Fayetteville and Western Plank Road was chartered January 27, 1849 and provided for a road from Fayetteville to Salisbury, and eventually beyond to Salem and Bethania. By the terms of the law the state would subscribe three-fifths of the stock and have three-fifths of the votes in the meetings of the company, so clearly the presence of the state's proxy was necessary for a meeting. *Laws of N. C., 1848-'49*, chap. LXXXIX, pp. 183-192 (January 27, 1849).

[203] George McNeill was a prominent merchant in Fayetteville who died in 1865. John A. Oates, *The Story of Fayetteville and the Upper Cape Fear* (Fayetteville, 1950), p. 851 (cited hereafter as Oates, *Story of Fayetteville*).

paper[204] as he has for several years years past, been the States proxy in Fayetteville & *Albemarle P R Co*[205] while *W. G. Broadfoot* [206] was the proxy in the Fayetteville & *Western* P. R. Co I merely make this statement to correct any error if it occurred— the F & Albemarle meeting was the latter part of *August* & Mr. McNeill represented the State in it— the 2nd. Thursday in Oct has been suggested as the Called meeting but it Can be Called to Suit your Convenience

[Raleigh]

[on reverse]

Ansd day appointed 2[d] Thursday Oct[207] G. L. [George Little]

[A. L. S. Governors' Papers (Vance),

State Department of Archives and History, Raleigh.]

From L. M. Allen[208]

Head Quarters Allens Legion
Camp McCowan
Knoxville Sept. 25. 1862

I have ordered Capt John B. Nelson[209] My Quartermaster to Proceed to Raleigh N. C. on official business connected with

---

[204] This announcement was printed in the Raleigh *North Carolina Standard,* June 25, 1862, saying that Governor Clark had appointed George McNeill as state proxy for the coming year.

[205] The Fayetteville and Albemarle Plank Road Company, formerly the Fayetteville and Center, was chartered in 1855 and amended in 1857. Directors were appointed by the governor in proportion to the stock subscribed to by the state. It was chartered to build a road from Little's River to Albemarle. *Laws of N. C., 1854-'55,* chap. 183, (February 14, 1855); *Laws of N. C., 1856-'57,* chap. 63, p. 32 (February 3, 1857). A brief account of the two roads is found in Oates, *Story of Fayetteville,* pp. 373-377.

[206] William G. Broadfoot who came from Petersburg, Va. to Fayetteville early in the century and was for many years the cashier of the Bank of Fayetteville, Oates, *Story of Fayetteville,* p. 558; Raleigh *News and Observer,* April 7, 1930.

[207] The date of the meeting was later changed to the first Thursday in November. *Fayetteville Observer,* November 3, 1862.

[208] Lawrence M. Allen was born in 1833 in Buncombe County, but settled in Marshall in 1853, just before it became a part of Madison County and just after the Vance family had moved from Marshall to Asheville. Allen became clerk of the superior court and was identified with the Democratic party, being a delegate to several state conventions. He volunteered at the beginning of the war, was commissioned a captain, and was among those captured at Roanoke Island in February 1862. After his exchange he was permitted to raise a legion which later became the Sixty-fourth North Carolina Regiment, and of which he became the colonel on July 20, 1862, and was sent to Edmund Kirby-Smith's command in East Tennessee. At Knoxville the regiment was drilled and used on guard duty for the city and as scouts for the surrounding country for about three months. In December 1862 his legion was disbanded and assigned to another regiment. Allen resigned on June 30, 1864. Colonel Allen was described as "not an attractive man—rather otherwise—but was chosen leader because he was known to be brave and fearless. Fighting was expected and his men had the utmost confidence in him." Clark, *N. C. Regts.,* III, 659-671; Moore, *N. C. Roster,* IV, 50; *Partisan Campaigns of Colonel Lawrence M. Allen* (Raleigh, 1894), which is an account of his exploits during and after the war.

[209] John B. Nelson, also of Marshall, N. C., was assistant quartermaster of the

this command I have requested him to call upon you. I hope
you will assist him & give him the proper instructions relative
to his Matters our Men are performing hard service & a great
Portion of them without shoes or clothing We desire our old
Beloved N Carolina to assist us—at least as far as the bounty goes.
I am proud to inform you that I now have twenty companys
tendered me— but few roles are yet prepared Capt Baird [210] is
doing well, Lucias [211] is performing his duty like a man. & I am
Much pleased with him as an Adjutant his health is now good
   I desire to hear from you
[Raleigh]
[A. L. S. Governors' Papers (Vance),
State Department of Archives and History, Raleigh.]

Anonymous

Columbus N. C. Sept 25th 1862
   I take the libbeter though a Stranger personally to drop you
a line respecting affairs in our county with regard to the Conscripts in the first place Ward [212] the oald Col is very obnoxious
to the masses and when he got badly beaten for Shff. he started
to make a company and has not got it full yet he is gitting some
accessions to it in this way he tells Maj. Liles [213] to arrest the
conscripts and than he goes and gets them to Joine his company
perhaps you may like to hear how Liles got to be Maj Ward
got one Capt & one Lieutenant in his office and elected Liles with
three votes and not one other capt nor any of the commission
officers knew any thing of the election it was not advertised as
the law directs and Ward can make liles do any thing he wishes
they have got some of the captains riding in every direction and
others will not go the people is willing to go under law full

Sixty-fourth North Carolina Regiment, commissioned July 15, 1862. When Allen's
legion was disbanded he became commissary of the Fifth Battalion (cavalry) which
was organized during the winter of 1862 at Jacksboro, Tennessee. Clark, *N. C.
Regts.*, IV, 271; Moore, *N. C. Roster*, IV, 50.
   [210] Alfred H. Baird of Buncombe County, a first cousin of Vance, who was captain
of a company of cavalry on outpost duty near Clinton, Tennessee. The company was
later combined with others and Baird became major of the Fifth Battalion, and
subsequently lieutenant colonel of the Sixty-fifth North Carolina Regiment (sixth
cavalry). Clark, *N. C. Regts.*, IV, 271-291; Moore, *N. C. Roster*, IV, 82.
   [211] Lucius H. Smith (1841-1904) of Yancey County, another first cousin of Vance.
He was commissioned in 1862 the adjutant of the legion, and was afterwards
adjutant of the Fifth Battalion. See p. 1, 4n; *Asheville Citizen*, March 20, 1923;
Clark, *N. C. Regts.*, III, 271; Moore, *N. C. Roster*, IV, 50; Cumming, "Reminiscence."
   [212] Johnson L. Ward who was commissioned colonel of the 105th Regiment of
North Carolina Militia, Polk County, on December 21, 1861. He was from Columbus
and afterwards volunteered. Militia Roster, pp. 462-464; Militia Letter Book, p. 180.
   [213] Robert Lyles, who is listed in Militia Letter Book p. 180, as having a colonel's
commission sent him on August 28, 1862. The record is further confused by the
fact that in Militia Roster, pp. 462-464, Lyles' commission as colonel bears date of
November 18, 1862, and further still by the fact that the record remarks that
"Col. Lyles died Aug 10, 1862". He is not listed at all as major.

officers but the people will not submit much longer to such
rule as Ward Mills & Com we beat them all out last Election
root & Branch and there is not a single Democrat in office in the
Country except this miserobel Liles & George Mills one of the
coart and we will set him out next march if time lasts Liles is
one of the worst of fools in every respect in dating an order to
Capt Hannons[214] he dates it 9862

You may think that I am medling but I wish to see harmony
but it is any thing but harmony in this County as I Stated
before Ward is one of the most obnoxious men in the County
to a very large magority he told Liles the other day that he
had orders from you to take all men liabel to Conscript & tie them
and bring them to Jail an carry them off in chains if necessary
and that he had printed orders to that effect printed the morning he left Raleigh they also tel the people that they have orders
from you also to take the men from 35 to 45 Ward when the
orders Came first for the Conscripts to enrole set his day to meet
at Columbus and instead of being there himself he gose off to
Richmong & the army Election & leaves Lils to manage affairs
Liles made arangements for transportation & had every thing
arranged & the peopel though perhaps all right but Ward come
back with new orders and then the Peopel began to think as before
of Ward all rong and there has bin at least one half dozen meetings by them since and it leaves room for the peopel to dout the
truth in any way that Ward & Liles may suggest or order Ward
is one of the most miserobel corrupt men in power in any way
in N. C. or any whare els an honest man in my county will
sustain me in what I say he is of the worst Stock ever raised
in our State his Father was whipe at the whiping post and Stood
in the Pillery at Rutherfordton dont believe me but ask Gen
Jones & John W. Hampton[215] for to sustain me in what I Say
and about what I have ritten to you & if there was orders for an
Election of pet officers in this the 105 the Regement N. C. melitia
I think all coul be mange sattisfactorily to the peopel
[Raleigh]

[A. L. S. Governors' Papers, (Vance),
    State Department of Archives and History, Raleigh.]

From James E. Hannon[216]

Columbus Polk County Sept 25 1862

As I am the oldest Capt in the Regiment I have to inform you
that we are with out field officers and I want you to order and

---

[214] James E. Hannon, captain of the second company in the 105th Militia. Militia
Roster, p. 462.

[215] John W. Hampton was active in the formation of Polk County, served on the
county school board, and was a justice of the county court. Griffin, Old Tryon and
Rutherford, pp. 217, 232, 236.

[216] See above, 214n. Hannon's commission bears date of October 25, 1861, and is
the oldest commission listed under the officers of the 105th regiment. Militia Roster,
pp. 462-464.

Election for field officers Col Ward [217] before he resigned HELL
AN Election for Mag and *only* Notified one Capt and one Lieu-
tenant Ward and them two officers Elected a Mag by giving three
Vots the other Capts and we being very much dissatisfied with
the Election from the fact he unfit for to fill the office of Mag
[Raleigh]
[A. L. S. Governors' Papers (Vance),
  State Department of Archives and History, Raleigh.]

From Eugene Grissom[218]

[Sept 26 1862]
Capt Eugene Grissom Co D 30th Reg N. C. T. respectfully represents to your Excellency that on the 25th June 1861 he rec⁰- from
the Military Secretary of N. C.[219] an appointment as Captain of
Infantry in the first Regiment of N. C. State Troops & that
under said appointment he raised enlisted & organized a company with Eugene Grissom Captain. Sol J Allen[220] 1st Liut, Allen

---

[217] See p. 227, 212n. John W. M. Turner had been the major but had volunteered
in the army. Lyles' irregular election was either over ruled, or he had died, for
Thomas M. Walker, former captain, was commissioned major on November 18,
1862. See p. 227, 213n and Militia Roster, pp. 462-464.

[218] Eugene Grissom (1831-1902) of Granville County who graduated in medicine at
the University of Pennsylvania in 1858 and also studied law and taught school. As
captain of company D of the Thirtieth North Carolina Regiment he was wounded
at the battle of Seven Pines, May 31, 1862; was promoted surgeon, February 23,
1863, and resigned his captaincy a month later. Meanwhile he was elected to the
House of Commons from Granville on the Vance ticket in 1862 and again in 1864,
where he was described as a member with a fine voice, excellent manners, and
remarkable self-composure, but modest withal. After the war he represented
Granville in the Convention of 1865. At the time Grissom wrote this letter to
Vance he had already been elected to the legislature but there was some question
as to his eligibility to his seat as he "joined the army under a requisition made by
the President upon the Governor of this State, and upon the reorganization of
the army, after the Conscript Act, he was re-elected to the Captaincy of his company." Robert B. Gilliam to William A. Graham, September 26, 1862, Graham
Papers CH. In 1868 Grissom was appointed Superintendent of the North Carolina
Insane Asylum because he "was satisfactory to both political parties," but he was
the center of a number of subsequent controversies, both medical and political.
He held many offices in medical organizations and wrote numerous articles, mostly
on insanity, for scientific and medical journals before his suicide in 1902. Grissom
had also written to Governor Clark about the date of his commission. Governors'
Papers (Clark), August 22, 1862; Connor, *N. C. Manual*, pp. 624, 881; Clark, *N. C.
Regts.*, II, 495, 498; Moore, *N. C. Roster*, II, 514; Jerome Dowd, *Sketches of Prominent Living North Carolinians* (Raleigh, 1888), pp. 153-155 (cited hereafter as
Dowd, *Sketches*).

[219] Warren Winslow, who was secretary of the Military and Naval Board which
had been authorized by the legislature in May of 1861, to advise and aid the
governor in appointments. The Board was abolished on August 20, 1861, but the
secretary continued for another month. Hill, *Bethel to Sharpsburg*, I, 155.

[220] Solomon J. Allen, of Wake County, whose commission bore the same date as
Grissom's, August 10, 1861. Moore, *N. C. Roster*, II, 514.

Bailey [221] 2ⁿᵈ Liut & Sidney S Abernathy[222] Junʳ. 2ⁿᵈ Leut— that on or about the first of August 1861 he came to Raleigh to tender said Company—ascertaining that the first Reg N C. State Troops was full & complete, he asked & obtained permission of His Excellency Gov Clark [223] to tender said Company for twelve months service which he did in its Organized form by presenting the rolls on the 10ᵗʰ of August 1861— He respectfully represents that his Commission should bear date & take rank from the 25th June 1861 instead of the 10th August 1861 [224]
[Raleigh]
[A. L. S. Governors' Papers (Vance),
    State Department of Archives and History, Raleigh.]

From W. W. Allen [225]

Olive N C
Sept. 26 1862

I see and appeal from you to the people of N. C. in behalfe of our Troops, for which I am under many obligations to you for it. But what is to be don? Many would respond to the call If it was not for the speculations & extortioners, who will not let them have the Leather for less than from $250 to 300 $ per lb and cotton yarn, at $6.00 and any thing else in perpotion, Have you not the power to stop this? If so, for Gods sake do it. They can sell Leather at $1.00 pr. lb. and cotton at $2.50 and make 75 per cnt, Janes cloth they are asken $5.00 pr yard, which the whole cost is a bout $ 75 pr. cnd
Sir how can we live at such rates? One more thing, some who are exempted by Law, are speculators post Masters who stand behine the Law in a little office, and are speculating and give the most of their time, and all most every case who are exemped are at it, even to the Preachers, I hear of some who have made from $5000 to $10.000 and say they are preachers, and are exempted, all this is doing the South more harme thane the enemy. We can not stand it much longer, I am a Methodist Preacher, bin

---

[221] Allen Benley, also of Wake County, commissioned August 10, 1861 and resigned December 10, 1861. Moore, *N. C. Roster,* II, 514.

[222] According to Moore, *N. C. Roster,* II, 514 Sidney S. Abernathy of Wake County was commissioned first lieutenant on April 1, 1863. He is not listed as having been second lieutenant, but G. S. Abernathy, also of Wake County, was commissioned second lieutenant on August 10, 1861, and afterwards promoted.

[223] See p. 133, 529n.

[224] Through his aide Vance replied that in his opinion Grissom ranked from the date of his commission and that since he had failed to raise his company in time for it to be placed in the first regiment that the appointment became void. David A. Barnes to Eugene Grissom, Raleigh, September 27, 1862, Governors' Papers (Vance).

[225] W. W. Allen was a Methodist minister of Iredell County.

in the conference for 30 years, and befor I will go into such a dark plot, I will beg. I will act as an Agent If you wish me, by refference to Rev W E Pell [226] or W W Holden[227] you can find out who I am, unless this speculating is stoped the poor must pearich and the army starved, please let us have more from your penn it may do good the people all through this county are ready to rise up against all such, but are waiting to see if you can not do something, this is a confidentual letter. May Heaven direct you in the right, and help you to take care of the poor, and bring you to the Kingdom of Heaven
[Raleigh]
[A. L. S. Governors' Papers (Vance),
State Department of Archives and History, Raleigh.]

From C. H. Wiley[228]

Greensboro N. C—
Septr. 26th- 1862—

It is my duty to inform you that the annual Meeting of the State Educational Association[229] will be held in Lincolnton on

---

[226] William E. Pell, a well known Methodist minister who had been editor of the Methodist paper, *The North Carolina Christian Advocate* until the outbreak of the war forced him to suspend publication. Having a large family to support and no resources to rely upon, he was forced to seek secular employment. At the time of this letter he had been with Holden on the *North Carolina Standard* for more than a year, where his services were described by Holden as "most valuable." Pell had no control over the policies of the paper, nor any responsibility for them. The *Raleigh Register*, a rival of the *Standard*, called Pell the "Financial, Political and, Ecclesiastical Assistant Editor of the *Standard*," but Holden claimed that Pell had never preached a political sermon. Raleigh *North Carolina Standard*, June 25, 1862.

[227] See p. 127, 499n.

[228] Calvin Henderson Wiley (1819-1887), of Guilford County, Superintendent of Common Schools. He studied at Caldwell Institute in Greensboro, graduated at the University of North Carolina in 1840, studied law and settled at Oxford, where for a time he edited the Oxford *Mercury* and wrote several novels and other literary compositions. But his principal interest became education, and in 1850 he returned to Guilford County and sought election to the legislature in order to sponsor educational reform. He was elected to the House of Commons as a Whig, and was re-elected in 1852. In the latter session a bill was passed authorizing the creation of the office of superintendent of common schools and in December 1852 Wiley, although a Whig in a Democratic legislature, was elected to the position which he held until October of 1865, when it was declared vacant; the office was abolished in 1866 because of lack of funds. Wiley studied theology privately, was licensed to preach in 1855, though not ordained until 1866, but he never held a regular charge. In 1869 he became general agent of the American Bible Society for Eastern and Middle Tennessee, and moved to Jonesboro. In 1874 he was transferred to Winston in a similar position, and lived there until his death. Robert D. W. Connor, "Calvin Henderson Wiley," Ashe, *Biog. Dict. of N. C.*, II, 427-440.

[229] The Educational Association of North Carolina was founded and organized by Wiley at a meeting in Salisbury in October 1856. The Association had held regular meetings every year since, usually well attended. The attendance at the Lincolnton meeting in 1862 was small, however, because of war conditions. It concerned itself primarily with school books, and adopted a resolution recommending a general convention of all the southern states to consider the problem. A committee was appointed to address the south on the importance of using southern textbooks and

Tuesday the 14th of October, Commencing at 7 o'clock, P. M.—
By reference to the Acts of Assembly, Session of 1860-61. Chap.
20th.[230] you will see that the Association is incorporated, with a
small annual appropriation to enhance its utility—& that to prevent abuses of its privileges certain safe-guards are thrown around
it, & among other provisions, its annual meetings are to be made
known -*Sect*. 5th-) fifteen days in advance to the President &
Directors of the Literary Fund—[231] Permit me to say that all the
provisions of the Act were proposed by myself, & that having
solely in view the permanent good of the State, I desired to make
the State Educational Association an efficient agency to that end;
& while adding to its means & powers for that purpose, to guard
zealously against their perversion— Allow me, also, to add, that
nothing would afford me greater pleasure than a careful personal
examination, on the part of the Chief executive Magistrate of
the State, & of the Members of the Legislature, of the various
means & appliances adopted by the Superintendent of Com-
Schools to harmonize, combine & advance *all* the educational interests of North-Carolina—. The first annual meeting of its character, after the acceptance of its charter in 1861, is to be held
in the midst of one of the most terrible wars of modern times; but
as the struggle, on the part of our people, is for the most sacred
rights of civilized man, no statesman can fail to see the infinite
importance of developing those moral elements which constitute
the true greatness & happiness of nations—
Unless the present generation be morally great it is in danger
of being overcome by the physical forces which it is creating,
on a vast scale, for its defence; & if the successors of the present
race are ignorant & vicious how long will they enjoy the liberty
won for them by priceless sacrifices of life, hardship & treasure?
Besides: the war forced on the Confederate States of America by
a proud & pharisaical enemy is one which boldly inpugns before
the whole Christian world, the civilization of our country. We
are charged, before the Bar of Nations, with being an inferior
people— necessarily inferior from a social system which, it is
falsely alleged, is inimical to the developement of moral power.
We are appealed to by every consideration which can influence
our pride, our patriotism & our manhood to vindicate our char-

---

to sustain and encourage southern literature. Among the seven members of the
committee were Wiley and Vance. *Report of the Superintendent of Common
Schools of North Carolina, for the Year 1862* (Raleigh, 1862), pp. 70-71 (cited
hereafter as *Report of Schools*); Raleigh *North Carolina Standard*, October 29, 1862.

[230] This law incorporated the Association for two years, but by act of February 5,
1863 it was extended for two more. *Public Laws of N. C., 1862-'63* adjourned session,
chap. 40.

[231] For the Literary Fund see p. 25, 115n. As governor, Vance was ex officio President of the Literary Board.

acter by diligent & ceaseless care in nourishing all the sources of inner national life, by keeping alive or rendering more & more efficient all the moral agencies of Society, & refusing to sacrifice for any illusive exigency of the moment the rights of freemen. If we will do this, building always on the Divine Law, & properly seeking Divine protection, we *never* can be conquered by an external power—for physical force can never overcome moral power which is in its nature eternal in duration & infinite in resources—External power may *wound*— it is the failing of inner life that causes *death*— these are very plain truths— yet in the confusion & weakness of the times many are in danger of being carried away by those old plausible errors which assume that the interests of freedom require its own destruction for the present. Your Excellency, called in the Providence of God, by an overwhelming popular vote, to preside over the destinies of a State most distinguished of all the Confederate sisters for promising elements of moral strength, cannot fail to see what an immensity of good may now be accomplished by the blessing of Heaven, by encouraging words from your high position— your fellow-citizens universally confide in your wisdom & honesty, & will respect your opinions; & while you are thus placed, behold the best interests now trembling in the balance in this glorious land of our birth; Other States boast of their materials resources, their great staples from a teeming soil, & of their commercial advantages: Nature, apparently more harsh, but really more generous to N. Carolina, locked up her material interests & gave the key to science. We could not be rich until we were morally great— & discovering this great truth a few years ago, every hill & valley, every mountain top & bog & swamp was lighted up with the cheerful radiance of a vast system of schools, & guided by these the iron tracks of commerce, & agricultural & mining enterprize were pervading the state— Most of all, in these Schools was, under God, created & enlarged that love for N. Carolina, that respect for her character, & that enthusiasm at the mention of her name which have made her sons the heroes of this war in every great battle from Bethel to the hills of Maryland—[232]

You cannot contemplate, without emotion, the possible drying up of the chief earthly source of so much good in the past & of such inestimable promise in the future to a State dear to you & to me as the place of our birth & the repository of the bones of our fathers— dear from the varied & beautiful scenery with which God has diversified its face, & the benignant climate in

---

[232] Bethel was the first battle of the war, fought near Yorktown on June 10, 1861; the last battle before this letter was in Maryland, at Sharpsburg on September 17, 1862. North Carolina soldiers were prominent in both battles.

which he has placed it—dear from the memory of past generations of free, modest & kindly men— dear to us on account of the sneers & slanders of its enemies, & for the battles we have fought in defence of its honor—

Please excuse the feeling with which I write & the length of a letter much longer than I intended when I began it— As I wrote I became impressed with a deep sense of the importance of the position which you now occupy— & ever feeling my own responsibility to God & to future generations I felt that I could not discharge my conscience by saying less than I have— No one can estimate the responsibilities of those now occupying influential positions in the Confederate States; & as the interests of education in N. Carolina have been partly committed to my care I am ever fearful that I shall not act up to the dignity & the wants of this great crisis— I do not pretend to think that I can enlighten you as to *your* duties.

My great concern is to use the position God has given me to maintain the right— You know as well as I do that every state always contains an element opposed to its true greatness: an element that would, on various plausibles pretexts, repress the elevation of the masses to preserve, in fact, a perpetual ascendancy for itself— This class will now be busy among us; & the people, led off from the real issue, by suggestions of necessity, may permit a deadly blow to be sruck at this future welfare before they know it—

Entertaining no doubt if *your* sentiments— Knowing that you understand the real dangers of the times, & that you belong to that class who would rather see equals in a free intelligent & prosperous population, than hold hereditery rule over a poor, ignorant & vicious people, I can freely call on you to utter, from your high place, sympathetic words of encouragement to the great cause of education in this State—[233] We cannot expect you to attend the coming meeting of our association— but may we not count on your sympathy & cooperation in our Counsels for the good of dear old North-Carolina?

[Raleigh]

[A. L. S. Governors' Papers (Vance),
   State Department of Archives and History, Raleigh.]

---

[233] In his message to the legislature, November 17, 1862, Vance reported the usual distribution to the schools, plus part of a back distribution, and added "There has been some disposition manifested to take this sum for war purposes. Should there really exist a *serious design* on the part of anyone to do this, which I hardly think probable, I earnestly hope you will promptly defeat it." *Legislative Documents, 1862-1863,* Document No. 1, p. 19.

From Jno. Thompson[234]

Thompsonville N. C.
Sep^t. 27 / 62

I have lately returned from a trip in an adjoining County[235] and have been informed of so many cases of men trying to avoid doing their duty to our common country under cover of the exemption Law— this as well as what I know in my own county has induced me to write you a few lines on this subject, not that I would presume to dictate to you, but believing that you cannot know the conduct of men in different Localities unless you were informed on the subject. I take the liberty to address you on this subject hoping that there might be some way to bring all such men to a sense of their duty and their interest in the great struggle now going on for the procurement of the Liberties of our oppressed and outraged people. I know some several men who are pretending to make Salt Petre for the Government and are claiming exemption from military duty on that account, and the whole company of six men dont make 12 lbs a month I know several men who are also claiming the same on account of age Some claim to be under 18 and some over 35 so as not to be subject to the conscript act and no measures have been instituted to correct these abuses I know also several Post Master who should be in the Army stout able bodied healthy men who are glorying in their exemption whose places could be as well or better filled by men too old for service. I know also several men who are pretending to carry on Government shops— Making shoes and guns & various other things who are no workman and have given large premiums to get employment to save them from the Army. "There is a Screw loose in the government Waggon some where" and it ought to be examined we want Patriotic men in office who will know their duty and perform it fearlessly and who are not Partizans or Speculators   •
There is the most Heartless specu [torn] going on in the prime necessaries of life, in Leather & shoes, in cotton Yarn and Domestic cloth, and many other articles, which the Poor are compelled to have or suffer, and it is high time our authorities had taken some action to regulate these things, this is, if not a military necessity at least a civil one and one of deep interest to many of our People.
I Hope that you will excuse me for these suggestions and would father say that you will find me always ready to aid in correcting

---

[234] John Thompson (1799-1881), one of large family of Scotch-Irish who descended from the pioneer John Thompson, who came to North Carolina about 1750.

[235] Thompsonville is in the southeast corner of Rockingham County, about equidistant from Caswell, Alamance, and Guilford. It is impossible to determine which adjoining county he may have had in mind, though his description of conditions probably fits Alamance better than either of the other two.

any abuse of law or privilege when called upon so far as I have
authority or may receive instructions to do so.

[Raleigh]

[A. L. S. Governors' Papers (Vance),
  State Department of Archives and History, Raleigh.]

From L. L. Polk [236]

Camp French Petersburg Va
Sept 27th 1862

I addressed you a letter about the 5th Inst. & it is probable you
did not receive it, I hope you did however, for I Can not, now,
trouble you with repetition of its contents.

Suffice it to say, that is contained a request of you,—to relieve
me, if consistent, from my present position. I did it, conscious of
the difficulties which attended it, & with a reluctance & embarrassment which I never experienced before in writing, or
in asking favors. And nothing, but the *annoying* & *disagreeable*
position in which I find myself placed, could have induced me to
write you on the subject. Since about that time I have been
suffering continuously & severely with rheumatism in my breast. I
am fearful that it will become permament, if I have to be so
much exposed through the winter, I cannot ask you to consider
my proposition through sympathy, nor to relieve me from the
service, for I expect to remain wherever my services are most
urgently demanded, I cannot now enumerate the causes which
conspire to render my position so very disagreeable, for I am
sorry to say that *great* dissatisfaction exists in our Reg[t]. & not
without cause.

---

[236] Leonidas LaFayette Polk (1837-1892), of Anson County, sergeant-major of the
Twenty-sixth North Carolina Regiment. Left an orphan at the age of fifteen, Polk
spent the year 1855-1856 at Davidson College, but returned to Anson County as a
farmer at the end of one year. He attained some local prominence, was elected to
the House of Commons in 1860, and again in 1864. In the meantime he had joined
the army and become sergeant-major in Vance's regiment, and when Vance left
the regiment to become governor Polk was chosen to present the sword which the
officers gave as a parting gift. But Polk was dissatisfied in the regiment and was
transferred, in February 1863, to the Forty-third Regiment, where he served as
second lieutenant until 1864, when he returned to the legislature. He was a Whig
who opposed secession until Lincoln's proclamation; after the war he became a
Democrat; still later a Populist. He represented Anson County in the Convention
of 1865; was the first commissioner of agriculture of North Carolina, 1877-1880; an
editor of the *Raleigh News* in 1880, when it was consolidated with the *Observer* to
form the *News and Observer,* a position he relinquished in 1881. In the eighties
Polk became an outstanding leader of the farmers' alliance movement, founded and
edited the *Progressive Farmer* in 1886, became vice-president of the National
Farmers' Alliance and Industrial Union in 1887, and its president two years later,
He died on the eve of the People's party convention in 1892, a few weeks before
he likely would have been nominated for president of the United States. Stuart
Noblin, *Leonidas LaFayette Polk* (Chapel Hill, 1949), especially chapter IV for
Polk's military experiences (cited hereafter as Noblin, *Polk*).

Should you favor & honor me with a favorable consideration, I shall exert myself to prove worthy of it, & no effort should be lacking to showing high appreciation of what I would consider, under existing circumstances, a high favor & honor.

I am with sentiments of very high esteem,

[Raleigh]

Ans[r]. Polk Serg[r]. Major of the 26th Reg. that I have no place in my gift at present It will give me great pleasure to serve him &c when I can. *An*

[A. L. S. Governors' Papers (Vance),
State Department of Archives and History, Raleigh.]

From E. A. Vogler[237]

Salem N C. Sep[t] 29th 1862

A few minutes ago, I read in the "Standard" Surgeon Gen E[d] Warren's appeal in behalf of our sick & wounded Soldiers in the Hospitals[238] It occurred to me that as there are a great many from this County sick in the hospitals at Winchester, Gordonsville, Richmond &c whom their friends & relations at home would gladly relieve & send many little necessaries of which they are now deprived, if they but had the chance of sending them with any assurance of their getting them, I would ask your Excellency what the chances would be of getting free transportation for such articles & perhaps occasionally for a person to go along if a quantity was gathered together.

Last year after the first battle of Manassas when so many of our brave boys were sick at Manassas, Thorough Fare & Front Royal Gov Clarke[239] gave me transportation for a Corps of Nurses & a lot of supplies which were forwarded from this place & subse-

---

[237] Elias Alexander Vogler (1825-1876), of Salem, jeweler, silversmith, merchant, and farmer who was long prominent in public life in the community. He was one of the earliest who concerned himself with assistance to families of needy volunteers; he often packed boxes at his own home and paid the freight to send the materials to soldiers in the army camps. He became the wheelhorse of the central committee of the county for the administration of relief, was the county agent for the distribution of salt among the population, and chairman of the relief organization. Raleigh *North Carolina Standard,* November 7, 1862, January 25, 1862, quoting the *Salem Press;* Charlotte *Western Democrat,* January 28, 1862; William Frank Entrekin, Jr., "Poor Relief in North Carolina in the Confederacy," (unpublished M. A. thesis, Duke University, 1947), pp. 121-124 (cited hereafter as Entrekin, "N. C. Poor Relief"); Moravian Records, Wachovia Historical Society, Winston-Salem, N. C.

[238] For Warren see p. 159, 647n. Just appointed surgeon general, Warren in a letter to the *Standard* appealed for goods for the sick and wounded, claiming there were more than 2,000 North Carolina soldiers in Richmond hospitals alone, and that by "universal consent" the number elsewhere was very large. He appealed to the generosity and humanity of the citizens and recommended the formation of relief associations in each county for the regular collection of relief supplies. An agency for the distribution of donations was already provided in Richmond by Governor Vance. The letter is in the Raleigh *North Carolina Standard,* October 1, 1862.

[239] See p. 133, 529n.

quently I forwarded several hundred Boxes of Clothing, Medicine Provision &c which were gathered together & packed at my House The County Court having ordered me for the time being to forward such necessaries at County expense. We shall have no county Court now until December without one is especially ordered to convene.

As Presd^t. of a "Board of Sustenance" my County has given me unlimited authority to provide & furnish the families with provisions &c when & where necessary, but do not feel at liberty to extend that to sending supplies to our sick at Hospitals.

If we had Court I believe it would be given as our Magistrates have been acting very liberally in supplying the brave men who have gone forth to fight our battles & up to this time I have disbursed between $25 & 30,000⁰⁰ for their benefit & those they left behind.

Fortunately some months ago, anticipating a rise & scarcity in the necessaries of life I purchased a considerable supply of Flour & Bacon & now am selling to such as need & are able to pay, or furnishing gratuitously to those who cannot- of all who now are, or have died in service-

Having thus daily & hourly I might say constant intercourse with the families of our soldiers from this section I feel satisfied that they would rejoice if such an opportunity was offered them, & would gladly embrace it & send many things to their fathers, brothers, or sons, that would gladden their hearts-prove a benefit to them & the Country- by sooner enabling them to recover & recruit their health- & perhaps save many a valuable life-
[Raleigh]
[A. L. S. Governors' Papers (Vance),
   State Department of Archives and History, Raleigh.]

From W. D. Pender [240]

Camp at Bunker Hill Va
Septr 29th 1862

I have the honor to ask that if there is any thing in your power that can be done to expedite the carrying out the Conscript Law that you will help some of us out. My officers went on just after the battles before Richmond they have not yet returned & the last I heard from them they did not know when could unless they came without the men. I have not only needed the conscripts, but the officers sent after them, I have had to fight in several battles with less than 300 men in my Brigade & without an officer in some of the companies. Two of my Regts have frequently been with only one & two Captains. My officers were amongst the lines [?] in their application for men.

---

[240] See p. 170, 26n.

One other subject I feel constrained to write your excellency about; the unauthorized absentees.[241] I know it to be a difficult question to deal with but if you could organize the civil officers of the state to take up any officer or men at home without leave & retain him in custody until his case could be reported I think it might be of some service. There are at least 500 men & officers & too large a proportion of the latter absent without any excuse or reason from my Brigade alone. My dear sir you can scarcely image what a scarcity of material we have had to work with. Help us if you can.

[on reverse]

Ans[s] that I am using every effort to get the conscripts in & orders have issued to the militia to arrest all absentees—Everything shall be done that is in my power &c

Z.B.V.

[Raleigh]
[A. L. S. Governors' Papers (Vance),
State Department of Archives and History, Raleigh.]

From John P. Nissen[242]

Waughtown N C   Sept 29. 1862

Recently I learned that some insiduous sneaking, Scoundrel had written a letter to Gov Clark [243] assailing me in a most false & slanderous manner impeaching my loyalty as a Southern man,

---

[241] Straggling and desertion had increased very markedly and very alarmingly during General Lee's invasion of Maryland in September 1862. The nature, causes, and extent are described in Douglas Southall Freeman, *R. E. Lee. A Biography*, 4 vols. (New York, 1934-1935), II, 358-359.

[242] John Philip Nissen (1813-1874), of Forsythe County, founder of a prominent wagon-making industry at Waughtown, near Salem, and a member of the House of Commons in 1862 and 1870. He and J. J. Nissen had government contracts for wagons and horseshoes. In the election of 1862, John P. Nissen was a candidate on the Vance ticket, having been a Union man in the 1860 crisis, and during the campaign in 1862 the Winston *Western Sentinel* reported one of his speeches to be for Union still and that Nissen "*declared himself in favor of a compromise with the North and in favor of Reconstruction upon honorable principles.* He said that the old government was good enough for him; that it had never deprived him of any just right &c." The *Sentinel* pointed out that Nissen was for Vance and that all men of similar sentiments were for Vance, though it admitted that many true men were for him also. The Winston *Western Sentinel*, quoted in Charlotte *Western Democrat*, July 29, 1862; Connor, *N. C. Manual*, p. 605; Hamilton, *History of N. C.*, IV, 60-61. W. J. Yates, editor of the Charlotte *Western Democrat*, wrote that Nissen and Keener, the other Forsythe representative elected on the Vance ticket, were tories, and he quoted Rev. Mr. Eberhardt, an Episcopal minister of Charlotte, as saying that Nissen was "as vile a traitor as there is anywhere" and that he had openly denounced the southern government and rejoiced when the south lost a battle. William J. Yates (?) to Edward J. Hale, August 18, 1862, Edward Jones Hale Papers, State Department of Archives and History, Raleigh, N. C. (cited hereafter as Hale Papers). The signature of the letter is marred, but it is from Charlotte and the handwriting is clearly that of Yates, as shown by other signed letters from him in the same collection.

[243] See p. 133, 529n.

and insisting that I should forthwith be deprived of the government Contract which myself & Son have to furnish wagons &c, for the Army. On hearing of this I at once went to Raleigh to see your Excellency & get the name of the writer but finding you absent from the city, I called on Genl Martin [244] who handed me a copy of the letter without any name which he had received from the Governor dated August the 11th, hence he was unable to furnish me with the authors name. I pronounced the charges contained in it of disloyalty to the South as a wicked and malicious falsehood in every Shape, Shade & manner & I desire to get the authors name, I have no doubt it was one of the miserable lying dogs who were assailing me while a candidate last summer and whom I denounced all over the county of Forsythe as unprincipaled & lying Scoundrels. & in which I was sustained by a majority of upwards of *five hundred* [245] of my fellow citizens, Some one of these miserable whipped dogs, smarting under the castigation which I gave them & the triumphant manner in which I have been Sustained, by as inteligent & as patriotic a people as the South contains, now secretly injuring my private business, & for this purpose writes this false & lying letter to Gov Clark.

I feel it due to my character and to my constituents whom he assails in assailing me, to respect fully ask of you the kindness to furnish me with the writers name & a copy of the letter, which I presume is on file in your office
[Raleigh]
[on reverse]
Ansʳ that no letters have been written me- those shown me by Gov Clark were written in a disguised hand & not signed-
Am glad to see his emphatic denial of such a base charge &c

Z.B.V.

[A. L. S. Governors' Papers (Vance),
State Department of Archives and History, Raleigh.]

From R. M. Henry [246]

Camp Near Zollicoffer [247] E Tenn
Sept 30, 1862

When I last saw you in Asheville you authorised me to bring

---

[244] See p. 113, 447n. There are no letters of such character now in the Clark Letter Book or in Governors' Papers (Clark).

[245] The vote for Nissen and Keener was 1020 and 1021 respectively, over opponents who received 518 and 496 votes. *Fayetteville Observer,* August 11, 1862.

[246] See p. 222, 187n. At the time of this letter Henry was captain of company D in the Sixty-second North Carolina Regiment.

[247] Also known as Bluff City. Three companies of the Sixty-second Regiment were detached in August 1862 from the headquarters at Haynesville (now Johnson City) and sent to Zollicoffer to guard the bridge spanning the Holston River and to prevent railroad communication from being disturbed. Clark, *N. C. Regts.,* III, 517-518.

to the Camp of Instruction, C. W. L. Edney [248] as a drill Master for my Company, promising to make the appointment as soon as you took your seat. I according informed Col Edney of what had taken place between us, and he came on to the camp on the 10th Inst, and has been ingrossed in drilling my company ever since. If you have made the appointment and forwarded it to me, I have failed to receive it. It may be that you have over looked it in the hurry of business, or forgotten it. Col Edney is here and is manifesting some uneasiness about the matter, unnecessarily as I think. You will oblige me and him by transmitting his appointment, at your earliest convenience. I also wrote to you transmitting a Recommendation for Henry H Turpin [249] to be appointed drill Master for Captain John Turpins [250] Company which I have not heard from.

I understand that an officer has been sent out to Knoxville, with the view of disbanding this Regt. and taking them on as Conscripts, Col Love [251] has been in Richmond to the War Department and procured a Recognition of the Regt and the War Department has accepted of it and numbered it 62nd. North Carolina Troops. Now Governor we in this Regt being from Western N. C. [252] and many of us having been your constant supporters for favor and position, think that you are nearly immortal [?] in the State, or at least that you can do a thing or two for or against us, and the most of the Regt being part of that large

[248] C. W. L. Edney was a native of Tennessee, born in 1810, who was a painter by trade and lived in Asheville. *Census,* Buncombe County, 1860.

[249] Henry A. Turpin, of Haywood County, a private in company C of the Sixty-second North Carolina Regiment. He enlisted on July 14, 1862, the date of the organization of the regiment, and was later transferred. Moore, *N. C. Roster,* III, 723.

[250] John Turpin, also of Haywood County, was captain of company C of the Sixty-second North Carolina Regiment. He was later captured and held prisoner on Johnson's Island. Moore, *N. C. Roster,* III, 721; Clark, *N. C. Regts.,* III, 515, IV, 700, 711.

[251] Robert Gustavus Adolphus Love (1827-1880), of Haywood County. He was educated at Washington College, Vance's old school in East Tennessee, was active in the political affairs of his county, and in 1858 became colonel of the militia. He was a member of the House of Commons from 1848 to 1854, and so served with Vance in his last term. In June 1861 he became lieutenant-colonel of the Sixteenth North Carolina Regiment, but he was not re-elected when the regiment was reorganized on April 26, 1862, possibly because of bad health which plagued him throughout his army days. On July 11, 1862, he was elected colonel of the Sixty-second; illness continued to cause frequent absences from his command, and he eventually resigned. General Frazer wrote in his report of the surrender of Cumberland Gap that "The Colonel (Love) was absent and soon after resigned and became an open advocate of reunion in his county." This is indignantly denied and refuted by the historian of the Sixty-second Regiment in Clark, *N. C. Regts.,* III, 525. See also Allen, *Centennial of Haywood,* pp. 68-69; Moore, *N. C. Roster,* I, 1, III, 716; Clark, *N. C. Regts.,* I, 751, III, 515, 525, IV, 137, 151; Connor, *N. C. Manual,* p. 647.

[252] There were ten companies in the regiment: three were from Haywood, two from Jackson, and two from Transylvania, with one each from Clay, Macon, and Rutherford. Moore, *N. C. Roster,* III, 716-741.

majority that you beat Avery [253] Coleman [254] and Johnston [255], look to you to use your power and influence to let us go and fight in this Regt, and not to suffer us to be disbanded, on account of the political sins of one or two of the Field officers,[256] whose political conceptions a large majority of the Regt hates as much as you do. These things we are satisfied would not have any influence with you if the public service required you to disband the Regt. and only throughed in by me for the purpose of letting off a little of the wroth that is within me to an old friend, we want you to keep us as we are if within your power, and especially as officers, and positions are hard to get for some of us that is unwilling to bow the knee to Democracy and original Secession.[257]

You will confer a great favor on an old and constant friend by making the appointment, above asked for and forwarding them to me at this office.
[Raleigh]
[A. L. S. Governors' Papers (Vance),
State Department of Archives and History, Raleigh.]

From R. C. Puryear [258]

Huntsville N C Sep ? 1862

My object in addressing you this note to ascertain if cirtain men in this county can be detached to work on an iron forge.

---

[253] See p. 55, 201n. Vance defeated him for Congress in 1858.

[254] See p. 19, 91n. Vance beat him for Congress in 1859.

[255] William Johnston (1817-1896), of Mecklenburg County, whom Vance defeated for the governorship in 1862. He was born in Lincoln (now Gaston) County, graduated at the University of North Carolina in 1840, studied law and settled in Charlotte in 1842, where he lived the rest of his life. He was president of the Charlotte and South Carolina Railroad Company and began in 1859 to construct the Atlantic, Tennessee and Ohio Railroad, having built to Statesville from Charlotte when the war interferred. He was a member of the Convention of 1861, commissary general of North Carolina with the rank of colonel, May to September 1861 and, after the war, headed the Charlotte, Columbia and Augusta Railroad, and a number of other banking and commercial enterprises. Johnston was a Whig in politics until 1861, coming to favor secession because he thought it could be peacefully achieved. His dignity, ability, polish, and sincerity were universally recognized, but he lacked the art of appeal to the multitude. Except for serving as mayor of Charlotte for five years he held no political office after 1861. Sherrill, *Lincoln County*, pp. 271-273; McCormick, *Personnel*, pp. 48-49; A. D. Smith, *Western North Carolina*. Historical and Biographical (Charlotte, 1890), pp. 211-221 (cited hereafter as Smith, *Western N. C.*); Alexander, *Mecklenburg County*, pp. 147-148.

[256] Henry probably refers especially to the major of the Sixty-second Regiment, B. G. McDowell of Macon County, later the lieutenant colonel. He was an ardent Democrat and a warm admirer of David Coleman, Vance's congressional opponent, in whose regiment he had first enlisted. His vehement support of original secession was well known. Clark, *N. C. Regts.*, III, 517.

[257] Henry, in the crisis of 1860-1861, had taken a leading part in opposition to secession in his home county. He spoke at a number of Union meetings, opposing secession resolutions and denouncing Democrats. Perhaps such memories explain the fact that he became a Republican after the war. Raleigh *North Carolina Standard*, January 8, 1861.

[258] Richard Clauselle Puryear (1801-1867), of Surry County. He was a native of

Capt W W Long James Myers and Henry Snow commenced building a forge some time in June and employed and depended mostly on hands now subject to the Conscript law These hands are ordered off and unless some of them can be detailed the forge will have to stop for want of hands

This forge will be of great benefit to this section of County, Iron is scarce and it is difficult to obtain a supply for farming purposes. The gentlemen engaged in erecting the forge Messrs Long Myers and Snow have not engaged in this enterprize for the purpose of Keeping hands from the service of the Country They are all brave and loyal men and would not do anything for their own benefit which would injure the cause of the South.

These gentlemen desire the following men detailed to work in their forge in Yadkin County N C Towit Calvin Norman Thomas Norman Henderson Spillman Thomas Spillman Abraham Joyner John Carter John Hinshaw and Henry Price & P. H. Fortner.[259]

Will you do me the favor to address Capt W W Long Huntsville N C upon the subject and inform him what can be done.

[Raleigh]

[A. L. S. Governors' Papers (Vance),
State Department of Archives and History, Raleigh.]

To Jno. M. Worth [260]

STATE OF NORTH CAROLINA
EXECUTIVE DEPARTMENT
Raleigh- Oct. 1st. 1862

Your monthly report is rec.d It is satisfactory in all respects, except the amount produced. In the present emergency it is desirable to have salt without regard to expense. The vast amount

---

Virginia but had become a planter near Huntsville, where he was a magistrate, colonel of the militia, and the representative of Surrry County in the House of Commons in 1838, 1844, 1846, and 1852, and in the State Senate in 1840. In 1853 he was elected to the United States House of Representatives as a Whig, and served until 1857. Subsequently he was a delegate to the Provisional Congress of the Confederacy in 1861, and to the Peace Congress in Philadelphia in 1866. He died at "Shallow Ford" in 1867. *Biog. Dir. of Am. Cong.*, pp. 1709-1710; Connor, *N. C. Manual*, pp. 816, 934-935.

[259] Only three of these men appear to have been in the army at any time. Thomas Norman of Yadkin County was in company A of the Forty-fourth North Carolina Regiment, but was transferred to company I of the Twenty-eighth, a Yadkin County company. He enlisted on February 13, 1862. Moore, *N. C. Roster*, II, 467, III, 230. Abraham Joyner enlisted on October 14, 1863 in company I of the Twenty-eighth North Carolina Regiment, Moore, *N. C. Roster*, II, 467. John A. Carter, also of Yadkin County, enlisted on June 18, 1861, in company F of the Twenty-eighth and was discharged on January 12, 1862. He enlisted again on May 2, 1862 in company A of the Fifty-fourth Regiment, and is listed as missing July 20, 1864. Moore, *N. C. Roster*, II, 454, III, 533.

[260] See p. 206, 144n, 145n.

of meat will be lost without the salt renders the price of it a small consideration. If therefore it be possible for you to increase the number of your Kettles to the extent of 1500 or 2000 bushels per day, it is my desire you should do so at once.

I can furnish conscript labor, any amount of it. I suppose the yellow fever will hardly trouble you on the coast. Let me beg you my dear Sir, to push forward this matter with the greatest possible rapidity. I will assist and sustain you to the utmost of my ability.

[Vance Letter Book, 1862-1863,
State Department of Archives and History, Raleigh.]

From E. W. Johns [261]

CONFEDERATE STATES OF AMERICA
Purveyor's Office
Richmond Va.,
October 3.^{d} 1862

I have the honor to represent that a large amount of Alcoholic stimulants are indispensable in the treatment of the sick & wounded of the Army, and that the duty of providing the said stimulants is devolved upon this Department.

Of the required amount according to an estimate made in this office, a considerable portion has been contracted for, but still remains a large quantity to be provided.

I therefore respectfully request that authority be granted to this Department, to contract for the manufacture & delivery of as much Whiskey & Alcohol as may be required, for the Army of Confederate States for Medical & Hospital purposes, and that the parties contracting for the delivery of the said Whiskey and Alcohol to this Department for the purpose aforesaid be exempted from the operation of any statute [262] or order, prohibiting the distillation of grain in the State of North Carolina [263]
[Raleigh]
[Vance Letter Book, 1862-1863,
State Department of Archives and History, Raleigh.]

---

[261] E. W. Johns was medical purveyor in the office of the surgeon general of the Confederacy, and was primarily concerned with obtaining medical supplies. Until February 25, 1863, senior surgeons, as medical directors of commands, reported directly to him and obtained supplies directly from his office; after this date reports were made direct to the office of the surgeon general, and instructions from medical purveyors emanated from his office. General Orders, No. 23, *O. R.*, Ser. IV, Vol. II, 410-411.

[262] The Convention, on February 21, 1862, had adopted an ordinance which prohibited the distillation of spirituous liquors from grains, the prohibition to last until January 1, 1863. *Convention Ordinances*, 3 session, No. 24. See p. 183, 75n.

[263] Through an aide Vance replied to this request by calling attention to the prohibition of the Convention, by stating that he had no authority to disregard such an ordinance, and by suggesting that brandy might make a good substitute. George Little to Dr. E. W. Johns, October 14, 1862, Vance Letter Book.

From R. D. Lunsford [264]

Camp Near Drewrys Bluff V. A.
Oct. 5th 1862

It is for the purpose of gaining information that I take the liberty of writing a very short letter to day. You will oblige me very much by informing me whether or not the conscripts from North Carolina are entitled to a bounty from the State or not.[265] And if so I would like very mutch to no when they can get it. My object for making the above inqirys is to be able to give my men correct & satisfactory information when they ask it of me. I have some conscripts in my company and they are about out of cloths & Shoes & if they are to have a bounty from the State I would be very glad if they could get it soon. So as to enable them to buy them some Shoes & Clotheing for unless they buy them some clotheing I do not think they will get any soon If I am alowed to Judge the future by the past. You will oblige me very mutch by taking notice of this as soon as possible.

[Raleigh]
[A. L. S. Governors' Papers (Vance),
State Department of Archives and History, Raleigh.]

From S. D. Thurston [266]

H.[d] Qrs. 3[d] N. C. State Troops
Bivouac near Winchester Va.
Oct 5/62

In accordance with the unanimous desire of my officers & men I beg leave Sir to return to you the colors entrusted to us by the State of N. Carolina at the commencement of this contest. When

---

[264] Robert Darius Lunsford, of Johnston County, captain of company C in the Fiftieth North Carolina Regiment. Clark, *N. C. Regts.*, III, 161, 202; Moore, *N. C. Roster*, III, 431.

[265] North Carolina bounties were authorized by two acts of the legislature in May 1861, but the payment was then, of course, confined to volunteers. The Convention, on February 10, 1862, extended the bounty to those who volunteered directly to the Confederacy. The Conscription Act had the effect of stimulating enlistment, especially as enlistment before conscription carried the bounty with it. The state bounty was $50. *Convention Ordinances*, 2 session, No. 16 and No. 23.

[266] Stephen D. Thurston, a physician of Brunswick County and major of the Third North Carolina Regiment. He began as captain of company B and rose to become colonel, but at the time of this letter had led the regiment upon the wounding of his superior officers in the recent battle of Sharpsburg. Before the secession of North Carolina he had led the "Smithfield Guards" in obtaining the surrender of Fort Caswell, but his action had been disavowed by Governor Ellis. On October 5, 1862, Thurston wrote a long letter to the newspapers in which he set forth the achievements of the Third North Carolina at Sharpsburg, and attached a long list of its casualties. He served throughout the war and was several times severely wounded. After the war he practiced medicine in Dallas, Texas for many years. Clark, *N. C. Regts.*, I, 178, 190, 227, V, 24, 25; Moore, *N. C. Roster*, I, 80, 85; Sprunt, *Chronicles*, pp. 232-235; Raleigh *North Carolina Standard*, October 31, 1862.

the Regt. was first attached to the "Army before Richmond" the Confederate "Battle Flag" was issued to it and all other colors ordered to be discarded.

Previous to the Battles in M.ᵈ [267] however, our Colonel,[268] at the request of both officers & men once more unfurled our No. Ca. colors, a special guard was detailed for its defence, & in addition to our "Battle Flag" carried this into the engagement at Sharpsburg. This is the only one in which it has ever been, & it bears evidence in its folds that it was in the very thickest, while our list of killed and wounded shows that we did not fail in our trust.

Two of its bearers were killed & as many seriously wounded, yet not once were its folds allowed to touch the ground, we have the satisfaction of knowing that it never left the field, until we received orders from those in authority- to withdraw.

We have flattered ourselves that it is worthy of a place among the relics of which the State may be proud & we send it to you Sir desiring that it may be kept ever sacred to the memory of those who fell upon the battlefield of Sharpsburg while engaged in the defence of home & liberty.

I entrust the colors together with a report of the engagement, & a list of casualities, to Lt. John Van Bokkelen:[269]

And in the name of my officers & men am Sir

[Raleigh]
[Vance Letter Book, 1862-1863,
State Department of Archives and History, Raleigh.]

From J. M. Worth [270]

Asheboro N C
Oct. 7ᵗʰ 1862

Yours of Oct. 1ˢᵗ was forwarded to me from Wilmington, I regret to report that the State Salt Works are almost entirely suspended. On the 22ᵈ of Sept. my son,[271] a youth of 17 was attacked

---

[267] i. e., battles of the Sharpsburg campaign in Maryland, September, 1862.

[268] The colonel was William Lord DeRosset (1832-1910), of Wilmington, who was severely wounded at Sharpsburg and as a consequence had to retire from the army a year later. He was a merchant in Wilmington after the war. Sprunt, *Chronicles,* pp. 296-297; Grant, *Alumni History,* p. 162; Moore, *N. C. Roster,* I, 80.

[269] John F. S. VanBokkelen (1842-1863), of Wilmington, who left Harvard in 1861 to become second lieutenant in company D of the Third North Carolina Regiment, of which he was afterwards captain. He died in 1863 of wounds received at the battle of Chancellorsville. "He was universally popular and almost idolized by his own men. He . . . was full of youthful ardor, intelligent, and with an acute conception of his duties and an indomitable energy in pursuing the line of conduct which a discriminating judgment dictated to him." Sprunt, *Chronicles,* pp. 363-364. Van Bokkelen was acting adjutant and reported that of 520 carried into action only 190 could be accounted for. This figure was greater than that reported by the division commander. Clark, *N. C. Regts.,* I, 226-227.

[270] See p. 206, 144n.

[271] James Madison Worth (1855-1862), who died in Fayetteville of yellow fever contracted in Wilmington. *Fayetteville Observer,* September 29, 1862.

with Fever. By the advice of Doct. Dixon[272] I left with him on a boat for Fayetteville. His case proved to be yellow fever and was fatal on the 5th day.[273] I was almost his sole nurse, and was by him night & day. I had been all this time exposed at Wilmington and altogether left me Sick & unable for business- I came home and am now just able for business. My brother T. C. Worth[274] remained in Wilmington, and with the Agents that I had employed did all they could to keep the work going. I would not have left but for the reason given. I inclose you a letter from my brother, which shows the conditions of things. I will do all I can to increase the work, and will be busy, while the fever remains, in looking up materials for the work. All the supplies used at the works have to pass through Wilmington and the salt shipped from there- Breaking up was a positive necessity.[275]
[Raleigh]
[Vance Letter Book, 1862-1863,
 State Department of Archives and History, Raleigh.]

From Rufus Barringer [276]

Martinsburg Va
Oct. 7, 1862

As a citizen of the State I deem it my duty to call your attention to the condition of this Regt.—which has cost her treasury

---

[272] Dr. James H. Dickson (1803-1862), a prominent Wilmington physician, twice president of the North Carolina Medical Society (1854 and 1855) and the president of the first Board of Medical Examiners of North Carolina. He was a victim of the fever in the same week that young Worth died. Sprunt, *Chronicles*, pp. 284-286; Raleigh *North Carolina Standard*, May 15, 1861; *Medical Transactions*, 1859, p. 15.

[273] That is, the fifth day of the fever; he died September 27. Upon his death the Fayetteville authorities suspended all intercourse between Wilmington and Fayetteville and instituted regulations of a strict sanitary nature. *Fayetteville Observer*, September 29, 1862.

[274] Thomas Clarkson Worth (1818-1862), who operated the Cape Fear Steamboat Company running between Fayetteville and Wilmington. He was also a victim of the yellow fever epidemic, dying on November 1, 1862. He was a partner of his brother, Barzillai Gardner Worth, in a shipping and commission business in Wilmington from 1853 until his death. Another brother, Joseph Addison Worth (1820-1893) was a merchant in Fayetteville. Samuel A'Court Ashe, "Barzillai Gardner Worth," and "Joseph Addison Worth," Ashe, *Biog. Hist. of N. C.*, III, 461-468.

[275] For the extent of the epidemic see Vance to Worth, October 10, 1862, p. 255, 304n.

[276] Rufus Barringer (1821-1895), of Cabarrus County, then captain of company F in the Ninth North Carolina Regiment (first cavalry). He attended Sugar Creek Academy, graduated from the University of North Carolina in 1842; studied law under his brother, D. M. Barringer, and Chief Justice Pearson at Richmond Hill, in Yadkin County. He was elected to the House of Commons in 1848 principally to secure a charter for the Charlotte and Danville railroad project, and was elected to the State Senate in 1850. In both bodies he was an ardent Whig; he was a presidential elector on the Bell and Everett ticket in 1860, and so was identified with Vance's party. He raised a company of cavalry in May of 1861 and rose, successively through all the grades, to brigadier general. In this capacity he served throughout

so much money & to which her people have heretofore looked with so much pride.

Of over 900 men belonging to it, not over 300 have for several weeks been on duty- Of over 1500 or 1600 horses purchased, not over 650 can now be found or accounted for- & of them not over 300 are fit for service- & they poor- many with Sore backs- & generally feeble. Of the large number of saddles, bridles, army & other equipments, many have been lost or thrown away- Up to six weeks ago, we had a large supply of cooking utensils, tools &c &c. We are now without anything of the kind. The men are nearly naked, without any adequate provision ahead against winter as far as I can learn. They have been badly fed all summer and Fall- especially when on marches & picket duty- The moral character of the Regt. is going down very rapidly & it will soon be worthless- unless some very decided steps are taken to arrest the present downward course of things-

It is for your Excellency to decide what should be done in a matter that so deeply concerns the public service & the interests of N. C. I only ask for one that the truth of these allegations may be promptly enquired into- Great blame attaches somewhere- The service we have done has been of an irregular & annoying kind, but not severe or exhausting - either to the men or horses.[277] I have no hesitation in saying that I, with many other officers, think the chief responsibility rests with the Col [278] Commanding

---

the war until his capture on the retreat to Appomattox, April 3, 1865. After the war he moved to Charlotte and practiced law in association with James W. Osborne, became a Republican, was a member of the Convention of 1875, was nominated by his party for lieutenant governor in 1880, but in 1888 voted for the Cleveland electors. E. T. Cansler, "Rufus Barringer," Ashe, *Biog. Hist. of N. C.*, I, 116-124.

[277] Recent service in the Maryland campaign had included almost daily contests with Federal cavalry before the engagements at Harpers Ferry and Sharpsburg in September. At Sharpsburg the brigade was cut off from the regular ford and had to seek a blind crossing which Barringer described as an experience "worse than fighting." Once afterwards the Federals had crossed the river and attacked their lines at Martinsburg, but had been driven off. Barringer in Clark, *N. C. Regts.*, I, 421.

[278] The colonel of the regiment at this time was Lawrence S. Baker, of Gates County. The first colonel had been Robert Ransom, but he was transferred to the infantry and promoted. Baker was a graduate of West Point in 1851, resigned from the army in 1861 and went to South Carolina, but became colonel of the Ninth North Carolina on April 3, 1862. In 1863 he was wounded and "permanently disabled for the field, and afterwards transferred to another branch of the service." In the last days of the war he returned to service and commanded the first Junior Reserves, with headquarters at Goldsboro. After the war he was a farmer and railroad agent for the Seaboard and Roanoke, and lived in Suffolk until his death in 1907. Ellsworth Eliot, Jr., *West Point in the Confederacy* (New York, 1941), p. 296 (cited hereafter as Eliot, *West Point in Conf.*); Clark, *N. C. Regts.*, I, 417, 425, 484, III, 464-465, IV, 11, 39, V, 269-284; Moore, *N. C. Roster*, I, 305; Cullum, *Biog. Register*, II, 471. Barringer's own history of the ninth regiment in Clark, *N. C. Regts.*, 417-443 does not mention the charges against Colonel Baker which he makes in this letter.

& his Q^r Master [279] & Commissary.[280] Col Baker has been warned by myself & others that the Regt. was fast going to ruin- but all to no purpose. He has relapsed into a former habit of hard drinking- my own self respect, duty to my country & justice to my men all demand that I should remain silent no longer. I bring the matter to the attention of your Excellency- unofficially- but with the expectation that you will use my name in any way in relation thereto that the public interests may require, I can only say in defence of Col Baker that he complains a good deal of Genl. Hampton [281] (Brigade Commander) but I do not think the difficulty lies in that quarter- It is due to myself & men to say that *we* have not lost the public property entrusted to us (excepting cooking utensils, tools &c through the mismanagement of others) I still have all my horses excepting a few that have died- 7 sold & 3 turned over to the QrMaster- So of my arms &c &c. But of the 89 horses belonging to my Co only some 45 are at all fit for service- the remaining 44 being reduced to skin and bones for the want of food- a Supply of shoes & other necessary articles for the Qr Mrs. department.

Regretting the necessity that prompts this communication, I am truly Your obt. Servt.[282]

[Raleigh]

[Vance Letter Book, 1862-1863,
State Department of Archives and History, Raleigh.]

To the Sheriff of Wake County [283]

State of North Carolina
Executive Department,
Raleigh, Oct. 8, 1862.

To the Sheriff of Wake County . . . Greeting

Whereas I have been officially notified that a vacancy has occured in the representation of said County, in the House of Com-

---

[279] John B. Neal, of Hertford County, originally second lieutenant in company I, but promoted captain and then major in the quartermaster's department. Moore, *N. C. Roster*, I, 335.

[280] Marcus D. L. McLeod, of Mecklenburg County, first lieutenant and captain of company C, and John W. Primrose, of Craven County, a private who was promoted to second sergeant and detailed to the commissary, were the commissaries of the Ninth Regiment. Clark, *N. C. Regts.*, I, 485; Moore, *N. C. Roster*, I, 313, 334.

[281] Wade Hampton (1818-1902), South Carolina legislator, governor, United States Senator, and planter, who became brigade commander under General J. E. B. Stuart on July 28, 1862. There were four other regiments in Hampton's brigade, but no other one was from North Carolina. Clark, *N. C. Regts.*, I, 420; J. Harold Easterby, "Wade Hampton," *Dict. of Am. Biog.*, VII, 213-215.

[282] Vance sent this letter to the Secretary of War with the remarks that he thought the blame for "the obvious and mortifying" failure of the regiment must rest with its officers, and that "No indulgence whatever is due to a man whose habits are such as Col Baker's are described to be." Vance to G. W. Randolph, October 14, 1862, Vance Letter Book.

[283] W. H. High was Sheriff of Wake County.

mons of the next General Assembly by reason of the death of Henry Watkins Miller,[284] one of the members elect in the last August election: Now, therefore, I, ZEBULON B. VANCE, Governor of the State of North-Carolina, do hereby command that an election be held according to law on THURSDAY, the 23rd day of October, A.D., 1862, for the purpose of filling said vacancy.[285]

In witness whereof, Z. B. Vance, our Governor, hath signed these presents, and caused the Great Seal of the State to be affixed.

Done at our City of Raleigh, on the 8th day of October, in the year of our Lord one thousand eight hundred and sixty two & in the eighty-seventh year of our Independence.
By the Governor:
    R. H. Battle, Jr.,
        Private Secretary.
[The *North Carolina Standard,*
  Raleigh, Oct. 14, 1862.
Vance Letter Book, 1862-1863,
State Department of Archives and History, Raleigh.]

To Maj. Mallett[286]
STATE OF NORTH CAROLINA
EXECUTIVE DEPARTMENT
Raleigh Oct. 10th 1862

Complaints are made to me every day that the men are not allowed to select their regiments- This is in violation of Gen. Martin's orders,[287] and is producing the greatest dissatisfaction. I thought it so important that I mentioned the matter to the President when in Richmond, he approved the suggestion & said it might be done.

---

[284] See p. 148, 604n.

[285] Very little time was provided for canvassing between this call for an election and the date set for voting. This was because of Vance's hope for a special session of the legislature at least two weeks before its regular date of November 17, 1862. According to a convention ordinance, soldiers could vote on the Thursday preceding the election at home. Returning officers were required to take the votes of qualified soldiers if they were received within twenty days after they were cast, and said returning officers were forbidden to make up their returns until the twenty days were passed. This meant that soldiers would vote in this special election on October 16, but no official return could be made before November 6. But Vance wished the legislature to meet on November 3, hence the haste. The special session was not forthcoming, however, as the Council of State provided no quorum when Vance attempted to secure its necessary authorization for a special session. See p. 197, 118n. Daniel Gould Fowle was elected to take Miller's place. *Convention Ordinances,* 4 session, No. 14 (May 8, 1862); Raleigh *North Carolina Standard,* October 14, 1862.

[286] See p. 175, 44n.

[287] See p. 186, 83n. The order, dated September 9, 1862, stated that men coming to camps "will be allowed to select the infantry regiments they wish to join, and unless full they will be assigned accordingly." *O. R.,* Ser I, Vol. XVII, 754.

I hope therefore you will do so in future. The men come up relying on the published order of Gen. Martin, & it is an outrage to deceive them in this way. I desire to sustain the Conft. Govt. with all my power, but certainly don't intend to assist it in duping the soldiers in defiance of its own published orders.
[Raleigh]
[Vance Letter Book, 1862-1863,
  Copy in Governors' Papers (Vance),
  State Department of Archives and History, Raleigh.]

From Jas. C. McRae [288]

Head Quarters
Camp Holmes, Oct. 10th 1862

Your letter of today to Major Mallett [289] has been handed to me as Commandant of the Camp in his absence. In reply I have the honor to transmit to you a copy of Telegram received from the Secretary of War dated Oct. 3d which directs Major Mallett to send all conscripts to Genl French [290] at Petersburg to fill up the Brigades from N. C. under his command. The Commandant of this Post has always been anxious to gratify the conscripts by allowing them the choice of Regts, but in some instances Regts. have already been filled and in others the authorities have deemed it of the highest importance to reinforce with conscripts certain Regts: first- such seems at present to be the case.

The Secretary deems it of vital importance to strengthen immediately the commands in and near Petersburg.

The Conscripts are allowed to choose any Regt. in Genl French's command, as the Commandant here is directed to send *all* to that command for the present, he is allowing the men choice of Regts as far as practicable. The undersigned feels no hesitation in expressing the great desire of Major Mallett to send the men to the Regts. to which they desire to be assigned. Many if not most of the men express themselves perfectly satisfied with

---

[288] James Cameron McRae (1838-1907), captain and assistant adjutant general, was a son of John McRae, postmaster at Fayetteville, and brother of Duncan McRae. He was educated at Donaldson Academy, taught school in North Carolina, read law with his brother and was licensed in 1860. He settled in Fayetteville until the war came when he enlisted as a private in company H of the First North Carolina Regiment. Later he was adjutant of the Fifth North Carolina, and commanded a battalion in western North Carolina as a major; then was assistant adjutant general for the eastern district of North Carolina until the close of the war. He became a member of the State House of Representatives in 1874-1875, a judge of the superior court, 1882-1890, and an associate justice of the Supreme Court, 1893-1895. He was an earnest advocate of prohibition and served as president of the State Prohibition Convention which met in Raleigh in 1881. Dowd, *Sketches,* pp. 121-122; Clark, *N. C. Regts.,* I, 117, 128, V, 271-282; Connor, *N. C. Manual,* pp. 447, 450.

[289] See p. 175, 44n.
[290] See p. 204, 142n.

the choice of some Regt. in this command. It will soon be filled
and we can resume the plan of sending them where ever they
desire, provided the Regt. has not been filled.

Acknowledging the very great assistance received from your
Excellency in the collection of Conscripts, and hoping that this
explanation may be sufficient, or that the matter can be satisfactorily arranged.

[Raleigh]
Copy of Telegram   Richmond Oct. 3rd 1862

Major P. Mallett
Send forward your Conscripts from both camps as rapidly
as possible to Genl French at Petersburg to be placed in Pettigrew [291] & Daniel's [292] Brigades, and the two (3) N. C. Regiments,
my object is to fill them immediately to their maximum. Acknowledge the receipt of this order by telegraph & state the probable
number you can send on.

                        (Signed) Geo. W. Randolph [293]
                              Secretary of War

[A. L. S. Governors' Papers (Vance),
  Vance Letter Book, 1862-1863,
  State Department of Archives and History, Raleigh.]

To G. W. Randolph [294]

                              EXECUTIVE DEPT. OF N. C.
                              Raleigh, Oct 10th /62

Allow me to call your attention to the subject of disposing of
the conscripts in this State.

When I entered upon the duties of my office I found the thing
at quite a low ebb: few ever coming into camp, & Maj^r. Mallett [295]
found the greatest difficulty in hunting them up. I immediately
took the matter into my own hands, issued a proclamation,[296]
& orders to my Militia Officers [297] and procured Gen Martin to
issue an order promising them all, that they might choose their
regiments if not already filled- The good effect of this was in-

---

[291] See p. 215, 165n. Pettigrew's original brigade had been broken up after its
commander had been captured at Seven Pines, May 31, 1862. Two months later
he was exchanged and a new brigade was formed and sent to Petersburg. It consisted of the Eleventh, Twenty-sixth, Forty-fourth, Forty-seventh, and Fifty-second
North Carolina Regiments. Clark, *N. C. Regts.,* IV, 555.

[292] See p. 109, 428n. Daniel's brigade was formed in the summer of 1862 and
consisted of the Thirty-second, Forty-third, Forty-fifth, and Fifty-third North
Carolina Regiments and the Second Battalion. Clark, *N. C. Regts.,* IV, 513.

[293] See p. 132, 524n. For the reply to his telegram see below, p. 253, 299n.

[294] See p. 132, 524n.

[295] See p. 175, 44n.

[296] For the proclamation, dated September 18, 1862, see p. 191 and *O. R.,* Ser. I,
Vol. XVIII, 753-754.

[297] See p. 186, 83n, 84n, for appeal to conscripts and orders to militia. General
Martin's order giving the men choice of regiments is given on p. 250, 287n.

stantly manifest, the number coming in was trebled and a cheerful spirit of alacrity prevailed everywhere. I mentioned the matter to the President in your presence & understood it to be approved by both; and yet on my return home I find Maj.ʳ Mallett has received orders to send all the conscripts to certain Brigades,[298] without regard to their wishes, or to the promises made them by a Confederate General.

This has produced the greatest dissatisfaction & rightly too— What the particular exigencies of the Services are I do not know, they must be great indeed to justify bad faith toward the soldiers on the part of the Government. If such is to be the policy, as I do not wish to become a party to such transactions, I shall countermand the orders issued to my Militia Officers and turn the whole over again to Major Mallett, and leave him to hunt up the Conscripts as best he can.

Allow me to say generally, that I think the Department commits a serious error in declining to receive the advice of any body save the General in command of the Department. With the management of the Army proper, I shall of course offer no advice, not pretending to be a military man, but in regard to such political movements as secure most effectually the support of the execution of the conscript Law, I do claim that I ought to be heard. In this respect I might safely assert of myself that which after all amounts to not much that I know more than all the West Pointers in the service. And yet So far as I am aware, no one Suggestion of mine or recommendation, has received the approval of the Department— So be it. Though the responsibility rests not with me, yet as I & my State are to suffer any evil consequences that may follow, I feel it my duty to write you fully & frankly in regard to all matters affecting North Carolina[299]
[Richmond]
[Vance Letter Book, 1862-1863,
  Copy in Governors' Papers (Vance),
  State Department of Archives and History, Raleigh.]

---

[298] See above, p. 252.

[299] Randolph did not reply to this letter but he did answer a protest made by General Martin to his order to Mallett. Martin had written: "Your telegram to Major Mallett . . . will . . . cause great complaint. I respectfully suggest that men not be forced into regiments, but be allowed the choice assured in my order." Randolph replied that a uniform execution of the law required control from the center rather than from department commanders, such as Martin. "The only objection to the order you propose," he continued, "is that it conflicts with the conscript act in restricting the maximum of infantry companies to a smaller number than is allowed by that act. The right to volunteer before enrollment is reserved by law, and the order to Major Mallett only applies to enrolled men." Martin to Randolph, October 5, 1862, O. R., Ser. I. Vol. XVIII, 752; Randolph to Martin, October 11, 1862, O. R., Ser IV, Vol. II, 115-116. Martin's order of September 9 authorized companies of infantry and heavy artillery of 100 men, but not exceeding it. The conscript law of April 16, section 12, provided for infantry companies of 125 men and field artillery companies of 150 men. O. R. Ser. IV, Vol. I, 1096.

From Nereus Mendenhall [300]

New Garden Guilford N. C.
10th day of 10[mo] 1862.   ,

I should be pleased to hear officially from the subject laid before the Governor by John Carter and myself—[301]

The question is are not members of the Society of Friends entitled to the benefit of the ordinance of the Convention[302] in their behalf as soon as they are taken hold of by an officer of the State acting under the authority of the Governor of the State?
[Raleigh]
Private:

I have been informed by John Maris a member of our society, that he had an interview with Gov. Vance partly in regard to the foregoing matter and that the Gov. told him that Friends should have applied long ago if they expected any thing from the ordinance— I have to say, that I saw Gov. Clark in relation to the same subject, as soon as the conscripts were called for and that he told me that *his* officers, as his officers, should respect that ordinance— but if they chose to act under Confederate authority he should not hinder them from so doing.—

N. M.

[A. L. S. Governors' Papers (Vance),
State Department of Archives and History, Raleigh.]

---

[300] Nereus Mendenhall (1819-1893), of Guilford County, teacher and civil engineer. He graduated from Haverford College in 1839 and also from Jefferson Medical College in Philadelphia in 1845, but gave up practice soon thereafter and became famous as a school teacher at the New Garden Boarding School. For reasons of health he became a civil engineer and aided in the survey of several North Carolina railroads. In 1860 he returned as principal of the New Garden School and was an outstanding leader of the Quakers around Guilford County. Later he taught at Haverford College and at the Penn Charter School in Philadephia. He represented Guilford County in the House of Representatives in 1874. L. L. Hobbs, "Nereus Mendenhall," Ashe, *Biog. Hist. of N. C.*, IV, 319-324; Connor, *N. C. Manual*, p. 635.

[301] Mendenhall and Carter, Quaker leaders, had been to interview Governor Clark in July with regard to Quakers and their status under the conscription laws. Clark had pointed out that he had never ordered militia colonels to arrest them or to enroll them, but that he had no objection to the colonels doing it if under Confederate authority. Militia Letter Book, July 21, July 29, 1862. This letter is sent to David A. Barnes.

[302] At the fourth session of the Convention, on May 12, 1862, an ordinance was adopted which exempted Quakers from military service, provided each member exempted paid $100 to the state. If a member was unable to pay, the governor was given power to detail him to assist in the manufacture of salt, or to work in the state hospitals. *Convention Ordinances*, 4 Session, No. 35. The first Exemption Act of Congress, adopted April 21, 1862, did not exempt Quakers. The second Exemption Bill, adopted the day after Mendenhall's letter was written, provided for their exemption upon the hiring of a substitute, or upon payment to the Confederacy of $500. Matthews *Public Laws of the Confederacy*, 2 session, 1 Congress, pp. 77-89; *O. R.*, Ser. IV, Vol. I, 1081, II, 166.

To J. M. Worth[303]

STATE OF NORTH CAROLINA
Raleigh, Oct. 10th. 1862

Your letter to Governor Vance informing him of the fact that you were compelled to suspend your operations of salt making in consequence of the appearance of yellow fever has been received. His Excellency deeply regrets this visitation upon our people, not only on account of its blighting effects upon one of our most important towns,[304] but particularly on account of the necessity which it imposed upon you to suspend the operation of salt making. This suspension if long continued must result in great public injury.

His Excellency entertains the hope that you will be enabled to resume your operations at an early day, and that you will in the meantime provide yourself with kettles and such other articles as will enable you to produce salt in a much larger quantity. You should be prudent as you doubtless will be, in your expenditures, but salt must be had at any cost.

[Vance Letter Book, 1862-1863,
State Department of Archives and History, Raleigh.]

To Messrs. F. & H. Fries[305]

Executive Dept. of N. C.
Raleigh Oct. 10th /62

I have Seen with regret and mortification your note to Capt Garrett[306] A Q M in which you say you cannot comply with

[303] See p. 206, 144n. This letter was written by David A. Barnes, aide to Vance.

[304] The yellow fever epidemic in Wilmington began in August and continued into November. The fever was brought in by the steamer *Kate* from Nassau, which arrived in July, and two of her crew died in Wilmington in August. For several weeks the press suppressed the severity of the epidemic, but by the last week of September it had reached such proportions that the suffering was openly admitted. As summarized by the *Wilmington Journal,* November 20, 1862, there were more than 1500 cases and about 441 deaths between September 19 and November 15, when the epidemic abated. Sprunt, *Chronicles,* p. 27, says the plague ran from August 6 to November 17 and resulted in 446 deaths.

[305] Francis Levin Fries (1812-1863) and Henry William Fries (1825-1902), of Forsythe County, woolen manufacturers. Francis L. Fries was born in Salem of a leading Moravian family, educated at Nazareth Hall in Pennsylvania, studied law under Emanuel Shober and practiced only briefly. His interest in business made him give up the law and join the Salem Manufacturing Company (cotton), and in 1846 to establish with his brother Henry the F. & H. Fries Company (wool). Henry William Fries was also born in Salem, studied at John Beck Institute at Lititz, Pennsylvania, and joined his brother as a full partner in F. & H. Fries Company on his twenty-first birthday. After the death of Francis Fries in 1863 his brother operated the business. Francis Fries was a member of the House of Commons in 1858 and a director of the North Carolina Railroad. He was a Democrat. Hamilton, *History of N. C.,* V, 1-2; Connor, *N. C. Manual,* p. 605; W. A. Blair, "Francis Fries," E. Rondthaler, "Henry William Fries," Ashe, *Biog. Hist. of N. C.,* III, 129-134, 135-137; H. Fries to T. D. McDowell, February 3, 1860, McDowell Papers.

[306] See p. 190, 96n. Garrett was responsible for making the contracts by which

the provisions of the Exemption Law requiring manufacturers to furnish goods at 75 per cent profit over the cost of production,[307] and therefore declining to sell the State any more cloth for supplying the wants of our brave soldiers in the field. It is melancholy in every sense. If the Standard of patriotism was no higher in the great mass of the people, we might treat with the enemy tomorrow and consent to be slaves at once & forever. Poor men, with large & often helpless families, go forth to bleed & suffer at $11 per month, supporting their wives & children God knows how, with flour at $20, shoes & cotton goods at fabulous prices and yet men who stay at home in protected ease to reap a harvest of wealth, which might be truly called a harvest of blood, from the necessities of the Country, cannot afford to take 75 per cent above cost for the garments in which his protectors stand guard & do battle for his liberties! What per cent, gentlemen, do you suppose the soldier is reaping, with a half starving family, a shattered constitution, ragged & barefooted, sleeping on the bare earth or languishing with gaping wounds or raging fever in loathesome hospitals? If he can incur personal and pecumiary ruin for his country's sake, cant you afford to eat good food, sleep in a warm bed every night on 75 per cent clear profit for the country's good also? Alas, Alas, that such a state of things should exist in North Carolina! I will not pursue the subject.

Suffice it to say that without the assistance of the manufacturers the State cannot clothe the troops & they must brave the severities of the coming winter naked. When men of intelligence and public spirit take such a position, we may expect suffering & ruin to overwhelm our country. There is only one remedy to arrest the evil which threatens us: and that is for the civil authorities to permit the military to put forth its strong arm & take what it wants. The Confederate authorities have desired my permission to seize the Mills of N. C. and work them

the state supplied its troops with clothing under the commutation agreement with the Confederacy. Holden charged that Garrett used political pressure in making these contracts and that he had worked against Vance in the election of 1862. He was succeeded in 1863 by Major Henry A. Dowd. Raleigh *North Carolina Standard,* February 6, 1863.

[307] Under the terms of the Exemption Law, adopted October 11, 1862 but the terms of which were already public knowledge, manufacturers were allowed to exempt conscripts as laborers "subject to the condition that the products of the labor of such exempts, or of the companies and establishments with which they are connected, shall be sold and disposed of by the proprietors at prices not exceeding seventy-five per centum upon the cost of production, or within a maximum to be fixed by the Secretary of War, under such regulations as he may prescribe." The penalty for violation was enrollment of exempted workers in the Confederate army. Matthews, *Public Laws of the Confederacy,* 2 session 1 Congress, pp. 77-79; *O. R.,* Ser. IV, Vol. II, 161.

for the benefit of the Army:[308] should it be formally asked of
me again I shall withdraw my objections & permit them to do
as they wish, unless they will make reasonable contracts with the
State.

I should state as a matter of justice that you have been quite
as liberal, & perhaps more so, with the State, as any others, but
no amount of company can render extortion justifiable or respectable.[309]

Salem

[Vance Letter Book, 1862-1863,
  State Department of Archives and History, Raleigh.]

From Edward Warren[310]

Staunton October 11th. 1862

I write you an informal note, with a pencil, as pen & ink can
not be procured, to give you some account of myself since we
parted in Richmond. I came off in the control cars, according to
orders, en route for the Army, the day after you left for Raleigh.
On reaching Gordonsville, I ascertained that there were only
about 30 patients in the Hospital at that place, and that there
were no North Carolinians among them. I then hastened to Char-
lottsville, where I found over 50 soldiers from our State, in a
condition of great destitution. Their delight at seeing me, &
learning that you had sent me to look after their wants cannot
be expressed in words. Many of them cried like children, and declared that they would never forget you. I supplied their most
pressing wants, and took my departure for this place in the afternoon. On my arrival here I found Shiply with the stores and went
immediately to the surgeon in charge to inform him of the
object of my visit & to secure his cooperation. He gave me free
access to the Hospitals, and I have been occupied ever since in
looking up our sick & wounded & attending to their wants. There
are at least 3000 soldiers in the Hospitals here & of the number
at least 1/4 are North Carolinians. I had supposed the condition
of the sick & wounded at Charlottesville bad enough, but it is
infinitely better than that of the poor creatures in these Hospitals.
Dirty, naked, without shoes, hats or socks, wounded in every
possible manner, utterly dispirited & entirely indifferent to everything they present a picture of wretchedness & misery which no
tongue or pen can describe. They are arriving at the rate of one
thousand a day from the Army in trains which consume a whole

---

[308] See Quartermaster A. C. Myers to Vance, September 17, 1862, above, p. 190 and
97n.

[309] For the Fries' reply to this letter see below, p. 262.

[310] See p. 159, 647n. Warren had become surgeon general of North Carolina on
September 13. He and Vance had visited Richmond during the first week in October.

week in making the journey, and in this way hunger is added to their other sufferings. Taking all things together, the condition of these poor unfortunates is enough to wring tears from hearts of stone, and to stamp the authorities of the Confederacy with a brand of unutterable disgrace. Thank God, I have been able to do something at least for the poor fellows from North Carolina. I have visited all the Hospitals & hunted up our soldiers in every ward— taking them by the hand & assuring them that their Governor remembered them in their sufferings & was resolved that they should not be entirely neglected. In this way I have distributed all the supplies brought from Richmond, & have purchased others to the extent of $300. for their benefit— mostly clothes to cover their nakedness. I only wish it was in my power to do more, for my heart bleeds for these unfortunate, but most worthy fellows— All that I have done was in your name, and on this very night you have the prayers & blessings of hundreds who have been made comparatively comfortable by your kindness. All the sick and wounded are being sent from Winchester to this place & from thence to Lynchburg & Richmond. Only a few in fact now remain behind. I have thought it unnecessary to go further, as the Army will assuredly *fall back within a few days.* As my supplies are exhausted, I shall return to Richmond by the way of Lynchburg. D[r]. Manson[311] is the very man for our Agency in R. & with your consent I will engage his services. I have found D[r]. Little[312] an invaluable assistant.
[Raleigh]
[Vance Letter Book, 1862-1863,
State Department of Archives and History, Raleigh.]

From S. H. Walkup[313]

Camp Near Winchester Va. Oct 11th 1862.
I lay before you for your consideration the destitute condition of our Regt with the hope that you, who have experienced some of the severe trials of a soldiers life, may hasten up the requisite relief—

---

[311] See p. 157, 641n.

[312] William Little, of Wake County, assistant surgeon. Moore, *N. C. Roster*, IV, 16.

[313] Samuel Hoey Walkup, of Union County, lieutenant colonel of the Forty-eighth North Carolina Regiment. He was formerly captain of company F in the same company and became its colonel on December 4, 1863. Walkup graduated from the University of North Carolina in 1841, became a lawyer, and served in the State Senate in 1858 and 1860. He was a trustee of the University from 1874 to 1877. As an officer he was considered very brave but "was often laughed at on dress parade and brigade drill for his awkwardness, but when in battle all that knew him were satisfied that Walkup was there and that his regiment would do its duty." Clark, *N. C. Regts.*, III 113-114, 123; Moore, *N .C. Roster*, III, 355, 376; Grant, *Alumni History*, p. 643; Connor, *N. C. Manual*, p. 825; Samuel H. Walkup's Diary, Southern Historical Collection, University of North Carolina, Chapel Hill, N. C. (cited hereafter as Walkup's Diary).

We have present Six hundred & nineteen men rank file in the 48th- Regt. N. C. Troops— There are of that number Fifty one who are completely & absolutely Barefooted— & one hundred & ninety four who are nearly as bad off, as Barefooted, & who will be altogether so, in less than one month. There are but Two hundred & ninety seven Blankets in the Regt among the 619 men present which is less than one Blanket to every two men. In truth there is one Compy (I) having 66 men & only Eleven Blankets in the whole company— The pants are generally ragged & out at the seats— & there are less than three cooking utensils to each Company— This sir is the condition of our Regt. upon the eve of winter here among the mountains of Va. Cut off from all supplies from home, & worn down & thinned with incessant marchings, fighting & diseases— can any one wonder that our Regt. numbering over 1250 rank & file has more than half its no. absent from camp, & not much over one third 449 of them fit for duty? The country is filled with strangers, deserters, & sick men & the hospitals are crowded from the exposures. A spirit of disaffection is rapidly engendering among the soldiers which threatens to show itself in general straggling & desertions if it does not lead to open mutiny.

Add to this that our surgeons have no medicines & dont even pretend to prescribe for the sick in camp, having no medicines & you have an outline of the sufferings & prospective trials & difficulties under which we labor.

What is said of the 48th- N. C. is equally true of other Regts in the service from N. C. & from other States too.— But you are aware how the matter stands with N. C. The State agreed to & did receive from the Confed. Govmt. The commutation money & assumed to furnish the Clothing, Shoes Blankets &c to the soldier.[314] This she has utterly failed to do, or to give the commutation money in lieu thereof. She has received the money & has failed to furnish the clothing for which she has been paid by the Confed. Govmt.— Our Regt. entered the service 1st- of April last They recd-*generally* one suit each except socks, & nearly all recd, one pair of shoes— Only about one third of them received any Blankets & very few of those who furnished their own blankets have been paid any money by way of commutation— We have passed six Months in the service & you well know we have seen hard service during that time. Our scanty clothing, which we had independent of the government of either N. C. or the C. S.

---

[314] By a law of September 20, 1861, the legislature agreed to receive commutation money from the Confederate government and to assume the obligation of clothing and shoeing her own troops. The state agreed also to sell all her surplus supplies to the Confederacy if all Confederate agents would be withdrawn from the state and leave the field to North Carolina. North Carolina was the only state to make such an agreement with the Confederate government. *Legislative Documents, 1862-1863,* Document No. 1, p. 6; *Laws of N. C., 1861,* 2 extra session, chap. 21.

has been lost for the want of the means of transportation; & finally all that we had, except what we had on our persons, was lost when we crossed the Potomac after the late battle of Sharpsburg, Septr. 17th-. This of course was no fault of N. C. but one of the misfortunes of war. I mention these things to show that our destitution is no fault of the Regt. It was in fact mainly the fault of the misfortune of the C. S. government in not furnishing us with sufficient means of transportation & the casualties incident to War. But what I do insist upon now is that North Carolina who always has maintained a character for the prompt & faithful performance of all her contracts, Should now exert herself to her utmost capacity with her most patriotic energy & zeal to supply these just & pinching wants of her own citizens & save them from the extreme sufferings now rapidly approaching & already felt in the coming winter— Just think of our *ragged* & *barefooted* men with *one* blanket only & scarcely one to any *two* men & having *no tents,* or even *flies* to shield them from the cold rains & winter blasts in this Northern clime, Having so few cooking utensils that their constant use cannot supply the demands of the Regt. & having no medical supplies. And having *no other* rations except of flour & *eternal* Beef— And think of the sick, who constitute nearly two thirds of our army, in such a condition. And surely, surely with these facts before them, the generous & patriotic State of N. C. will be just & faithful in fulfilling the engagements which she has made to & been paid for by the Confederate States.[315] She will thus alleviate the miseries likely to befal her *own sons,* and save them & herself from the disgrace that may otherwise obscure their fair fame, & darken her history now proudly standing forth among the brightest of the Southern States or of the nations of the earth.

What we most pressingly need just now is our full supply of *Blankets,* of *Shoes* & of *pants* & *socks.* We need very much all our other clothing too. But we are in the greatest need of these indispensable articles & *Must* have them, & have them *Now.* Otherwise how can the government blame the soldier for failing to render service, when it fails to fulfil its stipulated & *paid for* contracts? A contract broken on *one* side is broken on all sides & void.— If N. C. cannot fulfil her contract for clothing, blankets & shoes. She ought to rescind it & refund the money & let the C. S. Govmt. do it. Or measures should be immediately taken to give *free transportation,* with *security* from *loss by the way,* to such articles as the parents. wives & friends of the suffering sol-

---

[315] For the fiscal year ending September 30, 1862, the Confederate government paid to North Carolina for clothing her own troops $903,096.95, with a large amount still due. Because of the great increase in prices the amount allowed by law did not pay more than about half of the expense of the state in clothing her troops. Report of the Adjutant General, *Legislative Documents, 1862-1863,* p. 26.

diers would immediately & joyfully send from home to their relief; And the State should pay over the commutation money to those furnishing the supplies, which indeed they would generously furnish at any sacrifice, without pay, if they were assured the gift would reach the beloved objects of their bounty & not be lost on the way. The State should however promptly pay for it & thus relieve the destitute family of the soldiers for the sacrifice made to him in his necessities & thus doubly bless in both giving & receiving favours.

The soldiers of the 48th- N. C. & from all the State will patriotically suffer & bear their hardships & privations as long as those from any other State, or as far as human endurance can tolerate such privations, But it would not be wise to experiment to far in such circumstances as now surround us upon the extent of their endurance. With Lincolns proclamation promising freedom to the slaves,[316] what might be the suffering, exhausted, ragged, barefooted & dying *Non* slaveholders of the South, who are neglected by their government & whose suffering families at home are exposed to so many evils, begin to conclude? Would it not be dangerous to tempt them with too great trials?—

Dear Sir, you will please not to consider me obstrusive in this communication to your excellency. I feel the very earnest & solemn responsibility of my position as commander of this Regt. at this critical period & under these trying circumstances & wish to do all I can to remove from my Skirts the heavy responsibility by doing all that I can to remove the evils by seeking a speedy supply of Blankets Shoes & clothing. & therefore beg your earnest attention to the premises & your zealous & I hope efficient aid to supply our necessity—I send with this paper Lt. R. H. Stitt [317] of Co. A 48th Regt. N. C. in whose care any clothing &c. will be attended to in the promptest manner, & who also can give any further information required of the condition of this Regt. The Quarter Master, Capt. Hayne, is too sick to leave his post—

Hoping to hear a favorable response & receive a speedy supply I remain very Respectfully
[Raleigh]

[A. L. S. Governors' Papers (Vance),
State Department of Archives and History, Raleigh.]

---

[316] On September 22, 1862, Lincoln had published his preliminary emancipation proclamation to go into effect January 1, 1863. The gist was contained in the following sentence: "All persons held as slaves within any state or designated part of a state the people whereof shall be in rebellion against the United States shall be then, thenceforward, and forever free." Of course this did not immediately emancipate a single slave, but it did announce a policy for the future, and Lincoln admitted that it had "no constitutional or legal justification, except as a military measure."

[317] Robert H. Stitt, of Union County, who died in Richmond, December 27, 1862. Lewis C. Haynes, of Davidson County, formerly first lieutenant of company B who, on May 1, 1862, was promoted captain and assistant quartermaster. Moore, *N. C. Roster* III, 356, 360.

From F. & H. Fries[318]

Salem N. C. Oct 13, 1862

Your favor of 10th- inst came to hand yesterday morning & we are sorry to see that you have misunderstood our note to Capt. Garrett.[319] We do not object to taking the oath,[320] because we are not satisfied with 75 per cent profit, as we believe that to be a very liberal percentage.

If you will ask Capt Garrett or Capt. Sloan[321] they will tell you that we have never asked for an advance on goods, & we know we have furnished the State our goods for *much* less 75 per cent profit. We have left it to the Q. M. to say what would be a fair price & from last January to this time have furnished goods at the prices then agreed on, although wool & all materials have advanced at least 100 per cent & goods of the same quality have been sold from 50 to 100 per cent higher than the State paid us, & we could not now replace these goods for the money we got, without counting any-thing for profits.

Now this has nothing to do with taking the oath & we just mention it to show that it is not our desire to get all we can—

Some of the difficulties about the oath are these: We have some old fashioned notions about taking an oath — when we take an oath we want to swear to facts. How any man can conscientiously swear that goods cost just so much is more than we can see. We have been doing business over 20 yrs. & when prices were settled, we could tell very nearly the cost of goods, but now when all the stock & the findings for a mill have no established price & some things can not be replaced at *any* price, we certainly could not tell what it would cost. For instance; what shall we charge

---

[318] See p. 255, 305n.

[319] See p. 190, 96n. and p. 255, 306n.

[320] The provision against extortion in the Exemption Act of October 11, 1862, provided that "where application is made to exempt superintendents and operatives in wool and cotton factories . . . the proprietor of the business . . . shall make oath in writing that the said superintendents, operatives, managers, or mechanics, as the case may be, are skilled and actually employed in their vocations; that they are habitually working for the public; that they are absolutely necessary for the successful prosecution of the business of the concern; that the products thereof shall not be sold or exchanged or bartered during the said exception for a price exceeding the cost of production and 75 per cent profit thereon; that no shift, contrivance, or arrangement shall be made to evade the law or to secure a larger return or profit than it allows, and that exemption is not sought for a larger number of persons than is absolutely necessary for the successful prosecution of the business of the concern." *O. R.*, Ser. IV, Vol. II, pp. 166-167. This clause never worked well; it seemed never to have been desired and was often evaded. In the next exemption act it was dropped because it had proved unwise for the military, rather than the civil, authorities to see to it that the manufacturers cooperated under the law. Entrekin, "N. C. Poor Relief"; Charles W. Ramsdell, "The Control of Manufacture in the Confederate Government," *Mississippi Valley Historical Review* (1914—   ), Vol. VIII, No. 3 (December, 1921), pp. 231-249.

[321] See p. 190, 95n. See also James Sloan to William A. Graham, October 9, 1860, Graham Papers CH.

for wear & tear of machinery & what shall we rate the machinery at? or shall a man just swear at the pole & *say* it cost so much to make a yard of cloth or a pound of yarn. Such a loose way of swearing is unfortunately too common, but it does not accord with our notions of an oath & we can not swear that a thing is so, unless we *know* that is *so*. Any manufacturer that tries to make goods as cheaply as they can be made, is the loser, whereas one that buys materials at extravagant prices has the advantage. For instance; say we by close economy & strict attention, can make goods to cost $1. per yd. another manufacturer by paying any price for stock & for labor may make his goods cost him $2. per yd. Now because we do our best to get materials at reasonable prices & keep expenses within proper bounds are allowed 75 cts advance on the yard & this reckless manager is allowed $1.50 bringing his cloth to 3.50 & our only to $1.75 So you see, it is a direct loss to the consumer & to the prudent manufacturer, as it is to the interest of the latter to make his goods cost him as much as possible, knowing that he will be allowed 75 per cent on the cost of production.

If the Secretary of War will establish a maximum price for goods this might be avoided, & would be in favor of men that tried to do business right.

This whole matter of regulating prices is very difficult & it is hard to make a law that will do justice to all. This being the law however we will of course abide by it, & if we cant comply with the law by taking an oath that may be required, we can but submit to their taking the hands.[322] We wont forswear ourselves for 75 cts on the Dollar

It never was out intention to deprive the Government of the product of our mill,[323] provided we can have the hands to do the

---

[322] The Fries mills employed seventy-nine hands: twenty-nine white males, thirty-six white females, and fourteen black males. Thirteen of their hands were between the ages of eighteen and thirty-five years, and were therefore liable to conscription unless exempted, though the age limit was raised to forty-five years about the time this summary was made. They had a contract with the Confederate government for 20,000 pounds of yarn, due February 1, 1863, in addition to their state contracts. They estimated the cost of making jeans cloth at $1.67 a yard and sold it at $2.50. Statement of F. & H. Fries Company, Salem, N. C., November 6, 1862, Governors' Papers (Vance).

[323] Francis Fries claimed that "to the neglect of our customers and of our interest we have from the beginning of our troubles, made all our business yield to the demands of the army. This applies to the cotton and wool mills of F & H Fries as well as to the tanyard of Fries & Co. which belongs to me. Everyone has had to stand aside when the State and the Confederacy or parties making work for the army applied for anything we had." Francis Fries to Governor Henry T. Clark, November 18, 1861, Governors' Papers (Clark). Other troubles also plagued the Fries' business. In the spring of 1862 they had great difficulty getting any more wool from Texas because of the domination of the transportation facilities by the Confederate government. They said they could get wool from Virginia, South Carolina, and Georgia only by paying for it in yarns or cloth, and they asked permits to allow them to send such out of the state. Governor Clark wrote to

work, & will be willing to furnish the goods at what they can get them of others. Perhaps others can get at the cost of production. All we want is, that prices be uniform & that we may not be required to swear to matters, about which we not form a correct judgment.

The army has to be clothed to enable the Government to keep it together & we will at all times do all in our power to aid the authorities in getting up clothing, & for such as we furnish we do not fear to leave it to the honor of the present Quarter Master of N. C. to say what our goods are worth.

We have never extortioned yet, & the last part of your letter about extortion is entirely uncalled for.[324]

[Raleigh]

[A. L. S. Governors' Papers (Vance),
State Department of Archives and History, Raleigh.]

From Annie Terry & Others

Kinston N. C. Oct. 13th
1862/

Sir, though an entire stranger to me, I deem it not improper to address you on a subject of so great importance, to the inhabitants of Eastern Carolina, which part of the state has been so sadly neglected.

In regard to this matter, let me beseech you, to apply those, who have it in their power to send us aid, and let those Blood Thirsty Demons (The Yankees) be driven to their Rendezvous, so that the present inhabitants of this part of the state, may hence forth be free from molestation. A very small portion comparatively speaking of our *own brave Carolina Boys* will prevent them from repeating their previous outrages. In the name of God send forces and let them be repulsed in their *Diabolical* efforts They spare neither women or children; they are alike liable to their insults.

Families who are left almost destitute whose Husbands, Fathers & Sons have gone to shed their blood for their Country's rights, who have not the means by which to move are left without protection, and are compelled to bear the insults of those unrelenting Tyrants who "thirst for the life blood of those they most cherish."

Richmond to try to facilitate transportation for them. F. & H. Fries to Governor Henry T. Clark, April 18, 1862, Governors' Papers (Clark); Governor Clark to Judah P. Benjamin, November 30, 1861, Clark Letter Book, p 208.

[324] In his message to the legislature, November 17, 1862, Vance expressed gratification that the prospect of obtaining cotton cloths at reasonable prices was better than it had been. But he added: "The woolen factories seem more incorrigible. Some of them when asked to furnish their goods at 75 per cent. declined entirely, and others agreed to do so by fixing enormous profits on the cost of the raw material and then adding 75 per cent on the finished article, making their profits even greater than before. . . . I recommend them to your tender mercies gentlemen, . . ." *Legislative Documents, 1862-1863,* Document No. 1, p. 7.

Surely if the higher authorities were aware of the cruelties and outrages that have been manifested towards the daughters of Carolina, they would send resistance to avert the impending evil without delay, and the only means by which this can be done, is to send sufficient force to keep the enemy in New Berne.
Wives daughters & Sisters of Comp[325] A 40, Regt N C. T. Written by Annie Terry.
[Raleigh]
[A. L. S. Governors' Papers (Vance),
State Department of Archives and History, Raleigh.]

To G. W. Randolph[326]
State of North Carolina— Executive Department
Raleigh, October 15th. 1862
His Excellency Governor Vance has received applications from two or three loyal citizens of the State for permission to obtain a supply of salt in exchange for cotton & turpentine from within the enemies lines. Our people our suffering for this very necessary article and the supply has been greatly diminished by reason of the unfortunate appearance of the yellow fever at Wilmington, in the vicinity of which place large quantities were being made. If this privilege is not granted to certain persons in whom we can confide, it is to be feared that an illicit trade may be commenced by those who may injure our cause and may ultimately join the enemy.

His Excellency did not feel at liberty to grant this permission without consulting you upon its propriety. He would suggest that no public harm can arise if the privilege is confined to discreet persons who shall be subject to the supervision of the military authorities
[Richmond]
[Vance Letter Book, 1862-1863,
State Department of Archives and History, Raleigh.]

Proclamation
Raleigh, October 15, 1862
TO THE PEOPLE OF NORTH-CAROLINA
After the most strenuous exertions on the part of its officers, the State finds it impossible to clothe and shoe soldiers without again

---

[325] Company A of the Fortieth North Carolina Regiment (heavy artillery), organized in 1861 and captured at Hatteras August 28, 29, 1863, was from Lenoir County. It was reorganized early in 1862, after exchange, and was stationed at Fort Lane below New Bern until the fall of that place on March 14, 1862, when it fell back to Kinston. In April 1862 it was ordered to Wilmington and stationed at the forts guarding the mouth of the Cape Fear River. Most of its time during the remainder of the war was spent at Smith's Island. Moore, *N. C. Roster,* III, 113-117; Clark, *N. C. Regts.,* II, 747-748.

[326] See p. 132, 524n. The letter is written by David A. Barnes, aide to Vance.

appealing to that overflowing fountain of generous charity—the private contributions of our people. The rigors of winter are approaching, our soldiers are already suffering, and must suffer more if our sympathies are not practical and active. The Quarter Master's Department is laboring faithfully to provide for them but, owing to speculation and extortion, will fall short. The deficiency must be supplied by the people. We shall have an active winter campaign, and how can our troops, if ragged, cold, and barefoot, contend with the splendidly equipped columns of the enemy?

The articles most needed, and which the State finds it most difficult to supply, are shoes, socks and blankets, though drawers, shirts and pants would be gladly received. If every farmer who has hides tanning would agree to spare one pair of shoes, and if every mother in North Carolina would knit one strong pair of either thick cotton or woolen socks for the army, they would be abundantly supplied. A great lot of blankets also might yet be spared from private use, and thousands could be made from the carpets upon our parlor floors. With good warm houses and cotton bed clothing, we can certainly get through the winter much better than the soldiers can with all the blankets we can give them.

The Colonels of the Militia Regiments throughout the State are hereby appointed agents for the purchase and collection of all such articles as can be spared by our people, who, through their respective Captains, are ordered immediately to canvass every county and visit every citizen in the beats for this purpose. A liberal price will be paid for everything where the owner feels that he or she is not able to donate it; and active agents will immediately forward them to our suffering regiments. Expenses will be allowed the officers engaged in this duty, and transportation furnished the Colonels or their agents to bring the articles to Raleigh.

And now my countrymen and women, if you have anything to spare for the soldier, in his name I appeal to you for it. Do not let the speculator have it, though he offer you enormous prices; spurn him from your door and say to him, that our brave defenders have need for it and shall have it without passing through his greedy fingers. Do not place yourselves among the extortioners— they are the vilest and most cowardly of all our country's enemies, and when this war is ended and people come to view the matter in its proper light you will find that the most detested Tories are more respected than they. When they tempt you with higher prices than the State offers, just think for a moment of the soldier and what he is doing for you. Remember when you sit down by the bright and glowing fire, that the soldier is sitting upon the cold earth; that in the wind which is whistling so fearfully over your roof, only making you feel the more comfortable

because it harms you not, he is shivering in darkness on the dangerous out-post, or shuddering through the dreary hours of his watch. Remember that when you come forth in the morning well fed and warmly clad, leading your family toward the spot where the blessed music of the Sabbath-bells tells you of the peaceful worship of the God of Peace, the soldier is going forth at the same moment, perhaps, half fed, after a night of shivering and suffering to where the roar of artillery and shout of battle announce that he is to die, that your peace and safety may be preserved. Oh, remember these things generous and patriotic people of North-Carolina, and give freely of your perishable goods to those who are giving all that mortal man can give for your safety and your rights. Z. B. Vance.
[The *North Carolina Standard,*
  Raleigh, Oct. 17, 1862.]

From John H. Reagan[327]

CONFEDERATE STATES OF AMERICA
Post Office Department
Richmond October 17th. 1862

Your letter of the 14th. instant, inquiring whether Postmasters are liable to conscription under the recent acts of Congress, and whether it is intended to discontinue the offices of such as are taken into the military service, or fill them with non-conscripts or women, and making similar inquiries as to contractors for conveying mails has been received.

Such Postmasters as are appointed by the President and confirmed by the Senate, and such clerks in the large offices as are allowed by the Postmaster General, are exempt from conscription. All other postmasters and clerks in post offices are liable to conscription.[328] But there is no intenton to discontinue the post offices. They will be filled by the appointment of persons not liable to military duty, in all cases when postmasters are taken into the military service, as soon as the name of a suitable person is recommended to the Department.

---

[327] John Henninger Reagan (1818-1905), Postmaster General of the Confederacy. He was a lawyer who had been born in Tennessee and had begun his political career in Texas in 1847 as a member of the state legislature. Afterwards he became district judge, 1851-1856, a member of the United States House of Representatives, 1857-1861, 1875-1887, a member of the United States Senate, 1887-1889, and chairman of the Texas Railroad Commission, 1891-1903. Seth Shepard McKay, "John Henninger Reagan," *Dict. of Am. Biog.,* XV, 432-434.

[328] The language of the Exemption Law of October 11, 1862, after exempting certain officers of the Confederate and state governments, continued ". . . including postmasters appointed by the President and confirmed by the Senate, and such clerks in their offices as are allowed by the Postmaster-General, and now employed, and excluding all other postmasters, their assistants and clerks; . . ." *O. R., Ser. IV,* Vol. II, pp. 160-161.

Neither contractors nor mail carriers are on that account exempt from military duty, mail carriers and the drivers of post coaches were exempt under the old law.

Contractors who go into the military service will have to get Agents to act for them in fulfilling their contracts, and they will have to employ persons not liable to military duty, as riders & drivers.

Raleigh

[A. L. S. Governors' Papers (Vance),
 Vance Letter Book, 1862-1863,
State Department of Archives and History, Raleigh.]

From Jefferson Davis

EXECUTIVE OFFICE
Richmond, October 17. 1862

The resolutions[329] adopted at a meeting of the citizens of Onslow Co. N. C. referred to me by you were duly received and have occupied my serious attention.

I have not been unmindful of the condition of the Eastern portion of your State, and can make allowance for the anxiety felt by those who reside there. Efforts are industriously made to organize and instruct the new levies of mounted troops, that force being most relied on to protect your exposed districts; and you may be assured that the Government will do everything in its power to defend the citizens of Onslow against the depredations of the enemy.

With this view General French has received orders[330] to send

---

[329] The resolutions were adopted at a public meeting in Jacksonville, Onslow County, on September 27, 1862, as a result of a former meeting of citizens on September 1. The resolutions were sent to Vance by James H. Foy, a member-elect of the House of Commons from Onslow County, who also came to Raleigh to talk with Vance about the situation of the eastern counties. The resolutions called upon the state and Confederate governments to protect the riches and people of the county from incursions of the enemy; called upon the governor to convene the legislature and request that body to provide from 8,000 to 10,000 troops for the defense of the region; and concluded that "It is better to defend the porch than the altar, the door than the hearthstone." Vance transmitted the resolutions to President Davis and expressed the hope that something could be done, as he desired to avoid coming into conflict with the Confederate government. It was doubtless resolutions of this sort, with the conditions that produced them, which persuaded Vance to recommend to the November legislature the raising of 10,000 troops for the defense of the state, which recommendation did bring him into conflict with the Confederate government. For the resolutions and the Vance endorsement to Davis see *O. R.*, Ser I, Vol. LI, Part II, 629-630; James H. Foy to Vance, September 16, 1862, Governors' Papers (Vance).

[330] On October 15, 1862, Major General Gustavus W. Smith requested French "to send a small force there for the purpose of preventing marauding and protecting private property, . . ." On October 22 French reported to Vance that complaints had come to him because of the withdrawal of forces from Onslow County, but that "the same cavalry force is there under Captain Ward that has been there since the fall of New Bern except two companies of Partisan Rangers." *O. R.* Ser. I, Vol. LI, Part II, 630; Vol. XVIII, 760.

thither as soon as practicable, a force to prevent marauding expeditions and afford protection to private property.

The large and increasing numbers of the enemy at Suffolk[331] whence he threatens North Carolina & Virginia as well as our principal line of communication has rendered it necessary to concentrate our forces at a point where they can offer the most effective resistance, and in the success of that resistance I am sure that the intelligent citizens of Onslow Co as well as the rest of North Carolina will perceive how deeply they are interested.

I gratefully acknowledge the earnest & patriotic manner in which since your assumption of the Executive Authority in N. Car. you have labored to fill her battle-thinned regiments and recruit her armies in the field. I am happy in the confidence that you will continue to afford this Government your valuable cooperation, & beg to assure you of the deep interest I feel in all that relates to the security & welfare of your State.

[Raleigh]

[A. L. S. Governors' Papers (Vance),
Vance Letter Book, 1862-1863,
State Department of Archives and History, Raleigh.]

From Rich[d] Sterling [332]

EDGEWORTH FEMALE SEMINARY,[333]

Greensboro N. C. Oct. 18 1862.

I take the liberty of sending to your address, a copy of each of our publications, now ready for sale. We have one book still in the hands of the binders, & two in press, As soon as they are ready I will forward them all. Though still in our infancy as a publishing house, & with many difficulties in our way, we hope to do something for the intellectual independence of the Confederacy, while strong arms & brave hearts are contending for our political freedom.[334]

---

[331] Major General Gustavus Smith wrote President Davis that enemy concentrations at Suffolk, Va. made it unwise and impractical to detach a large force for the defence of Onslow County. Smith to Davis, October 15, 1862, *O. R.*, Ser. I, Vol. LI, Part II, 630.

[332] Richard Sterling, principal of Edgeworth Female Seminary in Greensboro, and head of the printing firm of Sterling, Campbell, and Albright. A graduate of Hampden-Sydney College, he became principal at Edgeworth in 1850 and remained in charge until the school closed in 1862 because of the war. Charles Lee Raper, *The Church and Private Schools of North Carolina* (Greensboro, 1898), p. 112 (cited hereafter as Raper, *Church and Private Schools of N. C.*)

[333] Edgeworth Female Seminary was founded by John Motley Morehead in 1840; it was built at his expense and was privately owned. From 1862 to 1868 there was no school, and the buildings were used during the war as a hospital. From 1868 to 1871 another school was operated there by Rev. J. M. M. Caldwell. It burned in 1872. Raper, *Church and Private Schools of N. C.*, pp. 113-114.

[334]The printing firm of Sterling, Campbell, and Albright was founded in 1861 largely to meet the needs of southern schools for textbooks. Sterling and Campbell, who was a professor in Sterling's school, prepared a primer, a speller, and a series of readers; others prepared an arithmetic and English grammar, and thousands of

We have been much delayed in our operations by the want of *papers*, & by the absence in the military service of the country of our partner J. W. Albright—[335] the only practical printer in our firm.

The demand for the books already published is greater than we can supply, owing to the difficulties mentioned above.

With plenty of paper, & a good practical printer in our office we would be able to meet the wants of our Schools in North Carolina, & other States where they have already been introduced. [Raleigh]

[A. L. S. Governors' Papers (Vance),
State Department of Archives and History, Raleigh.]

From A. S. Merrimon[336]

Asheville N. C.
Oct 20th- 1862.

Enclosed find duplicate of letter from Genl T. J. Jackson[337] to Genl. Cooper.[338] It explains itself and I send it at the request of

---

copies were sold during the war through their agents in Richmond and Columbia. The publishing house was closed when Federal troops entered Greensboro, April 20, 1865. Bettie D. Caldwell, "James W. Albright," *Founders of Greensboro*, pp. 289-290.

[335] James Washington Albright (1835-1917) was born and reared in Greensboro and at the age of sixteen became an apprentice printer in the office of the *Greensboro Patriot*. In 1856 he began a partnership with E. W. Ogburn and C. C. Cole as publishers of the Greensboro *Times*, an independent literary weekly. This venture lasted until the war, when Ogburn died and Cole entered the army, and Albright joined Sterling and J. D. Campbell in a new printing firm. In May 1862, he enlisted in the army and served throughout the war as an ordnance sergeant in the Fifth Battalion of Light Artillery. After the war he returned to Greensboro and to publishing: *The Patriot* and *Patriot and Times* (1868-1876); *The Beacon* (1880-1881), a Democratic Greenback weekly; and the *Daily Bugle* (1883-1884), an organ of the new tobacco interests. He was briefly city editor of the *North State* and the *Daily Record* (1890-1892) before he removed to Asheville in 1892, where he lived the remainder of his life, and where he was city editor of the *Morning Gazette* and then publisher of *The Ballot Box* (1894-1895), a publication journal. Bettie D. Caldwell, "James W. Albright," *Founders of Greensboro*, pp. 287-292.

[336] See p. 13, 65n. He was at this time solicitor pro-tem of the seventh judicial district.

[337] General Jackson's letter was written on September 4, 1862, and in it he said; "I respectfully recommend that Col. Bradley T. Johnson, late colonel of the First Maryland regiment, be appointed brigadier-general. While I was in command at Harper's Ferry, in the early part of the war, Colonel Johnson left his home in Maryland and entered our service, where he continued until his regiment was recently disbanded. I regarded him as a promising officer when he first entered the army, and so fully did he come up to my expectations that when his regiment was disbanded I put him in command of a brigade, and so ably did he discharge his duties in the recent battles near Bull Run as to make it my duty as well as my pleasure, to recommend him for a brigadier-generalcy. The brilliant service of his brigade in the engagement on Saturday last proved that it was under a superior leader, whose spirit was partaken of by his command. When it is so difficult to procure good general officers, I deem it due the service not to permit an opportunity of securing the services of one of such merit to pass unimproved." The letter is in Evans, *Conf. Mil. Hist.*, II, 177.

[338] Samuel Cooper (1798-1876), Adjutant and Inspector General of the Con-

Judge Saunders.[339] I learn that the only difficulty in the way of appointing Col. Johnston[340] Brig. Genl. is that M'd. has more field apps. now than that State ought in fairness to have. The Judge *would be glad* if you would *recommend* Col. J. if you could do so consistently with duty and obligations resting upon you towards others. The difficulty with you, it seems to me, touching the matter is, that it would seem that, if you were to recommend him that there would be an apparent, at least, neglect of our own State, but I learn that Col. J. will probably move to this State.

The letter is complimentary indeed, but I am not prepared to advise you what to do touching the matter. I would think we have many military officers who are fairly entitled to promotion. Consider of the matter and do what you think advisable and prudent. While I do not wish you to become my *electioneering* friend, if any of my friends should inquire about my wishes touching the Sol. which I now hold say to them, that I should be glad indeed, to be elected Sol. of this Circuit for the next four years.[341] If I am not greatly deceived all the members from this part of the State are for me.

---

federate army. A native of New Jersey and a graduate of West Point in 1815, Cooper had become southern in sympathy through his marriage to a granddaughter of George Mason and his residence in Virginia, and through his friendship with Jefferson Davis while Davis was secretary of war. Before 1861, when he resigned from the United States army, most of his duty had been as a staff officer and his wealth of experience along this line made him a natural choice to organize and administer the building of a new army. He became a full general when that rank was created by the Confederate Congress, and was the senior Confederate officer throughout the war. After the war he engaged in farming at his home near Fairfax, Virginia. Thomas M. Spaulding, "Samuel Cooper," *Dict. of Am. Biog.,* IV, 411-412; Cullum, *Biog. Register,* I, 150-151.

[339] See p. 194, 108n. Saunders was interested in recommending Johnson because he was his son-in-law, having married Jane Claudia Saunders on June 25, 1851.

[340] Bradley Tyler Johnson (1829-1903), politician and Confederate soldier, was born in Frederick, Maryland, graduated at Princeton in 1849, studied law, and was admitted to the bar. He became state's attorney, Democratic candidate for comptroller, state chairman of the Democratic committee, and delegate to the National Convention of 1860, where he supported the nomination of Breckinridge. He helped to organize the First Maryland Regiment for the Confederate army and served with it as major in the valley campaigns of J. E. Johnston and T. J. Jackson. He was left without a command through the disbanding of his regiment, of which he had become colonel, by the War Department. At second Manassas he was in temporary command of J. R. Jones' brigade, later served in the cavalry and was made brigadier general June 28, 1864, serving under Early in the Valley and in Maryland. In November 1864, he was sent to Salisbury, N. C. as commander of prisoners. After the war he practiced law in Richmond and represented railroad interests before the legislature. He was a member of the Virginia Senate, 1875-1879, where he led in drafting compromise measures designed to restore order to the tangled finances of that state. From 1879 to 1890 he practiced law in Baltimore, but spent his last years in Amelia, Va. W. C. Mallalieu, "Bradley Tyler Johnson," *Dict. of Am. Biog.,* X, 90-91; Evans, *Conf. Mil. Hist.,* II, 174-182.

[341] Merrimon was unanimously elected solicitor for the seventh circuit by the legislature on November 22, 1862. The total number of votes cast was 127. *Senate Journal, 1862-1863,* p. 33; *House Journal, 1862-1863,* p. 25.

Court week is just over here. I convicted five men of wilful murder and six of manslaughter. There are seventy persons on this circuit charged with capital crimes. Seven have already been convicted of murder misdemeanors are almost without number.

Nothing new of importance

[Raleigh]

[A. L. S. Governors' Papers (Vance),
State Department of Archives and History, Raleigh.]

From Ed. Stanly[342]

New Bern No. Ca.
October 21st. 1862

The strong affection which I have inherited & cherish for the people of my native State, has induced me to come here, by request of the President of the United States.

Nations like individuals, sometimes quarel because they misunderstand each other. This, I think, is now the case, between the Government of the United States and the State of North Carolina.

I confidently believe, I am in a situation to confer blessings upon the people of North Carolina, if the honorable gentlemen in high station, who now control her affairs will give me their assistance.

If it is not incompatible with your views of duty, I earnestly solicit the favor of an interview[343] with you, at such time or place, hereafter to be designated as may be agreeable to you.

[342] Edward Stanly (1808-1872), military governor of North Carolina under appointment of President Lincoln. He was born in New Bern, educated at Norwich University, studied law, and settled in Beaufort County to practice it. In politics he was an ardent Whig and served in Congress several terms, 1837-1843, 1849-1853. He represented Beaufort County in the House of Commons in 1844, and 1848, and was twice speaker. He was also attorney general of North Carolina from 1846 to 1848. In 1853, after his defeat for Congress by Thomas Ruffin, he moved to California, where he attained great prominence as a lawyer and joined the Republican party; he was nominated for governor of California in 1857. In 1862 President Lincoln appointed Stanly military governor of North Carolina and he came to New Bern on May 26 empowered by Secretary of War Stanton to perform all the duties of governor and with the purpose to "reestablish the authority of the Federal Government in the State of North Carolina, and to provide the means of maintaining peace and security to the loyal inhabitants of that State until they shall be able to establish a civil government." Stanly worked for the election of Vance in the occupied areas, but he encountered many difficulties, offended many people, both North and South, by his policies, and resigned, January 15, 1863. Stanly was still sympathetic with slavery and when he resigned he stated that the Emancipation Proclamation had crushed all his hopes for making peace and had altered the purposes of the war. He returned to California, broke with the Republican party over its reconstruction policies, and died in San Francisco in 1872. Warren, *Beaufort County History*, pp. 5-7, 13-15; Joseph Gregoire deRoulhac Hamilton, "Edward Stanly," Ashe, *Biog. Hist. of N. C.*, V, 370-378; Connor, *N. C. Manual*, pp. 444, 471, 498, 929-930; *Biog. Dir. of Am. Cong.*, pp. 1853-1854.

[343] President Lincoln himself had suggested to Stanly the desirability of an interview with Vance. *O. R.*, Ser. III, Vol. II, 845.

If the interview with yourself personally, for any reason be declined, then I ask that one or more good citizens, natives of, or residing in *North* Carolina, be authorized by you to confer with me.

My chief purpose is to see whether some measures cannot be adopted which may lead to an honorable peace.

If unfortunately this consumation so devoutly wished cannot be obtained, we may at all events do much to alleviate the inevitable sufferings that attend a War.

Authority has been given me, to negotiate for an Exchange of political prisoners.

I desire to do nothing in secret; will not stand upon any questions of etiquette, wishing only to be instrumental in doing good to my country, and to that brave & noble-hearted people who hitherto have conferred honor upon both of us; whose glory & welfare, I am as solicitous to protect, as any other son of North Carolina can be.

I hope to have an answer as soon as your convenience will allow.

I beg leave to tender you the assurance of my best wishes, for happiness and prosperity individually, and to express the hope, that millions of your countrymen will hereafter bless the day, on which the people of *North* Carolina, elevated you to your present position

[Raleigh]
[Vance Letter Book, 1862-1863,
  State Department of Archives and History, Raleigh.]

From S. G. French[344]

Head Quarters
Petersburg Va
Octo. 22ᵈ. 1862

I. I have the honor to acknowledge the receipt of your letter of yesterday. Let me first assure you that you have not the interest and welfare of the people of your State more at heart than I have.

II. That after the departure of Genl Lee to Northern Virginia N. C. was stript of all her available forces to meet the enemy on the Potomac.

III. That on the threatening advance of the enemy at Warrenton and lower Potomac I was directed to hold all the regiments at points on the line of the railroads to move up here and in this condition they now mostly remain. It was my wish to rapidly mass my forces and strike blows at different points where the enemy were in small force in different parts of yr State, but the requirements of General Lee, has together with the accumulation of the troops of the enemy at Suffolk, prevented my doing so.[345]

IV. Finding the Enemy not disposed to advance some days since I sent orders to Col. Martin[346] (17 Regt) to hold his troops ready to move on Plymouth — that Col Cantwell [347] would join him &c and not to disclose the movement to any human being. I did not know the Colonel was on leave.

The order to both him and Cantwell were on the outside marked "private" lest some Staff Officer should open them. The result was Martins "private" letter and Cantwells must have been forwarded to them, and neither being with their regiments nothing has been heard from them.

V. On the 20th. Radcliff's[348] regiment was ordered up in place of Cantwell's and Col Radcliff has been directed to move with his regiment and Martins on Plymouth, to drive out the enemy and give the people of Martin, Washington & Tyrell Counties an apportunity to bring out their provisions &c.

As secrecy is the Soul of Success in cases of this kind, I told no one except one Officer on my staff who did part of the writing for me. I presume Radcliff will move the last of this week or early

---

[345] See p. 269, 331n.

[346] William Francis Martin, lawyer and Democratic politician and brother of Adjutant General James G. Martin, was from Pasquotank County. He graduated from the University of North Carolina in 1842, studied law and, when the war came, was commissioned captain of company B in the Seventeenth North Carolina Regiment. He was captured at Hatteras; when he was exchanged he became colonel of the regiment. He was a trustee of the University from 1874 to 1879; he died in 1880. Grant, *Alumni History;* Moore, *N. C. Roster,* II, 39; Clark, *N. C. Regts.,* II, 1, IV, 556.

[347] Edward Cantwell, a Wilmington editor who had moved to Raleigh in the fifties, where he became a city commissioner and city attorney, and now lieutenant colonel of the Fifty-ninth North Carolina Regiment (cavalry). Cantwell had been clerk of the House of Commons, 1856-1860 and became, in 1874, a member of the State Senate from New Hanover County. He had been a Know-Nothing who later became a Democrat and favored secession. In December 1860 he wrote from the House of Commons "A Plan of Adjustment Through the Treaty Making Powers of the President and the Senate" to Charles Wilkes, captain of the United States Navy. In this tract Cantwell denied that he was a disunionist *per se,* but he appeared to be, in the language of the times, a conditional disunionist. He advocated the making of a treaty with South Carolina, thereby recognizing secession and avoiding war. A copy is in the Graham Papers CH, December 31, 1860. Early in 1862 Cantwell was made military governor of Norfolk and the *Standard,* quoting the Milton *Chronicle* claimed that the "true secret of all our reverses is appointment of such broken down politicians to offices of responsibility." Holden blamed old party prejudices and criticized President Davis for appointing only secessionists to office, using Cantwell as an example of what he styled inefficient results. On May 11, 1861, Cantwell had been elected lieutenant colonel of the Twelfth North Carolina Regiment but was transferred to the Fifty-ninth on September 28, 1862. Later in the war he was appointed by the president a judge of the military court for the third army corps at Petersburg, October 19, 1864; after the war he was professor of law and assistant professor of history at Georgia Military College in Savannah. Raleigh *North Carolina Standard,* March 6, 1861, March 29, April 5, 1862; Clark, *N. C. Regts.,* III, 456; Connor, *N. C. Manual,* pp. 423, 725.

[348] See p. 142, 579n. Radcliffe was now colonel of the Sixty-first Regiment, which had been organized in Wilmington in August 1862.

next week on Plymouth & I hope with successful results. About this you had better say nothing, for between gossip and the newspapers nothing can be done without the Enemy finding it out before it can be executed.

VI. There were some complaints come to me respecting the withdrawal of forces from Onslow County.[349] The Same Cavalry force is there under Capt Ward [350] that has been there since the fall of New Berne, except two companies of Partisan Rangers.[351] When these Rangers are disciplined in the Camp of instructions at Garysburg we will have a force for the position that can move rapidly from point to point.

VII. I have been anxious to have the rivers obstructed, but have had no means to do it. Finally Engineers have been sent to examine them. Had they been ordered to report to me, I should now have them on the Roanoke River at work. I can only say in conclusion that I will do all that can be done to protect the people— at the same time confront the threatening forces of the enemy when they are in large force. The force in Suffolk now are 25000 holds most of my troops from necessity here and at Franklin.

I will be most happy to confer with you at any time and will thank you to write to me freely your views on any matters concerning our common Welfare
Raleigh
[Vance Letter Book, 1862-1863,
    State Department of Archives and History, Raleigh.]

To Jefferson Davis

STATE OF NORTH CAROLINA
EXECUTIVE DEPARTMENT
Raleigh Octr. 25th. 1862

When in Richmond [352] I had the honor to call your attention in the presence of Mr Randolph to the subject of allowing the conscripts the privilege of selecting the regiments to which they should go. I understood you and the Secretary both to assent to it willingly. A few days after my return home therefore I was much surprised and grieved to find an order coming from the Secretary to Major Mallett to disregard an order to this effect

[349] See p. 268, 329n.

[350] George D. Ward, of Bertie County, captain of company I of the Fifty-ninth North Carolina Regiment (cavalry). Moore, *N. C. Roster*, III, 671.

[351] Partisan Rangers were authorized by act of Congress on April 21, 1862. The act prohibited the organization of new corps but new recruits were made possible through the partisan rangers by application through the commanding generals of the military departments where the said corps were to be employed. These were irregular service units and the act authorizing them was repealed on February 17, 1864. *O. R.* Ser. IV, Vol. I, 1095, 1098.

[352] Vance was in Richmond for a few days during the first week of October.

from Brig. Genl. Martin and to place all of them in certain brigades under Genl. French.[353]

I immediately addressed a letter to Mr. Randolph protesting against it and giving my reasons for so doing. To this letter after the lapse of two weeks I have rec^d. no reply.[354]

Last week about one hundred men were brought into camp from one county above from a region somewhat lukewarm who had been got to come cheerfully under the solemn promise made them by my enrolling officer that they should be allowed to join any regiment they desired according to the published order. Under the circumstances Genl Martin said they might yet have their choice, started them accordingly and wrote to Genl French begging his consent to the arrangement. He refused of course and according to a note received from him, the men were stopped at Petersburg and distributed equally to certain regiments as quarter Masters' stores or any other chattel property alleging that by not coming in sooner they had forfeited all claims to consideration.

Of the shortsightedness and inhumanity of this harsh course towards our people, I shall offer no comment. I wish not only to ask that more liberal policy may be adopted but to make it the occasion of informing you also of a few things of a political nature which you ought to have

The people of this State have ever been eminently conservative and jealous of their political rights. The transition from their former opinions anterior to our troubles to a state of revolution & war was a sudden & very extraordinary one. Prior to Lincoln's proclamation the election of delegates to our proposed convention exhibited a popular majority of upwards of 30000 against secession for existing causes.[355] The late election after sixteen months of War and membership with the Confederacy show conclusively that the original advocates of secession no longer hold the ear of our people, without the warm & ardent support of the old Union men No. Carolina could not so promply and

---

[353] For the order from the secretary to Mallett see p. 252.

[354] See p. 252 for Vance's letter to Randolph. Randolph's reasons for not answering Vance's letter were given on November 7, to President Davis: "The letter of Governor Vance was not answered because it imputed "bad faith" to the President and Secretary of War and could not be answered risking a breach between the Governor and the Department, which would be detrimental to the public service." O. R., Ser. IV, Vol. II, 148.

[355] It is difficult to say just how Vance arrived at this majority opposed to secession for existing causes in February of 1861. When the vote was taken for a convention or no convention, and delegates elected, the convention was defeated by a majority of 651 in a vote of 93,995. Of course many persons voted for the convention without thereby favoring secession, but it is impossible to say how many. A plurality of the delegates chosen were Unionists and a clear majority was against secession for existing causes, but the issue was so complicated that it is difficult to say just what majority for Union existed in the state at the time. See Sitterson, N. C. Secession, p. 223, 56n.

generously have been brought to the support of the seceding States and without that same influence constantly & unremittingly given the present status could not be maintained forty eight hours. *These are facts.* I allude to them not to remind you of any heretofore political difference (which I earnestly hope are buried in the graves of our gallant countrymen) but simply to give you information.

The corrollary to be deduced is briefly this that the opinions and advice of the Old Union leaders must be heeded with regard to the government of affairs in North Carolina or the worst consequences may ensue. I am candid with you for the causes' sake. I believe, Sir, most sincerely that the Conscript Law could not have been executed by a man of different antecedents without outbreaks among our people. And now with all the popularity with which I came into Office it will be exceedingly difficult for me to execute it under your recent call with all the assistance you can afford me. If on the contrary West Point Generals who know much less of human nature than I do of military service, are to ride rough shod over the people, drag them from their homes and assign them or rather *consign* them to strange regiments and strange commanders without regard to their wishes or feelings. I must be compelled to decline undertaking a task which will certainly fail. These conscripts are entitled to consideration. They comprise a number of the best men in their communities whom indispensable business large and helpless families poverty & distress in a thousand shapes have combined to keep at home until the last moment. In spite of all the softening I could give to the law and all the appeals that could be made to their patriotism, much discontent has grown up and now the waters of insubordination begin to surge more angrily than ever as the extended law goes into effect.[356] Many openly declare they want not another conscript to leave the State until provision is made for her own defence, others say it will not leave labor sufficient to support the women & children & therefore it must not be executed. Thousands are flying from our Eastern Counties with their slaves to the centre & West to devour the very short crops and increase the prospect of starvation. Gov Letcher[357] is threatening to deprive the

---

[356] The second Conscription Act, September 27, 1862, extended the age limit of those liable to military service from thirty-five to forty-five; and reduced exemptions followed in the law of October 11, 1862.

[357] John Letcher (1813-1884), Governor of Virginia. A graduate of Washington College in Lexington, Va., he studied law and settled there to practice. He became editor of the *Valley Star,* a Democratic paper supporting Jacksonian policies in a strong Whig county, and was elected to Congress as a Democrat, 1851-1859. In 1860 he opposed secession until Lincoln's proclamation, and supported Stephen A. Douglas for president. He became governor in 1859 and usually supported the Confederate administration. William G. Bean, "John Letcher," *Dict. of Am. Biog.,* XI, 192.

State of a contract we have for procuring Salt in Virginia.[358] And when the enemy pestilence abates, we shall have no assurance of obtaining it from any other source, hence I am importuned by many to defend our own coast myself. You see the difficulties that beset me. But through them all I have endeavored & shall endeavour to hold my course straight forward for the common good. It is disheartening however to find that I am thwarted in so small a matter as this which is yet a great one to the conscript.

I have thus spoken candidly & explicitly— I beg you will not in any matter misunderstand me or fail to appreciate my motives. I trust that whether on the field or in the council I have establish-ed claim to respect & confidence. I can do much towards increasing our armies if properly aided by the War Department. When the sowing of the wheat crop is completed fifteen or twenty thousand men can be got out in a short time, especially if an assurance can be given that an adequate proportion will be sent to the defence of our own coast & suffering people.

I should also be pleased to know what our Sister States are doing in support of the conscript law as a very general impression prevails that this State is doing vastly more than her share. A course of justice & fair treatment will do more than all besides in bringing our entire able bodied population into the field.

Earnestly trusting that my representation of things in No. Ca. may enable you to do that which is for the best & will most ad-vance the great cause for which the nation is suffering & bleeding.

I remain, with the highest respect

[Richmond]
[Vance Letter Book, 1862-1863,
  Copy in Governors' Papers (Vance),
  State Department of Archives and History, Raleigh.]

From H. W. Ayer[359]

Pleasant Hill Guilford Co
Octr. 25th. 1862—

I herewith continue my report of the condition of the mnf interests of N. C. which I hope will meet yr. approval. J Shelly &

---

[358] The Virginia legislature had just passed an act prohibiting the export of salt in certain contingencies. According to the law, if the supply of salt was not sufficient in Virginia the governor was given authority "to disregard any contract made with the separate states of the Confederate States" until Virginia was sup-plied. This was viewed as a tragedy in North Carolina, where the sea coast opera-tions had been interrupted by the yellow fever epidemic. Holden was bitter: "We give him blood, but he may refuse us salt." Raleigh *North Carolina Standard,* October 21, 1862. Letcher had protested to Governor Clark about the North Caro-lina embargo on cotton and woolen goods. Letcher to Clark, April 29, 1862, Gov-ernors' Papers (Clark).

[359] Hal W. Ayer, of Wake County, was an agent of the state employed to inspect manufacturing contracts and establishments on behalf of the government.

Son, Tho masville, Shoe Makers— work 25 hands— Whites 24, Males— 24 Females 1, Blks 00 No. of Conscripts 14. Contract unlimited with State & Gov^t. No stipulation pr month Average to the hand pr day 1½ pairs Delivered since Aug. 4th. 790 prs. by the 25th inst— would deliver 200 prs more, Saw Contract all Bona Fide Employees— Stitched Shoes— John T. Harris— *Eden P. O.* Randolph Co.— Makes Saltpetre, Whole No. hand 7, all Conscripts, Contract with State & Confe^d. date of Contract Sep^t. 6th. Amt. Do. 50 lbs to the hand, has delivered 46 lbs— and by the 6th Nov, will deliver 300 lbs. More— Doing the best they can— J. S. Steed Ashboro— Shoes— Contract with the State & Confed— work 6 hands 4 Whites 2 Blks— 2 Conscripts— Contract 75 pr, pr month, Has not Failed in a single instance— Cedar Falls Co— at Cedar Falls and Franklinsville— Cotton factories, To these Gentlemen I put some pretty close questions, thinking you would like to know all you could find out about them, as the prices are a little *taller* on their kind of goods than any other— They report, for both factories— the whole No. of Employees 106. Males 24, females 82 no blacks— 10 Conscripts, Amt of Contract with state & Gov^t. $10,000— worth pr month, Delivered last week $2644, Present cost of one Bundle, Cotton Yarn $1.70 selling price, $4.00, (in which you see the 75 pr. ct. business groaneth) Present cost of 1 yd sheeting, 17 cents, selling price 50c (*previous observations applies*) sheeting when make into shirts to fill Gvt. Contract, netts 30 cts Oznaburger in to drawers for Do— netts 32c Do, in Salt-Sacks, 33c Very heavy sheeting, made into grain sacks for Gvt Contract, netts 50c Post Office Twine for Gvt Contract, netts 30c not half (as they say) of actual cost.

No. yards sheeting produced in one months running (25 days) 32500 yds. Costs $5525-00 sells for $16250-00 No. Bunches Cotton Yarn made in one month (25 days) 1125 costs $1912 ^{50}--$_{100}$ sells for $4500^{00}- so that in these two items alone according to their own figures there is a nett profit pr month of $14322,50, that I think is a great deal better pay than being either soldier or Governor— and not one half the responsibility— About— 1/20 1/20th. of what they make goes out of the state into the hands of Speculators They include in their calculation of the actual cost of these articles, The interest on the original investment of capital, hire of labor, wear & tear of Machinery &c &c. in fact every thing they can get in, and also count 6 lbs of raw cotton to the bundle of yarn— which weighs only 5 lbs Occasionally they sell to the wife or widow of some poor soldier at ½ price— Deep River Manf Co— make the same report, except that their Bunch Yarn Costs $1.75— & their sheeting 18, which difference they say is oweing to their having a smaller factory, but having to emply the same No— of Overseers— *They* make pr month (25 days) 15500 yds— sheeting & 500 Bundles Yarn— about 1/20 goes out of the State, They both count their cotton at 20c but a part of it did not cost that much Messrs. Coffin Foust & Co, (Island Ford) also have a Cotton factory— but declined answering some of my questions, They report 57 operatives, 11 white males, 46 females— 4 Conscripts, Have no state or Gov^t. Contract, make in 26 days— 1170 bunches Cotton Yarn, 19968 yds of Sheeting— Sell Yarn at $4.00. Cloth at 50c but decline saying what it costs to produce it, I merely replied *"Good morning gentlemen"* But I thought they could tell if they would I visited several small contracts for shoes— N. Kivett,[360] A. M. Smith & P. C. Smith found their details and contracts all right, Gave Kivett a blowing up about not making more than one pr. pegged shoes pr day— and A. M. Smith for not making I pr. *sewed* shoes pr day to the hand, Kivet works 9 Conscripts & A. M. Smith 4. P. C. Smith has 7 Conscripts, doing well There has been 5 barns burned in Randolph & Chatham within the last two weeks— supposed to be the work of these renegrade Conscripts and deserters, A number of persons have been shot at also— and in every instance, the party suffering was one who had been engaged in trying to catch these miscreants, A part of this has been done in Col Worth's regiment,[361] and a part in Col, Fouchee's—[362] With one question now I will close Has the administrator of an estate a right to sell as a part of the estate, a contract to carry the mail, and is the contract sufficient, when thus obtained to exempt a man from the conscript law, Address me it Greensboro,

[Raleigh]

[A. L. S. Governors' Papers (Vance),
State Department of Archives and History, Raleigh.]

From Jas. Rhodes and Others

Oct the 26 / 62 (2)

campe hanes Mr vanes I am abecesente for mi commande a voute lef ande I am sorey that I done soe hite is the fiste defence

---

[360] The firm of S. W. & N. Kivett made shoes for the state at the factory at New Market, in Randolph County. They also owned a large tannery which was operated by steam power. Raleigh *North Carolina Standard*, October 21, 1862.

[361] See p. 206, 144n. Because of his duties as salt commissioner Worth resigned the colonelcy of the Sixty-third Militia and was succeeeded by Henry L. Steed, formerly captain, on December 20, 1862. Lieutenant colonel Hezekiah Fuller commanded the regiment until Steed was chosen. The jurisdiction of the Sixty-third was confined to the western portion of Randolph County, and Worth had been ordered to use force if a collision with deserters was inevitable, and to apply to Raleigh for more troops if they were needed. Militia Letter Book, October 1, 1862, p. 208; Militia Roster, p. 226.

[362] William F. Fouchee, colonel of the Sixty-fourth Regiment of Militia, which operated in the eastern portion of Randolph County. He lived at Reed's Creek, in Randolph, and had been colonel since February 25, 1862. Militia Roster, p. 230.

I evr was gilte of and ef you will parden me and sende me to mi commande I nevr will doo so no more I com hom to see mi famley I didente come to gate shete of the war I com to per vide for mi famley and I am her under garde at this time I didente lieowte in the wodes to excape from bin taken upe I will wate for your Dispaches yours re spectfull

Jas Rhodes
Bengeman Lovless
Drewey gren
Alberte toney
Gilferde ones
calvin ones
Th camell
Henrey ramsey

[Raleigh]
[A. L. Signed by same hand, Governors' Papers (Vance), State Department of Archives and History, Raleigh.]

From Jefferson Davis[363]

CONFEDERATE STATES OF AMERICA
Executive Department
Richmond, Va. Oct. 27. 1862

I am directed by the President to inform you that your letter of the 20th. inst.[364] suggesting the employment of heavy cotton stuffs for army harness and the devotion of leather to the exclusive manufacture of shoes, was referred to the Quartermaster General,[365] who reports:

That very inconsiderable contracts are made by the Q. M. Dept. for harness in North Carolina. The contracts to which you refer are probably for the Ordnance Bureau. The suggestion is a good one that the practice of using leather be discontinued as far as possible for the manufacture of anything else than shoes. But the Q. M. Genl. thinks that while cotton serves very well for plantation harness it is unfit for the wear & tear to which harness is necessarily subjected in the Army.

Your letter has been forwarded to the Secretary of War with directions to secure the leather of the country as far as practicable for shoes.

---

[363] The letter is written and signed by Burton N. Harrison, private secretary to President Davis.

[364] Vance's letter to Davis is printed in *O. R.*, Ser. I, Vol. XVIII, 758. In it Vance estimated that, because the price was better, two-thirds of the state's leather was made into harness instead of into shoes. If his suggestions were to be followed he expressed the belief that the production of needed shoes could be doubled.

[365] Abraham Charles Myers. See p. 150, 611n.

I have the honor, Sir, to present you the compliments of the President.
[Raleigh]
[A. L. S. (Harrison), Governors' Papers (Vance),
[Vance Letter Book, 1862-1863,
State Department of Archives and History, Raleigh.]

From Jas. Sinclair[366]

Private

Lumberton Oct 27th- 1862

This is entirely a *private* letter upon *private* business which I trust you will excuse, notwithstanding the claims upon your attention & time of higher and more important duties. I have been just informed by a letter from a friend that Col Cantwell [367] of the 51st- Regt. N. C. T. Stationed at Kinston has resigned, — Owing to the following circumstances It is said that for five consecutive days he was unfit for duty by reason of drunkenness and that of the most beastly character, And being about to be cashiered for the offence his resignation being tendered it was accepted and he is no longer in the service, It is alledged that even if Seniority was allowed to prevail in filling the vacancy in a Regt. so recently formed as the 51st- the qualities of the next officers in rank,[368] so far as excessive indulgence in ardent spirits is concerned utterly unfits him for the position, not to mention the fact that he is totally unacquainted with military matters, The next field officer

[366] See p. 121, 474n.

[367] John Lucas Cantwell, colonel of the Fifty-first North Carolina Regiment from its organization at Wilmington on April 13, 1862, until his resignation in October 1862. He was born in Charleston and lived in Columbia and New Orleans before moving to Wilmington in 1851, where he became colonel of the Thirtieth regiment of North Carolina Militia in 1855, clerk of the United States court for the Cape Fear District, and a magistrate of the county. As a colonel of militia he had achieved some notoriety in April 1861 when he obtained the evacuation of Fort Caswell by Major Hedrick and Captain Thurston, who had prematurely captured that Federal post. After his resignation from the Fifty-first he enlisted as a private in company F of the Third North Carolina Regiment, eventually being promoted to the captaincy from the ranks. He was captured at Spottsylvania Courthouse, May 12, 1864, and imprisoned at Morris Island until the close of the war. After the war he was agent of the Adams Express Company, a produce broker, secretary of the Wilmington Produce Exchange, and for many years secretary of the Wilmington Chamber of Commerce. He was a veteran of the Mexican, the Civil, and the Spanish-American wars; Sprunt describes him as a character who was, to say the least, quixotic. Evans, *Conf. Mil. Hist.*, IV, 420-421; Sprunt, *Chronicles*, 276-280, 300-302; Moore, *N. C. Roster*, I, 100-101, III, 447; Clark, *N. C. Regts.*, III, 205-206. For recommendations of Cantwell for high military positions at the beginning of the war see John D. Taylor to Clark, October 6, 1861; William George Thomas to Clark, October 7, 1861; Eli W. Hall to Clark, November 1861; and George Davis to Clark, November 1861, Governors' Papers (Clark).

[368] The next officer in rank was William A. Allen, of Duplin County, who was made colonel but who soon resigned, on January 19, 1863. Moore, *N. C. Roster*, III, 447; Clark, *N. C. Regts.*, III, 205-206.

is the Major, a young man of the name of McKethan,[369] a son of the carriage maker at Fayetteville of that name. Now I am burning to be in the service once more, will you not permit me to lift my arm, *one more time,* in defence of "the *Old North State."* Gov if you have not the power directly a word from you would secure my appointment at Richmond. I am aware that this may seem to be asking too much, and so it is in one respect, and there was a man living who knew the circumstances of my case, from beginning to end as you do, God is my witness that I would never have troubled you, But I have not, *therefore I appeal* to you as a man whom God in his providence has placed in your present elevation to do justice and vindicate the rights of the innocent and the oppressed, You know how I have been dealt with I ask you to assist me, not for anything I have done or may do for you, but for the sake of truth and right.

If I cannot get the command of the 51st. will you give me authority to raise a body of state troops for the defence of our own glorious North Carolina, I can do it, if you will but give me the authority Your obedient

servant & friend

[Raleigh]

[A. L. S. Governors' Papers (Vance),
State Department of Archives and History, Raleigh.]

From Jas. Sinclair[370]

Lumberton Rob. Co, N. C.
Oct 27th. 1862

I beg leave to inform you that agreeable to the conversation had with you in reference to Salt, inter alia, when last in Raleigh I have instituted the necessary inquiries as to the quantity of that highly indispensible commodity in Wilmington, and the person by whom it is held.

Exclusive of what has arrived in port recently, there was a few week ago between fifty & sixty thousand bushels of imported Salt in Wilmington and upon which no doubt the yellow fever has laid its embargo, so that the probabilities are that the full quantity mentioned above may be there still. Many of the merchants of that Town are refugees, residing for the present in this village, and I am aware that efforts are being made to send the most of it to Augusta Ga, where prices are still higher than

---

[369] Hector McKethan, of Fayetteville, originally captain of company I upon the organization of the regiment, then major, and made colonel on January 19, 1863. Moore, *N. C. Roster,* III, 447; Clark, *N. C. Regts.,* III, 205-206.

[370] See p. 121, 474n.

here, and where there is not so much of domestic Salt to compete in market with the imported, as at Wilmington.

The firms by whom the Salt is held are as follows,
Kidder & Martin
Harris & Howell
Geo, Myers
and the Worths

The above information may be relied on, as I have conversed personally with some of those who hold the Salt.

I have the honor   to be

[Raleigh]

[A. L. S. Governors' Papers (Vance), State Department of Archives and History, Raleigh.]

To Edward Stanly[371]

STATE OF NORTH CAROLINA
EXECUTIVE DEPARTMENT
Raleigh— Oct. 29th. 1862

Your communication of the 21st. inst.[372] has been recd, to which I proceed to reply—

It is "incompatible with my views of duty" to grant you a personal interview for the purposes mentioned for the following reasons

First. If the measures which you propose to discuss relate to a general peace between the Confederate States, and the United States, then it is needless for me to inform you that I have not the power to confer with you authoritatively. By the Constitution of the Confederate States to which the State of North Carolina has unanimously acceded, the power to make war & conclude peace has been delegated to the President & Senate— To their hands I am content to leave it.

Secondly—If your proposition (as it evidently does) has relation to a separate peace between the State of North Carolina & the United States, then it is still more inadmissable. North Carolina with great unanimity dissolved her connection with the old government and entered into a solemn compact with the new government of the Confederate States. Her obligations in this new relation are obvious & her honor is pledged to redeem all these obligations faithfully with the last dollar & the last drop of blood, for the general good.

Your proposition is based upon the supposition that there is baseness in North Carolina sufficient to induce her people to abandon their confederates & leave them to suffer alone all the horrors of this unnatural war, for the sake of securing terms for them-

[371] See p. 272, 342n.
[372] See p. 272.

selves — a mistake which I could scarcely have supposed any one so well acquainted with the character of our people as yourself could have committed.

North Carolina having committed the questions of war & peace to the authorities of the Confederate Government has now no cause to distrust their ability or their patriotism, or to withhold that generous support to their measures which has thus far characterized her.

The same remarks are applicable in reference to the negotiating for the exchange of political prisoners of whom North Carolina has none in custody.

Your prosposition that I should send Commissioners to hold an interview with you is also respectfully declined for the reasons set forth above.

Regretting, Sir. that it is equally beyond my province to treat with you in regard to doing anything to "alleviate the inevitable sufferings that attend the war," and assuring you that any proposition you may feel authorized to make for that humane purpose with be promptly forwarded to the proper authorities if intrusted to me,[373]
New Berne
[Vance Letter Book, 1862-1863,
State Department of Archives and History, Raleigh.]

From Jno. H. Peebles[374]

Goldsboro Octo. 31st 1862

Enclosed please find Check on Bank of North Carolina for $60. a contribution by my wife & daughters & the Citizens of Kinston & Vicinity as a Gun boat fund, which project Exploded after the fall of Several of our Sea port Towns & fort Dollenson,[375] the money was returned to my wife, to refund to the several contributors. We find in the Raleigh Standard an appeal from your Excellency to the citizens of North Carolina for Clothing Shoes &c for our brave Soldiers,[376] and as we cannot procure them in this section we have the consent of the several contributors to dispose of the funds in any manner we thought proper for the benefit of our Soldiers. Not Knowing whom to send the Check to, we have taken the liberty of Enclosing to you, Knowing that it will be

---

[373] Vance sent a copy of Stanley's letter, and of his own reply, to President Jefferson Davis, saying: "I think you should be aware of what is going on on our coast, and also because I did not know but that Stanly's proposition might foreshadow something of importance to our cause." Vance to Davis, November 1, 1862, Vance Letter Book, 1862-1863.

[374] See p. 130, 517n. He was now a refugee in Goldsboro.

[375] Fort Donelson, on the Cumberland River in Tennessee, was surrounded by forces under General Grant, and surrendered Feb. 16, 1862.

[376] For Vance's appeal see pp. 265-267.

properly attended to— you will please dispose of the proceeds of the Check for the benefit of our Sick & wounded Soldiers in Va. You will perceive that I am writing from Goldsboro where I am now living, for how long I cannot say, I deemed it imprudent to remain in Lenoir longer as every once in a while the Negroes were leaving for the Yankees, and my impression is that, they will come to Kinston this Winter and there will be a general stampede of the Negroes, and I am advising my particular friends to remove them up the country, and many of them are doing so— the blood & thunder fellows have long since done so, they you know, were to whip the Yankees in no time, but the first booming of the Cannon on our cost they took fright, and left the true men to protect the Country. Your patriotic course my dear Sir are extorting from your heretofore vilest enemies the highest praise, I hear it almost every day, and it does my very soul good. I hope when the legislature meets, some steps will be taken to defend this Section of the State, the present force is inadequate, I learn the Yankees are being reinforced at Newbern weekly there present force numbers between 8 & 10 thousand men. I shall be glad at your leisure to hear from you on the subject that I addressed you upon Sometime Since please acknowledge receipt of the Check that I may know it reached you safely.—

My Wife's Kind regard together with my own, to yourself & Mrs. V—
[Raleigh]
[A. L. S. Z. B. Vance Papers,
State Department of Archives and History, Raleigh.]

From J. A. Maultsby[377]

Whiteville N. C.
Oct^r- 31st 1862

As one of the Captains of the Militia you have made it my duty to get by purchase or otherwise sundry articles for the Army—[378] I can get w^l- socks *now* for 75 cts per pair for cash, shall I give it? I can also get common jeans for $3^{00} pr yd— no blankets, are to be had & but few quilts—
Our county people gave so liberally last year, that they have

---

[377] John Alexander Maultsby (1818-1887), captain in the Fifty-seventh Regiment of North Carolina Militia. He was a lawyer and merchant. He studied at the University of North Carolina, 1835-1839, but refused a diploma on the ground that he was unjustly denied first honor. In 1861 he was a tax assessor who administered oaths of allegiance before the controversy over the oath came up in the Convention. After the war he moved to St. Louis, Missouri, where he successfully practiced law. He was a member of the House of Commons in 1850. Grant, *Alumni History*, p. 420; Battle, *History of U. of N. C.*, I, 458-460; Raleigh *North Carolina Standard*, January 22, 1862.

[378] In the proclamation of October 15 Vance ordered officers to collect supplies from the citizens for relief of the soldiers. See p. 266.

nothing now to give or sell and cards & cotton yarns are so high that they can not make anything. I can not get leather or shoes for the rogues have taken off nearly all the leather of which there was not enough for home consumption before— I have just issued notices that 50 cts a pair will be paid for wool & 33 1/3 cts a pair for cotton socks— Shall I recall it or continue it? Good jeans will sell for $4. a yard— Shall I get any of it? As such things must be had & as I do not know how much of such things or at what prices you can get them in other parts of the State, I therefore ask the foregoing questions and hope to hear soon from you.
[Raleigh]
[A. L. S. Governors' Papers (Vance),
  State Department of Archives and History, Raleigh.]

CHAPTER III

November—December, 1862

To John White[1]

[Nov 1, 1862]

THE State of North Carolina to
Mr. John White, of Warren County, Greeting:
You are hereby appointed a Commissioner for and on behalf
of the State of North Carolina, to visit Europe and negotiate for
the sale of Cotton Bonds of the said State and of the Confederate
States of America, by virtue of authority vested in me by the
General Assembly of North Carolina to clothe and equip her
troops in the armies of the Confederate States,[2] and You are

---

[1] John White (1814-1894), a merchant of Warrenton who became state agent
for North Carolina in Europe. He was born in Kirkcaldy, Fifeshire, Scotland
and came to Warrenton when he was about fourteen years of age, where he
established a mercantile business with his brother Thomas. In 1845 Thomas
White moved to Petersburg, Virginia, where he died. In the fifties John White
had perhaps "the handsomest stock of dry goods and notions in North Carolina"
housed in three large brick buildings which he had constructed for the purpose.
Later the business was known as White & Thorne and, when his son-in-law was
admitted to it, as Arrington, White & Company. John White was a striking looking
man, Scottish in complexion and business-like in manner. For a while after the
war he located in Liverpool where he was associated with William Lamb's general
agency for the sale of cotton and the purchase of goods. He returned to Warrenton
later where he died. L. W. Montgomery, *Sketches of Old Warrenton* (Raleigh,
1924), pp. 85-86 (cited hereafter as *Sketches of Warrenton*); Circular
in Graham Papers CH, April 1866; Raleigh *News and Observer*, July 14, 1937.
White was chosen for the mission to Europe upon the recommendation of
Colonel Thomas Devereux, chief quartermaster, and of Major Thomas D. Hogg,
chief ordnance officer. Hill, *Bethel to Sharpsburg*, I, 333.

[2] This was a bold construction of authority from the act of the legislature of
September 20, 1861, whereby the governor was to raise and equip the North
Carolina troops and wherein he was instructed to collect from the Confederate
Government the yearly allowance due the North Carolina soldiers in lieu of
clothing and "to pay the same into the public treasury, to the end that the same
may be expended under his direction in providing suitable clothing for said
troops, together with such additional sums as may be needed to supply the same."
Public Laws of N. C., 1861, 2, extra session chap. 17, section 76. Adjutant General
Martin, upon whom the task of equipping the troops was laid, found that the
commutation money was insufficient because of the great rise in prices and managed
to secure a revision of the arrangement whereby the actual cost of the supplies
of clothing and shoes would be met by the central government. Martin suggested
sending an agent to Europe in an effort to obtain supplies that were more and
more difficult to obtain at home, and to those who questioned the legal authority
to initiate so bold an enterprise he argued that if he could, under the law, purchase
a wagon, why not a steamer? Vance consulted a number of advisers about the
project, among whom B. F. Moore and Holden opposed the venture, and decided
to launch the state on the business of running the blockade in order to obtain
supplies for the army. Martin undoubtedly deserves the credit for suggesting the
plan, but Vance took the responsibility and his judgment was decisive in determining the degree and scope of the venture in the months to follow. White sailed
from Charleston on the Steamer *Leopard* on November 15, was delayed in Nassau,
and finally reached London on January 5, 1863. Hill, *Bethel to Sharpsburg*, I,
329-335; Adjutant General's Letter Book, p. 321, for commission to White.

further authorized to purchase supplies with the money thus raised, or in any other way you may be able to do so. All your official acts, done in pursuance of this authority, will be valid and binding on the said State of North Carolina.
In witness whereof Zebulon B. Vance, our Governor and Commander-in-Chief hath signed these presents, and caused our *Great Seal* to be affixed thereto.
Done at our City of Raleigh on the First day of November, A. D., one thousand eight hundred and sixty-two.

[SEAL]

Zebulon B. Vance

By the Governor
    R. H. Battle Jr.
        Private Secretary

[on reverse]

John White's commission from Gov. Vance, to visit Europe on business for the State of N. Carolina Nov. 1st. 1862.

[L. S. Governors' Papers (Vance),
State Department of Archives and History, Raleigh.]

Form B.

[Nov. 1, 1862]

    The State of North Carolina
      To Mr. John White of Warren County, Greeting,
You are hereby appointed a Commissioner for and on behalf of the State of North Carolina to visit Europe and negotiate for the sale of Cotton Bonds of the said State, and of the Confederate States of America, by virtue of Authority vested in me by the General Assembly of North Carolina to clothe and equip her troops in the Armies of the Confederate States And you are further authorized to purchase supplies with the monies thus raised or in any other way you may be able to do so— All your official Acts in the pursuance of this authority will be valid and binding on the said State of North Carolina.
        In witness whereof Zebulon B. Vance, our Governor, Captn. General and Comander-in-Chief hath signed

these presents and caused our Great Seal to be affixed
thereto.

[SEAL]

Done at our City of Raleigh on the 1st. day of November A. D. 1862

By the Governor   Zebulon B. Vance
R. H. Battle Jr.
Private Secry.

I, Edgar Pinchback Stringer of No. 8 Austin Friars in
the City of London do make oath and say That the foregoing is a true Copy of the Warrant to Mr. John White
whereby he is appointed a Commissioner for the purposes therein mentioned.

Sworn by the above named
Edgar Pinchback Stringer at 61   (Signed) Edgar P. Stringer
Gracechurch St.
(Signed) Jas. Abbiss
Aldn. J. P.
[Copy, Governors' Papers (Vance),
State Department of Archives and History, Raleigh.]

From Geo. W. Randolph[3]

Richmond, Va. Nov. 1, 1862.
The communication referred to in your letter of the 28th
ult. presented by Mr. S. P. Arrington,[4] did not reach the Department.

The Confederate Government is very desirous of complying
with the recommendation of the Governors of the several
States of the Confederacy, whenever it can be done with a due
regard to the public interests, and this Department would gladly
embrace the opportunity to gratify your wishes by detailing Mr.
Arrington for the purpose designated, but I regret to say, that in
the present stage of the campaign, when the exigencies of the service are so pressing, it is deemed unsafe to detail men from regiments in the field, and especially from those in the immediate

---

[3] See p. 132, 524n.
[4] S. P. Arrington was from Warren County and was quartermaster sergeant in
the Twelfth North Carolina Regiment. Originally from Nash County, he had
married a daughter of John White of Warrenton, and became a partner with his
father-in-law in business. After the war he joined his father, Dr. John Arrington,
and his brother, Richard T. Arrington, in the cotton commission business in Petersburg, Virginia. About fifteen years later he returned to Warrenton and built up
a large business in bright leaf tobacco, dying there in 1893. Montgomery, *Sketches
of Warrenton*, pp. 319-320; Moore, *N. C. Roster*, I, 437.

front of the enemy, for any civil employment, unless such detail is requisite for the support of the Army itself.

[on reverse]

An^{sd}. Sec'y of War that Arrington was to be detailed to take the place of his father-in law, who has gone abroad as Agent of the State for Army supplies & that his services could not have been obtained but for this detail

Z B V

[L. S. Governors' Papers (Vance),
State Department of Archives and History, Raleigh.]

From John H. Kinyoun[5]

Lewisville, N. C.
Nov. 1st. 1862

I hope that you will pardon me for intruding myself upon you at present. I write you this letter to make some inquiries concerning some individuals up here, how we should treat them, I have been off in the Service for some eight months, and and was owing some individuals and being paid off in Confederate money of corse this is all the mony that I have to offer them and there are two individuals that absolutely refuse to take the confederate mony, and I would like to know what we are to do with such men, that strike Such blows at our Cause and Country—The two men, that refused to take the curancy are Thomas Springle and Solomon Transue of Forsythe Co. I hope Gov. that you will give me answer to this. that we may stop this distructive policy— I would refer you our representatives Mr Jarrett[6] or Mr Coles[7] from my County, (I have been Surgeon in the Hospitals at Richmond for some time past) Please refer to my representatives

[Raleigh]

[on reverse] I don't know any remedy. Z B V

[A. L. S. Governors' Papers (Vance),
State Department of Archives and History, Raleigh.]

From Jno Michael[8]

Lexington. Nov. 1st. 1862

Having sent forward my Resignation on account of Suffering

[5] John H. Kinyoun, of Yadkin County, commissioned a surgeon on June 5, 1862. He was detailed on a variety of special duties until August 1863. when he became surgeon of the Sixty-sixth North Carolina Regiment upon its organization at Kinston. Moore, *N. C. Roster,* IV, 107; Clark, *N. C. Regts.,* III, 685, IV, 642.

[6] Isaac Jarratt, of Ashe County, who represented the 44th senatorial district (Alleghany, Ashe, Surry, Watauga, and Yadkin counties) in the State Senate in 1862. Raleigh *North Carolina Standard,* July 30, 1862; Connor, *N. C. Manual,* p. 493.

[7] Andrew Carson Cowles, of Yadkin County, member of the House of Commons, 1860-1864, and of the State Senate, 1865, 1866, 1870, 1872. He was also colonel of the Seventy-fifth Regiment of Militia. Connor, *N. C. Manual,* pp. 844, 857-858; Militia Roster, p. 354.

[8] John Michael, of Davidson County, captain of company H of the Forty-eighth

from a Wound Recved at the last battle before Richmond and left our army near Winchester a few weeks ago and knowing its Condition my regment & Company among others having lost all their Blanketts in the Sharpsburg fight in *Md* I am now Canvassing My County for the purpose of getting up Some Blanketts Socks Clothing &c for My Company and those men in my Regment from my County and am happy to Say I find the Good people of Davidson willing to give liberly with the Inshurance that they will be forwarded to their Sons which is now in So great Need what I have promised to do or at least those in My Company & Regt they are not only ancious to furnish Clothing but Vegetables Such as potatoes onions &c If they Could have Some asurance that those whoom they desere to give to would get them and Some friend or Father of a Son would allwayes be willing to forward them free of Charg for their trouble If Transportation Could be furnished More Convenient the question has bin ask me why we could not have a Transportation office in Davidson as well as Guilford or Rowan I can only answer by Saying probably thare has bin No application made— I write this letter at the request of May Citizens and if You think in Your Wise Judgment it is worth Notice and would add to the Comfort of our Sufering Soldiers, to establish a quartermasters office at Lexington and will give me the appointment I will Serve in that Capacity and do every thing in my power to relieve the wants of our poor Soldiers

P. S. As to my Caracter or ability I only refer you to Such men as B. C. Douthit[9] E. D. Hampton[10] A Hunt[11] A Hargrave[12] J. M.

North Carolina Regiment. He was commissioned March 1, 1862, wounded and disabled June 25, 1862, at French's Farm, and resigned from the service February 10, 1863. After the war he was a member of the State House of Representatives in 1872, and Sheriff of Davidson County, 1880-1884. Moore, *N. C. Roster*, III, 383; Clark, *N. C. Regts.*, III, 114-115; Connor, *N. C. Manual*, p. 589; Jacob Calvin Leonard, *Centennial History of Davidson County North Carolina* (Raleigh, 1927), p. 44 (cited hereafter as Leonard, *Davidson County*).

[9] Benton Clemons Douthitt (1811-1873), of Davidson County, was a merchant who had been a member of the House of Commons in 1844 and of the State Senate in 1858. He also represented Davidson County in the Convention of 1861, having opposed secession until Lincoln's call for troops. His business was ruined by the war and he emigrated to Missouri, where he died at Kingsville in 1873. Connor, *N. C. Manual*, p. 588; McCormick, *Personnel*, pp. 32-33.

[10] E. D. Hampton was Sheriff of Davidson County from 1854 to 1860. Leonard, *Davidson County*, p. 44.

[11] Andrew Hunt, a merchant of Lexington who was one of the original charter members of the Bank of Lexington when it was chartered in 1859. Leonard, *Davidson County*, pp. 101, 173.

[12] Alfred Hargrave, president of the Lexington Manufacturing Company which built the first cotton mill in Davidson County in 1839. He represented Davidson County in the State Senate in 1840 and 1844, and died in Lexington in 1880. Leonard, *Davidson County*, pp. 91, 437; Connor, *N. C. Manual*, p. 588.

Leach[13] W. R. Holt [14] H. Walser[15] or if a petiton from the Citizens
is nesary it can be furnished
[Raleigh]
[A. L. S. Governors' Papers (Vance),
State Department of Archives and History, Raleigh.]

From Wm. Poisson[16]

Fayetteville N. C. Nov 1st 1862
There seems to be at present a great demand for salt which if
not supplied must tend to reduce our supply of bacon the coming winter which result would have a great effect on our Army
and people.
But the question is how shall we make it and how shall the
price be reduced? There are plenty of salt works and what they

[13] James Madison Leach (1815-1891), former colleague of Vance in the United
States House of Representatives. He was born in Randolph County, attended the
common schools, graduated from West Point in 1838, but studied law and was
admitted to the bar in 1842, moving to Lexington about 1845. He represented
Davidson County in the House of Commons, 1848-1856, and in the State Senate
in 1865, 1866, and again in 1879. He was a member of the United States House
of Representatives in 1859-1861 as an American colleague of Vance, and again
from 1871 to 1875 as a Democrat. He was a member of the Confederate Congress
in 1864-1865; captain and lieutenant colonel in the Confederate army; and was
prominently mentioned for the Democratic nomination for governor in 1876
before Vance was named. Leach was never a real student of law, but he was a
leader in politics, had a keen intellect, and was an old-style orator of real power,
being powerful in sarcasm and invective, and a campaigner of great effectiveness.
Biog. Dir. of Am. Cong., p. 1445; Connor, *N. C. Manual*, pp. 588-589, 936, 939;
Clark, *N. C. Regts.*, II, 144; clippings in Walser Papers, Mrs. Maude Alford
Carpenter to Z. V. Walser, March 16, 1925, Walser Papers; Jonathan Worth to
A. G. Foster, April 28, 1866, Marmaduke Robins Papers, Southern Historical
Collection, University of North Carolina, Chapel Hill, N. C. (cited hereafter as
Robins Papers).
[14] William Rainey Holt (1798-1868), a farmer and physician of Lexington. He
was active in the founding of Davidson County, served as justice of the peace,
tax assessor, and as a member of the State Senate from Davidson County in 1838.
He was a very strong and active Democrat, a blatant original secessionist, and at
one time a man of some wealth, gradually abandoning medicine for planting on
his estate at "Lindwood." For many years he was president of the state agricultural
society, succeeding Judge Ruffin, and carried on many experiments in agriculture.
An item of interest to Vance was the fact that Mrs. Vance's close Morganton friend,
Elvira Jane Holt Erwin, was his daughter. W. W. Pearson, "William Rainey
Holt," Ashe, *Biog. Hist. of N. C.*, VII, 172-180; Leonard, *Davidson County*, pp. 162-
166; Connor, *N. C. Manual*, p. 538. For some interesting observations of Holt to
Warren Winslow, chairman of the Military Board, on how to win the war see
Holt's quixotic letter of June 6, 1861 in Military Board Papers.
[15] Henry Walser, known as "the squire of politics" in Davidson County, who
represented the county in the House of Commons in 1842, 1846, 1848, 1854, 1858,
and 1862. A man of much prominence and influence and very active in public
affairs, he died in Lexington at the age of seventy-six. Hamilton, *History of N. C.*,
IV, 295; Connor, *N. C. Manual*, p. 588.
[16] William Poisson was a citizen of Wilmington, but was in Fayetteville because
of the yellow fever epidemic at his home. He was superintendent's clerk and ticket
agent of the Wilmington and Weldon Railroad Company.

mostly used is labor but hands are scarce and what are hired $30 to 35 per month & found has to be paid.

My ideas are that the free negroes should bear some part in this conflict and not be allowed to enjoy their rights and privileges quietly at home. I think free negroes should be enrolled and be sent to the state and private salt works and be compelled to work for soldiers wages as do our Bros. friends & kindred in the army This would help to increase the supply of salt and would lessen its cost as so much would not have to be paid by the proprietors of our salt works for labor and again it would strengthen our army; for good strong young men are going & have gone to the state salt works to prevent going into the army and it is no uncommon thing to see Randolph Co. wagons hauling salt with two strong young men to each wagon when one driver is enough. Let these men go into the army free negroes are capable of driving these teams and should be allowed soldiers wages. The State authorities should not assist strong young men to dodge the conscription act for such a trifial position or duty as hauling state salt. The legislature ought to regulate the prices of the common necessaries of life or there will much suffering. A Lieut recently returned from Virginia says the soldiers in our army are getting dissatisfied in reference to it. I am fearful if prices are not put down and speculation put an end to there will be a revolution in our army. Our brave soldiers will not contend with the enemy while their families are grined at home Speculators ought not to be allowed to purchase in our state for speculation in Ga. & Va. Markets.

I am of the opinion of that poor Lieut who says unless stopped it will deprive us of our independence. Just to think of flour being $30 per brl. Bacon 60c per lb. fresh pork 30c per lb. Who can live at such prices?

I have seen your patriotic appeal in behalf of our suffering army.[17] Many poor women would gladly weave a suit of clothes for their husbands & sons in the services but the factories are charging from $4 to 7 a bunch for warp which formerly sold at 90c but the poor creatures cant afford it   it is as much as they can do to live.

Please hand the enclosed to the proper person to address for state Bounty.

I have not as yet seen your proclamation setting a part a day of thanksgiving surely we are indebted to God for His goodness & should acknowledge it. A day of fasting and prayer is needed. If you have not appointed the state proxy to the Wilm & Weldon

---

[17] See pp. 265-267.

Road [18] I would suggest My father (M[r]. Jehu D. Poisson) [19] or our relative Hon Geo. Davis[20] they are both Whigs and opposed to the old administration of the road, My fathers address for the present is Prospect Hall P. O. Bladen Co. My relative's Mr Davis at Richmond

[Raleigh]

[A. L. S. Governors' Papers (Vance),
State Department of Archives and History, Raleigh.]

From Jefferson Davis

Richmond Nov. 1st. 1862

I have the honor to acknowledge favor of the 28th ult.[21] and regret the disappointment to which some of the recruits of North Carolina have been subjected. I concur with you as to the policy of allowing the conscripts as far as the State of the Service will permit to select the companies and regiments in which they are to serve. The right secured by law to the volunteer to select his own company was lost it is true, by enrollment,[22] but the policy was so obvious of associating men together who would best harmonize with each other, that it was my purpose to continue the privilege beyond the limits fixed by law.

The danger to the coast of No. Ca. and our inability to draw troops from the Army of N. Virginia rendered it proper that the greatest exertion should be made immediately to fill up the regiments in Gen French's command,[23] but this did not interfere

---

[18] Formerly known as the Wilmington and Raleigh; it became the Wilmington and Weldon in 1855. Finished in 1840, the road was originally without state aid, but had since been successful in obtaining state help, the state's vote being in proportion to its financial stake in the railroad. See *Laws of N. C., 1848-'49*, chap. LXXXVI (January 27, 1849); *Public Laws of N. C., 1854-'55*, chap. 235 (February 14, 1855); Connor, *North Carolina*, II, 35-39.

[19] Of Wilmington, but in Bladen County because of the fever in Wilmington.

[20] George Davis (1820-1896) of Wilmington, Confederate Senator. He was born in New Hanover County (now Pender), graduated with first honor at the University of North Carolina in 1838, studied law and was licensed in 1840. He was a prominent Whig leader, but rarely sought office. In 1861 he had counseled Union and moderation, but when Governor Ellis sent him as a delegate to the Peace Convention in Washington he was persuaded that the union could not last. He was elected by the Convention to the Confederate Senate and remained there until January 1864, when he became attorney general of the Confederacy. He remained essentially conservative despite embracing secession, and as attorney general was a strict constructionist in his opinions. In 1878 Governor Vance offered him the position of Chief Justice of the North Carolina Supreme Court, but he declined on the ground that he could not live off the salary. Samuel A'Court Ashe, "George Davis," Ashe, *Biog. Hist. of N. C.*, II, 71-81; Fletcher Melvin Green, "George Davis, North Carolina Whig and Confederate Statesman, 1820-1896." *North Carolina Historical Review*, Vol. XXIII, No. 4 (October, 1946), pp. 449-470; Sprunt, *Chronicles*, pp. 220-225.

[21] See p. 275. The letter is dated October 25 in Vance Letter Book.

[22] See Randolph to Martin, October 11, 1862, *O. R.*, Ser. IV, Vol. II, 115-116 for the point that the right to select regiments was reserved only to those who volunteered before enrolment, and above, pp. 250-252.

[23] For French's command see p. 204, 142n.

with allowing the conscripts to select among those regiments the one to which they would be assigned so long as vacancies existed in the companies chosen & that I expected would have been done. I will send your letter to the War Department [24] with a copy of this reply to you and hope for the future there will be no grounds for dissatisfaction & that as far as feasible the disappointment to which you refer may be corrected by transfer.

I feel grateful to you for the cordial manner in which you have sustained every proposition connected with the public defence and trust that there will always be such cointelligence and accordance as will make us to cooperate for the public good.

The Conscript Act has not been popular any where out of the Army. There as you are aware it served to check the discontent which resulted from retaining the 12 months men beyond the term of their original engagement and was fairly regarded as a means equitable to distribute the burthen of public defence, but the State authorities have no where offered any opposition to its execution or withheld their aid except in the State of Georgia and so far as the Cadets of the Military Institute are concerned in the State of Virginia.

I shall endeavor by judicial decision to settle the questions raised in those two States and in the mean time have been cheered by the evidence of a popular sentiment which supports any measure necessary to protect our Country and secure our political independence.

Like yourself I have hoped that party distinctions which existed at a former time would be buried in the graves of the gallant men who have fallen in the defence of their birthrights & that we should all as a band of brothers strike for the inheritance our fathers left us. With sincere regard, I am most respectfully & truly

Raleigh

[A. L. S. Governors' Papers (Vance),
Vance Letter Book, 1862-1863,
State Department of Archives and History, Raleigh.]

From L. B. Northrop[25]

CONFEDERATE STATES OF AMERICA
SUBSISTENCE DEPARTMENT
Richmond Nov. 2[d]. 1862

It is very desirable to exhaust the hogs, beeves, peas, beans and potatoes of that part of North Carolina which lies within

---

[24] Randolph's reply is explained on p. 276, 354n.

[25] Lucius Bellinger Northrop (1811-1904), commissary general of the Confederacy. He was born in Charleston, graduated from West Point in 1831, studied medicine

the lines of the enemy or accessible to them. The President called my attention to information derived from you on the subject and the representations made in response to inquiries have been of a discouraging nature. I venture to apply to you for action thereon. It is obvious, that, those charged with such an undertaking, should be reliable business men whose integrity and energy should be personally known to those among whom they are to operate. Neither myself nor any one in my office has such knowledge of the country or the people of lower North Carolina as to enable me to make the proper selections and the necessary arrangements to the above end.

That being the case, I write to ask if you will allow your Agency to be used in this matter by having the whole devolve upon you, except so far as existing arrangements go. They run thus far— Mr Jacob Parker[26] has a Contract for packing Hogs at Warrenton and has the following Counties allotted to him for purchase— viz: Franklin, Warren, Nash, & Halifax. In addition Maj. W. H. Smith[27] has made certain arrangements with Mr. H. Hays of Harrellsville, which he will detail to you. The balance of the district spoken of it is proposed to put under your charge with these remarks—1st- That as this Bureau has already more Captains & Majors than it ought to have, it is not expedient to appoint more, except in case of absolute necessity, but to operate by Agents whose Agencies can cease when their business with the Department closes. 2d- That the points of delivery of the hogs should be fixed with reference to the packing houses, both in and out of the State of No. Ca. so that such as can go conveniently to the packins which Maj Smith has established or will establish, may do so, and such as are more convenient to Petersburg, can go to that point whence they can be brought to this place. 3d. That it may be necessary to procure both bags and transportation to get out the peas & potatoes and any bacon that may be attainable.

at Jefferson Medical College in Philadelphia and practiced it in Charleston from 1853 to 1861. When the war began he was made commissary general by his friend Jefferson Davis and given the tremendous task of providing food for the armies of the Confederacy. He appointed state commissary agents under him and revealed some talents for pedestrian administration, but he was peevish, obstinate, condescending, and difficult, though he remained a special favorite of Davis' as long as the president lived. After the war he retired to a farm near Charlottesville, Va. Robert Douthat Meade, "Lucius Bellinger Northrop," *Dict. of Am. Biog.*, XIII, 567-568; Cullum, *Biog. Register*, I, 487.

[26] Jacob Parker was a merchant of Warrenton who owned a large mercantile supply house and who was also engaged in the cotton business. The firm was first known as Alston and Parker, but after the war Alston withdrew and Parker was joined by John Watson, the firm being known as Parker, Watson and Company. Parker was a native of Murfreesboro but had married a Warrenton girl, and had settled there. Montgomery, *Sketches of Warrenton*, pp. 82-83, 242-244.

[27] W. H. Smith was a militia officer who had been active in the collection of supplies from the occupied eastern counties and who had commanded a line of couriers to facilitate these operations. Clark, *N. C. Regts.*, IV, 646.

As to the transportation Mr Hayes in a letter to Maj Ruffin,[28] says, that a few teams & wagons can be bought in his region. If they can be bought at prices satisfactory to yourself you will be authorized to buy them, and when they are done with they can be disposed of in some satisfactory manner. As to the bags, it would be very desirable to secure the services of some of the factories of No. Ca. in order to get them. And as they have not been called on up to this time, it is to be hoped they will now be able to serve the needs of this Bureau. One of the greatest difficulties now is to get bags and there are not half enough. I have been induced to ask you to undertake the above service in consequence of your communication to the President and my notice of your address to the people of your State,[29] indicating a readiness to help the cause in general
Raleigh
[L. S. Governors' Papers (Vance),
  Vance Letter Book, 1862-1863,
  State Department of Archives and History, Raleigh.]

From John L Webb[30]

This the 2 off Novembr
I take the
          plasur off the kindness to you the govner to relait to you to let you know the situation I am in at this time I lern the call is maid up to forty and I am knone to be weakly and all so knowen to be and a mecanick serven prenis ship at the wages times I under stand the call is a public not to nelecp one pore breast com plaint person I servd prent isShip with A good old wokman others knows yet all A rond I have seekly famly not Able to wate on them self I took my brother famly to livie in my yard after he volentrd hesed heknowed hed was abler to go then me and I took his fam I have thwree brothers in the armey with other relatin tow We sotter is know man person belonging to the famleys ther is farther famly he is dis eable off waten on his self I dont have no Idey but thay wod suffer of I cant bage off I bage off you is I wod bage my maker and god I wod bin in the armey but my my friends advised me to stay they knowed I wase A frend to my nabors County and nabers wageon tade is very nessery and I ant eable to to do moe but my set off tools all so I

---

[28] Frank G. Ruffin, major and commissary of subsistence for the Confederate government. After the war he was an auditor for the Commonwealth of Virginia. Ruffin sent Parker to see Vance and to make arrangements for the more expeditious collecting of the supplies in eastern North Carolina. Ruffin to Vance, November 3, 1862, Vance Letter Book, 1862-1863.
[29] See pp. 265-267.
[30] John L. Webb does not appear in Moore, *N. C. Roster.*

am in gagend on the stage line leaden from danvile to greens-
borrow
Aneer theas fue line with kindness sure
[Raleigh]
[A. L. S. Governors' Papers (Vance),
State Department of Archives and History, Raleigh.]

From Elender Gibson

Nov. 3rd 1862
State of North Carolina
Caldwell County
this is to no of you whether ther should be any chance for me
to get my Two sons Discharged or furlowed home or not that is
Harrison[31] & Paton Gibsons[32] that formerly belonged to your
Regement they are both Sick and has been for along time not
able for Service and I am ferful they never will again if you
please instruct me how to Get them home if I had them home I
cold nurse them up and maybe save ther lives or Recrute them up
so they wold be able for service again my Boys has been in the
War over fifteen Months and have don all they cold in defince of
there contry of you please to assist me in tryin to get them home
for I am apoore widow woman Dependant on my boys for surport
I have don all I cold for the War I have in both Clothing and
provision, and I should vary Glad if I cold get to see my son for
a short time I want you to answer this letter if you please and if
ther is any chance you will no it in so doinge you will oblige your
humble servant
Direct you letter to Bucke Shoal P off Caldwell Co N. C.
[Raleigh]
[A. L. S. Governors' Papers (Vance),
State Department of Archives and History, Raleigh.]

From J. R. Neill[33]

Bald Creek N. C.
Nov 3d 1862
After my Compliments and good wishes for you and Your
Family.

---

[31] Harrison Gibson enlisted July 26, 1861, and was a private in company I of the
Twenty-sixth North Carolina Regiment. He was wounded July 1, 1863, at Gettysburg. Moore, *N. C. Roster*, II, 399.
[32] Peyton Gibson enlisted July 21, 1861, and was a private in the same company
with his brother. Both were from Caldwell County. Moore, *N. C. Roster*, II, 399.
[33] James R. Neill, of Yancey County. He enlisted September 16, 1861 and was
first sergeant in company E of the Twenty-ninth North Carolina Regiment. He
became assistant quartermaster on September 25, 1861, but resigned in 1862.
Moore, *N. C. Roster*, II, 473, 499. He became quartermaster of the 111th North
Carolina Militia June 1, 1862. Militia Roster, p. 422.

I hope You will excuse me for troubling You When You are So presed with business.

About fourteen Months ago I Vollenteered in the Servis of my Country was advised at the same time not to do so as my health was quite bad Col. R. B. Vance[34] promoted me to the office of Quartermaster of his Regt which I accepted and Served them faithfully for nearly a Year by taking the greatest care of my *Self* finely on account of bad health and nothing else I had to Resign my office and come home it was with great Reluctance that I left the Regt. for they cant be a better and Kinder man in the Army than *Col R* B Vance, he regretted very much to have to give me up but advised me to Resign, as he thought I could not stand it much longer.

I suppose in a short time all men to the age of Forty Years will be called out I am not quite that old it would make no difference with me about age If I could stand the hardships of camp *life*. if You Kneed any help in the way of Agents in this part of the State or any thing that you could give me to do that would release me I will be truly glad. *I do not want you to think* that I ask this of You merely because I was your warm and faithful friend in your Election for Governor I Vote for all men that went in to this troublesome war as *You did,* do me a faivour if you can and it will be highly appreciated by your many friends in This *section* Do Something if you can through the Legislature to put down the *Rascal extortioners,* excuse this bad letter and write me Soon *to Bald Creek P O N C*

[Raleigh]
[on reverse]
Ans[r]- that I will take great pleasure in giving him an agency in Yancey if I should need one there. If he can get me any leather and woolen cloth of consequence I will give him a temporary appointment right away
                    Z B V.
[A. L. S. Governors' Papers (Vance),
  State Department of Archives and History, Raleigh.]

From C. H. Wiley[35]

Greensboro N. C.
Nov: 3rd- 1862—

There are certain cases in this County & I suppose in others, which in my opinion, might safely be recommended to the President as of that class which deserve special exemptions by him, from

---

[34] See p. 2, 6n.
[35] See p. 231, 228n.

Military duty, on the ground of "equity & justice." [36] As you are aware, they will not keep confirmed lunatics in the Asylum— & idiots not cared for by private individuals have to go to the County poor house— In all countries, & in all ages of the world, the care of such persons is regarded as Sacred; & our Confederate Authorities never intended that we should be liable to reproach which cannot often be laid to the charge of even Savage tribes. Only teachers, Nurses &c in *Asylums,* are exempt by law; but Congress could not provide for every case, & therefore vested a large discretionary power in the President— Now I wish to know if President Davis will exempt those who have charge of incurable lunatics & of idiots, where there are no other white male members of the family but those seeking exemption— & as a letter from a private individual might not be attended to, I venture to request you to ask for information on the subject. I enclose a draught of a letter stating distinctly the kind of Cases to which I refer—. I intended to have seen you last week on matters connected with my department of the public Service, but have been quite sick, & you See evidence of my disability in my handwrite— Please enclose the President's answer to me,[37] if I do not see you before it comes to hand.

P. S. It is unnecessary to enclose any memorandum as you will know what kind of Cases are referred to— If there is but one sane white man in the family, & he has charge of an incurable lunatic or idiot, & has heretofore assumed this charge, & kept it from the County, ought he to be exempt—

My question refers only to those who have aways assumed the care of their lunatic or idiot friends, & kept them from the County.

[Raleigh]

[A. L. S. Governors' Papers (Vance), State Department of Archives and History, Raleigh.]

From D. W. Siler[38]

Near Franklin
Nov. 3rd. 1862

There are about enough men in Macon County between the

---

[36] At the end of a long list of specified exemptions the Act of October 11, 1862 added: ". . . and such other persons as the President shall be satisfied, on account of justice, equity or necessity, ought to be exempted . . ." *O. R.,* Ser. IV, Vol. II, 162.

[37] Vance recommended the exemption of such persons as Wiley describes in a letter to Davis of November 10, 1862. Davis declined on the ground that the clause quoted above was intended to operate on individuals and not on classes. Vance to Davis, November 10, 1862, Davis to Vance, November 29, 1862, Vance Letter Book, 1862-1863.

[38] David Weimar Siler (1822-1884), a farmer of Macon County. He was a political friend of Vance, having been both Whig and American, and a member of the House of Commons in 1850, 1856, and 1860. Connor, *N. C. Manual,* p. 688; D. W. Siler

ages of 35 and 40 to make one company.[39] We have an opportunity as I understand of getting into Col Folks[40] battalion. This is preferable to going as conscripts. I am requested by a number of our most respectable citizens who are between these ages to ask you whether in your opinion any other alternative will be presented than conscription or going to that battalion. We have no hesitation in believing that it is our duty to stay here and provide for the helpless while it is in our power to do so. Consultations were held and it was agreed in family councils who should go & what one should stay. Those on whom the lot fell to stay in many instances made the greater sacrifice of feeling. But we have taken on upon us charges and responsibilities that we cannot throw off until compelled to do so—or until there is a certainty that we will be so compelled. Having acted conscientiously in the matter we feel that we have done nothing to deserve the punishment of going to the Army discredited by conscription. Before we are taken to a Camp of instruction discredited and scattered to the four winds we ask the privilege of doing what we should have done long ago, had it not been for the earnest appeals of brothers who have fallen in the service to stay and take care of those left to our charge.

I shall venture on a suggestion tho' it may seem to come from a party interested. For every able bodied man taken from this county, there ought to be an able bodied man retained. We have a number of men in the field now falling very little below the number of voters in the county. Our people having poor facilities for communication with other sections have learned to subsist mainly on the immediate productions of their own labor. Deprive us of that labor [41] and the innocent & helpless must perish though their pockets were filled with current money. You know all about men and their powers of endurance of their wives and children. They can turn away from the graves of comrades and brothers firm in resolve to die as they have died for the sake of objects coming to their recollections with thoughts of home, But what

to William A. Graham, November 23, 1860, Graham Papers CH; Leona Bryson Porter, *The Family of Weimar Siler 1755-1831* (Franklin, N. C., 1951), p. 68 (cited thereafter as Porter, *Siler Family.*

[39] The recent Conscription Act of September 27, 1862, extended the age limit of those liable to military service from thirty-five years to forty-five years, but provided that if all within those ages were not called at once that those between the ages of thirty-five and any other age less than forty-five should be called first. The first calls came for those from thirty-five to forty. *O. R.*, Ser. IV, Vol. II, 160.

[40] See p. 81, 298n. Folk was now commander of the Seventh Battalion of Cavalry, later the Sixty-fifth Regiment, which had several Macon County companies. Clark, *N. C. Regts.*, III, 673, IV, 301.

[41] This labor problem was of particular importance because of the relative scarcity of negroes in the mountain counties. Macon County, in the census of 1860, had only 519 slaves in a population of more than 6,000 people, and this number of slaves was roughly twice as many as most of the small mountain counties possessed.

consolation or encouragement can come to a mans heart in an hour of trial from a home where the helpless are perishing for want of his hand to provide. We have but little interest in this connection about which we feel a very deep interest. We are opposed to negro equality. To prevent this we are willing to spare the last man down to the point where women & children begin to suffer for food & clothing. When these begin to suffer & die, rather than see them equalized with an inferior race will die with them.

Everything even life itself stands pledged to the cause. But that our greatest strength may be employed to the best advantage and the struggle prolonged let us not sacrifice at once the object for which we are fighting.

I have not thought it worth while to dwell in argument upon the question as to whether the mountain people can subsist after taking out every man between the ages of 18 & 40. It will be sufficient for any one acquainted with this section to pass in imagination through almost any neighborhood and consider the matter over, In a short distance of where I now write there are several families living on adjoining lands and the only man to be left for them all is ninety years old. I have mentioned this case to no one who has not been able to point out one similar to it. The usual means of subsistence seems to be cut off from great numbers. I shall only ask you to reply to the questions presented in the first few sentences. Knowing the press of important matters that must be upon you it is with reluctance that I have written at all. And was only induced to bring matters to your notice which are not immediately under your control, by the request of a number of citizens that I should do so.[42]

[Raleigh]

[Vance Letter Book, 1862-1863,

State Department of Archives and History, Raleigh.]

From Thos. J. Jarvis[48]

Camp 8th. N. C. Regiment
Kinston N. C. Nov. 3. '62

About one half of my company made their way out of the lines of the enemy and could not bring anything like blankets with

---

[42] Vance sent this letter to President Davis and suggested the propriety of exempting the region from any further call under the discretionary power invested in the president by the Conscription Act of September 27. Vance to Davis, November 12, 1862, Vance Letter Book, 1862-1863; O. R., Ser. I, Vol. XVIII, 771-773.

[48] Thomas Jordan Jarvis (1836-1915), first lieutenant of company B in the Eighth North Carolina Regiment. Jarvis was educated at Randolph-Macon College and was teaching school in Pasquotank County when the war came. He joined the Seventeenth Regiment, but soon became a lieutenant in the Eighth, becoming captain of his company on April 22, 1863. He was wounded at Drewry's Bluff in May of 1864. After the war he opened a store in Tyrrell County, studied law, and began a

them. I only have about thirty blankets in my company to serve the whole company— they consequently are suffering from cold. They unlike the rest of the Reg. cannot send to their homes for such things because their homes are far within the enemy's lines (Currituck County) For these reasons I have taken the liberty to address you this letter requesting you to send me a few blankets. I know there is a great scarcity of blankets, but I hope you will be able to send me a few. I have made requisition on the Q. M. time and again but cannot get them. If you cannot do something for them they must suffer

[Raleigh]

[A. L. S. Governors' Papers (Vance),
State Department of Archives and History, Raleigh.]

From R. L. Abernethy[44]

Marion, N. C.

Nov. 4th '/62/

Will your Excellency permit me a private individual, a Minister of the gospel of the grace of God; one who feels the greatest possible concern for the interest of your Excellency, as well as for the interest of the State at large, to address you in an unofficial way? If so, I proceed.

Your humble correspondent has always been an earnest and devoted friend of your Excellency; and though he has never enjoyed the privilege of seeing your Excellency but *once*, (when you past last through Marion to Asheville) yet he exerted all his limitted influence in putting your Excellency in the Chair of State, and now he desires to lay some facts before you, which he conceives to be of vast importance to the interests of the people of Western N. Carolina.

---

political career by representing Currituck County in the Convention of 1865 and in the House of Representatives in 1868. He moved to Pitt County, formed a law partnership with David M. Carter, represented Pitt in the Convention of 1875, and was elected lieutenant governor in 1876 when Vance was returned to the governorship. In the meantime he had been Speaker of the House in the important session of 1870. He succeeded Vance as governor in 1879 when Vance went to the United States Senate, and also succeeeded him as Senator upon Vance's death. He was governor from 1879 to 1885, then minister to Brazil, 1885-1889. Joseph Gregoire deRoulhac Hamilton, "Thomas Jordan Jarvis," *Dict. of Am. Biog.*, IX, 623-624; Samuel A'Court Ashe, "Thomas Jordan Jarvis," Ashe, *Biog. Hist. of N. C.*, 1, 330-340.

[44] Robert Laban Abernethy (b. 1822), Methodist minister and teacher, was a native of Lincoln County who became a Confederate tax collector in McDowell County and quartermaster pro-tem later in the war. He described himself as an Old Whig who was fixed in those principles. After the war he taught schools in various places, including Burke County, and became president of Rutherford College. He was a strong supporter of the prohibition movement and was once a candidate for the office of superintendent of public instruction. Later, in the eighties, he called himself a Democrat. Abernethy to Vance, March 15, 1864, Governors' Papers (Vance); Abernethy to Samuel McDowell Tate, January 14, 29, 1881, January 23, 1883, January 19, 1885, Tate Papers; Dowd, *Sketches*, pp. 207-209.

If it is Constitutional, and if your position as Governor of N. Carolina gives you the power to do so, in the name of *God,* of suffering humanity, of the cries of widows and orphans, *do* put down the Speculation and extortion in this portion of the State.

Here in Marion, beef is being sold to the poor wives of soldiers who get but $11 per month in the field, at the enormous price of 11 and 12 cents per pound! Leather at $4 per pound! Bacon at 40 & 50 cents per pound; Corn from the heap, at $1.50 per bushel! Salt at near 50 cents per pound! And every thing in proportion.

If this thing is not put down, our Country is *ruined* forever. Many children of the soldiers in the Camps are nearly barefoot and naked without the possibility of getting clothes or shoes.

Here in Marion, Messrs Maroney and Halyburton have a large Tannery, and the tanner is allowed to remain by virture of the Exemption Act, and yet one pound of leather cannot be bought of the concern by private purchase. The leather is put up in lots of 250 sides and sold to speculators at $4.00 & $4.50 per pound! Your correspondent went himself in person to the concern of these gentlemen, and though he laid his case before them, that he had 6 little barefoot children that must have shoes, and offered to give any reasonable price for leather— *just one side.* But the reply was, if we sell to one man privately we must sell to others, and we will not do it.

In the name of the Great Gov of the universe, what are we to do?

Pardon my presumption in addressing your Excellency, for I could not restrain.

[Raleigh]

[A. L. S. Governors' Papers (Vance),
State Department of Archives and History, Raleigh.]

From Samuel Forkner[45]

Mt. airy N. C. Nov. 4th 1862

I have seized on Some 400 lbs of Leather in the hands of Elisha Banner, he Claims that it is not the object of the 4th Artic[l] of Gen[l] Odire No 9[46] of Oct 25th under which I am acting, to interfere with former contracts, I have agreed to mak no disposition of the leather untile we herd from you

---

[45] Samuel Forkner, colonel of the Seventy-third Regiment of North Carolina Militia. He was formerly adjutant of the regiment, but the former colonel, Gabriel A. McCraw, had been promoted to brigadier general and Forkner became colonel on September 24, 1862. He was later charged with neglect of his duty in making arrests, but was exonerated by an investigation of the adjutant general. Militia Roster, p. 290; Militia Letter Book, pp. 294-296.

[46] The fourth article of General Orders, No. 9 provided that "Each Colonel will . . . pay particular attention to the purchase of shoes and leather, see that none go into the hands of speculators, and seize for the use of the soldiers any of these articles going out of the State, or in the hands of speculators for that purpose." Statesville *Iredell Express,* November 20, 1862.

Mr Banner[47] has made a Salt trade for which he has bought leather to Give in exchange, the object is Speculation

We have a County Contract with the Va Salt works which will suply this County if we can get it hauled with what the State works can do for us,

Were it not for Speculation many of our Soldiers Wifes & Children in this Section would have ben saved of going bare footed this Winter I wish to here from you Soon on the subject, likely there may be other contracts of a like nature[48]

[Raleigh]

[A. L. S. Governors' Papers (Vance),
State Department of Archives and History, Raleigh.]

From S. R. Mallory[49]

CONFEDERATE STATES OF AMERICA
NAVY DEPARTMENT

Richmond November 4th

Commander Cook[50] sent by me to North Carolina to obtain iron for plating the gunboats being built in and for the defence of the State, has returned without having accomplished this object. He reports that you have the control of a quantity of Rail road iron and I therefore address myself to you upon the subject.

To enable the boats to resist the guns of the enemy their Armour must be at least four inches thick, placed at an angle of at least thirty six degrees, this Armour from the limited power of our mills

---

[47] Elisha Banner said that he made a contract on October 7, 1862 with Stuart, Buchanan & Co., of Saltville, Va., whereby he agreed to deliver four hundred pounds of good leather to them before December 1, and for which Stuart, Buchanan & Co. agreed to pay one hundred bushels of salt. On November 3, 1862, Banner wrote to Vance inquiring whether his embargo on exports of certain materials applied to contracts previously made, and asked for a permit to show the militia colonel if his contracts were permitted to stand. Banner to Vance November 3, 1862, Governors' Papers (Vance).

[48] See below, Forkner to David A. Barnes, November 18, 1862, p. 376.

[49] Stephen Russell Mallory (1813-1873), of Florida, Confederate secretary of the navy. He was born on Trinidad Island, educated at Nazareth, Pa., and studied law in Florida, where he was admitted to the bar before 1840. President Polk appointed him collector of customs at Key West, and in 1851 he became United States Senator, was re-elected in 1857, and was chairman of the Senate Committee on Naval Affairs. In 1861 he favored secession but not war, but accepted the position in Davis' cabinet, where his wide experience and intense interest in naval matters kept him throughout the war. Afterwards he practiced law in Pensacola, which had become his home in 1858, until his death. Kathleen Bruce, "Stephen Russell Mallory," Dict. of Am. Biog., XII, 224-226.

[50] James Wallace Cooke (1812-1869). He was born in Beaufort County, N. C. and became a midshipman in the navy in 1828. When the war came he joined the Virginia Navy and soon afterwards became commander of the Confederate Ellis and led her in action at Roanoke Island in February 1862. In 1863 he superintended the construction of the ram Albemarle and on April 20, 1864, led her in action at Plymouth, N. C., after which he was promoted to captain that summer and placed in command of all the Confederate naval forces in eastern North Carolina. After the war he lived at Portsmouth, Va. Evans, Conf. Mil. Hist., IV, 446-448; Clark, N. C. Regts., I, xiv, V, 181, 303, 312, 323.

we are compelled to roll into plates two by seven inches and ten feet long and to put them on the vessels in two courses.

If you will let the Department have the rails and facilitate its transportation to Richmond, they will be immediately rolled into plates for the vessels in question and for such other defences as we may build in the waters of your State.

Commander Cook will remove the iron if you consent to its transfer and will arrange the compensation according to his instructions. Please telegraph your reply[51]
[Raleigh]
[Vance Letter Book, 1862-1863,
  State Department of Archives and History, Raleigh.]

From John L. Pugh[52]

Mouth of Wilson Gray[son] Co Va
Nov 5. 1862

I take this opportunity of writing you a note from information I understand that there has been orders issued for my arrest as a deserter from the 37 N C Regiment. I do not consider myself a deserter from the army from the fact that I am over the age of the conscript. and had not reenlisted and on the 16th. of July last I made application for a discharge and it was Refused me I still remained in campt untill the 20. of said month I being very sick at the time I thought it best to come home, I did so. On the account of my [illegible] which was bad at that time and has been ever since not being able to do anything since I came home I enlisted for only 12 months that time expired on the 15" of September last, as I did not reinlist I received no bounty, I furnished my own clothing for the whole time I was in the army and there being a bal due me from the Government of thirty Dollars shows that I am not in debt to the Government at this time. I therefore humbly request you not to enforce the orders Issued to F. J. MMillan[53] Col of 96 Reg N C M and request that you answer me through him the study of my case— and oblige Your fellow citizen
[Raleigh]
[on reverse]
I can not revoke the order— as he left Camp without leave—
        Z B V
[A. L. S. Governors' Papers (Vance),
  State Department of Archives and History, Raleigh.]

---

[51] There is no record of a telegraphed reply, but see Vance to Mallory, November 21, 1862, below, p. 382.

[52] John L. Pugh, of Alleghany County, first sergeant in the Thirty-seventh North Carolina Regiment, having enlisted September 15, 1861. He was wounded at Gettysburg. Moore, N. C. Roster, III, 43.

[53] Fields J. McMillan became colonel of the Ninety-sixth Militia Regiment on March 22, 1862. His post office was also at Mouth of Wilson, Grayson County, Va., but the regiment operated in Alleghany County, N. C. Militia Roster, pp. 474-475.

From Lydia A. Bolton

November the 5 1862

i set down to rite you a few lines and hope and pray to god
that you wil oblige me i ame a pore woman with a pasel of little
children and i wil have to starve or go naked me and my little children ef my husband is kept way from home much longer and i ask
you to lat him come home and burn cole for the state i dont want
him to come and do nothen for the confedracy but he can see to
his famely and burn cole and i beg you to tell him come tha
dont give me but thre dolars a month and fore of us in famely
and i cant cloth my children i have knit 40 pare of socks fo the
solgers and it takes all i can earn to get bred and i beg you in
the name of the lord to let him come my sister en law is nearly
as bad of as i ame and she wants her husban ef you can spare him
i hope that can serv the stat as such a burning cole as tha can
thear if you cud hear the crys of my litle children i think you
wod feel for us I am pore in this world but i trust rich in heven
i trust in god and hope if he wil cos you to have compaahion on
the pore

rote by James A Bolton[54] wife

he is at wilmington general french[55] Young[56] kartaken [?] company a Capt Lewes[57]

Joab Bolton[58] is my sister in law husband name he is at the same
place i umblr beg in the name of our father in heven to send
my husband home and i hope the lord wil reward you if not in
this world in heven is my prayer Sir hear the crys of the pore
i beg you

[Raleigh]

[A. L. S. Governors' Papers (Vance),
State Department of Archives and History, Raleigh.]

From O. F. Manson[59]

MOORE HOSPITAL

Richmond Va., Nov.[r] 5th 1862.

It is very important that I should receive from you a letter of

---

[54] James A. Bolton, of Davidson County, a private in company A of the Tenth
Battalion, a heavy artillery unit. In Moore, *N. C. Roster,* IV, 359 it is listed as the
Eighth Battalion. Clark, *N. C. Regts.,* IV, 315.

[55] See p. 204, 142n.

[56] Wilton L. Young, of Wake County, major of the battalion, which then consisted of only three companies. Moore, *N. C. Roster,* IV, 359; Clark, *N. C. Regts.,*
IV, 316-317.

[57] William R. Lewis, captain of company A. This company was composed of
men from Davidson County. Moore, *N. C. Roster,* IV, 360.

[58] Joab Bolton, also from Davidson County, enlisted on April 18, 1862, in the
same company as his brother. Moore, *N. C. Roster,* IV, 360.

[59] See p. 157, 641n. Dr. Manson had just been made head of the North Carolina
hospital in Richmond.

introduction to the Hon. Geo. W. Randolph[60] Secretary of War.
He is very favourably inclined to do everything in his power to
carry out your views and without his assistance I shall be beset
with obstacles. Please let me hear from you immediately & oblige
[Raleigh]
[A. L. S. Governors' Papers (Vance),
  State Department of Archives and History, Raleigh.]

From W. A. Houck[61]

Salisbury N. C. Nov. 6' 1862

Since the issuing of your stirring appeal [62] to the people of N. C.
in behalf of our destitute soldiers I have canvassed the greater portion of this County (Rowan) and have found the following to
be almost the universal feeling. First a unanimous desire to assist in relieving the necessities of the soldiers and a willingness to
share the last Blanket and the last change of clothing with our
brave boys, if they had any assurance that such articles as might
be contributed would ever reach their destined recipients. Without intending to be officious I would respectfully submit the following plan as the best means of securing the most liberal contributions from our people.
Let an agent properly commissioned visit every family and have
with him a blank book easily made with one page for each Regiment in which is any company from that particular County, for
instance the companies from this County are included if I mistake
not in about eight different Regts. consequently eight pages would
be necessary. Having such a book prepared let the Agent go to Mr
Smith and inform him as to his business and that he can send
it directly to his son or any friend he might select and the entry
in the book would show that Regt. and company and individual
the article is intended for Example
John Smith) 1 Blanket & pr Drawers to son James. Co A. 4' Regt.
James Brown) 1 Pr Shoes 2 pr Socks to A. B.   Co D 6' Regt.
At first glance this plan may look complicated and difficult of
execution but I deem it practically the best way to reach the
object desired only yesterdey one gentleman assured me he would
give freely 3 pr of shoes if he could send them to his friends.
I must beg pardon for troubling you with so lengthy a letter. I
will close by saying that a close acquaintance with the feelings of

[60] See p. 132, 524n.
[61] William A. Houck, formerly captain of company D and lieutenant colonel of
the Thirty-fourth North Carolina Regiment. Moore, *N. C. Roster*, II, 640, 651. In
November 1861 Houck wrote to Governor Clark informing him that he was
appointed to raise arms by purchase and wished advertisements made. He had
charge of repairs for prisoners in Salisbury. W. A. Houck to Clark, November 16,
1861, Governors' Papers (Clark).
[62] See pp. 265-267.

the people satisfies me that by the above mode four fifths of the soldiers from Rowan could be made comfortable at trifling expense to the State.

Should the plan suggested meet with your approbation, I would be pleased to canvass this County and if desirable would visit your city and complete and simplify the plan. Hoping that I will at least get credit for a sincere desire to aid in alleviating the sufferings of our Soldiers.

Raleigh

[A. L. S. Governors' Papers (Vance),
State Department of Archives and History, Raleigh.]

From J. M. Worth[63]

Asheboro N. C.   Nov 6th 1862

I have agreed with Jason C Harris[64] & James W. Wilborn at the Request of your friends Ralf Gorrel[65] & Jonathan Worth[66] to postpone arresting their Salt Peter hand until they can go and see you on the Subject, with the proviso that they take my letter to you and deliver the men at Camp if you decide they are not exempt the conscripts were enrolled here on the 8th of July and ordered to the Camp, the 15th you will find that they failed to go to camp and have been from that day to this evading and engageing in all sorts of work to get exempt. the main object in all the engagements is to get exempt, all the hands being conscripts they are asking for men to be detailed to make Iron when the Iron is all in its native Hills. John W Thomas[67] Esqr of Davidson and Mendenhall and Dick of Guilford[68] are contractors with the North Carolina Railroad for sills & wood &c and have a number of Conscripts from this regiment most of them engaged since you

[63] See p. 206, 144n.

[64] Harris and Wilborn lived at Caraway, in Randolph County.

[65] Ralph Gorrell (1803-1875), of Guilford County. A graduate of the University of North Carolina in 1825, he had represented Guilford in the House of Commons in 1834, 1835, and 1854, when Vance knew him, and was a member of the State Senate in 1856 and 1858, and of the Convention of 1861. As a lawyer he was respected and able and he had many friends who supported him for a judgeship from time to time. Robert P. Dick wrote of him that he was "honest, just, learned, poor, and upright." He was a Whig in politics, though he had come to act with the Democrats with regard to secession by the time the convention was authorized. McCormick, *Personnel,* p. 38; Connor, *N. C. Manual,* pp. 633-634, 882; R. P. Dick to Governor Clark, October 23, 1861, Governors' Papers (Clark).

[66] See p. 184, 79n.

[67] John W. Thomas was a member of the State Senate from Davidson County in 1842, 1848, 1854, 1856, and 1860, and of the House of Commons in 1831. Leonard, *Davidson County,* pp. 67-68; Connor, *N. C. Manual,* p. 588.

[68] Cyrus Pegg Mendenhall (1817-1884), of Jamestown. He was engaged in many varied business enterprises, among them being his association with James Dick and others in the Union Manufacturing Company. He was secretary-treasurer of the North Carolina Railroad Company in the fifties and mayor of Greensboro after the war. *Greensboro Record,* November 16, 1940.

ordered them to be arrested. I mention these cases to show the condition in which I am placed if they are allowed to hold them, it will be a bid to the next call to hide until they can get into some place to exempt them. Your order to me was to arrest all of them and send to Camp which I shall certainly do unless you countermand the order. I will wait in the case of Harris & Wilborn until I hear from you I believe if any are to be exempt they are entitled to it except that Wilborn has two or three men that are engaged in the last few days— yet I think it far the best that all hands in this and all other Counties that failed to go to camp at the proper time shall be required to go up The men never will go up promptly if they believe there is any chance to get off If you will stop all details of conscripts after these are enrolled, except from the Camp, you will save yourself and all the enrolling officers a great deal of trouble— I regret that this County gives you any trouble I am doing my best to get all hands to their post. [Raleigh]
[A. L. S. Governors' Papers (Vance), State Department of Archives and History, Raleigh.]

From Cass A. Marlow

November the 6th 1862

I take the present opportunity of droping you a few lines to inform you that we have a cooper in the twenty sixth regiment that went as a conscript that we cant well do with out he was all the man that followed this trade anywhere near in this neighborhood people depended on him for all kinds of vessels in our country he followed this for his trade mostly for the last six or seven years in particular people come from fifteen to twenty miles for his work he is a man that insures his work to be good and faithful to his word he is not very stout in his body at times with the rumatick pains he has had his back nearly brok by a fall and that injures him great eal at times from laboring only at his trade he is a splended shoemaker too so when he cant work at one trade he can at the other when needed we would be thankful for the Said Albert Marlow [69] to be exempted if it can be done it will be a great favor to this ninth district of Said county of wilkes he has favored the women and children all he could in their distress at their time of need since this war commenced he sent to the soldiers in the army all he could it has bin proposed to me that I should write to the said govener of north carolina that he should used all exertions to exempt said Albert Marlow with a free discharge if possible to come back to his usual trade he is one of our most useful men he was raised a poor farmers boy but he

---

[69] Albert Marlow, a private in company D in the Twenty-sixth North Carolina Regiment, is listed as having enlisted September 22, 1862, and as being from Wake County. Moore, *N. C. Roster*, II, 378.

took these trades in this rough mountainous country The said
Albert Marlow can do any kind of work that he is call on for he
is a very good carpenter when call on for furniture he makes his
own furniture without buying it the above Albert Marlow has
wrote to me that he would give all he was worth to be at home
at his usual trade Mr Govener I will forfeit and pay fifty dollars
in the Treasury for the said Albert Marlow to be discharge to
come home I dont do this because he is my loveing companion
it is the request of my friends and fellow citizens in this desolate
County of wilkes you need not think that I have rote you a lye
becaus he is my husband for that is one thing that I wouldent do
if I knew it because god has give his only son that the whole
world might live I believe on him as a savior and made my peace
with him some eight years ago the said Albert Marlow is in the
Twenty sixth regiment under captain Adams[70] Company D North
Carolina Troops he is thirty five this december the twenty second day his age was recorded in his infantile state I wish you
to do all you can to exempt him all other tradesmen is exempted
from the army not so much needed as those trades of his at times
for every thing is so high I expect to suffer for the want of his
trades being stop This to, Z. B. Vance governer from Miss Cass. A,
Marlow yours respectfully

[Raleigh]

[A. L. S. Governors' Papers (Vance),
  State Department of Archives and History, Raleigh.]

From Archibald Curlee[71]

Saturday Evening November 6th 1862
i comence this note not noing i Shall be able to Speak my minde
up on the Subject or not, as i am writing to One i never have seen
you will be informed that i am in Bad health and has bin ever
Since April last i Volenteered and went of to the army an Come
home in August just a live i've not seen nary well day since i have
bin in the army So i write these lines to you as we truely hope there
is sompthing i Can do that i Cold live out of the army for i assure
you i Cant live there long i Can put up as good Shoes an Boots as
any man, So i have folerd the trade Before i went off Some, & So
if you Can or will Git me out of the army and let me go to
makeing Shoes i Should do good eal more good and be of more
Benefit to the Confederacy So Mr Govenor if you Can Say or do

---

[70] T. J. Adams, of Wake County, who became captain of company D after the
capture of Oscar R. Rand at New Bern; Adams was later major and lieutenant
colonel of the Twenty-sixth and was wounded at Gettysburg. Moore, *N. C. Roster,*
II, 362, 376.

[71] Archibald Curlee was a private in company I of the Fifty-third North Carolina Regiment, having enlisted from Union County on March 20, 1862. Moore,
N. C. Roster.

any thing to my Case i Shall more than thank you a thousand times although you may give me a Short answer or nun, i am young and green about the law in these Criticle times, i want you to write to me an let me no whither Such Cold be dun or, no will inclose 10 cts male your Letter pleuse write to me as Soon as this you rece

Direct your Letter Olive Branch N. C.

[on reverse]

No power to detail him— Z B V

[A. L. S. Governors' Papers (Vance),
State Department of Archives and History, Raleigh.]

From H. W. Ayer[72]

Salem N. C. Nov. 6th. 1862.

Hearing of a little meanness & rascality in this neighborhood I came up here on yesterday, and the most important item I have to communicate is this. I have it upon the most reliable authority that a certain W. W. Long[73] 1 mile beyond Huntsville, (former Shff. of Yadkin Co.) has a *large quantity* of sole & upper leather on hand, for which he is asking the *blockade* price of $300 per sole and $350, for upper pr lb. He has sent out word to all his neighbors that if they will come up he will let them have all they want at that price, There are also in this town, two *bales* of factory sheeting belonging to a Mr Gibbony of Wythville, for which he has been offered 40 cts pr yd; (it cost him only 20), but he refuses to take it holding it at 75c I write these facts, so that you may know where to find the articles if you wish to press them, for the army—It is the *prettiest* chance I have seen— There is another Iron foundery near here, which I am going to see— as I understand, it is rather on the hum bug order— If you want the cloth and leather address either Col. Joseph Masten[74] 71 N. C. Militia at this place— or your humble and obt svt —at Greensboro.

[Raleigh]

[on reverse]

Referred to Maj Peirce[75] Z B V

[A. L. S. Governors' Papers (Vance),
State Department of Archives and History, Raleigh.]

---

[72] See p. 278, 359n.

[73] W. W. Long had been sheriff of Yadkin County until September of 1862.

[74] Joseph Masten was commissioned colonel of the Seventy-first Militia Regiment October 29, 1861. In the fall of 1862, he was often criticized for neglect of duty with regard to sending up deserters, and the adjutant general wrote him that Governor Vance would "no longer tolerate a continuance of this." Masten was ordered to use arms against deserters even "though life should be taken." Across from Masten's name on the Militia Roster in the adjutant general's office is written "Masten thrown out by Div" "Masten report Dec. 14, 1864 Absconded for the Yankees." Martin to Masten, December 8, 27, 1862, Militia Letter Book, pp. 288, 304; Militia Roster, pp. 270-271.

[75] See p. 142, 577n.

From W. A. H. Comer

New Market N C
Nov 6th 1862

in August last I applied to Capt Cha[s]. R. Barney[76] Agt of the Nitre and Mining bureau for the Confederate States of America at Greensboro for the district of N. C. for a Contract to Manufacture Nitrate of potasa for the Ordinance department for Tho[s] C Powell Alex Robbins W[m] Sawyer and Rash Briles of Randolph County N. C.[77] Capt Barney quoted the Contract and neither of the parties being present as a Matter of accommodation I assgned? the Contract Myself and promised Capt Barney that the hands should be keep constantly at their work I then had to travel to Wilmington N C. for Col John M Worth[78] to order detail as you know he is salt Commission for the State. He order their detail according to general Orders No. 41 [79] and 50 [80] of the War department   ? I stoped at Raleigh N C was introduced to Gov H. T. Clark[81] of N. C. by Comptroler Brogden[82] showed him My Contract and Order for the detail of the hands he told me that he had nothing to do with the Conscript law or the Nitre Bureau but if the hands were keep constantly at their work

---

[76] Charles R. Barney was sent as the agent of the Nitre and Mining Bureau, by the authority of the Chief of Ordnance and the Secretary of War, to North Carolina to supervise government contracts for the manufacture of nitre, and to make contracts with private parties as well. See Richard Morton to Vance, November 10, 1862, below, p. 326.

[77] Of these Alexander Robbins appears as a private in company B of the Fifty-second North Carolina regiment, having enlisted the day after this letter was written, November 7, 1862. He was from Randolph County, Moore, *N. C. Roster*, III, 476.

[78] See p. 206, 144n.

[79] General Orders, No. 41, issued May 31, 1862, provided for details to work nitre caves, the details to be made upon the requisition of the officer in charge of the Nitre Bureau in the War Department, and that such of the detailed men as left the works without permission were to be regarded as deserters. Section II of the order provided that "'All persons in the employment of the Nitre Bureau, whether contractors for manufacturing salt peter, or laborers in their employment, are exempt by law from enrollment." *O. R.*, Ser. IV, Vol. I, 1139.

[80] General Orders, No. 50, issued July 18, 1862, provided that "Conscripts engaged on Government work, either directly or by contractors, will not be taken from the work on which they are engaged, except for the purpose of enrollment, after which they will be returned on the certificate of the officer under whose charge the work is being performed, or with whom the contract is made. Such certificate will be presented to the enrolling officer, who will thereupon order the detail of the men specified for a period not to exceed sixty days. . . . Extension of these details will be made when deemed necessary, on application through the heads of departments or bureaus." *O. R.*, Ser. IV, Vol. II, 8.

[81] See p. 133, 529n.

[82] Curtis Hooks Brogden (1816-1901), of Wayne County, Comptroller of North Carolina, 1857-1867. He represented Wayne County in the House of Commons, 1838-1850, and in the Senate, 1868-1870. He was a member of the Convention of 1868, became a Republican and was lieutenant governor in 1872, succeeding to the governorship upon the death of Tod R. Caldwell, remaining governor until Vance was elected in 1876. He returned to the House of Representatives in 1887 for one term. George S. Wills, "Curtis Hooks Brogden," *Biog. Hist. of N. C.*, XI, 106-112.

he thought it right that they should be permitted to work for the Government in lieu of going to the army I promised him that they should be keep constantly at their work. He (Gov. Clark) gave me a letter of introduction to Maj Mallett [83] at Camp Holmes I went to the camp did not find Maj Mallett but left the certificate of Capt Barney and the order for a detail from Col Worth with his Agent— Come to Greensboro Capt Barney gave me another certificate and ordered me to put the to work which I did Since that date John R Beckerdite his been put in place of Rush Briles and Briles assigned to another Contract nearer his home. by Capt Barney. The hands has been constantly at their work and even boiled ther juice night and day sunday and Monday and have Made and deliver a large quantity of Salt Petre to Capt Barney at Greensboro N C and secured their pay from the government in Sept last the Congress of the Confederate of America passed an act entitled the exemption act exempting all persons working for Contractors for the government Manufacturing any of the Munition of War or Army supplyes of any kind on a certificate of the officer in charge that their services are necessary for the Contractor to carry out his contract this I have and have commited it to. T. C. Powell & charge who has doubless shown it to you before this time. Your Excellency will please examine my contract and the certificate of Capt Barney— approving the number of hands assigned to me. I could not come to Raleigh when Powell and Robbins were taken from their works by order of Col John M. Worth by his commisioned officers of Capt Chellcutt [84] and let them come home and go at this work again or it they must go into the army permit them to come home and prepare their affairs to leave and dispose of their Salt Petre works that are worth a hundred or two, Dollars. that did not even have a days warning by the Commission officers of there arrest please excuse this long letter as I wanted to explain the whole matter to you
Raleigh N C
P. S. Powell has a wife and children left in great distress by his sudden arrest who are beging me to come to Raleigh and see you
[A. L. S. Governors' Papers (Vance),
  State Department of Archives and History, Raleigh.]

From Mrs. M. B. Moore

Pine Hall, Stokes, N. C.
Nov. 7th- 1862

This cold wintry day reminds me of the destitution of our soldiers; and I hope you will not deem it too much trespas upon

---

[83] See p. 175, 44n.
[84] John B. Chellcutt, captain in the Sixty-third Militia.

your time and patience, if I drop you a line upon this subject.

We are told our brave boys are suffering for clothing; and more especially for *blankets*. We are told that it is the duty of southern women to supply these things. The *government* cannot supply them, because it can not *make* them. Woman must do the work: the State is willing to pay for it. I wish to inform you that there are a great many blankets yet in N. C. While many have spared the last one, others have more packed away from a dozen to fifty, good blankets. Most of these persons are Quakers some of Union sentiment. The former, you are well aware, are opposed to war in all its forms; and consequently will neither give nor sell articles for the army. I have good reasons to believe that if you were to press these things, many of them would really thank you, for the opportunity of assisting their county, with out violating the rules of their order. Thus much good would be affected by such a step; and public opinion, generally. would approve it. Those who have strained the last nerve preparing for the comfort of our dear brave soldiers; take it hardly to see so many others hording up those necessaries (to the soldiers) which they could so easily spare.

I am not disposed to dictate to your Excellency; but should you think proper take measures for securing these things, I will simply state, where you may find them in abundance. In the counties of Randolph & Guilford, you will find blankets most abundant. In Montgomery, Davidson, Forsythe Stokes Rockingham &c you will find some. I am not so well acquainted in the other counties; but have reason to believe that there is an abundant supply, if they are only collected.

For further information on this subject, I refer you to J. Worth,[85] member of the State Legislature & Rev. S. Branson[86] Raleigh N. C.

Pardon the liberty of an unpretending woman in addressing one in your position.

[on reverse]

The Govr- must decline to enter citizens houses to seize their goods, but thank the lady for her suggestions

Z B V

[Raleigh]

[A. L. S. Governors' Papers (Vance),
State Department of Archives and History, Raleigh.]

---

[85] See p. 184, 79n.

[86] Rev. S. Branson was a Methodist minister who had been forced out of eastern North Carolina by the fall of New Bern, and had come to Raleigh. He was formerly president of Lenoir Institute and then head of a seminary at Morehead City. See John S. Long to Governor Clark, April 2, 1862, Governors' Papers (Clark).

From Edw. Stanly[87]

New Bern 7th Nov. 1862

Your communication of the 29th- Ulto.[88] has reached me by flag of truce.

The rejection of the proposition made by me, renders it unnecessary to correspond further in relation to them.

But lest it should be inferred that by my silence I acquiesce in the justice of one remark in your communication, I am compelled to address you again.

After giving your first and second reason you use the following language.—"Your proposition is based on the Supposition that there is baseness in North Carolina Sufficient to induce her people to abandon their Confederates and leave them to suffer alone, all the horrors of this unnatural war, for the sake of receiving terms for themselves: A mistake which I would scarcely have supposed any one so well acquainted with the character of our people as yourself could have committed.

There is nothing in my letter, there is nothing I have ever said or written that can justify the imputation, that I ever supposed, the people of *North* Carolina, could be guilty of any "baseness." I may have mistaken the nature and extent of her obligations to what you call the "New Government" I have never seen the act, resolution or decree, by which the State "acceded to the New Government." For nearly twelve (12) months previous to my arrival here I had not seen a newspaper or letter from the State. I presumed, one in your position could have informed me, what your obligations were and could have referred my communication to any other authority, if your duty required it. With deference I still think this might have been done, without the unbecoming language I have quoted, entirely uncalled for, and especially ungracious, in reply to a courteous letter.

From the best information I could procure, I had believed that after several of the "Confederate States" had formed "a Campact" to Suffer "Alone", all the horrors of this unnatural war, the people of *North* Carolina deliberately voted by a large majority, against the proposition to call a Convention, to consider the "baseness" of Separating them from the United States.

From the best information I could procure, I had believed, that her people had aroused to revolution, under the idea, that wrong had been done, not to the "Confederate States," but to her alone. Acting under this belief and Knowing that the Government of the United States had never intended to do her any wrong,

---

[87] See p. 272, 342n.
[88] See p. 284.

I did indulge the earnest hope, that "consideration like an Angel" would come and prevail on her, to listen to terms of honorable peace, to be communicated by her to her Sister States.

I had been laboring under the belief that some of the "Confederate States" had averred they were at war, because they claimed the "Old Government" was a "Compact" between Soverign States, each one of which had a right to secede at pleasure. I Know that the people of *North* Carolina had always repudiated this heresy, with as much earnestness and sincerety as I understood you had. But I never imagined that *North* Carolina in "Attempting" to dissolve the Connection with the "Old Government" and to part with the "Mild Glories" that adorned her, had while delusively decked with the tawdry finery of a Soverign State, been so shorn of her strength, that her Chief Magistrate could declare, in Substance, that he presided only, over a territorial appendage to a Confederacy, and could neither negotiate for the exchange of any Son of hers taken prisoner, or treat in regard to doing *"anything"* to alleviate the evils of War!

When Commissioners were sent from other States, Making propositions, that *North* Carolina, should enter into their "Compact", though she declined to do so, they were treated respectfully and not discourteously accused of making "prospositions based on the supposition, that there was baseness in North Carolina.

If there was no "supposition of baseness" in their propositions, how can there be any in the proposition made by me, representing the Government of the United States, that I might confer with her authorities, to see whether some measures could not be adopted which might lead to an honorable peace?

Without multiplying arguments, allow me to call your attention to another instance.

The State of Maryland is inhabited by as noble and brave a race of people as lives on earth. Her people believe they are citizens of a great nation. They never dissolved their connection with the "old Government." They believe the doctrine, that a State has a right to secede when it pleases, is a ridiculous heresy. General Lee, the Commander of the forces that made the recent incursion in the State of Maryland, issued a proclamation[89] inviting the people to unite their destinies with the "New Government" and to disregard her Solemn obligations to the United States. Did he make "a proposition based on the supposition that there was baseness in Maryland sufficient to induce her people to abandon "her Sister States and leave them to suffer "alone"?

He went with the sword, in contemptuous disregard, of the

---

[89] For Lee's proclamation to the people of Maryland see *O. R.* Ser. I, Vol. XIX, Pt. II, 601-602.

regularly constituted Authorities of the State. I came with the
olive branch and approached you in the most respectful manner.

The one avows an intention to produce civil war, the other
asks, that he may be allowed to see "Whether some Measures
Cannot be adopted, which may lead to an honorable peace, or to
do something to mitigate the Sufferings that invariably follow war.
You have allowed many of *North* Carolina's gallant Sons to be
dragged away from their homes, their life blood poured out upon
the soil of Maryland. You approve the conduct of the General
referred to and yet, discourteously censure mine!

I will not intrude upon you by citing other Cases, as I have no
"intention to enter into a controversy, but merely to repel and
oppose the unfairness of an unprovoked and most unjust reflection upon myself.

There is nothing Sir, in your position or in mine, that justifies
you in using the language complained of to me. Though I am
not asking and can never ask for any favors at the hands of the
people of *North* Carolina; though my house is in a far and distant
land, my affection for her is unchangeable, my anxiety to Save her
unabated. I came on a "Mission of Love" to hold out the Olive
Branch of peace, "on terms such as brave people could honorable
accept." This has been my unvarying purpose often publicly
averred. I came to "provide the means of maintaining peace and
security to the loyal inhabitants" of the State. I command no
squadron in the field: if I had the skill to do so anywhere, I have
no disposition to do so here. Whether in answering the respectful
communication of our coming in such a spirit, you had forgotten
you were the Chief Magistrate of *North* Carolina, and had con-
descended to be only for a brief interval I hope— the mere agent
of the "proper authorities of the new Government." I leave to our
honest Countrymen to decide.

While I must deeply regret, I cannot have your assistance, I
thank Heaven, I represent a Government, which does not think
it "beyond my provence" to do "anything" to alleviate the inevitable Sufferings that attend the War. The widow and the orphan,
the defenceless and forsaken, have had protection and Support
through my humble instrumentality.

Without looking for your aid, I shall whenever I have the ability
continue to make every effort, consistent with duty, and patriotism
to protect the unfortunate and misguided, as well as the loyal
people of my native State, from the disastrous tyranny of your
"New Government."

[Raleigh]

[A. L. S. (copy) Z. B. Vance Papers,
  State Department of Archives and History, Raleigh.]

To L. B. Northrop[90]

STATE OF NORTH CAROLINA
EXECUTIVE DEPARTMENT
Raleigh 8th- Nov. 1862

Your communication to Gov. Vance[91] has been recd. in which you propose to avail yourself of his Agency in procuring a speedy removal of the hogs, beeves, peas, beans and potatoes from that portion of the State "Within the lines of the Enemy or accessible to them"

His Excellency directs me to say in reply that he will most cheerfully undertake the task which you propose to assign to him. He is of opinion that the energies of the Department should be directed to the removal of those articles from the counties which are threatened with immediate invasion. All the counties west of this place are at present safe and if a supply of Salt can be procured the hogs will be cured into bacon which can be procured at any time

[Richmond]

[Vance Letter Book, 1862-1863,

State Department of Archives and History, Raleigh.]

From A. A. Deweese[92]

Camp McCowan
Knoxville Tenn
Nov 9th 1862 To

There is one man in the Co of Madison by the name of B. J. S. McLean[93] who vol in my Company offered himself for 3d Leut in the Co was beeten he then said he was not going into the service claiming himself exempt from conscript by the state law exempting commissioned Militia officers he backed by others stands in defiance of authorities has made some considerable threats &c. I ask you whether he is subject to being taken or not. he being an officer in the Militia of this Co. Alltho volunteered in July last you will pleas condicend to answer me at Marchall N. C. as soon posable as we are trying to get out men all in camp.

[Raleigh]

[on reverse]

He is not liable as a Militia officer but if he signed the rolls of

---

[90] See p. 296, 25n. This letter is signed by David A. Barnes, aide to Vance.

[91] See p. 296.

[92] Arthur A. Deweese, of Madison County, commissioned July 16, 1862, was captain of company D in Allen's legion, afterwards the Sixty-fourth North Carolina Infantry Regiment. Moore, *N. C. Roster,* IV, 61.

[93] Bachus J. S. McLean, of Madison County, enlisted July 15, 1862, in company D of Allen's legion. He was defeated for the lieutenancy by William C. Harrison and Thomas Hunter, both of Madison County. Moore, *N. C. Roster,* IV, 61. He was a second lieutenant in the Gabriel's Creek District of the Madison County Militia, his commission bearing the date of May 15, 1862. Militia Roster, p. 428.

your Co & was sworn in, then he waived his office & can be arrested

Z B V

[A. L. S. Governors' Papers (Vance),
State Department of Archives and History, Raleigh.]

From J. M. Edwards[94]

N. C. Rutherford County
November the 9th 1862

His excellency Governor of North Carolina
Sir I have to refer to you for information: viz: an old gentleman
of South Carolina twelve months ago sold to a taner of North
Carolina 25 or 30 hids and made a verbal contract withe the
tanner to let him have enough leather this Fall of the same hides
for his own use the old gentleman came the other day and got 50
lbs of the leather and a captain of my Regiment seized it and has
the leather in possession at this time the old gentleman contends
for his leather, he sold the hids & buys the leather, I wish to know
if I must give the old man the leather, or take it to Raleigh. I
also wish to know if it is in violation of general order No 9th [95]
sent to me by the Adjutant General for a tanner of North Carolina to sell to a person of South Carolina a side or two of leather
for their own use and also if it is a violation for the ladies to
exchange cloth for spun thred withe the South Carolinians to get
thread for their own use.
please answer this as soon as possible as the old gentleman is comeing to see about the leather the 16th of this month.
Raleigh
[on reverse]
Let him have the Leather the Ladies can exchange of course

Z B Vance

[A. L. S. Governors' Papers (Vance),
State Department of Archives and History, Raleigh.]

From Theo. Edwards[96]

Goldsboro N. C. Nov 9th 1862
Desiring to raise a company of Infantry for the defence of
N. C. and also that you would grant authority to raise such Com-
panies East of the W. W W. Rail Road, I addopt this my only

---

[94] James M. Edwards, colonel of the 104th North Carolina Militia Regiment, his
commission bearing date of March 15, 1862. He lived at Webb's Ford, Rutherford
County. Militia Roster, pp. 306-307. His jurisdiction was the southern portion of
the county.
[95] See p. 305, 46n.
[96] Theophilus Edwards, who became first lieutenant of company C of the Sixty-
seventh North Carolina Infantry Regiment. Moore, N. C. Roster, IV, 136.

opportunity of communicating with you upon the subject I am prevented from communicating with you in person on acout of my being a Soldier and am unable to procure a furlough to visit Raleigh from the commandant of this post I send you two letters one from Capt Cha⁸. C. Clark⁹⁷ & Mr Ja⁸. H Everett ⁹⁸ whitch will give you an idea of my standing I would respectfully ask an answer to this as soon as convenient I remain with much respect your obedient servant
[Raleigh]
[A. L. S. Governors' Papers (Vance),
State Department of Archives and History, Raleigh.]

From Ervin Sluder⁹⁹

Asheville Nov 9/62

I have bin informed that President Davis has ordered out all men between the age of 35 & forty. I wish to if have the Rite to enrole myself in any Company I ma chose now and then would have the Rite to get a Substitute¹⁰⁰ in my place if I have that Rite you will confer a particular favour by giving me the power to do so. Please answer my letter— letter as early as possible for the Reason that I am so much engad at home in privt business that I would prefer to employ a substitute than to go my self and I now have a chance to engage a man that is over forty five that will be vary gladly Received
[Raleigh]
[on reverse]
By the law the conscripts have a right previous to their enrollment,

---

⁹⁷ Charles Cauthen Clark (1829-1911), of New Bern, who was a member of the House of Commons of 1860 and of the Convention of 1865. On November 27, 1862, he was elected solicitor of the second circuit. A lawyer and a former Whig, he had left New Bern when the Yankees captured the town in March of 1862 and was refugeeing in Goldsboro, from where he wrote Vance that Edwards was a "young gentleman of the best social position in his county, of irreproachable character" and that any statements he made could be relied upon. Clark to Vance, November 8, 1862, Governors' Papers (Vance); *North Carolina Booklet,* XXII (1923), pp. 57-61; Connor, *N. C. Manual,* pp. 572, 875; Raleigh *North Carolina Standard,* February 27, 1861; *House Journal, 1862-1863,* p. 43.

⁹⁸ James H. Everitt was a member of the House of Commons from Wayne County (Goldsboro) in 1865 and 1866. Connor, *N. C. Manual,* p. 849. He wrote Vance that Edwards was "a young man of character and standing" and that any statement he made could be relied upon. Everitt to Vance, November 5, 1862, Governors' Papers (Vance).

⁹⁹ Ervin Sluder is listed in the census of 1860 as a note shaver of Buncombe County, age thirty-six. He had therefore been exempt from conscription until the passage of the second act, Setember 27, 1862. Earlier he had acted as a quartermaster with W. A. Patton for McDowell's battalion, and had posted bond of $20,000. N. C. Quartermaster Contracts, Box 107.

¹⁰⁰ Substitutes were allowed by the ninth section of the Conscription Act of April 16, 1862, and continued under the second act. The War Department did not allow substitutes under eighteen, but only those over forty-five or, before September 27, over thirty-five. *O. R.,* Ser. IV, Vol. I, 1096, 1099.

to volunteer in any company formed previous to the 16th of April
& can then put in a Substitute Z. B. V.
[A. L. S. Governors' Papers (Vance),
State Department of Archives and History, Raleigh.]

From A. L. Corpening[101]

Macon County
Nov 9th 1862

These are times that pesters the mind of man to know where
he should start as a law abiding man I wish to know whether a
man is exempt from the army after he has been regular discharge
by a regular physician of the army, as a subject that is dieased
not able to stand exposier and I would like to kow whether
your Maliatia officers are still exempt the Capts more particular
I ask those queseions for others as well as my self I am as willing
to serve my country as any man in it if I can get to do it as
I can stand it I know that I cant stand camp life nor wet weather,
but if I had a position where I would not be exposed to the
weather too much I would do all that I could for the interes of
my country but I think that the western portion of N. C. has done
a very good part so fare in the war and think that your Excellency
should show some lenity to our part of the county as you know
that there is very few blacks in this part of the state. I hope that
I may here from you soon I will close
P S since I wrote the above i have received orders through our
Colonel [102] to get clothing for the soldiers. I am very near throug
the women in this part say if they could get thread they would
have done a great deal more for the soldiers, but owing to speculation they Could not get any thing to work on and earnestly
appeales to you to put down some of those things that we are
compeled to have such as thread and wool if it is in your power.
I done very well taking all things in to consideration I wait for to
here from you
[Raleigh]
[on reverse]
Militia officers not subject to conscription Certificate of a surgeon
does not necessarily exempt.[103] Gov. has called the attention of
the Legislature to speculation
[A. L. S. Governors' Papers (Vance),
State Department of Archives and History, Raleigh.]

---

[101] A. L. Corpening lived in Franklin, in Macon County. He does not appear as a
captain in the 114th Regiment of Militia in Militia Roster.

[102] No colonel is listed for the 114th Militia in Militia Roster. Captain LaFayette
Howard, commissioned March 1, 1862, appears to be the ranking officer of the
regiment. He was also from Franklin.

[103] This refers to a provision that "The fact that a person has been discharged
from service for physical disability or other cause does not of itself exempt from
enrollment as a conscript." O. R., Ser. IV, Vol. II, 166.

From Thos. Miller[104]

Pittsborough N. C.
Nov 10th 1862.

I hope you will not deem it amiss, or presumptious in me, from the slight acquaintance I have with you personally, although I may assure you, that I have by reputation been long acquainted with you, & that most favorably to submit my views to you upon one point particularly, for the good of the country, as we are all equally interested in the same cause—

It is, for the security of ourselves & our negro population, that instead of having the ordinary Patrol appointed by the Courts, I think that the Legislature should pass a law, establishing a Military Patrol. And let that Military Patrol be armed, & be subject to the same strict & rigid rules, as the military rules of the army— Let that be due by a law passed, — Let it embrace all men, between the ages of 45 & 65, & *all exempts*— under the present law of Congress, except the *Govr* & officers of State— I mean civil officers, at the time, on duty— let them be detailed day & night, in sufficient numbers, to do duty, as may be necessary in the opinion of the commanding officers— Now Sir, I deem this as the *only means* of keeping the country quiet— & secure, it is the best means to *keep the Negroes within our lines*— by day, & the best to keep them at their homes at night— Let it be the duty of this Military Patrol, to disperse all crowds of negroes assembled, for conversation, & *apparently for evil purposes,* & their duty *especially to arrest all negroes* by *night or by day going without a pass*— for now Sir, a negro in some sections, can go one hundred miles without being arrested, or asked for a pass, I have a Plantation perhaps over 100 miles from my Plantation near Wilmington, & my negroes have recently told me, that when passing from one place to the other, they are never asked for their pass— A regulation of this kind, has much greater influence with the negroes, than the ordinary Patrol—Why Sir, *ten bayonets to a negro* passing about at night, & in the day, has more terror than a thousand Cow hydes, & then if the Patrols are governed by a law, with the strictness of a military discipline then it will be kept up, & it will *last,* but the ordinary patrol is generally speaking strict for a week or two, & then entirely neglected & it has no moral effect at all— I have conversed with several intelligent influential Gentlemen upon this subject, in different parts of the Country, & they in variably think it advisable, & from the general approbation of others, & the full convictions of my own mind, I am induced to submit it to your consideration—

---

[104] Thomas Miller was a lawyer, planter, and railroad director whose home was in Wilmington, but who was a refugee in Pittsboro because of the yellow fever epidemic in Wilmington. Sprunt, *Chronicles,* p. 566.

Govr I belong to the Safety Committee of the Town of Wilmington, & I can assure you that we have *great confidence* in your *determination to defend* our Town, & the State— that is, that you will do all in your *power to cause the Confederate Govemt* to do it, for it is the duty of the *Confederate Govemt to do it*— We have done our duty as a State— and as a State we should be equally defended— Militia cant fight against regular trained troops.— Wilmington is as much entitled to be defended as Charleston—, but the Sun & the Moon must stand still till *South Carolina* is made satisfied when No Carolina is always neglected,— Wilmington is now the only out let that North Carolina has, for her salt & medicine & such things as are brought by vessels escaping the Blockade, & it is important to *North Carolina,* as Charleston is to South Carolina,—

I assure you the people of Wilmington knowing you to be a military man, feels great confidence that you will *insist* on the defence of place *by the President.*—

N. B.

I have no doubt but that we will be attacked at Wilmington as soon as the fever subsides, especially as they know that there are no troops there, & that will *be soon,* for the fever is now subsiding, & as sure as a few frosts come it will disappear--

[Raleigh]

[A. L. S. Governors' Papers (Vance),
State Department of Archives and History, Raleigh.]

From A. H. Jones[105]

Hendersonville N. C. Nov the 10th 1862

I have authority from Col Allen[106] signed by himself and A. G. Smith[107] to raise a company of inf or for artilery in

[105] Alexander Hamilton Jones (1822-1901). He was born in Buncombe County but moved in 1851 to Hendersonville, where he engaged in mercantile pursuits until the war. Politically he was a Whig and a staunch Union man who not only opposed the calling of a convention in 1861, but also opposed secession after Lincoln's proclamation calling for troops. When the war came he founded "Union Leagues" in western North Carolina and eastern Tennessee and helped men evade conscription in many ways. In 1863 he enlisted in the Union Army and was authorized by General Burnside to raise a loyal regiment in North Carolina. He was captured in Tennessee while attempting to raise it, was imprisoned in Asheville, Camp Vance, Camp Holmes, and in Libby prison in Richmond. He was conscripted in 1864 and placed in Lee's army, but deserted to the enemy and again joined the Union Army in 1864. After the war he returned to North Carolina and was elected a member of the Convention of 1865, representing Henderson and Transylvania counties. He was elected to Congress as a Republican in 1865, but was not permitted to qualify; he was again elected twice and served from 1868 to 1871, but was then defeated for re-election. He then lived in Wilmington until 1876, in Maryland until 1884, in Asheville until 1890, in Oklahoma until 1897, and in California until his death. Connor, *N. C. Manual,* p. 883; *Biog. Dir. of Am. Cong.,* p. 1384; and Alexander H. Jones, *Knocking At The Door* (Washington, 1866), which relates his own version of his war time adventures and his political beliefs.

[106] See p. 226, 208n.

[107] Lucius H. Smith, Allen's adjutant. See p. 1, 4n and p. 227, 211n.

Allens Legion and I dont wish (notwithstanding this is Gen Smiths[108] department) to commence to organize a company without consulting the Govr of my State not that its legality is doubted by any one, but is thought by some that this part of the State will or should not be called on for any more men i.e. no more conscripts should leave this part of the State.

I have no doubt that I can make a company and be ready in case they are called for. Shall I organize a company and be ready to report to Allens Legion of Partisan Rangers or Shall I organise and await orders from my State.

I have no doubt that you are pressed with business, but I hope that you will give this your attention and give me an early answers. Should the people of this section have to go into confederate or State service they would much prefer forming their own company by volunteering than to go without this privilege.

I consulted Col Stancil[109] in regard to authority he says doubtless my authority is good unless it would conflict with some late State arrangement I then told I would write you on the subject.

What I wish to know is will it conflict with State arrangements and if so shall I raise the company and hold it subject to orders by State authority.

I am certain if any man can raise a company in this county I can do so, and should I have to go I would like to situate myself the best I can, but I wish to do right and hence my object in addressing this to yourself.

[Raleigh]
[on reverse]
Write to raise his company & wait for orders from me. Allen has no authority to raise more troops   Z B V
[A. L. S. Governors' Papers (Vance),
  State Department of Archives and History, Raleigh.]

From Richard Morton[110]

CONFEDERATE STATES OF AMERICA
War Department
Nitre and Mining Bureau
Richmond Nov. 10th- 1862

You are aware that the great scarcity of powder in the C. S. had made it necessary to promote in every means possible the production of nitre from sources within our own limits, this branch of the advance service was made the speciality of *this*

---

[108] Edmund Kirby-Smith. See p. 177, 53n, for his command.
[109] Stark Stansill, of Hendersonville, was colonel of the 106 Regiment of North Carolina Militia. Militia Roster, pp. 418-419.
[110] Richard Morton was a captain attached to the Nitre and Mining Bureau of the Confederate government in Richmond.

Bureau, and under authority from the Chf. of Ordnance & the Secty of War Capr. C. R. Barney[111] has been sent as the agent of this Bureau to N. Ca. to put Gov. works for the manufacture of nitre and even to make contracts with private parties for the same, under the assurance, contained in Gen[l]. orders[112] which I enclose, that the parties so engaged should be exempt from Military duty; and up to this time he has been very successful; in a letter just received however he states that Col Worth,[113] of the N. C. Militia, of Randolph County has positively *refused to respect the Gen. orders from the Sec. of War alleging that you have instructed him to that effect.* This Bureau is now furnishing 4000 lbs *crude,* or 3000 lbs *pure nitre* per week to the *Raleigh powder mills,*[114] which were erected under the auspices of the State of N. C. and now I believe largely in debt to the same, and the debt is being paid by the manufacture of this nitre. I can but think therefore that Col Worth has entirely misapprehended your instructions and I respectfully request your immediate attention to this matter, for Capt Barney who is at Greensboro reports that Col Worth has already seized more of his men and is now hunting up others; it is impossible for any man to render more efficient service to his country at this time than by making nitre, this remark is caused by an intimate acquaintance with the wants of the service

Hoping your favorable and early action in this matter
Raleigh
[A. L. S. Governors' Papers (Vance),
State Department of Archives and History, Raleigh.]

[Nov. 10, 1862]
Memorandum of an agreement between Zebulon B. Vance Governor of North Carolina, contracting for and on behalf of the State of the One part and John White[115] of the town of Warrenton in said State of the other part.

The said John White covenants and agrees on his part to visit Europe and to use all skill energy and prudence in purchasing for said State such articles as the said Zebulon B. Vance may direct—

The said Zebulon B. Vance covenants and agrees for and on behalf of the State to pay all the necessary expenses of the expedition, to furnish the funds necessary to make such purchases and as a compensation to said White to pay him Five Thousand dollars in cash two and a half per cent commission on expenditures amounting to Five Hundred Thousand Dollars and one and

---

[111] See p. 314, 76n.
[112] General Orders, No. 41 and No. 50, issued May 31 and July 18, 1862. See p. 314, 79n, 80n.
[113] See p. 206, 144n.
[114] See p. 187, 87n.
[115] See p. 288, 1n.

a half *per cent* Commission on all sums between Five Hundred Thousand and One Million of Dollars.

In witness whereof the parties have hereunto set their hands in duplicate this the 10th day of November 1862

Z. B. Vance

Jnº. White

[Agreement: Gov: Vance & John White 1862]
[A. L. S.   Governors' Papers (Vance), 2 copies, State Department of Archives and History, Raleigh.]

From S. S. Satchwell [116]

General Military Hospital—[117] Wilson, N. C.
November 10th 1862

As the Legislature will convene in a few days, will you permit me to intrude upon your attention a few minutes, a suggestion that I should be pleased to see endorsed by you to that Body?

You will perceive my meaning in the following statement. I am a law and order man in respects my state and the Confederacy, but how myself and other Confederate officers like me can faithfully obey both as matters now stand is more than I can understand. For example, I am a Confederate Surgeon in charge of a large & important Confederate Military Hospital at this place. Last Spring at the request of the citizens and in deference to the wants of the Confederate service, Maj General Holmes[118] issued a special order to me to confiscate all liquor here belonging to those who retail the same. &c. I have executed this order as a Confederate officer each time. Recently, as there has been so much talk in & out of Congress on subjects pertaining to each proceedings, my authority to do so has been questioned, and I laid the whole matter before the Sec. of War. asking for instructions, &c. Receiving no answer from him, I then referred the matter

---

[116] Solomon Sampson Satchwell (1821-1892), physician and Confederate surgeon in charge of the Confederate hospital in Wilson. A native of Beaufort County, he attended Wake Forest College, 1839-1841, and graduated in medicine at New York University in 1850. He practiced medicine near Washington, N. C., 1850-1854, at Long Creek, Pender County, 1854-1860, and studied at the Sorbonne in Paris, 1860-1861. During the war he was surgeon of the Twenty-fifth North Carolina Regiment and head surgeon of the Confederate hospital at Wilson. He held many other honors in his profession: he was president of the State Board of Medical Examiners, of which he was a member, 1866-1872; president of the North Carolina Medical Society, 1877; editor of the *North Carolina Medical Journal;* first president of the State Board of Health, 1877-1884; and superintendent of public health for Pender County, 1892. He died of typhoid fever in Burgaw. *Medical Transactions,* 1899, pp. 172-174.

[117] The Confederate Military Hospital at Wilson was housed in Wilson Female Seminary, later called Wilson Academy, which had been chartered in 1859 and whose buildings were used for hospital purposes throughout the war.

[118] See p. 136, 541n.

to the General in Chief of this Department— Gen. G. W. Smith.[119]
He referred the matter to Gen. French,[120] but expressed the
opinion that the original orders of Gen Holmes should continue
in force, Gen French orders me to "rigidly enforce the order of
Gen Holmes & thus prevent the sale of intoxicating liquors in
this (your) vicinity."

As I said before I have enforced the order because I am satisfied the interests of the public service & the cause of the Confederacy are thereby promoted. When I ask the opinion of the
lawyers & judges of our State, as I have done they tell me I have
no authority to thus confiscate &c. but when I solicit the views of
Military men they tell me I have authority & that I must obey
the orders of my superior officers &c. Now this perplexes & em-
barrasses me, and my suggestion, if you will permit me to make
it, is that if you will recommend in your Message the passage of
a law forbidding the sale of liquor in the vicinity of Confederate
Military Hospitals in this State, the difficulty will be solved if
such a law is made. Detached Hospitals especially like this need
such a protection from the State as well as the Confederacy. Civil
Magistrates & citizens are down upon me if I obey the orders of
the Commanding Generals, & the latter and other Military officers
threaten me if I fail to execute them. If you will recommend the
passage of some such law as I suggest, I believe it will pass, much
good will result, and another of those vexed questions so unfortunately tending to conflicts between State & Confederate authorities, will be effectually disposed of.

I have the honor to remain, very Respectfully yr obt. Servt
[Raleigh]
[A. L. S. Governors' Papers (Vance),
State Department of Archives and History, Raleigh.]

---

[119] Gustavus Woodson Smith (1822-1896), who in August 1862, was made commander of a large military department between the Cape Fear and the Rappahan-
nock Rivers, with headquarters in Richmond. He was a native of Kentucky, a
graduate of West Point in 1842, a veteran of the Mexican War, and formerly street
commissioner of New York City, 1858-1861. Ill health sent him south in 1861 and
when his arrest was ordered by Federal authority as a disloyal person he offered
his services to the Confederacy and was made a major general in September 1861.
In the spring of 1862 he commanded a wing of J. E. Johnston's army defending
Richmond and was briefly commander of the army when Johnston was wounded,
May 31, 1862, and just before Lee took over the command. He was acting Secretary
of War between November 17 and November 20, 1862, and resigned his departmental
command in February 1863. Then he became the superintendent of the Etowah
Mining and Manufacturing Company in north Georgia, and major general of the
Georgia Militia, June 1864, in which capacity he fell back before Sherman in his
march through Georgia in the fall of 1864. In 1865 he commanded a sector in the
Department of South Carolina, Georgia and Florida until his surrender in April.
After the war he became general manager of the Southwestern Iron Company in
Chattanooga, 1866-1870, and the first Insurance Commissioner of Kentucky, 1870-
1875. The last fifteen years of his life he spent in New York. William M. Robinson,
Jr., "Gustavus Woodson Smith," *Dict of Am. Biog.*, XVII, 272-273.

[120] See p. 204, 142n.

From H. W. Ayer[121]

Bethania Forsythe County
Nov. 10th. 1862

I have been busily engaged since my last communication to you, but have not a great deal to show for it. Those iron works I alluded to in my letter from Salem have been visited and have an outward appearance of honesty, but there are some rumors afloat against them, which I could not trace up as true. The one owned by Stephen Hobson is situated in Yadkin County, he has at present 50 employees, detailed to him from Forsythe, Iredell Davidson and Yadkin Counties by the Cols. of the Regts to which they respectively belong. In addition to these he has 17 others, who have not been enrolled, being between the ages of 18 & 45 now, but were under 18 & over 35 at the last enrollment. He has no state or Govt. contract, further than a sub Contract, from Jno. P. & J. J. Nisson[122] of Waughtown, who have a Govt. Contract for wagons and horse shoes, which sub Contracts Hobson agrees to furnish 3000 lbs of iron every two weeks— He now runs two fires and one forge— is interested in 3 other new forges now being erected, and wishes to have some 38 hands more in addition to the 50 he now has detailed, Thinks he will be able then to furnish 1000 lbs iron pr day The opinion of some of his neighbors is that he is erecting the new forges for the purpose of screening some of his friends from the army, as he is a *Quaker*, but my own opinion is he is doing it for the dollars and cents he can make by it, as he employs these conscripts for $10, pr month He has a foundry also— and has been engaged in the manufacture of Iron with one forge for the last 20 years— You can make your own calculations whether the amt. which he now produces to the Govt. (3000 lbs. in two weeks with 50 hands) is a paying business or not, and whether it will pay to raise the number of operatives to 88 for the sake of 1000 lbs, pr day— Jesse Wooten near him has one forge completed and at work, & two others on the way— will be in operation in a few weeks— 15 conscript hands— a sub contract with Nisson— and furnishes 15000 lbs, every two weeks— at least that is his contract. Neither he or Hobson however quite reach the stipulated amt, Wooten has been at the business some eight years—and has as he says only the same number of hands that he always had— some of them are new however, oweing to the fact, that a part of his men went to the service in the early part of the war I would not have visited either of these establishments, had I not heard that they were frauds upon the Govt. Hobson has been heard to say "That he would *ease the conscience* of as many of the neighbors as he could, from fighting in the war. Both of

---

[121] See p. 278, 359n.
[122] See p. 239, 242n.

these establishments are in the bounds of the 75 N C M. Col.
Cowles—
I visited also the Shoe Shop of Messrs Kerner & Gentry at Kern-
ersville, Forsythe Co. find the working 13 hands— 12 whites,
1 Blk. 11 Conscripts, Contract with State, for 1000 prs pegged
and sewed shoes. Stipulation pr month 200 prs. Date of Contract
23 of May, Average pr day to the hand 1½ prs. was another contract just made with Q. M. Sloan,[123] for which he has not yet gotten the papers from Mr Sloan— Enclosed find if you please, the
report of Messrs Fries & Fries—[124] Salem, for woolen goods— and
Messrs Hine & Co— for Leather, The report from the Cotton
factory of Gray & Wilson Salem has not been made out yet
oweing to the absence of Mr Gray—It will reach me at Greensboro— and will be for^d. in my next. I am authorized and requested by Chief Justice Pearson,[125] to lay before your Excellency
the following facts, There is a man in Yadkin county near Mount
Nebo— 75 Regt, N. C. M. named Elkanah Willard, who openly
defied the law. First, By rescueing his brother who is a conscript
(he himself is not) from a guard who had him in custody by a
display of arms and open force Secondly, By putting Capt Flemming[126] of that district and the men accompanying him at defiance,
in such a way that they were obliged to shoot him down or rush
upon him armed as he was at the iminent danger of their lives
The Capt says he could have shot him down or at the risk of his
life have attempted to arrest him but as he was a man of most
desperate character and has 5 other brothers as bad as himself,
the better plan he thought was to let him alone— It is the opinion
of the well affected neighbors in order to avoid bloodshed that the
best policy would be to send an officer with 12 or 15 armed men—
to arrest him, supposing that this display of force would let them
see their resistance was hopeless and that they would surrender
without opposition Whereas if tampered with and not put down
at the start it may result in some dreadful evil. The effect of

[123] See p. 190, 95n.
[124] See p. 255, 305n.
[125] Richmond Mumford Pearson (1805-1878), Chief Justice of the Supreme Court
of North Carolina, 1858-1878. He was born in Rowan County, educated at John
Muchat's Academy near Statesville, and graduated from the University of North
Carolina with first honor in 1823. He read law under Judge Henderson and was
admitted to the bar in 1826. He was judge of the superior court, 1836-1848 and
associate justice of the Supreme Court, 1848-1858. He had sat in the House of
Commons from 1829 to 1832 as an Old Line Whig; he became a Republican in 1868
and was involved in the notorious Kirk-Holden war of Reconstruction days. During
the war he issued many writs of *habeas corpus* and was known as an arch defender
of states' rights against the encroachments of Confederate military authority. His
law schools at Mocksville and later at Richmond Hill, in Surry County, were
famous centers of legal instruction. Robert P. Dick, "Richmond M. Pearson," Ashe,
Biog. Hist. of N. C., V, 295-309.
[126] Flemming was a captain in the Seventy-fifth Militia Regiment, whose colonel
was Andrew Carson Cowles. See p. 291, 7n.

armed men in in the neighborhood, would be wholesome in many ways, as there is some disaffection in that part of the County. This man Willard has said that he would rather join the Federal Army than ours— The above statement are facts, vouched for by Judge Pearson Any thing else coming to my knowledge will be promptly reported to your Excellency [Raleigh]

[A. L. S. Governors' Papers (Vance),
State Department of Archives and History, Raleigh.]

From H. H. Best [127]

Greene Co.
Nov. 10th 1862

Recent demonstrations upon our lines, by the enemy, have alone induced us, the Representatives of this County to make this petition.

Knowing your Excellency to have *always* in consideration the welfare and propriety of your whole Country as it now exists, we Cannot but feel some embarrassment in making any suggestions in relation to this matter. *But,* at the sametime, we are not unremindful of the duty we owe to our Constituents, nor are we entirely ignorant of the many impositions likely to be practiced upon your Excellency as well as the Citizens of this Co., by applicants for posts of honor.

Taking these things in consideration, and endeavoring to keep upmost in our minds the important trust, imposed upon us by our fellow Citizens, *we*, in Compliance with our own feelings, heartily recommend to your Excellency's Consideration the qualifications of our young friend D. W. Edwards.[128] And I, H. H. Best, late Capt Co A. 3d- N. Cs. Troops, and Commoner elected to the Legislature of this State, do certify to this having served for nearly Twelve months in the ranks as a *private* and *never*, whilst in the enjoyment of good health, was he known to flinch any required duty.

Mr. Edwards desires to raise a company of the Citizens of this Co.

I recommend him to your Excellency, as a young man in every way qualified to fill the above named position.
[Raleigh]

[A. L. S. Governors' Papers (Vance),
State Department of Archives and History, Raleigh.]

---

[127] Henry H. Best, of Greene County, first lieutenant and then captain of company A of the Third North Carolina Regiment. He resigned when elected to the legislature, in which he served in 1862 and 1864. Moore, *N. C. Roster*, I, 81; Connor, *N. C. Manual*, p. 629.

[128] D. W. Edwards became captain of company C of the Sixty-seventh North Carolina Regiment on January 6, 1863. Moore, *N. C. Roster*, IV, 136.

From R. V. Blackstock[129]

Stocksville Nov. 10th 1862

At the request of Mr. Byers[130] I write to request of you to write a letter to the Secty. of War in regard to his Exemption from Military duty. Mr. Byers says you wrote such a letter to him while he was in the Hospital at Richmond but at the time he received it he thought he was likely to be transferred to the "Spirit land," (and I fear he is not much better yet), still he insists. I hope you will at Once write the letter and send it to me and I will send it on with his application and see what can be done for the poor fellow, as I think he can not live long. And now I would respectfully sugest an improvement in furnishing clothing for our soldiers who are fighting our battels. (US) for you to to empower some person officially to collect by contribution and purchais clothing in each section, let that be their business and make them give it their whole attention. One good efficient man can turn out and get more clothing than all the commissioned Militia officers in the State.[131] the people have not got confidence in those little Militia officers and the "Aaid Societies" in this part of the state arc doing but little good, as they cannot agree among themselves who to send their goods to, I know men who are willing to contribute 25 - 50 and some $100. but they want to give it to a responcible authorised agent of the State. this is the true state of affairs in my section One Agt could soon travall through all the counties west of the Ridge and in a short time would be able to send to the army a large quantity of clothing, what we need is Some Sistim and the right Kind of agents and the work would be done at Once. our Ladies bless them are ready and willing to make the garments for nothing if they had the cloth or make the cloth & Garments if they had the raw material Your Proclamation has had a good effect upon the people and there is considerable clothing ready made now all that is necessary to get that off is for there to be an authorised agent to gather it up and take it to the army thcr has ben so much clothing lost that the people are not willing to trust it to every one. I hope you will consider of these things and of there importance And if it meets your approbation to authorise some person in this section to

---

[129] See p. 39, 153n. Blackstock became one of the state's two appraisement commissioners.

[130] C. R. P. Byers, who enlisted in Vance's original company of volunteers on May 4, 1861. He was from Buncombe County and a private in company F of the Fourteenth North Carolina Regiment. His profession was that of a mechanic, and his detail was requested for the benefit of the community by his friends at Swannanoa. He died at Asheville in the fall of 1862. Moore, *N. C. Roster*, I, 528; William D. Fortune to Vance, September 15, 1862, Governors' Papers (Vance).

[131] Militia officers were ordered to perform this duty by Vance's proclamation of October 15, 1862. See above, p. 266.

collect & forward without delay all the clothing that our boys are suffering for if you think it necessary to have such an Agt. I would be willing to undertake myself although I have ben spoken to to take a situation at the Salt Lick but I think this more important. about who you appoint use your own pleasure all is well
Raleigh
P. S. My Respects to Mrs. V.[132] & Children
[A. L. S. Governors' Papers (Vance),
State Department of Archives and History, Raleigh.]

From Geo. W. Randolph[133]

CONFEDERATE STATES OF AMERICA
WAR DEPARTMENT
Richmond Va. Nov. 10th. 1862

In consequence of threatened attacks on our Rail Road connections in the Eastern portion of N. C. & Va and our inability at present to withdraw from the Army of Northern Va. reinforcements sufficiently large to secure those connections, it is considered very important to complete the Danville & Greensboro connection[134] as speedily as possible. The Piedmont R R Co is now working 800 hands on the Road & proposes to hire about 400 more— This is all that can possibly be obtained by the company: but it is not more than half the number that can be worked to advantage.

I shall give the company every assistance in my power by supplying at cost, rations, tools, horses, carts &c and under An Act

---

[132] See p. 16, 81n.
[133] See p. 132, 524n.
[134] The gap in the transportation line between Danville and Greensboro had long been a concern of the Confederate government, for if that forty mile gap could be closed with a railroad line a new line southwestward from Richmond to the upper Carolinas, seemingly more immune from Federal raids than the railroads in the eastern part of the state, would be assured. President Davis had advocated public assistance for the purpose of constructing the road in the fall of 1861 but Congress, with its states' rights proclivities in the ascendancy, had ignored the suggestion. But sentiment for the project developed even in North Carolina, where powerful interests had long feared that such a route would divert traffic from western North Carolina into Virginia. The State Convention, on February 8, 1862, approved a charter for the Piedmont Railroad Company, provided that the same be certified by the Virginia legislature. The charter allowed Confederate control of the route and invited Confederate aid. On February 10, 1862 Congress gave in and appropriated $1,000,000 in Confederate bonds for the purpose of building the road. On March 27, 1862, the Virginia legislature gave it formal sanction; by May construction agreements had been made and by June the company was organized. The greatest problems of the venture were never financial ones but the problems of material and labor. Robert C. Black III, *The Railroads of the Confederacy* (Chapel Hill, 1952), pp. 148-159 (cited hereafter as Black, *Confederate Railroads*).

of the General Assembly of Va, I can draft hands for the portion of the road in the State.

If your Excellency can supply hands[135] for the N. C. part of the road, I must ask you to do so and to inform me when and where they can be delivered to the Co.

Upon Conference with the Engineer[136] of the Company it has been determined to add 1900 hands to the force now employed and to appropriate them as follows,

Va. — 650 laborers and 100 mules
N C   1250   ”   500   ”

I am informed that the Planters of the Roanoke have hands, mules, and carts. If you can prevail upon them to hire them to the Co. it will enable us to complete the work by the 1st. of March. The owners of the hands drafted under the Va Act receive $16 per month and are taken under the ordinary responsibilities of hirers except they are to be paid for if they escape to the enemy.

The distance of the road from the scene of operations and the presence of a mounted patrol, which I shall organize to operate along the line will render the latter risk very small. Can you recommend a suitable person to raise the Mounted Company for local service as guards and patrols— He should be somewhat acquainted with Cavalry service. The company will be composed of non conscripts and be mustered into the service for six months..[137]

Raleigh
[on reverse]
Answ that the Govr will of course assist the Govt all he can, but is impressed with the fact that it is better to defend one road than build another. Thousands of slaves can be hired in the east if [illegible] will only try to get them. *Z B V*
[A. L. S. Governors' Papers (Vance),
[Vance Letter Book, 1862-1863,
  State Department of Archives and History, Raleigh.]

---

[135] The labor problem was the most acute aspect of building the road. The company sent a bevy of agents into the country to secure equipment and labor, but planters were loathe to part with their slaves. Soon the Piedmont Board began to buy slaves with its own funds, but this proved unsatisfactory. The Virginia law authorized the impressment of as many slaves as were necessary to finish the road within her own border, but as 90 per cent of the road lay in North Carolina, this was of limited help. Black, *Confederate Railroads*, p. 151.

[136] The engineer was Captain Edmund D. T. Myers, the son of Confederate Quartermaster General Abraham C. Myers. He was detailed as chief engineer and chief of construction by the War Department on June 16, 1862. Black, *Confederate Railroads*, p. 150.

[137] For Vance's reply to this request see his letter of November 17 in *O. R.*, Ser. I, Vol. XVIII, 779.

To Jefferson Davis

STATE OF NORTH CAROLINA
EXECUTIVE DEPARTMENT
Raleigh Nov. 11th. 1862

By the recent expedition of our Troops by the order of Gen French[138] into Eastern North Carolina some forty persons were arrested on suspicion of disloyalty and sent up to Salisbury[139] for safe keeping. As Governor of the State of which they are citizens it becomes my duty to see that they are protected in whatever rights pertain to them. First among them is undeniably the right of a trial of their alleged offences. A number of others it is proper to state have been there in confinement for some time past under similar circumstances. I should be glad to know what disposition is to be made of them or if there exists any grave public reason why their cases should not be investigated
[Richmond]
[Vance Letter Book, 1862-1863,
Copy in Governors' Papers (Vance),
State Department of Archives and History, Raleigh.]

From D. Stradley[140]

Hendersonville N. C.
Nov 12th- 1862

I was in Raleigh a few days ago and called to see you but you was not at home My business was to see about money to pay for janes socks &c &c for the Soldiers, there are so many persons here with money to pay for those articles as fast or before they are ready for market that we found it almost impossible to buy any without the money to pay down for them and so I thought to

---

[138] See p. 204, 142n. President Davis sent this letter to General French, who replied to Vance on November 16, saying that his instructions to his officers on the frontier were that they should not molest citizens unless they had positive proof of disloyalty. The men referred to were arrested by Colonel J. D. Radcliffe of the Sixty-first North Carolina Regiment, who had gone beyond Greenville into eastern North Carolina. French expressed regret that the men were carried beyond Tarboro and wrote to Radcliffe to make out charges against such as had committed offenses and to release the remainder and return them to their homes. French to Vance, from Petersburg, November 16, 1862, *O. R.*, Ser. I, Vol. XVIII, 778.

[139] The Confederacy established a prison at Salisbury in a former cotton factory, in November 1861. It was used for Confederates who had been arrested for alleged disloyalty, and for prisoners of war. Clark, *N. C. Regts.*, IV, 745.

[140] David M. Stradley, a lawyer of Hendersonville, was a son of James Stradley, an Englishman who had come to Asheville about 1850 and married a daughter of Samuel Patton. James Stradley was a blacksmith and carriage maker in Asheville during Vance's boyhood there, and David Stradley was one of his boyhood contemporaries, seven years younger than Vance. Years later Stradley was one of the leaders of the movement which led to the founding of the North Carolina Bar Association, in Hendersonville, in 1883. Patton, *Henderson County*, pp. 247-248; McLean, "Notebooks."

sugest a plan to you that you appoint an agent in each County and furnish him with money to pay for those goods, requiring him if thought necessary to give bond & security in that way a good deal of Cloth & socks could be bought in the mountains but unless the money is furnished we cant get along with any success—

an other thing a pair of men requested me to Call your attention to swindle on a small scale in the advertismt of the Fall Distribution of the School fund. Atkins[141] of the News makes his advertisement a third larger than in other papers in order as some think to make his bill a third larger you will notice this that it is set up in larger type than is usual for advertising I think his object is to swindle and when he presents his bill he should be docked if he attempts to swindle in any such way

P. S. The Magistrate's will have a meeting on the 21st to consult on some plan to carry out this object and I would like to here from you before that time if convenient D. S.

[on reverse]

Mr. Arledge[142] is entrusted with the purchase of articles for the soldiers in that section Z B V

[Raleigh]

[A. L. S. Governors' Papers (Vance),
State Department of Archives and History, Raleigh.]

From A. J. Battle[143]

Wilson Nov 12th- 1862

It is without doubt apparent to you, that those counties lying East of the Wilmington and Weldon R. R. are exposed to great loss & suffering to their citizens, by the inroads and depredations of our enemy. And there can be no doubt with those who know you, but that you do feel most deeply interested for the welfare of that portion of your constituents lying in this part of the State. And I feel assured that any suggestions from any source, tending in any degree to ameliorate the condition of those suffering people,

---

[141] See p. 18, 84n.

[142] Isaac Arledge was the sheriff of Henderson County. In the Governors' Papers (Vance) there are seven different petitions, signed by more than 100 citizens of Henderson County, protesting the appointment of Arledge as state agent because "his former course towards the orders of the Governor and the people of this county generally does not entitle him to such promotion while there are so many of our citizens worthy of the same." Petitions in Governors' Papers (Vance), November 27, 28, 1862.

[143] Amos Johnston Battle (1805-1870), of Edgecombe County, a wealthy planter who had been converted to the Missionary Baptists, became a preacher, and contributed to many Baptist charities at Wake Forest and in Raleigh. He was a brother of Judge William H. Battle, associate justice of the North Carolina Supreme Court. J. Kelly Turner and Jno. L. Bridgers, Jr., History of Edgecombe County North Carolina (Raleigh, 1920), pp. 418-419 (cited hereafter as Turner and Bridgers, Edgecombe County).

will meet with a respectful consideration at your hands; and therefore I am encouraged to submit a few thoughts to your reflection
on this very important subject. It strikes my mind as not good
policy, that after our citizens have toiled through the year to make
their crops, & now just as they are securing them in their barns &
store houses, to let our enemy drive our people from their homes,
& without resistance be allowed to carry off & destroy what has
been made; & which will be so much needed not only by themselves & families, but also their surplus produce will be so much
needed toward the suport of our armies, as well as to meet the
wants of a large portion of our people in other parts of our State,
who will need such a supply. Already the enemy is pushing his
way up our rivers unobstructed, & our people are fleeing their
houses and leaving their provisions at their mercy. The desire to
save their negro population is causing a great many to bring
them up out of reach of the enemy, to prevent their running
off or being forcibly carried off by the enemy, even before they
have housed what they have made. For the last five days thousands
of negroes have been brought out of those eastern counties, &
the provisions needed to support them left behind, & they being
carried into sections of the State where provisions are not so abundant, must lead to great suffering for food before the end of the
ensuing year, unless some plan can be adopted to bring out the
abundant supply of provisions already made in those eastern
counties, & conveyed to where they will be so much needed. I
am no Military man & can know but little about military management, but it strikes my mind that the thing is practicable, that
a System might be adopted by which a great many more negroes,
and great deal of those provisions might be saved. The following
suggests itself to my mind as worthy of consideration, & that is,
that you as Governor of the State might call out a force of all ages
over forty years without respect to their official position or professions, as a matter of necessity or the good of the state; & appoint
competent officers to organize them into three or more divisions,
expressly to act as a protection to lines of transport waggons, that
might be established to haul out the grain & meat from those
counties mostly exposed to the ravages of the enemy; and also
to drive out the stock of cattle hogs & sheep in these counties.
By the same authority & for the same necessity you might call
into service a full supply of waggons, teams & drivers from all
parts of the State, & put them into this service. I would suggest
that one such line of defence & communication might be established from Tarboro, leading into the counties of Martin, Washington, Tyrrell, Hyde & those portions of Beaufort & Pitt lying
north of Tar River. Another such line might be established
from this place or Goldsboro leading into the counties of Greene,

Lenoir & those portions of Pitt, Beaufort & Craven lying between
Tar river & the Neuse. A similar one from favorable points on
the Rail Road leading into those counties between the Neuse
& Cap Fear. I suppose something of this kind might also be done
for a part of the counties lying north of the Roanoke. I do feel assured that such a plan of operations could be made available to
the saving a great many negroes to their owners, which otherwise
will be lost not only to them, but also is a real loss to the strength
of the State as to its revenue. By such a plan a vast amount of
provisions might be saved, otherwise it will be lost to the owners,
& must be felt seriously by a large portion of the State, & result
in starvation in many instances. It is greatly to be regretted that
we have not had better Military management for coast defence in
the first instance. There appeared to be a great lack of comprehension on the part of the proper authorities to the vast amount
of resources to be protected, and the very great disadvantages
that would result to the Confederate cause by neglecting to defend our inlets at all hazards. Soon after the fall of Fort Hatteras,
I addressed a letter to President Davis,[144] & from my intimate
acquaintance with all the country east of the W. & W. R. R.
from Wilmington to the Virginia line, I took the priviledge of
minutely describing the country, & suggested the importance of
its defence. My letter was refered to the Secretary of War, Hon.
J. P. Benjamin,[145] then acting in the Department, acknowledged
its reception & thanked me for the information, & assured me that
it would be fully attended to. But I did not learn that any thing
of importance was done for such a defence· and the fall of Roanoke
Island [146] was done for the want of it has entailed upon the Eastern
Carolina an injury that fifty years of peace will not repair.

My dear Governor let us do something for the defence & protection of our dear old North State, & not wait for, nor look to
the Confederate authorities for help, whose movements are too
slow & inefficient to prevent the enemy from still further inflicting
irreparable injury upon our defenceless inhabitants.

Excuse the liberty I have taken by thus addressing you; the deep
interest I feel in this subject, & the very great sympathy I feel for
the continual stream of our fleeing & destitute people who continually throng my dwelling on their way to place of safety from

---

[144] His letter is dated September 30, 1861, and is found in *O. R.* Ser. I, Vol. LI,
Part II, 327.

[145] See p. 136, 541n.

[146] The Roanoke Island disaster in February 1862 forced Benjamin from the War
Department. A Congressional committee investigating the defeat blamed the secretary, who could not defend himself without revealing the weakness of the Confederate military resources. He took the criticism in silence and President Davis
promoted him to the State Department, knowing that Benjamin had had no
strength to send to Roanoke Island. But the public did not know this, and
Benjamin's unpopularity was increased.

the enemy, must be my apology. All I am & all I can do is at your service in this great emergency.— May God sustain you & bless all your efforts is the prayer of one of your earnest supporters & most respectfully

[Raleigh]

[on reverse]

Rev. A. J. Battle S.

Letter suggesting plan of removing provisions & from lines of the enemy.

Col B.[147] will ansʳ this & say that his suggestions will be laid before the Legislature. Z B V

[A. L. S. Governors' Papers (Vance),
    State Department of Archives and History, Raleigh.]

From Samuel James Guy[148]

No the 12 1862

dier Sir by request of my docter i drop you a few lines for information i have bin under his handes for several year and more so in the last six monthes   i suffer vary much with the rumatice in my hip and my liver he advised mee to get a discharge or be detailed to a farme to my one or some one elce i cold doo more good at that than eny thing elce for i warnt fit for services nor never wold bee a gain i have bin in servies for six month and has bin of now servies attall of eny importance dier sir if this meetes with you my request i will send you a stiffacite from my docter pleas grant mee this if you pleas as my health is vary feeble and I have five brothers in the same compenny and now one at home to cair on a farme i am now in fayeteville as garde but cant bee of much importence pleas ancier this and give mee your advice pleas excuse bad riting and bad spelling and I remain your truley until death Samuel James Guy to Governor Vance

Whauley N C Comberland County dire your ancier to fayetsville N C

[on reverse]

Gov no power to detail or discharge him

[Raleigh]

[A. L. S. Governors' Papers (Vance),
    State Department of Archives and History, Raleigh.]

---

[147] Colonel David A. Barnes, aide to Governor Vance.

[148] No Samuel J. Guy appears in Moore, N. C. Roster. There are a half dozen soldiers by the name of Guy and they are all from Cumberland County. They are possibly the brothers referred to in the letter. Moore, N. C. Roster, II, 721, III, 465, 536, 537.

To Jefferson Davis

STATE OF NORTH CAROLINA
EXECUTIVE DEPARTMENT
Raleigh Nov. 12th. 1862

I have accepted the proposition of Col Northrop,[149] Com. General to collect with my own Agents all the supplies possible in Eastern No. Ca. and my agents are already down there at work. Two of the richest counties in the State are Gates & Hertford and I am extremely anxious to strip them first. It is necessary however to have some protection and assistance from the troops. I therefore earnestly request that you will order Gen French to send Col Ferebees[150] Regt. 59th (who were raised in that section) with a section of Artillery to Winton on the Chowan. By so doing the whole County of Hertford could be stripped in their rear and much brought across the Chowan from Gates. It seems to me this can be done with great advantage to the service.[151]

[Richmond]
[Vance Letter Book, 1862-1863,
State Department of Archives and History, Raleigh.]

From W. R. Young[152]

Asheville N. C.
Nov 13th 1862

Enclosed you will find a list of employees engaged at the Armery at this place I could not obtain a list sooner owing to the absence of Col Pullian[153] and there was no one authorised in his absence to furnish a list.

---

[149] See p. 296, 25n.

[150] Dennis Dauge Ferebee (1815-1884), who became colonel of the Fifty-ninth North Carolina Regiment (fourth cavalry) on August 10, 1862. He was born in Currituck County, attended the Bingham School and the University of North Carolina, studied law under Judge Gaston, but was always more of a planter than a lawyer. He moved to South Mills, Camden County, and was a member of the House of Commons in 1846, 1848, 1856, 1858, and 1860, and represented that county in the Conventions of 1861 and 1865. He was a Whig and opposed secession before Lincoln's call for troops. Connor, *N. C. Manual*, pp. 534, 870; Grant, *Alumni History*, p. 195; McCormick, *Personnel*, pp. 34-35; Clark, *N. C. Regts.*, III, 456. These sources disagree as to the date of his death, the spelling of his middle name, and as to whether or not he was a member of the State Senate.

[151] President Davis referred this letter to General French, for whose reply see below, French to Vance, November 15, 1862, p. 364.

[152] William R. Young was colonel of the 108th Regiment of Militia, having been commissioned May 3, 1862. His regiment served the northern part of Buncombe County. Militia Roster, pp. 334-335.

[153] Robert W. Pulliam (1809-1886), prominent merchant of Asheville, who was organizer and superintendent of the Confederate Armory in that town. There some guns were made for the army and there, during the spring of 1862, Pulliam organized all the artisans into a military company to hold themselves in readiness for an emergency. Raleigh *North Carolina Standard*, April 30, 1862; *Census*, Buncombe County, 1850.

I have & will be able to get up several Hundred dollars worth of articles for the Soldiers Blankets Shirts drawers Socks & some Janes. I can get no Shoes or leather what articles I have to purches I will receive donations in money to fut the bill There are some persons purchasing all the wool they can get at enormous prices & Sending it out of the State if it can be stoped there are women here that will manufacture it into Jeans if thread can be obtained I have instructed the Captains in my Regt to Stop & cease all they find going out of the State You will give me some instructions in the premises There are four or five men from this Regt that have been dodging ever since the 8th of July 1862 and I learn that one or more off them are in Greenville district S C and I advertise them as deserters & have them brought to Justice

[Raleigh]
[A. L. S. Governors' Papers (Vance),
  State Department of Archives and History, Raleigh.]
[Enclosure]

LIST OF OPERATIVES AT THE C. S. ARMORY, ASHEVILLE, N. C.

November 13: 1862

NAME	OCCUPATION	AGE
A. W. King	Act'g Master Armorer	29
Z. L. Clayton	" Mil. Storekeeper	27
A. M. Kitzmiller	Clerk	51
E. Clayton	Foreman, Carpenters	58
W. D. Riley	" Filers	40
W. D. Copeland	" Barrels	43
J. Hildebrand Jr	" Mach.y	41
Jos: Reed	" Smiths	36
Geo. W. Whitson	" Stocking	36
Ashe, A. D.	Stoker	36
Boone, Erwin	Smith	30
Begg, James	Machinist	25
Baird, W. F.	"	32
Benson, M. C.	Filer	31
Bright, H. M.	Carpenter	28
Bechtler, C. S.	Capt Guard	21
Britt Geo	Collier	40
Ballew Robt A	Barrel Borer	35
Brank X	Pattern maker	33
Barnett W. A. J.	Polisher	37
Ballew Jno	Filer	28
Bechtler A	"	27
Buckner M. G.	"	29

Brank W. F.	Wood Chopper	24
Brank —	" "	19
Brank C. B.	Getting lumber for stock	35
Creasman L.	Teamster	40
Clark J. A.	Guard	30
Cordell Alsey	Wood Hauler	35
Dirigler J. J.	Guard	38
Ensley E.	Smith	23
Foard David	Asst. Founder	19
Frants Herman	Rifler	40
Francis H. N.	Filer	30
Fradey S. C.	Polisher	27
Gillispie W.	Filer	33
Goodlake Geo.	Hauling Charcoal	33
Gibson A. M.	Asst. Smith	37
Hamilton —	Getting stock lumber	25
Howard A. E. M.	Machinist	37
Hurdner James	Filer	26
Holesclaw R.	"	31
Hildebrand J Sen.	Barrel turner	52
Henly Jos.	Smith	26
Hopper A. W.	Asst Smith	16?
Hopper S. T.	Smith	37
Hamilton D. H.	Getting lumber for stocks	23
Jetton G. M.	Filer	18
Jacobs Noah	Pattern maker	46
Justus W. M.	Filer	23
Justus W. D. Jr.	"	35
Jordan L. M.	Smith	36
Kitzmiller Archd.	Machinist	23
Kitzmiller Jennings	Barrel Corer	16
Kirby G. S.	Armcaler	42
Keman Hugh	Hauling Wood	25
Lang J. M.	Grinder	28
Lick L. H.	Smith	33
Linfield J. W.	Filer	38
Ledgord J. M.	Carpenter	38
Miller L. T.	Smith	47
Miller J. F.	Shoptender	14
Miller Pink	" "	12
Miller Thomas	Barrel Corer	16
Maxwell R. R.	" "	28
McIntuff C. R.	Smith	26
Martin Wm.	Machinist	35
Mabers J. E.	"	19
Matthew John	Guard	45

Matthews C. C.	Wood Chopper	33
Roore J. J. A.	Asst Smith	18
Rowe John	Smith	39
Reichert H.	Stocker 40	40
Reed Jas. T.	Filer	32
Rhodes Abner	Stocker	34
Reid H. N.	Machinist	27
Ramsey E. D.	"	27
Rush C. C.	"	20
Reed W. R.	Filer	29
Reed, J. A.	Miller & Driller	28
Roberts H. C.	Asst. Smith	17
Reed S. M.	Filer	25
Rudisill W.	"	36
Ragland W R	Founder	29
Rilet C W	Miller & Driller	16
Rice J. L.	Hauling Charcoal	36
Sorrel J. T.	Guard	36
Seidell Carl	Shoptender	55
Staggs B. F.	Filer	35
Staggs G. W.	Miller & Driller	42
Stradley C	" " "	27
Snow Frost	Stocker	43
Stubbs E. W.	Machinist	28
Swanson S. U	Smith	30
Smith J. D.	Asst Smith	35
Swan T. W.	" "	26
Stradley Thos Jr.	Wood Chopper	35
Swanson J L	Smith	30
Sercey Riley	Teamster	34
Smith W. E.	Hauling Fire-wood	33
Trahthern Richard	Smith	40
Woods N. H.	Smith	33
Wing G. B.	Tool maker	29
Wilkie J. L.	" "	29
Westmoreland A.	Fernace man	37
Westmoreland J.	Shoptender	14
Walker N. E.	Asst. Smith	30

R. W. Pulliam

From Richd. H. Smith[154]

Scotland Neck
Nov. 13th 1862

Having failed in all my efforts to induce the Confederate
Authorities to extend adequate protection of the Roanoke Valley,

[154] Richard Henry Smith (1810-1893), of Halifax County, planter and lawyer. He

I am induced, as the last resort, to address you upon the subject, believing that you will exert all the power & influence that you possess, as the Executive of the State, in pressing the matter up on the attention of the Government in Richmond, as well as upon the legislature of the State soon to meet— with the history of the past before them it does seem to me that the Government has ben wilfully blind to the condition of things here— The fall of Roanoke island,[155] with the loss of the Albemarle region with its immense supplies of grain & meat was a heavy blow, & no doubt led to the evacuation of Norfolk & the Navy Yard—[156] yet the authorities were blind to its value & importance until it was lost—& I now predict that the loss of the Roanoke river & country will lead to the loss of Weldon & eventually of Richmond & our army compelled to retreat to central North Carolina—

The Roanoke & Tar river countrys are now the only portions of North Carolina from which abundant supplies of corn & meat can be procured & yet to judge from the past & from what is actually being done at the present time for the defence of this country it would seem as if the intention is, to give it up if vigorously pressed upon by the enemy. The recent raid,[157] (of which you are cognisant resulted in the Stealing of 800 or 1,000 negroes from the counties of Bertie, Martin & Halifax besides the destruction of property of other Kinds & after a visit from Major Gen French to Hamilton[158] *he* has decided (I learn), to leave but *one* regiment of infantry 1 battery of artillery & a company or two Cavalry to prevent a like visit in the future— what confidence can our people have in this small force? What inducement have our planters on the river to gather their crops of corn, when their *entire* personal estate is liable to be seized & carried off at any moment? I write, Sir, what I intend to do myself, & what I

---

graduated from the University of North Carolina in 1832 and read law under Judge Hall at Warrenton, but he was mainly a planter on the Roanoke. In politics he was a Whig who opposed secession until Lincoln's proclamation, represented his county in the Convention of 1861, where he was nominated for the Provisional Congress of the Confederacy but was defeated by William N. H. Smith, 76 to 28. He was a member of the House of Commons in 1848, 1852, and 1854, where he served with Vance as a Whig. Connor, *N. C. Manual*, pp. 641, 882; McCormick, *Personnel*, p. 76; Allen, *Halifax County*, pp. 209-212.

[155] Roanoke Island fell February 8, 1862 and doubtless led to the evacuation of Norfolk as claimed by Smith. General Wise thought the place the key to Norfolk and the Navy Yard saying that its capture "unlocked two sounds; eight rivers; four canals, and two railroads." *O. R.*, Ser. I, Vol. IX, 190.

[156] Norfolk and the Navy Yard were evacuated on May 9, 1862.

[157] The raid was conducted by a portion of General Foster's troops who came from New Bern to Washington, N. C., and thence raided the Roanoke valley by Williamston, Tarboro, and Hamilton. There were two engagements; one at Rawle's Mills, in Martin County, and the first at Little Creek. The Federal reports of these engagements are in *O. R.*, Ser. I, Vol. XVIII, 20-30.

[158] General French went to Hamilton and inspected the damage in the region, an account of which is given in a letter to General Gustavus W. Smith, commanding in Richmond. *O. R.*, Ser. I, Vol. XVIII, 778-779; Clark, *N. C. Regts.*, II, 336-339.

believe is the intention of nine tenths of the river planters &
that is, to abandon the crops & remove negroes & stock to the
interior of the State unless we can have more troops & better
defences for the river— Already many are leaving & with the
scarcity of food in the West, God only knows what the prices will
reach, when the population of the East is to subsist in addition—
with 3 or 4,000 troops & works on the river I believe this country
can be held— without them there is nothing to prevent the enemy
during the high waters of the Winter from passing up the river
to the Weldon bridge— destroying the corn barns on his way &
therby doing an incalculable injury to both people & government— I feel confident that there is a surplus of 500,000 bushels of
corn on the Roanoke will the Government need this or not?
if they will, is it not worth protecting? If it is lost, they may see
where corn is to be obtained, I can not—
My Dear Sir will you press this matter upon their attention— If
they can or will do nothing in the state to permit her people to
be spoiled in this way without an effort to prevent it— Call upon
the legislature to do its duty, by remonstrating against it & if that
fail, raise her own troops to defend her soil— (over)
I hope my Dear Sir, that you will pardon this freedom with which
I have written I would have prefered to have had a personal
interview with you (as I was requested to do by a public meeting
of this & the adjoining counties) but my presence has been constantly needed at home during the trying scenes of the last week—
Raleigh
P. S. The census returns of 1850 show the following Black population of Counties of Bertie Martin Halifax & Northampton—

	26,000	
Bushels of Indian corn raised——	2,565,000	Bus
Beans & peas——	254,000	"
wheat——	40,000	"
Potatoes——	435,000	"
Oats Rye &c——	105,000	"
Hay & Fodder——	15,000	Tons
Hogs——	132,000	Tons
Cattle & sheep——	77,000	
Horses & Mules——	9,000	

Value of negroes & live stock $18 million
Value " real estate   7   "

_____

25 millions

Tax of 1.5 of 1 pr ct——$50,000
Census returns of 1860 will give greater
[A. L. S. Governors' Papers (Vance),
  State Department of Archives and History, Raleigh.]

From A. J. Rogers[159]

Near Henderson Nov 13th- 1862

As North Carolina is now being invaded by a Merciless foe & gloom seems over shadowing our cause. You will please allow me to make following suggestions, knowing that your chief desire is to promote and defend as far as in you lies the Flag of the Confederacy and especially that of North Carolina.

Would it not therefore in the present State of affairs be well for you immediately order out the Militia between the ages of forty and forty five and bring them at once into the field, for the space of three or six months? I am of the opinion that you have the right to do this, and think it would be better not to wait for the Legislature; as that body generally indulges too freely in unimportant discussions in consequence of which the State might be seriously damaged by delay

The patriotism of our People has not faltered yet and am satisfied that they would not only sustain you in this act but respond cheerfully to your call I believe that many over fifty years of age would place themselves immediately in the Ranks at least for the period of three months which time would not interfear seriously with the far merging interests though if it did it would be a jusifyable interfearance on the part of the State Executive For if we ever need men in the field now is the time. In the event you should issue this call I will assist in any way that you may desire and accept any position which you may think fit to assigne me for the bettering of our cause. I think that it would be well instead of permitting our Citizens in the Vicinity Tarboro & Goldsboro to run off their available force for security— to Draft them for a few days for the purpose of placing obstructions in the Rivers before leaving. If you are not pressed with business at present I would be glad to get your opinions in a day or so.
[Raleigh]
My address for a few days is Henderson N C
[A. L. S. Governors' Papers (Vance),
State Department of Archives and History, Raleigh.]

From John Dawson[160]

[Wilmington, N. C.
Nov. 13, 1862]

The undersigned Citizens of Wilmington would respectfully represent to your Excellency that Mr. James L. Barnwell of

---

[159] A. J. Rogers, of Warren County, was captain of company D in the Eighth North Carolina Regiment. He had been in the army since May 16, 1861; he was later wounded at Fort Wagner in 1864. Moore, *N. C. Roster,* I, 283; Clark, *N. C. Regts.,* I, 387, 395.

[160] John Dawson, mayor of Wilmington, was a hardware merchant, a stockholder

Columbia S. C. now here, came among us bringing supplies for our sick and suffering people and tendering his own services in any capacity in which he could be useful. We would also represent that Mr. Barnwell has, while in Wilmington purchased some lots of Salt for Sale, as we are assured and believe, at actual cost and charges in Columbia S. C. and not in any way for purposes of speculation, and that of this Salt he has yet some Three hundred bushels unshipped.

Considering that Mr. Barnwell's mission here, has been one of mercy, and that his object in shipping the Salt is to afford relief to the poor in and around Columbia, we respectfully request your Excellency to withdraw any prohibition, Embargo, or other obstacle in the shipment of the lot of Three Hundred Bushels of Salt now held in this place by Mr. Barnwell—

[Raleigh]

I have thought that my own signature officially would be Sufficient to represents this case, if others are required they can be obtained.

[on reverse]

Ansr^d— that Gen Whiting[161] has been instructed to ship all salt purchased previous to the prohibition. I did not intend to violate any contract with citizens of other states Z B V

[A. L. S. Governors' Papers (Vance),
State Department of Archives and History, Raleigh.]

---

in the Wilmington and Weldon Railroad Company, and the leader of the anti-secession forces in Wilmington in the spring of 1861. Sprunt, *Chronicles,* p. 138; *Wilmington Journal,* February 9, 1861; Raleigh *North Carolina Standard,* February 27, 1861.

[161] William Henry Chase Whiting (1824-1865), Confederate brigadier general who, on November 8, 1862, was assigned to the defense of the Cape Fear River and told to report directly to Major General Gustavus W. Smith in Richmond instead of through General French at Petersburg. Whiting was born in Biloxi, Mississippi of parents who were from Massachusetts, was graduated at Georgetown College, D. C. in 1840 and at West Point in 1845, where his record was the highest ever made at the academy up to that time. When he resigned from the army in 1861 he had reached the rank of captain in the corps of engineers, and entered Confederate service as a major. He was promoted to brigadier general on the field of Manassas by President Davis, and became a major general on February 28, 1863. In 1856 Whiting had been assigned to the improvement of the defenses of the Cape Fear at Wilmington and had married Kate D. Walker, a daughter of Major John Walker of Smithville and Wilmington. In May 1864 he was sent to Petersburg, but soon returned to Wilmington at his own request. He made Fort Fisher "the most powerful defensive work of the Confederacy" and Wilmington a haven for blockade runners. Mortally wounded in the attack on Fort Fisher, January 15, 1865, he died at Fort Columbus, Governor's Island, New York. Sprunt, *Chronicles,* pp. 281-296; Joseph Mills Hanson, "William Henry Chase Whiting," *Dict. of Am. Biog.,* XX, 136-137.

From A. E. Hall [162]

Wilmington N C
Nov 13th 1862

Your request to the Rail Road companies of this place that they will not transport any more Salt out of the State is very properly respected by them. this operates very hard on parties who purchased Salt previous to the promulgation of the request.

I have on hand about 200 Bags for different parties in South Carolina sold & paid for by them from a week to a month ago, & awaiting transportation.

If your excellency is of the opinion that this Salt should go forward in justice to all parties I will feel very grateful if you will give me permission to ship the same also to enclose to me a permit to that effect.

Infer you to Major Mallett [163] of your city for my character and standing

I would here state that the most if not all of this Salt would have been sent forward in October but from the fact that the writer was down with the yellow fever & his clerk dead of same disease & office closed for five weeks.

[on reverse]
Ansr. that all salt paid for previous to order can go forward
Z B V

[Raleigh]
[A. L. S. Governors' Papers (Vance),
State Department of Archives and History, Raleigh.]

From Wm. J. Clarke [164]

Camp near Madison C. H. Va.
November 13th 1862

The last time I had the pleasure of conversing with you you promised me that if the time should ever arrive when you could assist me in procuring promotion you would cheerfully aid me.

That time has now arrived, and I feel that you need only be informed of it to obtain your recommendation.

I have lately been superceded by the appointment of Col. Iver-

---

[162] Avon E. Hall, a forwarding and commission merchant of Wilmington, formerly of Fayetteville. *Fayetteville Observer,* June 2, 1862; Sprunt, *Chronicles,* p. 341.
[163] See p. 175, 44n.
[164] See p. 143, 581n.

son,[165] a Georgian, commanding a N. C. Regt. Col. Cooke,[166] a Virginian, commdg, a N. C. Regt. and Col. Ramseur[167] all of them younger men, having less experience in actual service and holding commissions younger than mine. Why am I thus treated I know not, as both my personal and military record are untarnished.

There are strong efforts now being made to secure the promotion of Col. Matt Ransom[168] over me. Knowing me as you do,

---

[165] Alfred Iverson, Jr. (1829-1911), whose first American ancestors had settled at Wilmington but whose family had long been prominently identified with Georgia. His father had been an advanced "southern rights" man in 1860 and a prominent Democratic Senator in the United States Senate. Alfred Iverson, Jr. had served in the Mexican War at the age of seventeen, studied law briefly, but soon changed to a railroad contractor. In 1855 he received an appointment as first lieutenant in the First United States Cavalry, recruited a company and served in Kansas, Utah, and Indian Territory before he resigned his commission when Georgia seceded in 1861. He was appointed captain in the Provisional Army of the Confederacy and ordered to report to General Holmes at Wilmington, where he was put in command of companies at the mouth of the Cape Fear. Upon the organization of the Twentieth North Carolina Regiment, June 18, 1861, Iverson was elected colonel. All the other officers, and the men, were North Carolinians. In June of 1862, the regiment was placed in the brigade commanded by General Samuel Garland of Virginia, along with four other North Carolina regiments. General Garland was killed at South Mountain, September 14, 1862, and upon his death the command of the brigade devolved upon Colonel Duncan K. McRae, of the Fifth North Carolina, until both he and Colonel Iverson were wounded at Sharpsburg three days later. On November 1, 1862, Colonel Iverson was made brigadier general and put in charge of the brigade. He served in this capacity until after Gettysburg, when he was transferred to the west and was replaced by a North Carolinian, Robert D. Johnston of the Twenty-third North Carolina Regiment. After the war Iverson settled in Macon, Georgia, until 1877 and then moved to Florida, where he engaged in orange culture. Evans, *Conf. Mil. Hist.,* VI, 424-426; Clark, *N. C. Regts.,* II, 112, IV, 521-522.

[166] John R. Cooke was born in Missouri, but his father's family had Virginia connections. Cooke was a civil engineer and had no military education, but in 1858 he was appointed a second lieutenant in the United States army. In June of 1861, while stationed in the far west, he heard of the secession of his father's native state—Virginia—and joined the Confederacy, where he was appointed quartermaster and assigned to the staff of General Holmes. When he was elected colonel of the Twenty-seventh North Carolina Regiment, April 16, 1862, he was chief of artillery on General Holmes' staff, with the rank of major. He remained colonel of this regiment of North Carolinians until November of 1862, when he was promoted brigadier general for gallantry on the field at Sharpsburg though he was the junior colonel of the brigade. His brigade was composed of the Fifteenth, Twenty-seventh, Forty-sixth, and Forty-eighth North Carolina Regiments. Clark, *N. C. Regts.,* II, 504-512.

[167] Stephen Dodson Ramseur (1837-1864) was, of course, a North Carolinian, but he had become colonel of the Forty-ninth North Carolina Regiment before he was twenty-five years of age. He was promoted brigadier general on November 1, 1862, upon recommendation of General Lee. Ramseur succeeded General Anderson, who died of a wound received at Sharpsburg, September 17, 1862. Ramseur's brigade was composed of the Second, Fourth, Fourteenth, and Thirtieth North Carolina Regiments. Ramseur became a major general on June 1, 1864, and was mortally wounded at Cedar Creek, October 19, 1864, dying the following day at Winchester, Va. Samuel J. Heidner, "Stephen Dodson Ramseur," *Dict. of Am. Biog.,* XV, 341; William R. Cox, "Stephen D. Ramseur," Peele, *N. C. Lives,* pp. 458-494.

[168] Matt Whitaker Ransom (1826-1904), colonel of the Thirty-fifth North Carolina Regiment, who was not promoted brigadier general until June 1863, when he succeeded his brother, Robert Ransom, in command of the brigade of which his old regiment formed a part. Ransom played a conspicuous part at Sharpsburg and retired temporarily, October 14, 1862, on account of wounds. He received appointment as brigadier over the three senior colonels of the brigade, including William

and having served with me you will at once see the injustice of
this, and you will perceive that it forces me to resign. I hope to
be spared both the humiliation and the necessity of this step, and
I feel a strong assurance that if *you* will write to the President,
stating that you have served with me and what my conduct has
been in battle, that with representations made by others, it will
secure my promotion. I am, as you know, the senior Col. of the
Brigade, and the programme is to appoint Brig. Gen'l. Ransom,[169]
Major Gen'l of the Division (late Walker's),[170] and his brother is
working to be appointed over me in his place. He is now, or lately
was, in Richmond and will leave no stone unturned to effect his
object.—

Hoping that you will give this matter your *immediate* attention,[171] and assuring you that you will render me a great service,
I am,

[Raleigh]

[A. L. S. Governors' Papers (Vance),
State Department of Archives and History, Raleigh.]

From N. A. Waller

State of N C Granville County
November the 13 day 1862

I send you a few lines to ask of you what ought to be done with
aman who refuses to take Confederate notes in payment of
Debt [172] I and what corse the Law woods have with him and if

---

J. Clarke. Ransom's brigade then consisted of the Twenty-fourth, Thirty-fifth,
Twenty-fifth, and Forty-ninth North Carolina Regiments. Ransom was an important
political figure who was originally a Whig but who, refusing to become a Know-
Nothing, joined the Democrats, though not the secessionists. He was attorney general of North Carolina before the war and United States Senator for a quarter of
a century thereafter, for fifteen years of which Vance was his colleague. Samuel
A'Court Ashe, "Matt Whitaker Ransom," Ashe, *Biog. Hist. of N. C.,* I, 420-429.

[169] Robert Ransom. See p. 131, 518n.

[170] John G. Walker (1822-1893), a native of Missouri and a veteran of the Mexican
War, who was promoted a major general on November 8, 1862, and transferred to
the Trans-Mississippi area, where he served for the remainder of the war. Evans,
Conf. Mil. Hist., IX, 223-225.

[171] Vance had served with Clarke very briefly in the field, but their regiments had
been together in Ransom's brigade when it was ordered to Richmond in June
1862, where they skirmished at White Oak Swamp and fought at Malvern Hill.
Clark, *N. C. Regts.,* II, 272-274. Vance replied to Clarke that he was sorry to have
to say his "position with the President is such that a letter from me would hardly
be of any service to you. And I could scarcely do so consistently with self-respect,
inasmuch as I have made divers recommendations to him not one of which has received an appointment." But if Clark insisted he would write the letter, which he
could cheerfully and conscientiously do. Vance to Clarke, November 25, 1862, Clarke
Papers.

[172] By many of its actions the Confederate Congress irretrievably committed itself
to a paper money policy but, though it frequently debated the subject, it refused,
throughout the war, to make its notes legal tender. The controversy is treated in
John Christopher Schwab, *The Confederate States of America 1861-1865. A Financial and Industrial History of the South During the War* (New York, 1901), Chap.
V (cited hereafter as Schwab, *Conf. Finance).*

I cant do any thing with him I want you to urge it on the presant Legislator to do somthing that will compel such person to take Confederate notes[173] in payment of Debt I am owing aman som money and he refuses to take Confederate money inpayment of what I ow him and said that I could not git my not without the Goal & silver but that he did not demant of me I have bin to to the man I ow and have offered him both intrust and principal in the presence of three respectible witness and he refuses to tak it from me and give me up my note I think you ought to prees such men in to servis or cose them to loose the Debt for I consider such men and enemy to our country for if we had enough such men our Country would be ruined for the credit of the southern Confederacey would be ruined If you have the time I would like to have your vuse on the matter and urge it on the Legislator to do somthing with such men for they are and ingury to our country my adress is Knap of Reads Granville County [Raleigh]
[on reverse]
The Gov has no power to make Confederate
notes a legal tender as Congress refused to
do it— Z B V
[A. L. S. Governors' Papers (Vance),
State Department of Archives and History, Raleigh.]

To C. G. Memminger[174]

STATE OF NORTH CAROLINA
EXECUTIVE DEPARTMENT
Raleigh 13th- Nov. 1862
I applied two weeks ago for two hundred and fifty thousand in bonds to send abroad for the purchase of shoes &c. I thought I

---

[173] On February 26, 1862 the Convention adopted an ordinance which provided that Confederate notes be receivable for any and all state and local taxes in North Carolina, but it did not extend its provisions to private debts. *Convention Ordinances,* 3 session, No. 35. On November 24, 1862 a bill was introduced in the North Carolina Senate providing that when a debtor offered to pay his debts in current banknotes, State or Confederate Treasury notes, and his offer refused, interest upon his debt should cease. No action was taken upon this bill. On December 4, 1863 the North Carolina House of Commons rejected a bill to make Confederate notes a legal tender. *Senate Journal, 1862-63,* p. 35; *Senate Journal, 1863-64,* p. 30; Schwab, *Conf. Finance,* pp. 99-100. The Confederate Constitution forbade the states to make anything but gold and silver legal tender and to pass any law impairing the obligation of contracts. Though this clause was frequently violated by various states, most officials felt that it prevented the states making Confederate Treasury notes a legal tender, however much debtors might wish to pay their obligations in a steadily depreciating currency.

[174] Christopher Gustavus Memminger (1803-1888), secretary of the treasury of the Confederacy. He was born in Germany, educated at the South Carolina College, studied law and practiced it in Charleston. He opposed nullification in the thirties and separate state action in the fifties, but by December 1860 he had been won over

could certainly get them inasmuch as the Confederate Government owes this state near five or six million dollars.[175] I have sent two special agents[176] for them, but have been put off for the reason that the papers were not in form &c. As the vessel was about to sail in which my Agent was going, I instructed my Agent to ask for the bonds any how and to say that any papers would be signed afterwards that might be required by the forms of the Department. This was refused also and my Agent [177] has probably lost the vessel. I am compelled Sir to complain of such treatment, it displays either an incompetency on the part of your subordinates or an unwillingness to accommodate me with the bonds which I would not have and do not want after my Agent has gone. I would feel obliged Sir, if you would investigate the matter and see if there is any reason for the failure to accommodate me[178]
[Richmond]
[Vance Letter Book, 1862-1863,
State Department of Archives and History, Raleigh.]

---

to secession and was an active member of the South Carolina Convention. Appointed secretary of the treasury he faced the difficult task of financing the war, and when the credit of the government collapsed completely he was generally held responsible for the disaster, and resigned on June 15, 1864. Thereafter he lived at Flat Rock, N. C. and in Charleston, his chief public service being in behalf of the public schools, in which he had always been interested and active. Charles W. Ramsdell, "Christopher Gustavus Memminger," *Dict. of Am. Biog.*, XXII, 527-528.

[175] According to Secretary Memminger the requisition of the Secretary of War was made on November 2, and reached the Treasury Department on the next day. On November 11, Memminger wrote Vance, in reply to a telegram of inquiry of November 8, that he had "no information, previous to your telegram, that Captain Gulick had called for the bonds." On November 15, Memminger wrote again to explain that the requisition was not in favor of the State of North Carolina, or any authorized agent of the same, but in favor of Major W. W. Peirce, quartermaster at Raleigh, and it requested that the sum of $250,000 in bonds should be placed to his credit with E. C. Elmore, Treasurer of the Confederate States. "This was done on the day on which the requisition of the Secretary of War reached this Department. After it was placed to the credit of Major Peirce, no one had any control over its payment except Mr. Peirce himself, and I am informed by the Treasurer that the check of Mr. Peirce was paid as soon as presented." Memminger to Vance, November 11, 15, 1862, Z. B. Vance Papers.

[176] The two special agents were Peirce and Captain W. B. Gulick, who was assistant adjutant general of North Carolina, and appointed a special attorney to receive monies for the state. Vance Letter Book, October 22, 1862.

[177] The agent was Thomas M. Crossan who, with White, sailed from Charleston on November 15 to purchase supplies in Europe.

[178] Vance sent Memminger's replies to Major Peirce, who claimed that it had been expressly stated to him that the Treasurer would advise him when the amount was placed to his credit, and that he had never received any such advice. The Treasurer stated that the amount was placed to his credit on November 12. Peirce to Vance, November 21, 1862, Z. B. Vance Papers. But acting Treasurer T. Greene wrote Secretary Memminger that Gulick came for the bonds with a receipt from Peirce instead of a check, and that when Major Peirce's check arrived the bonds were delivered to Gulick on November 15. T. Greene to Memminger, November 21, 1862 (copy enclosed in Memminger to Vance, November 25, 1862) Z. B. Vance Papers.

From J. H. Flanner[179]

Wilmington N. C. 14 Nov. 1862

There is a notice posted on our Street Corner, signed by Ag[t]. W. M. R R[r].[180] say[g]"by request of Gov[r]. Vance" that no more Salt will be rec[d]. by that comp[y]., for transportation out the State.— I am Ag[t]. for the Salt "Convoy", recently arriv[d]. at Shallotte, N. C. from Nassau N T with cargo (ab[t]. 250 Sacks" Liverpool Sack Salt) belonging to Mess Cummins, Edwards & Co Shipped to them & it is now being lightened here for that purpose.

Will the embargo apply to this?— These Gentle[m]., & persons at Chlston, are expect[g]. Cargoes Salt, and our Coast is the only point along which they can dare to venture.—

I regret the appointm[t]. of M[r]. T. D. Meares[181] as proxy for the State at the annual meet[g]. of the W & M R R Co, he *I think*, has been unfavorable to y[r]. election, and being a connexion of the present President of that Comp[y]. "M[r]. Tho[s] D Walker" [182] (who *was bitter against* you in recent canvass, & who I do not think has *any qualification* for the office, as evidenced by votes of individual

---

[179] Joseph H. Flanner, of Wilmington, president of Wilmington Steamship Company. He had gained notoriety in the fifties as an ardent Know-Nothing who had killed Dr. William C. Wilkings, a prominent young physician and Democrat of Wilmington, in a duel. The quarrel arose over Wilkings' slurs upon Know-Nothing patriotism and his allegation that the Know-Nothing ticket was made up of merchants who would not hesitate to sacrifice the public interest, such as the quarantine, for the sake of a dollar. Flanner became the purser of the celebrated *Advance*, which so successfully ran the blockade during much of the war. He died a few years after the war, unhappy and under a cloud, in a foreign land. Sprunt, *Chronicles*, pp. 231-237; *Wilmington Herald*, as quoted in *Asheville News*, May 15, 1856.

[180] The Wilmington and Manchester Railroad, which had been chartered in 1847 to build a line from Wilmington into South Carolina. See below, p. 407, 360n.

[181] Thomas Davis Meares (1818-1881), of Brunswick County, who was a member of the House of Commons in 1856, 1858, and 1860, and a member of the Convention of 1861. He graduated from the University of North Carolina in 1839 and became a lawyer, but soon abandoned the bar and became a rice planter though he resumed legal practice after the war. In 1845 he married a daughter of Governor Iredell. The charge that he was opposed to Vance politically seems strange, as Meares was an ardent Whig in politics and opposed secession until Lincoln's call for troops. In the spring of 1861, when the legislature was debating the convention bill, Meares was a leading Whig advocate of a convention, but in this position he was joined by other prominent Whigs, such as Vance himself, who believed that a convention was the best way to defeat secession. Vance appointed Meares as state proxy, but he had to decline the appointment because of an accident to one of his sons that prevented his attending the meeting. See Meares to Vance, November 22, 1862, Governors' Papers (Vance); Connor, *N. C. Manual*, pp. 513, 869; Winston *Western Sentinel*, February 1, 1861; McCormick, *Personnel*, pp. 59-60.

[182] Thomas D. Walker, of Wilmington, lawyer and Democrat who had been president of the Wilmington and Manchester Railroad Company since 1858. If he did not please the stockholders, as Flanner charges, he had seemed to please the directors, for he had been unanimously re-elected president at the annual meeting of November 20, 1861. Sprunt, *Chronicles*, p. 187; *Proceedings of the Stockholders of the Wilmington and Manchester Railroad Co. at their 14th Annual Meeting Held at Wilmington North Carolina November 20th, 1861* (Wilmington, 1861), p. 10 (cited hereafter as *W & M Proceedings*).

Stockholders heretofore) may give the vote of the State for *him* unless otherwise instructed.—

Please excuse my digression from the Salt question.—
Raleigh
[A. L. S. Governors' Papers (Vance),
State Department of Archives and History, Raleigh.]

From D. K. McRae[183]

Head Quarters 5th. No. Ca. Regiment
Near Strausburg Virginia
Nov. 14th. 1862

I have this day tendered to the Adj General of the Confederate States the resignation of my commission recd. from the Governor of North Carolina as Colonel of the 5th Regt of her State Troops. I am constrained to do so, because consistently with my sense of dignity and self respect I can no longer serve the Govt. I have now been in the service about nineteen months with the exception of about twenty five days, sick. I have never been absent from the post of duty I have served under several commanders and have *never* in a single instance encountered a reproof. My division commander Maj. Gen Hill[184] endorses upon my resignation (in substance) "I have three times recommended Col M c Rae for promotion. No. Ca. had furnished more troops and had fewer General Officers than any other state. I approve Col McRae's resignation believing that his self respect requires it—" Lieut. Gen. Longstreet[185] & Brig Gens Early[186] & Rhodes[187] under all of whom I have served and all of whom are familiar with my conduct have recommended me in terms of compliment of of which I am justly proud. And there is not an officer of our grade in my division who does not freely concede to me a claim to promotion. My regiment has endured hardships, suffered privations, performed labors, executed marches, been exposed to peril and rendered service equal to any. Its actual loss in a single engagement while obeying immediate orders is not surpassed proportionately. Wherever it has encamped it has been remarkable for its orderly & honest deportment. It has constantly recd the approval of Gen-

---

[183] See p. 163, 2n.

[184] That is, Daniel Harvey Hill. See p. 181, 64n.

[185] James Longstreet (1821-1904) had been promoted to lieutenant general on October 11, 1862. McRae had served under him at First Manassas, July 21, 1861, when Longstreet was a brigade commander. Clark, *N. C. Regts.*, I, 282.

[186] Jubal Anderson Early (1816-1894). McRae had served under Early as brigade commander during the winter of 1861-1862, when his regiment was stationed at Union Mills on the Orange and Alexandria railroad.

[187] Robert Emmett Rodes (1829-1864), whose brigade was also in D. H. Hill's division, and who succeeded Hill as division commander when Hill was sent to North Carolina in January 1863. The Fifth North Carolina Regiment was attached to Rodes' division after the Maryland campaign.

eral Officers for its promptness and fidelity in responding to every call. The public journals of the enemy, country, the diaries of prominent officers found on the battlefield and private letters of other distinguished officers of the Army of the enemy[188] addressed to officers of my Regiment have contributed valuable testimony to its brave and gallant conduct in the fight. *So long as it retained* the material element which I had the honor to train and form it never faltered. I claim in some degree the reflection of the lustre it has shed upon the state. Much of the time I have been in the service I have commanded the Brigade.[189] This was the case in all of the hard trials of the retreat from Manassas— in the exposed service in the trenches of Yorktown[190] and in that retreat, in the battles of Maryland and since that period at the battle of "South Mountain" this Brigade tho' isolated from all support, numbering scarce a thousand opposed by a force of sixteen Regts. having all the advantage of position held the enemy in check for four hours, the fire of one regiment, the 23ᵈ. killing the Commanding General (Reno) [191] that of another the 20ᵗʰ. killing the enemys cannoniers and compelling the abandonment of his guns, while a third the 13ᵗʰ. under Lieut. Col. Ruffin[192] thrice cut its way through the enemys lines with desperate determination. Gen. Hill I learn applauds this fight, as one of the best of the War yet on several occasions I have been compelled to see junior officers promoted over me. Officers who had not and have not yet seen a battle. Shortly after the battle of "Seven Pines" State Brigades were organized— Genˡ Pender[193] and Anderson[194] were

---

[188] For example, Brigadier General Winfield Scott Hancock, of the Union army, who commanded the Federals in front of McRae's Regiment at the battle of Williamsburg, May 5 1862, said of the Fifth North Carolina and the Twenty-fourth Virginia: "They should have *immortality* inscribed on their banners." Clark, *N. C. Regts.,* I, 285.

[189] McRae commanded the brigade when Early was wounded at Williamsburg until he himself succumbed to severe illness. Again at South Mountain, when Garland fell, McRae took command of the brigade, until himself disabled. Clark, *N. C. Regts.,* I, 285-287.

[190] The retreat from Manassas was the withdrawal from that front to meet the advance of McClellan up the peninsula in the spring of 1862. Early's brigade was among the first to reach General Magruder on the peninsula, and was immediately put in the defensive works at Yorktown, where it remained until the evacuation on May 3, 1862, when the retreat up the peninsula began. McRae's Regiment was the last Confederate unit to leave the Yorktown defenses.

[191] Jesse L. Reno (1823-1862), Federal major general, who was killed at the battle of South Mountain, in Maryland, September 14, 1862. Cullum, *Biog. Register,* II, 262-264.

[192] Thomas Ruffin, Jr. See p. 172. 37n.

[193] William Dorsey Pender. See p. 170, 26n. Pender was promoted brigadier general on June 3, 1862 and given a brigade consisting of the Sixteenth, Twenty-second, Thirty-fourth, and Thirty-eighth North Carolina Regiments.

[194] George Burgwyn Anderson (1831-1862), formerly colonel of the Fourth North Carolina Regiment. He was promoted on June 3, 1862 to a brigadier generalcy and given a brigade composed of the Second, Fourth, Fourteenth, and Thirtieth North Carolina Regiments.

promoted and assigned to No. Ca. Brigades, while the Brigade in
which I was Sr Colonel was assigned to the command of General Garland [195] *of Virginia.* I refrained from resigning then because of the impending conflicts around Richmond, yielding to
the earnest solicitation of both Gen^ls. Hill and Garland. Since
that time Gen Garland has made the most favorable mention of
my conduct in the field and Gen Hill has renewed the recommendation for my promotion. The appointment of Brigadier to
this Command has just been announced in the person of Col
Alfred Iverson[196] of Georgia who since his entering on active
service last summer has been my junior in the Brigade and for
the last two months under my command. I could not consent that
a junior officer of my own command should be promoted to command me, when no allegation is made of my unfitness or unworthiness. But severe as is the trespass upon the individual pride of
No. Carolina officers who have lately been obliged to submit to
the promotion in several instances of citizens of other States to
the command of Brigades exclusively North Carolinians, the slur
upon the State is broader and demands the resentment of her
sons in the only mode they can manifest it. In the spirit of an
earnest protest against this injustice, individual and to my state I
resign my commission.[197]

I do not wish however to be idle so long as the foul steps of the
invader presses our soil. If your Excellency can make my services
available *in any capacity* however subordinate they are freely tend-

---

[195] Samuel Garland (1830-1862), of Lynchburg, Virginia, formerly colonel of the
Eleventh Virginia Regiment, Longstreet's brigade, who was promoted to brigadier
general after the battle of Williamsburg and given a brigade composed of the
Fifth, Twelfth, Thirteenth, Twentieth, and Twenty-third North Carolina Regi-
ments. Garland was killed at South Mountain, September 14, 1862. Evans, *Conf.
Mil. Hist.,* III, 595-597.

[196] See p. 350, 165n.

[197] Colonel McRae's letter was given to the press and published in the *Fayetteville
Observer.* Commenting editorially the *Observer* said that it had never supported
McRae politically, and had thought his appointment to the command of a regiment
"a fatal mistake," as it had also thought of the appointment of another North
Carolina politician of no military training, L. O'B. Branch, about the same time.
Both being civilians the *Observer* had doubted their fitness for command. "But in
his case, as in that of General Branch, we have lived to see our mistake, and to
find that they were both faithful and capable." Then the *Observer* contrasts their
treatment: Branch was petted and promoted by the Confederate administration;
McRae was neglected. "Gen. Branch was on the favored side in politics—he was a
Breckinridge man and a secessionist. Col. McRae, though also a secessionist, had
committed the unpardonable sin of being a Douglas man. Here lies the secret of the
different treatment of the two officers—Branch promoted before he ever smelt
gunpowder—McRae always *after* the fight recommended for promotion by the great
Generals who commanded him and knew his worth and his services, and always
rejected. It is but another exhibition of that great defect in the President's character
which has marked his course since the beginning of the war—where old political
differences exist, like the Bourbons, he forgets nothing and learns nothing." The
Observer concluded that McRae's treatment exhibited a case of injustice which
justified his resignation. *Fayetteville Observer,* November 27, 1862.

ered in any service which will not subject me to renewal of wrong.
I have felt bound to communicate with you, Governor the reasons
which have influenced me to surrender a commission which I
specially cherished because of the magnanimity accompanying its
bestowment by your predecessor Gov. Ellis.[198]

In order to be just to myself I have been obliged to dwell more
upon the subject than my inclination would prompt. I shall very
shortly file in Adj[t]. Gen[l]. Office a complete narrative of the part
borne by the 5th. in the events of the War, together with a list
of its officers and men, the fate of those dead and the whereabouts
of the survivors.
[Raleigh]
[Vance Letter Book, 1862-1863,
  State Department of Archives and History, Raleigh.]

From C. Henderson

[Franklin, N. C.]
N C Maken Nov the 15 1862
this is afew lines from your old friend Cannada Henderson i jest
want to let you no i am in good helth at this time hopin these
lines may finde you in the same blesin allso i can hear from you
often by persons and in knew's papers i saw in one it said Z B
Vance was a brave soldier hee could fite and hee knowed how to
doe it you war a good officer but i am glad your in the place you
are i would ruther you ware in Jf Daviss place i think you could
plage old abe till hee would drop the fite i must tell you how
myself and the sugar fork boys voted the first election for you
our prisink is over 100 strong you lost but 3 stinkin dimacrats
this last gov election you lost but 1 and it dident go aganst you
we provd him to like negro wimon and tha throad it aside your
friend John leeford his enfluence is good him others and myself
went ahead i do wish this war would come to a close for wimon
and children is suffrin and no men left to help them i have 3 sons
and son an laws gone one my sons dide at ritchmon there ante half
a dosin men left in the hole neighborhood mr Vance pleas gave
mee your opinion on this war when you think it will end what
will bee the consequence its a ruther a unfare qustion but i
no your jugment good and a nother little mater concernin dets
some sware tha wont pay for it will bee a strike off one wante nor
another wonte pleas gave mee your opinion on that so i will quit
my broken leter excuse mee and rite to mee if you pleas i would
like to read your lines   your friend till deth, to me govner Z B
Vance

[198] See p. 74, 281n.

[on reverse]
Col Little[199] will ansr. friend Hendersons letter, & tell him I hope
the war will end next spring &c. if we all stand firm & fight hard.
My thanks for his good will &c
Raughley
[A. L. S. Governors' Papers (Vance),
  State Department of Archives and History, Raleigh.]

From C. M. Andrews[200]
Head Qats. 19th. Regt. N. C. T.
Culpepper, Va.
Nov. 15th. 1862

I now appeal to you for a favor in another direction, 1st. My
Reason, I have been in the service from the 31st. day of May 1861.
I have been on duty almost all that time & most of the service has
been of a very severe kind.

My family is at Statesville, quite among strangers, and I am
unable to afford them any immediate aid. Mrs Andrews is a
Northern lady and she has no relations South.

She has so often besought me in her letter to return to my
former occupation that I have at length determined so to do, if
it can be accomplished without great trouble.

I have no desire, Gov. to quit the field: although I have been
on it often enough, in a very active way, but I feel that it is a
sacred obligation that I owe to my family. The citizens of Statesville, too, have petitioned me to resume my Military school there
& I feel that it will be only a change of service & not going out
of the service at all, for me to resume the charge of that school at
their request. Please inform me, Gov, whether you can free me
from all liability to the Conscript Act, if I can obtain an acceptance
of my resignation, or is it convenient for you to place me in a
position that will not call me so far away from my family. I am,
Governor, very respectfully
[Raleigh]
[A. L. S. Governors' Papers (Vance),
  State Department of Archives and History, Raleigh.]

[199] George Little, an active Whig and supporter of Bell and Everett in 1860,
who became an aide to Vance during his governorship. After the war he was president of the North Carolina Land Company, established for the transportation and
location of northern and European settlers in North Carolina, and for the sale of
real estate. In 1871 he was Commissioner of Immigration for North Carolina. He
also served as a United States marshal.

[200] Charles Milton Andrews (1829-1864), of Greensboro and Statesville, major in
the Nineteenth North Carolina Regiment (second cavalry). He had raised a company from Iredell County which became company B of that regiment. He was
at the University of North Carolina about Vance's time there, and a part of his
regiment had participated in the battle of New Bern under Vance. After Gettysburg Andrews became colonel of the regiment and died from the effects of a wound
in the thigh received at Davis' Farm, June 27, 1864. He had become major on
September 6, 1862. Clark, *N. C. Regts.*, II, 80, 99, 102, Grant, *Alumni History*, p. 14;
Moore, *N. C. Roster*, II, 113, 117.

From T. M. Crossan[201]

Received at Raleigh Nov 15 1862
By telegraph from Charleston 15 To Gov Z B Vance
Here in time, send Bonds as soon as possible— May be detained—
[Telegram, Governors' Papers (Vance),
    State Department of Archives and History, Raleigh.]

From J. J. Lawrence[202]

Wilson N. C. Nov. 15th 1862
I hereby tender you my services for N. C. Defence.
In the early part of the summer of /61— I raised a company—
and was stationed at Fort Macon— untill December when owing to
continued "Ill health" I "resigned" my Captaincy—
My health gettin better in the spring of /62— I raised a company
of Cavalry— and continued in service untill recently when I
resigned My commission in Col— Claibornes[203] Reg— "You are
already aware under what circumstances" (No one could have
done otherwise) If you think proper to grant it— I would like
to get the Appointment of Major— to raise a battalion of Infantry,
for N. C. service— The Battalion to be raised in Eastern counties
within thirty days? I can procure satisfactory Recommendations
from Col. White,[204] also from Gen¹. Clingman—[205] whom I was
under when Capt. Independent Co— P. R.[206] &c. &c.
I offer you my Services in any position that you may think pro-

---

[201] Thomas Morrow Crossan (1819-1865), of Warrenton, who was appointed with
John White to go to Europe on behalf of the state for the purchase of supplies, and
who later commanded the *Advance* for its first few trips. Crossan was of northern
birth, but had married Rebecca Brehan of Warrenton and settled there before the
war. He was formerly in the United States navy and joined the Confederate navy
in 1861, where as a lieutenant in the fall of 1861 he commanded the *Winslow*. At
the battle of New Bern, where Vance first fought, Crossan was in command of the
batteries on the river. Montgomery, *Sketches of Warrenton*, pp. 233-234; Clark,
N. C. Regts., I, 17, 30, V, 299, 312, 453; Raleigh *North Carolina Standard*, March 22,
1862; Marshall DeLancey Haywood, "Thomas Morrow Crossan," Charles L. Van
Noppen Papers, Duke University, Durham, N. C. (cited hereafter as Van Noppen
Papers).
[202] Joseph J. Lawrence, captain of company H in what afterwards became the
Seventy-fifth North Carolina Regiment (seventh cavalry). He was from Wilson
County. Moore, *N. C. Roster*, IV, 384.
[203] William C. Claiborne, colonel of the Seventy-fifth North Carolina Regiment
(seventh cavalry), who was commissioned May 10, 1862. He does not appear to have
been a North Carolinian: the companies composing his regiment were formerly the
seventh Confederate Cavalry and consisted mainly of Georgia troops. Moore, *N. C.
Roster*, IV, 373.
[204] Moses J. White, who was colonel commanding at Fort Macon during the fall
of 1861 when Lawrence was stationed there. Clark, *N. C. Regts.*, I, 489, 502.
[205] See p. 55, 200n.
[206] In the spring of 1862 there were several independent companies of mounted
troops raised in North Carolina with the understanding that they were to remain
in the state and were to be used only in its defense. A regiment of partisan rangers
was forming at Wilson during this time. Clark, *N. C. Regts.*, IV, 91; J. J. Lawrence to Governor Vance, from Wilson, October 24, 1862, Governors' Papers (Vance).

per to place me, that I can be of any use to North Carolina and
our cause—
Hoping to hear from you soon in relation to the matter—
[on reverse]
Ans⟨r⟩. Capt L—
that I shall be pleased
to accept his services
if occasion calls for
them
          Z B V
[Raleigh]
[A. L. S. Governors' Papers (Vance),
State Department of Archives and History, Raleigh.]

To John White[207]

Executive Department of N. C.
Raleigh November [15th] 1862.
In the execution of the trust reposed in you it is expected of
course that you will exercise a discretion as to the manner and
quantity of shipping to the goods purchased referring to the opinion of Capt Crossan who undertakes this part of the business more
especially. In regard to the date of the bonds, it is thought advisable that you should not permit a greater discount upon those
of the State than forty per cent and you should not suffer them
to sell at that unless after sufficient time passed in dilligent negotiations you shall find it impossible to buy anything without this
sacrifice I hope however you will not be asked to go any lower
than 75 cent upon the dollar and have strong hopes that you can
sell at 85 or 90. Try hard to get in the cotton delivered at return
of price or running the blockade if you do so at rates which would
be equal to the sacrifice of our bonds. Communicate with me by
every opportunity and do nothing in haste that involves comuni-
cations
     If compelled to Ship in different vessels I suggest an assortment
of each cargo so that one vessel in safely may bring something of
each most essential article &c &c.
[Copy in Governors' Papers (Vance),
State Department of Archives and History, Raleigh.]

[Nov. 15, 1862]
STATE OF NORTH CAROLINA
CONFEDERATE STATES OF AMERICA
At the opening of the Second Winter of the War between the
Confederate States and the United States of America The State

---

of North Carolina is under the necessity of applying in foreign markets for material with which to equip its citizens in the Army, especially for shoes and blankets.

In common with other southern States, North Carolina previously to this War relied for supplies of manufactured articles in a great measure upon the States with which it is now at War. Besides this the necessity the State is of throwing more than one half of its men into the Army has compelled it to reduce within the narrowest limits its labours in the various branches of peaceful industry. Under other circumstances North Carolina would have no difficulty in supplying all of its wants from its own resources. But now in addition to what is said above, the very great Naval superiority of the public enemy deprives its citizens of the usual resort of communities pressed by War, inasmuch as foreign merchants are debarred from that access to our markets which is usual. Which at the present time would be so abundant a source of accomodating and profitable trade.

The Authorities of North Carolina therefore recur to the extraordinary course of sending Commissioners abroad in order to purchase the articles which are needed. Being unable to procure exchange in quantities sufficient for their purpose, and the transmission of gold or cotton involving a double risk, they have decided to offer a pledge of the faith and credit of the State upon a loan of money to be obtained in Europe for the purpose above indicated.

It is presumed that the general character of North Carolina for solvency & honor has been repeatedly canvassed, and is now well established in the money markets of England where the State has repeatedly heretofore negotiated its bonds with success. During all the period of its connection with the United States, North Carolina was prompt in discharging every pecuniary liability. Although the present War has of necessity prevented the State from remitting with regularity, the interest accruing upon its public debt its respect for those obligations and determination to keep its faith untouched remains the same. The value of the property belonging to its citizens and within its borders is reconed as more than Five hundred millions of dollars ($500.000.000) in value of which the value of its slave property is about Two hundred millions of dollars ($200.000.000) The public debt is not quite Twenty one millions of dollars ($21.000.000)

The debt of North Carolina is upon a footing very different from that of the Confederate States, and its payment is by no means dependent upon the successful issue of the present War.

The returns of the Census of 1860, which are yet unpublished, exhibit a marked increase in the growth of cotton in North Carolina and it is probable there are within its limits belongng to its citizens Three hundred thousand Bales awaiting the re-opening of commerce. Besides it may reasonably be anticipated that the developement of its mines of coal and iron which have recently been opened, and the products of which are just finding their way to market will prove in future a very considerable item of wealth.

The State of North Carolina proposes to repay any money which it may borrow under the Commission herewith sent, with interest at   per cent payable semi-annually by remittance of cotton at market rates, to be effected at the earliest moment possible either during the War or after the return of Peace. Or the Credi-tors may have an option of funding his debt in bonds of the State with interest as above— Such bonds to be issued upon the return of peace and the option to be declared at the time of lending the money.

The Commission is intrusted to Messrs John White and T. M. Crossan[208] and in the absence of either of necessity to the other

Z. B. Vance

[L. S. Governors' Papers (Vance), filed under October 1862 ex-cept for the last paragraph.

Also in Vance Letter Book, 1862-1863, as printed here.

State Department of Archives and History, Raleigh.]

To S. R. Mallory[209]

EXECUTIVE DEPARTMENT

Raleigh Nov. 15th- 1862

His Excellency Governor Vance has received your letter[210] stating that he had the control of a quantity of rail road iron and asking his consent to have the same rolled into plate to be used upon Boats now being built in this State.

His Excellency presumes that your informant Commander Cook alludes to the iron of the Atlantic Road,[211] the state is but a Stockholder in the road a large portion belonging to private individuals. A meeting of the directors of the Company has been called and your proposition will be submitted to them. Their decision will be made known to you

[Richmond]

[Vance Letter Book, 1862-1863,

State Department of Archives and History, Raleigh.]

---

[208] See p. 360, 201n.
[209] See p. 306, 49n. This letter is signed by David A. Barnes, aide to Vance.
[210] See p. 306.
[211] That is, the Atlantic and North Carolina Railroad Company, whose line ran from New Bern to Morehead City.

From S. G. French[212]

HEAD QUARTERS PETERSBURG VA.
November 15th. 1862

Your letter to the President dated Nov. 12th.[213] has been by him referred to me.

Colonel Leventhorpe[214] some two weeks since was anxious to send a force to Winton and it would have been done only I was not satisfied it was safe to scatter his small force too much. Since then another Regiment has been sent him and he has been instructed to send four companies there with a section of Artillery and company of Cavalry, with a view to enable the people to send out their supplies.[215] When I was in Hamilton, from all the information I could learn, I think the people were remiss in not watching the enemy and reporting to General Martin[216] with more promptness and *certainty* the *strength* of the enemy. I purpose reporting to the President the wanton depredations of the enemy on private property and on innocent and unoffending citizens with a view to his considering the propriety of having Foster[217] and his officers proclaimed as robbers and outlaws and

---

[212] See p. 204, 142n.

[213] See p. 336.

[214] Collett Leventhorpe (1815-1889), colonel of the Eleventh North Carolina Regiment. He was born in Plymouth, England, and served a number of years in the British Army, in which he attained the rank of captain in the cavalry. He resigned his commission, came to Charleston, studied medicine there, and entered practice at Rutherfordton, N. C. He became a naturalized citizen of the United States in 1849. When the war came he became colonel of the Thirty-fourth North Carolina Regiment in October 1861; when the Bethel Regiment was reorganized in the spring of 1862 he became colonel of that celebrated unit. He was seriously wounded at Gettysburg, and captured. In September 1864, at Kinston, Governor Vance appointed him a brigadier general in the state forces and he commanded the Home Guards in eastern North Carolina for the remainder of the war. In February 1865, he was commissioned a brigadier by the Confederacy. He returned to Rutherfordton after the war, but shortly thereafter moved to New York, soon returned to England for an extended visit, where he collected some notable antiques, and came again to North Carolina, where he lived at "Holly Lodge" near Patterson, just north of Lenoir. The state convention of the Democratic party nominated him for state auditor in 1872, but he was defeated by the Republican candidate in a close race. About 1878 his health began to fail, he sold "Holly Lodge" and moved to the home of Mrs. Leventhorpe's sister, Mrs. W. D. Jones at "The Fountain," also in Happy Valley, Caldwell County. Clark, *N. C. Regts.*, I, xii, 586, 591, IV, 651, V. 7; Hickerson, *Happy Valley*, p. 32; *Asheville News*, May 8, 1856; Moore, *N. C. Roster*, I, 376, II, 640; Griffin, *Old Tryon and Rutherford*, pp. 293-295.

[215] The Eleventh was ordered from Wilmington to Franklin, Va. on October 1, 1862 and took, for the next two months, a prominent part in the defense of the Blackwater, engaging in numerous skirmishes with the enemy operating from Suffolk. They came to be known as the foot cavalry. Clark, *N. C. Regts.*, I, 587.

[216] See p. 113, 447n. This refers to Martin as brigadier general, not as adjutant general.

[217] John G. Foster (1823-1874), Federal commander of the Department of North Carolina since July 1, 1862, when Burnside was transferred. Cullum, *Biog. Register*, II, 256-260.

not entitled to the provisions of the Cartel for exchange of prisoners when any of them may fall into our hands.[218]
[Raleigh]

Rest assured Governor I will do all I can to protect the frontier & to getout supplies. Our difficulty is want of R. R. Transportation which I have had to remedy by calling on Col Fremont, to send cars on this end of the road.

                                                         S G F

[A. L. S. Governors' Papers (Vance),
Vance Letter Book, 1862-1863,
State Department of Archives and History, Raleigh.]

From Wm. Lamb[219]

                          H. Qrs. Fort Fisher N. C. Nov. 17th 62.
I take pleasure in sending you a sword & ensign captured from a party of Yankee officers & sailors who landed at Masonboro to destroy a Confederate vessel.

A kind Providence favored us with a tempestuous sea, that prevented our foe from retreating. & some gallant dragoons of the Scotland Neck Cavalry Company[220] under Sergt. Baker,[221] bagged the whole party in the regular Jno Morgan style.[222]

I send you these trophies from the Steamer Daylight, (a Yankee gunboat that had the audacity to fire on our State Salt works) as a manifestation of the cordial approval of this command of your noble & zealous efforts to protect the Old North State from any further invasion on the part of our unscrupulous enemy, & as a

---

[218] General French wrote to Major General Gustavus W. Smith describing the many evidences of wanton destruction he claimed he saw on a visit to the Roanoke River area. He described the burning of sixteen or eighteen private dwellings, forcible entries and general destruction. "They burned all bedding, all the ladies dresses, and stole, in one instance, money from the bosom of an aged lady by force. They, in pure wantonness, shot cattle and hogs by the roadside and in the fields. In Williamston they quartered their horses in the parlors of dwellings, and in that place also destroyed the jail and other buildings." General Smith advised French to write to General Foster regarding these charges and to determine if they were committed with his knowledge and sanction. French did this, and General Foster replied both to him and to General Martin, denying any wanton destruction by his order. French to Smith, November 17, 1862, French to Foster, November 27, 1862, Foster to French, December 4, 1862, Foster to Martin, December 4, 1862, *O. R.,* Ser. I Vol. XVIII, 466, 470, 471, 778-779. The Dix-Hill cartel for the exchange of prisoners may be found in *O. R.,* Ser. II. Vol. IV, 265-268 (July 22, 1862).

[219] See p. 202, 132n.

[220] The "Scotland Neck Mounted Riflemen" were from Halifax County and formed company G of the Forty-first Regiment (third cavalry). Clark, *N. C. Regts.,* 11, 771.

[221] John L. Baker, promoted to sergeant from private, was a member of company G. Most of the men were from Halifax County, but Baker was from New Hanover. Moore, *N. C. Roster,* III, 162.

[222] John Hunt Morgan (1825-1864) whose exploits as a Confederate raider were already famous. He had recently conducted daring and successful raids in the vicinity of Nashville, Louisville, and Cincinnati, after earlier exploits in Mississippi.

slight earnest of what you may expect from your brave countrymen whom I have the honor at present to command.

[Raleigh]

[A. L. S. Governors' Papers (Vance),
State Department of Archives and History, Raleigh.]

From G. W. Logan[223]

Rutherfordton, N. C.
17th Nov[r] 1862

some time since I wrote you respecting a Mr James Justice[224] a Justice of the Peace of this County who was in the army & have not rec[d]- any answer— Please drop me a line upon the subject.

Co[l]. [illegible] who has this note is going to the army and can attend to any matter then is necessary— Please write me when you can make any appointments that will embrace my Nephew J. F. Logan[225] & if necessary I will go to Raleigh

I hope you will pardon my troubling you so much

[Raleigh]

[on reverse]

Esq Justice can not be discharged the exemption law being construed prospectively. I can make his nephew an agent temporarily, or give him a commission in the State troops either

Z B V

[A. L. S. Governors' Papers (Vance),
State Department of Archives and History, Raleigh.]

From F. B. Satterthwaite[226]

Oak Dale
Pitt County N C
Nov 17th 1862

This will be handed you by Col S. T. Carrow[227] of Beaufort County who I ask leave to introduce to your acquaintance, Col

---

[223] See p. 86, 313n.

[224] James M. Justice (1835-1877), a carriage maker of Hendersonville who moved to Rutherfordton and studied law and was admitted to the bar. He was a member of the Rutherfordton city council from time to time, a representative to the Convention of 1875, and a member of the North Carolina House of Representatives as a Republican in 1868 and 1870. He was also presidential elector-at-large on the Grant ticket in 1872. Griffin, Old Tryon and Rutherford, p. 347, who says he was in the Sixty second North Carolina Regiment, company E, for a short time, but he is not listed in Moore, N. C. Roster.

[225] John Francis Logan, who enlisted May 9, 1861, in company G of the Sixteenth North Carolina Regiment and who had been wounded on September 13, 1861 at Valley River, Va. Moore, N. C. Roster, II, 21.

[226] Fenner Bryan Satterthwaite (1813-1875), of Pitt County, formerly of Beaufort County, which he represented in the House of Commons in 1836. He represented Pitt County in the House of Commons in 1848, and in the Conventions of 1861 and 1865. He was a Whig and as such was chosen a member of the Council of State by the legislature which convened the day he wrote this letter. McCormick, Personnel, p. 72; Raleigh North Carolina Standard, January 5, 1861; Connor, N. C. Manual, pp. 439, 498, 763, 895.

[227] T. S. Carrow was a country merchant of Beaufort County.

Carrow is My Neighbour (residing just below the County line) he is a gentleman, who has felt a deep interest in the Southern cause, and I *know* that he *has* made, and is *Still* making important contributions to help it on, but like myself he is now so completely at the mercy of the enemy, that what he does for the benefit of our soldiers he wishes done more secretly, than heretofore, for fear that it may provoke the enemy to arrest and imprison him, and to destroy his property

The enemy has already been out to his house, and seized a quantity of bacon, which he had purchased for the benefit of the Confederate Gov^t.—

Co^l. Carrow is a country merchant and has it in his power to get a great many articles of immense value to our soldiers (smuggled) through the enemies lines, such as shoes, hats, wollen goods Salt &c, and I *know* will take pleasure in doing all he can for our cause, if it can be so done as not to cause his own ruin, I send you by him a small box containing ten pairs of shoes thirteen pairs of socks and three counterpanes as a small contribution for the relief of our suffering soldiers— I regret that I am not able to send more, but my wife has sent off all the blankets that we can possibly spare and is devotedly at work providing as far as she can for the comfort of the soldiers under the immediate command of her sons

I hope to be able to visit Raleigh soon, when I shall have much to say to you about the defense of the eastern part of our State & I hope to be able to make some suggestions which may command your Excellencys favourable consideration

Wishing the most abundant success to all your efforts, in behalf of Southern Independence, and a successful administration of our State Government

[Raleigh]

[A. L. S. Governors' Papers (Vance), State Department of Archives and History, Raleigh.]

From B. Craven[228]

Trinity College[229]
Nov 17. 1862

Capt C. W. Garrett [230] sent me a list of prices this morning, part of which are utterly impracticable. Shoes cannot be made at $5.00 unless we had authority to press the leather. I could get some two

---

[228] Braxton Craven (1822-1882), president of Trinity College. He was a Methodist preacher, a graduate of Randolph-Macon College, an M. A. from the University of North Carolina during the year that Vance was there, and pastor of Edenton Street Methodist Church in Raleigh, 1863-1865, when he returned to Trinity College. Thomas N. Ivey, "Braxton Craven," Ashe, *Biog. Hist. of N. C.,* IV, 102-111.

[229] Trinity College was then in Randolph County, having been taken over by the Methodists from Normal College, which in 1851 had replaced Union Institute.

[230] See p. 190, 96n.

hundred sides to morrow, but they ask even for the Government $2.25 for sole and $2.75 for upper. Your state contractors will not furnish the army, they can do much better by selling to others There is a large amount of clandestine trade now going on, both shoes and leather are held up for higher prices. The agents that visit the tanyards generally know nothing about them. Capt Garrett says 40 to 60 for wool socks, I know Capt Sloan[231] is giving 75, I do not understand such discrepancy.

I have raised and sent a considerable amount,[232] and shall have a fine lot of carpet— blankets in a few days, but there is no use in going into the market so much below the current price. Soldiers shoes bring through all this part of the State from $10 to $18 per pair, wool socks 75 to 1.00 good blankets $5.00 to $12.00 There are yet large amounts of woolen coverlids and blankets, but they cannot be had at the prices proposed. Every sort of device is practiced. Soldiers are now sending word to their friends, that they are barefooted, and urging their friends to buy and send at any price.

I am making quilts, blankets and socks or rather having done through a large district of country, but cannot operate in any other article to much extent, because of the price proposed.
[Raleigh]
[A. L. S. Governors' Papers (Vance),
State Department of Archives and History, Raleigh.]

From M. J. McSween[233]

November 17th 1862
It may be proper to give you a brief statement of the condition of the N. C. Troops in Va whom I have recently seen—

---

[231] See p. 190, 95n.

[232] Craven had been appointed by Vance to purchase and transport supplies for the army. He reported that he could find a good deal to buy provided he could send it to specified persons and particular companies. Vance ruled that articles could be given to particular companies, but that the goods must pass through the hands of the quartermaster, either actually or through an order, so that some units would not obtain supplies from the state and from private hands as well. The materials collected by Vance's agents and by the militia were for general distribution, and any particular gifts for individual parties had to be so designated before they were turned in and paid for. See Craven to Major Peirce, November 20, 1862, with Vance's notation on it, Governors' Papers (Vance).

[233] Murdock J. McSween, a lawyer and journalist of Richmond County. He was left an orphan at an early age, but attended the University of North Carolina, 1857-1859, and joined a South Carolina unit early in the war. He appears in Moore, N. C. Roster, III, p. 64 as a private in Oliver H. Dockery's Company E of the Thirty-eighth North Carolina Regiment, but McSween claimed that he never joined the company but had only agreed to go with it and sustain himself while he assisted in drilling and training the men, while in the meantime Dockery was to assist him in getting offices as a drillmaster, or in some regimental position. "Failing in this I intended to join the company as private, should further acquaintance justify. Just then there was a great call for troops for the war and I got a recruiting appointment to go home and raise a company." He failed to raise the company but got an appointment as drillmaster at Camp Mangum. McSween said that the adjutant general informed him that since he left the regiment before it was transferred from

Our troops about Petersburg & Richmond are not in absolute need of many articles. Our soldiers in the Army of the Potomac need shoes, blankets & clothes very badly— The companies there average probably 30 effective men each. About one third are barefooted or the same as barefooted— I saw many men marching in the snow entirely without shoes or any substitute— There are perhaps 10 men in a company well shod— Very few men are amply supplied with blankets, many have none and others have only one thin blanket apiece. Our soldiers in the Army of the Potomac have been generally several weeks without changing their clothes having left or lost their baggage before their trip to Maryland.

state authority and got another appointment before reporting to the regiment that this promotion would supersede any supposed enlistment. Duncan G. McRae, who succeeded Dockery as captain of the company, charged McSween with desertion. William B. Gulick, assistant adjutant general of North Carolina, dismissed McSween as drill master for over-staying a furlough. McSween's controversy with Gulick and McRae became bitter and public, as all parties wrote letters to the press. Mc-Sween said that Gulick was a "native Yankee—a mere adventurer . . . now in power here to lord it over true Southerners and outrage their feelings with impunity." McSween thought that McRae's motives were obscure, but that he was partly insane, and so was excused from enmity and malice in his charges. Between the summer of 1862 and the spring of 1863, McSween appears to have been an unofficial journalist engaged in collecting information for a series of historical sketches on North Carolina's part in the war. He had met Vance personally at Statesville when Vance passed through that place on his way to Asheville just after his election as governor. Many of his articles appeared in the *Fayetteville Observer* under the pen name of "Long Grabs." In addition to his confused status in the Thirty-eighth Regiment, McSween was a private in Company C of Thirty-fifth North Carolina Regiment, of which Matt W. Ransom was colonel, and with whom McSween had a bitter controversy that resulted in his arrest and conviction before a military court and his sentence to twelve months of hard labor in the penitentiary, in February 1864. He was released from prison about June 1, 1864, and rejoined his regiment. He frequently appealed to Vance for redress of what he called his unjust and tyrannical treatment by Ransom and Colonel John G. Jones, who succeeded Ransom as colonel of the Thirty-fifth when Ransom became a brigadier general. Vance became involved in McSween's quarrels when Vance issued him a commission in the Home Guards in September 1863, but revoked it a few days later upon McSween's arrest by Ransom and Jones. McSween supported Vance in the election of 1862, but denounced him bitterly in 1864; but that fall he wrote Vance a long letter of apology, saying that he had seen the records of his case and therefore retracted any insulting statements he had made which had charged Vance with failure to support him in his trials. His military record is further confused by the fact that from the spring of 1863 until his enlistment in July 1863 in Ransom's regiment, McSween had some sort of vague relation to the Fifty-sixth North Carolina Regiment, but his name does not appear on its rolls. He claimed that Ransom promised him the position of adjutant or of lieutenant if he joined the regiment, and that Ransom went back on his promise. McSween appears to have been a sober and sensitive man, with a good deal of education and a flair for writing. He was also ambitious and persistent and hot-headed, and he remained a controversial figure throughout the war years. After the war he lived in Fayetteville, where he published the *Fayetteville Eagle,* beginning in 1872. He died on January 5, 1880. Moore, *N. C. Roster,* II, 683. III, 64; *Fayetteville Observer,* September 1, July 28, 1862; Raleigh *North Carolina Standard,* June 25, 1862; Andrew McMillan to Vance, October 17, Giles Leitch to Vance, October 18, Bettie Coleman to Vance, October 18, McSween to Vance, March 12, July 27, 30 (2 letters), July 15, August 30, October 3, 6, 28, 1863, February 17, May 3, 25, June 8, 1864, Governors' Papers (Vance); McSween to Governor Clark, March 6, 1862, Governors' Papers (Clark); McSween to Vance, November 21, 1864, Zebulon B. Vance Papers; Oates, *Story of Fayetteville,* p. 324.

They are of course ragged and dirty, and itch vermin and disease are very prevalent—Much of the baggage they left when starting on their march has been damaged, stolen or misplaced since they left— Nearly every soldier in the Regiments that have been through the battles in Northern Virginia and Maryland are without sufficient clothing, and a great majority of them are in very great need of all articles of clothing. The articles I think most necessary are shoes, blankets, pants and coats & should be supplied first— Many of the Quarter Masters are endeavoring to get supplies for the men, but they have to await the action of the Quarter Masters Department at Richmond— Col Myers[234] the Quarter Master General told me that the Government proposes to furnish the troops, but that it would be late before it could be done— He says he will be very seriously embarrassed in this arrangement if he cannot have control of the resources & manufacturers of North Carolina— From what I could ascertain I am satisfied the authorities at Richmond will be unable to supply all the troops properly—It will be certainly impossible for them to get shoes and blankets enough in time— Gen[1]. Lee says he does not wish the troops to have two or more supplies and hopes that economy and system will be practiced— He regards an over abundant supply as a useless waste of our scanty resources & a serious impediment to his movements & plans. I do not think overcoats strictly necessary, and they are certain to be lost if the army has to fight & march much— There is but little use for them on the march or in winter quarters— A good common suit with plenty of under clothing and a good large blanket is amply sufficient and as much as the soldiers can possibly carry & save— The soldier can generally buy socks & underclothing or get them from home, but outside clothing & blankets cannot be got by the privates generally.

Any sort of a hat or cap will do and they manage to make substitutes for gloves & socks from old clothing— It matters but little what is the color of the clothing— so it is not blue— It is very unfortunate so many of our men wear Yankees clothing and blue uniforms— It would be well if the coats were dyed another color— It would be to the interest of North Carolina & her soldiers if the state would retain control of her own manufacturers & resources till her own troops are supplied, for I have noticed that other States have furnished less & their troops in greater need than ours and thus her resources might be exhausted on others while her own sons are suffering— The hospitals are generally needy of supplies— I think it highly proper to have the hospital furnished with underclothing for the patients— These articles should remain at the hospitals & only be used by the soldiers while there— This change & cleanliness would no doubt have a very desirable effect—

[234] See p. 150, 611n.

Many a sick soldier lies for weeks in rags & filth and actually rots away with disease— When such is the case the citisens have been entirely robbed by the enemy or have exhausted their supply heretofore by furnishing the hospitals. The Government does not furnish these articles— The proper vegetables & nourishment for the sick are much needed especially in Richmond, Gordonsville & Culpepper & there is no way to get them. The State should assist in the manufacture & purchase of medicine.
Raleigh
[A. L. S. Governors' Papers (Vance),
State Department of Archives and History, Raleigh.]

From Celluda F. Pattilo[235]

Anderson's Store N. C.
Nov 18th 1862.

You have appealed, to the kind-hearted ladies of North Carolina, to make up clothing, and to contribute anything they can spare, for our suffering soldiers,[236] as the government cannot do it. Sir: The ladies of this county have done, are doing all they can with the means with which they are provided, they are still willing to do, if they could get a little help from the factories, but Sir we go there, and have to give six dollars for a bunch of cotton, to the tanyards, and give three dollars for a pound of leather. Who can pay such prices for themselves and soldiers too? Now the speculators are going round, buying up all the corn for the purpose of making *liquor,* and such as this will cause making a poor soldiers family to suffer from cold, and hunger. Why should this be, when it can be prevented by a few words from you, to the Honorable Legislature? In the name of all the ladies, and especially the soldiers families, I beg you to set a price on all these things.

I have no Father, nor brothers engaged in military service, but I feel very much for those who have, and will do all I can to make them comfortable.
[Raleigh]
[A. L. S. Governors' Papers (Vance),
State Department of Archives and History, Raleigh.]

From Young Jordan[237]

November the 18th 1862

Dear sir it Becomes my necessitated Duty to Address your Excellency By Way of Enquiry Dear Sir By A resent Proclimation to the colonels and Captains of the malitia of N. C. to Visit the

---

[235] Of Caswell County.
[236] See pp. 265-267.
[237] Of Iredell County.

respective familys, they were not only to gather By donation and Subscription for the Soldiers but they were to forward you A list of the Tanners and shoemakers in their respective Districts[238] Captain kerr[239] called on me and has taken my name as A Shoemaker and it is the opinion of Every one that all these men will Be pressed to work for the government Now I can inform you that I am A Regular minister of the gospel and I cannot discharge the duties of my Office if i am called Away from home therefore if I an Exemped from all military duty please sir Exemp me from being pressed to work for the government and notify your Subaltern officers to that Efect and Let me work for my neighbours at My trade through the week and labour for the Cause of Christe too days in Each Weak and for the good of souls Respectfuly

> P. S. in as much as there is no shoemakers in this parrt of Iredell county and Ministers very scarce

> [on reverse]

Raleigh

> Ans^r. that he will not interfered with.
>
> Z B V

[A. L. S. Governors' Papers (Vance), State Department of Archives and History, Raleigh.]

From R. N. Price[240]

Lenoir N. C. Nov. 18th 1862.

I write to introduce to your acquaintance Mr. J. H. Abernethy[241] a worthy citisen of this county, and a political friend of yours. He informs that he wishes to see you to ascertain whether you will send him to a camp of instruction as a conscript or not; as he wishes to know whether to sell out, and make his arrangement for service. He says Dr. Scroggs of this place has recommended him for exemption in consequence of a disabled arm. As to those matters, he will speak for himself. He is a useful citisen and has contributed considerably to the aid and support of soldiers

---

[238] These directions were embodied in General Orders, No. 9, issued from the adjutant general's (militia) office in Raleigh, October 25, 1862. Section 4 called for the list of shoemakers, tanners, and cloth manufacturers, with the probable amount produced by each. See p. 305, 46n.

[239] Nathaniel C. Kerr, captain of Snow Creek company of the Seventy-eighth North Carolina Militia, Iredell County. Thomas Holcombe was its colonel. Militia Roster, p. 218.

[240] See p. 69, 258n and p. 107, 414n.

[241] J. H. Abernethy does not appear on the rolls in Moore, N. C. Roster.

families. I bespeak for him any favor which he may ask that may be consistent with right & propriety.
[Raleigh]
P. S. Family all well. We leave about 8ᵗʰ Dec for Va. Provisions to high for a boarding school.

R. N. P.

[A. L. S. Governors' Papers (Vance),
State Department of Archives and History, Raleigh.]

From Ed. Cantwell [242]

Camp near Franklin Va—
18ᵗʰ- Nov 1862

unofficial

I trust you will succeed in the application for the services of this Regt in Eastern Carolina— I have talked with the Col [243] and our officers, & all are anxious to go, and I am persuaded can & will render efficient service in that country, We have already captured two lots nearly $10.000 worth of shoes &c in the last few days, and Dr Hutchings[244] reports forage and corn in abundance, and good winter quarters. Here we have only the little forage we get near Norfolk & the supply is getting scarce. We were out yesterday in force under Col Leventhorpe[245] I scanned the country for 5 or 6 miles below Carrsville had a fair shot with a Yankee Captain, & took two of his men. The approach of Graham[246] with his artillery and reinforcements, interrupted the sport of the Yankees "skedaddled." Genl Peck[247] seems angry. He has been firing artillery since daylight today. I have not yet found out, what at, Our Colonel (Ferebee)[248] sent out three companies to reconnoitre, They have already sent us 13 prisoners, two of them Massachusetts negroes, with a supply of excellent ammunition, sabres, pistols &c, all of which are exceedingly acceptable, some of our men say

---

[242] See p. 274, 347n. He had become lieutenant colonel of the Fifty-ninth Regiment, September 28, 1862.
[243] The colonel of the Fifty-ninth Regiment was Dennis D. Ferebee.
[244] John William Hutchings, surgeon of the Fifty-ninth Regiment, and formerly surgeon of the Fourteenth Regiment when Vance was a captain in it. He had resigned on June 25, 1862 and then was reappointed surgeon in the Fifty-ninth; on October 23, 1863, he became surgeon of the Sixty-eighth Regiment, resigning again on April 14, 1864. He was from Hertford County. Moore, *N. C. Roster*, I, 510, III, 653, IV, 147; Clark, *N. C. Regts.*, III, 457, 713, IV, 634, 641-642.
[245] See p. 364, 214n.
[246] John W. Graham, of Orange County, captain of company D of the Fifty-sixth North Carolina Regiment, who saw brief service with Leventhorpe's troops on the Blackwater. Graham became a major on September 1, 1863. Clark, *N. C. Regts.*, III, 321.
[247] John James Peck (1821-1878), major general in the Union army who was in command of Federal troops in Virginia south of the James River. Cullum, *Biog. Register*, II, 158-160. For his November operations on the Blackwater see *O. R.*, Ser. I, Vol. XVIII, 31-34.
[248] See p. 341, 150n.

that thay had toasted cheese for breakfast but as they did not invite me to the feast, I shall not report.—

I omitted in my interview with you the other day to call your particular notice to the fact, that this brigade composed almost wholly of N. C. Cavalry has been assigned to a Virginia Brigadier.[249] Col Ferebee is the senior Colonel and is eminently entitled to the post— He has made great sacrifices in this war, is a man of judgment and bravery and thoroughly acquainted with this country, I think it due to the State and to the Cause that his friends should bestir themselves in his behalf and demand his promotion as a debt of justice, If Col F had been a Virginian and did not labor under the misfortune of North Carolina diffidence and modesty it would not be necessary for me to make this suggestion to the Governor of North Carolina. I intend to write Gov Bragg[250] & Gen Clingman[251] on the subject, I am quite sure they will readily cooperate with you in this matter.

Please write us speedily & let us know the chances of going to the Chowan & Roanoke.

[Raleigh]

[A. L. S. Governors' Papers (Vance),
State Department of Archives and History, Raleigh.]

From Martha Coletrane

Nov the 18 1862

Stae of Northcarolina   Randolph Co

Dear sir this is a greate undertaking for me as i never wrote to a man of authority before necesity requires it of me as we are nonslave holders in this section of the State i hope you and our legislature will look to it and have justice done our people as well as the slaveholders i can tel you the condition of my family and you can judg for your self what its condition woul be if my husban is called from home we hav eight children and the oldest is not forteen years old and an old aged mother to support, which makes eleven in our family and without my husband we are a desolate and ruined family for extortion runs so hie here we cannot support and clothe our family without the help of my husband i hope

---

[249] Beverly Holcombe Robertson, of Virginia, a graduate of West Point in the class of 1849, formerly colonel of the Fourth Virginia Cavalry. He was promoted brigadier general in June 1862, and on September 5, 1862, was sent to the Department of North Carolina and given command of a brigade of cavalry there. Evans, *Conf. Mil. Hist.*, III, 650-658.

[250] Thomas Bragg (1818-1872), lawyer and Democrat of Warren County. After membership in the House of Commons in 1842 from Northampton County, to which he had moved, he became governor of North Carolina, 1855-1858, and United States Senator, 1858-1861. He was attorney general of the Confederacy from November 1861 until March 1862; after the war he practiced law in Raleigh. Samuel A'Court Ashe, "Thomas Bragg," Ashe, *Biog. Hist. of N. C.*, VI, 94-100.

[251] See p. 55, 200n.

you will look to the justice of the peepils of this section of the state and i trust you will hold the rane in your own hands and not let the confederate congress have the full sway over your State i appeal to you to look to the white cultivaters as strictly as cngress has to the slaveholders [252] and i think they men from 35 to 45 be hel as reserves at hom to support ther families if the are calld from home it is bound to leave a thoasn families in a starving condition in our county we trust in god and look to you for some help for our poor children so no more

[Raleigh]

[A. L. S. Governors' Papers (Vance),
State Department of Archives and History, Raleigh.]

From Geo. W. Randolph [253]

CONFEDERATE STATES OF AMERICA
WAR DEPARTMENT
Richmond, Va. Nov. 18[h] 1862

The communication referred to in your letter of the 28th ult. presented by Mr S. P. Arrington[254] did not reach the Department.

The Confederate Government is very desirous of complying with the recommendations of the Governors of the several States of the Confederacy wherever it can be done with a due regard to the public interest, and this Department would gladly embrace the opportunity to gratify your wishes by detailing Mr Arrington for the purpose designated, but I regret to say, that in the present stage of the campaign, where the Exigencies of the Service are so pressing, it is deemed unsafe to detail men from regiments in the field and especially from those in the immediate front of the Enemy, for any civil employment, unless such detail is requisite for the support of the Army itself.

[Raleigh]

[Vance Letter Book, 1862-1863,
State Department of Archives and History, Raleigh.]

---

[252] Among the numerous specified exemptions in the act of Congress of October 11, 1862 was a provision that "to secure the proper police of the country, one person, either as agent, owner or overseer, on each plantation on which one white person is required to be kept by the laws or ordinances of any State, and on which there is no white male adult not liable to do military service, and in States having no such law, one person as agent, owner or overseer, on each plantation of twenty negroes, and on which there is no white male adult not liable to military service: *And furthermore,* For additional police for every twenty negroes on two or more plantations, within five miles of each other, and each having less than twenty negroes, and on which there is no white male adult not liable to military duty, one person, being the oldest of the owners or overseers on such plantations; . . ." *O. R.,* Ser. IV, Vol. II, 162.

[253] See p. 132, 524n.

[254] See p. 290, 4n.

From Saml Forkner[255]

Mt. airy N. C. Nov. 18 1862

I have failed to comply with your instructions in regard to the Leatha in the hands of Elisha Banner[256] subject to Gov orders refered to in my letter of the 4th of Nov[257] in reference to former Contracts Said Contract no doubt was bonafide, but the object was to Sell at exorbitant prices any where the Salt Could be Sold for the most. I Claime Said leathe as coming under the Govs order for the use of the State Mr. Banner Claiming that it was not Subject being a former contract we agreed that it was not to be interfered with untill we herd from the Gov, then to be governed according to instructions, but in violation of contract between E Banner & myself he the said Banner at Mid Knight leaves while honest pepole Should have ben sleeping carried the leather to Va. the leather was gone at the time he wrote his letter to the Gov asking permission to comply with former Contract. After geting an answer to our letter he acknoledgs he sent the leather off and that the Salt was Sold at Salt Vill at a big price and he has the money for it a bigg pile and that we may help our selfs So I am at the end of my roe as fare as I know-
[Raleigh]
P. S. if there is eny way to reach sutch caces I would like to know it I write the within so you may know how things is going on by Speculators in our County   S F
[A. L. S. Governors' Papers (Vance),
State Department of Archives and History, Raleigh.]

From A. J. Hill[258]

Clinton
Sampson Co N. C.
Novr-19- 1862

As the Chief Magistrate of our State, I address myself to you to aid me in releasing my son[259] from Military Service- He has been, for the last two or three years in charge of my Rice Plantation, two miles distant only from Wilmington, and some sixty odd negroes- who have been left all this past summer without a Protector and he personally would perhaps resume this fidelity they being all family negroes, and much attached to him- I am over sixty years of age, and can not undergo the fatigue, and have besides in charge, two single daughters- My son, is a young man

---

[255] See p. 305, 45n. This letter is addressed to David A. Barnes, aide to Vance.
[256] See p. 306, 47n.
[257] See p. 305.
[258] Arthur J. Hill, who lived at Sans Souci, near Wilmington, after the war. Sprunt, *Chronicles*, p. 75.
[259] Arthur J. Hill, Jr., second sergeant of company C in the Fifty-ninth North Carolina Regiment, who enlisted July 17, 1862. Moore, *N. C. Roster*, III, 659.

of delicate constitution, entirely unfitted to the exposure of Camp life- unlike my grandson Charles M^c. Lean [260] who was with you at New Bern, and who I am please to have been himself [illegible] My son Arthur, attached himself to Cap.^{tn} M^c. Intire's [261] Rangers, from New Hanover, and when last heard from, was at or near Franklin V^a. and I think in Co^l Ferebee's [262] Regmy 59th - - As I only had the pleasure of meeting you personally in Morganton & now two summers since, I must refer you to my Nephew D^r. Tom Hill [263] in the Hospital there, my friend D^r. W. G. Hill [264] Gov Manly [265] and other friends I have known my dear Sir, of the perilous condition of our country- but my whole interest in life depends upon the result of the application I am making- I find many violent Democratic Secessionists staying at Home under various pretexts, or in some post office. But yet I would not to you sir, excite prejudices of this kind- Hoping that you can excuse me, I remain

P. S. I am awaiting Sir, the absence of Yellow fever to return Home- if the Enemy then will let us-

[Raleigh]

[A. L. S. Governors' Papers (Vance),
State Department of Archives and History, Raleigh.]

From Jno. D. Hyman

Asheville, N. C.
Nov. 19/62.-

I desire to know of you, to whom the Old "Spectator" [266]

---

[260] No soldier by the name of Charles McLean appears on Vance's rolls in Moore, N. C. Roster.

[261] Robert M. McIntire, who lived at Rocky Point, near Wilmington, and who in the spring of 1862 raised a cavalry company, afterwards company C of the Fifty-ninth Regiment. His uncle, Dr. Andrew McIntire, became the first captain, but Robert McIntire became captain on May 10, 1863. Clark, *N. C. Regts.*, IV, 701, 709; Moore *N. C. Roster*, III, 659.

[262] See p. 341, 150n.

[263] Thomas Hill (1832-1906), a physician who was in charge of the hospital at Peace Institute in Raleigh from May of 1862, until March of 1864. He was commissioned assistant surgeon in July 1861 and had served at hospitals in Fredericksburg, Va. and Goldsboro, N. C. before coming to Raleigh. After he left the general hospital in Raleigh he was surgeon of the Fortieth North Carolina Regiment, and in December 1864 was appointed chief surgeon of North Carolina reserves, on the staff of General Holmes. After the war he practiced medicine in Kenansville, Salisbury, Danville, Missouri and, after 1880, in Goldsboro. *North Carolina Medical Journal*, Vol. 54 (1906), p. 99; *Medical Transactions*, 1906, pp. 156-157; Clark, *N. C. Regts.*, II, 745, IV, 7, 37, 638; Sprunt, *Chronicles*, pp. 324-325.

[264] William G. Hill, of Raleigh, a prominent physician who had been active in the founding of the Medical Society of North Carolina. *North Carolina Medical Journal*, Vol. V (1880), p. 337.

[265] Charles Manly (1795-1871), a lawyer of Chatham County who was clerk of the House of Commons for a score of years, secretary and treasurer of the Trustees of the University of North Carolina, 1821-1848, 1850-1869, and governor of North Carolina, 1848-1850. He was a Whig, and a lawyer in Raleigh after 1850. Marshall DeLancey Haywood, "Charles Manly," Ashe, *Biog. Hist. of N. C.*, VI, 349-356.

[266] See p. 29, 128n. and p. 50, 181n. Hyman was associated with the *Spectator* from

office belongs? I have made inquiry of several persons, but they profess not to know. Supposing that you can give me the desired information, I write to request that you will do so. Mr. Byers, who last conducted the paper, I understand, has returned to Buncombe, but I do not know where he is. He remained in Asheville a very short time. I wish to know to whom the establishment belongs, and upon what terms, and for how much, it can be purchased- that is, if you are in possession of the information. If you are not, please be so good as to let me know who is, and the proper person with whom to negotiate-

The reason I make request for this information, is, because I think I can effect a sale of the establishment-[267] not that I propose to engage in the newspaper business myself. I have no such idea.

From what I learn, the presses must be in a bad condition, and if it is not sold soon, it become worthless. I have heard that a quantity of the type is scattered about town.

Allow me to say, Dear Governor, that I very much admire your late stirring appeal in behalf of our soldiers.[268] I know of nothing during the war, that has so forcibly and effectually struck the sympathetic cord of the popular heart. It has been followed, I feel well assured, by its appropriate fruition. God Speed the good work!

The times seem pregnant with future disaster to our cause. I know not how matters may appear to you and others, but to me the war clouds seem dark & dismal indeed. Of course, I fear no such thing as subjugation, but I do fear much more of distress and desolation to our people for the next six months, than we have hitherto experienced. I do hope, however, that the dark clouds I now see only portend the day-break of our independence.-

I regret that my wound is but little better than it was when you were here. I fear I will have to abandon the idea of re-entering the service.

Sir my kindest regards to Mrs. Vance.[269] We are looking for

---

1853, when he took over with James M. Edney the old *Highland Messenger* in Asheville, until he sold it in 1856 to Henry E. Colton and James L. Henry, who edited it from May 1857 until September 1858, when financial difficulties forced their abandonment. Vance was associated with Hyman in the editorship of the paper for about a year and a half in 1855 and 1856.

[267] Hyman sold the press to the commandant of the Confederate Armory in Asheville for $1400, and assumed in his letters to Vance that the money was to be applied to the payment of their bank debt. He described the condition of the type and the press as being very poor and estimated that he himself would not have given more than $500 for it, but the government was rich and could afford it. See Hyman to Vance, February 16, April 20, 30, 1863, Z. B. Vance Papers. The sale was made in April 1863.

[268] See pp. 265-267.

[269] See p. 16, 81n.

your message to-night.[270] Hoping, dear Sir., that your Administration may be honorable & glorious, as your previous career has been brilliant and successful, I subscribe myself, as ever,
[Raleigh]
[A. L. S. Governors' Papers (Vance),
  State Department of Archives and History, Raleigh.]

To G. W. Smith[271]

STATE OF NORTH CAROLINA
EXECUTIVE DEPARTMENT
Raleigh Nov. 19th- 1862

His Excellency Gov Vance received a communication from your immediate predecessor the Hon Geo. W. Randolph[272] in which he states, that "in consequence of the threatened attacks upon the RailRoad connections in the Eastern portion of No. Ca. & Va. & our inability at present to withdraw from the Army of Northern Va. reinforcements sufficiently large to secure those connections it is considered very important to complete the Danville and Greensboro connection as speedily as possible and asking him to aid in procuring hands to work upon that improvement.

His Excellency instructs me to say that he will most cheerfully give whatever assistance he can consistently with his sense of duty to further the speedy completion of this work- but at the same time he hopes it will not be improper to remark that the Government should at all hazards and at all times defend our present Rail Road connections at Weldon. That section of the country is of the utmost importance to the Government abounding in abundant supplies for the Army.

His Excellency must decline authorizing or recommending the Legislature to authorize the drafting slaves for this purpose. Vast numbers of slaves are leaving our Eastern Counties, threatened with invasion and their owners are anxiously seeking employment.

The Contrators upon the work can without the intervention of the public authorities obtain the most abundant supply of hands if they will offer fair and remunerating prices.
[Richmond]
[Vance Letter Book, 1862-1863,
  State Department of Archives and History, Raleigh.]

---

[270] Vance's message to the legislature was delivered on November 17, 1862. See *Legislative Documents, 1862-1863*, Document No. 1.

[271] See p. 329, 119n. General Smith served as acting Secretary of War from November 17 to November 20, 1862. This letter to him is signed by David A. Barnes, aide to Vance.

[272] See Randolph to Vance, November 10, 1862, above, p. 334.

To Jas. A. Seddon [273]

STATE OF NORTH CAROLINA
EXECUTIVE DEPARTMENT
Raleigh Nov 20th 1862

His Excellency Governor Vance applied to your immediate predecessor [274] asking him to detail Mr. S. P. Arrington [275] which was declined.

The ground upon which the application was made was this. Mr. John White [276] of Warrenton, N. C. an extensive merchant of that town had been appointed an Agent of the State to visit England for the purpose of purchasing Army supplies. It was necessary during his absence to leave some person in charge of his business who was familiar with its details. This knowledge was only posessed by Mr Arrington his partner and son in law.

Under these circumstances it was hoped that Mr. Arrington would have been detailed. Mr. White has gone to England and his Excellency renews the request that you will make the detail

[Richmond]
[Vance Letter Book, 1862-1863,
State Department of Archives and History, Raleigh.]

From Elizabeth Chamberlain

1862

state of N C yadkin county nov the 21
dear sir it is with a troubled heart an distressed mind and aflicted body that I now attimpt to write to you and I hope that you will not turn a deaf ear to my request Sir my husband has been forced from me to the army while he is deseased in different ways and I have understood that he was not allowed to stop to be examined but was sent right to the army and has to stay there dis-

---

[273] James Alexander Seddon (1815-1880), who became Secretary of War on November 20, 1862. He was born in Fredericksburg, Va., studied law and settled in Richmond to practice it. He became a member of the United States House of Representatives, 1845-1847, 1849-1851, when he returned to his estate in Goochland County to live the quiet life of a country gentleman. Always interested in politics, he was known as an ardent follower of John C. Calhoun. He was a member of the Peace Convention of 1861, where he defended the right of peaceful secession and led the secessionist element, and of the first Confederate Congress. He served as Secretary of War from November 20, 1862, until he was succeeded by John C. Breckinridge on February 4, 1865. He was capable, efficient, cold, and humorless, and he was loyal to Jefferson Davis, upon whom he had some influence in spite of the fact that Davis determined most of the policies of the war department. Seddon was crushed by the failure of the Confederacy and considered his life to have been a failure upon its collapse. Robert Douthat Meade, "James Alexander Seddon," *Dict. of Am. Biog.,* XVI, 545-546.

[274] This letter was written for Vance by David A. Barnes, his aide. For the former request see pp. 290-291.

[275] See p. 290, 4n.

[276] See p. 288, 1n.

eased and afflicted and has not been well since he has been there
and was not well when he left but he was taken away while others
well and sound was let of and I am left here desolate and weekly
I have neither father nor brother to assist me and I a poor woman
and one child to take care of and my request to you that you
will let my husband of so that he can come to my assistance that
me and child may not suffer and die deny me not I come as a
beging lazerous and as a weeping mary I come pleading for my
husband myself and my child that we may not perish and die
hear me in behalf of my husband and I hope that god will reward you for it my husband name is L L chamberlain [277]
From Elizabeth chamberlain
Governor vance
I had forgotten to state where he was 13th regiment N C troops
company G care of captain Hymen [278] answer my letter if you
please but dont put your name on the back for fear that I never
git it Hamptonville
[on reverse] Ans[r] this Lady that the Gov[r] has no power to release her husband & explain why   Z B V
[Raleigh]
[A. L. S. Governors' Papers (Vance),
State Department of Archives and History, Raleigh.]

From S. S. Carter [279]

Trenton
Nov 21st- 1862

You are aware that we W[m] Carter [280] & Sons have a contract of
making 50 prs Army Shoes per month for the Government. &

---

[277] L. L. Chamberlain was from Yadkin County and entered the army on September 27, 1862 as a private in company G of the Thirteenth North Carolina Regiment.
Moore, *N. C. Roster*, I, 495.

[278] J. H. Hyman, formerly captain of company G in the Thirteenth Regiment,
who became major in the same unit on October 15, 1862. In 1863 he was promoted
to the colonelcy and was wounded at Gettysburg, July 1, 1863. He was from Edgecombe County. Moore, *N. C. Roster*, I, 471, 494.

[279] S. Sidney Carter who entered the service in April 1861 as a private and was
elected second lieutenant from the ranks, July 10, 1862, of company A of the Eighth
North Carolina Battalion, which was composed of six companies of partisan rangers
from the eastern section of the state and was an independent command until
August of 1863, when his unit was combined with the Fourth Battalion to form
the Sixty-sixth North Carolina Regiment. Carter then became second lieutenant
of company F. Moore, *N. C. Roster*, IV, 118; Clark, *N. C. Regts.*, III, 685-686. On
November 28, 1862, from Goldsboro, Carter wrote the Secretary of War asking that
his resignation be accepted. It was endorsed as returned to be forwarded through
the proper channels. On January 3, 1863 Carter wrote to Vance asking for his help,
but Vance replied that his application had now been forwarded through the proper
channels and, the secretary having refused it, there was nothing more he could do
about it. Carter to Secretary of War, November 28, 1862, Carter to Vance, January
3, 1863, Governors' Papers (Vance).

[280] William Carter was Sidney Carter's father. The son claimed that the production
of shoes would be increased four-fold—to 200 a month—if he could be returned
to the business. Carter to Vance, January 3, 1863, Governors' Papers (Vance).

with my Manufacturing ability- combined with the - help I have at Home we could make 100 prs pr month & therefore I shall Resign & will also Tan Government Hides at their Pro Rater or prices & make all the work for the Army I can during the war & will not expect over 75 per cnt on any thing we do. I today Tender my Resignation as 3rd Lieut Co A 8th N. C. Battalion & ask you to advise the Secretary of War my usefulness at Home N B please Inquire into all the particulars of the 8th N. C. Battalion Maj. J. H. Nethercutt [281] Commanding and democratic Political Battalion

Your Bosom frind

[Raleigh]
[A. L. S. Governors' Papers (Vance),
State Department of Archives and History, Raleigh.]

To S. R. Mallory [282]

Executive Dpt. of No. Ca.
Raleigh Nov. 21st [1862]

Upon consultation with the Directors of the Atlantic & North C. R. R. Co.. I have concluded to let you have the iron for the Gun-boat, building on the Neuse River, if you will get it from the torn up portion of the road nearest the enemy.[283]

In consideration of the alarming condition of our main Roads, (the iron giving way &c,) it is deemed advisable that the iron taken from the Atlantic Road, which is nearly new, be exchanged with the other roads for their damaged rails, which I am told will answer for rolling as well as the other. The bolt iron of the destroyed bridges across the Neuse you can also have.

In regard to the other boat in the Tar or Roanoke, I think you ought to furnish with iron from the Roanoke and Sea Board road,[284] which is close on hand, and is principally the property, as I am informed, of an alien enemy.

Please let me know if these propositions meet your approval The R. R. Co. of course expect to accept your proposition for providing for a return of the iron.

[Richmond]
[A. L. S. Governors' Papers (Vance),
State Department of Archives and History, Raleigh.]

---

[281] John H. Nethercutt, of Jones County, who was captain of the partisan rangers known as the Eighth Battalion before the formation of the Sixty-sixth Regiment. Jones rose successively in rank from captain to colonel by June 3, 1864, and on March 15, 1865, he became commander of a brigade of Junior Reserves. He is described as a plain, blunt man, but every inch a soldier. He was assassinated at his home in Jones County after the war, presumably by some disaffected person desiring revenge, perhaps for some punishment received during the war. Moore, *N. C. Roster,* IV, 107, 118; Clark, *N. C. Regts.,* IV, 56, 302.

[282] See p. 306, 49n.

[283] See p. 306, Mallory to Vance.

[284] See p. 200, 123n.

From D. T. Ramseur [285]

Med: Purveyor's Office
Charlotte, N. C. Nov: 22nd: 1862

In view of the recommendation in your recent message [286] "that the existing prohibition against the Distillation of Spirits of all kinds from Grain be continued during the war-" I respectively beg to state-

That- the very limited supply of alcohol in the Confederacy creates the alternative of a further manufacture of alcohol, or a cessation of the Manufacture of Medicines for the Army for which we are now largely dependent upon our own resources-

That- at this Depot as well as at others, there have been collected during the past summer & fall by Order of the Surgeon General C. S. A. large quantities of indigenous Plants &c: to make Tincture & Extracts from Alcohol of which we are now in urgent need and unless supplied a suspension of the operations of this branch of the Med: Purveying Dept. must follow.

And that- as each Purveyor is restricted in his purchases to his own District, this Department cannot look beyond the limits of the State of North Carolina for its Supply.

I would, therefore, as Medical Purveyor in this District, respectfully represent the pressing necessity for such a modification in the Law referred to in your message, as has been made in the State of Virginia- Viz: the Distillation of Alcohol from Grain for Governmental purposes only- and fraud prevented by very heavy bonds, or by the appointment of a Government (State) Officer to oversee the Distillation.

Ten Thousand Gallons of alcohol- which could approximate a years supply for this Depot- could not consume one-twentieth of the corn annually raised in one of the adjacent counties.

---

[285] D. T. Ramseur was assistant superintendent in the office of the medical purveyor in Charlotte. There were thirty-two medical purveyors in the Confederacy employed in the procurement of medical and hospital supplies. Dr. M. Howard was the surgeon and medical purveyor in Charlotte. Dr. M. Howard to Governor Clark, August 5, 1862, Governors' Papers (Clark); H. H. Cunningham, "Organization and Administration of the Confederate Medical Department," *The North Carolina Historical Review*, Vol. XXXI, No. 3 (July, 1954), 385-409.

[286] In his message to the legislature, November 17, 1862, Vance recommended the continuation of the convention's prohibition of distilling on the ground that there was no grain to be spared for such purposes and that the medical needs of the army could be supplied by liquors made from the fruit crop. "Should even the supply for the army fail, it cannot be doubted that it is much better for the soldier to go without spirits than that his wife and child should be without bread." *Legislative Documents, 1862-1863*, Document No. 1, p. 18; *Convention Ordinances*, 3 session, No. 24 (February 21, 1862). The prohibition of the ordinance of the convention was to expire on January 1, 1863, but the legislature responded to Vance's message with a law on December 17, 1862, and amended on February 11, 1863, making it unlawful to distill any spirituous liquors out of specified grains. *Laws of N. C., 1862-'63*, chap. X; *Laws of N. C., 1863*, adjourned session, chap. 39.

Hoping that the above Statement will give you some immediate and favourable attention-
[Raleigh]
[A. L. S. Governors' Papers (Vance),
State Department of Archives and History, Raleigh.]

From John Roberts [287]

1862

Stat of for gined November the 22
Mr. gov ner Z B vance sir muste State to you my un for tunate con Dition in my presente health I have suffered with the liver com plaints since April 1859 So that I hante bin able to Doo an ny worke of en ny acounte I have sufered a heape with a breste com plainte I hante strenth to march to ceape up with my regmente when they wes march ing I am as tender as I can bee I man I was wonste as well a looking man as en ny an was as cante stand wet nor colde a tole yet I am a tolerable well looking Stoute a man as en ny my heath is now effected so that I am no acount in the servis of my country nor at home my sergione think be cause I looked well e nough for sirvis I was able am not ef I was I am as willing as man in my country so hope you will Reade these lines an call me to you an an have me examine before you so I hope you will not for git me I am in the hospital at Campe winder in the 70 warde my sergent here is Brown [288] in the 23 north Carolina Reg ment al Sergent is hicks [289] I you will not for git my con Dition Dear friend yours Respectfully
[Raleigh]
[A. L. S. Governors' Papers (Vance),
State Department of Archives and History, Raleigh.]

From R. L. Abernethy [290]

Marion, N. C.
Nov. 22.ᵈ/62

I write to inform your Excellency that I have one brother in Catawba County, who is a shoe maker, a splendid workman. and who has a wife and *nine little girls* dependant upon his daily labor for a support. He requested me to inform your Excellency that, if the leather &c were found, he would manufacture shoes for the soldiers at 75 cents per pair.

---

[287] John Roberts is listed in Moore, *N. C. Roster*, II, p. 267 as a private in company D of the Twenty-third North Carolina Regiment. He enlisted September 6, 1862, from South Carolina. Most of the company was from Richmond County.

[288] No sergeant by the name of Brown is listed in Moore, *N. C. Roster*, II, 264 among the non-commissioned officers of the company.

[289] Robert J. Hicks, of Granville County, surgeon of the Twenty-third Regiment. Moore, *N. C. Roster*, II, 252.

[290] See p. 304, 44n.

I humbly hope your Excellency will employ him to make shoes for the army, as his family is quite feeble, and none of them able to render him much aid in supporting the family.

His name and address are "Logan B. Abernathy, Jacob's Fork, P. O. Catawba Co., N. C."

I do humbly trust you will *at once* grant him permission through me, to go to work for the government, and I will see that the materials shall be got, and the shoes handed over to the proper authorities.

I request this, Governor, because my brother is an *honest poor man,* and because the extortioners have run grain of all kinds so high that the amount of work my brother can get, can hardly support his family; while the government contracts are sure pay and always plenty of work.

He has been a shoe maker sixteen years, and is 39 years old.

May God bless your Excellency, and speedily terminate these troublesome days.

P. S. If your Excellency grants my request, please send a certificate to that effect to me.

Yours- R. L. A.

[on reverse]

If leather can be bought so as the shoes shall not cost over Six dollars pr pair, he can make as many as he wishes- & we will pay for the leather-

Z B V

[Richmond]

[A. L. S. Governors' Papers (Vance), State Department of Archives and History, Raleigh.]

From Wm. H. Thomas [291]

Knoxville
Nov. 22. 1862

In the progress of the war men and circumstances change. At the commencement you were in Military I in Civil positions. Now my position is what your position was then. I find myself at the head of a Regment or Legion of Indians and mountaineers, entrusted with duties in East Tennessee and Kentucky. And as your duties relate principally to the defence of North Carolina permit me to submit for your consideration a few facts believed to be connected with the public services and the defence of the State.

1.st Would it not be advisable to make an arrangement to have able bodied negro men belonging to the counties in reach of the enemy employed by the State and transferred from their

---

[291] See p. 67, 249n.

present positions to work on the extension of the Railroad.[292] They could, I presume, be employed for the cost on ensurance and food and raiment. By this two objects would be gained. 1st every negro would be a saving of $1000, to the owner, 2d Every able bodied negro kept out of the hands of the enemy would lessen the number of troops we have to raise in defence, equal to a saving of at least $1000 per year. Thus if North Carolina employed ten thousand negroes on the road where a small force could keep them in subjection, $10,000,00 would be saved to the owners, and 10,000 men less would defend our cause.

One consideration now animates us all. What will ensure success not what would be most agreeable to us. The Legislature appropriated two millions of dollars to defend Eastern North Carolina and the Western frontiers.[293] Both are now in danger. The western Counties are in danger of being over run by deserters and renegades who by the hundred are taking shelter in the smoky mountains. The men between 35 and 40 west of the Blue Ridge should be furnished with arms and ammunition, and required to aid in guarding their homes And the Confederate should be required to place Military compys at every trap in the Smoky mountains from Ashe to Cherokee. As long as we can hold the Country encircled by the Blue Ridge and Cumberland mountains and their outside slopes we have the heart of the south, which commands the surrounding Plains. The loss of this country larger than England or France is the loss of the Southern Confederacy and we sink under a despotism

[Raleigh]
[A. L. S. Governors' Papers (Vance),
State Department of Archives and History, Raleigh.]

From Jos. J. Williams [294] and Others

November 22d 1862

The Undersigned Citizens of North Carolina residing in that portion of the Roanoke Valley lying South of Weldon respectively represent that the lands which they occupy are teeming with abundant crops of grain that at least one million bushels of corn,

---

[292] That is, the extension of the Western North Carolina Railroad, in which Thomas had long had an active interest.

[293] The legislature adopted this measure shortly after the fall of Hatteras had alarmed the legislators for the safety of the state. The sum was to be expended by the governor to secure the coast and frontiers, but only in case the Confederate authorities should fail to begin all necessary work for their effectual defense. *Senate Journal, 1861,* 2 extra session, pp. 94-95; *House Journal, 1861,* 2 extra session, 1861, p. 252; *Laws of N. C., 1861,* 2 extra session, chaps. 17, 21, 22 (September 20, 1861); Ashe, *History of N. C.,* II, 656.

[294] Joseph John Williams, of an old Halifax County family, whose ancestors had been prominent in Revolutionary affairs and had served in the legislature. Allen, *Halifax County,* pp. 25, 31, 35.

as many pounds of pork, large herds of beeves and other stock, great quantities of peas beans, potatoes and other supplies necessary for the support of the army and people of the Confederacy are now either gathered or ready to be gathered on their several plantations. They further represent that the plantations so situated, with the supplies upon them now lie completely exposed and at the mercy of the enemy, that in a recent marauding expedition of the abolitionists, large quantities of these supplies were destroyed & horses necessary to save the crops were stolen & carried off. in some cases plantations were entirely stripped of slaves, horses, hogs- stock of every description & the corn left standing upon the land. That since this expedition many citizens feeling the utter insecurity of their property have removed their negroes & stock, abandoned their plantations and crops & sought what they hope to be greater safety in the interior of the State. That numerous other Citizens are making preparations in like manner to remove their slaves preferring to abandon the crops of the present year to the entire loss of both negroes & crops. That the crops so abandoned are as completely lost to the army & the people as if the plantations on which they stand had been ravaged by the enemy, and unless some greater security is had this abandonment of property will go on until the loss will be beyond calculation & vast injury to the whole country. The undersigned further represent that this Country possesses natural advantages which the proper application of military skill can make easily defensible. That at Rainbow Bank [295] (a point on the Roanoke) by the construction of proper fortified works & the maintenance of a sufficient force, this wealthy section of the Confederacy can be certainly defended. That the people are & have always been willing & anxious to furnish the labor to construct these defences & do all in their power to assist in the work. They further represent that the force now at Rainbow Bank (the only force in the country) is totally inadequate to its defence, consisting as it docs of only one Regiment & one Light Battery numbering in all not more than 700 men (where there ought to be 5000) thus inviting rather than being able to resist aggression. And they do hereby *Protest* against this neglect & virtual abandonment of a country whose supplies are necessary to the support of the people & the maintenance of our armies, & they do hereby respectfully request that the proper works of defence be at once constructed & a sufficient force sent to defend & hold the country- The undersigned do further represent that by a recent order of Brig Gen *French* it is directed that all the Cotton found in the

---

[295] Rainbow Bank on the Roanoke River was near Hamilton, N. C. Fort Branch was built nearby.

East Side of the Rail Road be burned,[296] This singular method of *defending* a Country by burning up the sources of its wealth is something *new* in the annals of defensive warfare- & exhibits intention on the part of the commanding general to abandon the country whose crops are believed to be *necessary* to the army & the people and they do hereby indignantly *protest* against the execution of this order & demand its immediate repeal and that this matter be left to the loyalty of the people who are willing now as they always have been to make this and all other sacrifices to the honor & safety of the Country.

Nov 22[d]- 1862

Jos. J. Williams
Tho.[s] Ives
W R Smith [297]
John J. Bishop
P. E. Smith [298]
W. H. Phineas
J. W. Smith
Jos. Blount Cheshire [299]
Rich[d] H. Smith [300]
W. J. Hill
T. P. Devereux [301]
B. W. Edmondson
J. Devereux
[Raleigh]
[A. L. S. Governors' Papers (Vance),
State Department of Archives and History, Raleigh.]

---

[296] Vance and many others protested this order of General French. John A. Campbell, Assistant Secretary of War, wrote to Major General Gustavus W. Smith, suggesting that forces be very certain that destruction was necessary before it was wantonly done. *O. R.,* Ser. I, Vol. XVIII, 792.

[297] William Ruffin Smith (1803-1872), planter of Halifax County and a graduate of the University of North Carolina in 1824. Grant, *Alumni History,* p. 578.

[298] Peter Evans Smith (1829-1905), planter and civil engineer. He was born in Edgecombe County, educated at the Bingham School and the University of North Carolina, where he graduated in 1851, and became a planter for thirty years. In 1882 he became a civil engineer, indulging a passion for mechanical tinkering which he had long had. He invented several things, was a railroad builder of considerable note, and was the chief builder of the Confederate Ram *Albemarle* at Edward's Ferry. From 1896 to 1905 he was a land surveyor and mechanical engineer and lived at his home near Scotland Neck. Grant, *Alumni History,* p. 576; Allen, *Halifax County,* pp. 218-220.

[299] Joseph Blount Cheshire, of Edgecombe County, who for nearly fifty years (1842-1889) was rector of Calvary Church in Tarboro. He was the father of Bishop Cheshire. Turner and Bridgers, *Edgecombe County,* pp. 452-456; Hamilton, *History of N. C.,* V, 254.

[300] Richard Henry Smith. See p. 344, 154n.

[301] Thomas Pollock Devereux, co-reporter of the Supreme Court with William H. Battle.

To Joseph E. Brown [302]

STATE OF NORTH CAROLINA
EXECUTIVE DEPARTMENT
Raleigh Nov. 22.ᵈ 1862

Your communication through Mr. A. Stevens [303] has been received. My recent order does not prohibit the exportation of Salt purchased prior to its date. Nor was it my purpose to prevent citizens of other States making bona fide purchases for their individual use or to prevent purchases made by counties or towns for charitable distribution.

My only purpose was to prevent extortion and speculation in this important and necessary article. Genl Whiting [304] in immediate command of this order and has full instruction upon the subject.

[Milledgeville]
[Vance Letter Book, 1862-1863,
State Department of Archives and History, Raleigh.]

From Charlotte Rowell

Brunswick county N C nov the 23 1862

adress to the honerfle govener frome a old widow lady that has a grat many servents and other property and has no person to atend to enny bisness at tall for me I would be thanful to you if you would assist me you would a asist me agrate deal if you will have John N regester [305] detailed from scrves to at tend to bisness for me he is the best overseer that i in my noing all th men is gon from a bout her pretty much and there is noboddy that i can get to pertect my servents for me i can not doo with out someboddy and i rother have him then enny one elce i no of i have no boddy but myself and 2 daughters and sense he has been in servis, my property has ben goin to destruction no boddy to sea to it if you will have him sent home you will doo me grate favore he is the 51 N C redgment under Capt lippett [306] co g i must close with saying i put my trust in you as a friend to as asist me a cording to my request

[Raleigh]

---

[302] See p. 213, 160n. Brown had written to Vance on November 17 asking a relaxation of his policy, giving assurance that the salt was to be used for the benefit of the public and not for speculation. Brown to Vance, Vance Letter Book, 1862-1863.

[303] A. Stevens was a merchant of Augusta who had been unable to get his salt shipped from Wilmington on account of the yellow fever. Governor Brown said that Stevens had sold salt to the families of soldiers at half what it would command in the market. Brown to Vance, November 17, 1862, Vance Letter Book, 1862-1863.

[304] See p. 348, 161n.

[305] John N. Regester, of Brunswick County, is listed in Moore, *N. C. Roster*, III, 462 as having enlisted on January 10, 1863 in company G of the Fifty-first North Carolina Regiment. He was later wounded.

[306] James W. Lippett, of New Hanover County, commissioned captain of company G in the Fifty-first North Carolina Regiment on March 14, 1862. Moore, *N. C. Roster*, III, 461.

[on reverse]
Gov has no power to detail an overseer Z B V
[A. L. S. Governors' Papers (Vance),
    State Department of Archives and History, Raleigh.]

From S. G. French [307]

Head Quarters Petersburg Va
November 24th. 1862

When I joined our forces that were assembled near Tarboro I was forcibly struck with the want of positive and accurate information as respected the force of the enemy under General Foster,[308] as well as to the roads along which he was advancing and which important information I think could & should have been conveyed to General Martin [309] by the inhabitants residing along the line of his march. To remedy such or rather to provide for the ascertaining of all movements of the enemy on any future advances, permit me to suggest that you cause in all the Eastern Counties as far as practical the enrollment of all persons capable of bearing arms into companies (that are not conscripts) whose duty it shall be to watch the enemy, and on any movement taking place to hover on his line of march and give information and join our forces as guides and skirmishers. These on being enrolled to meet occasionally for drill and consultation under their officers as to what each shall do on the occasion and arrangement of places of rendezvous. The rolls of such companies to be sent to Richmond to put them in the Confederate service, but not to serve unless such occasion for local service be required. The sole object of putting them in Confederate service being- that should any be taken prisoners they can be *exchanged*. No troops in the service of any State when taken prisoners can be exchanged, the U. S. Government only dealing with the Confederate Government These men can and must remain at home just as though not in the service until their officers call them out on the approach of the enemy. All the details of these duties can be arranged by the men and officers when they assemble. The whole being more particularly to gain and give information and act as guides when necessary.

Such a company as this for local purposes I commanded in Mississippi long before secession and for domestic tranquility at home. A very heavy penalty was attached to any member who did not assemble with his gun and ammunition at *one* of the rendezvous, or at the nearest rendezvous to the point where his services might be required on notice from any member of the

---

[307] See p. 204, 142n.
[308] See p. 364, 217n.
[309] See p. 113, 447n.

company, consequently each knew he would meet the others there. By such a system as this all approach of the enemy could be made known and preparation be made to meet him more successfully by our Army.

I deem it much preferable to calling out Militia and taking them from their homes. Besides this is a revolution of the people and those out of the Army are as deeply interested as those mustered into service- All good citizens must aid.

I has been truly said- "That when a people are suddenly called to fight for their liberty and are sorely pressed upon, their last field of battle is the floors upon which their children have played: the chambers where the family of each man has slept: upon and under the roofs of which they have been sheltered: in the gardens of their recreation, in the streets or in the marketplace: before the altars of their temples and among their congregated dwellings, blazing and uprooted-" And if the people cannot do all or part of this, they can organize, and ambush the enemy by the way side and dog his steps and harass him at every swamp and crossing in these counties.

Some of the best and most influential citizens should by their presence and example be with the parties engaged in obstructing the rivers and not sit idle smoking the pipe of peace by their family firesides and calling solely on our poor soldiers to do all! We must all unite against a common and barbarous enemy who disregards most of the customs of civilized war

[Raleigh]
[Vance Letter Book, 1862-1863,
State Department of Archives and History, Raleigh.]

To E. Stanly [310]

Raleigh, Nov. 24th 1862.

Having received and read your letter of the 7th inst, [311] a proper sense of self-respect and of regard to the position I occupy compels me to return it herewith to its author.

I have only to say Sir, by way of conclusion to this correspondence, which I thought had ended with my reply to your first, that you should by this time have been convinced that your mission to North Carolina was a failure, miserable and complete.

Coming to the people who had often honored you, in the wake of destroying armies; assuming to be governor of the State by

[310] See p. 272, 342n.
[311] See p. 317. Stanly's letter of November 7, along with the previous correspondence, is published in *O. R.*, Ser. III, Vol. II, 845, with a covering letter from Stanly to Edwin M. Stanton, secretary of war, dated November 20, 1862, in which Stanly stated that he still believed that if the people of North Carolina were allowed free expression of their wishes and opinions that they would decide to abandon the Confederacy.

the Suffrages of abolition bayonetts red with the blood of your kindred and friends, how could you expect it to be otherwise?

Do you not Know sir, that your name is execrated, and only pronounced with curses in North Carolina. Could any sane citizen believe in the "blessings" which you propose to bestow upon the people whom you betrayed and seek to subjugate, or trust your professions of a desire to mitigate the evils of war, in the presence of the damnable atrocities every day committed almost under your very eye, upon a defenceless and unarmed people?

Are you aware Sir, of the shooting of a private citizen, of the burning of the villages of Hamilton and Williamston, turning naked women and children out upon the bare earth, and of the vandal destruction of property on the Roanoke by Gen. Foster's command recently?[312] Do you know the fact that two helpless females were recently, almost in gun-shot of the town of New Bern, seized by a brutal Soldiery

"With liberty of the bloody hand
And conscience wide as hell"

and forced to submit to the last and crowning outrage which can be inflicted on the Sex?

Are you informed Sir, lastly, that even the sleeping dust of the dead- of the great and good dead of North Carolina has been *robbed* of its covering in sight of that man who speaks of himself as a "son of North Carolina", "Solicitous for her honor", who comes to "Confer blessings" and who "thanks heaven that he is the representative of a government" &c?.

When you use your influence to suppress these outrages of your associates, nay when you avow yourself ashamed of them, then and not till then, will your professions be entitled to slightest credence.

No Sir, the people of North Carolina know all these things, and have learned well the character of their foes, and the nature of the "blessings" in store for them. Her "Chief Magistrate" too appreciates his position, and glories in the fact that he represents a people who are prepared for the worst and have sincerely resolved to endure all, even as their fathers did, which a merciless foe can inflict, for the sacred cause of liberty and independence

Dismiss therefore your hopes of the subjugation of North Carolina through the weakness and baseness of her people. She *may* be subjugated, you *may* reach her Capitol and take possession of her government, the fortunes of War are fickle. But I assure you upon the honor of a Son, who will follow as he has followed and maintained her, *whether right or wrong,* who has every means of Knowing the sentiments of her people, that you can only do so over the dead bodies of the men who once respected you,

---

[312] See p. 365, 218n.

through the smoking ashes of the homes which once greeted you with hospitable welcome, and through fields desolated, which once gladdened your eye, rich with the glorious harvest of peace. New Berne

[A. L. S. (Copy), Z. B. Vance Papers,
State Department of Archives and History, Raleigh.]

From J. W. McElroy [313]

Asheville Bla Mon
November 24th 1862

I received a letter from Col J. B. Palmer [314] last week in which he requested me to write to you and ask you to write to him and give the charges made against him in a petition sent you from Mitchell County as he is desirous of seting him self right before you and the community. I saw the Petition when in the hand of Solicitor Merrimon [315] and am fully satisfied that there were many false statements in it and I have understood many of the names forged that were to the Petition.

I wish to know if it is my duty to enroll Mens names as Conscripts from 18 to 40 years of age, without a special order from the Adjt Genel of our State. [316] We have no jail in our County and I find it will give me great trouble to take all the prisoners, one by one to the camp of instruction near Raleigh, and the number of deserters seems to accumulate rather than diminish, Please give me orders to lodge them in the nearest jail.

I hope you will write me soon on this subject and also tel me if a company was organized in this or in the county of Yancey If it would be received into the service of our state or the Confederate States.

Will you be so kind as to hand the enclosed two dollars to Mr. W. Holden [317] and tel him to send me his weekly Standard, and to commence at the beginning of the present Session. I am at Roberts [318] he is nearly well and will leave this week.

[Raleigh]

[A. L. S. Governors' Papers (Vance),
State Department of Archives and History, Raleigh.]

---

[313] See p. 96, 361n.

[314] John B. Palmer, of Mitchell County, colonel of the Fifty-eighth North Carolina Regiment. In 1864 he was detailed from his regiment, then in the Army of Tennessee, and succeeded Brigadier General Robert B. Vance, who had been captured, as commander of the district composing western North Carolina. Moore, *N. C. Roster,* III, 633; Clark, *N. C. Regts.,* IV, 371.

[315] See p. 13, 65n.

[316] By Special Orders, No. 245, October 20, 1862, the adjutant general in Richmond ordered officers commanding camps of instruction to extend enrollment of conscripts to all men not subject to exemption who were between the ages of eighteen and forty. *O. R.,* Ser. IV, Vol. II, 133.

[317] See p. 127, 499n.

[318] Robert B. Vance. See p. 2, 6n.

To Jefferson Davis

STATE OF NORTH CAROLINA
EXECUTIVE DEPARTMENT
Raleigh Nov. 25th 1862

In accordance with my recommendation the Legislature has determined to raise 10000 men to assist in the winter campaign.[319] I am requested by the Military Committee to write your Excellency to know if it will be possible to get any assistance in Arms & Munitions from the Confederacy. And also if your Excellency would object to the State organization embracing the remainder of the Conscripts under thirty five years of age.[320]

---

[319] In his message to the legislature, November 17, 1862, Vance recommended the "raising of at least ten regiments of reserves, to be accepted for three or four months, and dismissed in time to pitch their crops in the Spring." The troops were to be primarily for the defense of the eastern counties and for aid in withdrawing the abundant supplies therein. The justification was that in September 1861, just after the fall of Hatteras had alarmed the state, the legislature had, by the passage of several bills, authorized the governor to raise troops for the defense of the state. But difficulties had arisen—especially the passage of the conscript laws—and no troops for state defense had been raised. "It is for you, therefore to say, whether you will suffer our defences as heretofore, to remain exclusively in the hands of the Confederate authorities, or take steps to carry out the will of the last Legislature, and raise troops enough on State authority to strengthen the weak hand of the General Government on our coast." *Legislative Documents, 1862-1863,* Document No. 1, p. 2.

[320] The Ten Regiment Bill was introduced into the House of Commons on November 22, 1862, by James H. Foy, of Onslow County, who had talked with Vance about the situation in the eastern counties and who had been the agent of a special meeting of citizens, held on September 27, to bring resolutions calling upon the state for military aid to the notice of the governor. See p. 268, 329n. The legislature debated the bill for several weeks and sent a committee to Richmond to confer with President Davis concerning it. To those who argued that the previous legislature had authorized such a force, the answer was that circumstances had materially changed since September 1861, and what seemed a reasonable measure then seemed defiance of the Confederacy a year later, when two conscription bills laid claim to the very men from whom the ten regiments must largely come. Therefore several attempts were made to change the measure and to soften the intent and meaning of the proposed step. These efforts were usually led by Democrats, such as S. J. Person of New Hanover and M. Q. Waddell of Chatham. Person introduced a resolution that the regiments be composed of men "not called, nor liable to be called into the service of the Confederate States under the conscription law, which latter may be accepted and enrolled by the consent of the President of the Confederate States." This was defeated in the House of Commons by a vote of 37-61. *House Journal, 1862-1863,* pp. 94-95 (December 11, 1862). On December 15 M. Q. Waddell offered a preamble that "this Legislature . . . desire to be understood as offering no impediment to the operation of the Conscription Act of Congress, and disclaiming any intention to throw itself in conflict with the President of the Confederate States or the authorities at Richmond, but simply to carry out the provisions of an act of the General Assembly, by which a State force shall be organized." This effort was also defeated in the House of Commons by a vote of 41 to 44. *House Journal, 1862-1863,* pp. 109-110. On December 16 J. S. Amis tried to exclude persons under 40 who were liable to conscription, unless the conscript law was suspended. This also lost by a vote of 37 to 49. *House Journal, 1862-1863,* p. 119. The bill passed the House of Commons the same day by a vote of 53 to 36, but it later failed in the Senate. There was a great deal of discussion about the proposed measure in the press of the state, and in Richmond. The Richmond

The reason for asking the latter question is because it is thought that the State authorities could get out a considerable number of that class which the Confederate Officers would not be able to reach.

Please to answer at once, as the Committees action will wait your reply and time is everything

[Richmond]

[Vance Letter Book, 1862-1863,

State Department of Archives and History, Raleigh.]

From D. L. Swain [321]

Chapel Hill, 25. Nov. 1862

I fear that in your hurried interview with Prof. Fetter [322] yesterday, you had no opportunity to understand the importance to us of his application. No crib that you propose in your message to supply on the N. C. Rail Road will serve more pressing needs than ours.[323] A few of us have advanced more than $3000 for 650 barrels of corn below Goldsboro which is to be distributed in small lots, and will go into the hands of those mainly who have husbands, or sons in the army. The contract for the corn was made & partial promises obtained for its transportation 3 weeks ago. Corn subsequently purchased by private persons is understood to have been transported to Raleigh & Hillsboro- A great blunder (to use no harsher term) was committed, in locating the road, if we are allowed to receive it at all, we must haul it from Durham, 12 miles, and I trust that after individual liberality and enterprize have attempted to do for the university,

---

Enquirer, generally regarded as a mouthpiece of the president and administration, charged that the bill was in conflict with the Confederate laws and that "a plot exists in Raleigh to break the unity of the Confederacy, and point the path to anarchy and subjugation." Quoted in Raleigh *North Carolina Standard,* December 23, 1862. The Charlotte *Bulletin,* according to the same source, thought that the plot in Raleigh should be broken up by the president who "ought to send a regiment to Raleigh, and arrest and punish every man engaged in the damnable plot." Raleigh *North Carolina Standard,* January 13, 1863. Holden vigorously defended the measure and printed the bill, together with the substitutes attempted by Person and the Democrats, in the Raleigh *North Carolina Standard,* December 31, 1862.

[321] See p. 9, 45n.

[322] Manuel Fetter, professor of ancient languages and bursar of the University of North Carolina from 1838 to 1868. He was of German descent, was born in Lancaster, Pa. in 1809, and came to Chapel Hill from New York. Battle, *History of U. of N. C.,* I, 451.

[323] In his message to the legislature, November 17, 1862, Vance recommended the purchasing and storing of at least two hundred thousand bushels of corn and five hundred thousand pounds of pork to be sold to the wives and children of soldiers at moderate prices. Anticipating this measure, he had already "ordered the building of large cribs on the N. C. R. Road and made other preliminary arrangements for purchasing on a large scale." *Legislative Documents, 1862-1863,* Document No. 1, p. 5.

and the poor and needy around us, what the public propose to do for them on the immediate line of road, we are not to be thwarted in our purpose.

I know you are very busy, neither need, nor have leisure, to scan minute statements and therefore, I write briefly. I may be permitted to advert nevertheless to the fact that the State owns three fourths of the stock, and that no village in proportion to its means did more in seeking the original individual subscription of stock than Chapel Hill.

[Raleigh]

An intimation from you to Mʳ. Webb³²⁴ of your desire to have an accommedation will probably be effective. Mʳ. Mickle³²⁵ our agent is at Goldsboro waiting advices.

[on reverse] Ansʳ that I have arranged to bring up the corn. ZBV

[A. L. S. Governors' Papers (Vance),

State Department of Archives and History, Raleigh.]

From A. A. Harbin ³²⁶

Mocksville Nov. 25ᵗʰ 1862

Mr. Hendrix,³²⁷ of this County, who saw you a few days ago, was drafted in March & afterwards volunteered in a cavalry Company, but the Company was never organized. These being the facts in the case does he not come under the Conscript Law passed April 16ᵗʰ 1862? Please answer immediately.

[Raleigh]

[on reverse]

Certainly, if he is of the proper age   Z B V

[A. L. S.   Governors' Papers (Vance),

State Department of Archives and History, Raleigh.]

---

³²⁴ Thomas Webb (1827-1894), of Hillsboro, a lawyer who had become president of the North Carolina Railroad Company on February 7, 1862.

³²⁵ Andrew Mickle, a merchant of Chapel Hill, who was sent by thirty heads of families to make purchases for them. According to a calculation made in November 1862 by Charles Phillips, Mickle bought 383 barrels of corn, equal to 1921 bushels, for $1,897.95. The freight to Durham was $349.70; the cost of bringing it from Durham to Chapel Hill by wagon was $327.51. Mickle's expenses were $172.35. Adding minor expenses, the cost of the corn at Chapel Hill was $2,460.61, or $6.75 per barrel. It was distributed in varying amounts from two barrels upward, according to demand. President Swain took 33 barrels. Battle, *History of U. of N. C.,* I, 725.

³²⁶ Allen Alexander Harbin, colonel of the Seventy-seventh Regiment of North Carolina Militia, of Davie County. Militia Roster, pp. 282-283. He was afterwards a major in the Third Battalion of Home Guards. Clark, *N. C. Regts.,* IV, 650.

³²⁷ Probably N. G. Hendrix, of Davie County, who enlisted in company E of the Forty-second North Carolina Regiment on March 18, 1862. Moore, *N. C. Roster,* IV, 183.

From S. L. Fremont [328]

WILMINGTON AND WELDON RAIL ROAD COMPANY OFFICE CHIEF ENGINEER AND SUPERINTENDENT
Wilmington N. C. Nov. 25th- 1862

I learn from Mr Dickinson[329] that you complain of this Road for not hauling Cotton belonging to the State.

Lest you may not be informed of the facts I write this—

An agent of the State called on me with a letter from your Aid-de-Camp, Col. Little,[330] requesting transportation for 212 bales of Cotton from Wilson & 64 bales from Taboro all to Goldsboro—

I immediately agreed to transport this cotton as soon as it was placed on the platforms of the company— the cotton having been stored under sheds some distance from the Road—

This delivery was to be made & I was to be informed of the fact when I should have directed the cotton to be hauled to Goldsboro—

This information has not yet been furnished, hence the delay in hauling the cotton

I will now make an arrangement with Mr Whitford[331] of the

---

[328] Sewall L. Fremont (1823-1886), a native of Vermont, chief engineer and superintendent of the Wilmington and Weldon Railroad Company. He graduated from West Point in 1841 and resigned from the army in 1854 to accept his position with the railroad, where he remained until 1871, when he accepted the same position with the Wilmington, Charlotte, and Rutherford Railroad Company. When he retired from railroading in 1876 he became a rice planter near Wilmington for a year or so, then was the city surveyor of Wilmington, 1880-1881, and an architect in the service of the United States, 1881-1886. He was also the architect and, briefly, the superintendent of the North Carolina Asylum for the Colored Insane, near Goldsboro. When the war came he was nominated by Governor Ellis as adjutant and inspector-general of the state forces, but Warren Winslow, chairman of the Military and Naval Board, persuaded Ellis that Fremont, because of his army artillery experience, was needed more in that branch of the service. Fremont to Winslow, May 24, 1861, Winslow to Ellis (no date), Minutes of Military Board, May 22, 1861, pp. 17-18. Accordingly he was commissioned by the states to build special defence works in the engineer corps, and became colonel of artillery and engineers of the Cape Fear district. He was also colonel of artillery in the militia. When the state turned over its forces to the Confederate government no provisions were made for engineer officers, and Fremont continued to serve for some time without pay and without a commission. *Wilmington Journal*, August 15, 1876; Clark, *N. C. Regts.*, IV, 413, 416, 422; Militia Roster, p. 495; Cullum, *Biog. Register*, II, 82-83, which has the curious note that he was named Sewall L. Fish when he graduated.

[329] P. K. Dickinson, of Wilmington, lumber dealer and railroad promoter. He was a northern man by birth who came to Wilmington and was a leading spirit in promoting the Wilmington and Weldon Railroad, of which he was a director during his lifetime. The *Fayetteville Observer*, September 29, 1862, said that he declined the presidency of the road when Ashe died that month. Sprunt, *Chronicles*, p. 149.

[330] See p. 359, 199n.

[331] John Dalton Whitford, of New Bern, president of the Atlantic and North Carolina Railroad Company. He had long been interested and active in internal improvements; was a director of the Neuse River Navigation Company and of the railroad before he became president in 1854. He remained its president until removed by military authority after the war, but became president again upon the restoration of home rule. For a time during the war he was ordnance officer for

Atlantic & N. C. R R to take this cotton all the way to Raleigh if it meets with your approbation—

I addressed you a telegram from Rocky Mount on thursday last when I was en route to Richmond asking your cooperation to obtain some Engines from the A & C R R to assist in hauling out the crop from the Eastern counties now pressing us to our utmost & beyond our ability to remove—

The yellow fever has crippled our machinery to such an extent by scattering our mechanics that unless some aid is supplied from abroad the produce of the east will I fear in large part fall in to the hands of the enemy.

It behooves *us all to unite our energies* in a common cause & rescue this means of subsistence for our army & people—
Raleigh
[A. L. S.   Governors' Papers (Vance),
  State Department of Archives and History, Raleigh.]

From J. B. Fitzgerald [332]

Richland Valley
Haywood Co N. C.
Nov. 25th 1862

It is with some diffidence I presume to address you not being accustomed to corresponding with men in high position, however I hope your excellency may indulge me— "hear me for my cause" The object of this communication is to refer to our condition in this Country, of which you may have been apprised ere this, and beg of you some aid so far as you may think practicable and demanded. I suppose you are apprised of the murder of Nolande[333] and the conviction of Franklin[334] who was strongly ironed in our jail. On last Tuesday night a number of armed men attacked the jail & brok through and cut Franklin loose and marched off with him, threatening to burn up the Town, There were thought to be 30 or 40 in the crowd, and before a sufficient force could be

---

the state, with the rank of major in the transportation department of the Confederacy. In 1865 he established the shipping house of Whitford, Dill & Company, from New Bern to New York; from 1867 to 1871 he was financial agent for the Raleigh and Augusta Airline Railway, and from 1885 to 1888 was assistant engineer in charge of government work on Tar River. Politically Whitford held only a few offices: he was collector of customs at New Bern under President Taylor, was mayor of New Bern in 1853-1854, a member of the Convention of 1861, and of the State Senate in 1865. Connor, *N. C. Manual*, 572, 875; McCormick, *Personnel*, pp. 87-88; John D. Whitford Papers, State Department of Archives and History, Raleigh, N. C. (cited hereafter as Whitford Papers).

[332] John B. Fitzgerald, a lawyer of Haywood County, who abandoned legal practice after the war. Allen, *Annals of Haywood*, p. 166.

[333] The Nolande family was a prominent one in Haywood County. There is a good sketch of the family in Allen, *Annals of Haywood*, pp. 376-383, but there is no evidence to tell which one of the family is referred to in this letter.

[334] J. H. Franklin.

collected they were in the mountains beyond Jonathan creek. A number of our Citizens and Indians persued them to Tenn line and learned the force collected in these were too strong for them, stoped and sent for more force. The Malitia have been called out and troops have been sent for to Ten. to come up from the other Side. There are supposed to be several hundred deserters, Tories and rascals collected in them. We are apprehensive of a good deal of Troble. Our Citizens are very much excited. This state of things is likely to continue and grow worse during the war if not promptly met and force kept in these mountains between here and Ten. to keep them in check.

This trouble is not altogether with our citizens, for the body of whom are civil and law abiding men. You are aware then there is an extensive mountain country between here and Ten. through which are scattered inhabitants and some disaffected and unreliable, and a good many such on the Ten. side and when pressed on either side, run to the other.

Perhaps no section affords such advantages for concealment and evading law as this, and if not broken up, and its' found, such as get in there go with impunity, it gives encouragement to deserters from the army, tories and outlaws in the surrounding country, and such puts in jeopardy the homes, the property and even lives of our Citizens, for these scoundrels must live. They may penetrate the interior of our country, even in day light, unseen, by following some of the smaller mountains leading from the large ones, and off without much chance of being apprehended. Our citizens, if needed, deserve protection, for according to numbers and means have contributed well to the war. We haven't the means of defence and does seem that men can't all leave and the people live, for we have but few slaves to produce for us should in view of this and the circumstances refered to no more of our men ought to be called off from here

It is scarcely worth while to put them in jail if any are caught, without a standing guard. It does seem to me there ought to be a company or two ordered in here and one at least, remain and if necessary our men liable under the conscript law, be allowed to form a company to remain in these mountains and arms and ammunition provided, such would tend to quiet our folks, and to satisfy their friends in the army, for they can't remain in the army quiet, when their homes and property are unprotected. I am satisfied in the above I but speake the sentiment of our citizens and if necessary could get a petition from the whole county. Can't you do something or suggest for us? Your humble Sevt.
[Raleigh]
[A. L. S. Governors' Papers (Vance),
State Department of Archives and History, Raleigh.]

From W. F. Bason[335]

Nov. 25th 1862

As I am anxious to serve my country in this time of our extremity & believing I could be of more real service in mitigating the pains & suffering from bad Teeth in the Army, I beg leave most respectfully to call your attention to the propriety of a Dentist to our suffering soldiers.

I notice in the northern army they dignified Chiropedists to; or by giving them appointments in the mitigation of pain by removing excrescences from the feet; & as I have devoted the greater portion of my life to the Teeth, It would be humiliating to think, that my profession does not stand as high in the south, as operating upon the *toes* does in the N.

"A word to the wise is sufficient."

If you have forgotten me, I beg to refer your Honor to Gov. Swain,[336] Giles Mebane[337] Esqr & others— I would like an office in Raleigh or any place you think proper to call or send me.
[Raleigh]
[on reverse]

The Govr would like to see Dr Bason in Raleigh operating on Soldiers teeth, but can not give him an appointment with army for that purpose

Z B V

[A. L. S. Governors' Papers (Vance), State Department of Archives and History, Raleigh.]

From Jefferson Davis

Circular
Executive Department
Richmond Nov. 26th. 1862

The present condition of public affairs induces me to address this circular to the Government of the several States on a subject of vital importance to the people.

The repeated defeats inflicted on the Federal forces in their attempt to conquer our Country have not yet sufficed to satisfy them of the impossibility of success in their nefarious designs to subjugate these States. A renewed attempt on a still larger scale

[335] W. F. Bason was a well-known dentist who had been practicing his profession for nearly twenty years. He was a graduate of the Philadelphia Medical College and of the Baltimore Dental College, and had practiced in Mississippi, and in Salisbury and Graham, N. C. *Asheville News*, November 9, 1854; Raleigh *North Carolina Standard*, January 5, 1861; *Raleigh Register*, February 14, 1855.
[336] See p. 9, 45n.
[337] See p. 217, 171n.

is now in progress: but with manifest distrust of success in a warfare conducted according to the usages of civilized nations. The United States propose to add to the enormous land and naval forces accumulated by them, bands of such of the African Slaves of the South as they may be able to wrest from their owners, and thus to inflict on the non combatant population of the Confederate States, all the horrors of a servile war, super added to such atrocities as have already been committed on numerous occasions by their invading forces.

To repel such attacks conducted on so vast a scale, the most energetic action of every department of the Government is directed, but appreciating the great value of the cordial cooperation of the different State Governments and with unfaltering reliance on their patriotism and devotion to our cause, I earnestly appeal to them for all the aid it may be in their power to extend to the officers of the War Department in the discharge of their duties within the several States, and for their cooperation in the following important particulars.

1. In the enrolment of the Conscripts and the forwarding of them to the proper points of rendezvous.

2. In restoring to the Army all officers and men now within the States, absent without leave, or whose term of absence has expired, or who have recovered from disability and are now able to return to duty—

3. In securing for the use of the Army all such necessary supplies as exists within the State in excess of the quantity indispensible for the support of the people at home.

Prompt action in these matters will save our people from very great suffering: and will put our Army in a condition to meet the enemy with decisive results, and thus secure for us an early and honorable peace on the basis of recognized independence.

In addition to the above urgent matters I beg respectfully to ask the aid of the Executives of the several States in recommending to the several Legislatures such legislation as will enable the Governor to command the slave labor to the extent which may be required in the prosecution of works conducive to the public defence:[338] also the adoption of some means to suppress the shame-

---

[338] In his message to the legislature, November 17, 1862, Vance had anticipated this request and had recommended to that body that "Inasmuch as it may become necessary for slave labor to be employed on State defences, . . . I would respectfully recommend the propriety of the passing of an act whereby such authority may be vested in me, in case such urgent necessity should arise, as will justify it." *Legislative Documents, 1862-1863,* Document No. 1, p. 3. On December 20, 1862, the legislature passed an act carrying out the recommendation, and providing "That the Governor shall have power and authority to compel the services of any number of slaves in erecting fortifications and works for the defence of the state." The law also provided for compensation and for indemnity in case of loss to the enemy. *Public Laws of N. C., 1862-1863,* chap. 16.

ful extortions[339] now practised upon the people by men who can be reached by no moral influences and who are worse enemies of the Confederacy that if found in Arms among the invading forces. The armies in the field as well as the families of the soldiers and others of the people at home are the prey of these mercenaries and it is only through State action that their traffic can be repressed. Their condign punishment is ardently desired by every patriot.
[Raleigh]
[A. L. S. Governors' Papers (Vance),
State Department of Archives and History, Raleigh.]

From S. D. Wallace[340]

OFFICE WILMINGTON AND WELDON RAIL ROAD CO.
OFFICIAL BUSINESS
Wilmington, N. C. Nov 26th 1862

A friend of mine has just informed me that your Excellency had addressed me one or more letters relative to transportation of Cotton & that you thought proper attention had not been given thereto. The facts are that I was waited on at Warsaw by Mr Litchford with an order from Col Little[341] requesting the transpon. aforesaid— I replied that I would do all I could to facilitate it & advised him to proceed to the next station (Magnolia) & see

---

[339] In the same message Vance also spoke of extortion and recommended action especially against those who represented themselves falsely to be agents of the Confederate government in order to obtain provisions. He recommended the prohibition of the export of certain articles of prime necessity from the state except by regular agents of the government for the army, and except for contracts already made. "This is all the remedy I can suggest for the evils of extortion—history and common sense have taught us the danger of trying to force trade, which refuses to be governed by any but natural laws." *Legislative Documents, 1862-1863*, Document No. 1, pp. 4-5. On February 11, 1863, the legislature followed with an act which provided that any person who purchased certain specified articles by false representation that they were purchased for the army was guilty of a misdemeanor and fined $500 and six months in prison, as a minimum penalty. *Public Laws of N. C., 1862-1863*, adjourned session, chap. 56. Previously, on November 22, 1862, the legislature had adopted a resolution "That the Governor be authorized to lay an immediate embargo on all articles of . . . prime necessity, except articles held by properly authorized agents of this and the Confederate States, and any other State of the Confederate States; and this resolution shall have the force and effect of law, for the space of thirty days from and after its passage." *Public Laws of N. C., 1862-1863*, pp. 53-54.

[340] Stephen D. Wallace, of Wilmington, president of the Wilmington and Weldon Railroad Company, having been elected president after the accidental death of William S. Ashe in September 1862. Wallace had been for many years one of the officers of the road, having served as general ticket agent, assistant secretary, bookkeeper, and accountant. He was also chairman of the school board of Wilmington and in 1864 served as chairman of the Wilmington relief association. After the war he was a commission merchant in Wilmington. *Fayetteville Observer*, September 29, 1862; *Wilmington Journal*, September 7, 1864; S. D. Wallace to Calvin H. Wiley, February 23, 1864, Wiley Papers CH.

[341] See p. 359, 199n.

our Sup^t. Col. Fremont—^{342} he did so, & next morning returned with Col Fremont, when I was informed as soon as the Cotton was ready, notice was to be given us, & we would send a train for it— We have had a train hauling cotton & yours would have been transported had we been informed it was ready. I assure you Govr. that it is my desire to aid the State by every means I can, public or private.

It is only necessary to inform me as to your wishes— the order refered to is the only communication I have rec^d.
[Raleigh]
[A. L. S. Governors' Papers (Vance),
State Department of Archives and History, Raleigh.]

From C. W. Garrett [343]

Quarter Masters Department
Raleigh Nov 26, 1862

In consequence of the magnitude of donations for the benefit of our troops, many of which are special,[344] for the receiving of which and the proper distribution of the same according to the wishes of the donors requires so much labor and time, that I find it impossible to attend to the other duties of my department and bestow upon this that atention the importance of the case requires.

I would therefore suggest to your Excellency the necessity of appointing a commissioned officer, to continue until those donations shall cease, charged with the duties of receiving all contributions, as well as the purchases of Militia Officers; further, to make arrangements for forwarding all special donations by agents employed, according to the wishes of the donors, taking such agents, receipts and requiring them on delivery of the goods to get receipts from the proper or authorised officer of the Regiment or company to which the recipient may belong.

The additional expense to the State by such appointments can be but little, as I find the room I now occupy is entirely insufficient to do the business, while other and efficient services will also be required.

Hoping this suggestion will meet your approbation I am Sir
[Raleigh]
[A. L. S. Governors' Papers (Vance),
State Department of Archives and History, Raleigh.]

---

[342] See p. 397, 328n.
[343] See p. 190, 96n.
[344] Vance's appeal for gifts for the soldiers and his orders to the militia provided that supplies could be specified for particular individuals or units. See pp. 265-267, and General Orders, No. 9, p. 305, 46n.

From S. P. Arrington[345]

Warrenton N. C. Nov. 26th- 1862

I dislike to trouble you but situated as I am I feel it my duty to have something more definite. You are aware the understanding Mr. White[346] had with the Gov was that I was to remain at home during his absence, You are also aware the Sec of War refused to grant the detail recommended by the Gov. Mr. White before leaving Raleigh the last time mentioned to the Gov that my sick furlough had expired and I had nothing to show why I remained at home, his reply was to write to me stating he would be responsible for my absence and to remain at home until he could see the President when he thought there would be no difficulty in arranging the matter. The message sent by the Gov through Mr. W is probably all that is necessary, but I would feel much better satisfied if I had a paper directly from Hd. Quarters ordering me to remain. Will you be kind enough to make an arrangement that would exhonerate me from all blame in the matter if there should ever be any attached. I have the honor to be Very Respectfully Yr obt Servt

[Raleigh]

[A. L. S. Governors' Papers (Vance),
State Department of Archives and History, Raleigh.]

Proclamation

[Nov. 26, 1862]
By the Governor of North Carolina
A Proclamation

Whereas, in order to stop, if possible, the wicked system of speculation which is blighting the land & prevent the production of famine in the midst of plenty, the Legislature of North Carolina, by Joint Resolution[347] thereof ratified on the 22d. day of this month (November) have authorized me to lay an embargo upon the exportation from the State of certain articles of prime necessity, except to certain persons and for certain purposes.

Now therefore, I Zebulon B. Vance Governor of the State of North Carolina, do issue this my Proclamation, forbidding all persons, for the space of thirty days, from the date hereof, from carrying beyond the limits of the State, any salt, bacon, pork,

---

[345] See p. 290, 4n. This letter is addressed to George Little, aide to Vance.
[346] His father-in-law. See p. 288, 1n.
[347] See *Public Laws of N. C., 1862-1863*, pp. 53-54 and above p. 402, 339n. The comment of the Salisbury *Watchman* is typical of the reception of this proclamation: it said that large quantities of goods about to be shipped out of Salisbury marked "army supplies" but destined for private hands in Richmond to be sold on speculation, could now be seized. "'This document will fall among the speculators like a bombshell.'" Quoted in Raleigh *North Carolina Standard*, December 5, 1862.

beef, corn meal, flour, potatoes, shoes, leather, hides, cotton cloth, and yarn and woollen cloth. The following persons are alone to be exempted from this prohibition—viz.

All Quarter Masters and Commissary Agents of the Confederate Government, and of any State of the Confederacy exhibiting proper evidence of their official character. Also all Agents of any County, district, town or corporations of other States, who shall exhibit satisfactory proof of their authority to purchase such articles in behalf of such town, county districts, or corporation for public uses or distribution at cost and transportation and not for resale or profit: Also all persons who make oath before the nearest Justice of the Peace that the articles purchased are for his own private use and not for resale before they are removed. Also all persons non residents, who may have bought such articles before the dates hereof. The exception is to extend to salt made by non residents on the sea coast and in their own works and to cargoes entering any of our ports from abroad. Any of said articles that may be stopped in transit from our borders are to be confiscated to the use of the State. Until further orders the Colonels of Militia in the different counties are enjoined to see that this Proclamation is enforced.

Not intending or desiring to prevent the people of our Sister States from sharing with our own citizens whatever we can spare but to repress speculation so far as may be possible. I earnestly appeal to all good citizens to aid and sustain me in the enforcement of this proclamation for the common good.

In witness thereof Zebulon B Vance Governor Captain General and Commander in Chief hath signed these presents and caused the Great Seal of the State to be affixed.

Done at our City of Raleigh, this 26th. day of November A. D. 1862 and in the year of our Independence the 87th.

Z. B. Vance

By the Governor
    R. H. Battle
        Private Secretary
[Vance Letter Book, 1862-1863,
State Department of Archives and History, Raleigh.]

From John D. Whitford[348]

Goldsboro, Nov 27th 1862

Mr Wallace[349] goes up to-day. I will endeavour to get our train of cotton up the No. Ca. Road to-morrow But there will be a number of trains on that Road & I may have to keep it here until Sunday or Monday Morning— If you desire me to aid you on

[348] See p. 397, 331n.
[349] See p. 402, 340n.

getting your salt from Virginia I would suggest you send me a letter to that effect as my action on the matter might be questioned, as there are so many speculators about in these days of *patriotism*— I regret to see in the Raleigh papers this morning that the Confederate Administration had the cordial endorsement of No. Ca. or rather the Legislature[350] For one I am not willing to endorse the Administration while I would cheerfully sacrifice property & even my life to sustain & uphold the Government, What did the Legislature mean by their action? I am only asking as an humble citizen of No. Ca. & believe you do not approve their action— I understand the Secretary of the Navy intends to take over Rail Road iron with or without your consent,[351] I have as yet rec.d no notice from an official source if I do I will give you the information It would never be taken without your consent, if I had the power, without a fight. I desire no hasty action in this matter but No. Ca. has been in my opinion sufficiently kicked about—
[Raleigh]
[A. L. S.   Governors' Papers (Vance),
State Department of Archives and History, Raleigh.]

From William H. Oliver[352]

Nov 27/——
62

I wrote you a large portion of the Cotton of Mr P A Atkinson was in bad order and the quality not good. The Cotton was in

---

[350] The resolution was introduced by S. J. Person of New Hanover, and Jesse G. Shepherd of Cumberland moved that the rules be suspended and it passed its third reading without a roll call vote. *House Journal, 1862-1863*, p. 43 (November 27, 1862). The resolution said "That we have full confidence in the ability and patriotism of His Excellency President Davis, and that his administration is entitled to the cordial support of all patriotic citizens." Vance and his policies were also approved in the same resolution. *Public Laws of N. C., 1862-1863*, pp. 43-44. The meaning of the resolution was the subject of speculation. It was usually regarded as a gesture from the minority original seccession Democrats to invite conciliation and persuasion rather than antagonism. By some it was considered an answer to Holden and his party of "obstructionists." Ashe, *History of N. C.*, II, 758-759.

[351] On December 20, 1862, the legislature adopted a resolution on this subject. It declared that the Confederacy had no right to seize the iron, as it belonged to the state; that the governor was to transmit this protest to the secretary of war; and that while the right to seize was denied, at the same time, if the governor thought it necessary for the public defence he might allow the Confederate government to have it, provided it was returned in kind or a reasonable money compensation supplied, as might be agreed upon between them. *Public Laws of N. C., 1862-1863*, p. 46.

[352] William H. Oliver, a merchant of New Bern. He was now an agent of the state appointed to gather supplies and especially to purchase cotton for the state to ship out in its blockade running enterprise. He was known as Captain Oliver, but he was never a staff officer, occupying much the same position in the eastern counties that James Sloan did for the western ones. Oliver's special commission to buy cotton specified that he was to pay 25 cents a pound; he later testified that he purchased about 7,000 bales, beginning nearest the enemy lines in order to get

The oldest-known picture of Asheville, North Carolina, taken in 1851 shows this view of the town and the surrounding mountains. Conspicuous in the middle section are the old courthouse, the absence of paved streets, and the wooded condition of Battery Park Hill.

the cars at Goldsboro and I thought it best not to shp it. without orders to contrary I will have Mr Atkinson Cotton placed to itself and let its merits? be decided on hereafter.

I have as pr instruction from Genl Martin[353] and Colo Little[354] made arrangements for having shelter put up so the cotton may be carefully preserved. A few hundred dollars judiciously expended in protecting the Cotton will add vastly to its future value.

I will see Mr Sumner[355] and endeavor to get a train from him immediately. I will also write the President of the Wilmington road on the same subject.[356] Mr. Whitford[357] has put in one train which I presume he will keep running— Every effort shall be made to get good Cotton, in good order, and get it off as soon as possible

Raleigh

any comumnication to me addressed at Enfield for a few days will be received. after that a few days at Tarboro.

[A. L. S.   Governors' Papers (Vance),
State Department of Archives and History, Raleigh.]

From O. G. Parsley[358]

Wilmington N. C. Nov 28 1862

Your telegram of 26th duly recd and replied to today—[359] The meeting of stockholders of W & Manchester r r [360] was yesterday

---

that out first. Furthermore, "on account of the scarcity of railroad accommodation it was a tedious matter to get the cotton moved." He took much of it to Graham, N. C. for safe-keeping. After the war Oliver was treasurer of the Atlantic and North Carolina Railroad when Vance became governor again in 1877. See his letters in Carter Papers, July 12, 1873, and in Governors' Papers (Vance), December 7, 1878. See also Clark, *N. C. Regts.*, I, 24, 32 for Oliver's account of his wartime purchasing operations.

[353] See p. 113, 447n.

[354] See p. 359, 199n.

[355] T. J. Sumner, the agent of the North Carolina Railroad at Company Shops (Burlington). Since Oliver sent much of the cotton he purchased to Graham for safe-keeping, Sumner's cooperation was necessary.

[356] Stephen D. Wallace. See p. 402, 340n.

[357] See p. 397, 331n. Whitford was president of the Atlantic and North Carolina Railroad.

[358] Oscar G. Parsley, active Whig of New Hanover County, former commissioner of public schools in Wilmington, and a director in the Wilmington and Manchester Railroad, in which he owned 1142½ shares of stock in 1862. This was more than any other private individual held. The State of North Carolina had 2,000 shares. After the war he was president of the Wilmington and Manchester Railroad. Sprunt, *Chronicles*, pp. 152, 174, 213, 297; *W & M Proceedings*, 1861, p. 7.

[359] Parsley's reply, dated November 28, 1862, advised Vance that the meeting of the stockholders of the Manchester road had been adjourned until December and that he would "write explaining fully the position of matters." O. G. Parsley to Vance, November 28, 1862, Governors' Papers (Vance).

[360] The Wilmington and Manchester Railroad had been chartered in 1847 to build a line from Wilmington into South Carolina. Before 1851 it was fostered largely by the town of Wilmington and the interests in South Carolina. In 1851 the stockholders of the Wilmington and Manchester road accepted the subscription of the State of North Carolina of $200,000 to be paid in the stock of the Wilmington

adjourned until the 11th day of December; one week after the meeting of the W & Weldon road— It was proposed by our friends to have the meeting on next Tuesday the 4th two days before that of the other road but our opponents favourable to the present officials of the Weldon Road, fearing that some action would be taken by us which might operate against their plans overruled us— We cannot controul the election of President in the W & Weldon road *without* the cooperation of the Proxy of the W & Manchester road, and the President of the latter[361] who holds the proxy and is the son in law of Mr Dickinson,[362] one of the Directors of the former and who is *personally* interested and urgently advocates the election of Mr Wallace[363] will not cast the vote for any other unless a prety sharp rod is held over him— If his, Mr Walkers election was in jeopardy it might influence his action— The proxy of the State held by our friends, together with the individual stock under our control will enable us to elect any one as President of the Manchester road [364] and Mr Walker knowing this may be influenced to cooperate with us in the proposed change at the Weldon road— This would *certainly* have been the result if the Manchester meeting could have been held first.— If therefore it is desirable to make an inroad into the heretofore alliance between the officers of the two roads by which each one influenced the election of the other it must be done now, and if Mr Walker with the knowledge that a majority of his stockholders desire a change, which change can be made by his action and still persists in oppostion to their wishes, as much as I regard him personally and as willing and indeed anxious as I have been

and Raleigh Railroad, which became the Wilmington and Weldon Railroad in 1855. The stock was valued at par though the market value was about $60 a share. This arrangement meant that the treasurer of North Carolina exchanged 2,000 shares of Wilmington and Raleigh stock for a like number of Wilmington and Manchester. State aid was thus given to the road. *Laws of N. C., 1850-1851*, p. 518. Prior to this time the state had appointed two-fifths of the directors of the Wilmington and Raleigh road, or four out of ten. After this exchange of stock the matter of directors was adjusted by two acts of the legislature: one gave the state one director in the Wilmington and Manchester, and the other reduced the number of the state's directors in the Wilmington and Raleigh from four to three. *Laws of N. C., 1852-1853*, chaps. 145, 146; Brown, *Railroad Development*, pp. 40-43.

[361] Thomas D. Walker was president of the Wilmington and Manchester Railroad. See p. 354, 182n.

[362] P. K. Dickinson. See p. 397, 329n.

[363] Stephen D. Wallace, president of the Wilmington and Weldon Railroad. See p. 402, 340n.

[364] Walker was re-elected president, but no change was made in the Wilmington and Weldon Road, Wallace being unanimously re-elected at the December meeting, in spite of the fact that Parsley was the proxy for the state. But he was not a director of the Wilmington and Weldon and could only announce, as the state proxy, the three directors chosen, as provided by law, by the Board of Internal Improvement. *Annual Report of the President and Directors, and the Chief Engineer and Superintendent of the Wilmington & Weldon R. R Co., with the Proceedings of the General Meeting of Stockholders, December 4, 1862* (Wilmington, 1862), p. 13 (cited hereafter as *W. & W. Proceedings*).

to have him retain the Presidency of the Manchester road, I would
vote against him and put another in his place, equally competent,
but not tied down and to, other influences than those now pre-
dominent I shall leave town in the morning and return on Monday
when I hope to be able to indicate some suitable person to hold
and vote the state proxy. There are very few of our citizens yet
returned,[365] and as this whole matter is one requiring advisement
counsel and prudence and as the meeting of Manchester Stockholders does not take place until the 11th prox° I hope the delay
may not produce any *entanglements.* If the proxy were transferable
I would suggest Genl Alex McRae[366] as a proper person, but he is
in command of a company at Fort Fisher and might not be able
to attend or even to transfer— The question was raised at the
meeting yesterday as to the eligibility of a director to hold the
proxy but not decided— the charter does not forbid it
neither does any by law—[367] Mr W Wright[368] gave his opinion
when called upon as a legal gentleman that a director was
competent to hold and exercise the proxy, but I think the opinion
of many was that a large proxy was held by me, and the disposition
was to decide adversely— But for this I should have no objections
to taking the responsibility— Many are averse to taking the responsibility of holding and voting so large a proxy and against the
present Railroad influences— I myself have no such scruples— I
think the times and circumstances require and justify strong measures and unshirking decission— I do not desire or wish by any
means to have the proxy but if no one better can be appointed
I would take the burthen and exercise the right even if the
resignation of my directorship become necessary for a qualification— It will be important to know by 11 oclock Tuesday who
will hold the proxy in the Manchester, but I think it will be time
enough to telegram to you on Monday & receive reply. I hand
inclosed the communication to Mr Meares[369] placed in my hands

[365] Many citizens had left Wilmington on account of the yellow fever epidemic,
and their absence had prevented the regular meeting of the stockholders in
November.
[366] Alexander McRae, former president of the Wilmington and Weldon Railroad, 1847-1854, and one of its chief promoters. He had fought in the war of
1812; when the Civil War came he, though an old man over seventy, again took
the field in what was known as McRae's Battalion, a heavy artillery unit in
General Hebert's brigade. Sprunt, *Chronicles*, pp. 127, 150-151, 195, 320, 337,
where the name is spelled MacRae.
[367] Parsley himself held the state proxy and voted it at the meeting, *W. & W. Proceedings,* 1862, p. 13.
[368] William A. Wright, who was both an eminent member of the Wilmington
bar and a director of the Wilmington and Weldon Railroad on behalf of the
state. Sprunt, *Chronicles*, pp. 152, 187, 566. *W. & W. Proceedings,* 1862, p. 13.
[369] See p. 354, 181n. Meares had to decline to act as state proxy because of an
accident to one of his sons, which delayed him in Salisbury. See Meares to Vance,
November 22, 1862, Governors' Papers (Vance). Meares suggested Colonel Robert
H. Cowan as a good appointment in his place.

for delivery— as he was not here I retained and now hand it to you
[Raleigh]
[A. L. S. Governors' Papers (Vance),
State Department of Archives and History, Raleigh.]

From Asa I. Smith[370]

Newbern N-C
Nov 28th. 1862

On the thirtieth of last month a Yankee force arrested me on my plantation in Hyde County and carried me to Washington, from there they brought me to this place where I am detained as a political prisoner.

This evening I had an interview with Mr Edward Stanly—[371] he told me that I would detained during the war unless I took the oath of allegiance to the United States, or you agreed to an exchange of political prisoners.

Until disabled by sickness I belonged to the 18th. Reg. N. C. V. where I swore allegiance to the Confederate States and I cannot reconcile it to myself to take the Federal oath now.

Am I, on account of my loyalty to North Carolina, to remain in prison during this war? Or will you have me exchanged so that I can be of service to the State? I will be glad to reenter the service as soon as I am exchanged. Without seeking to influence your judgement I submit my case.
[Raleigh]
P. S. Mr Stanly says I can be paroled if I claim to be a soldier, but it would not be honorable for me to do so as I think I have been discharged.
[A. L. S. Governors' Papers (Vance),
State Department of Archives and History, Raleigh.]

From Jamima A. Thomas

Nov The 29 1862
NC Iredell Co

Ser it is with and aking hart and tremelous hand I seat my self this morning to inform you of my condition my only der son[372] voluntered and inlisted to fite for his country May the 2)

---

[370] Asa I. Smith was in a New Hanover company, company G of the Eighteenth North Carolina Regiment. He enlisted on April 21, 1861 and was discharged on June 1, 1862 for disability. After the war he was a planter at Sladesville, in Hyde County. Moore, *N. C. Roster*, II, 108; Carter Papers, February 28, 1869.

[371] See p. 272, 342n.

[372] Isaac H. Thomas, of Iredell, who enlisted as a private on June 13, 1861 in company H. of the Fourth North Carolina Regiment. Moore, *N. C. Roster*, I, 149.

1861 he rented my farm to Mr Shearer left my self and a sister in his car he dide last april I cold not get any person to tend my farm my dorters ar of delacate constitution my friends ar all in the army and the most of them ded my so en lar went with the recrutes in March and dide from the forteague of the battles around Richmon hour farms join he left 6 children his name was Edson he lost his life for his country my der son lives as far as I no I received a letter from him last weak he was in the valleys in Va ner strors Burge Gen Lees army & hedy N C A Troops co H car of capt Osburn[373] he is serlj in that co he is as Fin a soalder as ever lived he fort thru the battles around Richmon and in Mererland and agrate many more The God of battle has spared his life he is as tru a son as aMother ev er rased he oud 50 od dollars when he inlisted for which I was security for my land is now advertised for sale for That det he has bin Trying to pay that deat ev er since he left it has Taken all he cold get for my serport and to alorate his own sufferings The cost and in Trust on that det now amounts to ninty dollars pleas bee so condersendin as to bar with my weak partision as nesesaty compels me to apply I have made all exsersions during This awful war to do all I cold Towards cloathing the soalders tho it is hard to get much don at that the Specurlators will prove too hard for us as we have every thing to by and so little to by with som times I am all moast reddy to giv up the strugle as Thar is no ey to pitty or hand to suath her I li in a pore neighberhood Those That can as sist The nedy will not do so tha all have exceuse some say I cold of ccp't my son from going other say thars wold not have gon if it had not bin for him I had one side of bacon from the Goverment the summer after my son left is all I have hade I am in my 72 yer my husban served 6 months in the last wor he has binded 10 yer and I was left my son had age anuf to take car of this auffle war had oppresed me so I am foast to apply to you my condission is un none to my son I do not no What he wold do if he nu it pleas excuse bad speling and writing and help me if you pleas I canot see well I oald and nervus

[Raleigh]

[A. L. S. Governors' Papers (Vance),
State Department of Archives and History, Raleigh.]

---

[373] Edwin Augustus Osborne, who rose from captain of company H to colonel of the Fourth Regiment and was wounded at Seven Pines, Sharpsburg, and the Wilderness. After the war he was clerk of the superior court of Mecklenburg County, 1866-1875, practiced law in the firm of Osborne and Maxwell in Charlotte, 1875-1877, established the Thompson Orphanage and Training School in Charlotte in 1877 and was its superintendent for a decade, when he resigned his position and entered the Episcopal ministry, and became rector of Calvary Church at Fletcher, N. C. He was a nephew of superior court judge, James J. Osborne. "Address of Justice Heriot Clarkson," (1933); Alexander, *Mecklenburg County*, p. 65.

From A. S. Merrimon[374]

Morganton N. C.
Nov. 30th. 1862

I learn that the two Youngs, who escaped from the Jail in Cherokee County, have been re captured and returned to the jail. You
need not offer a reward as to them. You had better make the
reward for J. H. Franklin[375] two or three hundred Dollars. A
resolution has been introduced into the Legislature, inquireing
into the propriety of sending slaves from the eastern part of the
State to work upon our Railroad.[376] Allow me to suggest, that I
think the matter worthy of your attention. If you were to issue the
Bonds to which the Co. is entitled, they would be sold at a handsome premium and the road might be made ready to receive the
iron by the time the war closes. The slaves would be secured and
profitable to the State, if thus employed. Think of the matter.
You will be called upon to issue the Bonds if the work can go on,
I see no reason why you should not do so— Our little friend,
D[r]- Wallen[377] is the author of the Resolution. Give him a word
of encouragement. When the time to appoint new directors of
the W. N. C. R. Co. in behalf of the State,[378] if you will allow me
to suggest, I am satisfied that you ought to make a *change*. The
present directors are inefficient, or some of them are. You might
see D[r]. Powell,[379] the Pres. on the subject. He will tell you who
is active and who are not.— Don't let us loose sight of the Rail
road interests of the State! I venture to add a word, unsolicited,
in behalf of Hyman.[380] Poor fellow! What can be done for him?

[374] See p. 13, 65n.

[375] See pp. 398-399.

[376] The resolution was introduced on November 22 and provided "That the
Committee on Internal Improvements be instructed to inquire into the propriety
of authorizing the Governor to employ slaves on works of Internal Improvements
in the State." *House Journal, 1862-1863*, p. 22.

[377] Jesse Wallen, of Madison County, a physician who defeated the veteran Democrat, Colonel John A. Fagg, for the seat in August 1862. Nothing came of his
resolution in the legislature, as it was never reported out of committee. Connor,
N. C. Manual, p. 689; Raleigh *North Carolina Standard*, August 16, 1862; *House
Journal, 1862-1863*, p. 22.

[378] The state's financial interest in the Western North Carolina Railroad Company was twice that of the private stockholders. There were seven directors for
the state and four elected by the private stockholders. The state's directors included such prominent names as Nicholas W. Woodfin, W. H. Thomas, W. W.
Avery, and George F. Davidson, and some of them were now known as opponents
of the Vance—and Merrimon—wing of the Conservative party.

[379] Dr. A. M. Powell, who succeeded R. C. Pearson as president of the road in
1860. Powell was from Catawba County, the owner of the Long Island Textile
Plant and the Shoal Textile Plant, which were the first textile ventures in Catawba
County, dating back to 1839. After the war he joined with Samuel McDowell Tate
in the firm Powell & Company, manufacturers of cotton yarns and sheetings. In
the eighties he became president of the Catawba Manufacturing Company. Tate
Papers, *passim*; Charles J. Preslar, Jr., (ed.), *A History of Catawba County Compiled and Published by Catawba County Historical Association, Incorporated*
(Salisbury, 1954), p. 188 (cited hereafter as Preslar, *Catawba County*).

[380] See p. 50, 181n.

I am satisfied that he cant get the Solicitorship of the 7th. Circuit,[381] if the Ct. is made, and if he could, he has hardly experience enough to make an efficient officer. If you can, I am sure you will take care of him. I hope you will give him the first handsome position you have to dispose of, if he is qualified to discharge the duties of his office with credit to himself and benefit to the public. Pardon this liberty.

If I can serve you any way, write me.— By the by, you did not give me any definite instruction about the old press at Asheville[382] Did you write Hyman?

Keep out friends together Don't let them get out with each other and produce discord. I'm sorry indeed, they allowed the Resolution endorsing Davis to pass.[383] The effect of this ought to be counteracted by a resolution in reference to his illtreatment of our troops and brave and meritorious officers.— I hope the session will be strict, and it seems to me, the Ses. might properly adjourn to a future day, after finishing the work of immediate importance.

I remember that it is a *rumor*. that Wash. Hardy[384] Killed Dr. McDowell [385] and mortally wounded William McD.[386]— This is only rumor. I learn that Alfred Baird,[387] (Capt.) and Col Folk[388] fought some days since and the former hurt the latter. I learn this from young Hoppoldst [389] just from Tenn. I hope he is mistaken. No news—

[Raleigh]

[A. L. S. Governors' Papers (Vance),
State Department of Archives and History, Raleigh.]

---

[381] Hyman got six votes in the Senate for the solicitorship on December 12. In the House of Commons his name was withdrawn. W. P. Bynum was elected, Tod R. Caldwell being his principal opponent. *House Journal, 1862-1863*, p. 113; *Senate Journal, 1862-1863*, p. 102.

[382] See p. 378.

[383] See p. 406, 350n.

[384] See p. 43, 168n.

[385] Dr. Joseph A. McDowell, of Warm Springs, Madison County, who had been given authority to raise a battalion. Washington Hardy was then captain of a company of light artillery which became company A in the Sixteenth Regiment Joseph A. McDowell became colonel of the regiment when the battalion was enlarged. Hardy was a captain in it. Clark, *N. C. Regts.*, III, 473-474.

[386] William W. McDowell was captain of a company in the same battalion and became major of the regiment in which Joseph A. McDowell was colonel, being promoted over Hardy, whose commission outranked William McDowell's. After the battle of Murfreesboro there was an extensive reorganization of the regiment, Hardy became colonel, and the McDowells were dropped. Clark, *N. C. Regts.*, III, 473-474. See p. 63, 228n.

[387] See p. 227, 210n.

[388] See p. 81, 298n. Baird and Folk were commanders of two cavalry battalions which were later merged into one unit, the Sixty-fifth North Carolina Regiment, with Folk as colonel and Baird as lieutenant colonel. Both battalions were on scouting duty in East Tennessee and Kentucky in 1862. Clark, *N. C. Regts.*, III, 673.

[389] Probably J. M. W. Happoldt, a second class drill master who had served six months at Asheville in camp before illness forced him to stop. He was soon restored. He was a son of Dr. J. M. Happoldt, of Morganton. Dr. J. M. Happoldt to Governor Clark, June 12, 1862, Governors' Papers (Clark).

From J. R. Blanton[390]

Hanover Junction Va
Dec 1st. 1862

after my compliments to you, I wish you to bear with me while I make a statement of facts to your Excelency

I am, as you know a member of the 49th. Regt N. C. Troops, & have done good servis in the army for over eight months, and I feel it to be my duty to my family and allso to my God to make aplication got a Discharge from servis, as I am an Authorised Minister of the Gospel of the Baptist order, and wishes to return to My Aflicted family and also to attend to the Pastorial Cear of my Church, which is now Entirely without a Pastor, and while My Prayers has; and shall ever arise in Behalf of our Southern Confederacy, and though I feell duty Bound to the South, I still feel that God *Requires* me to Preach the gospil of his son I hope you will grant me this my humble Request, and will Ever Pray Pleas let me heare soon,

[Raleigh]
[A. L. S. Governors' Papers (Vance),
State Department of Archives and History, Raleigh.]

From S. W. Taylor

Hendersonville N C
December 1st- 1862

I arrived safe at home and am going to the discharge of My duty in making shoes for your soldiers. the appointment of Mr. Arledge[391] Assistnt Q. M. dos not meet with the approbation of Some of the Robble Maleitia &c But It will all come right in a short time there is some excitement & Miss Ripressentation Some of the Malisited men think they Should of had the appointnt but none of them would, of ben half as Suitable as the the Man apponted as thay neither have many or as Much Credit as Arledge nor not as enerjetic thay may get up a petertion and forward to you, for his removal from office Such a thing would be rong as the responsible part of the Community are well pleased at the appoint I hope you will not notice any effort that may be made Arledge as starting off. Some 6 or 8, 100 yd of Janes & Some 5 or 600 pr of Shoes in haste

[Raleigh]
[A. L. S. Governors' Papers (Vance),
State Department of Archives and History, Raleigh.]

---

[390] Joseph R. Blanton, fifth sergeant of company A in the Forty-ninth North Carolina Regiment, who enlisted March 24, 1862. He is not listed as a minister in Moore, *N. C. Roster*, III, 395. He was from Rutherford County.

[391] Isaac Arledge. See p. 337, 142n.

From A. C. Myers[392]

CONFEDERATE STATES OF AMERICA
QUARTER MASTER GENERAL'S DEPARTMENT
Richmond Dec 1st. 1862

I have the honor to acknowledge the receipt of your communication of the 29th ultimo.

It will afford me great pleasure to do anything in my power to further your views in regard to the subject of your letter: but, as you are aware, Congress has authorized the detail of a large number of shoemakers from the Army and it is not improbable that the stock obtained may have already been distributed, to a great extent, for manufacture.

I have, however, placed in the hands of Mr Shelly[393] an order directing Mjor Dillard A. Q. M. Columbus, Ga. to deliver, if practicable, One hundred thousand (100,000) pounds of leather to Major W. W. Peirce[394] Q. M. C. S. Army at Raleigh, to be manufactured into shoes in North Carolina
Raleigh
[Vance Letter Book, 1862-1863,
   State Department of Archives and History, Raleigh.]

From James A. Seddon[395]

CONFEDERATE STATES OF AMERICA
WAR DEPARTMENT
Richmond Va. 3d- Dec. 1862

Your letter to the President,[396] informing him of the prospect of a law for the "raising of ten thousand men in your State to assist in the winter campaign," and asking to be informed whether any assistance in arms and ammunition may be expected from the Confederation, and also to know whether objection would be entertained to the state organization embracing the remainder of the conscripts under thirty five years of age, has been referred by him to this Departmnt. In reply I have to say, that it is hoped the assurances, generally given a few days since to a committee of your Legislature in a conference with the President will have inspired the fullest confidence in the desire of the President and this Department to do all in the power of the Government for

---

[392] See p. 150, 611n.
[393] R. M. Shelly, who was an agent sent by James Sloan, who was charged with the collection of supplies for the army, to Alabama to try to find some leather for use by the shoe makers of North Carolina. Shelly found the leather and Sloan wrote to Vance suggesting that he make application to the quartermaster for a supply of it. James Sloan to Vance, from Greensboro, November 28, 1862, Governors' Papers (Vance).
[394] See p. 142, 577n.
[395] See p. 380, 273n.
[396] See Vance to Davis, November 25, p. 394.

the defence of your State;[397] and to that end, to cooperate with and advance the laudable effort of your authorities to add to existing forces. Still, while every disposition will exist in this Department to afford arms and munitions to such State force as may be raised, yet in view of possible contingencies under the exigencies of the service, the Department cannot feel certain of having arms and munitions at command, and can come under no positive engagement to supply them.

I am instructed to say that the President does not feel authorized under the existing provisions of the Conscript Law to relinquish claim on any of the persons who are made subject to its operation and liable to be called into the Confederate service. Only those beyond the prescribed age or exempt under the Law are by the intendment of that Law subject to be recruited and organized for retention in State Service, but most valuable assistance may and it is hoped will be rendered by the cooperation of the State authorities as well in enforcement of that Law, as by the employment of those not subject to conscription in swelling under State authority our means of defence.

With assurances of the highest respect and esteem
[Raleigh]
[A. L. S. Governors' Papers (Vance),
Vance Letter Book, 1862-1863,
State Department of Archives and History, Raleigh.]

From Tod R. Caldwell[398]

Morganton N C
4th Dec[r]. 1862

S. E. Poteet[399] of our County a good substantial citizen thereof

---

[397] A committee of the legislature visited the president to discuss the proposed Ten Regiment Bill with him. On December 2, 1862, the House of Commons went into secret session to hear the report of the committee, and invited Vance to be present. The legislature voted, on December 20, to pay the expenses of the committee on this trip for the public business. *Laws of N. C., 1862-1863*, p. 48; *House Journal, 1862-1863*, p. 63.

[398] Tod Robinson Caldwell (1818-1874), of Burke County, lawyer and Whig politician. He was a graduate of the University of North Carolina, read law with Swain, and entered politics in 1842, when he was elected to the House of Commons, being chosen afterwards for the same post in 1844, 1848, and 1858, and for the State Senate in 1850. After the war he became a Republican, was president of the Senate, 1868-1870, and governor, December 15, 1870-July 11, 1874. He was a life-long opponent in politics of W. W. Avery, staunch Democrat of Burke, though they were always warm personal friends. Tradition says that Caldwell turned Republican when he became embittered against the secessionists for the death of his son at Gettysburg. Statement of his brother, J. A. Caldwell, September 3, 1874, Walton Papers; Connor, *N. C. Manual*, pp. 419, 475, 522-523, 869; Raleigh *North Carolina Standard*, October 9, 1861.

[399] Sidney Erwin Poteat, second lieutenant in the Upper South Fork company of the 100th North Carolina Militia, Burke County. His record bears the curious statement "June 24, 1864-Oct. 4, 1862" Militia Roster, p. 350.

informs me that he has been elected 3rd Lieutenant in the Upper South Fork Company of the Burke Militia and that the Col has refused to send his name on for a commission alleging as a reason for this refusal that he will not send on the names of any one who is under 40 years of age- Mr. Poteet being 37 If there is any law which warrants the Col in this course I am not aware of it- tho' I admit that I am not familiar with the laws regarding the militia- The within certificate was handed to me by J. W. Carswell [400] the Capt. of the Upper Fork Company & he says that P. was regularly elected- I hope that if it be proper you will have a commission forwarded to the Lieutenant elect, he was a very warm & zealous friend of yours and belongs to the Holden[401] school of the Democracy & is very desirous to get his commission so much so that he was about to go to Raleigh to attend to in person, till I told him that I thought it unnecessary and that I would write to you on the subject- Please let me hear from you on this matter as soon as you can with convenience. I suppose you have heard that in the event of a new circuit being established I am a candidate for Solicitor-[402] Can't you forward my prospects some by speaking a good word for me to some of your acquaintances in the Legislature- I think I deserve that much at your hands.- With my best respects to Mrs. Vance

[Raleigh]

[on reverse]

Ansr. that his letter was recd. in my absence & mislaid until this morning. I can do nothing with the commission until the Col forwards certificate of election

                    Z B V

[A. L. S. Governors' Papers (Vance),
   State Department of Archives and History, Raleigh.]

To J. A. Seddon [403]

STATE OF NORTH CAROLINA
EXECUTIVE DEPARTMENT
Raleigh Dec 6th 1862

The State of North Carolina is purchasing some 15 or 20,000 bales of cotton & storing in the interior for purposes of obtaining credit abroad &c. The order to have all not removed west of

---

[400] Jonathan Wailsteel Caswell, captain in the 101st North Carolina Militia, Burke County. No officer higher than captain is listed for this regiment. Militia Roster, p. 352.

[401] See p. 127, 499n.

[402] The bill to create a new judicial circuit was introduced in the House of Commons on November 21, 1862, by John Burgin, of Buncombe. On December 12 Caldwell received eight votes in the Senate and twenty-nine in the House, but W. P. Bynum won. *House Journal, 1862-1863*, pp. 21, 103; *Senate Journal, 1862-1863*, p. 112.

[403] See p. 380, 273n.

the W. & Wilmington R. R. by the 16th inst. [burned] will embrace a large lot bought by the State.[404] Can you not order Gen French[405] to respect all such when the holders exhibit a contract of sale to the State. If so I will make arrangements to destroy it myself on the approach of the enemy.

I would respectfully suggest that the execution of that order will have a very unhappy effect on that portion of the country, not only producing great dissatisfaction, but even distress in many instances, where people have lost negroes & stock and having nothing left but their cotton to live upon.

I respectfully recommend that the order be generally delayed [Richmond]
[Vance Letter Book, 1862-1863,
State Department of Archives and History, Raleigh.]

From S. B. Erwin[406]

Marion N. C.
Dec[r]. 6th 1862

I have just understood that you might have the control, as Governor of our State, of a lot of Beef hides, & could let the same out to contract;[407] If so I would esteem it as a favor if you would give me a chance at them.

We have our Tannery ready (at last) & find it difficult to get Hides. And they have gone up so high, we would like to Tan on the shares, or by contract.

You will oblige me very much, if you have no control, to let me know what State officer has.

I wrote you several days ago on a matter personal to myself, hope you received it & can give a favorable answer. I see your "Councillors of State", are elected.[408] I know 3 of them, D[r]. Cal-

---

[404] The legislature also protested this order by means of a resolution adopted on December 9, in which the military order was called "unwise, unjust and impolitic, and if carried into effect will be a wanton and unnecessary destruction of property." Confidence in the patriotism of the people to the extent of burning their own cotton if necessary to prevent it falling into enemy hands was expressed. Governor Vance was directed to "earnestly protest against the execution of this order." *Laws of N. C. 1862-1863*, p. 53.

[405] See p. 204, 142n.

[406] Sidney Bulow Erwin, of Burke County, who later lived in McDowell County and in Asheville. He was a student at the University of North Carolina in 1841-1842, studied law, and entered railroad service after the war. Grant, *Alumni History*, p. 187 says that he was a member of the House of Commons in 1848, but he does not appear in Connor, *N. C. Manual*, or in the *House Journal, 1848-1849*. He died in 1908.

[407] See above, Myers to Vance, p. 415.

[408] Councillors of state were elected by the legislature and served as advisers to the governor upon his call. These were elected on December 2, 1862. Aside from the three mentioned below, the other members elected were: Jesse R. Stubbs of Martin County, Fenner B. Satterthwaite of Pitt County, L. Ethridge of Johnston County, and J. R. Hargrave of Anson County. *House Journal, 1862-1863*, pp. 62-63; *Senate Journal, 1862-1863*, pp. 66-68.

loway,[409] R. P. Dick,[410] & J. A. Patton,[411] I got very well acquainted with D[r]. Calloway in Washington City a good many years ago, was at College with Dick. When will you summon them to Raleigh? there is no news in this County.

Hoping to hear from you soon as to the Beef hides, particularly; I dislike to trouble you, but having always replied to, & attended to every thing I could when called upon I take the liberty of asking others the same favors. I know you are pressed for time; therefore excuse me for calling on you.

M[rs]- Erwin joins me in Love to Cousin Harriet [412] & yourself.
[Raleigh]
P. S.

I have finished cribbing my crop it is not as good as last year, though a fair one. All last summer & fall I sold corn to Soldiers families at $1. per Bushel when I was offered by others $1.50 & $2.00.

I have a bad lot of Hogs to Kill.

I understand that Corn is selling at $2.50 per Bush[l]. in Buncombe, too high entirely

Excuse this, as I write in a hurry Let me hear from you as to hides
[A. L. S. Governors' Papers (Vance),
State Department of Archives and History, Raleigh.]

---

[409] James Calloway (1806-1878), of Wilkes County, a doctor and politician. He was a son of Elijah Calloway who represented Ashe County in the House of Commons for many years. James Calloway graduated from Philadelphia Medical College and settled in Wilkes County, but he had a large practice over seven counties. He was a Whig member of the Convention of 1861; he opposed secession until Lincoln's proclamation, when he voted for it and gave his support to the Confederacy. As a large property owner he was hopelessly involved after the war; he moved to Kansas in 1870 but returned in 1872, broken in health and fortune, and died in Wilkesboro soon afterwards. He had married a sister of Abner Bynum Carmichael, Vance's friend. Hickerson, *Happy Valley*, p. 51; McCormick, *Personnel*, pp. 24-25.

[410] Robert Paine Dick (1823-1898), lawyer and politician of Guilford County. He graduated with honor from the University of North Carolina in 1843 and became a lawyer in 1845, settling in Wentworth until he moved to Greensboro in 1849. For many years he was active in the Democratic party, being a member of their national conventions in 1852, and of the Charleston and Baltimore conventions of 1860, where he supported Stephen A. Douglas for the nomination. He was Federal District Attorney for North Carolina, 1853-1861, and a member of the national executive committee of the Democratic party. In the crisis of 1861 he broke with the Democrats because he opposed secession, and so became identified with the Union, or Conservative, faction in North Carolina politics in the convention of 1861, of which he was a member. He split with this new allegiance in 1864, when he favored the peace movement. After the war he became a Republican, favored the Fourteenth Amendment, and became a member of the Supreme Court of North Carolina, 1868-1872, when he was appointed United States District Judge for Western North Carolina by president Grant. In 1878 he opened a law school with John H. Dilliard, which became creditably known over western North Carolina. His other political activities were as a member of the State Senate in 1864 and of the Convention of 1865. Obituary in *Greensboro Patriot*, September 21, 1898; McCormick, *Personnel*, pp. 29-30; Connor, *N. C. Manual*, pp. 439, 447, 635, 882.

[411] James Alfred Patton. See p. 19, 88n.

[412] See p. 16, 81n.

From D. K. McRae [413]

Wilmington
Dec 6th 1862

I reached here last night- This morning I have had conference with Cap[t]. Muse.[414] Who has Kindly placed me in communication with some of the citizens- who are thoroughly versed in the matters in which I am engaged-

The universal sentiment here as to the manner of effecting secure entrance with goods is that by Steamer- Cap[t]. Muse informs me that only in one instance has a steamer been lost, and that was the fault of the Captain.- He says and his opinion is concurred in that all the arms shipped by one steamer would be safer than to be distributed among 10 Sail vessels. and if Wilmington does not fall- He considers the chances much in favor of success If I understood M[r]. Saunders-[415] his idea as to the sail

---

[413] See p. 163, 2n. After his resignation from the army in November McRae agreed to act as an inspector of goods bought by North Carolina through a contract with George N. Sanders, who was about to leave for Nova Scotia and Europe to secure supplies through the sale of naval stores warrants issued by the State of North Carolina. McRae was to act not only as inspector of goods but as a commissioner of the state to verify the securities upon which the purchases were to be made, as it was deemed inadvisable to take them to Europe in negotiable form. Sanders and McRae engaged in a bitter controversy over the mission and the sale of the script when they reached Europe early in 1863. When Vance wrote McRae altering the goods to be purchased (because the legislature had decided not to pass the Ten Regiment Bill), McRae abrogated the contract with Sanders on his authority as agent. Sanders charged McRae with a fraudulent sale of the naval stores script and with the appropriation of an unknown profit to himself. George N. Sanders, Esq., *Appendix to the Life and Times of Duncan K. McRae* (Raleigh, 1864) is Sanders' defence of his own action and contains many letters having to do with the mission; it contains Sanders' contract with North Carolina, dated December 1, 1862; and an account of the relations between Sanders and McRae (cited hereafter as Sanders, *McRae Appendix*).

[414] William T. Muse, formerly of the United States navy. He was a native of Pasquotank County who resigned from the United States navy at the time of secession, was ordered to Norfolk by the Military Board to take charge of North Carolina vessels for the defence of the state, commanded the *Winslow,* the *Ellis,* and the *North Carolina,* and became a Confederate naval officer when North Carolina transferred her seven vessels to the central government, in August 1861. Muse was ordered to Wilmington in October 1861. Moore, *N. C. Roster,* IV, 443, 449; Clark, *N. C. Regts.,* V, 299-303; Sprunt, *Chronicles,* p. 353; Minutes of Military Board, May 16, 1861, p. 11.

[415] George Nicholas Sanders (1812-1873), promoter and adventurer, who had made a contract with Vance for the sale of naval script of the state and the purchase of war supplies. Sanders was born in Kentucky and participated in many promotional schemes in politics and finance throughout his life. In the fifties he was a leader of the "Young America" movement; in 1853 he received a recess appointment to the London consulship, where he plotted with continental revolutionaries who were in exile and failed to win confirmation to his post from the United States Senate. "Half idealist, half charlatan, impulsive and prodigal, he had the talent of making and keeping warm friends and bitter enemies." Merle E. Curti, "George Nicholas Sanders," *Dict. of Am. Biog.,* XVI, 334-335. Sanders had been on at least one mission to Europe for the Confederate government, from which he returned to Richmond in October 1862. On the return trip he stopped at Halifax, Nova Scotia and learned of the interest in naval stores as a basis of credit for purchases. In Richmond he met Duncan K. McRae, a former acquaintance, and told him of his belief as to what could be done with naval stores

vessels [416] was that they could coast in safety under a foreign flag outside the marine league until a favorable moment for coming in From the information derived here- I am satisfied he is mistaken in that point- The enemy overhauls *all craft*- without reference to the flag or distance from shore- so that the safety of a sail vessel will depend on escaping notice-

Capt Muse & others inform me that an English steamer can be bought or insured at or below the sum named for the insurance of the several schooners— of sufficient dimension to bring all the proposed purchases at one trip— I am expecting to meet this morning a Captain who is also the most reliable pilot about here Capt Muse recommends him in the highest terms before sending this letter I will give you the result of my interview My object in mentioning the information about the steamer— is to enquire whether if on communicating this to Mr S. he should be willing or should desire to change the plan in that portion Gov I shall have your authority to concur to the extent of the liability heretofore assumed—

You omitted to furnish me with necessary information to enable me to communicate with the signal corps which is very important please send it to me at Richmond Spottswood House—

Capt Muse informs me that Capt Crossin[417] did not procure a pilot and he fears for his success most on that score— If you think proper one may be secured to be put through with us— or to go out to him from Charleston I mention it to you because Capt Muse thinks it important— If this is rec^d- in time to send a dispatch in the course of the day to morrow— (Monday) it would reach me here— If you should determine to send such an one with me— it would be necessary to order an appropriation of funds to cover his expense from Halifax to Europe with— the address of Capt Crossin & Mr White[418]

I think I shall complete arrangements to leave here to morrow (Monday) night—

[Raleigh]

[A. L. S. Governors' Papers (Vance), State Department of Archives and History, Raleigh.]

script, and asked him to communicate with Governor Vance. The result was a telegram from Vance asking Sanders to come to Raleigh. This he did and laid before the governor his scheme, which received his unqualified approval. Accordingly an agreement was made that Sanders should go abroad — whether to Nova Scotia or to Europe is not clear — to purchase boots, shoes, ammunition, and clothing at fixed prices and the goods so purchased were to be approved bv North Carolina's agent before being shipped. McRae was this agent. A copy of the contract, with the schedule of fixed prices, is in Sanders, *McRae Appendix*, pp. 7-9 and the work includes Sanders' own account of his experiences which followed.

[416] Sanders proposed to share the expense of buying a schooner at Baltimore, load it with flour and other products, and leave the United States in this fashion. Sanders, *McRae Appendix*, p. 7.

[417] See p. 360, 201n.

[418] See p. 288, 1n.

From John McLaurin[419]

OFFICE GEN. TRANSPORTATION AGT.
WILMINGTON & MANCHESTER RAIL ROAD CO.
Wilmington, N. C. Dec. 6. 1862

Your proclamation of 28th.[420] ult., does not permit shipment of Flour which may have been on hand awaiting transportation previous to that date— For instance there were lying at Wilmington & Weldon R[l]. R[d]. Sundry lots of Flour, Hides &c, during the prevalence of Yellow Fever in this city, at which time it was impossible to obtain means of forwarding— Again parties claim that flour, or other articles shipped from Virginia by permission of Confederate Authorities, & therefore knowing or presumed to be for private disposal and not to be prohibited—

But the most difficult problem for solution, should you decide that articles conforming to above circumstances, may be exported is, whether previous contracts, for future delivery, are or are not prohibited, & if not, what means shall be taken, or requirements exacted to determine the nature & extent of such contracts— In conferring with Col Strange[421] of this county, on the subject, he expressed himself not authorized to go beyond the terms of the proclamation, & promised to ask further instructions— But parties here are pressing for transportation, & desirous as I am to accommodate shippers, while equally anxious to comply with the requirements of law, I have concluded to request of Your Excellency instructions on these point, for my guidance—

I omitted to ask, whether prohibited articles, known to be merely in transit through our state, are to be stopped within its borders.

An early reply is solicited
Raleigh
[A. L. S. Governors' Papers (Vance),
  State Department of Archives and History, Raleigh.]

To Gov. Letcher[422]

[1862]
Executive Dpt of N. C.
Raleigh Dec[r] 6th

I see a statement in one of our papers of a citizen of North Carolina, who called upon you for assistance in procuring transportation for some salt for his county, in which it is alleged, that he

---

[419] John McLaurin, of Wilmington, general transportation agent for the Wilmington and Manchester Railroad Company.
[420] See p. 404. The proclamation expressly excepted "all persons non residents, who may have bought such articles before the date hereof."
[421] Robert Strange, of Wilmington, an eminent lawyer and leader of the Wilmington bar, who had been solicitor in the fifties and a member of the House of Commons in 1852. He was a Democrat. Connor, *N. C. Manual*, p. 724.
[422] See p. 277, 357n.

The Governor's Palace, occupied by Zebulon Vance, was two-stories high with a classic portico facing Fayetteville Street in Raleigh. The edifice, completed in 1816, was abandoned by Governor Vance at the end of the War.

failed in his object because the authorities of Virginia resented my recent proclamation forbidding the exportation of certain articles from this State—[423]

I hope this is a mistake. I can see no reason why any one should complain of the proclamation except a speculator, as no one else is prohibited. It was put forth in accordance with a joint resolution of the General Assembly and is so liberal in its exceptions as to almost defeat its object: and although a doubtful and ungracious measure at best, we were compelled to resort to it to avoid suffering at home. So far from doing any thing offensive toward Sister States, it was and is yet my intention when I shall have a little further tried its virtues, to invite a similar one from their authorities, under the impression there is an abundance for all if prices can be kept in the reach of the poor.

Lest you may have not read it, I enclose a copy and ask your consideration upon it.

You will see that its provisions in regard to the most important article, salt, are more liberal even than the regulations prescribed in your state;[424] for whilst all citizens non resident can freely manufacture and carry off salt from our coast, county agents from North Carolina in addition to having their official character verified by the county seals have also to make oath of the fact, before they can remove their own salt from the states own works at Saltville. I am informed also, that private persons can not buy them even in small quantities for their own private use.

This State has now over thirty thousand bushels of salt at Saltville and it is constantly accumulating for want of transportation, whilst our people are feeding to their hogs their childrens bread. They can not slaughter until they get the salt. Special agents sent to see the Superintendents of your roads have returned with the intelligence that they refuse to enter into any arrangement for its removal. I can not believe it is done in retaliation, for I would earnestly invite instead of resist, a like action on your part; and yet it effectually deprives our people of meat for the next twelve months.

Earnestly desiring to preserve not only the very cordial relations existing with the state of Virginia, in whose defense our whole energies have been constantly exerted, but to preserve if possible our people form ruin at the hands of extortioners, I am anxious to have your valuable cooperation.

[Richmond]

[A. L. S. Governors' Papers (Vance),
State Department of Archives and History, Raleigh.]

---

[423] See p. 404.

[424] The proclamation provided that an exception be made for "non residents on the sea coast and in their own works and to cargoes entering any of our ports from abroad."

From W. H. C. Whiting[425]

H^d- Q^rs- Wilmington
Dec 6th- 1862

I send you herewith a copy of letters addressed to the War Department since my assignment to the defence of the Cape Fear, touching the importance of the matter in hand and the men and means required.[426]

I believe the Dept. to be fully impressed with the emergency of the case and aware of its necessities, but pressed so heavily at so many points, it has, so far, been unable to supply here, but a very small part of the number of Troops, I consider indispensible to a successful defence of Wilmington.

In the mean time I am Endeavoring to make the best use I can of the means at my disposal. In view of my small force, and the undoubted intention of the enemy to attack this place at no distant day, I recommend your Excellency to take speedy and strong measures to secure to your people the large supply of Salt now on hand in this City.

It should at once be placed, at the expense of the owners, out of chance of capture, by the 4 routes, W^m & Man. R. R. Charlotte & R^d. R. R. Cape Fear River & W. W. R. R.

Should the place fall (and I cannot say it will not unless I am heavily & speedily reinforced) the Salt Works must be lost. I shall do all in my power to aid in securing it.

The accompanying letter will explain to you the difficulty of this position.
Raleigh
[Vance Letter Book, 1862-1863,
State Department of Archives and History, Raleigh.]

From Sarah F. Smith

Cypress Creek N. Carolina
Dec 7th 1862

Sir with a hope of you complying with my request: I will endeavor to write you a few lines on this subject. I as well as 10 other Families are left here with any masculine protection at all, And do earnestly ask you to discharge John B. Smith[427] from the Service of the War, as he is or with the exception of one other & he is near 50 he is all the man in this vicinity to look to for protection or for any assistants what ever. He Mr Smith is 42 years old also he is & always was a true Southern rites man. He conducts himself well in every respect, And He is bouth honest

---

[425] See p. 348, 161n. Whiting had been sent to Wilmington on November 8, 1862.
[426] The letters are not enclosed, but may be found in *O. R.*, Ser. I, Vol. XVIII, beginning on November 14, 1862.
[427] No John B. Smith is listed in Moore, *N. C. Roster* as having been in military service.

& uprite Gov Vance I as well as the Ladies of those other Families do Unanimously ask you & let us prevale on you to send him a discharge, I will ask you and know that you will comply; as you are such a kind noble generous hearted man As for Mr Smith he has always expressed a willingness to go when called for, Although he had a wife and a large family of children, And if he has to go in service his Family as well as a great many others will have to shurely suffer.

I do this without Mr Smith knowing it Mr Smith is not related to me by Efinity or Consanguinity, My relation are all in Service & will be until the war ends as you know

I feel & know that you will discharge him and I will give you the name of his Post Office, Cypress Creek Bladen County, N. C. I will close by leaveing this to your discretion
[Raleigh]
[A. L. S. Governors' Papers (Vance),
State Department of Archives and History, Raleigh.]

From W. N. Pierce[428]

Wilkes County N. C.   Dec 7th. 1862
after my best respects to you I pray your honor grant me Twelve men clear of conscription together with my three Lieutenance for the purpose of taking up Deserters who are harbering in the mountains and being well equiped and als allow me some powder and caps and Twelve suficient Mukets. I think it will be very essential to keep a gard in these mountains as thare is every Day comeing in Deserter who are being harbed by union men these men to be able bodied men Who can stand fatigue over the mountains to be allowed me out of my own company, if nothing else pleas allow me some powder and caps. p's answer this soon
[Raleigh]
[A. L. S. Governors' Papers (Vance),
State Department of Archives and History, Raleigh.]

From W. B. Lovelace[429]

Moorsboro Cleaveland County N. C.
Dec the 7th. 1862
After My respects to You. I will inform you that I am Taning and Making shoes for the Government. I made my contract with Mr James Sloan[430] of Greensboro He said the Government had hides but he could not get them some of my neihbors who have

---

[428] William N. Pierce, captain in the Ninety-third Regiment of North Carolina Militia, company A, Reddie's River District, Wilkes County. Militia Roster, p. 386.
[429] The Lovelace family was prominent in the Mooresboro section of Cleveland County, but no mention of W. B. Lovelace has been found. See Griffin, *Old Tryon and Rutherford*, p. 491.
[430] See p. 190, 95n.

been in the Army about Kingston N. C. say that there is a great many hides there that belongs to government and they think the Brigade commissary has been selling of them.

I am getting my stock of leather pretty well worked out. and it is impossible to get many hides in this part of the Country The cattle has principally been sold and taken off I though it prudent in me to write to you and see if you would furnish hides for the State or Confederacy to be taned on the shares or anyway almost every letter that is sent from our soldiers say that there are a great many men barefooted in camp It is a heart rending thought if I had or could get the hides I could make leather in from 3 to 4 months with the improved system of taning that I now have in my yard and make better leather

But speculation is so great now that we can not buy what few hides we are buying for less than one dollar a pound

I hope you will make an arrangement to furnish me & others who are working at Government prices (instead of speculation) with good hides to tan or sell them to us at a fare price and we will make leather at a fare price and try to keep down speculation please answer this as soon as convenient give all information necessary I remain your most obedient servant—

[Raleigh]

N. B. If you wish any reference please call on Mr Beam[431] and Logan[432] members from this County.

[A. L. S. Governors' Papers (Vance),
State Department of Archives and History, Raleigh.]

From A. C. Myers[433]

CONFEDERATE STATES OF AMERICA
QUARTER MASTER GENERAL'S DEPARTMENT
Richmond Dec 8th. 1862

On the 17th September, I had the honor to address a communication to you, a copy of which is herewith transmitted, in which I suggested that all contracts and arrangements made by the State of North Carolina for the manufacture of Army clothing, should be transferred to the Confederate States.[434]

[431] David Beam (1818-1903), a farmer who was born in Rutherford County, served in the militia during the Cherokee removal of 1838, and in the House of Commons from Cleveland County in 1862 and 1864. He also served one term as clerk of the superior court and represented Cleveland County in the Convention of 1865. He was a large property owner in both Cleveland and Rutherford counties and wielded a large influence. Later he moved over the county line into Rutherford County and was elected to the House of Representatives in 1876. Connor, N. C. Manual, pp. 563, 799; Griffin, Old Tryon and Rutherford, p. 346.

[432] John R. Logan, of Cleveland County, member of the House of Commons in 1860, 1862, and 1865, and colonel of the Ninety-first North Carolina Militia from April 26, 1861 until December 8, 1863. Connor, N. C. Manual, p. 563; Militia Roster, pp. 406-407.

[433] See p. 150, 611n.

[434] See Myers to Vance, p. 189.

Since that date Congress has passed an Act which repeals the law allowing commutation for clothing to soldiers, and provides that the clothing prescribed by the Army Regulations should be issued *in kind* after the 8th. of October 1862.[435]

Inasmuch, as under the operation of this Act, no allowance can be made for clothing commutation to soldiers, the State of No. Carolina cannot be reimbursed in money for such clothing as it may supply to its troops, nor can any arrangement between the State or the C. S. Government similar to that heretofore existing be continued. As this Department is required to provide clothing for issue in kind to the troops, it is essential that every facility for obtaining supplies, should be at its disposal, and I therefore beg to repeat the application that all the contracts for Army Clothing made by the authorities of No. Carolina, may be turned over to this Department.

If this be done, I propose that, arrangements be made for for the manufacture of clothing in No. Carolina. And Major Pearce[436] Q. M. at Raleigh will be instructed to establish a manufacturing depot in that city, at which the material supplied by the resources of the State, my be made up into clothing.

In conclusion, I beg to request an early decision upon the subject of this communication.

Raleigh

[Vance Letter Book, 1862-1863,
State Department of Archives and History, Raleigh.]

From S. C. Wilson and Others

December the 8th 1862

we the under Seigned implore your exelancy to intercede for us the citizens of Burk County with the Legislature to pass an act for the more sure prompt and cheap Supply of Salt for the County of Burk Thomas G. Walton[437] got in as Salt agent for the County he advertised the people to come in to Morganton thursday the 4th of December to receiv their Salt the people had their hogs fat redy to kill and Corn Scarce but Thomas G. Walton refused to let them have more than three pounds for each member of the familey and the people could not git Salt to Salt their poark and

---

[435] Congress passed such an act on October 8, 1862. It repealed previous provisions for commutation money and required the secretary of war to "provide in kind to the soldiers, respectively, the uniform clothing prescribed by the Regulations of the Army of the Confederate States; and should any balance of clothing be due to any soldier at the end of the year, the money value of such balance shall be paid to such soldier, according to the value of such clothing fixed and announced by order from the War Department." Matthews, *Public Laws of Confederacy*, 2 session, 1 Congress, chap. XXX. The War Department added rules and details for the administration of the law. These may be found in *O. R.*, Ser. IV, Vol. II, 229-231.

[436] See p. 142, 577n.

[437] See p. 88, 321n.

here was Sharks that thought the had the people pend so that they ware bound to let them have their poark for lack of Salt and let thir own famileys Suffer but that was not all the evil of the Strategem here Stood Women thinly Clad the wives of our Suffering Soilgers in the mud in front of Thomas G. Waltons Salt House from early in the morning till near night eightteen miles from home awaiting till Thomas G Walton could weigh out Salt for a hole County and that is not all the evle Thomas G Walton will hire a wagoner to hall fifty Buishels of Salt he gives him ten Buishels for halling the fifty now the Salt at Salt Ville Va is $1.50 per Buishel but Thomas G. Walton prices the Salt $5 per Buishel then Says he paid $50 for halling forty Buishels then ads that fifty to the $60 that the forty Buishels cost at Salt Ville makes $1.10 thn Sells the Salt at five dollars per Buishel which makes the 40 Buishels Bring $200 that leves Thomas G Walton $90 to put in his own pocket for weighing 40 Buishels But I would Suggest a better plan for the poor of Burk County that is to count the cost on ten Buishels at Salt Ville on ten Buishels fifteen dollars on the ten Buishels paid to the waggoner add that fifteen dollars to the 60 that the 40 Buishels cost at Salt Ville Va makes the Salt worth $187 1/4 per Buishel in Burk County now add 12 1/2 cents on the Buishel for waistage that makes the Salt worth two dollars per Buishel now add 25 cents for the trouble of the Salt agent on each Buishel that makes the Salt two dollars and twenty five cents per Buishel and the Waggoner Still got his ten Buishels of Salt for halling the 50 Buishels now the wagoner is as well off and the people pays two dollars and 25 cents in place of five dollars per Buishel now pass an act for the people to elect a County Salt agent for the County whoes duty it Shall be to take bond and Security of School district agents who shall be elected by the people of the district and be Bound to have a Supply of Salt for their district against the first of December then the people will have a Supply of Salt in their own districts and have it at two dollars and twenty five cents per Buishel now we pray your execlency to have an act passed [438] to accomplish the above plan and you will doe much for the poor of Burk County

S. C. Wilson
James G Lanes
Joseph S turner
W F Gibbs
Joshua Gills
Joseph Shooke
[Raleigh]
[A. L. S. Governors' Papers (Vance),
  State Department of Archives and History, Raleigh.]

---

[438] The legislature passed an act concerning salt on December 20, 1862. This

From Henry T. Farmer[439]

Flat Rock No Ca
Dece nbr 8ᵗʰ 1862

The immediate attention of Your Excellency is respectfully solicited to the consideration of a case the facts of which are substantially as following

One James B Fitzgerald [440] a citizen of Haywood County, owning and having in his possession a lot of cattle some forty-nine head, was overhauled at Green River in the County of Henderson some three miles from the South Carolina line by Major Joseph Holbert [441] commanding in the absence of the Col & Lieut Col [442] the 106 Regt No Ca Milia, that the cattle were on the way to a market in South Carolina there can be but little doubt, for having past the toll gate at Flat Rock five Miles short of the point at which they were seized, they left behind them all roads leading to any other place than South Carolina, Fitzgerald declares however that he had no disposition to evade the law, and in justice to him I must say that I have every reason for believing him ignorant of the existance of your Excellencys proclamation at the time of his departure from home Viz the 2ᵈ of December,[443] being called upon officially decide what was to be done, and knowing no better course, I advised Fitzgerald to give a bond for the delivery of the

---

legislation continued in force the contract made by Governor Clark with Stuart, Buchanan and Company at Saltville, Va., and gave the governor power to appoint a superintendent, or to retain the one already in charge of the North Carolina interests there. The duties of the superintendent were defined as being those of manufacturing salt and furnishing it to the several counties of the state in proportion to population. The state agent at Saltville (N. W. Woodfin) could sell only to county agents selected by the justices of the counties to purchase and distribute the salt. The county agents were by law prohibited from purchasing a larger quantity than necessary for their counties, "nor shall they purchase any for their own use, nor sell the same at higher prices than the cost of the article when delivered, and any such agent violating the provisions of this act, may be indicted in any of the courts of this State having jurisdiction thereof, and on conviction, shall be punished as a misdemeanor." *Public Laws of N. C., 1862-1863*, chap. 22.

[439] Henry Tudor Farmer (1817-1888), manufacturer and construction contractor of Henderson County, and chairman of the county court. He was a son of Dr. Henry Tudor Farmer, a poet, and one of four nephews brought to Flat Rock by Mr. and Mrs. Charles Baring. As a contractor he built the hotel at Flat Rock and the Presbyterian Church in Hendersonville. He operated a furniture factory and a wood-working plant. He was chairman of the Henderson County court in 1846 and represented the county in the House of Commons in 1848 and 1850. Connor, *N. C. Manual*, p. 648; Patton, *Henderson County*, pp. 140, 180, 214-215, 217. For Farmer's earlier interest and concern with speculation and embargo see his letter to Governor Clark, April 17, 1862, Governors' Papers (Clark).

[440] See p. 398, 332n.

[441] Joseph Holbert, commissioned major on September 6, 1861, in the 106th North Carolina Militia Regiment. Militia Roster, p. 418.

[442] The colonel of the 106th Regiment of North Carolina Militia was Stark Stansill. See p. 326, 109n. The lieutenant colonel of the same regiment was William D. Justice. Militia Roster, p. 418.

[443] See pp. 404-405. The proclamation was dated November 26, 1862.

cattle at the end of ten days, Fitzgerald consenting a bond was executed on the same of Two Thousand dollars the worth of the cattle conditioned that the horned stock be forthcoming at the end of ten days to abide the decision of Your Excellency in the premises, May I suggest that it would be well to give us more explicit instructions as to the disposal of property seized, shall it be sent to Raleigh if not to whom are we to deliver it, does the driving of cattle on a road leading only to South Carolina make the parties guilty we want all the light to be had, determined as we are to execute the law, we fear we run ahead of the rabbit, and therefore appeal to you for instructions, does your Excelsy proclamation allow the passage of sheep, Would not it be well to authorize the County Court to appoint some suitable person living on the high ways leading into other state Most of the Militia Officers of Henderson live off the public roads and have but little knowledge of what may leave the State, Is there ay chance of getting a little powder for the people I take it there is not ten pounds within [?] the county— I have tried very hard to obtain a supply but so far without success

With the best wishes for the continued good health of your Excellency I have the Honor to be

[Raleigh]

[on reverse]

Ans^r. Mr Farmer that his letter was not rec^d until yesterday, and I presume there is no necessity for action now Z. B. V.

[A. L. S. Governors' Papers (Vance),
State Department of Archives and History, Raleigh.]

From R. H. Gray[444]

Camp near Fredericksburg Va.
Dec. 9, 1862

I learn from a reliable source that the N. C. Legislature has passed an Act to raise five Regiments of troops for State Service and that you have the appointment of the Field Officers to them: [445] I would most respectfully ask your Excellency to consider my Claims to a Colonency of one of these Regiments.

In connection with this, I would merely state that I have been in service since June 1861, have had command of this Regmt.

---

[444] Robert H. Gray, of Randolph County, lieutenant colonel of the Twenty-second North Carolina Regiment. He had entered service as captain of company L in the Twenty-second Regiment in June 1861, and was promoted lieutenant colonel after the battle of Seven Pines. Gray was in delicate health and died on March 16, 1863. Moore, *N. C. Roster*, II, 208, 247; Clark, *N. C. Regts.*, II, 162-163, 169, 170, IV, 157.

[445] See p. 394, 319n and 320n. The bill had not passed the legislature but was under debate in the House of Commons, which adopted it on December 16. The Senate refused to concur and the proposal was never implemented.

(22d N. C. T.) for more than six months (the Col being wounded) [446] have led it in some half dozen pitched battles besides numerous skirmishes, and as to how I have acquitted myself, I beg leave to refer you to Maj. Gen. A. P. Hill, comdg Light Division,[447] Brig. Genls. W. D. Pender[448] & Archer[449] of this Division —and Brig. Genl. J. J. Pettigrew.[450] I could multiply references but deem it unnecessary. As to my politics I refer you to Ex Gov. Morehead,[451] Hon. J. A. Gilmer[452] Maj. J. P. H. Russ[453] Secty. State, A. G. Foster,[454] esqr. & Dr. R. S. Beall,[455] all of whom are well acquainted with me.

Should you deem it consistent with the good of the service and your duties to consider my claims favorably I shall feel myself under lasting obligations to you personally.

[Raleigh]

[A. L. S. Governors' Papers, (Vance),
State Department of Archives and History, Raleigh.]

---

[446] The colonel was James Connor of South Carolina, who was wounded and resigned from the service in August 1863. Moore, *N. C. Roster*, II, 208.

[447] Ambrose Powell Hill (1825-1865), a graduate of West Point and a major general in the Confederate army. He was formerly colonel of the Thirteenth Virginia Regiment, but rose rapidly to the command of a division; later he was a lieutenant general. Gray had been complimented by Hill after the battle of Gaines' Mill in June 1862. The appellation "Light Division" was given because of the reputation for fast marching, and was proudly borne by the unit.

[448] See p. 170, 26n.

[449] James J. Archer (1817-1864), a native of Maryland and brigadier general in A. P. Hill's division. Archer had been made a brigadier after Seven Pines, and Gray had fought under Archer at Gaines' Mill, where Hill had complimented Gray. Evans, *Conf. Mil. Hist.*, II, 171-172.

[450] See p. 215, 165n. Pettigrew was the original colonel of the Twenty-second Regiment.

[451] See p. 98, 371n.

[452] See p. 62, 224n.

[453] John P. H. Russ, of Wake County, who had just been elected secretary of state of North Carolina by the legislature on November 25. He was a member of the State Senate at the time, having defeated Moses A. Bledsoe in a bitter local campaign in August 1862, some of which was fought out in the press. Russ was also colonel of the Wake County militia. When elected secretary of state Russ moved from his home, which was eighteen miles from the city, to Raleigh. He was, of course, a Conservative. *House Journal, 1862-1863*, p. 34; *Senate Journal 1862-1863*, p. 40; Raleigh *North Carolina Standard*, July 26, 30, 1862, January 2, 1863.

[454] Alfred Gaither Foster (1826-1866), lawyer and legislator from Davidson County. He was a graduate of the University of North Carolina in 1844 and a member of the House of Commons from Davidson County in 1850 and from Randolph County in 1856; he also represented Randolph in the Convention of 1861, and became a member of the Council of State in 1864. Foster had been born in Iredell County, moved to Lexington, and then to Randolph County to take charge of a large farm of his father. Connor, *N. C. Manual*, pp. 439, 588, 771, 895; McCormick, *Personnel*, p. 35; Grant, *Alumni History*, p. 204.

[455] Robert Lamar Beall, then a member of the House of Commons from Davidson County. He was a graduate of the University of North Carolina in 1852, having been in Chapel Hill with Vance, became a physician, planter, and bee cultivator, and later moved to Lenoir in Caldwell County. His medical study was taken at Jefferson Medical College in Philadelphia. He died in 1891. Connor, *N. C. Manual*, p. 588; Leonard, *Davidson County*, p. 439; Grant, *Alumni History*, p. 41; Battle, *History of U. of N. C.*, I, 804.

From J. A. Campbell[456]

Richmond, Va. Dec. 9 1862

Your letter of the 6th Ins't has been rec'd [457]—The department will give directions to the Genl commanding the district of North Carolina to exercise caution in the destruction of any property under the stress of necessity, & to abstain as long as possible from the destruction of that belonging to the State of North Carolina

Also, to take counsel, with yourself & your officers in relation to the same from time to time

Your Excellency will bear in mind, the strong language of the act of Congress of the 17th March 1862 on this subject [458] & the responsibility that would be thrown upon the department by any default on this subject.

Raleigh   By order of Secy of War

[A. L. S. Z. B. Vance Papers, State Department of Archives and History, Raleigh.]

From D. K. McRae[459]

Richmond
Dec 10th

I have just recd through Mr Hall the scrip as specified in your contract with Mr Saunders for $228,000—[460] Two hundred and twenty eight thousand dollars

I would still suggest its extension to $310 000 if at all practicable as the present sum limits the operation to so small a venture

I consulted several gentlemen in Wilmington among them Capt Muse[461] & Genl Whiting[462] all concur that the scheme is

---

[456] John Archibald Campbell (1811-1889), assistant secretary of war. Campbell was born and educated in Georgia, but moved to Alabama in 1840, where he served two terms in the state legislature and was a delegate to the Nashville Convention in 1850. In the meantime he had become one of the outstanding lawyers in the country, and was appointed an associate justice of the United States Supreme Court in 1853. He became assistant secretary of war for the Confederacy in October 1862 and served in that office, with special duty as administrator of the conscription laws, until the end of the war. After the war he settled in New Orleans and won another national reputation at the bar, arguing many famous cases before the Supreme Court. Blanton Fortson, "John Archibald Campbell," *Dict. of Am. Biog.,* III, 456-459.

[457] See Vance to Seddon, p. 417.

[458] The law was entitled "An act to regulate the destruction of property under military necessity, and to provide for the indemnity thereof" and provided that military commanders were authorized and directed to destroy cotton, tobacco, military and naval stores and other property of any kind which might aid the enemy when necessary to prevent such from falling into enemy hands. Owners were to perpetuate their testimony according to law and were entitled to indemnity out of the proceeds of property sequestered and confiscated under Confederate laws. Matthews, *Public Laws of the Confederacy,* 1 session, 1 Congress, chap. V.

[459] See p. 163, 2n, and p. 420, 413n.

[460] See p. 420, 415n.

[461] See p. 420, 414n.

[462] See p. 348, 161n.

feasible and they do not doubt its success— but *all* recommend a Steamer instead of vessels I wrote you to this effect from Wilmington but have recd no authority to substitute a Steamer I fear my letter miscarried [463]— Let me know if I will have this authority in the event Mr S. should desire to do so M[r] S expects to be ready by Saturday— So if you determine to send men script or further authority you can do so to reach here by Friday or Saturday Capt Muse suggested that the advantage of a Steamer is that success is almost sure with one and that you can sell her for 3 to 4 times her cost without difficulty I rec[d]. this morning also the certified authority & Mr S wishes a *certified* copy of his contract with the States I have secured the services of Capt Guthrie[464] who is the most skillful pilot at Wilmington

[Raleigh]

[A. L. S. Governors' Papers (Vance),
State Department of Archives and History, Raleigh.]

From Catherine White[465]

Edenton December 1862

Last spring my husband Baker White[466] on his return from a fishing trip down the Albemarle Sound was overtaken by a Yankee

---

[463] See McRae to Vance, December 6, 1862, p. 420.

[464] John Julius Guthrie, who was a lieutenant in the Confederate navy, later captain of the *Advance,* and a member of Vance's staff at the end of the war. Clark, *N. C. Regts.,* I, 59, V, 471.

[465] This letter is undated, but is included here because it is approximately the date at which it was probably written, and because of the letter which follows.

[466] Baker P. White was charged with having deserted from the Chowan militia draft, joining the enemy, and acting as a pilot for the Yankees on a gunboat at the time of the fall of Roanoke Island in February 1862. He remained away from Edenton until the first few days of May, when he returned to visit his family and was arrested by Confederate cavalry and taken to Suffolk, Richmond, and eventually to Salisbury prison. His arrest occurred on May 2 or May 3; the morning after his arrest Colonel Howard, of the Union army, landed at Edenton and demanded an interview with the town commissioners. On May 17 the town was picketed by Federal troops and the commissioners were arrested and taken to Roanoke Island by order of General Burnside, but after some days were released. On July 1 Joseph G. Godfrey, a citizen of Edenton and assistant commissionary for the Fifth Regiment of North Carolina Militia, was arrested in Edenton by Federal troops under Commodore Rowan as a hostage for Baker White. Godfrey, a merchant of Edenton, was taken to the Federal jail in New Bern, from which place he wrote to Governor Clark asking that he be exchanged for White. In November Godfrey came to Raleigh under a parole and a directive from Stanly to see Vance, having already failed to obtain exchange on a similar trip to Richmond. None of the Confederate authorities appears to have doubted that Baker White was a deserter; Governor Clark endorsed Godfrey's letter with the comment that Baker White was an excellent Albemarle pilot who had joined the Yankees; John A. Campbell, assistant secretary of war, refused to exchange White for Godfrey, called White a deserter from the Confederate army, and insisted that there was no right in the rules of war to seize persons not in the armed forces as hostages for prisoners. Clark thought, in September 1862, that Godfrey had been released, but Campbell did not write his refusal until November 24, when Godfrey was still a prisoner in New Bern. White's name was inclosed on a list of civilians held prisoner at Salisbury which President Lincoln

steamer the yankies insisted upon his getting on board this promising to Land him at Edenton when the steamer came to an anchor in Edenton Bay he took the boat left there and came ashore This was his statement at the time, the yankies have since made the same statement to some of our citizens it is further confirmed by the fact that he had in his boat at the time all such clothing covering and cooking utensils as he was in the habit of carrying with him on his fishing excursion as soon as he landed he was seized by the confederate pickets and carried off I understand during most of the time since he has been imprisoned in Salisboury there I suppose he now is

Govner Vance I am a strainger to you but I know you will excuse the liberty I take in addressing you in his behalf When I state that myself and 2 small children are dependant upon my husband for support I have no earthly friend to look too but my husband I have no father no Brother and no one in this life but my husband to befriend me and my poor little children and to be deprived off him my only friend I shall be ruined for ever fishing was the only Way that he had to make a living he had no other trade and all that know him can tell you the same he Was drafted and he thought he Would make one trip a fishing before he Was ordered in to Baricks and Was not notified ontill after he Was gone Govinor Vance I humbly beg and becach of you to have mercy upon me and my poor little Children and seake forgiveness for my husband if his being With the yankies Was a crime it Was not Wilful and intentional and that he has certainly suffered enough for being in their company ignorant as he was that it was Wrong as a Wife and a mother I appeal to you to inquire into his case oh Sir have not the claims of justice ben fully Satisfied by his long separation from his family Cannot mercy and forgiveness not be granted I implore of you a merciful consideration of his case Which I believe will result in his release and return home if you are a man of family make a self case of it what would be the feelings of your Wife and Children have not the enemy extorted enough of Wives tears and Children cries Shall natives of North Carolina be prosecuted to death by their own people I earnestly implore mercy and forgiveness for him if you can so use your official influence as to secure forgiveness for him my prayers and those of my children shall ascend for heavens choicest blessings to rest upon you and yours I have Writen you before but I fearing that

---

sent to his secretary of war and asked him to preserve it. The list was dated May 24, 1862, though Lincoln's note was not sent until September 18, 1862. J. R. B. Hathaway to Governor Clark, May 19, 1862, Joseph G. Godfrey to Governor Clark, July 23, 1862, Governors' Papers (Clark); A. Lincoln to Secretary of War, September 18, 1862, *O. R.*, Ser. II, Vol. IV, 528; John A. Campbell to Judge Heath, November 24, 1862, *O. R.*, Ser. II. Vol. IV, 951-952; R. R. Heath to Vance, November 14, 1862, Governors' Papers (Vance).

you have never Received my Letter I though I Would Wright you again I hope kind sir that you Will pity me and my poor Little Children and secure forgiveness for my husband and Let him return home once more to his poor Little Children I hope you Will excuse my bad Written Letter for I am in so much trouble I dont know one half of my time What I am saying pity pity I humbly beceach you a poor heart broken Woman kind friend allow me to call you so I would go to see you myself but I am not able I have nothing only what my husband toiled hard for he has all Ways bin a very hard Working man all his Life he toiled hard to support his family be a friend to me and my poor husband I pray

Oh have mercy and forgive my husband very humbly and Respectfully

[Raleigh]

[A. L. S. Governors' Papers (Vance),
State Department of Archives and History, Raleigh.]

From R. S. Mitchell [467]

Edenton Dec. 12. 1862

I have no sympathy with persons really guilty of the offences, with which Baker White,[468] of this place, stands charged; but it is right, that all the facts should be made known in such cases. I feel it incumbent upon me, as at that time Liut. Colonel, now Colonel, of this county, to state such information as I have obtained in regard to him, leaving it to you to use this communication, as you may deem right and proper.

1st. From the declarations of the Sergeant, I feel sure, no lawful summons to report as a *drafted militia-man,* was served upon him; a *verbal message* only being left with his wife in his absence.

2nd. From information received through various resources, he left home only on one of his ordinary fishing excursions, intending on his return to report himself for duty. Why he altered his purposes (if he did so), or how he came to be on board of a Yankee gun-boat, I am unable to say. The Yankees have declared to our citizens, that they overtook him on the Albemarle Sound, & made him get on their boat to be landed at Edenton.

I feel it my duty to make these statements as an act of justice to the said Baker White, and as an aid to those who may try him in

---

[467] R. S. Mitchell, colonel of the Fifth Regiment of North Carolina Militia, Chowan County.

[468] See p. 433, 466n.

finding out the precise degree of his criminality, With great respect

[Raleigh]
[L. S. Governors' Papers (Vance),
State Department of Archives and History, Raleigh.]

From George Tait[469]

Fort Fisher N. C. 12th Dec 1862

A vacancy has recently occured in my company caused by the resignation of 2d Lieut Jas. C Kelly—[470] In the election which is to take place, the probability is that a man who is totally unfit for the office will be elected, over a man who entered the service on the 15th April /61 & has been in the army ever since. the other having stayed at home until after the passage of the conscription act— The one is an educated man & a thorough soldier. the other though a very fair private, has no business capacity about him & in my opinion would never make an officer— Would your Excellency be kind enough to inform me whether an appointment can be made, or whether in the event of the men making an improper election, there is any way to prevent the commissioning of the successful candidate[471] A sincere desire for the welfare of my men alone prompts me to make this request—

[Raleigh]
[A. L. S. Governors' Papers (Vance),
State Department of Archives and History, Raleigh.]

From Nereus Mendenhall [472]

New Garden N. C.
12 mo 13. 1862

I understand that an order from the Governor is necessary to enable the people to get corn brought up by Railway. I have 35

---

[469] See p. 204, 139n. At this time Tait's company was attached to the Fortieth North Carolina Regiment (artillery) as company K.

[470] James E. Kelly, who was commissioned second lieutenant in company K of the Fortieth Regiment on May 6, 1862. The date of his enlistment or of his resignation is not given in Moore, N. C. Roster, III, 142. Kelly was succeeded by James W. Dickson, who was promoted from first corporal, and who had enlisted on May 6, 1862. Dickson is also listed as having been promoted first lieutenant on December 1, 1861, but this is manifestly an error as the company was not formed at that time. Moore, N. C. Roster, III, 142. Confederate States of America War Department List of Artillery Officers (Richmond, 1864), p. 129 says that Kelly was succeeded by first corporal James W. Dickson in December 1862.

[471] General Orders, No. 36, issued May 17, 1862, provided that when the qualifications of an officer for the position under consideration should be questioned a board of examiners should be convened by the brigade commander in order to determine the fitness, efficiency, and perfect sobriety of the person in question. O. R., Ser. IV, Vol. I, 1122-1123.

[472] See p. 254, 300n.

bushels at Boone Hill,[473] designed for my own use and which I am now needing— that I should be glad to have an order for.

If proper I wish the order to embrace the privilege of bringing 100 bushels.. It will require 50 for my own family, and some others have spoken to me to assist them in getting corn, and if procured will be furnished to them at cost—

[Raleigh]

[A. L. S. Governors' Papers (Vance),
State Department of Archives and History, Raleigh.]

From Alexander Dickson[474]

Jefferson N C
13th Decr 1862

As assistant Quarter Master for Ashe County I have intercepted and taken into my posession a load of bale cotton and cotton cloth on its way into the State of Tennessee.[475] The goods was the property of one James Culbert and he purchased them of the Eagle Mills factory Iredell county— And he was taking the property to Tennessee for the purpose of speculation.

Culbert has been a regular speculator in yarn & cloth since the war commenced. Culbert says he paid 7 pr bunch for his yarn & 75 cts per yard for the cloth and paid for the same in tallow butter & some cash— Now I wish to know what disposition to make of these articles and my whole duty in the matter— There are frequent opportunities to stop articles going into Tennessee to supply as it is thought the union men there, and for speculation and I would like to have from you instructions how to proceed in such cases— I have purchased for the use of the army about 400 $ worth of blankets &c & will start them next week—[476] Have advanced my own money for the same— But hope it will be all Right.

[Raleigh]

[A. L. S. Governors' Papers (Vance),
State Department of Archives and History, Raleigh.]

---

[473] Boone Hill was in Johnston County.

[474] Alexander Dickson is not listed as assistant quartermaster of the Ninety-seventh Regiment of North Carolina Militia, Ashe County. J. M. Gentry of Jefferson was colonel. Militia Roster, p. 88. In September Vance had ordered Colonel Gentry and Colonel William Horton of Watauga County militia to occupy the gaps into Tennessee in order to enforce the orders to the militia concerning deserters and transportation of goods out of the state. Militia Letter Book, September 19, 1862, p. 194.

[475] Militia officers were charged with the enforcement of Vance's embargo proclamation of November 26, 1862. See p. 404.

[476] Militia officers were authorized to purchase goods by Vance's proclamation of October 15, 1862. See p. 266.

From Wm. Preston Johnston[477]

Richmond, Va. Dec. 15 1862

Your letter of Dec[r] 8th- to the President, enclosing Joint Resolutions of N. C. General Assembly[478] relative to the burning of cotton has been received in the absence of the President. On his return it will be laid before him, unless you advise me to refer it at once to the consideration of the Secretary of War.

Raleigh

[A. L. S. Z. B. Vance Papers,
State Department of Archives and History, Raleigh.]

From J. A. Reves[479]

Ashe County N. C.
Dec the 15th 62

After compalyments & Respects to you I can in form you that I am well & my most Earnest Desire is this line may find you & family all well Govener in the first place I will inform you of our suffering condishion in ashe for the want of sault the salt that we are geting from Mr Woodfin[480] is comparitive nothing to our wants We have a large surplus of hogs in ashe if we could get salt to save them & thare is thousands of bushels at Saltville Va & we cant get it & we the Citisons of ashe has com to the conclusion to go & take it by force if the oners of it wont let us have it for a fare price & the people of this county has Requested me to Write you on the subject & we wish your advice & whether we can be seriously punished or not we are willing to pay a fare price for the salt we are compeled to have salt while it can be had or we will fite for it I can get from 3 to 4 hundred men in one days notice to starte

they have a nuf salt at the works at this time to salt all the hogs in the confederacy sir I wish your cincear advice on the sub-

---

[477] William Preston Johnston (1831-1899), aide-de-camp to President Davis with the rank of colonel. He was a son of General Albert Sidney Johnston, was born in Kentucky and educated at Yale, from which he graduated in 1852. He studied law at the University of Louisville, and settled in Louisville. After service in the First and Second Kentucky Regiments he became, in May 1862, an aide-de-camp to Jefferson Davis with the duties of inspector and confidential staff officer who bore many messages and instructions to generals in the field. He served in this capacity until the end of the war, when he became professor of history and English literature at Washington College in Lexington, Va., 1867-1877. In 1880 he became president of Louisiana State University, and in 1884 president of Tulane University, where he remained until his death. Melvin J. White, "William Preston Johnston," *Dict. of Am. Biog.*, X, 153-154.

[478] The resolutions are summarized on p. 418, 404n.

[479] Probably Jesse A. Reeves, formerly second lieutenant in company A of the Twenty-sixth North Carolina Regiment when Vance was its colonel. Moore, *N. C. Roster*, II, 363.

[480] See p. 92, 347n. Woodfin was the agent of the state at Saltville, Va.

ject at as Early a day as practible I am your most Obedent survent
& well wisher

[Raleigh]

[A. L. S. Governors' Papers (Vance),
State Department of Archives and History, Raleigh.]

From S. Cooper[481]

Adjt. & Ins Genls. office
Richmond Dec[r] 18th. 1862

The pressure of public business has prevented an earlier reply
to your letter of the 8th. inst. addressed to the Secretary of War.
The Secretary considers that he has no power under the Conscript
Laws to comply with your suggestions. And that it would be better
if the conscripts at Raleigh were distributed among the North
Carolina Regiments, where they could render efficient service. If
formed into a separate regiment, they would only have the value of
new levies, which as you know, are liable to lose confidence in
action. I may add that I do not see where Col Mallett can obtain
trained officiers for a regiment of conscripts— and no other officers
will answer— but if he can obtain any such, it would be well to
use them as enrolling officers, and thus supply his requisitions
upon this office Under all the circumstances it has been considered
best to refer your letter to Genl. G. W. Smith[482] to carry out these
suggestions and he has accordingly been authorized to call on
Maj. Mallett [483] for conscripts for the purposes indicated.

[Raleigh]

[A. L. S. Governors' Papers (Vance),
State Department of Archives and History, Raleigh.]

Commission to W. M. Shipp[484]

[Dec. 19, 1862]

State of North Carolina
To William M. Shipp greeting

We reposing special trust and confidence in your prudence,
integrity, ability and learning in the law do commission you a
Judge of the Superior Courts of Law and Equity of this State
(you having been thereunto appointed by the joint vote of the
two houses of the General Assembly) and do authorize you after
taking the oath prescribed by law, to enter upon the duties of
said Office and to exercise and perform its authorities of duties

---

[481] See p. 270, 338n.
[482] See p. 329, 119n.
[483] See p. 175, 44n.
[484] See p. 71, 268n. Shipp was elected a judge of the superior court by the legislature on December 12, 1862. He was a member of the legislature at the time.
Senate Journal, 1862-1863, p. 113.

& to receive and enjoy the salary and compensation thereunto annexed.

> In witness thereof, His Excellency Zebulon B. Vance our Governor, Captain General and Commander in chief hath with his hand Signed these presents & caused the Great Seal to be affixed thereto.
>
> Done at our City of Raleigh on the nine-teenth day of December in the year of our Lord, One thousand eight hundred & Sixty two & in the Eighty Seventh year of our Independence.
>
> Z. B. Vance

By the Governor
> R. H. Battle Jr
>> Private Secretary

[Vance Letter Book, 1862-1863,
State Department of Archives and History, Raleigh.]

From H. C. Jones, Jr.[485]

> Camp of the 57th Reg N. C. T.
> near Fredericksburg Dec 19th 62

I have learned with much pain that the Regiment to which I formerly belonged & to which I am still much attached is fast being demoralized & ruined by faction among its officers[486] and although I am aware that in addressing you upon this subject I may be guilty of an impropriety still I hope that the interest I feel in the regiment and all that concerns it will be a sufficient excuse for the liberty I am about to take— In the first place I think that the contest between the two rival candidates for the

---

[485] Hamilton Chamberlain Jones, Jr. (1837-1904), lieutenant colonel of the Fifty-seventh North Carolina Regiment. His father had been a prominent Whig leader of Salisbury for several decades; the son graduated from the University of North Carolina in 1858, studied law and began the practice of it in Salisbury in 1859. In 1860 he was defeated as a Whig candidate for the legislature, and supported the Bell and Everett ticket with Vance. In 1861 he became captain of company K in the Fifth North Carolina Regiment, of which Duncan K. McRae was colonel, and was wounded at Williamsburg. In July 1862 he was commissioned lieutenant colonel of the Fifty-seventh North Carolina Regiment and fought at Fredericksburg, Chancellorsville, and Gettysburg. On November 7, 1863, he was captured and remained a prisoner until February 1865, when he rejoined his regiment as colonel until again wounded near Petersburg, March 25, 1865. After the war he moved to Charlotte in 1867, where he was a fellow member of the bar with Vance, and where he formed a law partnership with Robert D. Johnston. Under President Cleveland he became United States District Attorney for Western North Carolina, 1885-1889. In 1870 he had represented Mecklenburg County in the State Senate. He was also president of the North Carolina Bar Association and a trustee of the University of North Carolina. Connor, *N. C. Manual*, p. 701; Grant, *Alumni History*, p. 328; Evans, *Conf. Mil. Hist.*, IV, 579-580.

[486] This controversy is discussed in a number of letters given above. See Thomas M. Garrett to Vance, pp. 163-167; W. N. H. Smith to Vance, pp. 168-170; D. K. McRae to Vance, pp. 170-171.

Colonelcy, Garrett [487] and Sinclair,[488] will decide the qu
whether the regiment is to continue as it has heretofore b⸱
one of the best in the service, or whether it is to become an unma⸱
ageable mob— a long an intimate acquaintance with it enables
me to speak with confidence when I say that Garrett alone can
restore the regiment to what it was six or eight months ago— He
commands the admiration and esteem of every one with whom
he is associated and is justely esteemed by them as one of the very
best officers from the State— He is a man of fine talent, excellent
judgment and most unflinchable courage. In him the regiment
has the utmost confidence and under his command I am confident
it will prove a credit to the State; under Sinclair I fear the result
would be disastrous—Unable to command respect he will hardly
be able to command obedience— Appoint him and the *esprit-de-
corps* for which this regiment was so greatly celebrated under the
leadership of the Gallant, high-toned Chivalrous McRae[489] will
have vanished— of Col Sinclair I will only say that I believe him to
be morally and mentally incapable of commanding the regiment
with any assurance of credit or usefulness to the State or Country—
    Having an interest in this matter beyond the deep interest I
feel in the regiment I have volunteered this information knowing that your object is fill the officies with the best men the state
affords, and knowing this I feel that my motives will be appreciated by you.[490]
[Raleigh]
[A. L. S. Governors' Papers (Vance),
  State Department of Archives and History, Raleigh.]

From George Richards[491]

Monroe Union County N. C. Decr 19 1862
    After my respects to you, I would say that I have had a long
& sevear spell of sickness, allmost ever since our retreat from
Malvern Hill,[492] My recovery has allmost been a miracle. When
I became convalescent & received a sick furlough to visit this place
where my brothers & sisters live hoping that good nursing & kind
attention would restore my broken health & shattered constitution,
and it is with pleasure I state, that my fondest hopes have been
realized, & I hope soon to be able to join my Regt the gallant Old
26th N. C. that still look with fondness on you, their gallant leader.

---

[487] See p. 163, 1n.
[488] See p. 164, 5n.
[489] See p. 163, 2n.
[490] Garrett was made colonel and Sinclair resigned in January 1863.
[491] George Richards, of Union County, fourth sergeant in company B of the
Twenty-sixth North Carolina Regiment, who enlisted June 5, 1861. Moore, *N. C.
Roster*, II, 367.
[492] July 1, 1862.

To day I have witnessed a rich & extraordinary seen, To wit, The enrolment of conscripts from 18 to 40, and just here I wish to inform you of the many subterfuges adopted by some of those who are— subject to the act. First & foremost I believe there is a collution between the Malitia Capt [493] & some of his favorites, with whome the most flimsey excuse is suficient to pass them over & lay them on the Shelf.

One man by name of John W. Rose[494] a man of some property about 35 or 36 years of age, who attempts to get out by buying an interest in a contemplated tannery, just started build a house for that purpose, or rather, to avoid going into service— No Mechanic himself but purely a Speculator in every sense of the word, ever since the war broke out.

The next is one Marshel Broadway a very stout able young man about 24 or 25 years old who bot out a little mail contract carried on horse-back once a week 10 or 12 miles, and he in his turn, hires another conscript one Moses Gordon very stout & able about 35 or 36 years of age to ride for him, so this little 10 mile mail, (formerly carried by a little boy) once a week deprives the service of 2 very stout able men,

The next is one John Shute a speculator about 36 or 37 who has Managed to get 2 or 3 neighbors to pretend to have him as an Overseer but realy attends to speculating & not to their business, & one of those persons pretending to hire him is only 35 or 36 years of age, but he is a Post Master,— So this favorite slips the noose—

The next one is one John Holm, with a little sore on his leg that no one heard of before, got a certificate from a hired Physician of disability and he slips through also, The next, a pretended "Doctr" Henry Tribble who never obtained diploma or perhaps never heard a Medical lecture a man of Very limited education a near-quack, who has been trying to practice physic in a very obscure neighborhood no more than 3 or 4 years & he too runs through. There are 2others John Irby & William Woolf what they feign, I have not heard, All the above, with one exception are in the little Town of Monroe Union County N C.—

The name of the Capt of this Beat is Stanly Austin.

Perhaps there are many others who never came under my observation I saw enough however to disgust a member of the Old 26th N C

---

[493] Robert G. Stanly Austin, captain in the Eighty-second Regiment of North Carolina Militia, which operated in the eastern portion of Union County. *Militia Roster*, p. 394.

[494] None of the men named in this letter appear in Moore, *N. C. Roster* as ever having been in the Confederate army.

I hope all the above will be attended too by an impartial officer as well as many others who are trying to evade the Conscript Raleigh

[A. L. S. Governors' Papers (Vance), State Department of Archives and History, Raleigh.]

From Jno. F. Miller[495]

In Camp near Fredericksburg Va
Decr 20/62.

I have the honor most respectfully to ask of you a position in the service of my native state, N. C. In a late Raleigh paper I notice that you & the Legislature have determined to raise 10.000 troops for State defense, & as these troops will require Officers in the various Depts, I would be greatly obliged could I be transfered to one of these Regts soon to be organized.[496]

I've been in the service unremittingly since 22ⁿᵈ April / 61 — a period of twenty months, with a loss of "Leave of absence" by reason of sickness & other causes of only 27 days. I'm in a Brigade & Div that is second to none in the service— Pender's[497] of A. P. Hill: [498] Div.; but the service is exceedingly hard, & if the State service be any easier, I would much prefer it on account of my health & reasons of a domestic character. My position is that of Surgeon of 34ᵗʰ N. C. Regt, & if it be not in yr power to give me a similar position somewhere in the State, I would accept that of Post or Regtl Qr. M. Since the battles before Richmond my exposures have been great, much of the time being compelled to live without a tent; but in the State service I imagine the troops will be mostly stationary & will not have a *"Stonewall" Jackson* to march after. If there be a position in any Hospital in the State that I could get I would prefer it. I refer to Confed. Bd. Med. Examiners as to competence. I presume there would be no difficulty with the Confederate authorities relative to a transfer. Yr. attention to this will be greatly appreciated. I have the honor to be, sincerely,

[Raleigh]

---

[495] John F. Miller (1834-1906), surgeon of the Thirty-fourth North Carolina Regiment. He was a native of Cleveland County, a graduate of the University of North Carolina, studied medicine at The Medical College of South Carolina and graduated at Jefferson in Philadelphia in 1858. He became assistant surgeon of the First North Carolina Regiment before he was made surgeon of the Thirty-fourth. In 1864 he was appointed inspector of hospitals in Virginia, and afterwards was chief surgeon of the department of eastern North Carolina and southern Virginia. In 1865 he moved to Goldsboro, and was superintendent of the State Hospital at that place from 1888 until his death in 1906. *Medical Transactions*, 1906, pp. 159-160. Moore, *N. C. Roster, II,* 640.

[496] See p. 394, 319n.

[497] See p. 170, 26n.

[498] See p. 431, 447n.

[on reverse]
Ans^r- the D^r that I will remember him if the State troops are raised. Z B V
[A. L. S. Governors' Papers (Vance),
State Department of Archives and History, Raleigh.]

To Jefferson Davis

EXECUTIVE DEPARTMENT
STATE OF NORTH CAROLINA
Raleigh Dec. 24th. 1862

In accordance with the request of the General Assembly of this State, I have the honor to send you herewith by the hand of A. C. Cowles [499] Esqr a joint resolution[500] of that body in relation to the seizure of one R. J. Graves[501] a citizen of North Carolina and his

---

[499] Andrew Carson Cowles, the member of the House of Commons from Yadkin County, who was appointed by Vance to bear the resolutions to Richmond. President Davis was absent from Richmond visiting the armies in the west, and Cowles dealt with the secretary of war, James A. Seddon. See p. 291, 7n.

[500] The resolution was introduced by William A. Graham, senator from Orange County, the home of R. J. Graves. The resolutions were adopted on December 20, 1862, by a unanimous vote and requested the governor to "demand of the authorities at Richmond . . . that he be immediately returned to this State, to the end that he may be delivered over to the civil authorities here . . . for examination, . . ." The essence of the complaint was that Graves had been arrested by the military authorities without a warrant and without a definite charge, and had been transported outside the state for trial by a military court, though Graves himself was not a member of the armed forces. *Public Laws of N. C., 1862-1863,* pp. 47-48.

[501] Rev. Robert J. Graves, pastor of the Bethlehem Presbyterian Church at "The Oaks" in Orange County. According to William A. Graham, also of Orange County, Graves was born in England. When very young he came to Massachusetts, practiced law for a year or so in Albany, New York, and then moved to Virginia, where he graduated from William and Mary College, taught school for a few years, and then graduated from Union Theological Seminary in Prince Edward County, Va. After his graduation he accepted a call to the Bethlehem church in Orange County. In 1862 he appears to have applied for a pass to go north for private reasons, among them being the necessity of an operation upon his throat which he wished done in New York. According to his story he was arrested by the Yankees and detained at McClellan's headquarters at Harrison's Landing, being confined for about two weeks, and refusing to take the oath of allegiance to the Union, which was urged upon him. Eventually he was released, made his journey north, and returned to his charge in Orange County. While in the north he was greatly impressed by the evidences of a serious war effort on the part of the Federal government, which seemed to belie the general opinion in the south that the north was war-weary and filled with anti-war sentiments. Upon his return to Orange County he told friends of his general impressions learned while in the north and, again according to William A. Graham, wrote his famous letter to the Richmond *Enquirer* at the request of William J. Bingham, the famous schoolman of Orange County, who was a member of Graves' church. Bingham's idea was that the letter would serve as an antidote to overconfidence in the south and arouse the south from its lethargy. But because of the letter, and because of other reports that came to the attention of the war department, Captain Mc-Cubbin, chief of the Richmond detective force, was sent to Orange County to arrest Graves, presumably for treason. McCubbin came one Sunday morning and sat quietly in a pew and heard Graves preach, and then arrested him and took him off to Richmond, where he was confined in Castle Thunder. Vance, about

transportation beyond the limits of the State.

An answer to the demand therein contained at your earliest convenience will oblige

[Richmond]

[Vance Letter Book, 1862-1863,

State Department of Archives and History, Raleigh.]

From J. W. McElroy[502]

Burnsville Yancy Co. Med
December 26th 1862

I send by Captain J. R. Neil[503] my Agent the articles collected by the Captains in my regiment the supply is much smaller than I could have wished but there had been Agents from all the Companies from that County in the 29th Reg and collected good supplies for their Companies is the great cause of no more being collected on your call[504] and another reason is the inefficiency of many of the Captains of my Regiment. If Captain Neil had been appointed for the whole county our success would have been much greater and if the destitution of our army continues I would recommend that he be appointed Agent for this County Mitchell and Watauga and if he could make any arrangement to barter Spun threads for Cloth Socks Clothing &c he could in my opinion collect a large amount through the year I suggest this for your consideration Neil is an energetic man and what he undertakes to do he does it with all his might Captain Neil is Authorised by me to receive and recepted for all money that may be coming for the articles & collections in this Regiment.

I am sorry to state that our mountains are full of Deserters and Tories and I fear their numbers will be augumented by the last enrollment of Conscripts. I am confident that many will go to the mountains before they will go to the war and I fear that they will do us much mischief will be done to our helpless inhabitants

---

to leave Raleigh, was advised of the episode and asked the mayor of Raleigh to stop the party, but the mayor was unable to find them on the train and the next they heard of Graves he was in jail in Richmond. The North Carolina press gave great publicity to the incident and most of the papers seemed to presume Graves' innocence, but most also pointed out that even if he were guilty the military authorities still had no right to arrest him and take him out of the state for trial. See *Fayetteville Observer*, December 15, 1862; Raleigh *North Carolina Standard*, December 23, 31, 1862, January 20, 30, February 6, 1863; George Davis to E. J. Hale, January 16, 24, E. J. Hale to George Davis, January 19, 1863, Hale Papers; and Seddon to Vance, below, pp. 449-452. Graham's speech on the matter is reported in the Raleigh *North Carolina Standard*, January 30, 1863.

[502] See p. 96, 361n.

[503] See p. 299, 33n. After his resignation from the army Neill became quartermaster of the 111th Regiment of North Carolina Militia, being commissioned June 1, 1862. This was a Yancey County regiment, and McElroy was its colonel. Militia Roster, pp. 422-423. Neill was a member of the State Senate from Yancey County in 1883. Connor, *N. C. Manual*, p. 859.

[504] See p. 266 for the orders to the militia.

when our best men are all gone as there has been many thefts committed by the acct byers all readdy. I suppose about half the men on the last call in this County Volunteered in old Companies the bal was enrolled as conscripts on the last call over one Hundred has been enrolled as conscripts and for other companies it leaves us a small number at Home and there being so few slaves it will make it hard on those who are left, but we must do the best we can believing that we have a Man at the Head of our State Government that will do Justice to all as far as lies in his power.

I wrote you a few weeks ago from Asheville in the letter I enclosed two dollars the Subscription money for the weekly Standard and requesting you to hand it to Holden and tel him to send me his paper first number to include the organization of the present Legislature. I have not yet recd the paper and suppose you have not recd my letter nor money I was writing to you on some Matters of Col J. B. Palmer by his request please write to me and say if you recd the letter or not. I wrote from Asheville in Nov the day before Col R. B. Vance returned to his Regiment.[505]

There was a man in this County collecting Articles for the Soldiers who represented himself as an Agent appointed by you for that purpose he bought a great deal of Jenes cloth Socks &c he was here buying the week before I recd your order his name I dont recollect.

I hope you will write me if you have the time
[Raleigh]
[on reverse]
See if Holden got the money
[A. L. S. Governors' Papers (Vance),
State Department of Archives and History, Raleigh.]

From Giles Leitch[506]

Lumberton N. C. Decr 26 A. D. 1862

In anticipation of the passage by the Legislature of the Military Bill [507] now before that body certain certain of my friends in Robeson County commenced raising a company to volunteer for state defence and have succeeded in enlisting nearly a sufficient number to form a company and are sanguine in the expectation and belief that they can succeed but recent events has rendered the

[505] The letter is dated November 24, 1862. See p. 393.

[506] Giles Leitch was a member of the State Senate from Robeson County, at home for the Christmas recess of the legislature. He was a lawyer who represented Robeson County in the House of Commons in 1856 and Richmond and Robeson counties in the State Senate in 1862, 1864, and 1865. He was born in 1827, a graduate of the University of North Carolina in 1851, and a planter. Connor, *N. C. Manual*, p. 781; Grant, *Alumni History*, p. 361.

[507] See p. 394, 319n.

passage of that Bill improbable. Most of the men thus enlisted are subject to conscription This is at their request to inquire of you if they can organize and as a company (with officers of their own selection) enter the service either confederate or State They would be pleased if an arrangement of that kind could be effected, They desire to go together as a company and to be controled by Officers of their own selection. You would confer a favor by replying to this at your earliest convenience directed to me at this place with such suggestions pertinent to their case as may occur to you Would they be received as a company under their own organization in Malletts[508] Battalion They officers they would choose have nearly all been in service as last twelve months Your attention to this will oblige

[on reverse]

I fear I can not receive them without the Legislature will pass the bill— Do not let them disband however until they hear further   Z B V

Raleigh

[A. L. S. Governors' Papers (Vance),
  State Department of Archives and History, Raleigh.]

To A. C. Myers[509]

STATE OF NORTH CAROLINA
EXECUTIVE DEPARTMENT
Raleigh 26th. Dec. 1862

I beg leave to call your attention to a subject of vital importance to the people of this State. The vast amt. of Salt belonging to the State of North Carolina at Saltville Va., I am afraid is destined to be of little use to us unless some aid is afforded by your Department. Nearly the whole locomotive power on the South Side[510] & Tennessee R. Roads,[511] I am informed, is controlled by the Government. And I am prevented from sending Engines & Cars from the Roads in this State, because the gauge of the several roads is different.[512] Under this condition of things, I am constrained

[508] See p. 175, 44n.

[509] See p. 150, 611n.

[510] The South Side Railroad ran from Lynchburg through Burkeville and Petersburg to Suffolk, Va., where it joined the Seaboard and Roanoke into Norfolk. At Petersburg the South Side crossed the Virginia extension of the Wilmington and Weldon Railroad, and so afforded a transportation route into North Carolina. This was the only route by which to bring salt from Saltville into North Carolina by rail until the Piedmont Railroad, which crossed the South Side at Burkeville, was finished later in the war. This could bring salt from Lynchburg to Burkeville, and thence on the Piedmont to Greensboro, N. C.

[511] The Virginia and Tennessee Railroad ran from Bristol to Lynchburg. Saltville was very near this line, and not far from Bristol.

[512] The gauge of both these Virginia roads was five feet; the North Carolina roads were all four feet, eight and one-half inches, except for the Wilmington and Manchester Railroad, which was useless for this purpose.

to request you to give us some relief: either by furnishing Engines & Cars, or by making an exchange of some Engines fitted to the gauge of the Virginia Roads, for Engines in this State which can be turned over to your Agents at any moment in their place.

The season is now far advanced, and the condition of every class of our people will be truly deplorable, unless salt is brought to them. Independent of that, the supply for the Army, will be seriously diminished. A large amount of pork is now waiting for salt, to be packed, and unless it is received very soon, an immense loss will ensue, which in the end will be a Serious public calamity. I cannot therefore too earnestly impress upon you the importance of this matter; and the importance of prompt action in our behalf. The result will be of immeasureable benefit to our people and in the end, will be to the Government itself.[513]
Richmond
[Vance Letter Book, 1862-1863,
State Department of Archives and History, Raleigh.]

Proclamation

[December 26, 1862]
By the Governor of North Carolina
A Proclamation
Whereas, the time limited in my Proclamation[514] forbidding the Exportation of Salt, Bacon, Pork, Beef, Corn, Meal, Flour, Potatoes Shoes, Leather, Hides, Cotton Cloth, and yarn and Woollen Cloth Cloth, is about to expire and the same necessity exists now as then for prohibition.

Now, therefore I Zebulon B. Vance Governor of North Carolina, do issue this Proclamation continuing the said prohibition, with the same restrictions and exemptions as were contained in said proclamation, for thirty days from the date hereof.

In testimony whereof, Z. B. Vance, Governor hath Signed these presents, and caused the Great Seal of the State to be affixed.

Done at the City of Raleigh, this 26th day of December A. D. 1862 and in the 87th. year of our Independence.
Z. B. Vance
By the Governor
R. H. Battle Jr
Private Secretary
[Vance Letter Book, 1862-1863,
State Department of Archives and History, Raleigh.]

---

[513] On December 30, Myers replied to the effect that he had written the superintendents of the South Side and the Virginia and Tennessee Railroads invoking their aid in the transportation of salt into North Carolina, and that he would acquaint Vance of their answers as soon as he received them. Myers to Vance, Vance Letter Book, 1862-1863.

[514] See pp. 404-405.

From James A. Seddon[515]

CONFEDERATE STATES OF AMERICA
WAR DEPARTMENT
Richmond Va [Dec 27/62]

In the absence of the President, now on a visit to the Armies of the West and South, your letter of the 24th. Inst,[516] communicating a Preamble and Resolution of the General Assembly of North Carolina relative to the seizure and transportation from the State of R. J. Graves[517] a citizen of Orange County & making in conformity with the resolution a demand for the return of the said R. J. Graves to the State for the delivery to the authorities there, for examination & if sufficient cause appear, for commitment, & trial, has been handed by A. B. Cowles,[518] Esqr. to me as Secretary of War for my action thereon.

It will doubtless be matter of regret to you and the General Assembly of your State, as it certainly is to me, that the matter cannot receive the more satisfactory consideration and determination of the President, and as the subject shall on his return be promptly submitted to his revision, it is not improbable he may deem it worthy of further special communication from himself. Still the imposing source of the application, and the gravity of the subject demanding from its nature prompt action in my estimation impose on me the responsibility of exercising my imperfect judgment in rendering a decision.

Some brief statement of the connection of the Department with the detention of Mr Graves and of the circumstances of his case will naturally and appropriately preced and explain both the action heretofore taken and the conclusion arrived at in his case.

On some few days since, was I informed as Head of this Department of the detention of Mr Graves in one of the Military prisons of the City to which he had been consigned by the order of Brig General Winder[519] Military Commandant of the District and Acting Provost Marshall of the City. When apprised of the fact, I enquired briefly as to the grounds of charge and was assured by Genl Winder that he was charged and held as a spy, and that he did not consider it safe that he should be dismissed. I then

---

[515] See p. 380, 273n.

[516] See pp. 444-445.

[517] See p. 444, 501n.

[518] See p. 291, 7n. and p. 444, 499n.

[519] John Henry Winder (1800-1865), military commandant of the district and acting provost marshall of the city of Richmond. He was a native of Maryland, a graduate of West Point, and a former major of artillery in the United States army. In 1861 he was appointed brigadier general and made provost marshall and commander of the prisons in Richmond. In this thankless position he drew much criticism and even his defenders, which were numerous and qualified, admitted that he "was no respector of persons" and that his "manners and mode of speech were perhaps naturally somewhat abrupt and sharpe." Robert Douthat Meade, "John Henry Winder," *Dict. of Am. Biog.*, XX, 380-381.

directed he should be examined by the Command. Mr Sidney
Baxter,[520] a lawyer of high repute, charged with the duty of en-
quiring into the cases of prisoners in the military prisons, and of
either discharging them or handing them over to the proper
tribunals for trial. A day or two afterwards on the application
of the Rev Mr. Brown of No. Carolina, learning that the examination had not been then had, I reiterated the order, and being informed that the cause of delay had been the absence of a
soldier and Officer in the Army, who were wanted as witnesses, I
immediately directed they should be ordered from the field here.
Thus the matter stood to day, on the delivery of your letter. On the
further investigation then immediately made of the circumstances
of the arrest and of the grounds on which it was based, I learn
from General Winder that on the 6th November last there appeared in the Richmond Enquirer a long letter[521] written by the
Rev. R. J. Graves, proffered as giving to our people just views of
the purposes of our enemies, a number of the paper containing
the letter will be submitted to you with this. Without pretending to judge the real intent or probable effect of this letter,
it is sufficient to say it seemed to many well calculated to cause mis-
trust & discouragement among our people, as to the result of the
War and that the loyalty of the writer was greatly doubted. Not
very long after the publication of this article two letters addressed
to the Editor of the Enquirer elicited by the distrust which this
letter had aroused as to the character and purposes of the writer,
were submitted by that Editor to General Winder. Copies of
these two letters are transmitted herewith. One was from Capt.
T. E. Upshaw,[522] a gallant officer of the Army giving the intelligence derived from one of his soldiers a returned prisoner vouched
as entirely truthful that the Revd. Gentleman (Mr Graves) who
had come down with the flag of truce to Harrisons Landing, while
there was heard by him giving information to the enemy of all he

---

[520] Sydney S. Baxter, appointed by Secretary of War Judah P. Benjamin to examine
prisoners and to report as to whether they should be discharged, or tried and
punished. Baxter was appointed on December 10, 1861, served without any pay, and
made numerous reports to the War Department about the prisoners, but no report on Graves is preserved. O. R., Ser. II, Vol. II, 1403-1404.

[521] For the substance of the letter and the reasons Graves wrote it see p. 444,
501n.

[522] T. E. Upshaw was captain of company C of the Thirteenth Virginia Cavalry.
A copy of his letter to the Enquirer, written from Culpepper, Va. on November
3, 1862, is in Governors' Papers (Vance). The man in his company who reported
Graves' activities was named Parker, and was described by Upshaw as "uneducated
but entirely truthful." He did not remember Graves' name until he heard it mentioned in connection with Graves' letter to the Enquirer. Upshaw asked that his
letter not be published, but said that either he or Parker would be forthcoming
if needed. He confessed that he "did not like the tone of the Article in the
Enquirer, thought it over wrought, and if Graves is the man whom Parker saw
and heard he is a traitor." The meeting between Graves and the Federal provost
marshall, which Parker saw and heard, took place on August 3, 1862.

knew "about our matters at Richmond, and especially about the Gunboat Richmond" in respect to which "so elaborate were the discussions and explanations that the drawings and plans of the Monitor were brought and shown to him." Other particulars tending to strengthen suspicion and identify the Rev. Mr Graves, are given, on which as you will have the letters, it is needless to dwell. In this connection it may be added that subsequently it has been ascertained that after his return from the North, the Rev. Mr Grave voluntarily stated to a leading clergyman of this City (Mr Norwood) [523] that finding difficulty interposed to his going North, he had obtained his permit to proceed by affecting to give information which he believed would be of no avail to the enemy and had among other topics made statements respecting the Gun Boat Richmond. This attitude confessed by himself of a minister of the Gospel for an end of private advantage affecting to act the Spy is certainly not calculated to diminish the suspiciousness of his conduct, while it identifies him with the person charged by the soldier and confirms the general accuracy of his statement. The other letter laid before Gen. Winder, signed an old citizen, but submitted by a Mr Geo. P. Miles appears to have been written by a zealous citizen of No. Ca. fully acquainted with the origin and antecedents of the Rev. Mr Graves and characterizes him as a Northern man, a Yankee undeserving of trust and of more than doubtful loyalty, having neither home nor people in North Carolina. On applying to Gen Winder for a passport, at the time of his trip to Harrisson's Landing, Mr Graves had represented himself as a New Yorker desirous of returning to the North. Other oral suggestions, Gen Winder informs me were made from various sources against this man, but the letter constituted the main grounds of his action. He sent an officer[524] under his command to No. Carolina, had him arrested and brought to this City. You will observe his information was that the Rev Gentleman had acted the Spy and might naturally be expected to continue the same line of conduct. He did not know him to be a North Carolinian, but believed him to be an alien enemy (being discribed as a Yankee without a home in the State) and as such being charged with giving information to the enemy, he considered him as a Spy, to be arrested anywhere in the Confederacy and brought for examination and trial to the Military District within which his alleged offences had been committed. Genl Winder in the judgment of the Department acted with over zeal in not first fully satisfying himself that the party charged was not a citizen of

---

[523] Rev. William Norwood (1806-1887), an Episcopal minister of Richmond. He was a native of Orange County, N. C., a graduate of the University of North Carolina in 1826, received an M. A. in 1832, and a D. D. in 1851. Grant, *Alumni History*, p. 462; Battle, *History of U. of N. C.*, I, 627.
[524] The officer was Captain McCubbin. See p. 444, 501n.

North Carolina. As such while amenable to arrest on sufficient grounds as a Spy, or even as a trator, he could with no propriety or legality be removed from the State, but should be handed over to the appropriate authorities military or civil, in the State to be dealt with according to law. While doubt on the subject of the citizenship of this party may have been on the information posessed pardonable heretofore, now that the assurance of his citizenship is afforded by the deliberate action of the General Assembly of North Carolina there can be neither prudence nor justification for not promptly admiting the error committed by his removal and rectifying it by his immediate return and delivery under your Excellency's demand.

He will accordingly be cheerfully and at once placed at the disposal of Mr Cowls[525] or at his option sent under the escort of an Officer to be delivered in Raleigh to such authority as you may direct.

Should any proceedings be instituted against him requiring the presence of witnesses, I need not add that all facilities will be afforded by the Department here, to secure their due attendance.

While regretting the mistake committed in this case, I find compensative satisfaction in evincing the sincere respect entertained by the Department for the rights of citizenship and the sovereignty of the States, & avail myself of the opportunity to assure your Excellency and through you the General Assembly of North Carolina that the Department so far from countenancing infringement on either, regards it as its highest privilege as well as plainest duty by the utmost efforts of its powers to preserve them both inviolate against all enemies.[526]

[Raleigh]
[Vance Letter Book, 1862-1863,
State Department of Archives and History, Raleigh.]

From J. R. Waugh [527]

Camp near Fredericksburg V. A.
December 28th 1862

I would like very much if you think it would be compatible with the interest of N. C. to receive the appointment of Lieut

---

[525] Cowles brought Graves back to Raleigh, where they arrived on December 28, and turned Graves over to Vance, who confessed that he did not know what to do with him. Raleigh *North Carolina Standard*, December 31, 1862. See below, p. 454.

[526] In his message to the legislature when it reconvened in 1863 Vance had high praise for Seddon's letter and expressed great approval of his answer. *Legislative Documents, 1862-1836*, Document No. 19, p. 3.

[527] James R. Waugh, of Surry County, captain of company A in the Second North Carolina Regiment. He was formerly captain of company H in the Twenty-first Regiment, but was transferred to the Second on September 19, 1862, having been defeated for re-election. He died May 28, 1863 of wounds received at Chancellorsville. Clark, *N. C. Regts.*, I, 47, 158; Moore, *N. C. Roster*, II. 195; J. G. Hollingsworth, *History of Surry County or Annals of Northwest North Carolina* (n. p., 1935), p. 230 (cited hereafter as Hollingsworth, *Surry County*).

Col or Major among those for the defence of the State.[528] I think I have Some claims as I have been a soldier ever since the war commenced.

I was a captain in a Volunteer Company from Surry for nearly twelve months was in several battles during the time, and trust did not act dishonerable but was always at my post never being absent during the time. At the reorgination was beaten and in Sept last received the appointment as Captain in this the 2nd Reg N. C. T. I have been engaged since the appointment at Fredericksburg yet without the opportunity of doing much

I can give a recommendation if necessary from Lieut Col Graves[529] of 21st Reg or Major Rankin[530] of the same Regiment to which I belonged 12 months And also from the field officers of this Reg

I would like to hear soon

[Raleigh]

[on reverse]

Say that I have as yet no authority to raise troops. Will give him a chance should it be done   Z B V

[A. L. S. Governors' Papers (Vance),
State Department of Archives and History, Raleigh.]

From Thos. Lilly[531]

Camp French
Dec 29th 1862

Pardon me for the liberty assumed in addressing you upon a subject which doubtless you have already been or will be much troubled. I am very desirous of a position in the "State Troops" [532] which I presume are now being raised— I can furnish you very satisfactory recommendations from Col's Burgwyn,[533] Lane,[534]

---

[528] See p. 394, 319n.

[529] Barby Y. Graves, also of Surry County, lieutenant colonel of the Twenty-first North Carolina Regiment. He enlisted as a captain, and became lieutenant colonel on August 28, 1862; he was wounded at Second Manassas immediately thereafter and resigned from the service March 12, 1863. Moore, *N. C. Roster*, II, 175, 181; Hollingsworth, *Surry County*, p. 226.

[530] W. S. Rankin, of Guilford County, who became lieutenant colonel on March 12, 1863, upon the resignation of Graves. Rankin was wounded and taken prisoner at Gettysburg. Moore, *N. C. Roster*, II, 175.

[531] Thomas Lilly, of Anson County, fourth corporal of company K in the Twenty-sixth North Carolina Regiment, who had been promoted to first lieutenant while Vance commanded the unit. He afterwards became captain of the company upon the resignation of Captain McLauchlin, and was killed at Five Forks, April 1, 1865, while in command of a brigade of sharpshooters. Clark, *N. C. Regts.*, II, 393, 419; Moore, *N. C. Roster*, II, 402.

[532] See p. 394, 319n.

[533] See p. 121, 473n. Burgwyn succeeded Vance as colonel of the Twenty-sixth.

[534] John R. Lane, of Chatham County, who succeeded Burgwyn as colonel of the Twenty-sixth after Burgwyn's death at Gettysburg. Born in 1835, he enlisted as a private and fought throughout the war, after which he was a merchant and planter in Chatham County. Clark, *N. C. Regts.*, II, 408-410.

and Capt. McLaughlin[535] as to the faithful discharge of my duties as 1st Lieut in Co "K" I would be happy to receive the appointment as Commander of Company Commissary, or Adjutant of a Regiment— I do not make this request thinking that I will get rid of my work by no means but am fully aware that that is the place for constant and hard work— which I'm perfectly willing to [illegible]

If this request, Governor, meets your approbation I warrant you shall never have cause to regret it, as I shall constantly strive to do my whole duty—

[Raleigh]

[on reverse]

Ansr that the Gov would do so with pleasure but the State has not yet formed   Z B V

[A. L. S. Governors' Papers (Vance),
    State Department of Archives and History, Raleigh.]

To M. E. Manly[536]

Executive Office
Raleigh Decr. 30th./62

I send herewith the body of R. J. Graves, returned from Richmond to the State authorities according to a joint resolution of the General Assembly.[537]

Not knowing exactly what to do with him, I have concluded by advice to send him to his own county to be bailed, that he may appear to answer any charge made against him. I hope therefore that you will oblige me by taking surety for his appearance at

---

[535] John Calvin McLaughlin (1835-1906), of Cumberland County, who became captain of company K at the reorganization in April 1862, having formerly been second lieutenant. He was wounded at Malvern Hill and disabled at Gettysburg, and resigned. He was an honor graduate of the University of North Carolina in 1857, became a lawyer after the war, moved to Wadesboro, and was clerk of the superior court of Anson County for more than twenty years. Clark, *N. C. Regts.*, II, 418-419; Moore, *N. C. Roster*, II, 402; Grant, *Alumni History*, p. 396; Battle, *History of U. of N. C.*, I, 675.

[536] Matthias Evans Manly (1801-1881), associate justice of the Supreme Court of North Carolina. He was born in Chatham County, a son of Basil Manly and a brother of former governor Charles Manly. He graduated from the University of North Carolina in 1824, studied law, located in New Bern, and married Hannah Gaston, a daughter of Judge William Gaston. He had a long political career: he represented New Bern in the House of Commons in 1834 and 1835; was judge of the superior court, 1840-1859; then went to the Supreme Court for six years. He was a member of the House of Commons and of the Convention in 1865, was president of the State Senate in 1866, when he was elected United States Senator to succeed John Pool who had been elected for the short term, but the state was denied representation in Congress. Afterwards he was presiding judge of the county court and mayor of the town of New Bern. While on the Supreme Court Manly was more friendly to Confederate claims than was the Chief Justice, Richmond M. Pearson. Samuel A'Court Ashe, "Matthias Evans Manly." Ashe, *Biog. Hist. of N. C.*, VI, 357-365.

[537] See p. 444, 500n and 501n.

the Court House in Hillsboro in such sum & at such time as you may deem best, for examination into his case, giving time sufficient to notify the Confederate authorities to produce witnesses &c.[538]

This is the only course I can fall upon in the matter, I should have required him to enter into bond here, but for the difficulty of procuring sureties out of his own County.

I send also copies of the evidence upon which he was arrested, sent me from Richmond, together with the letter of the Secretary of War, Mr. Seddon.[539]
Hillsboro
[Vance Letter Book, 1862-1863,
State Department of Archives and History, Raleigh.]

From James G. Ramsay[540]

Palermo Rowan Co N. C.
Dec 31st 1862

I write to commend to your favorable consideration Thomas J. Foster[541] of Salisbury. I have long known Mr Foster. He is a gentleman of fine business qualities and habits and will do excellent service in any business agency you may wish to fill. He

---

[538] The case was set for a hearing in January, but was postponed on Vance's order. When it was again scheduled for February 3 Vance wrote to Secretary Seddon and invited the appearance of any witnesses against Graves, and especially requested Norwood's appearance. He also wrote to inform George V. Strong, Confederate District Attorney, and to urge him to be present at the hearing in Hillsboro. When the hearing occured Graves was bound over to Confederate authorities in Richmond to be tried for treason. See Vance to Seddon, January 2, 10, 1863, Vance to Strong, January 1, 1863, Vance Letter Book, 1862-1863; Raleigh *North Carolina Standard*, January 20, February 6, 1863.

[539] See p. 449.

[540] James Graham Ramsay (1823-1903), then a member of the State Senate from Rowan County. Ramsay was born in Iredell County, graduated from Davidson College in 1841 and from Jefferson Medical College in 1848, and then settled at Palermo in Rowan County, where he took over the practice of his brother-in-law, Dr. Richard T. Dismukes, who had just died. He was then an ardent Henry Clay Whig, was defeated for the House of Commons in 1854, but defeated Charles F. Fisher for the Senate in 1860, when Ramsay opposed secession and supported the Bell and Everett ticket in the national campaign. He spoke in Salisbury with Vance at the celebrated Union meeting there on October 11, 1860. He was a member of the Senate from 1856 to 1862, and again in 1883. Ramsey was a supporter of the Vance administration until 1863 when he began to break with it over the civil rights issue and the peace movement, on which ticket he became a member of the Confederate Congress in 1864. After the war he became a Republican, was an intimate of Holden, and was defeated for Congress by Henderson in 1884. In 1894 he moved to Salisbury. Obituary in *Salisbury Herald*, January 10, 1903; *Greensboro Daily News*, January 4, 1925, Raleigh *North Carolina Standard*, December 9, 1863; *Alumni Catalogue of Davidson College*, p. 45; Robert D. W. Connor, "James Graham Ramsay," Van Noppen Papers; Connor, *N. C. Manual*, pp. 793-794.

[541] T. J. Foster, a business man of Salisbury who became, after the war, a partner of C. F. Baker and E. B. Neave in C. F. Baker and Company, dealing in stoves, tinware, and house furnishings. James S. Brawley, *The Rowan Story 1753-1953. A Narrative History of Rowan County, North Carolina* (Salisbury, 1953), p. 239 (cited hereafter as Brawley, *Rowan County*).

can give any reference about Salisbury or adjoining counties
substantiating the above statements
[Raleigh]
[A. L. S. Governors' Papers (Vance),
State Department of Archives and History, Raleigh.]

From Officers of Second N. C. Battalion

Hd. Qrs. 2nd- No- Ca- Battalion.
Camp near Drewry's Bluff.
Dec. 1862

In compliance with an order from the Secretary of War, the
Companies composing the 2nd- No- Ca- Batt. on the 25th- of Sept.
1862 proceeded to an election of Company Officers. The Officers'
elect then in pursuance of an order emanating from the same
source proceeded to an election of Field Officers, which resulted
as follows: W. H. Wheeler,[542] Lt. Col. L. H. Andrews,[543] Major.
While acting in their respective capacities, gave universal satisfaction. After an interview with Gen Daniel,[544] Brigade Commander,
they were assured at a very early day this Battalion would be increased to a Regiment. Lt Col. Wheeler would then by promotion,
have been Colonel; which position he neither desired, nor would
have accepted. In consideration of the above assurance from Genl-
Daniel, that the Batt. would very soon be made a Regt., Col.
Wheeler resigned the Lt. Colonelcy; then by his influence induced
a large majority of the Officers to sign a petition which he drew
up. placing the right of appointment in the hands of Genl Daniel;
with the understanding however, that Capt. Chas. E. Shober,[545]
W. H. Wheeler, & L. H. Andrews would be the Officers appointed.

---

[542] W. H. Wheeler, of Forsythe County, who was commissioned captain of company G in the Second Battalion on January 16, 1862, but he is not listed as ever
having been lieutenant colonel. Moore, *N. C. Roster,* IV, 226. In the reorganization
he was chosen lieutenant colonel in place of Wharton J. Green, who was "opposed
to it on principle as calculated to introduce politics into camp, and although from
the peculiar constitution of this command, it could have been avoided, nevertheless
when it became obvious that such was the desire of a number of the officers, no
obstruction was interposed on my part." Clark, *N. C. Regts.,* IV, 252.

[543] H. L. Andrews, of Randolph County, commissioned captain of company F in
the Second Battalion on November 30, 1861; promoted lieutenant colonel June 6,
1863; killed at Gettysburg, July 1, 1863. Moore, *N. C. Roster,* IV, 217, 224.

[544] See p. 109, 428n. Daniels was formerly colonel of the Fourteenth North Carolina
Regiment when Vance was a captain in it.

[545] Charles Eugene Shober (1827-1877), lawyer and banker, who was from Salem
but who then lived in Greensboro and had represented Guilford County in the
House of Commons in 1860. He was commissioned captain of company B in the
Forty-fifth North Carolina Regiment on February 15, 1862; was promoted major on
September 1, 1862; and, according to Wharton J. Green in Clark, *N. C. Regts.,* IV,
252, became lieutenant colonel of the Second Battalion shortly after Wheeler was
chosen and resigned, but he does not appear as lieutenant colonel in Moore, *N. C.
Roster,* III, 258, 262. Shober resigned from the Second Battalion shortly before
Gettysburg and later became colonel of the Seventy-seventh North Carolina Regi-
ment of Senior Reserves. After the war he was a lawyer and banker in Rome, Ga.
Connor, *N. C. Manual,* p. 634; Grant, *Alumni History,* p. 561.

We regarded this petition as equivalent to an election, from the fact of its expressing the wishes of a large majority of the officers. This agreement was entered into by us with great reluctance, until after we had been assured by Col Wheeler, he did not desire the Colonelcy. Feeling confident that the above conditions would be complied with, we gave ourselves no uneasiness. But, to our utter astonishment, we have been informed that Your Excellency has recommended [546] a M^r- B. R. Moore[547] for the Lt. Colonelcy of this Battalion, which if complied with we assure Your Excellency will create very decided & great dissatisfaction both with the Officers & the men. We therefore very respectfully ask Your Excellency to revoke the request for the following reasons; first; we have no doubt but what Your Excellency's recommendation was obtained by misrepresentation; second: in our opinion it would be a very dangerous precedent to establish, bringing a man from one division of the Army to another, to fill a position which he could not get by *an election* in the Reg^t- to which he was attached; over officers his senior in rank. Such a precedent would be calculated to demoralize the best Reg^t in Service, moreover, we feel as if very great injustice had been done us, in appointing a man over us, who is not in the slightest degree identified with the interests of the men we represent, only so far as getting the position he desires, which he knows well he could not get by an election. We assure your Excellency there is nothing so well calculated to utterly demoralize this Battalion, as the appointment of B. R. Moore to the Lt. Colonelcy. There is not a single man in it, that desire he should have a position in the Battalion, save the one that would entitle him to a *"Musket and Eleven Dollars per Month."* In the name of Justice & Right to men that have long been in service, & have the approval of their Commanding Officers, we very respectfully beg of Your Excellency, not to insist upon the appointment of a man for Lt. Col. of this Battalion who is only for self aggrandisement identified with it, in preference to

---

[546] In Special Orders, No. 278, dated November 27, 1862, the office of the adjutant and inspector general announced that "at the request of his Excellency the Governor of North Carolina, a regiment will be formed of the 2d Battalion North Carolina Volunteers, and the Conscripts at Raleigh North Carolina, *Benjamin R. Moore* late Adjutant 16 North Carolina Volunteers to be Lieutenant Colonel of said Regiment. By command of the secy of war." Copy in Z. B. Vance Papers.

[547] The records are very confusing with regard to Moore. Benjamin F. Moore, of Rowan County, is listed in Moore, *N. C. Roster,* II, 1 as adjutant of the Sixteenth North Carolina Regiment, but his commission bears the date of April 26, 1863. This would appear to eliminate him as the person spoken of unless his commission is dated in error by a year. Benjamin Roger Moore (1834-1894), who was born in Person County and lived in Wilmington as lawyer, solicitor of the criminal court of New Hanover County, 1877-1894, eventually became lieutenant colonel of the Forty-first North Carolina Regiment (cavalry) in 1864, but he is not listed as having been adjutant of the Sixteenth. See Moore, *N. C. Roster,* III, 146; Clark, *N. C. Regts.,* II, 769; Sprunt, *Chronicles,* p. 308. Vance admitted that he recommended Moore under a misapprehension. See Vance to Seddon, February 4, 1863, Vance Letter Book, 1862-1863.

men that have labored for its success, & the welfare & comfort of the men composing it. After presenting the views herein set forth, which as Officers of the Confederate Army we felt constrained to do as an act of simple justice to ourselves & men. If compatible with Your Excellency's feelings to let this matter remain in the hands of Gen[l]- Daniel, in whose wisdom & discretion we have unlimited confidence, if the request we have presumed to make meet Your Excellency's approbation, we sincerely hope you will comply with it.

If not we most earnestly ask that you should recommend an election of the Field Officers, when this Battalion is increased to a Regiment. We assure Your Excellency that in presenting this memorial we are actuated by what we conceive to be the interest of the cause we are engaged in, & the welfare of the men we command, all of whom would very gladly subscribe to the views herein expressed.

Van Brown[548] Capt Co (H)

S A Lusk[549] I Lieut   ”

J. N. Ducketts[550]

L. J. Norman[551] 1st. Lieut Co. B.

J. W. Askew[552] 2nd. Lieut Co H.

Jos. Sayars[553] 2d Lt Co. B.

Ralph Gorrell [554] 3rd Lt Co G—

J. C. Wheeler[555] 1st Lieut Co. G.

Joseph Gordon[556] 2nd Lieut Co B.

Milton Smith[557] Capt Co (A)

Lut N P G Smith[558] Co A

Lieut Edwin Smith[559] Co A

Wm. H. McClure[560] 1st Lt. Co. D

---

[548] Van Brown, of Madison County, who was promoted first lieutenant September 25, 1862. Moore, *N. C. Roster,* IV, 228.

[549] S. A. J. Lusk, of Madison County, who was promoted first lieutenant September 25, 1862. Moore, *N. C. Roster,* IV, 228.

[550] J. N. Ducketts does not appear as an officer of the battalion.

[551] Lacy J. Norman, of Surry County, who was promoted captain of company B on December 1, 1862. Moore, *N. C. Roster,* IV, 220. He was afterwards wounded at Gettysburg.

[552] Joseph W. Askew, of Madison County.

[553] Joseph Sayars, of Surry County, who was promoted first lieutenant on December 1, 1862. Moore, *N. C. Roster,* IV, 220.

[554] Ralph Gorrell, of Forsythe County. Moore, *N. C. Roster,* IV, 226, 228.

[555] Henry C. Wheeler, who enlisted as a private January 15, 1862, and was promoted to captain March 15, 1863. Moore, *N. C. Roster,* IV, 226, 228.

[556] Joseph Gordon, of Surry County; he resigned in February 1863. Moore, *N. C. Roster,* IV, 220.

[557] Milton Smith, of Stokes County. Moore, *N. C. Roster,* IV, 218.

[558] N. G. Smith, of Stokes County, second lieutenant. Moore, *N. C. Roster,* IV, 218.

[559] Edwin Smith, also of Stokes County, second lieutenant, wounded at Gettysburg. Moore, *N. C. Roster,* IV, 218.

[560] William H. McClure, see Clark, *N. C. Regts.,* IV, 245.

A number of the Officers are absent who would very gladly signed it.

[Raleigh]

[A. L. S. Governors' Papers (Vance),
  State Department of Archives and History, Raleigh.]

A

Abernathy, G. S., mentioned, 230n.

Abernathy, Logan B., mentioned, 385.

Abernathy, Sidney S., mentioned, 230n.

Abernethy, Robert Laban, sketch of, 304n; writes Vance, 304-305, 384-385.

Adams, Charles Francis, mentioned, 77n.

Adams, T. J., identified, 312n.

"Ad-Vance," mentioned, lii, liii.

Albright, G. M. G., identified, 217n.

Albright, James Washington, identified, 270n.

Alexander, James M., identified, 109n.

Allen, Lawrence M., mentioned, 325; sketch of 226n; writes Vance, 226-227.

Allen, Solomon J., identified, 229n.

Allen, William A., identified, 282n.

Allen, W. W., identified, 230n; writes Vance, 230-231.

Allison, John B., identified, 94n.

Allman, N. G., identified, 115n; receives letter from Vance, 115-117.

Anderson, George Burgwyn, identified, 356n.

Anderson, Joseph R., mentioned, 131n.

Anderson, Robert, discussed, 89n.

Andrews, Charles Milton, brief sketch of, 359n; writes Vance, 359.

Andrews, H. L., identified, 456n.

Archer, James J., identified, 431n.

Arledge, Isaac, brief sketch of, 337n; mentioned, 414.

Arrington, S. P., brief sketch of, 290n; mentioned, 375, 380; writes Vance, 404.

Ashe, Samuel A., reference to, 13n.

Asheville, armory personnel of, listed, 342-344.

Askew, Joseph W., identified, 458n.

Atkin, Thomas W., identified, 18n; mentioned, 337.

Austin, Robert G. Stanly, identified, 442n.

Avery, William Waightstill, mentioned, xxvi, xxxiv, xxxv, xxxvi, 56, 242, 412n; sketch of, 55n.

Ayer, Hal W., identified, 278n; writes Vance, 278-280, 313, 330-332.

B

Badger, George Edmund, identified, 33n; mentioned, xxxi.

Badham, John C., brief sketch of, 169n.

Baird, Adolphus Erwin, identified, 2n, 68n, 118n.

Baird, Alfred H., identified, 227n; mentioned, 413.

Baird, Harriet N., identified, 7n.

Baird, James Samuel Tazewell, brief sketch of, 29n; dispute with Vance, 29-30, 30n; writes Vance, 29-30.

Baird, Loretta T., identified, 2n.

Baird, Sarah Ann, mentioned, 11n.

Baird, Zebulon, mentioned, xix.

Baker, John L., identified, 365n.

Baker, Lawrence S., identified, 248n; mentioned, 249n.

Banks, Nathaniel Prentiss, identified, 139n.

Banner, Elisha, mentioned, 305, 306n, 376.

Barnes, David Alexander, identified, 224n-225n; mentioned, 195n, 255n, 265n, 340.

Barney, Charles R., identified, 314n; mentioned, 315, 327.

Barnwell, James L., mentioned, 347.

Barringer, Rufus, sketch of, 247n-248n; writes Vance, 247-249.

Bason, W. F., identified, 400n; writes Vance, 400.

Bates, Edward, mentioned, 69n.

Battle, Amos Johnston, brief sketch of, 337n; writes Vance, 337-340.

Battle, Kemp Plummer, mentioned, xxiv, 127n.

Battle, Richard Henry, mentioned, xxiv, 154n, 405; sketch of, 156n-157n; writes Vance, 167.

Battle, William Horn, brief sketch of, 8n; mentioned, xxiii, 337n, 338n.

Battle of New Bern, discussed, 121, 121n, 140, 140n, 141.

Baxter, John J., mentioned, xxvi, 28n, 50n; sketch of, 83n; writes Vance, 83.

Baxter, Sydney S., identified, 450n.

Beall, Robert Lamar, brief sketch of, 431n.

Beam, David, brief sketch of, 426n.

Beauregard, Pierre Gustave Toutant, identified, 111n; mentioned, 139n.

Beckerdite, John R., mentioned, 315.

Bell, John, identified, 34n; mentioned, 69n.

Benjamin, Judah Philip, identified, 136n; mentioned, 137, 339n.

Benley (Bailey), Allen, identified, 230n.

Best, Henry H., identified, 332n; writes Vance, 332.

Biggs, Asa, mentioned, xxxiv, 40n, 55n.

Blacknall, G. W., mentioned, 141n.

Blackstock, Nehemiah, mentioned, xxi.

M